Global Issues

Global Issues

2012 EDITION

Los Angeles | London | New Delhi
Singapore | Washington DC

SELECTIONS FROM **CQ RESEARCHER**

Los Angeles | London | New Delhi
Singapore | Washington DC

FOR INFORMATION:

CQ Press
An Imprint of SAGE Publications, Inc.
2455 Teller Road
Thousand Oaks, California 91320
E-mail: order@sagepub.com

SAGE Publications Ltd.
1 Oliver's Yard
55 City Road
London EC1Y 1SP
United Kingdom

SAGE Publications India Pvt. Ltd.
B 1/I 1 Mohan Cooperative Industrial Area
Mathura Road, New Delhi 110 044
India

SAGE Publications Asia-Pacific Pte. Ltd.
3 Church Street
#10-04 Samsung Hub
Singapore 049483

Printed in the United States of America

Library of Congress Control Number: 2012937014

This book is printed on acid-free paper.

SFI label applies to text stock

Acquisitions Editor: Elise Fraser
Associate Editor: Nancy Loh
Production Editor: Laura Stewart
Typesetter: C&M Digitals, Ltd.
Cover Designer: Judy Myers
Marketing Manager: Jonathan Mason

12 13 14 15 16 10 9 8 7 6 5 4 3 2 1

Contents

Annotated Contents

CONFLICT, SECURITY, AND TERRORISM
Rising Tension Over Iran

Successive U.S. presidents have insisted that a nuclear-armed Iran is "unacceptable." Iran's Islamic leadership insists that its nuclear program is for peaceful purposes only, but even as U.N. inspectors headed to Tehran in late January 2012, the body of evidence from earlier inspections raised nagging questions that the Iranians have failed to answer, such as why facilities for a peaceful program would be buried hundreds of feet underground. A nuclear Iran would alter the strategic balance in the tense Middle East and, some say, possibly trigger a regional atomic arms race. Although the United States and Europe have imposed tough economic sanctions on Iran, the Iranians have not stopped enriching uranium or begun operating their nuclear program with more transparency. But with Israel reportedly considering a pre-emptive strike on nuclear facilities in Iran — which has vowed to destroy Israel — the question of the sanctions' effectiveness may be moot.

Emerging Central Asia

Since emerging from the Soviet Union's orbit 20 years ago, the five nations of Central Asia — Kazakhstan, Kyrgyzstan, Tajikistan, Turkmenistan and Uzbekistan — increasingly are popping up on geo-political radar screens. Given the proximity of the "Stans" to Afghanistan, where NATO continues to wage war on Al Qaeda and the Taliban, Western powers are ardently wooing Central Asia's leaders in an effort to maintain military bases in the region. There are also rich resources at stake. Kazakhstan and Turkmenistan's abundant oil and gas reserves have made them magnets for foreign investors, especially from energy-hungry China, as well as from Europe and the United States. Central Asia also faces a daunting array of domestic challenges, from bloody ethnic clashes and Islamist terrorist attacks to criminal gangs that traffic in drugs and human beings. Meanwhile, some experts wonder if Central Asia, with its repressive, dictatorial leaders and weak but deeply corrupted governments, will soon see its own version of an "Arab Spring" — a popular uprising that will sweep away its aging regimes.

Future of the Gulf States

Known for their towering, ultramodern skyscrapers and jaw-dropping energy reserves, the six Arab monarchies of the Gulf Cooperation Council (GCC) are striving to improve regional stability amid the turmoil of the Arab Spring. The economic and security coalition — made up of Bahrain, Kuwait, Oman, Qatar, Saudi Arabia and the United Arab Emirates — celebrated its 30th anniversary in 2011with huge fiscal surpluses that are financing, among other things, construction of state-of-the-art facilities for higher education and international sporting events. However, the six Sunni-led Muslim countries — key U.S. military allies — face ongoing unrest from a Shiite majority in Bahrain, uncertainty about the intentions of Shiite regimes in neighboring Iran and Iraq and an unstable Yemen, home to Al Qaeda-linked terrorists. The GCC countries also are struggling to balance their overdependence on foreign labor with the need for more jobs for their huge, youth populations.

Resolving Land Disputes

Conflicts over land ownership are intensifying around the globe, as population growth, climate change and food insecurity make land an increasingly scarce resource. Private investors and governments are scrambling to purchase vast tracts of arable land. Such "land grabs" have increased more than 10-fold in the from 2009 to 2011. However, because up to 70 percent of the planet's land remains potentially in dispute because of the lack of clear titles, indigenous owners often end up losing their land to big investors. Meanwhile, long-festering land issues slow poverty reduction, and land disputes are at the root of social conflicts in countries from Cambodia to Colombia. Early land reform efforts in Latin America are eroding, and Asian land redistribution projects are causing tension between farmers and urban tenants. While some countries are successfully addressing land policy issues, experts say the need to grow economies and feed growing populations will only increase land disputes worldwide, potentially triggering more violence.

Weapons in Space

The more than 1,000 active satellites orbiting the Earth present vulnerable targets to hostile nations, and attacks could cause wide-ranging damage: Weather satellites help predict hurricanes; communication satellites support telephones and other electronics and satellite-based navigation networks provide myriad services worldwide. Moreover, an attack on a satellite also would add to the more than 12,000 pieces of potentially dangerous space junk already orbiting the Earth at speeds exceeding 17,000 miles per hour. So far, weapons have not been deployed in space that threaten satellites, nor has a satellite been deliberately destroyed by hostile action. But both the United States and China have shown they can target and destroy satellites. Some U.S. military leaders have pushed for the United States to achieve "space superiority," in part by developing a controversial system that could destroy incoming enemy missiles. Because such a missile defense system could also target satellites, many countries want it outlawed. But international negotiations to ban or regulate anti-satellite and other space weapons have been stalled for years.

U.S.-Pakistan Relations

On May 2, 2011, U.S. Navy Seals raided a house in Abbottabad, Pakistan, and killed Osama bin Laden, mastermind of the September 2001 terror attacks. While Americans hailed the Al Qaeda leader's death, some Pakistanis and Americans, including members of Congress, saw it as yet another betrayal in the rocky alliance between the two nations. Pakistanis considered the U.S. raid as a clear violation of their country's sovereignty; Americans say that bin Laden's ability to take refuge in a major Pakistani city — perhaps for as long as five years — reflected the country's duplicity. Some in Congress have called for ending aid to Pakistan — nearly $5 billion in fiscal 2010 — on the grounds that Pakistan has undermined the U.S. fight against terrorism. But others warn that halting aid could push nuclear-armed Pakistan further into chaos, thus opening a power vacuum that militants could fill.

Foreign Aid and National Security

The Sept. 11, 2001, attacks and subsequent wars in Iraq and Afghanistan prompted U.S. leaders to increase U.S. aid in the belief that improved global stability ultimately undergirds U.S. security. Secretary of State Hillary Clinton is among those calling for elevating international development assistance and diplomacy to the same status as defense. But budget debates on Capitol Hill could block aid-reform efforts. The Republican-led House calls for drastically reducing international affairs funding, but the Democratic-led Senate and the Obama administration are resisting. Complicating the arguments are questions about the efficiency of America's aid bureaucracy and, ultimately, the effectiveness of the aid itself. While aid supporters point to improved accountability, it's unclear whether future aid requests can withstand the pressure of budget cutters.

Russia in Turmoil

As Russians go to the polls on March 4, 2012 to choose a new president, there's little doubt about the outcome. Vladimir Putin, who has been president or prime minister since 1999, is considered a shoo-in. Yet, despite years of rapid economic growth fueled by boosted oil and gas exports, Putin's efforts to extend his authoritarian rule are facing a new and destabilizing challenge. Tens of thousands of people have taken to the streets since December 2011 to protest pervasive corruption and alleged electoral fraud. In the past, Putin has dealt firmly with political opponents — many of whom have been exiled, imprisoned or died in mysterious circumstances. But now many are wondering if Russia's winter of protests will mark the start of a "Snow Revolution," inspired by the "Arab Spring" movement that toppled dictators across the Middle East in 2011. The upheaval has strained relations with the West — as has Russia's recent support for the repressive Syrian regime — leading to questions about what lies ahead for Russia, a nuclear power and the world's second-largest oil producer.

INTERNATIONAL ISSUES

Sharia Controversy

To Westerners, the Arabic word Sharia often conjures up images of amputations for Muslim thieves and stonings of adulterous women. But the term actually encompasses all Islamic religious precepts — including how to pray — and its interpretation differs from region to region. Only a few Muslim countries, including Saudi Arabia and Iran, carry out such harsh Sharia penalties today. And, some Muslim countries, such as Tunisia and Morocco, have passed progressive laws giving women equality with men — in the name of Sharia. In recent years, imams at English mosques have been adjudicating hundreds of requests from Muslim women seeking religious divorces. Critics say these Sharia tribunals constitute a parallel legal system that discriminates against women. But researchers say they mainly free women to remarry in keeping with their faith. After recent electoral gains by Islamist parties in Egypt, Morocco and Tunisia, human-rights advocates worry that new governments may reject progressive interpretations of Sharia for the harsher, Saudi- or Iranian-style versions.

Peacebuilding

Peacebuilding is the international community's newest approach to ending cycles of conflict in hot spots around the world. It recognizes that even if conflict has officially ended, the risk of violence often remains ever-present. In fact, roughly 40 percent of post-conflict countries have faced renewed violence within a decade. Peacebuilding tries to improve the prospect for lasting peace by helping to stabilize societies, strengthen institutions and reinforce governments. Since 2005, the United Nations has spent $250 million on peacebuilding projects in 19 countries — most of them in Africa but also in Nepal, Sri Lanka, Haiti and Kyrgyzstan. But does this approach work, and can it be replicated in countries with drastically different histories and cultures? Is a democratic society a prerequisite for lasting peace? Critics of peacebuilding say it will take more than a new philosophy to fix the world's most fragile states. Proponents say it is the best attempt yet at dealing with the aftermath of conflict.

Gendercide Crisis

An estimated 160 million babies in China, India and other Asian countries have been aborted or killed over the last 30 years — just because they were girls — in a phenomenon some are calling "gendercide." A strong cultural preference for sons has existed for centuries in Asia. But in recent decades anti-female bias has combined with falling fertility rates, China's coercive one-child policy, new, high-tech prenatal gender-detection tools and widespread access to abortion to produce unprecedented gender imbalances in the region. An alarming shortage of females is changing the fabric of societies, with many villages so devoid of women the men cannot find wives. Governments are struggling to reverse societal attitudes toward daughters, but the changes will be too late for the 30-50 million Chinese men who over the next 20 years won't be able to marry. The gender imbalance already has led to increased kidnapping and trafficking in women and higher prostitution rates in the area. And experts worry that having so many unmarried men could threaten stability and security, because studies show that having large numbers of unattached young males leads to "the criminalization of society."

Saving Indigenous Peoples

Indigenous peoples in lands conquered by white Europeans — the Americas, Australasia and the Arctic — face a wide range of environmental, cultural and social problems. The world's native populations have rebounded numerically since the early 1900s, when many had been decimated, often by harmful assimilation policies. Australia and Canada have formally apologized for their earlier assimilation policies, and many indigenous groups today are seeking — and being granted — legal recognition of their political, economic and cultural rights. But uncertainty hangs over the survival of native cultures. Fewer young people speak their mother tongues and traditional customs are dying out. Moreover, native peoples often face daunting social problems, including dramatically lower life expectancies and significantly higher rates of poverty, suicide, alcoholism and domestic violence than among nonindigenous populations. Now, native groups face perhaps one of their biggest challenges: governments and private developers encroaching on their ancestral lands to exploit energy and other natural resources.

INTERNATIONAL POLITICAL ECONOMY
Future of the Euro

Portugal has become the third eurozone government to seek a bailout loan from the European Union, which is struggling to prevent a debt crisis from crippling its poorest members and spreading to richer euro countries. Historically impoverished nations such as Ireland, Portugal and Greece experienced a surge of wealth in the 1990s after adopting the euro. But in the wake of the worldwide economic crash and recession, that wealth proved to be an illusion based on cheap credit from Germany and other stronger economies. The euro's defenders say the crisis has created a new determination to fix the eurozone's defects, particularly its lack of strong centralized governance. But the rise of nationalist parties in richer countries opposed to bailouts could hamper a solution. And despite years of rhetoric about European unity, critics say individual nations will never give up enough of their sovereignty — especially their right to tax and spend on liberal social programs — to become part of a United States of Europe.

The Resource Curse

Ever since dozens of countries gained independence after World War II, scholars have been trying to understand why some new countries were able to grow and prosper while others stagnated. One prominent theory, known as the "resource curse" or the "paradox of plenty," holds that developing nations with valuable oil, gas or mineral reserves are less likely to thrive than their resource-poor neighbors. Proponents say revenues from extractable resources can distort economies, promote corruption and shore up autocratic leaders who waste or steal public money. The resource curse concept is hotly debated, and many analysts see no direct link between mineral wealth and economic growth. But anti-poverty advocates and citizens' groups widely support it and say extractive industries and governments should disclose the amount of money a government receives for its nation's natural resources. That's the best way for citizens to ensure their leaders are sharing the wealth and spending it wisely, they say.

Rising Food Prices

Global food prices reached record highs early in 2011, sending millions around the world into poverty and contributing to starvation in East Africa. Many blame the government-subsidized growth in the market for biofuels, such as ethanol. Biofuels are expected to consume 40 percent of the year's corn crop from the world's largest producer — the United States. Others say commodities speculators caused food prices to ricochet wildly. Europe is considering adopting restrictions on speculation similar to a new U.S. law, but Wall Street is lobbying hard to weaken the American regulations. Perennially high food prices may be the first sign that changing climate is handicapping agriculture. To feed the world's growing population, experts say farmers must double their food output by mid-century — a tall order to fill without destroying more rain forests and further boosting planet-warming carbon emissions. The solution may be a combination of two warring philosophies: high-tech agriculture and traditional farming methods that are kinder to the environment.

Youth Unemployment

Across the globe, the economic crisis has led to soaring youth unemployment — above 50 percent in Spain, nearly that high in Greece and above 30 percent in many other countries. The crisis also has exacerbated already-high levels of youth unemployment in the Middle East and North Africa, where frustrated, unemployed college graduates were at the forefront of last year's Arab Spring revolutions. Angry, jobless youths have taken to the streets in other countries, as well, including the U.K. Countries are grappling with the problem, but solutions remain elusive. Youth unemployment is seen both as a matter of demographics — disproportionately higher numbers of young people in many countries — and structural problems in labor markets, such as laws protecting older workers' jobs. Many observers believe if the issue isn't addressed, further upheavals will occur, while others worry that the world could be facing a "lost generation" of discouraged workers whose earnings will be diminished for decades.

Preface

I n this pivotal era of international policymaking, scholars, students, practitioners and journalists seek answers to such critical questions as: Are high food prices here to stay? Does peacebuilding work? Is there a place for Islamic law in western countries? Students must first understand the facts and contexts of these and other global issues if they are to analyze and articulate well-reasoned positions.

The 2012 edition of *Global Issues* provides comprehensive and unbiased coverage of today's most pressing global problems. This edition is a compilation of 16 recent reports from *CQ Researcher,* a weekly policy brief that unpacks difficult concepts and provides balanced coverage of competing perspectives. Each article analyzes past, present and possible political maneuvering, is designed to promote in-depth discussion and further research and helps readers formulate their own positions on crucial international issues.

This collection is organized into three subject areas that span a range of important international policy concerns: conflict, security and terrorism; international issues; and international political economy. Fifteen of these reports are new to this edition.

Global Issues is a valuable supplement for courses on world affairs in political science, geography, economics and sociology. Citizens, journalists and business and government leaders also turn to it to become better informed on key issues, actors and policy positions.

CQ RESEARCHER

CQ Researcher was founded in 1923 as *Editorial Research Reports* and was sold primarily to newspapers as a research tool. The magazine was renamed and redesigned in 1991 as *CQ Researcher.* Today, students are its primary audience. While still used by hundreds of journalists and newspapers, many of which reprint portions of the reports, *Researcher*'s main subscribers are now high school, college and public libraries. In 2002, *Researcher* won the American Bar Association's coveted Silver Gavel Award for magazine excellence for a series of nine reports on civil liberties and other legal issues.

Researcher staff writers — all highly experienced journalists — sometimes compare the experience of writing a *Researcher* report to drafting a college term paper. Indeed, there are many similarities. Each report is as long as many term papers — about 11,000 words — and is written by one person without any significant outside help. One of the key differences is that the writers interview leading experts, scholars and government officials for each issue.

Like students, staff writers begin the creative process by choosing a topic. Working with *Researcher*'s editors, the writer identifies a controversial subject that has important public policy implications. After a topic is selected, the writer embarks on one to two weeks of intense research. Newspaper and magazine articles are clipped or downloaded, books are ordered and information is gathered from a wide variety of sources, including interest groups, universities and the government. Once the writers are well informed, they develop a detailed outline and begin the interview process. Each report requires a minimum of ten to fifteen interviews with academics, officials, lobbyists and people working in the field. Only after all interviews are completed does the writing begin.

CHAPTER FORMAT

Each issue of *CQ Researcher,* and therefore each selection in this book, is structured in the same way. A selection begins with an introductory overview, which is briefly explored in greater detail in the rest of the report.

The second section chronicles the most important and current debates in the field. It is structured around a number of key issues questions, such as "Can sanctions stop Iran from building a nuclear weapon?" and "Should China rescind its one-child policy?" This section is the core of each selection. The questions raised are often highly controversial and usually the object of much argument among scholars and practitioners. Hence, the answers provided are never conclusive, but rather detail the range of opinion within the field.

Following those issue questions is the "Background" section, which provides a history of the issue being examined. This retrospective includes important legislative and executive actions and court decisions to inform readers on how current policy evolved.

Next, the "Current Situation" section examines important contemporary policy issues, legislation under consideration and action being taken. Each selection ends with an "Outlook" section that gives a sense of what new regulations, court rulings and possible policy initiatives might be put into place in the next five to ten years.

Each report contains features that augment the main text: sidebars that examine issues related to the topic, a pro/con debate by two outside experts, a chronology of key dates and events and an annotated bibliography that details the major sources used by the writer.

CUSTOM OPTIONS

Interested in building your ideal CQ Press Issues book, customized to your personal teaching needs and interests? Browse by course or date, or search for specific topics or issues from our online catalog of *CQ Researcher* issues at http://custom.cqpress.com.

ACKNOWLEDGMENTS

We wish to thank many people for helping to make this collection a reality. Thomas J. Billitteri, managing editor of *CQ Researcher,* gave us his enthusiastic support and cooperation as we developed this edition. He and his talented staff of editors and writers have amassed a first-class collection of *Researcher* articles, and we are fortunate to have access to this rich cache. We also thankfully acknowledge the advice and feedback from current readers and are gratified by their satisfaction with the book.

Some readers may be learning about *CQ Researcher* for the first time. We expect that many readers will want regular access to this excellent weekly research tool. For subscription information or a no-obligation free trial of *Researcher,* please contact CQ Press at www.cqpress.com or toll-free at 1-866-4CQ-PRESS (1-866-427-7737).

We hope that you will be pleased by the 2012 edition of *Global Issues.* We welcome your feedback and suggestions for future editions. Please direct comments to Elise Frasier, Acquisitions Editor for International Relations and Comparative Politics, College Publishing Group, CQ Press, 2300 N Street, NW, Suite 800, Washington, DC 20037; or send e-mail to *efrasier@cqpress.com.*

— *The Editors of CQ Press*

Contributors

Brian Beary, a freelance Irish journalist based in Washington, specializes in European Union (EU) affairs and is the U.S. correspondent for the daily newspaper, *Europolitics*. Originally from Dublin, he worked in the European Parliament for Irish MEP Pat "The Cope" Gallagher in 2000 and at the EU Commission's Eurobarometer unit on public opinion analysis. Beary also writes for the Brussels-based *Parliament Magazine* and *The Globalist*. His last report for *CQ Global Researcher* was "Saving Indigenous Peoples." He also authored the recent CQ Press book, *Separatist Movements, A Global Reference*.

Nellie Bristol is a veteran Capitol Hill reporter who has covered health policy in Washington for more than 20 years. She now writes for *The Lancet, Health Affairs* and *Global Health* magazine. She recently earned a master's degree in public health/global health from The George Washington University, where she earned an undergraduate degree in American studies.

Marcia Clemmitt is a veteran social-policy reporter who previously served as editor in chief of *Medicine & Health* and staff writer for *The Scientist*. She has also been a high school math and physics teacher. She holds a liberal arts and sciences degree from St. John's College, Annapolis, and a master's degree in English from Georgetown University. Her recent reports include "Income Inequality" and "Financial Industry Overhaul."

Roland Flamini is a Washington-based correspondent who specializes in foreign affairs. Fluent in six languages, he was *Time* bureau chief in Rome, Bonn, Beirut, Jerusalem and the European Common Market and later served as international editor at United Press International. While covering the 1979 Iranian Revolution for *Time*, Flamini wrote the magazine's cover story — in which Ayatollah Ruhollah Khomeini was named Man of the Year — and was promptly expelled because authorities didn't like what they read. His books include a study of Vatican politics in the 1960s, *Pope, Premier, President.* His most recent report for *CQ Global Researcher* was "Turmoil in the Arab World."

Sarah Glazer, a London-based freelancer, is a regular contributor to *CQ Global Researcher.* Her articles on health, education and social-policy issues also have appeared in *The New York Times* and *The Washington Post.* Her recent *CQ Global Researcher* reports include "Radical Islam in Europe" and "Social Welfare in Europe." She graduated from the University of Chicago with a B.A. in American history.

Konstantin Kakaes is a former Mexico City bureau chief and science writer for *The Economist.* He also was a fellow at the International Reporting Project at Johns Hopkins School of Advanced International Studies, where he researched the links between nuclear energy technology and nuclear weapons, and a Knight Science Journalism Fellow at MIT, where he studied the origins of the computer. He has a degree in physics from Harvard University. On June 20, he was selected as a Bernard L. Schwartz fellow at the New America Foundation, where he is studying the causes and consequences of technological innovation.

Reed Karaim, a freelance writer living in Tucson, Arizona, has written for *The Washington Post, U.S. News & World Report, Smithsonian, American Scholar, USA Weekend* and other publications. He is the author of the novel, *If Men Were Angels,* which was selected for the Barnes & Noble Discover Great New Writers series. He is also the winner of the Robin Goldstein Award for Outstanding Regional Reporting and other journalism honors. Karaim is a graduate of North Dakota State University in Fargo.

Robert Kiener is an award-winning writer whose work has appeared in the *London Sunday Times, The Christian Science Monitor, The Washington Post, Reader's Digest,* Time Life Books, Asia Inc. and other publications. For more than two decades he lived and worked as an editor and correspondent in Guam, Hong Kong, Canada and England and is now based in the United States. He frequently travels to Asia and Europe to report on international issues. He holds an M.A. in Asian Studies from Hong Kong University and an M.Phil. in International Relations from Cambridge University.

Jennifer Koons teaches journalism at Northwestern University's satellite campus in Doha, Qatar. Previously, she was a Washington, D.C.-based journalist writing about national politics and legal issues, including cases before the U.S. Supreme Court, the 2008 and 2004 presidential campaigns and congressional action on Capitol Hill. Her work has appeared in *The New York Times, The Washington Post, San Diego Union Tribune* and *Inside Mexico,* among other publications. She earned a master's degree in journalism from Northwestern's Medill School of Journalism and a master's degree in law from Northwestern's School of Law. She was the McCormick Journalism Fellow at the Reporters Committee for Freedom of the Press in Rosslyn, Va.

Jason McLure is a New Hampshire-based correspondent for Thomson Reuters. Previously he was an Africa correspondent for Bloomberg News and *Newsweek* and worked for *Legal Times* in Washington, D.C. His writing has appeared in publications such as *The Economist, The New York Times* and *BusinessWeek.* His last *CQ Global Researcher* was "Sub-Saharan Democracy." His work has been honored by the Washington, D.C., chapter of the Society for Professional Journalists, the Maryland-Delaware-District of Columbia Press Association and the Overseas Press Club of America Foundation. He is also coordinator of the Committee to Free Eskinder Nega, a jailed Ethiopian journalist.

Jina Moore is a multimedia journalist who covers human rights and foreign affairs from the United States and Africa. Her work has appeared in *The Christian Science Monitor, Newsweek, Foreign Policy, The Columbia Journalism Review* and *Best American Science Writing.*

Her report for the May 2010 *CQ Global Researcher*, "Confronting Rape as a War Crime," received an honorable mention in the Best Reporting on a Significant Topic category of the American Society of Journalists and Authors' 2010 awards.

Jennifer Weeks is a Massachusetts freelance writer who specializes in energy, the environment and science. She has written for *The Washington Post, Audubon, Popular Mechanics* and other magazines and previously was a policy analyst, congressional staffer and lobbyist. She has an A.B. degree from Williams College and master's degrees from the University of North Carolina and Harvard. Her recent *CQ Researcher* reports include "Gulf Coast Restoration" and "Energy Policy."

Global Issues

1

Rising Tension Over Iran

Roland Flamini

Two Iranian protesters try to pry a British coat of arms from the wall surrounding the British Embassy in Tehran, as rioters stormed the facility on Nov. 29, 2011. The assault recalled the 1979 attack and hostage-taking at the American Embassy in the same city. The November mob was protesting Britain's agreement to support beefed-up Western sanctions on Iran over its disputed nuclear program.

AP Photo/Vahid Salemi

From *CQ Researcher*, Feb. 7, 2012

When angry students, upset that London had cut off financial ties with Iran, attacked the British embassy in Tehran last November, Amb. Dominick Chilcott could only stand by, holding his quivering dog Pumpkin as attackers rampaged through offices and grounds. The marauders smashed furniture and portraits of Queen Elizabeth II, tore up documents and torched parked cars. Iranian riot police also watched, making no move to halt the destruction. [1]

An outraged British government withdrew its diplomats and closed the embassy in protest. [2]

Inevitably, the assault revived memories of the 1979 U.S. hostage crisis, when hard-line supporters of Iran's new Islamic Revolution stormed the American Embassy and took 52 staffers and Marine guards captive for more than a year. Since then the United States has had no diplomatic relations with the regime — a theocracy ruled by conservative Shiite clerics, surrounded by mostly Sunni Arab neighbors.

The striking similarities between the two embassy attacks reflect Iran's reputation for irrational behavior, fanaticism and disdain for the rules of international conduct — all of which helps explain why the possibility that Iran may be building nuclear weapons has caused consternation in the international community.

In November the U.N.'s nuclear monitoring organization said Iran probably has a nuclear weapons program. Iran has carried out activities "relevant to the development of a nuclear explosive device," the International Atomic Energy Agency (IAEA) said. "These activities took place under a structured programme" before 2003 and "may still be ongoing." [3]

1

Tensions Rise in Volatile Gulf Region

The wars in Iraq and Afghanistan have garnered most of the world's attention in the past decade. But with the fighting in those countries winding down, the spotlight is turning to their neighbor — Alaska-size Iran. The Western powers worry that Iran is developing weapons at its numerous nuclear facilities, some buried deep underground, which Iran says are strictly for peaceful purposes. In an effort to force Iran to halt its nuclear program, the European Union on Jan. 23 voted to join with the United States in embargoing Iranian oil exports. Iran responded by threatening to close the crucial Strait of Hormuz, located in the Persian Gulf on Iran's southern border, through which nearly 40 percent of the world's seaborne oil is shipped.

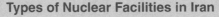

Types of Nuclear Facilities in Iran

Source: map by Lewis Agrell

The West has long suspected that Tehran's ruling ayatollahs were trying to develop nuclear bombs. Now, the IAEA report "destroys Iran's pretention that its nuclear activities have been purely peaceful," says Mark Fitzpatrick, director of the Nonproliferation and Disarmament Program at London's International Institute of Strategic Studies (IISS). Now that suspicion "has the imprimatur of the IAEA."

If Iran develops a nuclear weapon, it would violate the U.N. Nuclear Nonproliferation Treaty (NPT), which Tehran signed in 1968, and change the strategic equation in the Middle East, an unstable region on which the industrialized world depends for its oil lifeline. "This is not a question of [Middle Eastern] security," declared German Foreign Minister Guido Westerwelle recently. "It is a question of the whole world." [4]

Israel, the Middle East's sole nuclear power, strongly opposes Iran joining the nuclear club, given Tehran's open hostility to the Jewish state. Indeed, Israel sees a nuclear-armed Iran as an existential threat. On Feb. 3, Iran's Supreme Leader Ayatollah Ali Khamenei denounced tightening oil sanctions and renewed Israeli threats of an attack on his nation's nuclear facilities by vowing to retaliate in a way that "would be 10 times worse for the interests of the United States" than for Iran. In an unusually blunt warning, Khamenei said Iran would support militant opponents of Israel. His speech came one day after Israel's leaders delivered their own blunt warning that they might pre-emptively strike Iran's nuclear enrichment sites, possibly as soon as this spring. Israel has long contended that if the West waits to see if sanctions work, Iran will have time to bury key nuclear facilities deep inside mountain bunkers, making them inaccessible to even the most powerful bombs. [5]

Moreover, the United States apparently hasn't ruled out a strike of its own. Concerned for the stability of the region and pressured by Israel and its supporters in Congress, two successive U.S. presidents have repeatedly said a nuclear Iran was "unacceptable" and that — as President Obama warned during his Jan. 24 State of the Union address —"no options" are off the table.

Iran at a Glance

The Islamic Republic of Iran is the size of Alaska but with a population that is three times that of Texas. It has a predominantly Persian population and a Shiite theocracy, surrounded by mostly Sunni-dominated countries with Arab populations. Iran's per capita income is on a par with South Africa's.

Quick Facts About Iran

Area: 636,371 sq. miles (about the size of Alaska)

Population: 77,891,220* (about the same as Turkey, or three times the population of Texas)

Chief of state: Supreme Leader Sayyid Ali Khamenei (since June 1989)

Head of government: President Mahmoud Ahmadinejad (since August 2005)

Government type: Theocratic republic; Supreme Leader appointed for life by the Assembly of Experts; president elected by popular vote for up to two four-year terms; legislative members elected by popular vote for four-year terms

Ethnic groups: Persian 61%, Azeri 16%, Kurd 10%, Lur 6%, Baloch 2%, Arab 2%, Turkmen and Turkic tribes 2%, other 1% (2008 est.)

Religion: Muslim (official religion) 98% (Shiite 89%, Sunni 9%), other (includes Zoroastrian, Jewish, Christian and Baha'i) 2%

Infant mortality rate: 42.26 deaths/1,000 live births (60th in the world)

GDP: $818.7 billion**

GDP per capita: $10,600** (about the same as South Africa)

Unemployment rate: 13.2%**

Industries: petroleum, petrochemicals, fertilizers, caustic soda, textiles, cement and other construction materials, food processing, metal fabrication, armaments

July 2011 estimate

** 2010 estimate*

Source: The World Factbook, Central Intelligence Agency, 2012, *https://www.cia.gov/library/publications/the-world-factbook/geos/ir.html.*

And in a U.S. presidential election year, talk of military action and war with Iran provides sound-bite ammunition for the various candidates. Republican Mitt Romney vowed, if elected, to "do everything in my power to assure that Iran doesn't become a nuclear nation [and] threaten Israel, threaten us and threaten the entire world." [6]

Going nuclear would boost Iran's ambition to be a major international player. Some argue that it also would

Iranian Women Lost Rights Under the Mullahs

One Million Signatures Campaign seeks major changes.

During the Arab Spring uprisings last year, Iranian women's groups circulated a cautionary video, "Message from Iranian Women for Tunisian and Egyptian Women." The film depicted how Iranian women's lives changed dramatically after the Islamic Revolution of 1979 and warned Tunisian and Egyptian women that the same thing could happen to them if the religious party, the Muslim Brotherhood, gained majorities in their countries. [1]

During the reign of Shah Reza Pahlavi, Iranian women had made progress in the traditionally male-oriented region. They wore whatever they wanted in public and have been allowed to vote since 1963.

Under the ayatollahs, however, the *hijab* — the head-scarf worn by Muslim women — immediately became mandatory, and Islamic law was introduced and strictly enforced. [2] For example, the minimum age of marriage for women was changed from 18 to nine — although it has since been raised to 13 after protests by activists.

Polygamy has increased, as has the so-called temporary marriage (*mut'a*), a verbal, short-term relationship for a pre-determined period, with no divorce necessary to end it. Permitted under Shiite Muslim law, the *mut'a* is seen by many as prostitution under another name, because a dowry is one of its prerequisites.* [3]

The changes helped to spark the One Million Signatures Campaign, a grass-roots Iranian feminist effort to convince Iran's parliament to change marriage, divorce, custody and inheritance laws that discriminate against women.

The movement also wants to improve the legal position of women who are sex-crime victims. A married Iranian woman who is raped is considered to have committed adultery and can be stoned to death. If she kills her aggressor, she can be

* Depending on the culture, a dowry is the money or property that a bride's family pays to the groom's family or that a groom pays to a bride.

tried for murder. If she is unmarried, she could end up being killed by a male family member to avoid bringing shame on the family name. Such so-called honor killings are more a patriarchal custom than a practice condoned by the Quran. [4]

But that's not the full picture, according to Sussan Tahmasebi, an American-born Iranian who helped launch the campaign. "We have female doctors, we have politicians, MPs (members of parliament)," she said. "It's paradoxical that, despite these achievements, discrimination against women is embedded in the legal system, and that lawmakers justify it by saying it's based on religion." [5]

However, CNN broadcaster and columnist Fareed Zakaria says Iranian women fare better than women in Saudi Arabia. He was struck while on a recent visit, he writes, "by how defiantly [Iranian] women try to lead normal and productive lives. They wear the headscarves and adhere to the rules about covering their bodies, but do so in a very stylish way. They continue to go to college in large numbers, to graduate school and to work." [6]

Iranian women can vote, he added, while women in Saudi Arabia —"another country . . . run along strict Islamic lines" — cannot. And in Saudi Arabia, he noted, women "are not well integrated into the workforce or mainstream life." [7]

Even so, Iranian women face a litany of constraints. A daughter still needs her father's permission to marry; a wife must obtain her husband's written permission to travel abroad or get a passport. An Iranian woman can't sing in public or attend sports events where men are present.

In 1979, thousands of women protested in the streets against the shah — only to be repressed by Ayatollah Ruhollah Khomeini as soon as he assumed power. In 2009, women were a strong presence in the "Green" protests against the disputed re-election of President Mahmoud Ahmadinejad. Neda Agha Soltan, a 26-year-old music student, was shot dead in a Tehran street during the demonstrations. The bloody video of her death went viral on the

enable Iran to wreak havoc, by, for instance, giving a portable nuclear device to one of its proxies, such as the Lebanese Shiite fundamentalist movement Hezbollah or the radical Palestinian Sunni party, Hamas, which controls the Gaza Strip — both listed as terrorist organizations by Washington.

Neighboring Arabs aren't crazy about the idea of the region's two non-Arab countries having the only nuclear weapons in the Middle East. If Iran gets the bomb, warned Prince Turki Al-Faisal Al Saud, former head of Saudi Arabian intelligence, it would "unleash a cascade of [nuclear] proliferation that would significantly destabilize the region." [7]

Internet, making her what *The New York Times* called "the public face" of those who died in the protests. [8]

In 2002, the European Union lobbied to help persuade the Iranian courts to declare a moratorium on death by stoning, of either gender. The moratorium was extended in 2008 — although according to reports, four men and one woman were executed by stoning, a method usually reserved for convicted adulterers. In 2008, a spokesman for the judiciary confirmed that two of the men had been stoned, saying that the moratorium had no legal weight, and judges could ignore it. However, draft legislation to abolish death by stoning is being considered. [9]

The United Nations also has pressured Iran to reform its discriminatory laws, most of which violate the U.N.'s 1979 Convention of the Elimination of All Forms of Discrimination Against Women, which the mullahs say undermines Islamic teaching. [10]

The regime is particularly vigilant with regard to cultural activities. In 2011, the Iranian actress Marzieh Vafamehr was sentenced to a year in jail and 90 lashes for her role in the film "My Tehran for Sale," an internationally acclaimed underground movie about life in Tehran. She was never lashed, however, and was released after serving three months. [11]

It was a case of life imitating art. Vafamehr played a young theater actress trying to pursue her career against the backdrop of Iran's repressive regime. But the film's director, the Australian-Iranian poet Granaz Moussavi, says the movie, which was filmed in Iran, actually had the regime's approval.

"Nobody can deny that we are working with restrictions when it comes to writing and film making," she says. "But in Iran, and especially in Tehran, everything can be risky, even crossing the road."

— *Roland Flamini*

AFP/Getty Images/Atta Kenare

Female supporters of Mir Hossein Mousavi, Iran's reformist candidate in the 2009 presidential election, show off their fingers and nails — painted green, the color of Mousavi's campaign — during a Tehran rally on June 9, 2009. Iranian women, who have been able to vote since before the 1979 Islamic Revolution, played a big part in the so-called Green Movement — anti-government demonstrations that challenged Mousavi's defeat by President Mahmoud Ahmadinejad. The movement was brutally suppressed by the government.

[1] Dina Sadek, "Women in Egypt Heed Warning From Iranian Women on Rights," Global Press Institute, Jan. 10, 2012, www.globalpressinstitute.org/global-news/africa/egypt/women-egypt-heed-warning-iranian-women-rights.

[2] For background, see Sarah Glazer, "Sharia Controversy," *CQ Global Researcher*, Jan. 3, 2012, pp. 1-28.

[3] Donna M. Hughes, "Women in Iran: A look at President Khatami's first year in office," *Z Magazine*, October 1998, www.uri.edu/artsci/wms/hughes/khatami.htm.

[4] For background, see Robert Kiener, "Honor Killings," *CQ Global Researcher*, April 19, 2011, pp. 183-208.

[5] "Fighting for Women's Rights," Human Rights Watch, Oct. 11, 2011, www.hrw.org/news/2011/10/31/fighting-women-s-rights-iran.

[6] Fareed Zakaria, "Zakaria: Comparing the status of women in Iran and Saudi Arabia," CNN.com, Dec. 27, 2011, http://globalpublicsquare.blogs.cnn.com/2011/10/27/zakaria-comparing-the-status-of-women-in-iran-and-saudi-arabia%E2%80%A8/.

[7] *Ibid.*

[8] Nazla Fathi, "In a death seen around the world, a symbol of Iranian protests," *The New York Times*, June 22, 2009, www.nytimes.com/2009/06/23/world/middleeast/23neda.html.

[9] "Chaknews" (Iranian human rights blog), undated, www.chaknews.com/English/print.php?type=N&item_id=365.

[10] Christina Hoff Sommers, "Feminism by Treaty," American Enterprise Institute, June 1, 2011, www.aei.org/article/society-and-culture/race-and-gender/feminism-by-treaty/.

[11] "Concerns Iran film star Marzieh Vafamehr 'to be lashed,' " BBC News, Nov. 11, 2011, www.bbc.co.uk/news/world-asia-pacific-15262071.

But while the Sunni Saudis would certainly want to match the nuclear capability of their Shiite regional rival, most experts believe an arms race would be unlikely. "No countries went nuclear after Israel went nuclear, so why would they want to now?" asks Iran specialist Vali Nasr, a professor of international politics at the Fletcher School of Law and Diplomacy at Tufts University in Medford, Mass.

Defense Secretary Leon Panetta said recently that a nuclear Iran was a "red line" for the United States and for Israel. But he seems to differentiate between being *capable* of making nuclear weapons and actually *making*

Most Iranian Oil Ends Up in Asia

Nearly two-thirds of the 2.2 million barrels of oil exported daily by Iran goes to Asia, with one-fifth of it destined for China. Asian buyers have not signed onto new, tougher sanctions against Iranian oil purchases — imposed by the European Union on Jan. 23. For that reason, some observers doubt that the new restrictions will succeed in forcing Iran to halt its uranium enrichment program, seen as a possible precursor to the development of nuclear weapons.

Destinations of Iranian Oil Exports, 2010

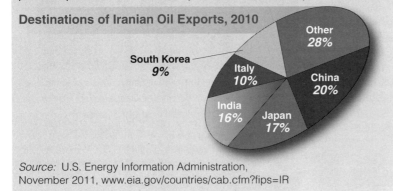

Source: U.S. Energy Information Administration, November 2011, www.eia.gov/countries/cab.cfm?fips=IR

them. "Are [the Iranians] trying to develop a nuclear weapon?" Panetta asked, rhetorically, on CBS's "Face the Nation" on Jan 8. "No. But we know that they're trying to develop a nuclear capability. And our red line to Iran is: Do not develop a nuclear weapon. That's a red line for us." [8]

The Iranians consistently have denied trying to do either. Last year, Iran's foreign minister, Ali Akbar Salehi, told Euronews that Supreme Leader Khamenei had decreed that holding, producing or using nuclear weapons "is against the principles of our religion." And a decree by the supreme leader, Salehi pointed out, "is both religious and governmental." [9]

Iran insists it is enriching uranium for only peaceful purposes, such as power generation. According to the IAEA, the Iranians now have enough 3 percent enriched uranium that, if further enriched to weapons-grade 90 percent strength, would allow them to make at least two nuclear bombs. Some uranium already has been converted to 20 percent strength — a higher level than is needed for civilian use. The report also warned that Iran may have other "undeclared nuclear facilities and material." [10] Iran also is moving at least one of its uranium-processing facilities to a location deep underground, an odd thing to do if the program's purpose is peaceful.

The West reacted to the report by ratcheting up long-running economic sanctions in an effort to force Iran into serious negotiation about halting its enrichment program. On Dec. 31, President Obama signed a law that "cuts off from the U.S. financial system foreign firms that do business with Iran's central bank." [11] Then on Jan. 23, the 27 members of the European Union (EU) agreed to embargo Iranian oil imports — starting in July — and froze the Iranian central bank's assets in Europe. [12]

Iran reacted by threatening to close the Strait of Hormuz, the Persian Gulf bottleneck through which up to 40 percent of the world's seaborne oil is shipped. [13] Washington said it would be forced to act to keep the vital shipping lanes open. Experts said Iran's belligerence indicated sanctions are pushing the country's economy into a nosedive. [14]

Frederick W. Kagan, a defense and security specialist at the conservative American Enterprise Institute, a Washington think tank, contends there is no question Iran wants the bomb. "The Iranian regime intends to acquire nuclear weapons," he says, "and it's bizarre that we continue to say, 'Well, maybe they don't mean it.' "

Still, others aren't so sure. David Aaron, who tracks Iran developments for the RAND Corporation think tank in Palo Alto, Calif., says, "The picture is one of a country that has technology and some physical capacity to produce nuclear weapons, but they still haven't taken the next step of stockpiling material capable of being turned into nuclear weapons. There seems to be internal disagreement in the Iranian leadership on the issue." He cites Khamenei's recent declaration that nuclear weapons are *haram*, or forbidden in Islam, and the fact that the influence of President Mahmoud Ahmadinejad, who talks the most about developing a nuclear program, "seems to be in decline."

The regime's insistence that its program is for peaceful purposes has "helped to build up support domestically for the nuclear program, and everyone is committed as a matter of national pride," says Riccardo Alcaro, a foreign policy analyst at the Italian Institute of International Affairs in Rome. "If the regime was now seen to be producing nuclear weapons, it would lose credibility with its own people. Crossing that threshold would be difficult — unless Iran were attacked. In that case Iranians would be much more understanding."

As 2011 ended, Iran's navy announced that it had successfully tested long- and short-range missiles, but they weren't able to carry nuclear payloads. [15]

"Iran is very dangerous," Israeli President Shimon Peres said, but "there's no need to get hysterical about the threat that it poses." Israel's nuclear arsenal, he implied, would deter the Iranians from bombing Israel. [16]

Experts say the international sanctions — along with the killings of at least five Iranian nuclear scientists and a 2010 cyber attack that temporarily crippled the nuclear program's computers — have delayed Iran's nuclear program. It would now take anywhere from less than two to as long as five years to produce a bomb, experts say.

As the West and Iran's neighbors fret over the nuclear threat posed by the Iranian regime, here are some of the questions being debated:

Can economic sanctions stop Iran from building a nuclear weapon?

On Jan. 23 the 27 members of the European Union, striking at what *The Guardian* newspaper called "the Islamic republic's lifeblood," agreed to embargo Iranian oil imports. The EU also froze the Iran central bank's assets in Europe and banned transactions involving gold, precious metals and diamonds. The measures amounted to "an unprecedented package of sanctions on Iran," said a joint statement issued by the British, German and French leaders.

"Until Iran comes to the table, we will be united behind strong measures to undermine the regime's ability to fund its nuclear programme," the statement said. [17]

"To avoid any military solution, which could have irreparable consequences, we have decided to go further down the path of sanctions," Alain Juppé, France's foreign minister, told reporters. "It is a good decision that sends a strong message and which I hope will persuade Iran that it must change its position, change its line and accept the dialogue that we propose." [18]

A month earlier, the United States had passed legislation making it illegal for any U.S. bank to do business with any foreign institution transacting business with Iran's central bank.

Whether the latest round of sanctions will achieve what earlier constraints have not remains to be seen. The United States first launched sanctions against Iran in 1979 and has been tightening the economic screws ever since. In 2006, in an effort to force fuller compliance with the IAEA, the U.N. Security Council adopted the first of four economic sanctions resolutions.

Iran today finds it increasingly difficult "to do business with any reputable bank internationally" or to conduct transactions in either euros or U.S. dollars, said White House national security official Tommy Vietor. [19]

Moreover, "the oil and gas sectors are not drawing anywhere near the international capital they need," wrote William C. Ramsay, energy adviser at the French Institute of Foreign Affairs (IFRI) in Paris. [20]

Yet Iran's nuclear program is well advanced, and progress — while slow at times — has never halted for very long. "Sanctions haven't failed in squeezing Iran and making it suffer, but they have failed in their objective" to halt Iran's enrichment program, says Middle East specialist Nasr of Tufts University.

That's because many countries enforce the sanctions poorly or refuse to abide by them — creating holes in the sanctions net big enough to drive an oil tanker through. For instance, despite a raft of U.S. and U.N. sanctions, EU trade with Iran in 2010, totaled $33.4 billion ($14.6 billion in European exports and $18.8 billion in imports). [21] The same year, about 60 companies in Germany — Iran's second-largest trading partner after the United Arab Emirates — registered to attend an international gas and oil refining convention in Tehran, an action that "violated international law," according to a German official. In addition, German Chancellor Angela Merkel's retired official jet, embarrassingly, was somehow sold to the sanctioned Iranian airline Mahan. [22]

Under pressure from the U.S. and Israeli governments, Berlin last year began to tighten controls on its Iran trade, according to *Der Spiegel* magazine. The Israelis provided the names of companies and individuals who "help prop up the Iranian regime," and some German exports were being used "for dubious purposes," the article said. When the Israelis showed that Daimler heavy trucks were being converted into rocket launchers, Berlin banned exports of heavy trucks. [23]

AFP/Getty Images/Atta Kenare

Demonstrators hold portraits of assassinated Iranian nuclear scientist Majid Shahriari during a protest in front of the British Embassy in downtown Tehran on Dec. 12, 2010. At least five Iranian nuclear scientists have been killed in recent years in an apparent effort to slow Iran's nuclear program. Iranians have blamed the killings on British, U.S. or Israeli intelligence services.

Taken together with Washington's latest sanctions, Europe's strong action on Jan. 23 raised the stakes dramatically, prompting Iran's sharp response. "If any disruption happens regarding the sale of Iranian oil, the Strait of Hormuz will definitely be closed," declared Mohammed Kossari, deputy head of Iran's parliamentary Foreign Affairs and National Security Commission. [24]

But even if the EU action succeeds in plugging European gaps in Iran's sanctions net, it's still riddled with Asian holes. For example, the new rules will not affect Iran's trade with China, which imported a fifth of Iran's oil exports in 2010, nor will it disrupt trade with Japan, which bought 17 percent of Iran's oil in 2010. India bought another 16 percent and South Korea, 9 percent. By comparison, Italy bought 10 percent in 2010. [25]

Indeed, skepticism is rife that the sanctions won't work. "Sanctions tend to punish citizens more than they do the regime," observes Kuwait-based Alanoud Al Sharekh, corresponding senior fellow for Middle East politics at London's International Institute of Strategic Studies.

But that's partly the point, said a senior administration official. "The question is whether people in the government feel pressure from the fact that there's public discontent," the unnamed official told *The Washington Post* recently. [26]

That isn't happening, according to Al Sharekh. "In spite of the problems, there's belief in the [Iranian] leadership and the ideology," she says.

Russia, which opposes the sanctions, called the latest EU action a mistake. "Under this kind of pressure, Iran will not agree to any kind of concessions or change in its policies," the Russian Foreign Ministry said in a statement. [27]

Would a nuclear Iran trigger an arms race in the Middle East?

Saudi Prince Turki's belief that a nuclear-armed Iran would lead to "a cascade of nuclear proliferation" in the Middle East is widely held. British Foreign Secretary William Hague said in a recent interview that an Iranian breakthrough in producing nuclear weapons "threatens the whole region with nuclear proliferation."

The U.S. National Intelligence Council expressed the same concern in its "Global Trends 2025" report. A nuclear Iran, it said, could well encourage other nations "to consider their own nuclear ambitions." [28]

Shmuel Bar, director of studies at the Institute of Policy Studies think tank in Herzliya, Israel, asked the question: Could "a polynuclear Middle East be avoided in the wake of Iran's acquisition of nuclear weapons?" The answer, he concluded, "seems to be clearly negative." Rather, he wrote, a nuclear Iran would "undoubtedly intensify the drive of other states in the region for nuclear weapons." [29]

Not so, counters Tufts University's Nasr. The threat of nuclear proliferation is "more a talking point than a reality," he says. "No Middle East countries went nuclear when Israel went nuclear. Egypt and Turkey would have no motivation to follow suit. Besides, it takes time to build up a nuclear arsenal of say 20 to 30 nuclear warheads — perhaps 10 years or more."

Some experts point out that when Communist China went nuclear in the 1950s, Beijing's neighbors were dissuaded from following suit because the United States offered to protect them from a nuclear attack. The same thing happened after North Korea developed nuclear weapons.

But that approach was less likely to work in this instance, argues Bar, because of "the decline of American stature in the region after the withdrawal from Iraq" — and Washington's apparent failure, at least so far, to keep Iran from developing nuclear weapons.

C H R O N O L O G Y

1950s-1960s *U.S. consolidates influence in Iran by helping to remove nationalist leader and installing pro-Western monarch.*

Aug. 20, 1953 After Prime Minister Mohammed Mossadegh nationalizes Iran's oil industry, he is overthrown with help of U.S. and British intelligence agencies. . . . Shah Mohammed Reza Pahlavi is put in power.

January 1963 Shah launches campaign to modernize Iran, including land and economic reform and improving conditions for women — which alienates religious clergy.

1970s-1980s *Rising discontent forces shah from office. Shiite Islamic theocracy is established. Hostage- taking at U.S. Embassy sours U.S.-Iran relations for decades. Iraq and Iran go to war.*

1978 Civil unrest against shah's dictatorial rule breaks out, inflamed by taped sermons by exiled Shiite clergyman Ayatollah Ruhollah Khomeini. Shah imposes martial law.

1979 Shah leaves Iran on Jan. 16. . . . Khomeini returns, and Islamic republic is established following referendum.

Nov. 4, 1979 Iranian militants storm U.S. Embassy in Tehran, demanding shah's return to Iran to stand trial. Fifty-two Americans are taken hostage and held for 444 days, leading to ongoing animosity.

September 1980 Iraq attacks Iran, triggering eight-year war.

Aug. 20, 1988 U.N. brokers peace in Iran-Iraq war.

1990s-2000s *Iran resumes abandoned nuclear program. West suspects Iran wants to develop nuclear weapons and imposes sanctions to pressure Iran to accept U.N. inspections. Iranian regime suppresses reform.*

Aug. 25, 1992 Iran re-starts nuclear program begun under shah's rule.

1995 U.S. imposes oil and trade embargo because of Iran's efforts to acquire nuclear arms, hostility toward Israel and alleged sponsorship of "terrorism." Iran denies the charges; says its nuclear program is for peaceful use.

Aug. 15, 2002 Iranian exiles say Iran is building two secret nuclear sites — a secret uranium-enrichment plant at Natanz and another in Arak.

Nov. 12, 2003 Iran agrees to suspend uranium enrichment, allows tougher U.N. inspections. International Atomic Energy Agency (IAEA) finds no evidence of weapons program.

Nov. 14, 2004 Britain, France Germany and Iran sign Paris accord, reaffirming Iran's commitment not to acquire nuclear weapons.

Nov. 16, 2005 Iran reverses course and resumes enrichment program, breaking IAEA seals at Natanz nuclear facility.

Dec. 23, 2006 U.N. Security Council imposes sanctions on Iran's trade in nuclear materials and technology.

Oct. 25, 2007 U.S. slaps toughest-yet sanctions on Iran.

2009 Five Security Council members plus Germany offer to enrich Iran's uranium. Iranians refuse. Government cracks down on protests over disputed presidential election.

2010-Present *Despite persistent U.N. requests for more transparency in its nuclear program, Iran remains defiant and evasive. West increases sanctions. Danger rises of possible military intervention to halt Iran's uranium enrichment.*

2011 Iran strongly denies IAEA report saying it could be secretly trying to develop nuclear weapons. . . . United States bars any foreign bank that does business with Iran Central Bank from dealing with U.S. financial institutions.

2012 European Union agrees on Jan. 23 to embargo Iranian oil imports, starting in July. . . . Tehran threatens to block critical Strait of Hormuz oil-shipping lanes if Europeans put sanctions in place.

Decades of Sanctions, But No Surrender

Some companies still find ways to get around them.

" A *nation boycotted is a nation that is in sight of surrender. Apply this economic, peaceful, silent, deadly remedy, and there will be no need for force.*"

The speaker was not President Obama grappling with the Iran conundrum, or even one of his immediate predecessors. It was President Woodrow Wilson, who believed "no modern nation could resist" the power of economic sanctions. [1]

But in reality, sanctions have a poor record of bringing recalcitrant nations to heel. Sanctions failed to topple the late Iraqi leader Saddam Hussein, former Serbian President Slobodan Milosevic or longtime Libyan dictator Moammar Gadhafi. And although the West has been piling on sanctions against Iran for more than 30 years, the regime doesn't seem to be in sight of surrender — at least not yet. [2] Some say sanctions worked in ending apartheid in South Africa because they hurt the middle class, which was able to pressure the government. But there were other factors at play, as well, such as frustration at being excluded from international sporting events, a younger generation more sensitive to the injustices of the system and political pressure from the British Commonwealth.

The Obama administration retains its faith in sanctions, coupled with diplomacy, to convince the Iranians to halt their uranium enrichment effort and agree to more transparency for their nuclear program. "The path we're on — the economic sanctions and the diplomatic pressure — does seem to me to be having an effect," Gen. Martin Dempsey, chairman of the Joint Chiefs of Staff, said recently. "It's premature to be deciding that the economic and diplomatic approach is inadequate." [3]

Sanctions also have been imposed on Iran by the U.N. Security Council, Canada and the 27-member European Union.

After the American Embassy in Tehran was seized along with 52 hostages more than 30 years ago, President Jimmy Carter froze all Iranian assets in U.S. banks. In 1984, after Iran was implicated in bombings of French and U.S. military bases in Beirut that killed 299, export controls were imposed on dual-use products and a long list of products, from helicopters to scuba gear. [4]

Tougher U.S. trade restrictions were imposed when Iran appeared interested in developing nuclear weapons: the Iran-Iraq Arms Non-Proliferation Act of 1992 and the Iran, North Korea and Syria Nonproliferation Act of 2000. Taken together, they banned the transfer of equipment or technology that could be used to "make a material contribution to the development of weapons of mass destruction." [5]

In 1995, President Bill Clinton banned U.S. trade and investment with Iran, making it virtually impossible for American companies to do business in Tehran. Then the Iran and Libya Act (ILSA) of 1996 banned energy investments in either country by foreign companies. Libya was removed from ILSA after it renounced its nuclear program in 2003.

The U.S. Treasury Department administers the American sanctions program. Its website lists sanctions covered by successive laws, executive orders and other decisions, right down to a ban on importing Persian carpets. It also lists scores of banks and other organizations affected by the sanctions. [6]

Many companies have figured out ways to get around the sanctions, even tlthough the United States imposes prison sentences and fines of up to $100 million on convicted "sanction busters."

The United States recently listed four shipping companies in the Mediterranean island-state of Malta that allegedly fronted for the Islamic Republic of Iran Shipping Lines. [7] The Gulf emirate of Dubai has long been a transit point for goods to Iran, legal and otherwise, but Dubai calls the process "re-exporting" rather than "sanctions busting." Iranian firms open offices in Dubai and import the prohibited goods ostensibly to the emirate. But then cargo planes and Gulf freighters transport the goods across the water to nearby Iran. [8]

In one of the highest-profile cases against sanction violators, Britain's Lloyds TSB Bank paid the U.S. government

$350 million in 2009 to settle a case involving cash transfers out of the country for clients in Iran, Libya and Sudan. [9] Sanctions were imposed on Sudan in 1997 for its alleged support of terrorism and persecution of its Christian minority.

The United States also has frozen the financial assets and property of members of the elite Iranian Revolutionary Guard Corps, Quds commando forces and several leading military officers. On Dec. 31, the United States went one step further and banned financial institutions from doing business with the Iran central bank.

International Sanctions

Since 2006, the U.N. Security Council has passed four resolutions imposing sanctions on Iran — each tied to requests for better access for IAEA inspectors and the halting of Iran's uranium enrichment. The first banned the shipment of arms, nuclear materials or technology to Iran. The second and third — in 2007 and 2008, respectively — froze the assets of organizations and some individuals involved in Iran's nuclear program.

But the toughest sanctions came in 2010, when the Security Council tightened the arms embargo, banned international travel for those involved in Iran's nuclear program and froze the funds, businesses and other assets of the Iranian Revolutionary Guard and the Islamic Republic of Iran Shipping Lines. [10] The Security Council listed 41 Iranian individuals subject to travel bans and assets freeze and of 75 entities subject to assets freeze. [11]

As for the European Union, in June 2008 it moved away from a policy of negotiation with Iran and froze the assets of 40 individuals and entities doing business with Bank Melli, Iran's biggest bank. This began what the Congressional Research Service, Congress' nonpartisan research arm, called "a narrowing of past differences between the United States and its allies on the issue." [12]

By June 2010, the EU had adopted many of the major U.S. sanctions, including a ban on investment in the Iranian oil and gas industries and doing business with the Iran central bank. It also published the names of 442 entities on its sanctions list.

Then in January the EU embargoed crude oil, petroleum and petrochemical products from Iran, starting in July. Contracts concluded before Jan. 23, 2012, were allowed to be executed — but only until July. [13]

Given that the EU is Iran's second-largest trading partner — some observers ask: If European sanctions don't bring the Iranians to the table, what will? [14]

— Roland Flamini

[1]Barry C. Hufbauer, "Economic Sanctions: America's Economic Folly," Council on Foreign Relations, Oct. 10, 1997, www.cfr.org/trade/economic-sanctions-americas-folly/p62.

[2]Simon Jenkins, "Why is Britain ramping up sanctions against Iran?" *The Guardian*, Jan. 3, 2012, www.guardian.co.uk/commentisfree/2012/jan/03/britain-ramoing-sanctions-against-iran-washington.

[3]Elad Benar, "Obama: Our Sanctions on Iran 'Had a Lot of Bite,' " IsraelNationalNews.com, Jan. 27, 2012, www.israelnationalnews.com/News/News.aspx/152169#.TybRi9VLaf8.

[4]Greg Bruno, "The Lengthening List of Iran Sanctions," Council on Foreign Relations, Nov. 22, 2011, www.cfr.org/iran/lengthening-list-iran-sanctions/p20258.

[5]"Iran, North Korea and Syria Nonproliferation Act Sanctions," www.state.gov/t/isn/inksna/index.htm.

[6]"An Overview of OFAC Regulations Governing Sanctions against Iran," U.S. Treasury, www.treasury.gov/resource-center/sanctions/Programs/Documents/iran.pdf.

[7]"Malta companies on Iran sanctions busting list," *Times of Malta*, Aug. 27, 2010, www.timesofmalta.com/articles/view/20101027/local/us-lists-malta-based-companies-individuals-involved-in-iran-sanctions-busting.333387.

[8]Raymond Barrett, "Sanctions busting is in Dubai's DNA," *The Guardian*, April 20, 2010, www.guardian.co.uk/commentisfree/2010/apr/20/iran-sanctions-busting-dubai.

[9]Gil Montia, "Lloyds TSB settles US sanctions case with $250 million," *Banking Times*, Jan. 11, 2009, www.bankingtimes.co.uk/tag/sanctions/.

[10]Kenneth Katzman, "Iran Sanctions," Congressional Research Service, Jan. 6, 2012, www.fas.org/sgp/crs/mideast/RS20871.pdf.

[11]"Individuals and entities designated as subject to travel ban and assets freeze, etc.," United Nations Security Council, August 2010, www.un.org/sc/committees/1737/pdf/1737ConsolidatedList.pdf.

[12]Kenneth Katzman, "Iran Sanctions," Congressional Research Service, April 9, 2010, http://fpc.state.gov/documents/organization/141587.pdf.

[13]"EU publishes updated list of sanctions on Iran," Kuwait News Agency, Jan. 30, 2012, www.kuna.net.kw/ArticleDetails.aspx?id=2217118&language=en.

[14]Najimeh Bozorgmehr and Geoff Dyer, "China overtakes EU as Iran's top trading partner," *Financial Times*, Feb. 8, 2010, www.ft.com/intl/cms/s/0/f220dfac-14d4-11df-8f1d-00144feab49a.html#axzz1l6Bbzi00.

Al Sharekh of IISS contends that a nuclear Iran "doesn't make much difference to the Gulf Arabs. There's a lot of antagonism towards Iran in the Gulf, but Iran is the 'frenemy,' " she says, meaning a friend who can still create problems. "We share a waterway, and we're too close to be a nuclear target. This is a very crowded neighborhood. From the neighbors' point of view, a nuclear Iran is more a flexing of the muscles." [30]

There's also a cost factor, she says. "At the end of the day it's also an economic issue. Kuwait is still paying for the [1991] invasion of Iraq, and we're in the middle of a world-wide recession." [31]

However, many think the predominantly Sunni Saudis would likely want to assume a more responsive posture to a nuclear-armed Shiite Iran. In June, Prince Turki told NATO officials that if Iran developed nuclear weapons, Saudi Arabia would have no choice but to do likewise, according to a British press report. [32]

That wouldn't necessarily mean the kingdom would have to produce its own bombs, says Kagan of the American Enterprise Institute. "It could order them from Pakistan," he says. "The Saudis financed the Pakistani stockpile," which amounts to having "purchased" them.

Is military action against Iran inevitable?

"No doubt there is a danger there, but the Obama administration doesn't want to go there," says Iran expert Nasr, at Tufts University. And anyway "we may have passed the point" when attacking the Iranian nuclear facilities will make any lasting difference. The danger, he says, is from "the chances of war happening as a result of escalating the sanctions."

Both the Obama administration, with its action against the Iran central bank, and the European Union with its Iran oil embargo, have ratcheted up the sanctions to a level that might cause too much economic pain, potentially forcing the Iranians to take military action.

Tehran's threats to close the Strait of Hormuz are one result, says Nasr. Not that the Iranians would deliberately take on the U.S. Navy: Some covert action through surrogates in Afghanistan or Pakistan is more likely. But an incident in the strait could spark a shooting war; and mines and small gunboats could do a lot of damage before American warships asserted their superiority.

Furthermore, U.S. spy chiefs warned Congress on Jan. 31 that, if pushed hard enough, Iran might launch terrorist attacks inside the United States. They said the alleged plot, uncovered last October, to assassinate the Saudi Arabian ambassador in Washington might foreshadow other attempts.

"Sanctions were once enthusiastically embraced because they were free and stable, but they have become a factor of instability," Nasr says.

Others recommend more aggressive action by the West. The United States should "conduct a surgical strike against Iran's nuclear facilities, pull back and absorb the inevitable round of retaliation and then seek to quickly de-escalate the crisis," says Matthew Kroenig, an assistant professor of government at Georgetown University and a fellow of the Council on Foreign Relations. Prior to the attack, he adds, the United States would embark on a diplomatic effort to assure the Iranians that the strike was not an attempt to destroy the regime.

But even he concedes that military action is unlikely to halt Iran's nuclear program. At best it will "significantly" set it back from three to 10 years, "buying a lot more time for diplomacy."

For the Israelis, however, waiting for sanctions to succeed means time is running out for a pre-emptive strike. "It is still possible from the Israeli point of view to launch an attack within a few months," says Israeli military commentator Ron Ben-Yishai. While the nuclear facility in Natanz is vulnerable to air assault with penetration bombs, a newer facility near the holy city of Qom — built up to 450 feet deep inside a mountain —"is not so susceptible to air strike," he says, even with bunker-busting bombs. And the Iranians are moving their main uranium-enrichment operation to that underground site.

Unlike the Iraqi or Syrian nuclear facilities — both of which the Israelis bombed out of existence — a unilateral attack on the Iranian facilities would not be "an easy option," says Nasr, because Iran's facilities are widespread and would require "sustained aerial bombing."

Indeed, Iran's nuclear program is spread across a country the size of Britain and Germany combined, says Alcaro, of the Institute of International Affairs in Rome. Thus, no one thinks an attack will destroy the program, he says. Rather than deterring the Iranians, "The program is more likely to go forward underground," he contends.

Should the United States and/or Israel attack Iran, they likely would become locked into "a cycle of facing the same problem every three to 10 years," Alcaro adds.

The only reason to attempt an attack would be to weaken the regime so as to create the conditions for a coup or insurrection that would install a government more responsive to U.S. demands, he says. But that probably won't happen, he adds, because, "the nuclear program is an issue of national pride; even a reformist government acceptable to the West would still want one."

Thus, a surgical strike, says Nasr, would probably only "encourage the Iranians to accelerate their program."

And Denis Bauchard, Middle East specialist at the French Institute of International Relations, points out that Iran's determination to establish its "nuclear sovereignty" is total, leaving little hope for a negotiated solution.

"History teaches that engagement and diplomacy pay dividends that military threats do not," Thomas R. Pickering and William H. Luers, two former senior U.S. diplomats, wrote recently. "Deployment of military force can bring the immediate illusion of 'success' but always results in unforeseen consequences and collateral damage that complicate further the achievement of America's main objectives." [33]

BACKGROUND

Persian Roots

Persia was the center of Sunni learning until the rise of the conservative Safavid empire, a militant Shiite theocracy that governed the country from 1501-1732 and established a Shiite branch of Islam as the official religion. The predominantly Sunni population had no choice but to convert or leave. [34]

When the empire ended in the 18th century, Shiism survived as the dominant religion. For the next 200 years the country "lay in decay" as "[b]andit chiefs and feudal lords plundered it at will, [and] people yearned for strong central rule and stability." [35]

In 1921 Reza Khan Pahlavi, a Persian army officer, overthrew the reigning house, set up secular dynastic rule and — to differentiate his people from their Arab neighbors — changed the name of the country to Iran, which means Land of the Aryans.

The Shiite clergy "accepted the legitimacy of the rule of monarchs so long as they did not violate religious law [or] harm Shiism," explains Tufts' Nasr. [36]

The discovery of oil in Iran early in the 20th century drew the interest of the British and Americans. Until the early 1950s, the dominant Western presence in Iran was British. The Anglo-Iranian Oil Co. gave the British a majority interest in Iran's oil, and London exercised considerable political influence in Tehran. But in 1951, Iran's popular, newly elected liberal-democrat prime minister, Mohammad Mossadegh, nationalized the oil industry, at considerable financial loss to British interests. [37] Two years later, he was ousted in a coup organized jointly by the CIA and British Intelligence, mainly to safeguard Anglo-American oil interests. [38] America's role in Mossadegh's removal generated anti-American feeling in the region for the first time.

Shah Mohammad Reza Pahlavi gained control over the country, with growing U.S. support. During the 1950s, Iran was a frontline state in America's Cold War with the Soviet Union and the most important U.S. ally in the Middle East. About the size of Alaska, Iran shared a 1,200-mile border with the Soviet Union and served as an Allied listening post into the Soviet bloc. It also was one of the few Muslim countries to recognize Israel and to sell it oil. U.S. military aid to Iran increased from $10 million in 1960 to its highest level of just over $5 billion in 1977. [39]

But the Pahlavi regime was autocratic and tightly controlled by SAVAK, the nation's hated, CIA-trained, national security organization, notorious for its arrests and torture of political opponents and dissidents. The shah did introduce some reforms — agrarian reform, increased literacy, greater participation by women in society — but corruption was rife, and most citizens did not benefit from the country's oil wealth.

Shiite Radicalism

Social unrest grew, fomented by the Shiite clergy, which opposed Iran's secularization. Cassettes of anti-government sermons by exiled cleric and spiritual leader, Ayatollah Ruhollah Khomeini, were sold in the bazaars. Khomeini's violent rhetoric called the shah "the Jewish agent, the American serpent whose head must be smashed with a stone." [40]

By 1978, mosques had become centers of opposition to the regime. Huge anti-regime demonstrations erupted across the country, and up to a million protesters swarmed the streets of Tehran, including many women in chadors, the head-to-toe black covering mandated by the mullahs.

President Jimmy Carter pressured the shah to avoid bloodshed, so the army did not intervene. Even after some demonstrations turned into violent clashes with security forces, the Carter administration continued to urge the shah to try to ease tensions by bringing moderate opposition figures into the government and calling for elections.

On Jan. 16, 1979, the shah left Iran — ostensibly to seek medical treatment abroad. He would never return. Instead, Khomeini came home in triumph less than a month later, and Iran was declared an Islamic republic, with Khomeini as its supreme leader. Within less than a year, all members of the secular government had been purged, and the clerics were in control. A new age of Shiite radicalism had begun.

On Nov. 4, 1979, a group of student followers of Khomeini stormed and occupied the U.S. Embassy in Tehran, in retaliation for President Carter allowing the deposed shah to enter the United States for cancer treatment. [41] Khomeini publicly approved the takeover, calling the embassy "a nest of spies."

Eventually, 52 American diplomats, staff and Marine guards were held captive for 444 days, despite a failed rescue attempt in April 1980. [42] Negotiations to free the hostages — mediated by Algeria — continued, even as the Carter administration froze $8 billion in Iranian assets in U.S. banks and embargoed Iranian oil exports — the first of a long series of sanctions. The United States has not bought Iranian oil since.

On Jan. 20, 1981, the hostages were released within minutes of President Ronald Reagan's inauguration as Carter's successor, a move designed to cause Carter the most humiliation. In return, the United States agreed not to interfere in Iranian politics. [43] By then, the shah was dead, and Iran had been attacked by Iraq in a conflict that was to last eight years.

War With Iraq

The previous September, Iraqi leader Saddam Hussein had taken advantage of Iran's domestic turmoil to take possession of Shatt al-Arab, a waterway disputed by both countries that flows into the Persian Gulf, and some adjacent oil fields. Centuries-old Sunni-versus-Shia and Arab-versus-Persian religious and ethnic tensions contributed to the outbreak of hostilities, as did a personal animosity between Saddam and Khomeini. Ten years

earlier, Saddam had expelled the ayatollah after he had taken refuge in Iraq. [44]

Iran threw waves of young men and boys against Saddam's heavy armor in a conflict that developed into trench warfare reminiscent of the bloody fighting in World War I. And, like the Germans in WWI, Saddam even used mustard gas against the Iranians. In Tehran, fountains ran water dyed red to symbolize the blood of martyred Iranian soldiers.

In 1988, exhausted, economically battered and deadlocked, both sides agreed to a U.N.-brokered cease fire. Iraq's territorial gains were returned to Iran. More than a million soldiers and civilians perished in what was essentially an exercise in futility.

As the war was winding down, two incidents served to further sour U.S.-Iranian relations. In 1988, the *USS Samuel B. Roberts*, an American frigate, hit an Iranian mine in the Strait of Hormuz. In retaliation, U.S. forces destroyed two offshore oil platforms, sank two Iranian frigates and damaged a third. "The aim was to teach the Iranians a lesson," the BBC recalled in a recent analysis. "The conclusion was clear — Iran's conventional naval forces were no match for U.S. sea power in a straight fight." [45]

Weeks later, the *USS Vincennes*, a guided missile cruiser, shot down an Iranian commercial jet carrying 290 passengers and crew. Washington said the *Vincennes* mistook the plane for a military aircraft, and refused to apologize or admit any wrongdoing. [46]

Driven by anti-U.S. sentiment and its perceived mission to spread Shiism, Iran between 1980 and 1996 strongly supported Islamist terrorist groups such as Hezbollah (in Lebanon), Hamas, Palestinian Islamic Jihad, the Supreme Council for Islamic Revolution in Iraq (SCIRI), the Afghan Northern Alliance and its precursors and groups in Bahrain, Saudi Arabia, Kuwait, Egypt, Algeria and elsewhere. But since then, as Iran's revolutionary fervor has dissipated somewhat, Tehran's support for terrorist organizations has became more focused on its own strategic interests. By the mid- and late-1990s, the Iranians had reduced their support to Hezbollah and Hamas. [47]

That may have been in part because Iran was at a kind of political cross-roads. In the summer of 1989, Ayatollah Khamenei had succeeded Khomeini as supreme leader, and progressives were making inroads in

Iranian politics. In 1997, the moderate Mohammad Khatami won the presidential election with 70 percent of the vote, beating the conservative ruling elite.

Stronger Sanctions

Beginning in the mid-1990s, Iran's efforts to resume its stalled nuclear program would escalate tensions between Tehran and the West.

In 1995, President Bill Clinton imposed new, stricter sanctions on Iran, arguing that Iran supported international terrorism, was trying to undermine the Middle East peace process and was acquiring weapons of mass destruction. [48] The new restrictions blocked trade in technology, goods or services to or from Iran and prohibited U.S. citizens from investing in Iranian projects.

In August 1996 Congress tightened the screws even further by passing the Iran-Libya Sanctions Act (ILSA), which extended restrictions on energy-related investments to foreign-owned companies. The new law, said a report by Chatham House, a British foreign affairs think tank, was designed to force foreign companies to decide whether they wanted to "do business with Iran and Libya or the United States." [49]

Despite the sanctions, U.S.-Iran relations appeared ready to thaw a bit in September 2000, when Iranian President Khatami remained in the hall at the annual opening of the U.N. General Assembly to listen to President Clinton address the body. [50] Later, Clinton reciprocated, breaking a tradition since 1979 of U.S. officials leaving the chamber when an Iranian leader spoke. Some American import restrictions were removed, including on Iranian carpets, but not on oil. And Secretary of State Madeleine Albright met with the Iranian foreign minister Kamal Kharrazi — the first such meeting since the United States broke off diplomatic ties with Tehran in 1979.

Then, after the Sept. 11, 2001, terrorist attacks in the United States, Iran quietly offered support for the U.S. campaign in Afghanistan, for example, by blocking the retreating Taliban from crossing into Iranian territory. That November, Secretary of State Colin Powell shook hands with Kharrazi — a simple yet historic gesture.

But in his Jan. 29, 2002, State of the Union address, President George W. Bush declared Iran a member of "an axis of evil" (along with North Korea and Syria) that was "arming to threaten the peace of the world." [51] Two days later, National Security Adviser Condoleezza Rice said, "Iran's direct support of regional and global terrorism and its aggressive efforts to acquire weapons of mass destruction belie any good intentions." Her statement was reinforced by a CIA report claiming that Tehran was "attempting to develop a domestic capability to produce various types of weapons — chemical, biological and nuclear — and their delivery systems." [52]

Nuclear Program

Iran has always claimed it needed nuclear power in order to shift from its over-reliance on oil for domestic energy. With oil exports accounting for 50-76 percent of the Iranian government's revenues, the country prefers to sell as much oil as possible rather than burn it for electricity. [53]

With the help of the Germans and the Americans — before the revolution — and the Russians after it, Iran built a nuclear power station in Bushehr on the Persian Gulf. Enriched uranium is needed to run a nuclear power station, but only enriched to single-digit percentage levels. To make a nuclear weapon, uranium must be enriched to 90 percent or higher. Although Iran has not yet enriched uranium to weapons-grade levels, it has enriched some up to 20 percent of the strength needed, according to the IAEA.

In short, for nearly a decade Western governments have tried using negotiations, threats and U.N. sanctions to persuade the Iranians to either import their enriched uranium from elsewhere or make their enrichment operation more transparent. So far, the Iranians have refused to comply.

Talks between Iran and Britain, France and Germany got off to a promising start in 2004, when the Iranians agreed to suspend all uranium enrichment activities while negotiations continued and to allow the IAEA to inspect its nuclear sites. Some observers linked Tehran's concessions to the U.S. invasion of Iraq the previous year. The Iranian leadership had been cowed into cooperating by the proximity of a strong U.S. fighting force across the border, they said.

The most optimistic moment came in March 2005, when the United States joined the negotiations, and the Western team became known as 3+1 (and eventually as 3+2 when Russia was added, and then 5+1 with the inclusion of China). As a goodwill gesture the United States offered to supply spare parts for Iran's civil aviation fleet.

EU Trade with Iran Rose, Despite Sanctions

Even though the United States and the U.N. had imposed sanctions on trade with Iran, the European Union (EU) increased its trade with Iran more than 17 percent between 2009 and 2010. In January, the EU adopted its own sanctions against trade with Iran, increasing international pressure designed to stop the regime from enriching uranium, considered a precursor to the production of nuclear weapons.

Value of EU Trade (Imports and Exports) with Iran, 2009-2010

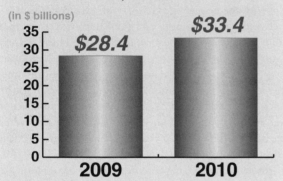

Source: "Iran: EU Bilateral Trade and Trade With the World," Directorate General for Trade, European Commission, January 2012, trade.ec.europa.eu/doclib/docs/2006/september/tradoc_113392.pdf

Then the Iranians insisted on resuming uranium enrichment as a condition for continuing negotiations, and the talks collapsed. [54]

The election of Ahmadinejad, then mayor of Tehran, as president in 2005 — when negotiators had hoped for the more pragmatic Akbar Hashemi Rafsanjani — further hardened Iran's position.

The battle then moved to the U.N. Security Council, which between 2006 and 2010 passed four resolutions, starting with an IAEA resolution demanding more inspections. Each subsequent resolution piled on more economic sanctions and restrictions, including freezing the assets of the Republic of Iran Shipping Lines and the powerful Iranian Revolutionary Guard Corps and authorizing the inspection and seizure of shipments violating the sanctions.

The Iranian facilities in question included the nuclear plant at Bushehr, the Isfahan plant, where "natural" uranium is converted into uranium hexafluoride — a gas used in centrifuges to create weapons-grade uranium — and Natanz, an enrichment facility where the Iranians were said to be installing centrifuges. In 2009, Iran revealed the existence of another heavily fortified plant near the holy city of Qom, where the Iranians told the IAEA it was transferring its operations to enrich uranium to 20 percent levels.

In 2009, the world reacted with shock when the Iranian regime brutally suppressed huge "Green" protest demonstrations that erupted after Ahmadinejad, who had trailed badly in the polls, somehow won an overwhelming re-election victory over his progressive challenger, Mir Hussein Mousavi. [55] Youthful supporters of Mousavi called for a more stable economy, greater freedom at home and a friendlier foreign policy.

The Obama administration had remained aloof from the international chorus of criticism of the regime. "We do not interfere in Iran's internal affairs," Obama said at the time. But in December 2011, as his re-election campaign began heating up, his GOP challengers criticized Obama for not supporting the Iranian protesters in 2009. The White House promptly issued sanctions against two senior members of the Iranian military for their part in "the violent crackdown in the summer of 2009." [56]

Inevitably, Iran's nuclear ambitions have spurred war talk. Both the United States and Israel are rumored to have contingency plans for a military strike against Tehran's nuclear facilities. For some years the accepted version of events was of Washington restraining an increasingly apprehensive Jerusalem and urging that sanctions be given a chance to work.

"Everybody says a military attack should be a last resort," says Ben-Yishai, the Israeli military affairs expert. "The question is, 'When is the last resort?' " The notion of a nuclear Israel and a nuclear Iran creating a system of mutual deterrence doesn't wash in Israel because of Iran's declared hostility to the Jewish state's very existence.

"Deterrence worked during the Cold War, because both sides were rational and responsible centers with fresh memories of World War II," argues Ben-Yishai.

"The Iranian leaders are fanatic clerics with visions of martyrdom. We don't know what they'll do, and we can't live under the threat of doomsday."

Tensions rose again in November, when the IAEA reported for the first time that the Iranians could be working on a nuclear explosive device — although the agency did not say they were already capable of producing a bomb. [57]

"The Americans and the Europeans . . . have succeeded in turning Iran's nuclear program into an issue of international security," says Alcaro of the Italian Institute of International Affairs. What happens next, he adds, will depend largely on whether the Americans and Europeans can maintain a united front with Russia and China.

"Under pressure from all the major powers, Iran may be willing to give in on the question of enriching uranium — provided a mechanism can be found to save appearance," Alcaro says.

CURRENT SITUATION

Tightening Sanctions

IAEA inspectors were in Iran in late January for their first visit in three years, during which time the Iranians have refused to even discuss allegations that they were developing nuclear weapons. "We're looking forward to the start of a dialogue," the agency's deputy director, Herman Nackaerts, declared, "a dialogue that is overdue since very long." [58]

The three-day visit — during which the IAEA team was expected to inspect several locations, including the new underground facility deep inside a mountain near Qom, could greatly influence the direction and urgency of the U.S.-led efforts to halt Iran's nuclear program.

Both the Obama administration and the EU have followed up their most robust economic moves so far against the Iranian regime with a strong barrage of rhetoric on both sides of the Atlantic.

Obama used his State of the Union address to warn that "America is determined to prevent Iran from getting a nuclear weapon, and I will take no options off the table to achieve that goal." He added, however, that, "A peaceful resolution of this issue is still possible." [59]

And in a rare joint statement, German Chancellor Angela Merkel, French President Nicolas Sarkozy and Prime Minister David Cameron of Britain cautioned that Tehran would face economic isolation unless it "immediately" abandoned its nuclear ambitions. "We will not accept Iran acquiring a nuclear weapon," they said emphatically. [60] Meanwhile, U.S., British and French warships steamed into the Strait of Hormuz, testing the freedom of passage.

Faced with rising tension, Major Gen. Mohammad Ali Asoudi of the Islamic Revolution Guards Corps said Iran's armed forces "are at the height of their powers and military prowess, and threats by the U.S. and Israel are (part of) a psychological warfare campaign." [61]

Meanwhile, Ahmadinejad played down the impact of the EU oil embargo: "Today, we have attained a status that we need not sell oil to Europe, and we are following our path determinedly," he said. And the freezing of the Iran central bank's European assets, he continued, would have minimal effect, because only $24 billion of Iran's $200 billion in foreign exchange are in Europe. [62]

Economic Pain

The Iranian economy is in shambles because the U.N. sanctions block outside investment and development. In the last three months, the value of the Iranian rial has plunged 40 percent against the dollar, according to the French newspaper *Le Monde*. [63]

Several European countries had been worried that an embargo would cause oil prices to spike, exacerbating the EU's serious economic problems. But the EU governments fell into line, in part because they have good prospects for alternative supplies.

"The French strategy is to confront Iran with a choice: The future of the regime, or the nuclear bomb," said *Le Monde*. [64]

But will it work? Turkey, China and India — major importers of Iranian oil — say they will not honor the embargo, although Japan agreed to cut back its Iranian oil purchases after a personal visit by U.S. Treasury Secretary Timothy Geithner. While Beijing "adamantly opposes Iran developing and possessing nuclear weapons," Prime Minister Wen Jiabao declared recently, it will continue to import Iranian oil. [65]

In December, Obama wrote to Ahmadinejad urging him to resume negotiations with the 5+1, after nearly a year-long break. The daily *Tehran Times* said Obama's request "announced readiness for negotiation and the

Is Iran planning to build nuclear weapons?

YES
Frederick W. Kagan
Resident Scholar and Director Critical Threats Project American Enterprise Institute

Written for *CQ Global Researcher*, February 2012

Iran's leaders are seeking the ability to produce an arsenal of atomic weapons. No other explanation fits their behavior. Claiming that Iran needs nuclear power to meet its energy needs in order to strengthen its economy and raise its people's quality of life, the Iranian leadership has brought crushing sanctions on its country.

In addition to constraining Iran's economy, the sanctions have badly undermined its currency and harmed its population. The international community — including Russia, one of Iran's most trusted allies — has offered to provide Iran with nuclear fuel, yet the regime persists in its enrichment program. If the regime sought to improve Iran's economic well-being, it would have abandoned the nuclear program long ago.

The regime claims it has a right to the full nuclear fuel cycle, however, and insists that its program is nothing more than the pursuit of that right. Indeed, Iran could develop a nuclear program in accord with the international laws its leaders cite — if it complied fully with the inspections regime established by those laws and embodied in the International Atomic Energy Agency (IAEA).

Instead, the regime has consistently refused to answer questions from the IAEA, let alone provide the agency with full access and transparency to its program, which other signatories do.

The Iranian regime is not only pursuing a nuclear program to the enormous detriment of its people but it is doing so in violation of the very treaties it claims allow it to pursue the program in the first place.

One could add the disturbing fact that Iran has buried an enrichment facility (which it did not declare until others discovered it) under a small mountain — not the behavior of a regime seeking peaceful nuclear power. Numerous reports also show that Iran has tried to acquire and build atomic weapons devices, detonators and testing facilities and already has a large arsenal of ballistic missiles ready to have atomic warheads fitted.

But the reality already should be clear. The facts support only one rational explanation: Iran's leaders are building a nuclear program to support an arsenal of atomic weapons. All other explanations are rationalizations.

NO
Riccardo Alcaro
Research Fellow, Istituto Affari Internazionali, Rome and Fellow, European Foreign and Security Policy Studies Program

Written for *CQ Global Researcher*, February 2012

It is true that Iran has gone the extra mile to divert international checks on its nuclear program, but uncertainty still clouds its ultimate objective. Meanwhile, there simply is not enough evidence to argue that Iran is determined to leave the Nuclear Non-Proliferation Treaty, test a nuclear device and declare itself a nuclear state.

If Iran were to go openly nuclear, it would have a hard time persuading its mostly opportunistic partners (like China) to resist American and European demands to isolate it. In theory, Iran could go nuclear without telling anyone. In practice, however, keeping the construction of a nuclear arsenal secret is an increasingly difficult, costly and risky option, and Iran is under almost unprecedented scrutiny from the International Atomic Energy Agency (IAEA) and Western powers.

Iran's behavior so far has seemed to fit the strategy of approaching but not crossing the nuclear threshold. While resisting what it considers excessive intrusions into its nuclear program, it has avoided severing ties with the IAEA. Defiance of Western pressure — as well as of IAEA and U.N. Security Council resolutions — seems to have paid off for the Iranian leadership. Domestically, it has given the regime a narrative around which popular support could coalesce. Internationally, it has forced a re-appraisal of Iran's role in the strategic calculus of the United States. And thanks to the nuclear dispute, Iran potentially is in a better position to extract concessions from what Ayatollah Ruhollah Khomeini labeled the "Great Satan" than it was before the nuclear standoff.

From that point of view, the nuclear program is more a means to get U.S. acceptance of the clerical regime and recognition of Iran's regional interests than an end in itself. If that is the case, there still is room for settling the nuclear dispute, as Iran may decide that compromise rather than continued defiance can ultimately deliver its strategic objective of climbing the region's hierarchy.

However, if it has no way out but bowing to U.S. demands or — worse — if attacked by the United States and/or Israel, Iran might instead calculate that isolation with an H-bomb is better than isolation without it. Grownup diplomacy, not teenage muscle flexing, can spare the world another unnecessary crisis.

resolution of mutual disagreements." However, the last session, in January 2011, lasted only a day-and-a-half and ended without agreeing on either an agenda or a date for another session.

Each side accuses the other of delaying the start of new talks. The Iranians insist there should be no preconditions. In a separate account the *Tehran Times* quoted Iranian Foreign Minister Salehi as saying, "If the West has a sincere intention, a date should be decided, and negotiations should start." [66]

Yet, when Salehi said on Jan. 18 that, "Negotiations are going on about venue and date. We would like to have these negotiations," an EU spokesman denied that any discussions were under way on new talks. [67]

Ray Takeyh, a senior fellow at the Council on Foreign Relations, said skepticism abounds regarding Tehran's sincerity. "By threatening the disruption of global oil supplies, yet dangling the prospect of entering talks," he wrote recently, "Iran can press actors such as Russia and China to be more accommodating." But any concessions made by Iran at a negotiating table "are bound to be symbolic and reversible." [68]

Meanwhile, Israel says the window of opportunity for a successful military operation is rapidly closing. "There's a very vivid and very bitter dispute going on between the Israeli and U.S. governments" over timing, says the Israeli commentator Ben-Yishai. "It is still practicable, from an Israeli point of view, to launch an attack, but the Americans say, 'Give sanctions time to work.' " Isareli Defense Minister Ehud Barak, however, said recently that any decision on attacking Iran is "very far off." [69]

Some say a covert war to derail Iran's nuclear program already is underway. On Jan. 11, Iranian chemist Mostafa Ahmadi Roshan, head of the Natanz enrichment facility, was killed after a motorcyclist attached a magnetic bomb to his car in Tehran's rush-hour traffic. He was the fifth Iranian nuclear scientist killed in the past two years. The Iranians blame his killing on U.S. and/or Israeli intelligence agents, but the United States adamantly denied any role in the killing.

In 2010, work had to be suspended for a while at the Natanz nuclear facility after a computer worm called Stuxnet caused large numbers of centrifuges to malfunction. The operating system was restarted a few days later, but the centrifuges remained less efficient. [70]

No one took credit for the cyber attack.

OUTLOOK
Diplomacy and Provocation

"The next few months will look pretty much like the last few months," predicts Takeyh, at the Council on Foreign Relations. "There'll be diplomacy, incremental gains and, occasionally, a degree of provocation, with all parties invested in not having full-scale conflict."

However, he believes Iran would be open to "an arrangement with the United States," under "certain circumstances." For instance, if Iran were allowed to join the World Trade Organization, it could mean a quantum leap in the Iranian economy. [71]

The EU oil embargo won't begin until the summer, allowing European importers time to organize alternative suppliers, such as possibly Libyan oil production, badly damaged during the civil war. Saudi Arabia also is expected to fill the gap, despite Tehran's warning not to increase capacity for its defecting clients.

As for the effectiveness of the oil embargo, experts say the international oil market is too complex, with too many options. "History is littered with failed oil embargoes ranging from Cuba, Rhodesia [today's Zimbabwe] and South Africa to the Arab oil embargo [of 1973], and the embargo against Iraq in 1990," Paul Stevens of London's Chatham House wrote recently. [72]

Moreover, he continued, "some form of [Iranian] retaliatory action against the EU countries . . . could also be expected. There could even be a Lockerbie-type response prompted by elements from within Iran," he continued, referring to Libya's 1988 bombing of a Pan American jet liner over Scotland. [73]

The endgame, according to Julian Lee, an energy expert at the London-based Centre for Global Energy Studies, is to get the Iranians to agree to "proper monitoring of their nuclear industry. The sanctions aren't an end in and of themselves." [74]

Meanwhile, Israel's intentions are unclear, and there is uncertainty about how the Iranian regime will respond to the latest sanctions. The more immediate concern is Iran's threat to close the Strait of Hormuz, which could easily spark a broader conflict. As for hopes of a breakthrough in the negotiations, "No amount of sanctions can pressure Iran into U-turning on its nuclear program," The *Arab News* commented recently. [75]

"Iran knows where the whole world stands; we know where Iran stands; the situation will continue that way," Saudi Prince Turki said recently. "None of us want to engage in military conflict, and I think the Iranians themselves . . . fear that they will be the target of military strikes either by Israel or the United States or both." [76]

In Israel, meanwhile, talk of war rises and subsides. "There's no realistic hope in Israel that the Iranians will suspend their enrichment program altogether," says commentator Ben-Yishai. "If the sanctions work, they might say, 'We suspend enrichment at 20 percent.' That, in itself, would be a big gain."

NOTES

1. "British ambassador: "I had to leave my dog in Iran," BBC News, Dec. 2, 2011, www.bbc.co.uk/news/uk-16009838.

2. Robert F. Worth and Rick Gladstone, "Iran Protesters Attack British Embassy," *The New York Times*, Nov. 29, 2011, www.nytimes.com/ 2011/11/ 30/world/middleeast/tehran-protesters-storm-british-embassy.html.

3. "Implementation of the NPT Safeguards Agreement and relevant provisions of Security Council Resolutions in the Islamic Republic of Iran," International Atomic Energy Agency, Nov. 8, 2011, p. 10, http://isis-online.org/uploads/isis-reports/documents/IAEA_Iran_8Nov2011.pdf.

4. Don Melvin, "EU formally adopts Iran oil embargo," *Arab News*, Jan. 23, 2012, http://arabnews.com/ middleeast/article567075.ece?comments=all.

5. Ronen Bergman, "Will Israel Attack Iran?" *The New York Times Magazine*, Jan. 29, 2012, p. 22. Robert F. Worth, "Iran's Supreme Leader Threatens Retaliation Against Attack," *The New York Times*, Feb. 3, 2012; and Joel Greenberg and Joby Warrick, "Israel: Iran must be stopped soon," *The Washington Post*, Feb. 3, 2012, p. 1.

6. "Remarks by the President in State of the Union Address," Office of the Press Secretary, The White House, Jan. 24, 2012, www.whitehouse.gov/the-press-office/2012/01/24/remarks-president-state-union-address. Also see "Remarks by Mitt Romney," The Israel Project, www.theisraelproject.org/site/apps/nlnet/content2.aspx?c=ewJXKcOUJlIaG&b=7721235&ct=11521353#.TyNrUWNSSkM.

7. Ghazanfar Ali Khan, "Attack on Iran would have 'calamitous' consequences, says Prince Turki," *Arab News*, Dec. 13, 2011, http://arabnews.com/saudi-arabia/article547026.ece.

8. Transcript, "Face the Nation," CBS News, Jan. 8, 2012, www.cbsnews.com/8301-3460_162-57354647/face-the-nation-transcript-january-8-2012/.

9. "Iran's foreign minister on protests and nukes," *Euronews*, March 3, 2011, www.euronews.net/2011/03/03/interview-with-irans-foreign-minister/.

10. "Implementation of the NPT Safeguards Agreement and relevant provisions of Security Council Resolutions in the Islamic Republic of Iran," *op. cit.*

11. "Obama signs Iran Sanctions Bill into Law," BBC News, Dec. 31, 2011, www.bbc.co.uk/news/world-us-canada-16376072.

12. Stephen Castle and Alan Cowell, "Europe and U.S. Tighten Vise of Sanctions on Iran," *The New York Times*, Jan. 23, 2012, www.nytimes.com/2012/01/24/world/middleeast/iran-urged-to-negotiate-as-west-readies-new-sanctions.html?ref=world.

13. Dan Murphy, "Iran's Threats over Strait of Hormuz? Understandable, but not easy," *The Christian Science Monitor*, Dec. 28, 2011, www.csmonitor.com/World/Backchannels/2011/1228/Iran-s-threats-over-Strait-of-Hormuz-Understandable-but-not-easy.

14. Fareed Zakaria, "Iran: Growing state of desperation," *The Washington Post*, Jan. 4, 2012, www.fareedzakaria.com/home/Articles/Articles.html.

15. Armin Arefi, "Iran-Etats-Unis: jusqu;ou iront les deux meilleurs ennemis?" Le Point.fr, Jan. 2, 2012, www.lepoint.fr/monde/iran-etats-unis-jusqu-ou-iront-les-deux-meilleurs-ennemis-02-01-2012-1414517_24.php.

16. "President Shimon Peres says 'Iran is very dangerous, but there is no need to get hysterical,' " Youtube,

Dec. 27, 2011, www.youtube.com/watch?v=x3e8QgAHv9g.

17. "PM, Merkel, Sarkozy: We call on Iran to suspend nuclear activities and abide by international obligations," Number 10 (official site of the British Prime Minister's Office), Jan. 23, 2012, www.number10.gov.uk/news/iran-sanctions/.

18. *Ibid.*

19. V. Vera, *et al.*, "Sanctions on Iran: Reactions and Impact," *AEI Iran Tracker*, Nov. 1, 2011.

20. William C. Ramsay, "Punish Iran Not Each Other," French Institute of International Relations, September 2009, www.ifri.org/?page=detail-contribution&id=5412&id_provenance=97.

21. Indira A. R. Lakshmanan, "Bank Tejarat Banned by U.S., EU Move Stifling Iran Trade," Bloomberg News, Jan. 24, 2012, www.bloomberg.com/news/2012-01-24/bank-tejarat-banned-by-u-s-eu-in-move-stifling-iran-s-trade.html.

22. Kristen Allen, "Iranian Airline Buys Chancellor Merkel's Retired Jet," *Der Spiegel*, Nov. 21, 2011, www.spiegel.de/international/world/0,1518,798973,00.html.

23. Bastian Berlner, "U.S. and Israel Demand Greater Measures against Israel," *Der Spiegel*, Nov. 14, 2011, www.spiegel.de/international/europe/0,1518,797570,00.html.

24. Hossein Jaseb and Justyna Pawlak, "WRAPUP 3: Iran slams EU oil embargo, warns could hit U.S.," Reuters, Jan. 23, 2012, www.reuters.com/article/2012/01/23/nuclear-iran-idUSL5E8CN22320120123.

25. "Iran exports by country, 2010," United States Energy Information Administration, www.eia.gov/countries/country-data.cfm?fips=IR.

26. Karen de Young and Scott Wilson, "Public ire is one goal of sanctions against Iran, U.S. official says," *The Washington Post*, Jan.11, 2012, www.washingtonpost.com/world/national-security/goal-of-iran-sanctions-is-regime-collapse-us-official-says/2012/01/10/gIQA0KJsoP_story.html.

27. Castle and Cowell, *op. cit.*

28. "Global Trends 2025: A Transformed World," National Intelligence Council, November 2008, www.dni.gov/nic/PDF_2025/2025_Global_Trends_Final_Report.pdf.

29. Shmuel Bar, "Can Cold War Deterrence Apply to a Nuclear Iran?" *Strategic Perspectives*, Jerusalem Center for Public Affairs, November 2011, www.jcpa.org/text/cold_war_deterrence_nuclear_iran.pdf.

30. "Saudi Arabia may need nuclear weapons to fend off threat from Iran and Israel, says former intelligence chief," *Daily Mail*, Dec. 6, 2011, www.dailymail.co.uk/news/article-2070704/Saudi-Arabia-need-nuclear-weapons-fend-threat-Iran-Israel-says-prince.html#ixzz1kOpRWhKh.

31. For background, see Patrick G. Marshall, "Calculating the Costs of the Gulf War," *Editorial Research Reports*, March 19, 1991, pp. 145-155, available in *CQ Researcher Plus Archive.*

32. "Saudi Arabia may need nuclear weapons to fend off threat from Iran and Israel, says former intelligence chief," *op. cit.*

33. William H. Luers and Thomas R. Pickering, "Military action isn't the only solution to Iran," *The Washington Post*, Dec. 30, 2012, www.washingtonpost.com/opinions/military-action-isnt-the-only-solution-to-iran/2011/12/29/gIQA69sNRP_story.html.

34. "History of Iran, Persian Empire," http://docmv.co.uk/Documents/History%20of%20iran.pdf.

35. See "Safavid Empire (1501-1722)," "Religions," BBC online, www.bbc.co.uk/religion/religions/islam/history/safavidempire_1.shtml.

36. Quoted in Mike Shuster, "Shia Rise Amid Century of Mideast Turmoil," Part 2 of the series, "Partisans of Ali," NPR, Feb. 13, 2007, www.npr.org/templates/story/story.php?storyId=7371280.

37. David Painter, "The United States, Great Britain, and Iran," Georgetown University Institute for the Study of Diplomacy, 1993, www.princeton.edu/~bsimpson/Hist%20725%20Summer%202006/The%20US%20and%20Mossadegh%201951-1953.pdf.

38. Mark Gasiorowski and Malcolm Byrne (eds.), "Mohammed Mossadeq and the 1953 Coup in

Iran," National Security Archive, June 2004, www
.gwu.edu/~nsarchiv/NSAEBB/NSAEBB126/index
.htm. "The CIA, with help from British intelligence,
planned, funded and implemented the operation."

39. "Arms exports to Iran," Stockholm International
Peace Research Institute, http://armstrade.sipri.org/
armstrade/page/values.php.

40. "Ruhollah Mousavi Khomeini, Part 3: Life in Exile,"
Medlibrary.org, http://medlibrary.org/medwiki/
Ruhollah_Mousavi_Khomeini#Life_in_exile.

41. "The American Experience: The Iranian Hostage
Crisis," PBS, www.pbs.org/wgbh/americanexperience/
features/general-article/carter-hostage-crisis/.

42. "On This Day, 1980: Tehran Hostage Rescue Mission
Fails," BBC, April 25, 2005, http://news.bbc.co.uk/
onthisday/hi/dates/stories/april/25/newsid_
2503000/2503899.stm.

43. "Timeline: U.S.-Iran Contacts," Council on Foreign
Relations, March 9, 2007, www.cfr.org/iran/timeline-
us-iran-contacts/p12806.

44. "Iran-Iraq War (1980-1988)," Global Security, Nov. 7,
2011, www.globalsecurity.org/military/world/war/
iran-iraq.htm.

45. Jonathan Marcus, "Is a U.S.-Iran maritime clash
inevitable?" BBC News, Jan. 10, 2012, www.bbc
.co.uk/news/world-middle-east-16485842.

46. Lionel Beehner, "Timeline: U.S.-Iran Contacts,"
Council on Foreign Relations, March 9, 2011, www
.cfr.org/iran/timeline-us-iran-contacts/p12806#p5.

47. Mark Gasiorowski, "Evidence to the National
Commission on Terrorist Attacks Upon the United
States: Iranian Support for Terrorism," National
Commission on Terrorist Attacks Upon the United
States, July 2003, www.9-11commission.gov/hearings/
hearing3/witness_gasiorowski.htm.

48. B. J. Rudy, "The Future of U.S. Unilateral Sanctions
and the Iran-Libya Sanctions Act," Chatham House,
Feb. 12-13, 2001, www.google.com/search?q=
chatham%20house%3A%20clinton%20administra-
tion%20imposes%20sanctions%20on%20
iran&ie=utf-8&oe=utf-8&aq=t&rls=org.mozilla:en-
US:official&client=firefox-a&source=hp&channel=np.

49. *Ibid.* Libya was removed from ILSA after Libyan
leader Moammar Gadhafi renounced the development of nuclear weapons.

50. Scott McLeod, "Diplomacy: Clinton and Khatami
Find Relations Balmy," *Time*, Sept. 18, 2000, www
.time.com/time/magazine/article/0,9171,997984,00
.html.

51. "Bush State of the Union Speech," CNN transcript,
Jan. 20, 2002, http://edition.cnn.com/2002/
ALLPOLITICS/01/29/bush.speech.txt/.

52. "How Iran entered the Axis," PBS "Frontline,"
undated, www.pbs.org/wgbh/pages/frontline/shows/
tehran/axis/map.html.

53. "Firms Reported in Open Sources as Having
Commercial Activity in Iran's Oil, Gas, and
Petrochemical Sectors," Government Accountability
Office, April 22, 2010, www.gao.gov/products/
GAO-10-515R.

54. "Iran 'ready for nuclear talks,' " BBC News, June 8,
2006, http://news.bbc.co.uk/2/hi/middle_
east/5059322.stm.

55. "Ahmadinejad wins Iran presidential election," BBC
News, June 12, 2009, news.bbc.co.uk/2/
hi/8098305.stm.

56. Joel Gehrke, "894 days: Now Obama stands up for
the Greens," *The Examiner*, Dec. 14, 2011, http://
campaign2012.washingtonexaminer.com/blogs/
beltway-confidential/894-days-now-obama-stands-
green-revolution/257116.

57. "Q and A: Iran nuclear issue," BBC News, Nov. 9,
2011, www.bbc.co.uk/news/world-middle-east-
11709428.

58. "IAEA nuclear inspection gets under way in Iran,"
Daily Telegraph, Jan. 31, 2012, www.telegraph.co.uk/
news/worldnews/middleeast/iran/9048556/IAEA-
nuclear-inspection-gets-under-way-in-Iran.html.

59. "Obama uses State of Union speech to warn Iran to
'change course' as Europe sends battleships to Gulf,"
Daily Mail, Jan. 25, 2012, www.dailymail.co.uk/
news/article-2091450/Obama-uses-State-Union-
speech-warn-Iran-change-course-nuclear-ambitions.
html.

60. *Ibid.*

61. "US, Israeli threats are empty: IRGC official," *Tehran Times*, Jan. 25, 2012, http://tehrantimes .com/politics/94816-us-israeli-threats-are-empty-irgc-official.

62. *Ibid.*

63. "Le EU décide de geler les avoirs de la Banque Central d'Iran," *Le Monde*, Jan. 18, 2012, www .lemonde.fr/proche-orient/article/2012/01/18/l-ue-decide-de-geler-les-avoirs-de-la-banque-centrale-d-iran_1631366_3218.html.

64. Natalie Nougayrede, "Paris redoute des frappes sur Iran pendant l'ete," *Le Monde*, Jan. 19, 2012, www .lemonde.fr/proche-orient/article/2012/01/19/ paris-redoute-des-frappes-sur-l-iran-pendant-l-ete_1631865_3218.html.

65. "Chinese Premier Wen Jiabao defends Iran oil imports," *Daily Telegraph*, Jan. 19, 2012, www.telegraph.co.uk/ news/worldnews/middleeast/iran/9024517/Chinese-Premier-Wen-Jiabao-defends-Iran-oil-imports.html.

66. "Tehran-5+1 dialogue should start if West has intention — Salihi," *Tehran Times*, Jan. 21, 2012, http:// tehrantimes.com/politics/94724-tehran-51-dialogue-should-start-if-west-has-sincere-intention-salehi.

67. Robin Pomer and Ramin Mostafavi, "Iran says it is in touch with powers on new talks, EU denies," *News Daily* (Reuters), Jan. 18, 2012, www.newsdaily .com/stories/tre80h15z-us-iran/.

68. *Ibid.*

69. *Ibid.*

70. Julian Borger, "West's previous attempts to derail Iran's nuclear program," *The Guardian*, Nov. 2, 2011, www.guardian.co.uk/world/2011/nov/02/previous-attempts-iran-nuclear-programme?intcmp=239.

71. "The Manama Dialogue," Fifth Plenary Session, International Institute of Strategic Studies, Dec. 4, 2010, www.iiss.org/conferences/the-iiss-regional-security-summit/manama-dialogue-2010/plenary-sessions-and-speeches/fourth-plenary-session/ fourth-plenary-qa-session/.

72. Paul Stevens, "An Embargo on Iranian Crude Oil Exports: How likely and with what Impact?" Chatham House, January 2012, www.chatham house.org/sites/default/files/public/Research/ Energy,%20Environment%20and%20Development/ 0112pp_stevens.pdf.

73. *Ibid.*

74. Stephen Mufson, "Oil prices, Iran are increasingly sources of concern," *The Washington Post*, Jan. 14, 2012, www.washingtonpost.com/business/economy/ increasing-concern-over-oil-prices-iran/2012/01/13/ gIQAP98PzP_story.html.

75. Linda Heard, "U.S. and Iran: Wheels within wheels," *Arab News*, Jan. 17, 2012, http://arabnews .com/opinion/columns/article564103.ece.

76. "Fifth Plenary Session — HRH Prince Turki Al Faisal: The Changing Nature of Regional Security Issues," 7th IISS Regional Security Summit, The Manama Dialogue, The International Institute for Strategic Studied, Dec. 4, 2010, www.iiss.org/con ferences/the-iiss-regional-security-summit/manama-dialogue-2010/plenary-sessions-and-speeches/ fifth-plenary-session/hrh-prince-turki-al-faisal/.

BIBLIOGRAPHY

Selected Sources

Books

Brumberg, David, *Reinventing Khomeini: The Struggle for Reform in Iran*, University of Chicago Press, 2001.
An associate professor of government at Georgetown University examines Ayatollah Khomeini's often contradictory ideas about government and how they led to competing institutions and ideologies in today's Iranian leadership.

Kamrava, Mehran, *Iran's Intellectual Revolution*, Cambridge University Press, 2008.
The director of Georgetown University's Qatar-based Center of International Studies examines the strengths and weaknesses of the three major intellectual currents in Iran — religious conservative, religious reformist and secular modernist.

Nasr, Vali, *The Shia Revival: How Conflicts Within Islam Will Shape the Future*, W. W. Norton, 2006.
A noted authority on the Arab world and a professor of international politics at the Fletcher School of Law and

Diplomacy at Tufts University argues that Operation Iraqi Freedom set the scene for a "new" Middle East fueled by the sectarian struggle between the majority Sunnis and minority Shiites.

Takeyh, Ray, *Hidden Iran: Paradox and Power in the Islamic Republic*, Times Books, 2006.
A senior fellow for Middle Eastern studies at the Council on Foreign Relations in Washington explains why we fail to understand Iran and offers a new strategy for redefining this crucial relationship.

Wright, Robin, ed., *The Iran Primer: Power, Politics and U.S. Policy*, United States Institute for Peace Press, 2010.
A distinguished American foreign correspondent well versed in Middle Eastern affairs pulls together 50 seasoned experts from around the world to compile a comprehensive primer on Iran today — its politics, society, military and nuclear program.

Articles

Bergman, Ronen, "Will Israel Attack Iran?" *The New York Times Magazine*, Jan. 29, 2012, p. 22.
An Israeli journalist and author of *The Secret War With Iran* concludes, along with several other Israeli politicians, that Israel will attack Iran in 2012.

Escobar, Pepe, "The Myth of 'Isolated' Iran," *Le Monde Diplomatique*, Jan. 24, 2012, http://monde-diplo.com/openpage/the-myth-of-isolated-iran.
An Al Jazeera analyst says Tehran, which is adept at "Persian shadow play," has no intention of provoking a suicidal Western attack.

Esfandiary, Dina, "It's Time to Deal With Nuclear Iran," *The Huffington Post*, Nov. 16, 2011, www.iiss.org/whats-new/iiss-experts-commentary/its-time-to-deal-with-nuclear-iran/.
A research analyst and project coordinator at the Non-Proliferation and Disarmament Programme at London's International Institute for Strategic Studies warns against jumping to conclusions about a 2011 IAEA report on Iran's nuclear ambitions.

Gelb, Leslie H., "Leslie H. Gelb on How President Obama Should Handle Iran," *The Daily Beast*, Jan. 30, 2012, www.thedailybeast.com/articles/2012/01/30/leslie-h-gelb-on-how-president-obama-should-handle-iran.html.
A former strategic arms reduction negotiator during the Carter administration says President Obama should offer a robust peace proposal now that toughest-ever sanctions are pressuring Iran to halt its nuclear program.

Kahl, Colin, "Not Time to Attack Iran," *Foreign Affairs*, Jan. 17, 2012, www.foreignaffairs.com.
An associate professor in security studies at Georgetown University explains why a military intervention to halt Iran's nuclear program would be ill-judged.

Kroenig, Matthew, "Time to Attack Iran," *Foreign Affairs magazine*, Jan/Feb 2012, www.foreignaffairs.com.
A nuclear security fellow at the Council on Foreign Relations says attacking Iran is the "least bad option."

Reports and Studies

Fitzpatrick, Mark, "Iran's Nuclear, Chemical, and Biological Capabilities —A Net Assessment," Institute of International Strategic Studies, Feb. 3, 2011, www.iiss.org/publications/strategic-dossiers/irans-nuclear-chemical-and-biological-capabilities/.
The London-based institute's detailed technical assessment of Iran's weapons of mass destruction programs concludes that Iran does not have a nuclear weapon and, "won't have one tomorrow, or next week, or next month or a year from now."

Kerr, Paul, "Iran's Nuclear Program: Tehran's Compliance with International Obligations," Congressional Research Service, Dec. 21, 2011, http://fpc.state.gov/documents/organization/180686.pdf.
A specialist reviews Iran's nuclear program and details the legal basis for actions taken by the IAEA and U.N. Security Council.

Pletka, Danielle, *et al.*, "Containing and Deterring a Nuclear Iran," American Enterprise Institute, December 2011.
Experts from the conservative think tank contend that Iran already is a nuclear state and outline a containment strategy.

For More Information

Chatham House, The Royal Institute of International Affairs, 10 St. James's Square, London SW1Y4LE, United Kingdom; 44 207 957 5710; www.chathamhouse.org. A leading source of independent analysis on global and domestic issues.

Council on Foreign Relations, The Howard Pratt House, 58 East 68th St., New York, NY 10065; 212-434-9400; www.cfr.org. An independent think tank that "promotes understanding of foreign policy and America's role in the world."

International Atomic Energy Agency, P.O. Box 100, 1400 Vienna, Austria; 431 2600-0; www.iaea.org. The U.N. agency charged with promoting the development of "safe, secure, peaceful nuclear science and technology."

King Faisal Center for Research and Islamic Studies, P.O. Box 51049, Riyadh 11548, Saudi Arabia; 966 1 465 2255; www.kff.com. Furthers Islamic civilization by supporting continuing research and cultural and scientific activities in a variety of fields.

National Iran-American Council, 1411 K St., Washington, DC 20005; 202-386-6325; www.niacouncil.org/site/PageServer?pagename=NIAC_index. A nonprofit, nonpartisan organization dedicated to furthering the interests of the Iranian-American community and providing information about Iran.

University of Tehran, 16 Azur St., Tehran 14174, Iran; 9821 664 05047; www.ut.ac.ir/en. Offers courses in most academic fields, including foreign policy.

Voices From Abroad:

BENJAMIN NETANYAHU

Prime Minister, Israel

A threat to all

"The significance of the (IAEA) report is that the international community must bring about the cessation of Iran's pursuit of nuclear weapons, which endangers the peace of the world and of the Middle East."

Al Jazeera (Qatar), November 2011

ALI AKBAR SALEHI

Foreign Minister, Iran

A peaceful program

"We have repeatedly announced that we are just after a peaceful use of the nuclear energy and we consider production or use of nuclear bombs as Haram (religiously banned). The European Union should think about the real threat of the atomic bombs stockpiled in Europe instead of presenting a deceitful and unreal image of Iran's peaceful nuclear program."

Fars News Agency (Iran), October 2011

MAHMOUD AHMADINEJAD

President, Iran

Building other things

"The Iranian nation is wise. It won't build two bombs against 20,000 [nuclear] bombs you (the West) have. But it builds something you can't respond to: ethics, decency, monotheism and justice."

National televised speech, November 2011

VLADIMIR EVSEYEV

Center for Public Policy Research, Russia

Japan's footsteps

"Iran is likely to follow Japan's way now, that is, it creates the opportunities for the production of nuclear weapons, but it does not produce it. It creates technical potential,

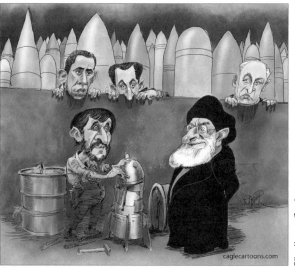

Riber Hansson/Sweden

which can allow it this. But it is difficult to restrict the creation of this potential."

Trend News Agency (Azerbaijan) May 2011

JOSCHKA FISCHER

Former Vice Chancellor, Germany

Endangering balance

"An Iran armed with nuclear weapons (or one political decision away from possessing them) would drastically alter the Middle East's strategic balance. At best, a nuclear-arms race would threaten to consume this already-unstable region, which would endanger the NPT, with far-reaching global consequences."

Korea Times (South Korea), December 2011

AFZAL BUTT

President, National Press Club, Pakistan

Double standards

"Iran will go ahead with its nuclear activities which are the country's right. They (the United States) cannot see a Muslim state following independent policy and not paying any attention to American threats. They must stop adopting dual standards against Iran . . . [the] U.S. knows that Iran is not developing a weapon-oriented nuclear program."

Philippine News Agency, February 2011

MEHDI GHAZANFARI

Minister of Industries, Mines and Commerce, Iran

Meaningless sanctions
"Some people think that sanctions have reached a damaging point and if the sanctions include the Central Bank, Iran will be finished off. But we think differently because this is their last ploy and test, and after this, sanctions will become meaningless."

Mehr News Agency (Iran), January 2012

UZI EILAM

Senior Research Fellow, Institute for National Security Studies, Israel

Uncertainty
"If they have enough . . . enriched uranium, they (Iran) will have to come up with a good design for the bomb. Then again, nobody knows how far they went in this field."

Trend News Agency (Azerbaijan), December 2011

AYATOLLAH SEYED AHMAD KHATAMI

Senior cleric, Iran

The U.S. is finished
"Today Iran is mighty, strong and powerful and retaliates against any plot so powerfully that it would become a lesson for others. . . . [T]he United States is a finished superpower . . . an empty drum."

Sermon during the Muslim Feast of Sacrifice, November 2011

2

Emerging Central Asia

Brian Beary

Kazakh Muslims pray outside a mosque in Almaty, the largest city in Kazakhstan, during Eid al-Adha (Feast of the Sacrifice), which follows the annual pilgrimage to Mecca. Since the 1980s, when the Soviet Union began relaxing curbs on religious freedom, Central Asia has seen a revival of Islam — viewed with suspicion and hostility by the region's Soviet-style secularist governments, which fear Islamic terrorism.

From *CQ Researcher*, Jan. 17, 2012

S ince the Sept. 11, 2001, terrorist attacks against the United States, the Central Asian republics have probably received more attention from the West than they did in the previous five centuries.

As neighbors of Afghanistan, the five countries known as the "Stans" — Kazakhstan, Kyrgyzstan, Tajikistan, Turkmenistan and Uzbekistan — play a key tactical role in the NATO-led offensive in Afghanistan against Al Qaeda and its Taliban allies. For example, they host Western military bases and act as crucial hubs for transporting troops and materiel to the battlefield. [1]

The Stans are critical allies to the West for economic reasons too: The petroleum-rich region is a preferable alternative to unreliable Russia as an energy supplier.

The five former Soviet republics are strategically located, bordered by China to the east, Russia to the north, Afghanistan and Iran to the south and Europe further to the west. Dubbed the "Roof of the World" by legendary 13th-century traveler Marco Polo, the region boasts the famed Pamir and Tian Shan mountain ranges. [2]

But running through the rugged region is the fertile Fergana Valley, a densely populated swath 200 miles long and 70 miles wide, where festering ethnic tensions frequently erupt among the overwhelmingly Muslim population. Apart from the Tajiks, who are Persian, Central Asians are predominantly Turkic peoples, with significant minority populations of Russians.

Since the 1980s, when the Soviet Union began relaxing curbs on religious freedom, the region has seen a fervent revival of Islam. In Kyrgyzstan,

A Hotspot Within a Hotspot

Once conquered by Genghis Khan and Tamerlane, Central Asia today is a hotspot within a hotspot. The rugged region's five nations are surrounded by China, Russia, Afghanistan and Iran — some of the world's most powerful or volatile nations. The so-called Stans have been courted by both their influential neighbors and by the West, either for their oil and gas reserves or because of their proximity to Afghanistan, where the United States and NATO need nearby air bases to help them wage war against radical Islamists. Lucrative oil and gas reserves have brought wealth to Kazakhstan and Turkmenistan, but it is concentrated among the ruling elite. Kyrgyzstan is freer and more democratic than the others, but its future is threatened by ethnic strife, poverty, political instability and corruption. Uzbekistan, the most populous of the five, is controlled by an oppressive regime, while fragile Tajikistan is still recovering from a civil war in the 1990s.

The Five Central Asian Republics

Source: map by Lewis Agrell

for example, only 47 percent of Kyrgyz citizens self-identified as Muslims in 1996; by 2008, 80 percent did.[3]

The rise of Islam is viewed with suspicion and hostility by Central Asia's governments, which are firmly rooted in Soviet-style autocratic secularism. Uzbekistan, for example, forbids anyone other than clerics from wearing religious clothing such as Islamic headscarves, and in 2010 the

government allowed only 5,000 Uzbeks to make the *hajj* pilgrimage to Mecca, out of the official quota of 25,000.[4]

In Marco Polo's time, the region was a key transit point on the famed Silk Road, a web of trade routes crisscrossing Europe and Asia used to transport porcelain, minerals, spices, silks and carpets. But in the 1600s, as it became cheaper to move goods by sea, Central Asia's golden age

Central Asia at a Glance

Kazakhstan

Area: 1.1 million sq. mi.
Population: 16 million
GDP per capita: $13,060
Global share of proven petroleum reserves: 2.9%
Global share of proven gas reserves: 1%
Government: republic; authoritarian presidential rule
President: Nursultan Nazarbayev, in power since 1990
Ethnic breakdown: 63.1% Kazakh, 23.7% Russian, 2.8% Uzbek, 2.1% Ukrainian, 1.4% Uyghur, 1.3% Tatar, 1.1% German, 4.5% other
Religion: 47% Muslim, 44% Russian Orthodox, 2% Protestant, other 7%
Human Development Index score: 0.745*

Kyrgyz Republic (Kyrgyzstan)

Area: 77,000 sq. mi.
Population: 5.3 million
GDP per capita: $2,380
Government: republic; parliamentary system
President: Almazbek Atambaev, in power since 2011
Ethnic breakdown: 64.9% Kyrgyz, 13.8% Uzbek, 12.5% Russian, 1.0% Ukrainian, 6.8% other
Religion: 75% Muslim, 20% Russian Orthodox, other 5%
Human Development Index score: 0.615

Tajikistan

Area: 55,800 sq. mi.
Population: 6.9 million
GDP per capita: $2,040
Government: republic
President: Emomamil Rakhmon, in power since 1992
Ethnic breakdown: 79.9% Tajik, 15.3% Uzbek, 1.1% Russian, 2.6% other
Religion: 90% Muslim, 10% other
Human Development Index score: 0.607

Turkmenistan

Area: 190,000 sq. mi.
Population: 5 million
GDP per capita: $7,519
Global share of proven gas reserves: 4.3%
Government: republic; authoritarian presidential rule
President: Gurbanguly Berdymukhamedov, in power since 2006
Ethnic breakdown: 85% Turkmen, 5% Uzbek, 4% Russian, 6% other
Religion: 89% Muslim, 9% Eastern Orthodox, 2% other
Human Development Index score: 0.686

Uzbekistan

Area: 174,500 sq. mi.
Population: 27.4 million
GDP per capita: $3,294
Global share of proven gas reserves: 0.8%
Government: republic; authoritarian presidential rule
President: Islam Karimov, in power since 1990
Ethnic breakdown: 80% Uzbek, 5.5% Russian, 5% Tajik, 3% Kazakh, 1.5% Tatar, 5% others
Religion: 88% Muslim, 9% Eastern Orthodox, 3% other
Human Development Index score: 0.641

* United Nations measurement of a country's life expectancy, literacy, education and standard of living on a 0 to 1 scale, with 1 being the most developed.

Sources: BP Statistical Review of World Energy, June 2011; IMF World Economic Outlook, September 2011; The World Factbook, Central Intelligence Agency, October 2011; U.N. Population Division, 2010 Revision Population Database, June 2011; Jim Nichol, "Central Asia: Regional Developments and Implications for U.S. Interests," Congressional Research Service, October 2011

came to a precipitous end. The landlocked region fell into economic decline, during which the five nations succumbed to Russian and later Soviet domination, before re-emerging from the ashes of the Soviet Union in 1991.

Kazakhstan has had the strongest growth, thanks largely to its abundant oil and gas reserves. But the recent discovery of the world's second-largest natural gas field has intensified outside interest in Turkmenistan. [5]

All five republics have dismal ratings from pro-democracy and anti-corruption organizations. Turkmenistan and Uzbekistan jointly place 177th (with Sudan) out of 182 countries in Transparency International's corruption perception index. [6] Turkmenistan is known as the country whose late leader built a giant golden statue of himself, which revolves with the sun. Uzbekistan gained notoriety in the early 2000s, when the British ambassador in

Russian Exodus Transforms Central Asia

"There is no future for young Russians."

In September, 138 Kazakh politicians and cultural workers signed a letter demanding an amendment to the constitution making Kazakh the nation's official language. At first glance, the request might seem reasonable in a country where the population is mainly Kazakh.

But less than a generation ago most citizens were neither ethnic Kazakh nor fluent in the language. The remarkable turnaround has come about partly because millions of ethnic Russians have left Kazakhstan, mostly migrating to Russia.

The pattern has been repeated in Kyrgyzstan, Tajikistan, Turkmenistan and Uzbekistan.

Yulia Savchenko, a Washington-based Russian broadcast journalist who has traveled extensively in Central Asia, explains, "There is no future for young Russians, as they cannot get normal employment without the necessary language skills. In Soviet times, Russian was the main working language, but not anymore." And in poorer Central Asian countries, such as Tajikistan and Kyrgyzstan, the worsening economic situation provides "no incentive to learn a language they cannot use in any other country."

The Kazakh government, which hopes to increase the share of Kazakh speakers from 64 percent to 95 percent by 2020, is requiring all public-sector workers to be fluent in Kazakh, putting Russians at a huge disadvantage. [1] However, some fear that the precipitous decline of Russian speakers could fracture the society along ethnic lines, because in a country with 130 ethnic groups, Russian served as a unifying bond. [2] In late 2011, a spate of terrorist attacks hit Kazakhstan, surprising many, given the country's relative stability. Rather than being ethnically motivated, however,

the attacks were thought to have been perpetrated by militant Islamists. [3]

Despite the exodus, Russians still make up 25 percent of the Kazakh population, by far their highest share among the five Central Asian republics. [4]

Tajikistan, meanwhile, is "a sad story," says Shokhin Asadov, a Tajik who worked at the U.S. embassy in Dushanbe, the capital, before moving to the United States recently to teach Tajik. "The Russians began arriving in the 1930s. Their influence grew right up to the Gorbachev era," he says. "In Dushanbe University, where I taught English for 20 years, I saw the change begin in 1989, when a pro-Tajik language law passed, and Russians started to leave."

Although Russians had "a disproportionate influence in the city and would look down on the locals," he says, "it was sad to see them leave so abruptly."

The downgrading of the status of the Russian language also makes it harder for the 1 million or so ethnic Tajiks who have emigrated to Russia to get a good job, he points out, because they do not speak Russian fluently so they are more vulnerable to exploitation. In Turkmenistan, the climate is even less welcoming, with the government insisting that its residents with dual Russian-Turkmen citizenship choose one or the other.

Russians first populated Central Asia in the 1700s, when a mix of soldiers and peasants arrived — escaping serfdom or fleeing religious persecution. Russian migration increased during World War II, when hundreds of Soviet factories were moved to Central Asia to keep them from falling into the hands of the invading German army.

Tashkent, Craig Murray, claimed the Uzbek regime systematically tortured political dissidents, including boiling at least one to death. The allegation embarrassed the U.K. and U.S. governments, who were closely collaborating with the Uzbeks in efforts to capture and interrogate Islamist terrorists based in the region. [7]

The countries "have all used the Western need for basing or airspace rights for military operations in Afghanistan to deflect criticism of human rights abuses," according to Minority Rights Group International, a

Britain-based advocacy organization for indigenous peoples. Moreover, the group added, authoritarian regimes in Turkmenistan and Kazakhstan have "successfully leveraged international thirst for their oil and gas reserves to avert significant pressure for human rights improvements and democratization." [8]

The flood of petrodollars to the region has created massive income inequality. During a recent diplomatic meeting in Ashgabat, the Turkmen capital, Struan Stevenson, a Scottish member of the European Parliament, recalls "in the

Despite steady influxes until the 1970s, Russians' share of the population gradually decreased due to the higher birthrate of non-Russians. The Russians began returning home in the 1970s, when Soviet leader Leonid Brezhnev encouraged the promotion of Central Asians to high political positions as part of his "indigenization" policy.

But the mass exodus did not start until the Soviet Union collapsed in 1991. Other minorities, including Germans, Poles, Ukrainians and Greeks also left in large numbers at the time as they felt marginalized in the new, more nationalist-oriented political climate. As a result, the region is now much more ethnically homogenous. [5]

Today, many of Central Asia's Russians feel bitter about their treatment. There is "strong resentment of Russia," writes Sebastien Peyrouse, a senior research fellow at the Washington-based School for Advanced International Studies at Johns Hopkins University. "They often portray it as a country unconcerned with its 'compatriots,' which prefers to get along with the Central Asian political regimes rather than defend the rights of Russian minorities or help them return." [6]

For instance, Moscow has not stood up against the Turkmen government's refusal to allow Russians to keep dual nationality. And there are other changes too, notably the rise of Islam, gangs and the growing influence of China on the region, all of which "contribute to the sentiment among Russians that they do not have a future in Central Asia." [7]

— *Brian Beary*

---

[1]Matthew Naumann, "Central Asia," in Joanna Hoare, ed., "State of World's Minorities and Indigenous People 2011," Minority Rights Group International, July 6, 2011, pp. 126-36, www.minorityrights.org/10848/state-of-the-worlds-minorities/state-of-the-worlds-minorities-and-indigenous-peoples-2011.html.

[2]Georgiy Voloshin, "Language Controversy In Kazakhstan Sparks Social Anxiety," *Central Asia-Caucasus Institute Analyst*, vol. 13, no. 18, Oct. 5, 2011, www.cacianalyst.org/?q=node/5640.

Russian Minorities Are Dwindling

The number of Russians in Central Asia has declined significantly over the past twodecades.

Russians as a Share of Total Population, 1989-2007

Source: Sebastian Peyrouse, "The Russian Minority in Central Asia: Migration, Politics, and Language," Woodrow Wilson International Center for Scholars, 2008, www.wilsoncenter.org/sites/default/files/OP297.pdf.

[3]Jacob Zenn, "Rising Terror Group Exploits Kazakh Unrest," *Asia Times*, Dec. 21, 2011, www.atimes.com/atimes/Central_Asia/ML21Ag01.html.

[4]"World Population Prospects: The 2010 Revision," U.N. Population Division, June 28, 2011, http://esa.un.org/unpd/wpp/Excel-Data/population.htm; and Sebastien Peyrouse, "The Russian Minority in Central Asia: Migration, Politics, and Language," Woodrow Wilson Center for International Scholars, 2008, www.wilsoncenter.org/sites/default/files/OP297.pdf.

[5]Peyrouse, *Ibid.*

[6]*Ibid.*

[7]*Ibid.*

---

old part of the city people were standing in unpaved muddy squares that had only a single cold-water tap and cooking their meals on charcoal burners. From there, I could see gleaming skyscrapers occupied by civil servants."

Indeed, numerous roadblocks physically separated rich and poor areas in the city, he says, while his delegation's meetings with ministers were filmed and the images later projected onto a screen in the city square as pro-regime propaganda.

Visitors to resource-rich Kazakhstan paint a similar picture of a country with extremes of rich and poor. Kate

Watters, executive director of Crude Accountability, an independent U.S.-based nongovernmental organization that addresses damage caused in the Caspian Sea region by the petroleum industry, says visiting the newly built capital, Astana, is "so surreal" that it is akin to "arriving at Oz," with its ubiquitous golden buildings, extravagant fountains and massive squares. Meanwhile, other parts of Kazakhstan remain mired in poverty.

Vast oil and mineral reserves have boosted Kazakhstan's per capita GDP from $1,000 to $12,500 over the past

Jihadist Groups Operate in Central Asia

Several groups in Central Asia advocate the creation of an Islamic state, similar to groups in other predominantly Muslim nations. Some of the groups, such as the Islamic Movement of Uzbekistan, promote their agenda through violent means. Others, such as Tabligh Jamaat, prefer more peaceful tactics.

Prominent Islamist Groups in Central Asia

Islamic Movement of Uzbekistan — Uses violence to advocate the creation of an Islamic state or caliphate based in Central Asia's Fergana Valley region. Operates largely out of Afghanistan.

Juno Al-Khilafah — Militant Kazakh-based group that calls for Islamic state in Central Asia.

Hizb ut-Tahrir — Officially nonviolent but has used harmful tactics to push its anti-Western, anti-Semitic agendas. Advocates the creation of a worldwide caliphate.

Tabligh Jamaat — Peaceful, nonpartisan missionary group based in India, with branches in 150 countries.

Source: "Annual Report 2011," U.S. Commission on International Religious Freedom, May 2011, www.uscirf.gov/images/book with cover for web.pdf

decade, and the country now rates "high" on the U.N.'s Human Development Index; the other four republics rate "medium" rankings. [9]

Joblessness has been a chronic problem across Central Asia, leading millions to migrate to Russia in search of work. [10] Tajikistan and Kyrgyzstan have been especially affected, since they lack petroleum reserves and are more uniformly poor than Kazakhstan and Turkmenistan. Their rivers, which they harness for hydropower, are their primary natural resource, but dams they built create major tensions with their downstream neighbor, Uzbekistan, which has severe water shortages.

In Uzbekistan and Turkmenistan, irrigation canals built during Soviet times created an environmental catastrophe: The Aral Sea, once the fourth-largest lake in the world, has shrunken to a fraction of its former size due to over-draining, turning massive swaths of land into desert and dramatically reducing water supplies.

Central Asians' longtime colonial master, Russia, has seen its influence wane since independence, just as China's influence has grown. In 2000, only 4 percent of Central Asia's trade was with China and 27 percent with Russia. By 2010, China's share had risen to 24 percent,

while Russia's had slipped to 20 percent. [11] China also has provided massive loans to Central Asian governments — often linked to their purchasing Chinese products or hiring Chinese workers. [12]

China uses its economic weight to persuade Central Asian governments to repress the Uyghurs, a Turkic Muslim minority living mostly in western China, according to Jana Brandt, a German who works as a project coordinator for the Munich-based World Uyghur Congress. China has accused Central Asia-based Uyghurs of plotting against the Chinese state and then pressured the governments to extradite them back to China, she says.

Alisher Khamidov, a Kyrgyz who serves as a Washington-based consultant for the World Bank, calls the situation "a pain in the neck." The Kyrgyz people, he told a seminar on Central Asia at Johns Hopkins University's School for Advanced International Studies on Nov. 9, 2011, "have to convince China that we are not supporting the Uyghurs, even though our people have ties and sympathies with them through marriage."

As the world pays ever-closer attention to this obscure part of the world, here are key questions being asked:

Is Central Asia becoming more democratic?

The scorecard for Central Asia on democracy is mixed, with no discernible trends, according to the Washington-based democracy advocacy group Freedom House.

Between 2007 and 2011, Turkmenistan and Uzbekistan improved, the group says, but Kazakhstan, Kyrgyzstan and Tajikistan slipped backwards. During the previous four years, the situation had been flipped: The Kazakhs and Kyrgyz did better between 2003 and 2007, and the Turkmen and Uzbeks fell back. [13]

In its 2011 report, Freedom House notes how the Tajikistan government, "citing the need to curb extremism, urged or compelled the return of students obtaining a religious education abroad." [14] The same year in Kazakhstan, the government "stepped up its suppression of the political opposition through dubious prosecutions and incarcerations, among other means," Freedom House reported. [15]

Jeff Goldstein, a specialist on human rights in Central Asia for Open Society, a Washington-based advocacy group financed by billionaire philanthropist George Soros, says, "The trend since the late 1990s has been downhill. It picked up speed when Vladimir Putin became president of Russia in 2000, and they copied his style of rule."

However, he continues, after the 9/11 attacks, "governments justified their repression by saying 'we're fighting extremists just like the U.S.' " In fact, Uzbek President Islam Karimov is on his third term, having simply ignored the country's two-term limit. Meanwhile, Turkmenistan "is in the same league as Burma, Cuba and North Korea," he says. [16]

After three months in Uzbekistan, Brandt, of the World Uyghur Congress, says, "you really feel the oppression. You see policemen every 300 meters — in the market, at the theater, in the subway. During a five-hour car journey from the Uzbek-Kyrgyz border, we passed 16 different checkpoints where they registered us."

In addition, she says, "Religion is almost forbidden. There are very few mosques. You do not hear imams calling people to prayer, because they are not allowed. It feels strange in an overwhelmingly Muslim country."

As for Turkmenistan, an expatriate who asked not to be identified out of concern for her family back home, says, "My country is like George Orwell's *1984*. All opposition is either in jail or outside of the country. There is no culture of questioning. During Soviet times, you could discuss politics openly, but not now."

And because the budget is not published, she says, "the average citizen knows nothing about where the state's money goes." Global Witness, a nongovernmental organization that tackles the causes of conflict and poverty, for example, revealed that the former leader, Saparmurat Nyazov, who died in 2006, stashed $3 billion overseas, $2 billion of it at Deutsche Bank. [17]

And Tajikistan, according to the International Crisis Group (ICG), an independent organization focused on conflict resolution, is "a kleptocracy centered on the presidential family. . . . All institutions have been hollowed out, leaving a state with no resilience to cope with natural disasters, economic crises or political shocks." [18] Yet Tajikistan is the only Central Asian country that allows a political party based on religion. The Islamic Renaissance Party typically wins less than 10 percent in elections, although analysts say it would win around 25 percent if elections were free and fair.

A Kyrgyz soldier casts her ballot in the presidential election on Oct. 30, 2011. Kyrgyzstan is often seen as more democratic than its autocratic neighbors in Central Asia. Deemed "mostly fair" by international observers, the election was aimed at overcoming tensions that sparked deadly antigovernment clashes during the previous year. Prime Minister Almazbek Atambayev, a pro-Russian former government official, received 63 percent of the vote.

AFP/Getty Images/Vyacheslav Oseledko

Stevenson, the EU Parliament member, says the situation is improving in Kazakhstan. "They have made greater progress than the others but still have a long way to go," he says. While on an election-monitoring mission, Stevenson recalls, Kazakh President Nursultan Nazarbayev told him: "We have no history of democracy, only of strong leaders like Genghis Khan and Tamerlane." He joked that he had to invent opposition parties, "because if I win 98 percent of the vote, no one will believe me." Then he shrugged, "I can't help it if I'm popular."

Meanwhile, Kyrgyzstan is often described as the exception to an overall preponderance of autocracy in Central Asia. Jana Aray, a Kyrgyz who works for a nongovernmental organization that promotes youth and volunteer programs in the capital, Bishkek, says things are moving in the right direction.

"There is not as much pressure on people as there used to be," she says. "After having endured several corrupt

AFP/Getty Images/Viktor Darchev

AFP/Getty Images/Vyacheslav Oseledko

Aftermath of Violence

Ethnic Uzbeks in Osh dine on Oct. 7, 2010, amid the ruins of their home, destroyed during ethnic clashes (top). The June 2010 violence between Uzbek and Kyrgyz communities in the south left more than 400 people dead and some 411,000 displaced, according to international reports. The violence had been sparked by accusations that Uzbeks had raped Kyrgyz women, bringing dishonor on their families and communities. Last June, Kyrgyz men, wearing traditional hats, pray at the "Mothers' Tears" monument in Osh during a ceremony to mark the anniversary of the violence (bottom).

presidents, we have decided to become a parliamentary republic."

Aray attended a Western-oriented school funded by philanthropist Soros. But her positive portrait of Kyrgyzstan is contested by Yulia Savchenko, a Russian broadcast journalist who lived in Kyrgyzstan for five years. "There has not been a movement toward genuine democracy," says

Savchenko. Newly elected President Almazbek Atambayev "is very much part of the system in which corruption and nepotism are [part] of everyday life. I am not hopeful in any way about the future of democracy in Kyrgyzstan."

Nicolás de Pedro, a Spanish researcher on Central Asia for the Barcelona Center for International Affairs, points out that the region's strongest links are with Russia and China, neither of which makes demands for democracy.

"The Central Asian governments' agendas have not changed much," he says, adding, "Europe and the United States do not have much leverage, so it is hard for them to push for democracy — although they should be doing more than they are."

Is Central Asia unstable?

The resurgence of Islam in Central Asia has led some to wonder whether the region will follow the path of some Arab countries, such as Egypt and Algeria, where government suppression of Islamic political parties has further strengthened the Islamists.

For instance, the Islamic Movement of Uzbekistan (IMU) is fighting to create an Islamist state, or caliphate, based in the Fergana Valley, to be carved out of numerous existing states. After being repressed in Uzbekistan, the IMU moved its base to Afghanistan in the late 1990s, where it is allied with both the Taliban and Al Qaeda. [19]

The Uzbek authorities also have imprisoned at least 5,000 people for associating with Hizb ut-Tahrir (HT), an Islamist group that aims to create a caliphate stretching from West Africa to western China. However, "according to international and Uzbek human rights activists, the only 'crime' of many of these individuals is independent practice and independent study of Islam." [20] HT is not overtly violent, although it is virulently anti-Western and anti-Semitic.

"HT is more popular than the IMU," says Noah Tucker, a U.S.-based Central Asia analyst who writes for registan.net, an independent website. "It has an active membership probably in the thousands in each of the five countries." HT is outlawed, however, so it cannot form a political party, and its supporters are often prosecuted, he notes.

Robert Blake, the U.S. State Department's assistant secretary for South and Central Asian affairs, believes Islamic militants pose "a continued, very serious threat." He adds, "It is important for the U.S. to support these governments in countering these threats."

Neighboring China is also afraid rising Islamic extremism could stir up more political dissent among its Uyghur minority, who share the same religion and have the same ethnic roots as Central Asians. [21] And the International Crisis Group has reported that the "disappearance of basic services" provided by the government during the Soviet era "will provide Islamic radicals, already a serious force in many Central Asian states, with further ammunition against regional leaders and openings to establish influential support networks." [22]

But others say the Islamist threat is overstated. "This idea of the Fergana Valley being a boiling pot of religious fervor is not reflected by events on the ground," says Tucker. "Yes, there are some Islamists and militants, but there is very little popular support for Islamism."

Instead, he says, there is "a religious revival, especially in Uzbekistan, Kyrgyzstan and Tajikistan. This is natural given how religion was repressed by the Soviets. Some people are choosing to explore this religious revival. Others — such as the urban intelligentsia who were Russified in the Soviet era — are not."

Uyghur advocate Brandt agrees. "The people in these countries practice a moderate form of religion. Their governments exaggerate the extent of Islamism as an excuse to crack down on religion — just like China says the Uyghurs are a threat to their national security."

"It is crucial not to confuse a return to faith with Islamism and terrorism," says Marlene Laruelle, a research professor of international affairs at George Washington University in Washington. "The international community must not accept Central Asian authorities' attempts to blame 'religious extremists' for all of the region's problems and the instability affecting the countries." [23]

A variety of other, widely acknowledged problems threaten the region's stability, but they don't involve religion, according to the International Crisis Group. Drug-trafficking, for example, poses a huge challenge for Tajikistan, a well-known conduit for drugs being smuggled from Afghanistan to Russia and China. [24]

Turkmenistan is a major source for human traffickers. Many Turkmen end up being trafficked to Turkey, where the men often work illegally on construction sites and the women in textile sweat shops, as domestic servants or as prostitutes. [25] And, while no Central Asian government has nuclear weapons, large quantities of nuclear waste were left behind in Central Asia by the Soviets. Plus, states like Kazakhstan and Uzbekistan could begin to exploit their abundant uranium deposits, fueling a nuclear threat.

Russian soldiers based in Tajikistan display more than a ton of heroin, with a street value of about $300 million, seized near the Tajik-Afghan border. Drug trafficking poses a huge challenge in rugged, sparsely populated Central Asian countries such as Tajikistan, widely known as a conduit for Afghan drugs smuggled to Russia and China.

Should the West forge closer ties with Central Asia?

Some analysts question whether Western democracies should strengthen their links with the region, given Central Asia's poor rankings on democracy, human rights, rule of law and corruption.

Crude Accountability's Watters, whose organization focuses on the environmental problems caused by the Kazakh and Turkmen energy industries, questions the wisdom of closer ties. "Turkmenistan is one of the most oppressive governments in the world. Kazakhstan is not much better," she says.

Oil revenues are enriching the ruling elite while the wider population languishes in poverty, she contends, pointing out that Turkmen President Gurbanguly Berdymukhamedov recently pushed through a law strengthening his control of the petroleum sector by placing 80 percent of revenues at his discretion.

In Kazakhstan, "the standard of living has risen inexorably," says EU parliamentarian Stevenson. While wealthy

AP Photo

Chinese and Central Asian leaders gather on Dec. 14, 2009, to celebrate the opening of a natural gas pipeline to China from Turkmenistan's Samandepe gas field. The pipeline will run through Uzbekistan and Kazakhstan on its way to western China. Shown, from the right, are presidents Nursultan Nazarbayev (Kazakhstan), Hu Jintao (China), Islam Karimov (Uzbekistan) and Gurbanguly Berdymukhamedov (Turkmenistan). Beijing's share of Central Asian trade has grown from only 4 percent in 2000 to 24 percent in 2010.

oligarchs have emerged, he points out, some of the oil wealth has trickled down. "I have seen improvements: roads being paved, new sanitation, more hotels and shops, including Western chains like Starbucks and McDonalds."

Oil and gas are not the only reasons why the West should engage with Central Asia, he says. With a quarter of Afghanistan's heroin being trafficked through Central Asia, he says, "We should be helping the governments stop the traffickers." [26] The governments are sincere in wanting to clamp down on the drug trade and are not linked to the traffickers as some allege, he believes. "If the West pulls up the drawbridge by cutting off contact, we will be cutting off our nose to spite our face," he says.

The U.S. and EU governments seem to share Stevenson's view. One of their pet projects is construction of the 2,000-mile-long Nabucco pipeline to move Caspian gas to Turkey and on to Eastern Europe and Austria — crucially bypassing Russia. Given its large gas reserves, Turkmenistan has emerged as a preferred source, although the Nabucco project is far from fruition. [27]

The U.S. special envoy and coordinator for international energy affairs, Carlos Pascual, says "a number of different pipeline options may be developed." However, he adds,

"The critical point is to be able to provide export routes for the very significant amounts of gas available in the Caspian area. The U.S. has provided full support for that." [28]

China and Iran also have been eyeing this energy and have built pipelines with Turkmenistan. And the new Trans-Afghanistan Pipeline (TAPI) project would transport Turkmen gas to Afghanistan, Pakistan and India.

Juan Miranda, director general of the Department of Central and West Asia at the Asian Development Bank in Manila, Philippines, says the international community should be helping to connect the landlocked region with the large, surrounding commercial centers. "Unless we develop connectivity, the region will not get out of poverty," Miranda says. Among other things, he says, the region needs the infrastructure to exploit its natural resources. "If minerals and hydrocarbons are a means to an end, then infrastructure is the means to those means," he says. [29]

Russian journalist Savchenko says, "The West should engage, because otherwise who is going to come? If they become Islamic states, they will move closer to countries like Iran."

But she also feels the West should be smarter about how it engages with Central Asia and should clearly prioritize its needs. "If it is just energy, they should keep doing what they are doing," she says. "But if they want long-term stability, they should have a clearer agenda on democracy, human rights and stopping the spread of radical Islam."

During a recent trip to Central Asia, U.S. Secretary of State Hillary Rodham Clinton struck a similar chord.

"We have learned over the years that after a while, after you've made your strong objections, if you have no contact, you have no influence," she said. And referring specifically to the repressive political climate in Uzbekistan, she said, "other countries will fill that vacuum who do not care about human rights." [30]

BACKGROUND

Invasions and Trade

Central Asia long served as a buffer zone between major empires. For centuries it marked the dividing line between the Turkic and Mongol empires of northern Asia and the Persian Empire of southern Asia.

CHRONOLOGY

500 B.C.-1500s *Persian, Mongol and Turkic peoples settle in Central Asia. Silk Road connects Asia and Europe.*

500 B.C. Darius I, a Persian king, expands his empire to include what is now Uzbekistan and Tajikistan.

A.D. 400s Turkic tribes from Mongolia and western China settle in Central Asia.

650 Arabs arrive from the Arabian desert and introduce Islam.

1218 Genghis Khan and his Mongol warriors defeat the Turkic Seljuks, later develop the Silk Road, a major trade route linking Europe to Asia.

1500 Uzbeks establish Bukhara as their capital; Uzbek gradually becomes region's dominant language.

1600s-1917 *Region declines economically, falls under Russian domination.*

1600s Maritime routes eclipse Silk Road, undercutting the region's prosperity.

Early 1700s Russian empire expands into Kazakhstan, rest of Central Asia.

Late 1800s Britain and Russia clash over influence in the region, a rivalry known as "The Great Game."

1914 Russia drafts Central Asians into the army in World War I, provoking a revolt that is brutally suppressed.

1918-1991 *Soviet communist rule leads to repression of nationalism and Islam in the region.*

1918-29 Attempts by Central Asian nations to assert nationhood are squelched by the communist Red Army as they become fully integrated into the Soviet Union, the successor to the Russian Empire.

1930s More than a million Central Asians are killed, starve or flee to China as the Soviets forcibly reorganize individually farmed lands into collectives.

1941-1945 Soviet leader Josef Stalin relocates Germans, Chechens and others to Central Asia.

1979 Soviets occupy neighboring Afghanistan. Some Central Asians, drafted into the Soviet army, later switch sides and oppose the Soviets.

1985 Soviet leader Mikhail Gorbachev liberalizes the Soviet Union, triggering a resurgence of Islam in Central Asia.

1991 Failed coup against Gorbachev precipitates dissolution of the Soviet Union into 15 independent countries, including five in Central Asia: Kazakhstan, Kyrgyzstan, Tajikistan, Turkmenistan and Uzbekistan.

1992-2012 *Autocratic regimes become entrenched in Central Asia. . . . Oil and gas enrich Kazakhstan and Turkmenistan; Tajikistan and Kyrgyzstan suffer from poverty and instability. . . . Uzbekistan becomes an important base and conduit for NATO mission in Afghanistan.*

Early 1990s Region suffers massive economic shock in transitioning to a market economy. Autocratic leaders consolidate their power, except in the more democratic but chaotic Kyrgyzstan.

1997 Peace agreement ending civil war in Tajikistan sparks first legally constituted Islamic political party.

Sept. 11, 2001 Islamic terrorist attacks on the United States prompt Western countries to establish military bases in Central Asia to support NATO's mission in Afghanistan.

2005 Popular uprising in Andijan, Uzbekistan, is brutally suppressed.

2010 Turkmenistan begins operating its first offshore natural gas well.

2011 Multicandidate presidential election in Kyrgyzstan brings peaceful transition of political power, highly unusual for the region.

2012 Customs union between Kazakhstan, Russia and Belarus takes effect. Russian Prime Minister Vladimir Putin pressures other Central Asian states to join it.

Where Dynasty — Not Democracy — Rules

Turkmenistan's Nyazov renamed months after relatives.

It is a curious coincidence that Central Asia has had two leaders who were raised in state-run Soviet orphanages: Islam Karimov, the only president Uzbekistan has had since independence, and Saparmurat Nyazov, Turkmenistan's president from 1990-2006. [1]

The two also have something else common: their iron-fisted rule, which in Karimov's case extended to boiling at least one political dissident to death, according to the British ambassador to Uzbekistan from 2002-2004, Craig Murray, who was dismissed for his whistle-blowing. [2] Karimov is now in his mid-70s, but no successor is in sight.

If Uzbekistan follows Turkmenistan's example, Karimov's dentist — yes, his dentist — could get the job. Gurbanguly Berdymukhamedov, a dentist who rose meteorically through the political ranks during the 1990s before deftly slipping into Nyazov's shoes after his unexpected death, quickly replaced Nyazov's cult of personality with his own. Berdymukhamedov's portrait now hangs in schools, universities, on aircraft and at markets, and he is building a new palace to surpass the grandiose one Nyazov built. [3] He also calls himself "Arkadag," or "protecter."

It was Nyazov who started the name-changing trend by bestowing upon himself the title of Turkmenbashi, or "father of Turkmen." During his regime, "newscasts began with the pledge that the announcer's tongue would shrivel if he defamed the nation or Turkmenbashi," according to *The Moscow News.* [4] Nyazov elevated his dead mother to cult status, renamed the calendar months after relatives and replaced the Koran with the Ruhnama, a book of personal philosophy, he claimed to have written. [5]

It remains to be seen if Berdymukhamedov will reach the heights of Nyazov's eccentricities.

In Tajikistan Emomali Rakhmon, in office since 1992, is not as repressive as Karimov and Berdymukhamedov, but his government is said to easily equal them in levels of corruption. "From the president down to the policemen on the street, government is characterized by cronyism and corruption," said a leaked U.S. embassy diplomatic cable. [6] "Rakhmon and his family control the country's major businesses, including the largest bank."

A journalist driving through Tajikistan reported how "full-color billboards with his portrait seemed to appear every 10 minutes. Here he is standing tall in a field of cotton, here he is lecturing with a pointer on the construction of the world's tallest planned dam. . . . Here he is in a business suit walking through a new monumental arch. In that shot, the angle makes him look as if he were wearing a crown." [7]

In Kazakhstan the cult of personality and repression may not be as extreme, but few doubt that Nursultan Nazarbayev could be president for life if he wanted. Earning fame in his school years as a traditional wrestler, Nazarbayev rose to become president of Kazakhstan in 1990 and has maintained a firm grip on power ever since. [8] In recent months, however, his regime has been shaken by a surprising and unprecedented wave of Islamist terrorist attacks and violent clashes between police and disaffected oil industry workers. [9]

Kyrgyzstan is the outlier in this sea of autocracy. It now has its fourth president since independence, after two previous leaders were driven out of office in popular uprisings. And yet Kyrgyz leaders have not been averse to corruption and nepotism. Former President Almazbek Akayev, who fled office in 2005, put his wife Meerim in charge of a lucrative market outside the capital, Bishkek, while his successor, Kurmanbek Bakiyev, allegedly was grooming his son Maxim to succeed him when he suddenly was ousted in 2010. [10]

Neither Nazarbayev nor Karimov has sons, but their daughters are prominent public figures. Gulnara Karimova cuts a glamorous swath in the country as a jewelry designer, singer and owner of a fashion house. And until recently she was the country's ambassador to Spain. Nazarbayev's eldest daughter, Dariga, was a powerful player in the business and political arena, although recently she has fallen out of favor with her father.

The legendary traveler Marco Polo (c. 1254-1324) wrote about the region's terrain and people. "So great is the height of the mountains that no birds are to be seen near their summits," Polo wrote. Pakistani-based journalist and regional expert Ahmed Rashid has written how "the harsh, sparsely populated landscape made Central Asia ripe for conquest but difficult to rule; empires rose and fell periodically throughout its history." [31]

In around 500 B.C., King Darius I expanded his Persian empire to include modern-day Uzbekistan and

The International Crisis Group, a nongovernmental organization focused on conflict prevention and resolution, has urged all the region's leaders to "cease using their countries' resources as a source of fabulous wealth for themselves and their families and create a meritocracy with decent pay that would free officials from the need to depend on corruption to make ends meet." [11]

While such calls may fall on deaf ears, the leaders are aware that they must maintain some popular support. They can look no further than Kazakhstan for inspiration. Nazarbayev is generally viewed as the most successful Central Asian leader, both by generating considerable wealth for his people and by cultivating strong allies abroad.

The key to Nazarbayev's success, Australian journalist Bruce Loudon writes, "is the way he has used his country's wealth to build a middle class even while feathering his own nest. [That] is an important survival lesson for embattled autocratic rulers elsewhere." [12]

— *Brian Beary*

During the rule of Turkmenistan's quirky late leader, Sapamurat Nyazov, newscasters began their programs with the pledge that their tongues would shrivel if they defamed the nation or the president. Besides renaming the calendar months after relatives, Nyazov erected a giant golden statue of himself in the centre of Ashgabat, the nation's capital and largest city.

[1]Ahmed Rashid, *The Rise of Militant Islam in Central Asia* (2002), p. 81.

[2]Craig Murray, "How a Torture Protest Killed a Career," consortiumnews .com, Oct. 24, 2009, www.consortiumnews.com/2009/102409b.html.

[3]"Turkmenistan: Briefing Note for the European Parliament Foreign Affairs Committee and Central Asia Delegation on Turkmenistan," Human Rights Watch, April 26, 2011, www.hrw.org/print/news/ 2011/04/26/turkmenistan-briefing-note-european-parliament-foreign-affairs-committee-and-central.

[4]Jim Brooke, "Taking a cue from Central Asia," *The Moscow News*, Oct. 6, 2011, http://themoscownews.com/russiawatch/20111006/189101308.html.

[5]Rashid, *op. cit.*

[6]"Tajikistan: The Changing Insurgent Threats," Asia Report No. 205, International Crisis Group, May 24, 2011, www.crisisgroup.org/-/ media/Files/asia/central-asia/tajikistan/205%20Tajikistan%20-%20 The%20Changing%20Insurgent%20Threats.pdf.

[7]Brooke, *op. cit.*

[8]Rashid, *op. cit.*

[9]Peter Leonard, "Kazakhstan's Interior Minister police chief defends use of live rounds as protests simmer," The Associated Press, Dec. 18, 2011, http://ca.news.yahoo.com/police-fire-rioters-tense-western-kazakhstan-1-killed-112319550.html.

[10]"The Pogroms in Kyrgyzstan," *Asia Report No. 193*, International Crisis Group, Aug. 23, 2010, www.crisisgroup.org/en/regions/asia/ central-asia/kyrgyzstan/193-the-pogroms-in-kyrgyzstan.aspx.

[11]"Central Asia: Decay and Decline," *Asia Report No. 201*, International Crisis Group, Feb. 3, 2011, www.crisisgroup.org/en/regions/asia/ central-asia/201-central-asia-decay-and-decline.aspx.

[12]Bruce Loudon, "Dictator with a difference wins massive vote," *The Australian*, April 14, 2011, www.theaustralian.com.au/news/world/ dictator-with-a-difference-wins-massive-vote/story-e6frg6ux-1226038670909.

Tajikistan. Later, waves of conquerors swept through the region, including the ancient Greeks, led by Alexander the Great (356-323 B.C.).

As the Huns migrated westward from Asia to Europe in the 5th century A.D., Turkic tribes from Mongolia and western China moved to Central Asia to fill the vacuum.

Around 650 Arab forces arrived and introduced Islam. In 751, an Arab army defeated the Chinese at Talas in Kyrgyzstan, ending Chinese ambitions in

Central Asia Rates Low on Freedom, Corruption

Kyrgyzstan has the most favorable "freedom" ranking among the five Central Asian countries. Kazakhstan has the most favorable "corruption" ranking. The other three countries are ranked as both "not free" and with high corruption perception rankings.

Freedom and Corruption Status, 2011

	Freedom Status	Corruption Index*
Kyrgyzstan	Partly free	164th
Kazakhstan	Not free	120th
Tajikistan	Not free	152nd
Turkmenistan	Not free	177th
Uzbekistan	Not free	177th

*Out of 182 nations; the lower the number, the less corruption

Sources: "Corruption Perceptions Index 2011," Transparency International, December 2011, cpi.transparency.org/cpi2011/results/; "Freedom in the World 2011," Freedom House, January 2011, www.freedomhouse.org/images/File/fiw/FIW_2011_Booklet.pdf

Central Asia and consolidating Islam as the dominant religion. While the Arabs did not establish a major kingdom, the Fergana Valley became a center for Islamic learning, with Osh (in modern-day Kyrgyzstan) and Bukhara and Samarkand (in today's Uzbekistan) emerging as important Islamic cities.

In 1218 Genghis Khan (c. 1162-1227) led his fearsome "Mongolian horde" to victory at Bukhara, defeating the Turkic Seljuks. Khan developed the Silk Road — a web of routes providing safe passage for traders carrying goods by camel caravan between Europe and Asia. It eventually stretched from Istanbul to Beijing and became a conduit not just for products but also for new ideas, religions and technologies, such as papermaking, gunpowder production and silk weaving. Khan's empire encompassed most of European Russia before collapsing in the 14th century, leaving behind smaller principalities, called khanates, across Central Asia.

In the late 1300s the great conqueror Timur, also known as Tamerlane (1336-1405), from the Samarkand region of modern Uzbekistan, built an empire comprising Central Asia, India, Persia, Arabia and parts of

Russia. One of the great political leaders of his era, Tamerlane transformed Samarkand into one of the architectural marvels of the world, bringing "artisans and architects from all the conquered regions."

Tamerlane made the region "the center for Turkic influence in Central Asia and of resistance to Persian cultural and political domination," and replaced Persian with his own Turkish dialect, Jagatai, as the court language. [32]

In 1500 the Shaybani Uzbeks, descendants of Genghis Khan, defeated Tamerlane's descendants and moved the capital to Bukhara, leading to a flourishing of the Uzbek language and literature. The Uzbeks' most famous poet, Mir Alisher Navai (1441-1501), created the first Turkic script, which supplanted Persian as the region's dominant written language. (Uzbek is a Turkic language.)

After 1600 the Silk Road went into a long period of decline as new maritime routes linked Europe, Africa and India. The Shaybani Empire gradually disintegrated, too, as income diminished along with trade flows.

Russian Rule

In the early 1700s, Russia began expanding its empire into Central Asia, beginning with Kazakhstan. By the late 1800s Russia's supremacy was being challenged by the British, who had colonized the Indian subcontinent. Afghanistan, on the southern border of Central Asia, was the buffer state in the Russo-British rivalry for regional domination — known as "The Great Game."

Between 1865 and 1876 Russian armies captured much of Uzbekistan, Turkmenistan and Tajikistan and created a province called Turkestan, with Tashkent as its capital. Russians then immigrated in significant numbers and planted large swaths of territory with cotton in order to consolidate their control. During World War I, the Russian authorities tried to draft Central Asians into Tsar Nicholas II's army, triggering a revolt that was brutally suppressed.

After the war, as the empire collapsed and a Bolshevik-led civil war raged in Russia, a series of nationalist uprisings broke out in Central Asia between 1918 and 1921. At the same time, ethnically based nation states were being created across Eastern Europe from the remnants of the Austro-Hungarian and Ottoman empires. Central Asia's Turkic and Persian people tried to assert their identity, too, but were thwarted by the Bolsheviks. By 1929 all the nationalist revolts had been suppressed and a new Russian-dominated state, the Soviet Union, had been created from the remnants of the Russian empire.

In an effort to tame nationalist sentiment, Soviet leader Josef Stalin redrew the borders of the five Central Asian Soviet republics, deliberately mixing up ethnicities and exacerbating ethnic tensions. The Tajiks, for example, deeply resented Bukhara and Samarkand being made part of the Uzbek Soviet Republic.

In the 1930s, when the Soviets forcibly reorganized farmlands into collective settlements, the nomadic Kazakhs, Kyrgyz and Turkmen suffered terribly, along with Russia's *kulaks*, or landed peasants. Several million were murdered, starved or fled to China. The Soviets also closed mosques, forbade women from wearing veils and banned children from reading the Koran. Soviet rule brought some benefits, such as universal education and health care.

During World War II, Stalin deported other nationalities from western Russia to Central Asia. For instance, ethnic Germans from the Volga region, who originally came to Russia in the 1700s during the reign of Catherine the Great, were moved to Kazakhstan. The move was designed to keep the ethnic Germans beyond the reach of the German military, which was sweeping through the Soviet Union as part of Operation Barbarossa. About 500,000 Chechens from the Caucasus also were relocated to Central Asia.

Soviet repression began to ease in the 1960s. By the 1980s, Soviet leader Mikhail Gorbachev's liberalizing policies had spurred a religious revival. Thousands of mosques were built, and Islamic literature was imported from Saudi Arabia and Pakistan. When the Soviets occupied neighboring Afghanistan in 1979, some Central Asian draftees into the Soviet Army switched sides after being taken prisoner by Afghan rebels.

Meanwhile, ethnic tensions began to flare up, with Uzbeks and Kyrgyz, for example, clashing in March 1990. [33] Gorbachev's responses to the political unrest varied. In Kazakhstan and Uzbekistan he restored order by appointing strongmen who quickly solidified their grip on power. In Kyrgyzstan he did not intervene, and the political establishment later fragmented, setting the three nations on the divergent paths they still follow today. [34]

The Soviet Union's final collapse began with a failed reactionary coup against Gorbachev in August 1991. The presidents of the Soviet republics of Russia, Ukraine and Belarus signed the Treaty of Minsk on Dec. 8, 1991, which effectively disbanded the Soviet Union, replacing it with a Commonwealth of Independent States, which included most former Soviet republics. But when the five Central Asian republics formalized their independence on Dec. 21, "the mood amongst the Central Asian leaders was one of mourning rather than celebration," wrote Pakistani journalist Rashid.

"By millions of threads, from electricity grids to oil pipelines to roads and military bases, the Central Asian states were tied to Russia," he noted. [35]

Independence Dawns

After independence, Central Asia became more visible on the global stage. The five countries' similarities and differences often can be overlooked. For instance:

- The Kazakhs and Kyrgyz are the most closely related ethnically, although the Kazakhs' longer exposure to Russian domination has made them less Islamic than the Kyrgyz.
- The Turkmen, like the Kazakhs and Kyrgyz, historically were a nomadic people. Since independence Turkmenistan has pursued a much more isolationist path than the Kyrgyz or Kazakhs.
- The Tajiks and Uzbeks are descended from more settled cultures with deep-rooted attachments to Islam. [36]

Despite being products of the Soviet system, most of the new Central Asian leaders were not interested in re-unifying their countries. In fact, they tightened border controls and introduced visa requirements. As

AFP/Getty Images/Kevin Lamarque

During a stop in the Tajik capital of Dushanbe on Oct. 22, 2011, U.S. Secretary of State Hillary Rodham Clinton speaks at a "Town Hall with Women, Youth, and Civil Society." Clinton was promoting her new Silk Road Initiative, designed to link the economies of Tajikistan and Uzbekistan with those of Afghanistan, Pakistan and other Central Asian countries. The effort reflects long-term plans to boost regional peace and stability.

AFP/Getty Images/Vyacheslav Oseledko

U.S. soldiers from the 234th Infantry Division in Fort Riley, Kansas, prepare to depart for Afghanistan from the U.S. Transit Center in Manas, near Bishkek, Kyrgyzstan, on April 15, 2011. Because of their strategic location near Afghanistan, Central Asian governments have attracted foreign financial aid, sometimes in exchange for the use of military bases, especially as U.S. relations with nearby Pakistan have soured. U.S. assistance to Central Asia has totaled $5.27 billion since 1992.

they transitioned to a market economy in the 1990s, each suffered from several years of hyper-inflation. Kyrgyzstan and Kazakhstan liberalized their economies the most, while Uzbekistan, Turkmenistan and Tajikistan

retained stronger state control of economic planning. The Kazakh economy emerged the strongest, with GDP growing at 10 percent a year between 2003 and 2007. [37]

Meanwhile, millions of Central Asians — especially Tajiks, Kyrgyz and Uzbeks — migrated to Russia seeking jobs. The remittances they sent home became vital revenue sources, accounting for as much as half of Tajikistan's GDP. Although this flow took a hit during the great global recession of 2009, when the Russian economy dipped sharply, it has since rebounded. [38]

Tajikistan is the only one of the Stans to have experienced a full-scale war since the end of the Soviet era. The conflict erupted in September 1992 after a coalition of nationalist, Islamic and democratic forces tried to take power, and regional elites — backed by Uzbekistan and Russia — launched a counter-offensive. In the ensuing five-year civil war, 50,000 people were killed. The 1997 peace accord legalized the Islamic Revival Party, making Tajikistan the only Central Asian country to permit a religion-based political party.

In Uzbekistan, Islamist groups have carried out sporadic suicide bombings, including the July 2004 bombing of the U.S. and Israeli embassies. [39] Islam is tightly controlled in all five Central Asian republics through such measures as restrictions on traveling to Mecca, bans on publishing Islamic literature and punishments for any religious activity that has not been approved by the state. [40]

However, disillusionment with government-sanctioned Islam has grown, and some people have embraced more conservative forms of their religion, including traveling to Turkey to pursue religious studies. At the same time, Christian missionaries such as Jehovah's Witnesses and evangelical Protestants have been coming to the "Stans," and governments have tended to be hostile toward Christian churches.

Afghan War

The U.S.-led invasion of Afghanistan in 2001, which later morphed into a NATO mission, opened a new chapter in Central Asia's history, as the world's top military powers competed to establish bases there.

From 2001 to 2005, Uzbekistan allowed the United States to use its K2 airbase as a transit hub. And the United States handed over some terrorist suspects captured in Afghanistan to Uzbekistan, where they were tortured before being flown to the U.S. prison in Guantánamo Bay, Cuba, according to former British ambassador to Uzbekistan Murray. [41]

But the cozy relationship cooled considerably in 2005, after Washington criticized the government's brutal suppression of an uprising in the Uzbek city of Andijan, in which hundreds of civilians were killed. Uzbek officials asked the U.S. military to leave, which it did in November 2005. [42] The German military, which was less vocal about events in Andijan, was allowed to keep its military base in Termez in southern Uzbekistan. [43]

In Kyrgyzstan money poured in from U.S.-based democracy foundations, such as the National Democratic Institute and International Republican Institute, which wanted to make Kyrgyzstan a democratic beacon for the region. That dynamic changed, however, when the U.S. military began using Manas airport, and the Kyrgyz government began profiting from air base rent and contracts to supply gasoline to the U.S. military.

Growing charges of government corruption sparked demonstrations in March 2005, which forced President Askar Akayev from power. [44] Russian journalist Savchenko insists "this was not a democratic revolution. People had just grown disillusioned with the Akayev clan because of their rampant corruption and increasing brutality." But Akayev's successor, Kurmanbek Bakiyev, followed the same path of corruption and nepotism, she says.

In June 2010, violence broke out between ethnic Uzbeks and Kyrgyz focused in the southern Kyrgyz city of Osh, with pogroms perpetrated against the Uzbek minority by some Kyrgyz, sparked by accusations that Uzbeks had raped Kyrgyz women, bringing dishonor on their families and communities. At least 418 people were killed and about 100,000 Uzbeks fled to Uzbekistan, although most returned several weeks later. [45]

Turkmenistan has been the most closed of the five republics since independence, first under President Nyazov from 1991-2006 and more recently under President Berdymukhamedov, who took power when Nyazov died. The Turkmen government has clamped down on independent media and political opposition but has successfully attracted foreign investment and expertise to the country's rapidly growing gas industry.

Its first offshore gas production plant and onshore gas terminal opened in July 2011. [46]

In foreign relations, Central Asian governments have successfully attracted financial support from foreign powers by playing their trump card: their strategic location. For instance, Russia's infusion in early 2009 of more than $2 billion in loans and grants to Kyrgyzstan was believed to have been conditioned upon the Kyrgyz evicting the United States from the Manas airbase.

But while Kyrgyzstan took the Russian money, it never expelled the Americans and in July 2009 signed a new lease for Manas. [47] U.S. foreign assistance to Central Asia has totaled $5.27 billion since 1992, with aid in 2011 alone estimated at $149.3 million. [48]

CURRENT SITUATION

Energy and Foreign Relations

Both Turkmenistan and Kazakhstan are forging links with foreign governments and companies interested in helping them develop their oil and gas sectors. The Kazakhs are farther along in the process, having been open to the outside world since their independence. Foreign interest in once-isolationist Turkmenistan, however, is high, so the country is opening up to foreign investors.

In Kazakhstan, the economy continues to perform strongly, but there are signs of growing social unrest. During the summer, there were mass protests by oil sector workers in the Mangystau region of western Kazakhstan — where most Western oil companies are based — who complained of low salaries and bad working conditions. [49] When 2,000 workers were fired in the dispute, tensions continued to rise, culminating in December with violent clashes in Zhanaozen, where 16 people were killed after police opened fire on protesters. [50] President Nazarbayev responded by imposing a curfew until the end of January. [51]

Meanwhile, a homegrown militant Islamist group, Jund Al-Khilafah (JaK), has claimed responsibility for a spate of terrorist attacks carried out since the summer, including some in Afghanistan that targeted U.S. forces. [52] JaK strongly opposes a law signed by Nazarbayevin 2011 that tightened censorship of religious literature, restricted the opening of new mosques and banned prayer in public buildings. Asked why he thought the sudden bout of

Does the revival of Islam in Central Asia pose a problem?

YES
Umed Babakhanov
Editor-in-Chief, Founder, Asia Plus (media group), Tajikistan

Written for *CQ Global Researcher*, January 2012

The rapid revival of Islam in Central Asia became a reality during former Russian President Mikhail Gorbachev's *perestroika* (restructuring) program and continued after the creation of newly independent states in the region in the early 1990s. It is a natural process that will continue to grow in the future.

However, Islamic society can take many forms. It may be modern, tolerant and open to the world or radical, militant and closed. Unfortunately, the second form is on the rise in Central Asia, due to several factors:

- Poverty, widespread corruption and social injustice have driven more people to the mosque, where they are taught that only an Islamic society can guarantee their rights and solve their problems.
- The region's poorly educated young people can be easily manipulated. Uneducated people are more easily convinced that their troubles are caused by people from other religions and nations or some other "hostile force," so intolerance has increased in the region.
- With an acute shortage of educated clergy, religious education is of a poor quality, which can be dangerous. Poorly educated imams can wrongly interpret Islam's provisions to the public.
- Authorities' unreasonable pressures on Islam often contribute to the growth of radical and extremist sentiments in Central Asia's Islamic communities. Local governments competing against political Islam often mistakenly spread their fight to ordinary Muslims. Bans on the *hijab* (headscarves) in schools and mosque attendance by young people as well as the closure of *madrassas* (Islamic schools) and other "secular extremist" government measures increase Islamic extremism in the region.
- Recent developments also indicate that Islamic extremism from abroad threatens to strengthen in the region. The unsettled conflict in Afghanistan and intensification of the supply of U.S. goods through the U.S.-supported Northern Distribution Network increase the likelihood that extremists' military operations and their militant ideology can be brought into Central Asia, where they could find fertile soil.

The tendency for Islam to strengthen in Central Asia is a natural and irreversible process. The nature of future Islamic communities here will depend largely on the factors mentioned above.

NO
Kamoludin Abdullaev
Independent Historian from Tajikistan

Written for *CQ Global Researcher*, January 2012

The alarming rhetoric about Islamic terrorism stemming from the rise of Islam in Central Asia is based on a belief that this region is part of the global "Muslim village" that confronts America, and that local militants here are linked to jihadis in Pakistan and Afghanistan. However, even though Central Asia borders Afghanistan and Pakistan (dubbed AfPak) — the world's most dangerous place — the region has remained relatively peaceful during the 10 years since the U.S. engagement in Afghanistan began.

That is due partly to the Soviet legacy of zero tolerance for organized violence and weapons possession. Plus, there are no uncontrolled territories in Central Asia that could attract jihadis willing to relocate from AfPak, and no Tajik or Uzbek Taliban has emerged similar to the Pakistani or African Taliban. Indeed, the radical Islamists who have penetrated into Tajikistan, Uzbekistan and Kyrgyzstan from Afghanistan since the 1990s have not received strong support from local Muslims in a jihad aimed at building a global caliphate.

Moreover, Central Asia has not been "occupied by infidels" as in Chechnya, Afghanistan, Xinjiang or Kashmir. Muslims here live in independent nation-states that preside over communal societies, which then advocate for a strong association between religion and nationalism, culture, language, etc. Today Tajikistan is the only Central Asian state with an Islamic movement that — after 10 years of open confrontation — has chosen to participate in the political process within quasi-democratic structures. Tajikistan's experience proves that political Islam and a national awakening could develop in a parallel fashion when juxtaposed within the framework of the legal political process.

Contemporary Central Asian society is becoming increasingly Islamized, with more people observing Islamic rituals and ceremonies. But gradual and voluntary Islamization — in contrast to forcefully imposed Soviet atheism — is a positive sign of emerging pluralism and reinterpretation of Islam by Central Asians. Muslims here are negotiating their identity in this globalized world, and the world should appreciate that.

Thus, one should be skeptical of Central Asian authorities' interpretation of "terrorist activities" in the region. The major security threat in Central Asia lies not in the radicalization of Muslim policies but in the failure of political and economic transformation, growing authoritarianism, mismanagement, widespread corruption and other political, social and economic ills unrelated to religiosity or the situation in Afghanistan.

unrest was taking place in his country, the Kazakh ambassador to the United States, Erlan Idrissov, says, "I would not make any link" between the oil worker riots and the Islamist attacks. "For 20 years we have been very lucky, which is why it is a major shock for us that this is happening now." [53]

In this tense atmosphere, parliamentary elections were held on Jan. 15 in which President Nazarbayev's Nur Otan party won 81 percent of votes cast, with two other parties exceeding the 7 percent threshold for parliamentary representation for the first time. While the election was cited by Nazarbayev as evidence that he is pushing his country in a democratic direction, European election observers criticized the ballot, noting genuine opponents of the President were barred from competing. [54]

The Kazakh government, meanwhile, continues to strengthen its energy ties with China, agreeing at a summit in Astana in June 2011, for instance, to construct a third branch of the Turkmenistan-China gas pipeline, which has been operational since 2009. [55]

President Nazarbayev has been equally successful in cultivating good relations with the United States, Europe and Russia. He also has forged friendships in some surprising places. Spanish-Kazakh economic ties have flourished, for example, due partly to the personal friendship that has developed between Nazarbayev and Spain's King Juan Carlos.

Kazakhstan's oil wealth has enabled it to provide development aid to Afghanistan, supporting projects to improve the Afghans' water supply, infrastructure and education system. [56]

In Kyrgyzstan, presidential elections on Oct. 30 were deemed by international observers as "mostly fair," albeit with "procedural flaws." Prime Minister Almazbek Atambayev, who served for several years in the Kyrgyz government and is perceived as pro-Russian, emerged the clear winner, with 63 percent of the vote. [57] Outgoing President Roza Otunbayeva was prohibited from running under a law she helped draft to prevent leaders clinging to power indefinitely.

"We are grateful that she did not cancel that law. She is a person of good wisdom," says Aray, the Kyrgyz who works for a youth-oriented NGO.

In a bid to curry favor with Russia, Atambayev pledged to close the U.S. military base at Manas. Russian Prime Minister Putin has been pressuring Kyrgyzstan to join the customs union formed by Russia, Belarus and Kazakhstan,

A Kazakh policeman detains a protester during a rally by striking oil workers in Almaty on Dec. 17, 2011. The regime of Nursultan Nazarbayev — who has been in power since 1990 — has been shaken in recent months by an unprecedented wave of Islamist terrorist attacks and violent clashes between police and disaffected oil industry workers.

AFP/Getty Images/Anatoly Ustinenko

which went into effect in January and allows goods, services and labor to move freely between member countries. [58]

Aray is not sure the free-trade zone is a smart move. "We are almost being forced to enter it even though many experts are really opposed. We are already in the WTO [World Trade Organization]. That should be enough," she says.

The West continues to hope that the Kyrgyz will become a model of democracy for the region. But Russian journalist Savchenko says the pro-democracy funds the country gets from Western countries "are a big waste of money. It ends up being spent on lavish conferences that are just big money-spinners. NGOs learn the rules of this game, and many of them turn it into a business of extracting money from foreigners," she says.

And if some in the West view Kyrgyzstan as a shining example, the other four Central Asian governments view it "as a pariah" that absolutely should not be emulated, says Kyrgyz World Bank consultant Khamidov. They associate it with political instability, institutional weakness, poverty and ethnic strife.

In Tajikistan, the World Bank has been pressuring the government to delay construction of the new Rogun

Kyrgyz President Almazbek Atambayev greets supporters during his inauguration ceremony in Bishkek on Dec. 1, 2011. Until the recent election, the violence-scarred country had not seen a peaceful transition of presidential power since the fall of the Soviet Union two decades ago.

hydroelectric dam until an environmental impact assessment is completed. The project also has strained relations with neighboring Uzbekistan, which fears it will adversely impact its water supply. [59] The Tajiks believe the project could help them become a significant exporter of electricity. Currently, seasonal changes in water levels result in wintertime power blackouts, despite summertime hydropower surpluses.

In September, after Russian President Dmitry Medvedev visited Tajikistan, the Tajiks agreed to allow Russian military bases to remain rent-free in return for Russian aid to the Tajik military. [60] In October, Secretary of State Clinton visited the country in a similar bid to forge closer ties. Clinton noted that the United States has provided nearly $1 billion to Tajikistan since independence. [61]

Western aid to Tajikistan has focused on projects aimed at boosting state structures, such as law enforcement and border security, and supporting local pro-democracy NGOs. The U.S. does not have a military base in the country.

Repression Continues

The Tajik government continues to suppress all religious activity not subject to state control, even as the outward signs of observant Islam grow "perceptibly and rapidly," according to the International Crisis Group. Even in the capital city of Dushanbe, "streets empty out and traffic is reduced to a trickle during Friday prayers, something that did not happen a few years ago," the group reported. "Several popular singers have abandoned their careers, deeming singing un-Islamic." [62]

In Turkmenistan, the government continues to repress civil and religious rights. For example:

• In August President Berdymukhamedov ordered the removal of all satellite dishes, claiming they spoil the appearance of buildings. Citizens were using the dishes to access foreign channels as an alternative to the five state-owned channels. [63]

• In October a court sentenced Radio Free Europe/Radio Liberty freelancer Dovletmyrat Yazkuliyev to five years in prison in a "sham trial" on the "absurd charge" of abetting an attempted suicide of a family member, the news outlet said. Before his arrest, the government had warned him not to continue blogging on sensitive issues. He had reported on deadly explosions in the town of Abadan. [64]

• Police regularly confiscate religious literature; Muslims are banned from traveling abroad for religious education and women are barred from studying Islamic theology. [65]

Presidential elections are scheduled for February, with eight candidates registered to participate by early January 2011, including the incumbent Berdymukhamedov. [66] Meanwhile, the government is accumulating great wealth from gas exports, much of it being channeled into grandiose projects like the $1 billion new resort city on the Caspian, Awaza, which has a riverside restaurant reserved solely for the president. [67]

Although Uzbekistan remains deeply autocratic, it is trying to improve its image.

> *"You really feel the oppression [in Uzbekistan]. You see policemen every 300 meters — in the market, at the theater, in the subway. . . . Religion is almost forbidden. There are very few mosques. You do not hear imams calling people to prayer, because they are not allowed. It feels strange in an overwhelmingly Muslim country."*
>
> *— Jana Brandt, Project Coordinator*
> *World Uyghur Congress*

In July 2011 the Parliament held hearings on the need for democracy and economic liberalization. [68] President Karimov claims to be redistributing power from the executive branch to the legislature, but his claims have been met with skepticism since there still is no opposition party in parliament.

Meanwhile, the United States is forging closer ties with the Uzbeks. In September Congress lifted restrictions on military aid to Uzbekistan, which it wants to use as a conduit for military supplies and personnel to the Afghan war. In October Secretary Clinton visited Uzbekistan to discuss the issue with Karimov. [69] A key rail line passes from the Baltic countries, which are NATO allies, through Uzbekistan en route to Afghanistan. The United States has been using Pakistan as a transit route, but that has become more difficult as U.S.-Pakistani relations have soured.

The Uzbeks are happy to cooperate, however, since the United States, in return, has agreed to lift an embargo on selling military equipment to the regime. [70] About three-quarters of Afghanistan-bound NATO cargo now travels via Uzbekistan, compared to a third in 2010. [71]

Human rights groups have slammed the United States for cozying up to such a repressive regime. According to Steve Swerdlow, an Uzbekistan researcher at Human Rights Watch, "doing business with extremely abusive dictators is not a smart policy from the perspective of human rights or security." Instead, it "sends the detrimental message to ordinary Uzbeks that despite its pronouncements on the Arab Spring and democratic change, the Obama administration is more interested in narrow security interests in Afghanistan than in supporting the fundamental human rights of the Uzbek population." [72]

OUTLOOK
Remaining Nonaligned

While the economic outlook for Central Asia is positive, the region's economy relies heavily on petroleum exports and remittances from migrant workers. [73]

"The three oil and gas producers in the region — Kazakhstan, Turkmenistan and Uzbekistan — are showing signs of the 'resource curse,' under which energy-rich nations fail to thrive or develop distorted, unstable economies," the International Crisis Group has noted. [74] To avoid the "curse," they should create more jobs, reduce corruption and rebuild education and health systems gutted after the Soviet Union collapsed, the organization says.

There is cause for optimism. The World Bank and Asian Development Bank are sponsoring long-term projects to develop roads, electricity and energy. For instance, a highway interlinking all five countries with Afghanistan is due for completion by 2016.

Kazakh Ambassador Idrissov promises his country will lead in regional integration. "We are, by nature, a strong supporter of integration. In the 1990s, it was Kazakhstan who came up with the Eurasian Union idea," he says, referring to the customs union between Russia, Belarus and Kazakhstan. [75] With just 15 percent of current Central Asian trade being intra-regional, there is room for improvement. [76]

Key environmental problems still must be addressed, such as an unevenly distributed water supply, growing desertification and an abundance of unsecured nuclear waste left over from Soviet days. Much of the nuclear waste is concentrated in Kazakhstan, where the Soviets tested hundreds of nuclear bombs between 1949 and 1990. [77]

China's dramatic economic growth poses another challenge. "Enormous projects have been started on the building of canals, reservoirs, hydroelectric stations" in western China, depleting Kazakhstan's water resources, Stevenson, the Scottish member of the European Parliament, said. China is also emitting pollutants such as heavy metals and oil products into its rivers, which flow into Central Asia. [78]

The major world powers are expected to continue forging closer ties with the region. "There are more and more Chinese coming — maybe because they need some space," notes Aray, the Kyrgyz NGO worker, while the United States wants to maintain a presence in Kyrgyzstan, because it's "a good corner for keeping an eye on Russia and China." The Shanghai Cooperation Organization — an intergovernmental body (dubbed Asia's NATO) set up in 2001 among four of the five Central Asian republics and China and Russia — also could become an influential player. [79] (Nonaligned Turkmenistan is not a member.)

Russian journalist Savchenko believes the Central Asian governments do not have deep-rooted allegiances to any particular power: "Their priority is to keep their independence. They will ally themselves with whoever supports this."

Politically, the key question is whether Central Asia will experience its own Arab Spring.

"Despite the appearance of political calm, these are brittle regimes," *The Economist* has written. "After all, the leaders of Kazakhstan, Tajikistan and Uzbekistan all face a problem that flummoxed their counterparts in Egypt, Libya and Tunisia: how to remain guarantors of stability and not [be] the main threats to it." [80]

Spanish researcher de Pedro says Western governments should prod the regimes to make democratic reforms now, because it is very uncertain what will happen once the incumbents leave office. [81]

Aray predicts that Kyrgyzstan will be the outlier in the democracy stakes. "We are nomads and have always fought for our freedom," she says. "But I do not think we will see the same thing happen in any other Central Asian country — at least for the next 20 years."

NOTES

1. Jim Nichol, "Central Asia: Regional Developments and Implications for U.S. Interests," Congressional Research Service, Oct. 12, 2011.

2. Ahmed Rashid, *The Rise of Militant Islam in Central Asia* (2002).

3. Professor Eric McGlinchey, associate professor of government and politics, George Mason University, presentation at Wilson Center for International Scholars, Nov. 17, 2011, Washington, D.C.

4. "Uzbekistan," in the "Annual Report of the United States Commission on International Religious Freedom," U.S. Commission on International Religious Freedom, May 2011, www.uscirf.gov/images/book%20with%20cover%20for%20web.pdf.

5. Peter Leonard, "Turkmenistan gas field is now said to be world's 2nd largest," The Associated Press, May 25, 2011, www.usatoday.com/money/industries/energy/2011-05-25-turkmenistan-natural-gas-field_n.htm.

6. "Freedom in the World 2011," Freedom House, Jan. 13, 2011, www.freedomhouse.org/template.cfm?page=363&year=2010. Also see "Corruption Perceptions Index 2011," Transparency International, http://cpi.transparency.org/cpi2011/results/.

7. Craig Murray, "How a Torture Protest Killed a Career," consortiumnews.com, Oct. 24, 2009, www.consortiumnews.com/2009/102409b.html.

8. "World Directory of Minorities and Indigenous Peoples — Overview of Asia and Oceania/Central Asia," Minority Rights Group International, www.minorityrights.org/?lid=499.

9. Bruce Loudon, "Dictator with a difference wins massive vote," *The Australian*, April 14, 2011, www.theaustralian.com.au/news/world/dictator-with-a-difference-wins-massive-vote/story-e6frg6ux-1226038670909. Also see "Human Development Index and its Components," United Nations Development Program, 2011 Report, http://hdr.undp.org/en/media/HDR_2011_EN_Table1.pdf.

10. Suhrob Majidov, "Iran Increases Influence In Tajikistan At Russia's Expense," *Central Asia-Caucasus Institute Analyst*, Vol. 13, No. 17, Sept 21, 2011, www.cacianalyst.org/?q=node/5632.

11. "Managing Instability on China's Periphery," Council on Foreign Relations, September 2011, www.cfr.org/china/managing-instability-chinas-periphery/p25838?cid=nlc-news_release-news_release-link5-20110923.

12. *Ibid.*

13. "Freedom in the World 2011," *op. cit.*

14. *Ibid.*

15. *Ibid.*

16. See Barbara Mantel, "Democracy in Southeast Asia," *CQ Global Researcher*, June 1, 2010, pp. 131-156.

17. "It's A Gas: Funny Business in the Turkmen-Ukraine Gas Trade," press release, Global Witness, April 2006, p. 4, www.globalwitness.org/sites/default/files/library/its_a_gas_april_2006_lowres.pdf.

18. "Tajikistan: The Changing Insurgent Threats," *Asia Report No. 205*, International Crisis Group, May 24, 2011, www.crisisgroup.org/~/media/Files/asia/central-asia/tajikistan/205%20Tajikistan%20-%20The%20 Changing%20Insurgent%20Threats.pdf.

19. *Ibid.*

20. "Annual Report of the United States Commission on International Religious Freedom," *op. cit.*, p. 183.

21. Richard Weitz, "Central Asian Worries in Beijing," *Central Asia-Caucasus Institute Analyst*, Vol. 13, No. 17, Sept. 21, 2011, www.cacianalyst.org/?q=node/5626.

22. "Central Asia: Decay and Decline," *Asia Report No. 201*, International Crisis Group, Feb. 3, 2011, www .crisisgroup.org/en/regions/asia/central-asia/201-central-asia-decay-and-decline.aspx.

23. Marlene Laruelle, "Central Asian Islamism in the spotlight," Centre for European Policy Studies, *Commentary No. 13*, June 1, 2011, www.ceps.be/ book/central-asian-islamism-spotlight.

24. "Tajikistan: The Changing Insurgent Threats," *op. cit.*

25. "Trafficking in Persons Report 2011," U.S. State Department, 2011, www.state.gov/g/tip/rls/tiprpt/2011.

26. "Tajikistan: The Changing Insurgent Threats," *op. cit.*

27. Mina Muradova, "Competition for Caspian Gas Transit Intensifies," *Central Asia-Caucasus Institute Analyst*, Vol. 13, No. 12, July 6, 2011, www.cacianalyst .org/?q=node/5598.

28. Comments made at news briefing, Foreign Press Center, Washington, D.C., Nov. 21, 2011.

29. Remarks made at the conference, "The U.S.'s 'New Silk Road Strategy': What Is It? Where is It Headed?" at Central Asia-Caucasus Institute Silk Road Studies Program, School for Advanced International Studies, Johns Hopkins University, Washington, D.C., Sept. 29, 2011.

30. Hillary Rodham Clinton, U.S. Secretary of State, "Town Hall with Women, Youth and Civil Society," Ismaili Center, Dushanbe, Tajikistan, Oct. 22, 2011, www.state.gov/secretary/rm/2011/10/175985 .htm.

31. Unless otherwise noted, information in this section is from Ahmed Rashid, *The Rise of Militant Islam in Central Asia* (2002), p. 17. Also see Kenneth Jost, "Russia and The Former Soviet Republics," *CQ Researcher*, June 17, 2005.

32. Rashid, *op. cit.*

33. "The Pogroms in Kyrgyzstan," *Asia Report No. 193*, International Crisis Group, Aug. 23, 2010, www.crisis group.org/en/regions/asia/central-asia/kyrgyzstan/193-the-pogroms-in-kyrgyzstan.aspx.

34. See Eric McGlinchey, *Chaos, Violence and Dynasty: Politics and Islam in Central Asia* (2011).

35. Rashid, *op. cit.*, p. 47.

36. *Ibid.*

37. Table A4, "World Economic Outlook," International Monetary Fund, September 2011, p. 182, www.imf .org/external/pubs/ft/weo/2011/02/pdf/text.pdf.

38. "The Pogroms in Kyrgyzstan," *op. cit.*

39. Nichol, *op. cit.*

40. "Annual Report of the United States Commission on International Religious Freedom, *op. cit.*

41. For further details, see Amb. Murray's website, www .craigmurray.org.uk/documents/.

42. Abu-Ali Niyazmatov, "Ceremony to close U.S. military base held in Uzbekistan," Russian News and Information Agency (RIA Novosti), Nov. 21, 2005, http://en.rian.ru/world/20051121/42166025.html.

43. Bernardo Teles Fazendeiro, "Uzbekistan's 20th Anniversary: Independence and Relations with the United States and Germany," *Central Asia-Caucasus Institute Analyst*, Vol. 13, No. 18, Oct. 5, 2011, www.cacianalyst.org/?q=node/5636.

44. Jost, *op. cit.*

45. Matthew Naumann, "Central Asia," in Joanna Hoare, ed., *State of World's Minorities and Indigenous People 2011*, Minority Rights Group International, July 6, 2011, pp. 126-136, www.minorityrights.org/10848/ state-of-the-worlds-minorities/state-of-the-worlds-minorities-and-indigenous-peoples-2011.html.

46. "Turkmenistan launches commercial offshore gas production," State News Agency of Turkmenistan, July 13, 2011, http://cci.gov.tm/en/index.php?option= com_content&view=article&id=351:turkmenistan-launches-commercial-offshore-gas-production-&catid =38:news-2011.

47. "Kyrgyzstan: A Hollow Regime Collapses," *Asia Briefing No. 102*, International Crisis Group, April 27, 2010, p. 5, www.crisisgroup.org/en/regions/asia/central-asia/kyrgyzstan/B102-kyrgyzstan-a-hollow-regime-collapses.aspx.

48. Nichol, *op. cit.*

49. Georgiy Voloshin, "Post-Nazarbayev Succession Becoming Most Discussed Issue In Kazakhstan," *Central Asia-Caucasus Institute Analyst*, Vol. 13, No. 14, Aug. 3, 2011, www.cacianalyst.org/?q=node/5605.

50. Peter Leonard, "Kazakhstan's Interior Minister police chief defends use of live rounds as protests simmer," The Associated Press, Dec. 18, 2011, http://ca.news.yahoo.com/police-fire-rioters-tense-western-kazakhstan-1-killed-112319550.html.

51. "Kazakhstan president extends Zhanaozen town emergency," BBC News, Jan. 4, 2012, www.bbc.co.uk/news/world-asia-16408229.

52. Jacob Zenn, "Rising terror group exploits Kazakh unrest," *Asia Times*, Dec. 21, 2011, www.atmes.com/atimes/Central_Asia/ML21Ag01.html.

53. Comments made at a press conference, National Press Club, Washington D.C., Dec. 21, 2011.

54. Kathy Lally, "Observers criticize Kazakhstan election," *The Washington Post*, Jan. 16, 2012, www.washingtonpost.com/world/europe/observers-criticize-kazakhstan-election/2012/01/16/gIQAHLl22P_story.html.

55. Georgiy Voloshin, "China and Kazakhstan Praise Strategic Relations and Strengthen Regional Co-operation," *Central Asia-Caucasus Institute Analyst*, Vol. 13, No. 11, June 22, 2011, www.cacianalyst.org/?q=node/5588.

56. Marlene Laruelle, "Involving Central Asia in Afghanistan's future — what can Europe do?" Centre for European Policy Studies, Policy Brief No. 20, August 2011, www.fride.org/publication/937/policy-brief.

57. Fred Weir, "Kyrgyzstan elections: Unity top priority for Atambayev," *The Christian Science Monitor*, Oct. 31, 2011, www.csmonitor.com/World/Asia-South-Central/2011/1031/Kyrgyzstan-elections-Unity-top-priority-for-Atambayev.

58. "Putin proposes the creation of a 'Eurasian Union' by bringing together former Soviet states," *Irish Times*, Reuters, Oct. 5, 2011, www.irishtimes.com/newspaper/world/2011/1005/1224305256273.html. Also see Tai Adelaja, "Russia Is Recreating the Soviet Union, One Little Step at a Time," Russia Profile.org, Jan. 4, 2012, http://russiaprofile.org/business/52457.html.

59. Suhrob Majidov, "World Bank Advises Tajikistan To Halt Construction Of Hydropower Station," *Central Asia-Caucasus Institute Analyst*, Vol. 13, No. 16, Aug. 31, 2011, www.cacianalyst.org/?q=node/5624.

60. Suhrob Majidov, "Iran Increases Influence in Tajikistan at Russia's Expense," *Central Asia-Caucasus Institute Analyst*, Vol. 13, No. 17, Sept. 21, 2011, www.cacianalyst.org/?q=node/5632.

61. Clinton, *op. cit.*

62. "Tajikistan: The Changing Insurgent Threats," *op. cit.*

63. Alima Bissenova, "Turkmen leader wages war on satellite dishes," *Central Asia-Caucasus Institute Analyst*, Aug. 31, 2011, www.cacianalyst.org/?q=node/5625.

64. "Turkmenistan Convicts RFE/RL Correspondent In 'Bogus' Trial," Radio Free Europe-Radio Liberty, Oct. 5, 2011, www.rferl.org/content/turkmenistan_convicts_rferl_correspondent_in_bogus_trial/24350279.html.

65. "Annual Report of the United States Commission on International Religious Freedom," *op. cit.*

66. "Turkmenistan's 'Protector' Registers For Presidential Election," Radio Free Europe-Radio Liberty, Jan. 4, 2012, www.rferl.org/content/turkmen_president_registers_for_election/24442383.html.

67. Richard Orange, "Awaza, Turkmenistan: the most ill-conceived resort ever built?" *The* (London) *Daily Telegraph*, June 11, 2011, www.telegraph.co.uk/travel/travelnews/8567575/Awaza-Turkmenistan-the-most-ill-conceived-resort-ever-built.html.

68. Farkhod Tolipov, "Uzbekistan Experiments With Checks and Balances," *Central Asia-Caucasus Institute Analyst*, Vol. 13, No. 16, Aug. 31, 2011, www.cacianalyst.org/?q=node/5617.

69. Background briefing after Sec. Clinton's meeting with Islam Karimov, president of Uzbekistan, in

Tashkent, Uzbekistan, Oct. 22, 2011, www.state.gov/r/pa/prs/ps/2011/10/175988.htm.

70. Erkin Akhmadov, "U.S. Lifts Military Embargo On Uzbekistan," *Central Asia-Caucasus Institute Analyst*, Vol. 13, No. 18, Oct. 5, 2011, www.cacianalyst.org/?q=node/5641.

71. Laruelle, *op. cit.*

72. Justin Elliott, "Obama cozies up to Central Asian dictator," *Salon.com*, Sept. 17, 2011, www.salon.com/news/politics/war_room/2011/09/17/uzbekistan_afghistan.

73. "World Economic Outlook Database," *op. cit.*

74. "Central Asia's Energy Risks," *Asia Report No. 133*, International Crisis Group, May 24, 2007, www.crisisgroup.org/en/regions/asia/central-asia/133-central-asias-energy-risks.aspx, pp. 80-84. For background, see Jennifer Weeks, "The Resource Curse," *CQ Global Researcher*, Dec. 20, 2011, pp. 597-622.

75. Comments made at a seminar, "Central Asia, Afghanistan and the New Silk Road: Political, Economic and Security Challenges," Jamestown Foundation, Nov. 14, 2011.

76. Presentation by Ana Lucía Coronel, division chief, International Monetary Fund, Middle East and Central Asia Development, at conference entitled "IMF's Latest Economic Outlook for Central Asia-Caucasus and the Role of Wider Trade Relations," Central Asia-Caucasus Institute Silk Road Studies Program, School for Advanced International Studies, Johns Hopkins University, Washington, D.C., Nov. 30, 2011.

77. Struan Stevenson, "Crumbling regimes teach global nuclear lesson," *The Scotsman*, Sept. 6, 2011, www.indigopr.com/newsroom/crumbling-regimes-teach-global-nuclear-lesson.

78. Struan Stevenson, "China is depriving Kazakhstan of water," www.StuartStevenson.com, May 9, 2008, www.struanstevenson.com/media/article/china_is_depriving_kazakhstan_of_water/.

79. Yichen Dai, "The SCO at Ten: Time for Europe to engage?" *Commentary No. 15*, Centre for European Policy Studies, July 2011, www.ceps.be/book/sco-ten-time-europe-engage.

80. "Banyan: More black tea than jasmine," *The Economist*, March 5, 2011, www.economist.com/node/18285625.

81. See Nicolas de Pedro, "The Nazarbayev Consensus and its Limits. Kazakhstan: An irreversible road to democracy?" CIDOB — Barcelona Centre for International Affairs, May 31, 2011.

BIBLIOGRAPHY

Selected Sources
Books

Hermann, Werner, and Johannes Lin, eds., *Central Asia and the Caucasus: At the Crossroads of Eurasia in the 21st Century*, Sage Publications India, 2011.
Five authors explore how rivalry, trade and transport and oil and gas drilling affect Central Asia as well as, the impact of the 2008 financial crisis.

Marat, Erica, *The Military and the State in Central Asia: From Red Army to Independence*, Routledge, 2009.
A Central Asia analyst from Kyrgyzstan examines the role of the army in building state processes in contemporary Central Asian states.

McGlinchey, Eric, *Chaos, Violence, Dynasty: Politics and Islam in Central Asia*, University of Pittsburgh Press, 2011.
An associate professor of government and politics at George Mason University explains why Central Asian states evolved as they have since independence, focusing on Kazakhstan, Kyrgyzstan and Uzbekistan.

Rashid, Ahmed, *The Rise of Militant Islam in Central Asia*, Penguin, 2002.
A Pakistani journalist gives a concise history of the region from the early Mongol and Turkic invasions up until 2002, with a focus on Islam's influence on society.

Articles

Gessen, Keith, "Nowheresville; How Kazakhstan is building a glittering new capital from scratch," *The New Yorker*, April 18, 2011, www.newyorker.com/reporting/2011/04/18/110418fa_fact_gessen.
The reporter tours Astana, the capital of Kazakhstan since 1997, which is adorned with lavish new buildings financed by the country's oil boom.

Laruelle, Marlene, "Central Asian Islamism in the Spotlight," The Centre for European Policy Studies, Commentary No. 13, June 1, 2011, www.ceps.be/book/central-asian-islamism-spotlight.
A visiting research fellow at the School of Advanced International Studies at Johns Hopkins University discusses the threat Islamist militant groups pose in Central Asia.

Peyrouse, Sebastien, "The Russian Minority in Central Asia: Migration, Politics, and Language," Woodrow Wilson Center for International Scholars, 2008, www.wilsoncenter.org/sites/default/files/OP297.pdf.
An academic paper explains why millions of Russians have left Central Asia since the Soviet Union's collapse in 1991.

Stevenson, Struan, "The Aral Sea environmental tragedy," entry on personal blog struanstevenson.com, Oct. 20, 2010, www.struanstevenson.com/media/speech/the_aral_sea_environmental_tragedy/.
Environmental catastrophes in Central Asia, such as the shrinking of the Aral Sea, are described by a European Parliament member who has travelled the region extensively.

Weitz, Richard, "Central Asian Worries in Beijing," *Central Asia-Caucasus Institute Analyst,* Vol. 13, No. 17, Sept. 21, 2011, www.cacianalyst.org/?q=node/5626.
The director of the Center for Political-Military Analysis at the Hudson Institute in Washington explains how China views Central Asia.

Winn, Howard, "Central Asia's new great game draws a player with an eye for oil and gas," *South China Morning Post,* May 9, 2011, www.tethyspetroleum.com/media/Article/20110519/EN_US/SCMP%20Monday%20Face%20DR.PDF.
Oil and gas companies from around the world are increasingly investing in Central Asia, lured by abundant petroleum reserves.

Reports and Studies

"2011 Annual Report," United States Commission on International Religious Freedom, May 2011, www.uscirf.gov/images/book%20with%20cover%20for%20web.pdf.
A U.S. government-funded agency tasked with reporting on the state of religious freedom around the world sounds alarms for several Central Asian countries.

"Central Asia: Decay and Decline," International Crisis Group, Asia Report No. 201, Feb 3, 2011, www.crisisgroup.org/en/regions/asia/central-asia/201-central-asia-decay-and-decline.aspx.
A report charts the challenges Central Asia faces to rebuild its infrastructure, health and education systems, which declined precipitously when the Soviet Union collapsed.

"Managing Instability on China's Periphery," Council on Foreign Relations, September 2011, www.cfr.org/china/managing-instability-chinas-periphery/p25838?cid=nlc-news_release-news_release-link5-20110923.
Five authors describe how Central Asia could become a source of friction between global rivals China and the U.S.

Nichol, Jim, "Central Asia: Regional Developments and Implications for U.S. Interests," Congressional Research Service, Oct. 12, 2011.
The geostrategic importance of Central Asia to the United States is explained in a report commissioned by the U.S. Congress.

For More Information

A Asian Development Bank, Central and West Asia Department, 6 ADB Avenue, Mandaluyong City 1550, Metro Manila, Philippines; 63 2 632 4444; www.adb.org. Operates numerous projects aimed at building up Central Asia's infrastructure and better integrating it with the regional economy.

Central Asia-Caucasus Institute, School of Advanced International Studies, Johns Hopkins University, Nitze Building, 1740 Massachusetts Ave., N.W., Washington, DC 20036; 202-663-5600; www.sais-jhu.edu. Center for scholars on the region; organizes seminars and publishes articles.

Crude Accountability, P.O. Box 2345, Alexandria, VA 22301; 703-299-0854; www.crudeaccountability.org. A nongovernmental organization working on environmental challenges around the Caspian Sea basin, notably damage caused by the coal, oil and gas industries.

Forum 18, Postboks 6603, Rodeløkka, N-0502 Oslo, Norway; www.forum18.org. Religious freedom and human-rights advocacy group focused on the former Soviet Union and Eastern Europe.

Human Rights Watch, 350 Fifth Ave., 34th Floor, New York, NY 10118-3299; 212-290-4700; www.hrw.org. Researches and about human-rights conditions in Central Asia.

Office for Democratic Institutions and Human Rights, Ul. Miodowa 10, 00-251 Warsaw, Poland; 48 22 520 06 00; www.osce.org/odihr. An arm of the Organization for Security and Co-operation in Europe that supports election monitoring, democratic development, human rights, tolerance and rule of law.

Program on Central Asia and the Caucasus, Davis Center for Russian and Eurasian Studies, Harvard University, 1730 Cambridge St., Room S301, Cambridge, MA 02138; 617-495-4037; http://centasia.fas.harvard.edu. Promotes an understanding of the social, cultural, political and economic issues facing Central Asia.

Transparency International, Alt-Moabit 96, 10559 Berlin, Germany; 49 30 3438 20 0; www.transparency.org. A nongovernmental organization that fights corruption and produces an annual ranking of countries according to corruption levels.

United States Commission on International Religious Freedom, 800 N. Capitol St., N.W., Suite 790, Washington, DC 20002; 202-523-3240; www.uscirf.org. An independent, bipartisan government commission that provides data and analysis on religious repression and intolerance around the world.

Voices From Abroad:

ABDULWAHID SHAMOLOV

**Director, Institute of Philosophy,
Tajik Academy of Sciences, Tajikistan**

We are not Europe
"Someone wants to build democracy in 20 years here, but we are not Europeans but Tajiks, and we have our specifics and national features. A society having its national rules and traditions cannot switch to European democracy immediately."

*The Times of Central Asia (Kyrgyzstan),
September 2011*

The Khaleej Times, UAE/Paresh Nath

AZHDAR KURTOV

**Senior Researcher, Russian Institute
of Strategic Studies, Russia**

Power over society
"Over the years of Nazarbayev's rule, attempts have been made in Kazakhstan to deliberately cultivate outdated and atavistic types of behavior, because they come in really handy in strengthening the authority of the nation's leader. In a traditional Oriental society, institutions of power dominate over society."

*Ferghana News Agency (Russia),
January 2011*

GURBANGULY BERDIMUHAMEDOV

President, Turkmenistan

No alliances
"As a neutral state, Turkmenistan does not join any military alliances and blocs, produce or supply weapons of mass destruction and take part in any local or regional conflicts."

Gundogar (online newspaper, Russia), January 2011

RAJAB MIRZO

**Leader, Democratic Party of
Tajikistan, Tajikistan**

Depending on resources
"[Uzbekistan] is a democracy whose lifetime is measured by the length of gas, oil and water [resources]."

Ozodagon (Tajikistan), February 2011

BAKHADIR MUSAEV

Independent sociologist, Uzbekistan

Lies and myths
"We're seeing unbridled nationalism of the most primitive kind, and you're talking about sprouts of democracy. It's a lie. And these [leaders] have been called pioneers in building a parliamentary republic. It's a myth. They are nobodies, blank spaces. They are being manipulated by someone who wants this piece of land for geopolitical reasons."

*The Times of Central Asia (Kyrgyzstan),
November 2011*

DAVID TRILLING

Central Asia Editor, *EurasiaNet*, Kyrgyzstan

Divisions remain

"Though the country has approved a new constitution and held parliamentary elections . . . the process has exposed deep divisions between the more developed, Russified north, and the rural, impoverished south."

Al Jazeera (Qatar), October 2011

ROZA OTUNBAYEVA

President, Kyrgyzstan

Drawing upon the past

"[Kyrgyzstan needs] to draw a lesson from the two revolutions, the main causes of which were the disagreements between the authorities and the public, the driving force of revolutions being the people striving for justice."

The Times of Central Asia (Kyrgyzstan), March 2011

GRIGORIY KARASIN

Deputy Foreign Minister, Russia

Russia's role

"Russia does not claim to play an exclusive role in Central Asian affairs and is open for cooperation. The actions of all players there should be predictable and transparent."

Interfax News Agency (Russia), April 2011

3

Future of the Gulf States

Jennifer Koons

Shiite protesters camp out on Feb. 16, 2011, in Bahrain's capital Manama under the towering Pearl Roundabout monument, which became the symbol of recent opposition to the monarchy. The majority Shiite population says it is not represented in the Sunni-ruled government and suffers from widespread discrimination. The demonstrators were dispersed violently the next day by government forces, who eventually demolished the monument. Despite a government crackdown, protests have continued almost daily.

From *CQ Researcher*,
Nov. 1, 2011

For weeks last February, thousands of pro-democracy demonstrators — inspired by the protests in Cairo's Tahrir Square — occupied the Pearl Roundabout, a landmark traffic circle in the heart of Bahrain's capital, Manama. [1]

At 3 a.m. on Feb. 17 the protesters suddenly were roused from their makeshift tents surrounding the circle's towering iconic monument to the six-nation Gulf Cooperation Council (GCC). Dozens of police in armored vehicles surrounded the encampment and began firing rubber bullets and tear gas into the crowd. "We were sleeping," said a man who asked to be identified only as Hussein. "There were guys, kids, schoolchildren, women, and suddenly they just attacked us with tear gas [and] stun bombs." [2] When the attack ended, at least two of the protesters were dead, and the others had scattered.

The demonstrators had declared a "day of rage" three days earlier, on the ninth anniversary of the day the island-state off the northeastern coast of Saudi Arabia adopted its constitution. Bahrain's King Hamad bin Isa Al Khalifa, a Sunni, oversees a Shiite majority in the tiny Gulf kingdom, population 1.2 million.* The mostly Shiite protesters — who have continued their demonstrations on and off since February — decried unemployment, corruption and discrimination.

---

* Shiites broke away from mainstream Islam after the death of the Prophet Muhammad in A.D. 632 over who should be his chosen successor. Unlike Sunnis, they believe Islam's leader should be a direct descendant of the prophet. Sunnis say leaders can be chosen by consensus.

Gulf Monarchies Face Regional Threats

Saudi Arabia is the largest — in size, population and wealth — of the six monarchies that make up the Gulf Cooperation Council (GCC), a coalition formed in 1981 to promote coordination, security and unity in the region. Located on the oil-rich Arabian Peninsula and bordered on the east by the Persian Gulf and the Gulf of Oman, the GCC has accepted bids from the monarchies of Jordan and Morocco to join the coalition, but no decision has been made on when the countries will actually join. The Sunni-led Gulf monarchies also are concerned about the intentions of their Shiite-run neighbors Iran and Iraq on their northern and eastern borders and rising political unrest in Egypt and Yemen, on their western and southern flanks.

Gulf Cooperation Council Members

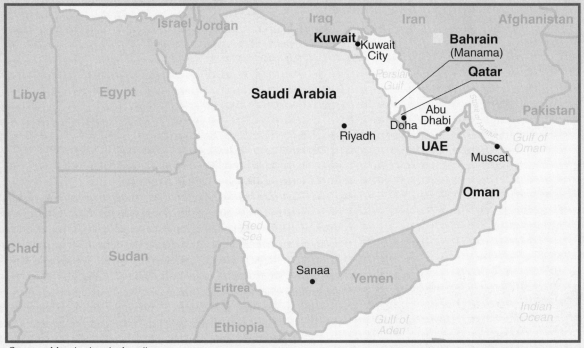

Source: Map by Lewis Agrell

Since then, the monarchy has silenced dissent aggressively. The government declared a three-month state of emergency, imposed martial law and razed the roundabout's famous sculpture of six buttresses supporting a giant concrete "pearl." [3] Officials also prosecuted and imprisoned doctors and lawyers who treated or represented detainees and arrested a founder of Bahrain's major independent newspaper *Al-Wasat*, who subsequently died in custody. [4] Hundreds of mostly Shiite workers were dismissed from public- and private-sector jobs for "absenteeism" during the demonstrations. [5]

In July, an international inquiry was launched into alleged human-rights abuses against the protesters by the government. But in late October, the Bahrain Independent Commission of Inquiry said it would delay release of its findings until "every testimony, complaint and item of evidence is considered and examined." The panel, which has the support of the Khalifa government, already has reviewed more than 8,000 complaints, testimonies and documents pertaining to alleged abuses. [6]

Popular challenges to Bahrain's stability and long-term success are a microcosm of issues facing the

Gulf States at a Glance

The six Gulf Cooperation Council members are mostly Sunni-dominated monarchies with high per-capita incomes due to vast energy wealth shared by small populations. Saudi Arabia has the region's biggest population and highest gross domestic product (GDP). Bahrain has the only majority-Shiite population, but its leaders and government officials are Sunni.

Bahrain

Head of state: King Hamad bin Isa al-Khalifa
Government: constitutional monarchy (Sunni minority rules over Shiite majority)
GDP: $29.7 billion (2010 estimate)
GDP per capita: $40,300 (2010 estimate)
Population: 1.2 million (July 2011 estimate)
Infant mortality rate: 10.4/1,000
Ethnic groups: Bahraini 62.4%, non-Bahraini 37.6% (2001 census)
Religions: Muslim 81.2% (Shiite 65-75%), Christian 9%, other 9.8% (2001 census)
Industries: petroleum processing and refining, aluminum smelting, iron pelletization, fertilizer, banking, insurance, ship repair, tourism
Average years in school: 14

Kuwait

Head of state: Emir Sabah al-Ahmad al-Jabir al-Sabah
Government: constitutional emirate
GDP: $136.5 billion
GDP per capita: $48,900
Population: 2.6 million (July 2011 estimate)
Infant mortality rate: 8.1/1,000
Ethnic groups: Kuwaiti 45%, other Arab 35%, South Asian 9%, Iranian 4%, other 7%
Religions: Muslim 85% (Sunni 70%, Shiite 30%), other (includes Christian, Hindu, Parsi) 15%
Industries: petroleum, petrochemicals, cement, shipbuilding and repair, water desalination, food processing
Average years in school: 12

Oman

Head of state: Sultan and Prime Minister Qaboos bin Said al-Said
Government: monarchy
GDP: $75.8 billion (2010 estimate)
GDP per capita: $25,600
Population: 3.0 (July 2011 estimate)
Infant mortality rate: 15.5/1,000
Ethnic groups: Arab, Baluchi, South Asian (Indian, Pakistani, Sri Lankan, Bangladeshi), African
Religions: Ibadhi Muslim 75%, other 25% (includes Sunni Muslim, Shiite Muslim, Hindu)
Industries: oil and natural gas production, construction, cement, copper, steel, chemicals
Average years in school: 12

Qatar

Head of state: Emir Hamad bin Khalifa al-Thani
Government: emirate
GDP: $150.6 billion (2010 estimate)
GDP per capita: $179,000
Population: 848,016 (July 2011 estimate)
Infant mortality rate: 12/1,000
Ethnic groups: Arab 40%, Indian 18%, Pakistani 18%, Iranian 10%, other 14%
Religions: Muslim 77.5% (Shiite 10%), Christian 8.5%, other 14%
Industries: gas and oil production, ammonia, fertilizer, petrochemicals, steel reinforcing bars, cement, ship repair
Average years in school: 12

Saudi Arabia

Head of state: King and Prime Minister Abdallah bin Abd al-Aziz Al Saud
Government: monarchy
GDP: $622 billion (2010 estimate)
GDP per capita: $24,200 (2010 estimate)
Population: 26.1 million (July 2011 estimate)
Infant mortality rate: 16.16/1,000
Ethnic groups: Arab 90%, Afro-Asian 10%
Religions: Muslim 100% (Shiite 10-15%, living mostly in the east)
Industries: oil production and refining, petrochemicals, ammonia, industrial gases, fertilizer, plastics, construction
Average years in school: 14

United Arab Emirates

Head of state: President Khalifa bin Zayid al-Nuhayyan
Government: federation, with certain powers delegated to the federal government
GDP: $246.8 billion (2010 estimate)
GDP per capita: $49,600 (2010 estimate)
Population: 5.1 million (July 2011 estimate)
Infant mortality rate: 11.9/1,000
Ethnic groups: Emirati 19%, other Arab and Iranian 23%, South Asian 50%, other expatriates (includes Westerners and East Asians) 8%
Religions: Muslim 96% (Shiite 10-16%); other (includes Christian, Hindu) 4%
Industries: petroleum and petrochemicals; fishing, aluminum, cement, fertilizer, ship repair, boat building, textiles
Average years in school: 13

Source: "The World Factbook," Central Intelligence Agency, 2011, https://www.cia.gov/library/publications/the-world-factbook/; "Mapping the Global Muslim Population," Pew Forum on Religion & Public Life, October 2009, pewforum.org/Muslim/Mapping-the-Global-Muslim-Population(6).aspx

UAE Arrests Prominent Democracy Activists

"I refuse to play the role written for me."

Although the United Arab Emirates (UAE) did not experience the same widespread protests that swept other Arab countries this year, officials at the federation of seven emirates have cracked down harshly on an attempt to question their absolute authority.

In April five pro-democracy activists were arrested after joining more than 130 leading academics, political activists and human-rights supporters in signing a March 9 online petition calling for a fully elected parliament and universal voting rights.[1] In June, the men were charged under Article 176 of the emirates' penal code, which makes it a crime punishable by up to five years imprisonment to publicly insult "the State President, its flag or national emblem."

Six months later, they remain on trial on charges of incitement and insulting the UAE's rulers.

One of the accused, Nasir bin Ghayth, an economics professor at the Abu Dhabi branch of Paris' Sorbonne University, served in the UAE air force and was a legal adviser for the armed forces. He was arrested along with blogger Ahmed Mansour, a member of Human Rights Watch's Middle East advisory committee, and online activists Fahad Salim Dalk, Hassan Ali Khamis and Ahmed Abdul Khaleq.

To protect itself from political upheaval, the emirates have announced new "benefits and handouts," bin Ghayth wrote in an article posted on the blog www.darussalam.ae on April 11 — less than a week before his arrest. They are "assuming their citizens are not like other Arabs or other human beings, who see freedom as a need no less significant than other physical needs. No amount of security — or rather intimidation by security forces — or wealth, handouts or foreign support is capable of ensuring the stability of an unjust ruler."

This fall, Human Rights Watch published a statement from bin Ghayth in which he says he and his fellow defendants have decided to boycott their trial. "I have reached an unshakeable conviction that this court, measured against international norms of justice, is merely a farce and facade meant to legitimize and make credible verdicts and penalties that may have already been decided. It is purely an attempt to punish me and those with me for our political opinions and our stances on certain national issues. Thus, I refuse to play the role written for me or to participate in this trial that does not rise to the standards of a fair trial."[2] The three-judge Federal Supreme Court panel hearing the case offers no right of appeal. The families of the men recently petitioned the court to drop the trial, writing that their loved ones have "suffered the bitterness of prison and the violation of their basic right to have a fair trial."[3]

Meanwhile, the government on Sept. 24 increased the number of UAE citizens permitted to vote in the country's second-ever election, which chose 20 members of the 40-member Federal National Council. The 20 other members are directly appointed to the council, which serves as an advisory board and has no legislative powers. Since the April arrests, the government has increased the number of eligible voters from about 7,000 in 2006 to 129,000, or 12 percent of the national population. No explanation was given as to how the voters were selected.[4]

Some 28 percent of those eligible actually showed up at the polls on Election Day in September.[5]

— Jennifer Koons

[1] "5 UAE activists held for 'opposing government,' " The Associated Press, April 25, 2011, http://arabnews.com/middleeast/article372546.ece.

[2] "Statement from Emirate detainee Dr. Nasir Bin Ghayth," Human Rights Watch, Oct. 1, 2011, www.hrw.org/news/2011/10/01/statement-emirati-detainee-dr-nasir-bin-ghayth.

[3] "UAE: A call for Help," Human Rights Watch, Oct. 9, 2011, www.hrw.org/news/2011/10/09/uae-call-help.

[4] Maysa Ghadeer, "Turnout in UAE's second election low at 28 percent of handpicked voters," Al Arabiya News, Sept. 24, 2011, www.alarabiya.net/articles/2011/09/24/168394.html.

[5] Ibid.

five other oil-rich GCC states. The six mostly Sunni-dominated monarchies — Bahrain, Kuwait, Oman, Qatar, Saudi Arabia and the United Arab Emirates (UAE) — share rising concerns about the strategic and ideological threats posed by neighboring Shiite-majority Iran and Iraq and a shortage of meaningful employment for their growing young populations. They formed the GCC coalition in 1981 to promote political and economic coordination, unity and security.

Home to some of the world's richest oil and gas reserves, the relatively young countries have a combined gross domestic product (GDP) of nearly $1 trillion and boast the globe's tallest building; a man-made island in the shape of a palm tree, used for luxury condominiums; and Islam's two holiest sites, Mecca and Medina.

Gregory Gause, director of the Middle East Studies Program at the University of Vermont, categorizes the GCC countries as "the super-rich per-capita states" such as Qatar and the UAE, "the super rich with relatively large populations" such as Saudi Arabia and the "moderately rich" states such as Oman and Bahrain.

Although all six are run by Sunnis, they all have Shiite minorities, except Bahrain, which has a Shiite majority. Saudi Arabia's Shiites make up a majority in the kingdom's eastern Gulf Coast province, which produces and exports most of the country's oil. All are run by tribal families that exercise near absolute political control, with limited personal liberties and strict adherence to Islamic social norms.

The monarchies initially were considered immune to the types of social and economic pressures that triggered the recent uprisings in Tunisia, Egypt and Libya. With 45 percent of the world's oil reserves, they were historically protected from having to democratize or curtail their close relationships with the West because Gulf citizens enjoy far better living standards than neighboring, non-oil-producing states. The ruling families share their oil wealth, providing citizens with annual stipends and free college educations and health care.

But in early February Gulf citizens began to challenge the monarchs' legitimacy, empowered by the Arab Spring uprisings in Tunisia and Egypt. Minor protests in every country but Qatar primarily targeted the absolute power wielded by the royal families. The families responded by spreading around more money.

In Kuwait, the emir distributed $4 billion to citizens, along with free food for 14 months, to celebrate the country's 50 years of independence. Some said he was "paying off" the citizenry to quiet the protests. In Saudi Arabia, King Abdullah announced a financial-aid package of about $36 billion for Saudi citizens, promising more jobs, pay hikes and student scholarships, among other things. Worried about unrest from the Shiite-majority in the eastern province, the government banned all protests. Protests also broke out in the UAE — mostly in the form of an online petition campaign — but the government cracked down hard, and there were no further demonstrations.

In Oman, several peaceful demonstrations protested government corruption. Protesters emphasized support for the ruling family but called for salary hikes and the removal of corrupt ministers. In response, the sultan promised to create 50,000 new government jobs and reshuffled his cabinet.

Even though the protests were tamped down, the GCC states still face some hard realities about their economic and labor models. To a large extent, the region's future development depends on the success of efforts to educate and employ its large population of young people. In 2010, a quarter of Saudi youth were unemployed — nearly double the global average. [7] In the five other GCC states, youth unemployment averaged 22.8 percent. [8]

Most GCC citizens resist working in low-level fields such as construction, so more than 80 percent of the private workforce consists of foreign workers. Foreigners hold key positions in airline, media, real estate and financial service companies, says Christian Koch, director of the Gulf Research Center Foundation in Dubai. The locals, however, lack the training for high-skilled jobs, where demand is growing fastest. If employed at all, most nationals work in the well-paying, but increasingly bloated, public sector.

Some governments — such as Saudi Arabia — have introduced "nationalization" schemes aimed at pushing their public employees into the private sector. [9] But most Gulf rulers have found it difficult to break a culture of easy-come government jobs and to prepare citizens for the private sector.

Other sheikdoms — especially those planning aggressive modernization programs that will require thousands of new foreign workers — are raising government salaries in an effort to keep unrest at bay. In Qatar, for instance, where native-born citizens make up only 5 percent of the private workforce, the ruling family in September announced 60 percent raises for all government employees and a 120 percent pay hike for military personnel. [10]

But that tactic can only work for so long, says Gause. "In the wealthier countries like the UAE and Qatar, nationals can work for the government," he says. However, there is "a certain ceiling you hit as ruling families get bigger and take up a larger and larger portion of

Futuristic skyscrapers create a striking skyline in Doha, Qatar, one of the glittering Gulf capitals known for their innovative and eye-popping architectural designs. Like the other energy-rich Gulf states, Qatar is investing in huge projects that depend heavily on foreign construction workers from developing countries. But growth is expected to slow in 2012, and Qatar and other Gulf states must deal with high unemployment rates among native-born citizens.

the population. The ruling al-Thani family in Qatar, for example, makes up one-third of the Qatari population."

In Bahrain, the government has long subdued its Shiite majority, which has been involved in efforts to overthrow the government since 1981, when an Iran-backed Shiite group attempted a coup. During anti-government street protests in August 2010, the government detained hundreds of Shiites, many of whom claimed they were tortured while in jail. [11] In the run-up to the Oct. 23, 2010, parliamentary election, government officials blocked the opposition party's website and banned local news coverage of the arrests. [12]

Neighboring Gulf countries remained largely silent during Bahrain's violent crackdown in February. But by March, as fears of growing Iranian influence grew, the GCC sent in roughly 2,000 troops to help restore order and demonstrate a show of strength. [13]

"If there is one thing the GCC monarchies dislike, it is uncertainty, and therefore the decision was made to support Bahrain reestablishing stability within the country," Koch says. "The feeling was unless such stability is restored, not only could the monarchy fall, but Iran could use the opportunity to increase its interference and ultimately level of control inside Bahrain." The intervention

made clear that an attempt to upset the political balance within a GCC country would not be tolerated."

As governments, academics and workers debate the region's future, here are some of the questions being debated:

Can the Gulf monarchies survive in their current form?

In the Gulf, families rule. The king or emir sits atop the pyramid, with family members filling important positions in the cabinet, the military and government agencies. Until recently, the system was mostly accepted without question, partly because citizens are content to enjoy high standards of living and partly because the democratic alternatives posed elsewhere in the Middle East were seen as unrealistic.

Since popular unrest swept the region this year, however, questions have been raised about the long-term viability of the autocratic model. While monarchies probably will survive in the short term, says the Gulf Research Center Foundation's Koch, "in the medium- to long-term it's unlikely, given that economic handouts only go so far. GCC citizens are increasingly globalized and aware of what is happening elsewhere and are beginning to ask for more than simply the opportunity to be rich."

Thus, he predicts, "For now, the monarchies continue to enjoy a high degree of legitimacy" and could "prolong their rule for some time to come" if they play it right.

But a push for more political representation and accountability likely will continue in Bahrain and Kuwait, which have the region's most democratic systems. Kuwait was the first Gulf country to adopt a constitution and the first to set up an elected parliament. The parliament can make laws, but the emir still has absolute authority over all decisions, and political parties are banned. Essentially, the parliament serves in an advisory capacity since the emir can overrule it and pass his own legislation by royal decree.

"The existing social contract — in simplest terms, trading political participation for material well-being — has been fraying for years, and it may now be more consciously doubtful," says J. E. Peterson, a historian and political analyst at the Gulf Research Center. "The situation is most acute in Bahrain, of course," where Shiite-Sunni sectarian tensions have been longstanding, and where "calls for a republic have spread to an unprecedented degree, particularly since the excesses of the regime in cracking down are unprecedented."

Calls for change are growing louder in Kuwait as well. The first Gulf state to establish a directly elected parliament, Kuwait has a 50-member National Assembly that can question and dismiss ministers, including the prime minister. Although formal political parties are banned, there are various interest groups.

"The rapid rise in oil prices and the accompanying oil boom [have] fueled corruption in Kuwait," said a 2006 U.S. Embassy cable released by Wikileaks. "Kuwaitis are increasingly beginning to ask where all this money is going." [14]

In June, thousands of young protesters in the streets of Kuwait City called for disbanding the parliament, new elections and the ouster of Prime Minister Sheikh Nasser Mohammad al-Ahmad al-Sabah. "The people want to topple the prime minister," chanted the more than 3,000 demonstrators, according to "Al Jazeera English." [15] In the past five years, the Kuwaiti prime minister has resigned six times, and parliament has been dissolved three times, amid accusations of corruption and infighting among the royal family.

Energy Reserves Enrich Gulf States

The proven oil reserves of the six members of the Gulf Cooperation Council account for more than one-third of the world's total, with Saudi Arabia leading the way. The states have more than one-fifth of the globe's natural gas reserves, led by Qatar, which ranks third worldwide behind Russia and Iran. Bahrain has the least oil and gas of the six.

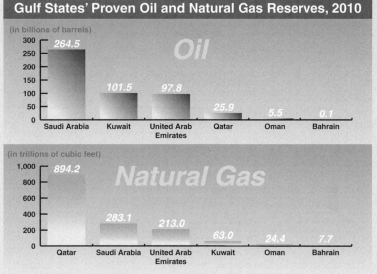

Gulf States' Proven Oil and Natural Gas Reserves, 2010

Source: "BP Statistical Review of World Energy," BP, June 2011, www.bp.com/assets/bp_internet/globalbp/globalbp_uk_english/reports_and_publications/statistical_energy_review_2011/STAGING/local_assets/pdf/statistical_review_of_world_energy_full_report_2011.pdf

To help buttress the oil-rich monarchies against future uprisings, the GCC on May 10 announced it was inviting Jordan and Morocco to join the security coalition. [16] Experts say the GCC was conveying to the world that monarchies are a stable form of government in the region and that since they face similar threats, they must band together. [17]

"In essence it was an attempt to gather strength from gathering all monarchies together, with an assumption that financial aid to the poorer ones would be both helpful and welcome," says Gerd Nonneman, dean of Georgetown University's School of Foreign Service in Qatar. "I doubt very much whether anything beyond associate membership will actually happen — if that."

The key to the monarchies' longevity lies in their ability to continue to meet the demands of their citizens, he added.

"They'll need to adjust, some more than others, and some earlier than others — with Bahrain at the fore," says Nonneman. "But if they do, gradually, then they should have many decades of monarchical rule ahead of them."

Reform won't be easy, he continues, because it will involve "economic demands on the populations if long-term sustainable economies are to be created; such demands will undermine the traditional social contract even further and are bound to bring demands for transparency and participation."

Gulf economies rely heavily on payments they collect for their crude oil exports, so they do not have strong domestic production sectors. And because the oil payments go directly to the rulers, there is little incentive to develop diversified economies that would provide expanding job opportunities for citizens.

AFP/Getty Images/Karim Sahib

Tennis superstar Roger Federer of Switzerland serves to India's Somdev Devvarman during their Dubai Open tennis match in the United Arab Emirates (UAE) on Feb. 22, 2011. The UAE is one of several Gulf states building world-class sports facilities in an effort to become a destination for major international events. Neighboring Qatar, for instance, has submitted a bid to host the 2020 Summer Olympics, and Dubai will compete for the spot four years later. Qatar also is hosting the 2022 soccer World Cup.

"At the risk of sounding tautological, the Gulf States are likely to endure because they have endured already," Gause, of Vermont's Middle East Studies Program, argues. "Over a few short decades, they have faced down successive challenges of modernization, radical pan-Arab nationalism and Islamic revivalism. They have demonstrated that they possess the qualifications necessary for survival."

Should the Gulf states diversify their economies to depend less on oil exports?

State-owned oil and gas industries are the single largest economic sectors in the GCC states, which nationalized their energy industries in the 1960s and '70s. Today about 80 percent of the Gulf countries' export earnings and revenues come from oil and gas. [18]

Saudi Arabia has one-fifth of the world's oil reserves, and Qatar has the world's third-largest gas reserves. During the uptick in oil prices in 2002-06, the GCC countries earned an estimated $327 billion per year — more than double their average yearly revenues for the preceding five years, according to the Carnegie Endowment for International Peace. [19]

But what goes up must come down. And the global financial crisis — coupled with a worldwide softening in

oil prices as economies slowed down — demonstrates that the GCC countries cannot count on consistently high oil prices forever. Already, countries with relatively limited oil and gas resources, such as Bahrain and Oman, are finding it increasingly difficult to sustain past levels of public spending.

On the other hand, Saudi Arabia faces another structural problem. Despite its huge oil production, the Saudis' per-capita oil-production rates are stagnant, due in part to a rapidly increasing population. The UAE and Qatar have per-citizen production rates that are nearly six times that of Saudi Arabia. [20]

All the GCC states are looking to develop non-oil sectors in order to diversify their economies. "They've realized this need long ago and pursued various strategies to that end, but have real difficulties in achieving it," the Gulf Research Center's Peterson says.

Some are investing in educational reforms so GCC nationals can get jobs in knowledge-intensive industries. Others are turning to energy-intensive manufacturing, converting a portion of their raw crude into value-added refined products, such as petrochemicals and plastics, for export. Some are using funds from the oil boom to enhance and market their tourism, hospitality and aviation industries.

While challenges remain, experts say the outlook for non-oil growth is positive. Over the next decade, the share of Gulf state wealth that comes from the oil sector will gradually decline. Non-oil growth is forecast to average 5.1 percent per year, versus 3.3 percent for the oil and gas sector. [21]

Qatar and Dubai (one of the seven emirates) are preparing bids to host major international sports championships, such as the 2020 Summer Olympics. Qatar will host the 2022 soccer World Cup, with huge infrastructure projects already under way. The early commitment reflects the kind of bold endeavor they are willing to undertake to secure their long-term survival in the post-oil era.

But some countries are taking a more proactive approach than others. "For mid-income countries like Saudi Arabia, Oman and Bahrain, there is a pressing need to diversify in order to create national employment and reduce long-term dependence on oil income," says Steffen Hertog, a lecturer at the London School of Economics and an adviser to the Gulf Research Center. "For the other three, it's more a choice of which kind of country and society they want to be — in principle they could live off of their oil rents for a long time, but in practice there is an ambition to diversify."

Not everyone, however, thinks economic diversification is a pressing concern. "As long as their reserves are ample and global oil demand is stable, oil and, in the case of Qatar, gas, will continue to dominate these countries' economies," according to Laura El-Katiri of the Oxford Institute for Energy Studies. "But this does not mean that their economies won't be more diverse; if a job can be found by most residents, then that is already a lot of progress."

While the GCC states rely heavily on foreign construction workers and laborers, they also want to limit how long the foreigners can stay. At the same time, the Gulf states' bloated public sectors employ significant proportions of the national labor force and offer a generous welfare system to their nationals.

Experts say generous government handouts — such as free health care and education and subsidized food and utilities — discourage Gulf citizens from working. Expatriates dominate the banking, law and technology fields. Yet Gulf countries want to build up their skilled private-sector workforces, so they must figure out how to reduce the culture of dependence without alienating the citizenry.

The Arab Spring presented a setback, of sorts, in that it encouraged Gulf rulers to try to avoid discontent by offering even greater handouts in order to buy political allegiance. "Whether the handouts are sustainable or not differs from country to country," Gause, at the University of Vermont's Middle East Studies Program, says. "They seem very sustainable in Kuwait, Qatar and the UAE, as long as there isn't a drastic drop in oil and gas prices. In Saudi Arabia they seem sustainable for some time, but not forever. In Bahrain and Oman, not as sustainable."

Gause and others remain unsure to what degree the state-cushioned economies inhibit diversification.

"They do inhibit shifting the private sector labor profile away from foreign workers," he says. "If citizens can expect a relatively comfortable living from the state sector, there is that much less incentive to take private-sector work." In addition, there is still plenty of support for large numbers of foreign workers, he says, because local businesses prefer them. "They can pay them less and control them more directly."

Are the Gulf states threatened by radical Islam or instability in Yemen?

GCC governments have watched warily as neighboring Yemen has been rocked by violence and political unrest. Inspired by the demonstrations in Egypt and Tunisia, protesters have spent the last six months calling for President Ali Abdullah Saleh to resign, blaming him for unemployment, economic conditions and corruption. In June Saleh was injured in a bomb attack at his palace compound in Sanaa and spent three months in Saudi Arabia receiving treatment before returning to Yemen in September.

Even before the recent unrest, the country teetered on the verge of becoming a failed state, with a weakened central government, a crippled economy, a young population and multiple insurgencies, including Al Qaeda in the Arabian Peninsula (AQAP).

"Numerous extremist activities have been carried out from Yemeni territory including, for example, the attempted assassination of Prince Mohammad Bin Nayef, the Saudi deputy minister of Interior," says Koch at the Gulf Research Center Foundation in Dubai. "The threat of a further disintegration of Yemen was one of the reasons the GCC put forward its initiative to enact a transfer of power from Saleh. But again the GCC did not want to push too hard, given that one consequence could have been more chaos in the country. Unless the political solution is clearly visible, the current sort of state of limbo is acceptable to deal with."

To combat terrorism, the GCC and the United States have tried to strengthen the Yemeni government and its people, who often are targeted by attempted AQAP attacks. Nonetheless, after Saleh's repeated violent reprisals against mass protesters, the GCC has begun to publicly call for his ouster.

"Yemen is very important to the GCC, and stability there is of great concern, particularly to neighboring Saudi Arabia," says Abdulkhaleq Abdulla, a professor of political science at United Emirates University, in Al Ain, Abu Dhabi. "It's a huge headache for them. They are doing everything to avoid Yemen becoming a failed state — they are investing and paying close attention and working toward a peaceful solution. But so far it's not working."

Qatar Has Highest Per-Capita Income

Qataris are the wealthiest population — when viewed on a per-capita basis — in the oil-rich Gulf region, with an average gross domestic product (GDP) of $179,000 per person. Saudi Arabia has the lowest per-capita income — $24,200 — even though it is the region's wealthiest country overall. Its total GDP is $622 billion (more than four times Qatar's $150.6 billion). But Saudi Arabia has the region's largest population — more than 26 million — compared to just 850,000 residents in Qatar. The United Arab Emirates, Kuwait and Bahrain are the middle-income Gulf states — with $40,000-$50,000 per-capita GDP. The per-capita GDP of the United States is $47,200.

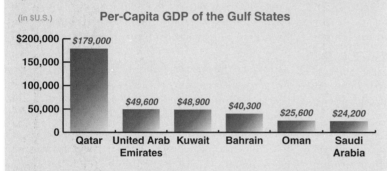

Per-Capita GDP of the Gulf States (in $U.S.)

- Qatar: $179,000
- United Arab Emirates: $49,600
- Kuwait: $48,900
- Bahrain: $40,300
- Oman: $25,600
- Saudi Arabia: $24,200

Source: "The World Factbook," Central Intelligence Agency, 2011, https://www.cia.gov/library/publications/the-world-factbook/

The GCC-backed deal calls for the formation of a unity government, with Saleh transferring power to his vice president, Gen. Abed Rabbo Mansour Hadi. Saleh would submit his resignation to parliament within 30 days, followed two months later by a presidential election. So far, however, Saleh has refused to sign off on the proposal, and the violence has continued. [22]

As recently as Oct. 22, at least 10 people were killed in fighting between Yemeni forces and opposition fighters in Sanaa, even as the government said it was ready to "deal positively" with a U.N. Security Council resolution approved the day before urging Saleh to step down in exchange for immunity. [23]

Nonneman, of Georgetown University in Qatar, doubts that even if Yemen dissolves into chaos it would harm the GCC countries. "The collapse of the state of Yemen can pose some threat of strikes but not of an overthrow of the system — at least not for the foreseeable future," he says.

Moreover, while there are some radical elements in other GCC countries, such as Saudi Arabia, he does not

think they pose an existential threat. "There is, of course, a good deal of fairly radical sentiment in Saudi Arabia, in particular, among sections of the population and some preachers, but it would take a collapse of regime legitimacy and control for this to take hold. By and large, Saudi Arabia's own anti-AQAP campaign has, since 2004, been quite successful, combining 'hearts-and-minds' [operations to win the public's support] with very effective security operations."

Abdulla says that since the Arab Spring uprisings began, domestic security concerns have surpassed terrorism as the major source of worry. Terrorism is "less of a concern now than before," he says, but "it's still a concern. I don't think anybody wants to downplay it.

"Having a front like Yemen as a fertile ground for radicals and jihadists is a concern," he continues. "However, there are a bunch of these unstable places that could breed extremist organizations."

Nonetheless, a State Department memo released by Wikileaks highlights the Gulf states' failure to block funding for groups like Al Qaeda and the Taliban. Individuals and charities in four Gulf states — Saudi Arabia, Qatar, Kuwait and the UAE — are the leading sources of funding for those terrorist organizations, according to the memo. "While the Kingdom of Saudi Arabia (KSA) takes seriously the threat of terrorism within Saudi Arabia, it has been an ongoing challenge to persuade Saudi officials to treat terrorist financing emanating from Saudi Arabia as a strategic priority," the memo stated. [24]

In May, GCC ministers announced they were creating a blacklist that would bar terrorists or anyone with suspected terrorist ties from entry into the six countries. [25] GCC members also have called upon the United Nations to set up an international center to fight the spread of global terror. [26] The ministers are concerned that a terrorist attack could disrupt the stability of the rapidly expanding and modernizing monarchies.

But Gause at Vermont's Middle East Studies Program says Al Qaeda in Yemen and Saudi Arabia poses more of a security threat than a serious political threat. "They're weaker in Saudi than they were five years ago," Gause says, adding, "They could take advantage of the chaos in Yemen, but I think they're really on the decline in terms of an ideological alternative. Yemen is a mess, but it's always been a mess, so that's pretty much a constant."

In September, a U.S. drone strike killed U.S.-born cleric Anwar al-Awlaki, a U.S. citizen living in Yemen and a leading AQAP member. He had been linked to several recent attempted attacks against the United States, including an unsuccessful plot last fall to send mail bombs on planes from Yemen to the United States. [27]

Meanwhile, Saudi Arabia — where the ultra-conservative Wahhabi form of Sunni Islam is the state religion — is prosecuting 17 alleged terrorists — 16 Saudis and a Yemeni. A Saudi Ministry of Justice spokesman said the defendants were charged with committing terrorist attacks and targeting oil wells in Saudi Arabia with mortars. "They are also charged with planning to assassinate a prominent Shiite cleric, with the aim of creating sectarian sedition in the country and distracting the authorities from the hunt for Al Qaeda operatives," according to *Al Arabiya*. [28]

BACKGROUND
Breaking British Ties

While the Gulf states were never occupied as colonies, they did enjoy long-standing "protectorate" status with Britain, which lasted from 1829 through 1971. The British first entered into a trade agreement with Oman, designed to limit piracy in the area by securing the shipping routes used between Britain and India. [29]

Abu Dhabi and Dubai, which would later become part of the UAE, and Bahrain signed similar treaties with the British in 1935. Kuwait entered into a similar arrangement in 1899 and Qatar in 1916. The British-Saudi relationship was more fraught, since the kingdom looked to expand into Oman. In 1915, the two countries signed a treaty expressly forbidding Saudi Arabia from acquiring territory in Bahrain, Oman and Qatar. The British provided military support and infrastructure development throughout the region but left traditional Arab monarchies in complete control over domestic affairs. [30]

In 1968, Great Britain announced its decision to end the treaty relationships by 1971, saying it could no longer afford its defense commitments. [31] That cleared the way for the United States to become the pre-eminent military and geopolitical power in the Gulf, a role it has strengthened and expanded ever since.

The GCC states are relatively young. The United Arab Emirates was created in 1971 as a loose federation of six separate emirates. A seventh joined in 1972. Qatar and Bahrain emerged in 1971 as independent entities after rejecting membership in the UAE.

Oman and Kuwait, independent from British protection since 1951 and 1961, respectively, continued to seek British guidance during the 1970s. Saudi Arabia had been recognized as a state in 1932, when King Abdul Aziz Al Saud declared rival tribal regions unified as the Kingdom of Saudi Arabia. [32]

The GCC was established in response to the tumultuous events of 1979-80, when the ayatollahs seized power in Iran, the Soviet Union invaded Afghanistan and war broke out between Iran and Iraq — sending shock waves through the Gulf states.

Before the 1979 Islamic revolution, Iran had been the region's de facto leader. But the ayatollahs took a radically different stance. [33] The Grand Ayatollah Ruhollah Khomeini called for the overthrow of what he considered the pro-American Gulf monarchies and even announced that Bahrain was historically and legally part of Iran. This prompted the Gulf nations to support Iraq's 1980 invasion of Iran.

When the Iran-Iraq War ended eight years later and Ayatollah Khomeini died in 1989, tension between the neighbors eased a bit, until Mahmoud Ahmadinejad's election in 2005. Under his presidency, Iran resumed uranium enrichment, which concerned the Gulf states as much as it did the United States and Israel.

On Feb. 4, 1981, the foreign ministers of the six nations signed a declaration creating the GCC. Security concerns, the catalyst for forming the organization, proved to be a unifying force as conflicts erupted throughout the region in the 1980s and '90s. The council moved to set up a joint defense force, the Peninsula Shield, in 1984. However, the GCC countries have remained dependent on British and later U.S. security guarantees, as the first Gulf war demonstrated.

"As small states living in a dangerous zone next to ambitious regional powers, you need regional protection," says Abdulla, of United Emirates University. "There was no other credible and willing foreign protector to provide you with a shield except for Britain and later the United States of America."

Forming U.S. Ties

The first Gulf War marked a turning point in the strategic military relationship between the United States and the GCC.

In 1991 the United States deployed more than 500,000 U.S. troops to Kuwait to combat an Iraqi invasion and occupation. [34] In the years immediately following the invasion, Bahrain, Kuwait, Qatar and the UAE all became joint signatories with the United States in separate bilateral defense cooperation agreements that allowed the United States to pre-position military equipment within their territories. Oman had entered into a defense "access" agreement with the United States more than 10 years earlier, allowing U.S. troops access to certain Omani military facilities.

The United States and Saudi Arabia have a long-standing military and strategic relationship, which began shortly before the start of the Cold War in the late 1940s and early '50s, when the U.S. government pledged to protect the kingdom from the Soviets. [35] The relationship was bolstered after U.S. forces pushed Iraq out of Kuwait. Roughly 5,000 U.S. military personnel remained in Saudi Arabia after the war, primarily to enforce a "no-fly zone" over southern Iraq.

After the Sept. 11 terrorist attacks in 2001, the U.S.-GCC relationship frayed, particularly when it was learned that 15 of the 19 hijackers were from Saudi Arabia. [36] In addition, Al Qaeda leader and 9/11 instigator Osama bin Laden, a Saudi, said the presence of U.S. troops in Saudi Arabia was one reason America was attacked on 9/11. The United States closed its bases in Saudi Arabia in 2003 and transferred the troops to Qatar and Bahrain.

The two countries remained in official agreement on larger security concerns, sharing a fear that Afghanistan was a terrorist breeding ground. However, those concerns diverged in March 2003 when the U.S. invaded Iraq.

"Trust in America is at its lowest point because of the disastrous showing in Iraq and Afghanistan, but it's still the only insurance company that we have in town," says Abdulla, of United Emirates University.

At the time, the White House maintained that removing Iraqi dictator Saddam Hussein from power and destroying Iraq's ability to produce weapons of mass destruction would eradicate its threat to the region. But the resulting sectarian infighting, which enabled the Shiite majority to take control for the first time in decades, and the rise of homegrown terrorism have been major causes of concern.

"Clearly, there has been a sea change with the removal of Saddam Hussein's regime and the rise of the Shia there," Nonneman of Georgetown University's School of Foreign Service in Qatar says, using an alternative form of the word Shiite. "Iraq is also the one place where Iran has been actively present, even though the vast majority of the Iraqi Shia, too, don't actually want Iranian control or an Iranian-style system."

Nevertheless, outside of Iran (which is Persian), this was the first time Shiites had dominated an Arab state.

"Baghdad has emerged as a center of Arab Shiite power," Juan Cole, a professor of Middle East history at the University of Michigan, said in 2007. "This is a new thing." [37]

Since the second Iraq War, the GCC has acted as a united body on military and strategic matters and focused on economic integration. The six members set up a customs union in 2002, a common market in 2007 and have had long-standing talks about adopting a single currency. But economic integration has yet to become a reality.

Women in Politics

Political participation has been primarily a 21st-century phenomenon for Gulf women. Although Qatar allowed women to vote in 1998, Bahrain did not enfranchise women until 2002, followed by Oman in 2003 and Kuwait in 2005.

In September, Saudi Arabia's Abdullah announced that women would be allowed to vote in the next election cycle, in 2015. [38] Women also will be appointed to the Majlis Al-Shura, an advisory council that can make public-policy recommendations. [39]

Abdullah had made small concessions to women in the past. In 2009, for instance, Noura al-Fayez, a former teacher and education administrator, was appointed

C H R O N O L O G Y

1960s-1970s *Bahrain, Kuwait, Oman, Qatar and the United Arab Emirates form independent states.*

1961 British protectorate in Kuwait ends. Iraq renews its claims on Kuwait but backs down after British military intervention. . . . Saudi Arabia's King Saud bin Abdul-Aziz Al Saud is deposed by his brother, Crown Prince Faysal Bin-Abd-al-Aziz Al Saud.

1968 Britain says it will withdraw its forces from the Persian Gulf, which it does by 1971.

1971 Bahrain declares independence and signs a treaty of friendship with Britain. . . . Abu Dhabi, Ajman, Dubai, Fujayrah, Sharjah and Umm al-Qaywayn form the United Arab Emirates (UAE), a federation of six city states. . . . Qatar becomes independent. . . . Bahrain agrees to allow the U.S. to rent naval and military facilities.

1972 After infighting in the ruling al-Thani family, Qatar's Khalifa bin Hamad al-Thani takes power in a palace coup. Ra's al-Khaimah becomes the seventh emirate to join UAE.

1973 Saudi Arabia leads an oil boycott among Arab members of the Organization of Petroleum Exporting Countries against Western countries that supported Israel in the October war against Egypt and Syria. Oil prices quadruple.

1975 Saudi Arabia's King Faysal is assassinated and is succeeded by his brother, Khalid bin Abdul-Aziz Al Saud.

1979 After overthrowing the Shah, ayatollahs establish a Shiite theocracy in Iran; call for overthrow of Gulf monarchies.

1980s-1990s *Six countries form Gulf Cooperation Council (GCC); Iraq-Iran War lasts for eight years; first Gulf War breaks out.*

1980 Iraq invades Iran, the start of an eight-year conflict.

1981 Responding to regional instability, Bahrain, Kuwait, Oman, the UAE, Qatar and Saudi Arabia form the GCC.

Aug. 2, 1990 Iraq's Saddam Hussein invades Kuwait; the United States responds by leading a coalition of 33 other countries, who invade Iraq. War ends when Iraq leaves Kuwait.

2000s *Constitutional reforms begin; 9/11 attacks occur in the U.S.; Gulf women are allowed to vote.*

2001 On Sept. 11, terrorists hijack airliners and ram them into New York's World Trade Center and the Pentagon; 15 of the 19 hijackers are Saudi citizens. . . . Bahrain becomes constitutional monarchy, allows women to stand for office. . . . Kuwaiti Parliament allows women to vote and run for parliament; first woman cabinet minister is appointed. . . . Qatar's first written constitution allows some democratic reforms.

2007-08 The global recession saw a fall in oil prices but the GCC states rebounded far quicker than the rest of the world by stepping up spending.

2010-2011 The protests that swept the Arab world beginning in Tunisia and Egypt also impact the GCC states, particularly Bahrain.

2010 World's tallest tower, Burj Khalifa, opens in Dubai. . . . Qatar wins bid to host 2022 FIFA World Cup (soccer).

2011 Tunisian and Egyptian protests lead to protests across the Gulf region. Protesters in Oman demand jobs, political reforms. . . . Saudi troops are called into Bahrain to quell protests over inequality and corruption; martial law is declared. . . . Qatar and the UAE join international military operations to back the rebels in Libya. Five political activists are arrested in the UAE. Jordan seeks to join GCC (May 10); Morocco is invited to join. . . . State of emergency in Bahrain is lifted. Bahrain convicts doctors who treated protesters. . . . An International organization launches investigation into whether Bahrain committed human-rights abuses against protesters. . . . Libyan leader Moammar Gadhafi is killed near his hometown of Sirte. . . . Fighting continues in Yemen even as embattled President Ali Abdullah Saleh said he welcomes a U.N. Security Council resolution urging him to sign a GCC-brokered deal to leave office.

Gulf States Pursue Academic 'Gold Rush'

But a critic says high school for all should come first.

Members of the Gulf Cooperation Council (GCC) are investing so heavily in Western-style university systems that some say the region is undergoing an "academic gold rush." Some countries are even building major branch campuses of elite American and European universities — such as New York University and the Sorbonne. Saudi Arabia, with a $15 billion annual higher-education budget, has created more than 100 universities and colleges since 2003, while the United Arab Emirates and Qatar have opened 40 foreign branches of Western universities during the same period. [1]

But Hana A. El-Ghali, senior program coordinator for the Issam Fares Institute for Public Policy & International Affairs at the American University in Beirut, Lebanon, tells reporter Jennifer Koons, in their question-and-answer interview, below, that importing education from abroad may not be the best way to prepare the GCC's growing youth population for success. [2]

JK: How would you characterize primary- and secondary-school educational opportunities throughout the Gulf region?

HE: As in most countries in the Arab region, primary and secondary education still faces an epidemic of rote learning . . . depending on memorization and preparation for national examinations. This graduates students who are not well prepared to tackle university education nor enter the labor market and address real-life challenges. Furthermore, equity is a major challenge for there is a discrepancy in the quality of education in public primary and secondary schools and private institutions. With better quality at the private schools, tuition fees become an obstacle for enrollment, and thus the inequity. Therefore, primary- and

secondary-school opportunities in the region can be described as backwards and limited. However, there has been an increase in female school enrollment at both the primary and secondary levels.

JK: Are there universal challenges?

HE: Major challenges include low enrollment rates and unaddressed dropout rates, particularly at the secondary level. One questions the goals set forth by the government when they invest in the tertiary-education system in the country rather than secure universal secondary education first.

JK: In what ways are the imported U.S. and European approaches to education lacking?

HE: Some argue the "academic gold rush" has been imported by the local governments themselves; others argue it was imposed by the international community. Either way, I strongly think interests on both sides allowed this transnational crossing of education to occur.

A number of institutions marched across a red carpet into the region while others had to put in a few dollars to enter. On another note, there hasn't been any formal evaluation of these approaches to the internationalization of higher education within the region.

I think that these endeavors are not culturally sensitive nor are they addressing the needs of the local community they are serving. There are a number of examples where the curriculum itself is not compatible with the local culture on several minute details that are considered taboo.

We have already witnessed a number of failures in the region, such as the George Mason University in Ras Al Khaimah. [3] I caution against labeling the remaining institutions

deputy minister for girls' education. But, as the Gulf's most religiously conservative country, where women still are not allowed to drive, Saudi Arabia remains the GCC state with the least female participation in public life.

Bahrain's King Hamad bin Isa al-Khalifa had led the way among GCC states in 2000, when he appointed five

women to the nation's 40-member upper house of parliament. [40] A year later, a royal decree enfranchised women in city council elections, although none of the 31 women who ran for office in May 2002 was elected. [41]

The February 2002 constitution gave women the right to vote and run for office in parliamentary elections. Eight a success, since it is still too early to judge their impact on the local communities.

JK: How important is a quality education to youth in the GCC states?

HE: As foreign institutions of education raided the region, quality became one of the victims. There are a number of reasons why the quality of education of these foreign institutions is not put to question, but it could be that because they are Westernized they are granted the face value of a quality education.

Quality education is increasingly significant as the youth population today is suffering more and more from a lack of opportunity post graduation. So, if these young people are not receiving the right education currently in demand within the local and global labor markets, then the nation will suffer.

JK: How would you characterize educational outcomes and performance in these countries?

HE: Educational outcomes are reflected within the students leaving the university and entering the labor market. Unfortunately, the rates of youth unemployment in these countries are among the highest in the world. These rates are not decreasing any time soon. Other indicators include the human-development index, which is always lagging behind in the GCC countries compared to the rest of the world.

JK: Where can improvements be made? And where are things being done that countries throughout the world may want to emulate?

HE: The Arab Gulf countries were pioneers in importing higher-education services to provide first-class educations to their citizens who decide not to leave the country. Some of the GCC countries managed to succeed in this endeavor.

Elementary school girls line up for classes in Dubai on Sept. 27, 2009. Members of the Gulf Cooperation Council (GCC) are investing heavily in Western-style university systems in what some call an "academic gold rush." But critics say the GCC's first priority should be reforming primary and secondary education, which they say relies too heavily on rote learning and preparation for national examinations.

However, there were a number of failures along the way. Furthermore, it remains to be determined what the result of these investments will be.

A closer look must be taken at the needs of the local society and labor market in order to reform not just higher education system but the whole education system. These reforms should take into consideration the K-12 culture in which they are embedded. Unless these factors are considered, the education system in the GCC countries will continue to present a one-size-fits-all approach, when in reality more customized solutions are needed.

[1]Vincent Romani, "The Politics of Higher Education in the Middle East: Problems and Prospects," Brandeis University's Crown Center for Middle East Studies, May 2009, www.brandeis.edu/crown/publications/meb/MEB36.pdf.

[2]Interview has been edited for space.

[3]Peter Stearns, "Closing the RAK Campus," Office of the Provost, George Mason University, Feb. 27, 2011, http://provostblog.gmu.edu/archives/56.

female candidates competed in a field of 190 during the October 2002 parliamentary elections, but none was elected. [42] Hamad later appointed six women to the upper house, the Consultative Council.

In the 2010 "Gender Gap Index," issued by the World Economic Forum, Bahrain ranked fourth from the top among Arabian countries but 110th internationally in gender inequality — up from 116th in 2009. [43] The report attributed the improvement to women moving into legislative and senior ministerial positions. [44] This year, three women were elected in Bahrain's special parliamentary elections on Sept. 24 and Oct. 1, bringing their total to four. [45]

AFP/Getty Images/Adam Jan

A Bahraini woman casts her vote in parliamentary elections on Oct. 1, 2011. Political participation has been primarily a 21st-century phenomenon for Gulf women. Qatar allowed women to vote in 1998, followed by Bahrain, Oman and Kuwait in 2002, 2003 and 2005, respectively. In September, Saudi Arabia's King Abdullah announced that women would be allowed to vote in the next election cycle, in 2015.

Meanwhile, in Kuwait — which has the region's most democratic political system — efforts to bring women into politics have stalled. Women received the right to vote in 2005, but none were elected to parliament until 2009, when four women were voted into the 50-member national assembly. [46]

In Qatar, women competed as independent candidates in municipal elections as far back as 1999, but none were elected. The first woman was elected to public office in April 2003 — as a member of the 29-seat municipal council. Eight years later, three out of four female candidates failed to win seats in the May 2011 municipal council elections.

Nevertheless, women have been appointed to several higher-profile positions, albeit in typically "female" fields, such as education and social affairs. Sheikha bint Ahmad al-Mahmud became the country's first female minister of education in 2003, having served as undersecretary since 1996. [47] The president of the University of Qatar and the dean of the Faculty of Sharia Law and Islamic Studies are also women. [48]

CURRENT SITUATION

Influential Actor?

Amid the tumult that is shaking the Middle East, the GCC continues to display unity and project itself as an influential regional actor.

In Yemen the council has tried to engineer an orderly transition from Saleh's rule. It has backed the NATO-led intervention in Libya, providing an Arab cover to Western intervention in the internal affairs of an Arab state. Finally, it has announced that it would accept membership bids from Jordan and Morocco, which would elevate the GCC from a subregional bloc into more of an international alliance.

With its preeminent position in world energy markets and buoyed by large budget surpluses — $19.6 billion in 2009 and $189 billion in 2008 — the Gulf states have shifted gears and sought to interact with nations throughout the world in unprecedented ways. It's part of an effort to explore new relationships and mechanisms to contribute to regional stability. [49]

As a result, the GCC's global involvement is being defined more by the member states themselves than by outside actors imposing decisions on them. For example, the involvement of Qatar and the UAE in the operations against Libya in March 2011 symbolized the new determination to shape policy instead of being shaped by it.

And Saudi Arabia — the 800-pound gorilla in the GCC living room — has tried to step into the power vacuum created by the turmoil in Iraq and Egypt. With 70 percent of GCC nationals and 88 percent of its total land area, Saudi Arabia's security and stability affect the well-being of the entire region. While the kingdom has avoided much of the unrest sweeping the Arab world, it has seen some clashes in its Shiite-dominated eastern region.

Fourteen people were injured in October when clashes erupted in the eastern town of Awamia. The government made a thinly veiled accusation against Iran for causing the unrest. "A foreign country is trying to undermine national security by inciting strife," said an Interior Ministry statement. [50] Saudi police had opened fire to disperse protesters in the same province last March, a day before planned countrywide anti-government protests. The protesters, all Shiite, were demanding the release of prisoners they said had been held without charge. Protesting is illegal in the kingdom.

Is Shiite influence from Iran and Iraq growing in the region?

YES
Taufiq Rahim
Visiting Scholar, Dubai School of Government

Written for *CQ Global Researcher*, November 2011

After the end of the brutal Iran-Iraq war in 1988, a growing détente existed between Iran and its Arab neighbors, especially during the presidency of Mohammad Khatami in 1997. Particular progress was made in strengthening diplomatic relations between Iran and Saudi Arabia, helping to bring a sense of calm to the Gulf Cooperation Council (GCC).

However, beginning with the U.S. overthrow of Saddam Hussein in March 2003, a renewed sense of concern arose among traditional Sunni political leaders in the region. In 2004, King Abdullah of Jordan warned that Iran was trying to establish a "Shiite crescent" slicing through the region. That same year, the United States revealed that Iran was pursuing an aggressive nuclear program. In 2005, firebrand Iranian President Mahmoud Ahmadinejad came to power. In 2008, Hezbollah swept through Beirut in a show of force and in early 2011 brought about a government of its allies. In Yemen, a minority Shiite population launched a renewed rebellion in 2009-2010. King Abdullah's warning appeared to be coming to fruition.

Leaked diplomatic cables published by Wikileaks have shown that GCC leaders increasingly are worried about what they see as a growing threat from Iran, exercised through its perceived Shiite proxies. In fact, Saudi and Emirati enthusiasm for a military option against Iran appeared to surprise even President Barack Obama when he visited Riyadh in 2009.

Concern reached a new level after the "Arab Spring." It was no longer just a contest for influence in the wider region but an existential threat to the domestic leadership of GCC countries. In Bahrain, with its majority-Shiite population, the overthrow of the monarchy was prevented only by the deployment of forces from neighboring countries. Every other GCC country has a minority-Shiite population, and the fear is that Iran will try to exploit this to further destabilize existing power structures, such as in the eastern province of Saudi Arabia.

Iran's influence is likely overstated when compared to the reality; many of the aforementioned Shiite movements have independent sources of legitimacy and power. In Bahrain, for example, pro-democracy and anti-monarchial movements have occurred for decades and are very much rooted in domestic circumstances.

Yet, the perception of the threat is very real, as is Iran's saber-rattling. The continued hostility between the GCC and Iran is likely to escalate and lead to further instability in the region in the near future.

NO
Marina Ottaway
Senior Associate, Carnegie Endowment for International Peace

Written for *CQ Global Researcher*, November 2011

Iran has emerged as the all-purpose scapegoat for Gulf countries that do not want to face their domestic problems and, more generally, for all Arab countries with sizable Shiite populations.

There is no doubt that Iran is a difficult neighbor for anybody to have and that its foreign policy seeks to capitalize on Shiite discontent. But there is no doubt either that by blaming all manifestations of discontent on Iran's machinations, Arab countries are making the situation more difficult. This is particularly true of Saudi Arabia and Bahrain.

Shiites in Saudi Arabia have good reasons to be dissatisfied. They are a minority, and they are considered heretics by their intolerant Wahhabi compatriots. They have problems obtaining permits to build Shiite mosques and are not treated as equal to other Saudi citizens.

The situation in Bahrain, a Shiite-majority country ruled by a Sunni monarchy, is worse. Discrimination against Shiites is rife, because a frightened government seeks to keep them out of government posts, the military and the police. The government is even trying to change the composition of the population by giving citizenship to Sunnis from other countries, including Pakistan.

Most Shiites support the al-Wefaq political society, which wants a constitutional monarchy. The government's harsh response to the demonstrations that started in February and continue to this day risks turning many al-Wefaq supporters toward the radical groups that believe Bahrain should become a republic. To Sunni governments in the region, that can mean only one thing: Iran is behind the unrest, and its goal is to transform Bahrain into an Islamic Republic in Iran's image.

The Gulf countries' policy toward Iraq shows the same unwillingness to face up to reality. Iraq is a Shiite-majority country, and any election-based system inevitably favors the Shiite population. Saudi Arabia and other Gulf countries go one step further and jump to the conclusion that Iran thus now controls Iraq through its Shiite majority, that Prime Minister Nouri al-Maliki, a Shiite, is Tehran's puppet and that U.S. intervention served Iraq to Iran on a silver platter. As a result, Gulf countries maintain their distance from Iraq, making the situation worse.

Iran is a dangerous neighbor, but the policies of the Gulf states make the situation more dangerous. Indeed, their obsession with Iranian influence on the Shiites risks becoming a self-fulfilling prophecy.

Discord has existed for decades between the kingdom's Sunni monarchs and the Shiite minority in the key oil-producing eastern provinces. Shiites, who make up 10 percent of the kingdom's 26 million citizens, complain they are barred from key military and government positions and are not given an equal share of the country's wealth.

Meanwhile, the Saudi government has led the charge to prevent unrest on a broader scale, particularly in Bahrain and Oman. In March, the GCC pledged $20 billion in financial aid to be split evenly over 10 years between Bahrain and Oman. [51] Oman experienced a series of protests against government corruption in February and March. Sultan Qaboos bin Said reshuffled his cabinet and fired a third of its members in response to demands from protesters. [52]

Domestically, the Gulf states have launched economic measures to ease the potential for future unrest. Saudi Arabia ordered roughly $37 billion pumped into programs targeting the kingdom's lower-income population. [53] The United Arab Emirates called for spending $1.55 billion to upgrade the electrical grid and water connections in the federation's less-developed emirates north of Dubai. [54] In Oman, the sultan called for 50,000 new government jobs, a new government advisory committee and higher unemployment benefits.

Iranian Threat

For the Gulf's monarchs, Shiite-ruled Iran is a concern both strategically and ideologically. But the seriousness of the threat posed by Iran remains a subject of debate among experts on the region.

"I come down in the middle on this," says Gause of the Middle East Studies Program at the University of Vermont. "People who deny it are as blinkered on this issue as people who say it's all Iran. It's obviously not all Iran. There are very real domestic social issues involved in Bahrain. A vast majority of Shiite are happy to be Bahraini and don't want to be Iranian. That being said, there are certainly sympathizers with Iran and those who have contact with various Iranian security services." Such people, he says, "are increasingly susceptible to Iranian arguments as their own rulers further the sectarian divide."

Georgetown University's Nonneman says Iran's actions and ability to act have been "very limited" so far.

"Of course, it is always possible to create self-fulfilling prophecies by wrong-headed policies," he adds, but, objectively, the most dangerous threat related to Iran would be "that a military attack by Israel or the U.S. would bring Iranian retaliation" and call into question the Gulf states' ability to defend themselves.

Concern about the real or imagined threat posed by Tehran is shared by the United States with the Gulf monarchies, especially in Bahrain — home to the U.S. Navy's Fifth Fleet. Major airfields in Qatar and the United Arab Emirates and a large base in Kuwait also serve as key points in a defensive arc around Iran.

Unrest in Bahrain puts the United States in a "precarious position," says Koch of the Gulf Research Center Foundation in Dubai. "It is unlikely that the U.S. military presence in Bahrain would be endangered due to a sudden shift of power, . . . but the U.S. will likely find itself having to defend its support for the al-Khalifa family," which is plagued by continued reports of "human-rights abuses and a possible re-escalation of protests in the country."

U.S. military involvement in the region remains critical, says United Emirates University's Abdulla. "Apart from Saudi Arabia, these are small states living in a dangerous zone next to ambitious regional powers, and they need regional protection," he says. "At this moment, there's no other credible and willing foreign protector to provide you with a shield except for the United States."

And the leadership in Iran will remain a pivotal — albeit perennial — issue for the GCC states. "Iran has always been a difficult neighbor, but it's not going to go away, and we're not going to run away either," Abdulla says. "Sometimes it's more difficult and sometimes less difficult. These days, it's twice as difficult, trying to go nuclear and expanding into the region, especially into Iraq. But the next time around, there could be a different [Iranian] president who is more modest. You just never know."

Having Morocco and Jordan join the GCC fold will further enhance its anti-Iran bloc, since both are Sunni-dominated monarchies with economic and political structures similar to the rest of the Gulf states. It would also increase the GCC's geographical size from 9.7 million square miles to 12.7 million and nearly double the number of its citizens — from 39 million to 77 million — about the same as Iran. [55] It is considered extremely likely the two countries will join the coalition.

"The GCC is solidifying into a loose security alliance, dominated by Saudi Arabia," wrote Shadi Hamid, director of research at the Brookings Doha Center. "Jordan, in particular, has much to offer in this domain, boasting one of the region's best-trained militaries and intelligence services."

As the GCC faces growing discontent, Hamid continues, such services may prove particularly helpful. "This 'new' GCC, if it ever comes to fruition, would bear resemblance to the old alliances of the Cold War, such as the Baghdad Pact, adopted in 1955, which aimed to contain Soviet influence." [56]

OUTLOOK

Expanding Global Ties

To ensure their long-term stability and security, the GCC member states must figure out how to deal with rapid population growth and inadequate job opportunities. They already have among the world's youngest and fastest-growing populations, which will increase by 42-80 percent by 2050. [57]

"The youth of today will need jobs," says Abdulla, of United Emirates University. "Right now, the GCC is pouring money into the more advanced sectors, but the local population — and, particularly, the young people — are not keeping up with the demands of these economies that are going global and post-modern and attracting the best of international standards. It's become very tough for the younger generation to keep up."

Nevertheless, the push for international influence is likely to grow. "The GCC states have already begun to be taken more seriously internationally, both economically and diplomatically," says Nonneman, of Georgetown University in Qatar. "This will continue over the next decade. One testing point will be implementation of announced mega-plans. Much can, of course, go wrong, and much will rely on expatriate labor and management." [58]

The Gulf Research Center Foundation's Koch suggests the GCC countries will try to broaden their influence by expanding their economic and political ties to central and Southeast Asia. "The importance of the GCC states has risen significantly in the last 10 years and is likely to continue to do so. From an energy and economic perspective, these countries play a vital role, and we are unlikely to see a significant lessening of the dependence on the region in these fields," Koch says.

Moreover, he adds, the GCC states also are re-defining their own national interests "to take advantage of their increasing clout," as the shift towards Asia implies. In the end, he expects "a continued rise in relevance."

Without a doubt, the GCC will continue to use its enormous wealth to seek global prominence. Less than a year after surprising many observers by winning its bid to host the 2022 soccer World Cup, Qatar is already pushing to host the 2020 Olympics, the 2017 World Athletic Championships and the Grand Départ for the 2016 Tour de France. [59] Meanwhile, Dubai announced it plans to compete for hosting the Olympics in 2024. [60]

But with these lofty global ambitions come increased scrutiny. In Qatar and the UAE, the international spotlight likely will be focused on how foreign laborers are treated. And Bahrain and Saudi Arabia will continue to face criticism of their human-rights records and — in the case of Riyadh — their treatment of women. Meanwhile, Oman and Kuwait already have garnered international attention for their widespread political corruption.

When he announced Dubai's decision to drop out of competition for the 2020 Olympics, Sheikh Hamdan bin Mohammed bin Rashid Al Maktoum referenced the unrest in much of the Arab world, including in neighboring Oman and Bahrain. "Our energy needs to go first and foremost to achieving a just and lasting peace for our youth as the bedrock to a future bid, which is most likely for the 2024 Olympic Games," he said. [61]

An International Monetary Fund report in October suggested a dip in economic growth for Saudi Arabia and Qatar next year, in part because of the recent softening in world energy prices. [62]

It remains to be seen how much current and future regional unrest will affect GCC growth and limitless ambitions.

"It is anybody's guess at this stage," Abdulla said. "2011 has been full of surprises at every turn. It is still an ongoing thing. There is no way to predict who is going to suffer today or tomorrow or the next month. It's a region in flux, and it's going to stay like this for a while."

NOTES

1. For background, see Roland Flamini, "Turmoil in the Arab World," *CQ Global Researcher*, May 3, 2011, pp. 209-236.

2. "At least 2 people dead after police move on protesters in Bahrain," CNN, Feb. 16, 2011, http://articles.cnn.com/2011-02-16/world/bahrain.protests_1_police-move-protesters-security-forces?_s=PM:WORLD.

3. Ethan Bronner, "Bahrain Tears Down Monument as Protesters Seethe," *The New York Times*, March 18, 2011, www.nytimes.com/2011/03/19/world/middleeast/19bahrain.html.

4. "Bahrain Arrests Prominent Lawyer, Doctors: Opposition," Reuters, April 16, 2011, www.reuters.com/article/2011/04/16/us-bahrain-arrests-idUSTRE73F0ZP20110416. See also "Al-Wasat Founder Dies in Custody in Bahrain," Committee to Protect Journalists, April 15, 2011, www.cpj.org/2011/04/al-wasat-founder-dies-in-custody-in-bahrain.php.

5. "Bahrain: Revoke Summary Firings Linked to Protests," Human Rights Watch, July 14, 2011, www.hrw.org/en/news/2011/07/14/bahrain-revoke-summary-firings-linked-protests.

6. "Independent commission in Bahrain delays report on protest unrest until late November," The Associated Press, Oct. 20, www.washingtonpost.com/world/middle-east/independent-commission-in-bahrain-delays-report-on-protest-unrest-until-late-november/2011/10/20/gIQAMm5D0L_story.html.

7. "MENA: The Great Job Rush," Al Masah Capital Management Limited, June 24, 2011, www.almasahcapital.com/uploads/media/MENA_Land_of_Job_Creation_Report__24-June-11_.pdf.

8. *Ibid.*

9. Eman El-Shenawi, "Saudization plan could be a big boon for Qatar, says Philippines ambassador," *Al Arabiya News*, July 13, 2011, www.alarabiya.net/articles/2011/07/11/157084.html.

10. Habib Toumi, "Pay hike: Expatriates and Qataris in private sector feel left out," *Gulf News*, Sept. 8, 2011, http://gulfnews.com/news/gulf/qatar/pay-hike-expatriates-and-qataris-in-private-sector-feel-left-out-1.863178.

11. Ian Black, "Bahrain's Elections Overshadowed by Crackdown on Shia Protesters," *Guardian*, Oct. 22, 2010, www.guardian.co.uk/world/2010/oct/22/bahrain-elections-overshadowed-crackdown.

12. "Bahrain: Elections Take Place Amid Crackdown," Human Rights Watch, Oct. 20, 2010, www.hrw.org/en/news/2010/10/20/bahrain-elections-take-place-amid-crackdown.

13. "Peninsula Shield Force: Gulf troops move in as Bahrain protests escalate," Agence France-Presse, March 15, 2011, http://tribune.com.pk/story/132454/saudi-troops-enter-bahrain-as-protests-escalate/. Also see Ethan Bronner and Michael Slackman, "Saudis, Fearful of Iran, Send Troops to Bahrain to Quell Protests," *The New York Times*, March 15, 2011, http://query.nytimes.com/gst/fullpage.html?res=9505E6DA133EF936A25750C0A9679D8B63&ref=michaelslackman.

14. Liam Stack, "Corruption Inquiry Rocks Kuwait," *The New York Times*, Sept. 21, 2011, www.nytimes.com/2011/09/22/world/middleeast/corruption-inquiry-rocks-kuwait.html.

15. "Kuwait protesters demand PM's removal," *Al Jazeera*, June 4, 2011, http://english.aljazeera.net/news/middleeast/2011/06/20116493343254151.html.

16. Randa Habib, "Jordan, Morocco Could Boost GCC 'Monarchy Club," *Middle East Online*, May 11, 2011, www.middle-east-online.com/english/?id=46079.

17. Joshua Teitelbaum, "Circling the Wagons: Middle Eastern Monarchies Confront the 'Arab Spring,'" Hoover Institution, June 13, 2011, www.advancingafreesociety.org/2011/06/13/circling-the-wagons-middle-eastern-monarchies-confront-the-arab-spring/.

18. "The GCC in 2020: Broadening the Economy," Economist Intelligence Unit, 2010, http://graphics.eiu.com/upload/eb/AVIVA_%20GCC_to_2020_Economic_diversification_in_GCC_WEB.pdf.

19. Ibrahim Saif, "The Oil Boom in the GCC Countries: 2002-2008," Carnegie Endowment for International Peace, 2009, www.carnegieendowment.org/files/cmec15_saif_final.pdf. Also see "Saudi Arabia, U.S. Energy Information Administration, www.eia.gov/countries/country-data.cfm?fips=SA.

20. *Ibid.*

21. "Gulf states aim to go beyond oil — which sectors have real economic potential?" *Economist Intelligence Unit*, Oct. 29, 2010, http://viewswire.eiu.com/index.asp?layout=ib3Article&article_id=1037551888&pubtypeid=1132462498&country_id=1450000345&rf=0.

22. "GCC Leaves Yemen Without a Deal," United Press International, Sept. 22, 2011, www.upi.com/Top_News/Special/2011/09/22/GCC-leaves-Yemen-without-a-deal/UPI-43061316712724/.

23. See Mohammed Sudam, "Heavy fighting in Yemen after U.N. resolution," Reuters, Oct. 22, 2011, www.reuters.com/article/2011/10/22/us-yemen-idUSTRE79L0WP20111022?feedType=RSS&feedName=topNews.

24. David Morgan, "Wikileaks: Saudis Largest source of Terror Funds," CBS News, Dec. 5, 2010, www.cbsnews.com/8301-503543_162-20024653-503543.html.

25. Habib Toumi, "GCC Ministers Agree on Terror Blacklist," *Gulf News*, May 11, 2011, http://gulfnews.com/news/gulf/bahrain/gcc-ministers-agree-on-terror-blacklist-1.806372.

26. Sunny Peter, "GCC Call to Tackle Global Terror," *Foreign Policy Blogs*, Dec. 8, 2010, http://foreignpolicyblogs.com/2010/12/08/gcc-call-to-tackle-global-terrorism/.

27. "Yemen Says Al-Qaida-Linked Cleric Al-Awlaki Killed," The Associated Press, Sept. 30, 2011, http://news.yahoo.com/yemen-says-al-qaida-linked-cleric-al-awlaki-092634554.html.

28. Mohamed Al-Youssi, "Saudi Arabia resumes trial of terrorist cell, members face 97 charges," *Al Arabiya News*, Oct. 4, 2011, http://english.alarabiya.net/articles/2011/10/04/170129.html.

29. "Neo-Piracy in Oman and the Gulf: The Origins of British Imperialism in the Gulf," MERIP Reports, April 1975, p. 4, www.jstor.org/stable/3011439?seq=2.

30. *Ibid.*

31. James Onley, "Britain and the Gulf Shaikhdoms, 1820-1971: the Politics of Protection," Center for International & Regional Studies, Georgetown University School of Foreign Service in Qatar, 2009, p. 20, http://exeter.academia.edu/JamesOnley/Papers/335324/_Britain_and_the_Gulf_Shaikhdoms_1820-1971_The_Politics_of_Protection_2009_.

32. "Background Note: Saudi Arabia," U.S. Department of State, May 6, 2011, www.state.gov/r/pa/ei/bgn/3584.htm.

33. For background, see the following Editorial Research Reports, available at *CQ Researcher Plus Archive*: D. Teter, "Iran Between East and West," Jan. 26, 1979; Mary H. Cooper and J. Hamer, "Persian Gulf Oil," Oct. 30, 1987; William V. Thomas, "American Military Strength Abroad," Feb. 15, 1980.

34. Kenneth Katzman, "The Persian Gulf States: Post-War Issues for U.S. Policy," CRS Report for Congress, July 14, 2003, www.fas.org/man/crs/RL31533.pdf. For background, see Patrick G. Marshall, "Calculating the Cost of the Gulf War," *Editorial Research Reports*, March 15, 1991, pp. 145-155, available at *CQ Researcher Plus Archive*.

35. Sharon Otterman, "Saudi Arabia: Withdrawal of U.S. Forces," Council on Foreign Relations, May 2, 2003, www.cfr.org/saudi-arabia/saudi-arabia-withdrawl-us-forces/p7739.

36. *Ibid.*

37. Mike Shuster, "Iraq War Deepens Sunni-Shia Divide," NPR, Feb. 15, 2011, www.npr.org/templates/story/story.php?storyId=7411762.

38. Neil MacFarquhar, "Saudi Monarch Grants Women Right to Vote," *The New York Times*, Sept. 25, 2011, www.nytimes.com/2011/09/26/world/middleeast/women-to-vote-in-saudi-arabia-king-says.html?pagewanted=all.

39. *Ibid.*

40. "Women to make debut in Bahrain's consultative council," *Al Bawaba*, Sept. 26, 2000, www.albawaba

.com/news/women-make-debut-bahrains-consulta-tive-council.

41. Neil MacFarquhar, "In Bahrain, women run, women vote, women lose," *The New York Times*, May 22, 2002, www.nytimes.com/2002/05/22/world/in-bahrain-women-run-women-vote-women-lose .html?pagewanted=all&src=pm.

42. *Ibid.*

43. "The Global Gender Gap Report 2010," World Economic Forum, www3.weforum.org/docs/WEF_ GenderGap_Report_2010.pdf.

44. "Global Gender Gap: Bahrain No. 4 in Arab World and 110 in the World," *Bahrain Monitor*, http:// bahrainmonitor.org/reports/p-022-01.html.

45. Habib Toumi, "New milestone for Bahraini women as two more win in elections," *Gulf News*, Oct. 2, 2011, http://gulfnews.com/news/gulf/bahrain/new-milestone-for-bahraini-women-as-two-more-win-in-elections-1.883335.

46. Robert F. Worth, "First women win seats in Kuwait Parliament," *The New York Times*, May 18, 2009, www.nytimes.com/2009/05/18/world/middleeast/ 18kuwait.html.

47. "Qatar launches first Constitution," BBC News, June 9, 2004, http://news.bbc.co.uk/2/hi/middle_ east/3789731.stm.

48. "Qatar," Freedom House, www.freedomhouse.org/ template.cfm?page=181.

49. Khatija Hague, "GCC 2011: Macro Outlook Onwards and Upwards," Shuaa Capital, PSC, Jan. 23, 2011, www.shuaacapital.com/Files/GCC2011 MacroOutlookOnwardsandupwards.pdf; also see Ali, Jasmin, "Managing budget surpluses GCC focus," *Gulf News*, April 25, 2010, http://gulfnews .com/business/opinion/managing-budget-surpluses-gcc-focus-1.617177.

50. Summer Said, "Saudi Blames Foreign Country for Unrest," *The Wall Street Journal*, Oct. 5, 2011, http:// news.google.com/news/story?client=safari&rls=en&-q=saudi+arabia+unrest+iran+arab+spring&oe=UTF-8&um=1&ie=UTF-8&ncl=dkiDLBMCPE7aKHM &hl=en&ei=nz6MTuuHEYT00gHUs5jRAQ&sa= X&oi=news_result&ct=more-results&resnum=1&ved= 0CCoQqgIwAA.

51. "GCC Pledges $20 billion in aid for Oman, Bahrain," Reuters, March 10, 2011, http://gulfnews .com/news/gulf/saudi-arabia/gcc-pledges-20billion-in-aid-for-oman-bahrain-1.774648.

52. "Oman's Sultan Shuffles Cabinet for Third Time," Voice of America, March 7, 2011, www.voanews .com/english/news/middle-east/Omans-Sultan-Shuffles-Cabinet-for-Third-Time-117533293.html.

53. "Saudi King back home, orders $37 billion in hand-outs," Reuters, Feb. 23, 2011, www.reuters.com/ article/2011/02/23/us-saudi-king-idUSTRE71M22V 20110223.

54. "New water and electricity projects in UAE gets Dh5.7 billion," gowealthy.com, www.gowealthy .com/gowealthy/wcms/en/home/news/economy/ New-water-and-electricity-projects-gets-Dh5b.html.

55. Anne Allmelling and Johannes Krug, "Analysis: How would Jordan and Morocco change the Gulf Cooperation Council?" *Al-Arabiya News*, June 9, 2011, http://english.alarabiya.net/articles/2011/ 06/09/152623.html.

56. Shadi Hamid, *The National*, May 16, 2011, www .thenational.ae/thenationalconversation/comment/ a-new-security-strategy-but-not-necessarily-a-new-gcc.

57. Ragui Assaad and Farzaneh Roudi-Fahimi, "Youth in the Middle East and North Africa: Demographic Opportunity or Challenge," Population Reference Bureau, 2007, www.prb.org/pdf07/YouthinMENA .pdf.

58. Nadim Kawach, "IMF revises up UAE real growth to 3.5%," Emirates 24/7 Business, April 30, 2011, www.emirates247.com/business/economy-finance/ imf-revises-up-uae-real-growth-to-3-5-2011-04-30-1.386981.

59. "Qatar bets on future as sports mecca," Reuters, Sept. 7, 2011, http://nbcsports.msnbc.com/id/ 44424034/ns/sports-soccer/.

60. "Dubai opts out of 2020 bid, targets 2024," Reuters, July 29, 2011, http://in.reuters.com/article/2011/ 07/29/idINIndia-58521120110729.

61. "Dubai rule out bid for 2020 Olympics but remain keen to host event four years later," *MailOnline*, July 29, 2011, www.dailymail.co.uk/sport/othersports/

article-2020134/Dubai-bid-2024-Olympics-2020
.html#ixzz1c0l0hxda.

62. "Regional and Economic Outlook: Middle East and
Central Asia," International Monetary Fund,
October 2011, www.imf.org/external/pubs/ft/reo/
2011/mcd/eng/pdf/mreo1011.pdf.

BIBLIOGRAPHY

Selected Sources
Books

*The New Arab Revolt: What Happened, What It
Means, and What Comes Next*, **The Council on
Foreign Relations/Foreign Affairs, 2011.**
This collection includes more than 60 articles, inter-
views and op-eds on the 2011 unrest in the Arab world.

Cooper, Andrew Scott, *The Oil Kings: How the U.S.,
Iran, and Saudi Arabia Changed the Balance of
Power in the Middle East*, **Simon and Shuster, 2011.**
A journalist and human-rights advocate looks at how oil
came to dominate U.S. domestic and international
affairs by examining the country's relationship with Iran
and Saudi Arabia.

**Legrenzi, Matteo, "The GCC and the International
Relations of the Gulf: Diplomacy, Security and
Economic Coordination in a Changing Middle East,"
Library of International Relations, I.B. Tauris & Co.
Ltd, 2011.**
A Gulf expert from the University of Ottawa looks at the
GCC's structure and role within the larger Middle East.

Articles

**"Concerns over Iran may push GCC to expand military
presence," Reuters, May 20, 2011, www.thenational.ae/
news/worldwide/middle-east/concerns-over-iran-may-
push-gcc-to-expand-military-presence.**
The article explores how fears over Iranian interference
may be shaping the GCC's evolving military strategy.

**Allam, Abeer, and Roula Khalaf, "Club of monarchs
to extend Gulf reach," *Financial Times*, May 11,
2011, www.ft.com/intl/cms/s/0/bbd079cc-7bf7-
11e0-9b16-00144feabdc0.html#axzz1bDSxB9at.**
The article examines the impact of Jordan and Morocco
joining the GCC.

**Ashour, Omar, "From 9/11 to the Arab Spring," The
Brookings Doha Center, Sept. 7, 2011, www.brookings
.edu/opinions/2011/0907_arab_spring_ashour.aspx.**
Intelligence operations, drone attacks, transformations
within jihadi ranks and the Arab Spring have severely
undermined Al Qaeda in the region.

Kinninmont, Jane, "The maybe greater GCC," *Foreign
Policy.com*, **May 16, 2011, http://mideast.foreign
policy.com/posts/2011/05/16/the_maybe_greater_gcc.**
The GCC is projecting itself as a unified regional actor in
four very different initiatives in a post Arab-Spring world.

**Koch, Christian, "How the GCC Can Rediscover that
Vital Spirit of Unity,"** *The National*, **Dec. 13, 2009.**
The director of the Gulf Research Center Foundation calls
on GCC member states to develop a more unified strategy.

**McGeehan, Nicholas, "Let Qatar 2022 not be built on
brutality,"** *Guardian*, **Dec. 6, 2010, www.guardian
.co.uk/commentisfree/libertycentral/2010/dec/06/
qatar-world-cup-human-rights.**
After hearing that Qatar will host the 2022 World Cup
finals, the columnist criticizes the country's human-
rights record.

**Vali, Nasr, "Will the Saudis Kill the Arab Spring?"
Bloomberg News, May 24, 2011, www.bloomberg.com/
news/2011-05-23/will-the-saudis-kill-the-arab-spring-
.html.**
Saudi Arabia has tried to stem unrest in the Gulf region.

Reports and Studies

**Kapiszewski, Andrzej, "Arab vs. Asian Migrant Workers
in the GCC," U.N. Department of Economic and
Social Affairs, May 2006, www.un.org/esa/population/
meetings/EGM_Ittmig_Arab/P02_Kapiszewski.pdf.**
A shortage of home-grown workers has given rise to a
labor dilemma in the GCC.

"The GCC in 2020: Broadening the Economy," *The
Economist Intelligence Unit*, **Oct. 31, 2010.**
A background report examines whether the GCC economic structures are likely to change over the next
decade.

"Gulf Security: Changing Internal and External Dynamics," Kuwait Program for Development, Governance and Globalization in the Gulf States, London School of Economics and Political Science, 2009.
Both "traditional" and "new" security challenges in the Gulf will affect ongoing efforts toward political and economic liberalization and diversification.

Carothers, Thomas, Abdulaziz Sager and Marina Ottaway, "Political Reform in the GCC States," Carnegie Endowment for International Peace, Sept. 23, 2004, http://carnegieendowment.org/2004/09/23/political-reform-in-gcc-states/286.

The authors take a look at future prospects for political reform in the GCC.

Shikara, Ahmad, "The Changing Strategic Balance of Power in the Middle East," The Henry Jackson Society, March 18, 2010, www.henryjacksonsociety.org/stories.asp?pageid=49&id=1414.
A researcher at the Emirates Centre for Strategic Studies and Research in Abu Dhabi discusses the causes and potential consequences of the shifting balance of power in the contemporary Middle East.

For More Information

Brookings Doha Center, P.O. Box 22694, Saha 43, Bldg. 63, West Bay, Doha, Qatar; 974- 4422.7800; www.brookings.edu/doha.aspx. A project of the Saban Center for Middle East Policy at the Brookings Institution; undertakes independent, policy-oriented research on the socioeconomic and geopolitical issues facing Muslim-majority states and communities.

The Cooperation Council for the Arab States of the Gulf, www.gcc-sg.org/eng/. The official web site of the Gulf Cooperation Council.

The Emirates Centre for Strategic Studies and Research, P.O. Box 4567; (971) 2-4044444; www.ecssr.ac.ae/ECSSR/ appmanager/portal/ecssr?_nfpb=true&_pageLabel=HomePa geECSSR&lang=en. An Independent research institution in the UAE.

Gulf Research Center, 187 Oud Metha Tower, 11th Floor, 303 Sheikh Rashid Road, Dubai, United Arab Emirates; 971-4-324 7770; www.grc.ae/index.php. An independent research organization focused on the Gulf Cooperation Council.

Sheba Center for Strategic Studies, zwww.shebacss.com/en/index.php?mod=home. An independent nonprofit think-tank that addresses strategic, political, economic and social issues related to Yemen and the region.

Voices From Abroad:

ANWAR AL-RASHEED

Coordinator, Gulf Civil Society Forum, Netherlands

Anticipating democracy

"We hope that the ruling families in the Gulf realise the importance of democratic transformation to which our people aspire. The Gulf peoples look forward for their countries to be among nations supporting freedom, the rule of law and civil and democratic rule, which have become a part of peoples' basic rights."

Kuwait Times, February 2011

MANOUCHEHR MOTTAKI

Foreign Minister, Iran

Shared power and growth

"Our [Iran's] power in the region is your power, and your power in the region is our power. Our growth will only pave the way for others to grow."

The New York Times, December 2010

WILLIAM HAGUE

Foreign Secretary, United Kingdom

Change begins in Yemen

"The problems of Yemen are a vital issue for us in foreign and security policy. Economic and political reform are crucial to the long-term stability of Yemen. Yemen is a long-standing ally in fighting international terrorism and it is here, in Yemen, that reform in the Arab world can begin."

Daily Telegraph (England), February 2011

THEODORE KARASIK

Director of Research and Development, Institute for Near East and Gulf Military Analysis, United Arab Emirates

Emerging capitals

"The GCC city-states are today regarded by most people as the emerging world capitals of globalisation,

The Ottawa Citizen/Cardow

despite the financial crisis. The scale of reform and changes on all levels that have taken place in these cities exceeds most countries in the region and even the world."

Gulf News (United Arab Emirates), November 2010

SHEIKH SALMAN BIN HAMAD AL-KHALIFA

Crown Prince, Bahrain

Looking forward

"At the present time the country's [Bahrain] entire attention is focused on building a new national dialogue for Bahrain. . . . Our nation's priority is on overcoming tragedy, healing divisions and rediscovering the fabric that draws this country together."

Kuwait Times, February 2011

SULTAN AL-QASSEMI

Columnist, National (newspaper), United Arab Emirates

Ahead of its time

"Kuwait is decades ahead of any Gulf state. Kuwaiti women several years ago won the right to vote and run in the parliament through democratic means. Kuwait is two or three decades ahead of any other Gulf states."

Al Jazeera (Qatar), March 2011

AYATOLLAH ALI KHAMENE'I

Supreme Leader, Iran

Islam's reign

"The recent huge uprisings in the Islamic world are preliminary steps toward greater evolutions and the reign of Islam. The position of the supporters of the [General Assembly of the] Household of the Prophet, peace be upon them, is supporting these Islamic uprisings."

Fars News Agency (Iran), September 2011

ABD-AL-AZIZ BIN-UTHMAN BIN-SAQR

Chairman, Gulf Research Center, Switzerland

Nukes not welcome

"The existence of nuclear weapons in the region, whether in Israel, Iran or in any other place, is a red line for the GCC member states. This creates two main problems. The first problem is the escalation of tension in the region, and [the second problem] is the encouragement of a nuclear arms race. The Gulf does not need this, because it does not need a new fourth war in the region."

Al Jazeera (Qatar), January 2011

4

Resolving Land Disputes

Jina Moore

Policemen in the town of Chengdu in China's Sichuan province detain a woman who tried to retrieve belongings from a building being demolished to make way for a new highway. China has made several efforts to reform its property laws and halt illegal land grabs, which have accelerated as the economy expands and farmland is gobbled up for industrial parks and skyscrapers. Land disputes are a major cause of social unrest in China.

From *CQ Researcher*,
Sept. 6, 2011

Korkesi Jabateh is a landowner — one of the lucky ones — in Ganta, a bustling Liberian border town. He was able to reclaim his property after Liberia's civil war — without resorting to violence.

When the war ended in 2003, about two dozen local families whose homes had been destroyed built makeshift shelters in the parking lot of Jabateh's gas station and lived there for years. Then Jabateh came back from neighboring Guinea, where he'd fled during the war. Like thousands of his fellow countrymen, he wanted to restart his life, on his own land. But unlike most returnees, Jabateh had the one thing he needed: the deed to the land.

"My father took his deed to Guinea when he fled," Jabateh explains. "It was the only thing he took with him."

Since the war ended, Liberia has seen thousands of similar complications over land ownership escalate into violence. More than 20 people were killed in land disputes in six Liberian villages in 2008, according to the International Crisis Group. And in Nimba County, where Jabateh lives, ethnic divisions have inflamed the controversies. Like many other merchants in Ganta before the war, Jabateh is a Muslim and belongs to the Mandingo people. But when he and other businessmen fled to Guinea, members of other ethnic groups took over their property.

Although many of Jabateh's fellow Mandingo were threatening to violently evict squatters, Jabateh chose a different path: He decided to compensate his squatters, even though legally he owed them nothing. But in a community where similar land conflicts divide neighbors along ethnic lines and rhetoric can quickly turn into violence, Jabateh felt he had no choice. If he had rejected a

"Land Grabs" Are on the Rise

Conflicts over land ownership are intensifying around the globe, often triggered by so-called land grabs — purchases of vast tracts of arable land in the developing world by governments and private investors. In the last two years, such acquisitions have increased at least 10-fold worldwide, according to the International Land Coalition, often resulting in indigenous land- owners losing their land. Ownership of up to 70 percent of the planet's land is potentially in dispute due to unclear or non- existing titles. Some of the largest purchases have occurred in Mozambique, where more than 10 million hectares were sold.

Total Purchases of Big Tracts in Selected Countries

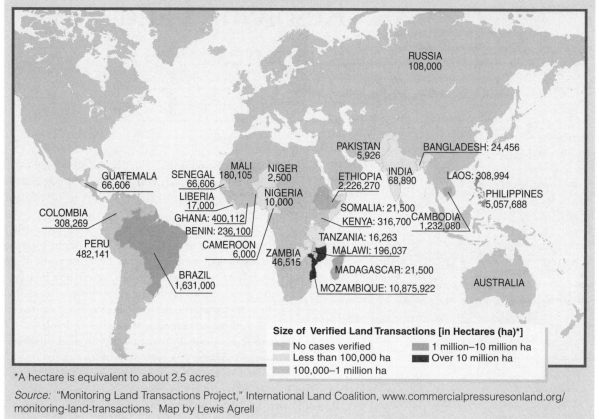

*A hectare is equivalent to about 2.5 acres

Source: "Monitoring Land Transactions Project," International Land Coalition, www.commercialpressuresonland.org/monitoring-land-transactions. Map by Lewis Agrell

nonviolent solution, he says, "There will be tension, and who will be the cause of that tension? They will say, 'Mr. Jabateh, he is the cause of that tension.' "

Land experts endorse his approach. While Liberia's civil wars were fought for bigger stakes — such as control of the country's rich rubber forests and diamond mines — observers and analysts worry that today's small land disputes, especially if ethnically or religiously tinged, could become the spark for tomorrow's civil war, and not just in Liberia.

Wars have been waged for millennia over territory and national boundaries, and land disputes have triggered recent conflict around the globe — from Guatemala to Sudan to Afghanistan. Almost 75 percent of major civil conflicts since 1990 have been fought over land, according to Liz Alden Wily, a leading expert on global land issues and a visiting fellow at Van Vollenhoven Institute in the Netherlands. [1] And even when land isn't the motivation for war, it often becomes a crucial post-war issue. [2]

"Many of the most entrenched conflicts have to do with different priorities and perspectives on how land and natural resources should be used," says Michael Taylor, program manager for global policy at the International Land Coalition in Rome, an alliance of 83 civil society and nongovernmental organizations. "People who haven't traditionally worked on land issues but are interested in how you resolve conflict are realizing they have to understand land tenure" — the rules by which people gain access to or use of land.

Around the world, conflicts over land tenure and ownership are intensifying, largely due to climate change, the skyrocketing global population and increasing biofuel production. Those and other factors are changing land use patterns and causing new conflicts over who owns land and how it can be used. Food prices are also rising, putting pressure on farmland prices and encouraging rampant land speculation.

Governments and private investors alike are scrambling to purchase vast tracts of arable land. In just the last two years, large-scale acquisitions by governments and corporations have increased more than 10-fold, to at least $25 billion. [3] These so-called "land grabs" often put indigenous owners and small-scale farmers at risk of losing their land to foreign investors or major landowners, which is forcing governments to try to clarify land ownership rules.

"Only 30 to 50 percent of the land globally is actually registered," leaving the rest of the world's territory potentially in dispute, says Mohamed El-Sioufi, a senior adviser on human settlements with UN-HABITAT, a United Nations agency based in Nairobi, Kenya.

But an even more fundamental issue is exacerbating tension over land. While it may represent power or profit for politicians or investors, for ordinary people around the globe a small plot represents survival. "Land is the means for livelihood," says Robin Nielsen, a lawyer with Rural Develoment Institute, headquartered in Seattle, Wash. "It's power. It's status. It's security. It's the most powerful asset people have."

Falling Farm Aid Makes "Land Grabs" More Likely

Money for agricultural development amounted to only 5 percent of the aid provided to developing countries by governments and multilateral institutions between 2006 and 2008, down from 17 percent in the 1980s. And less than 20 percent of the agricultural aid was earmarked for fragile, conflict-affected countries. When governments lack funds to develop agricultural infrastructure, such as farm-to-market roads, they often sell off vast tracts to foreign investors and governments that have funds for infrastructure, but small-scale landowners often lose their land in the process.

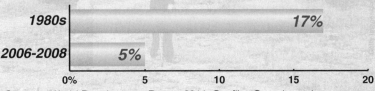

Share of Government Aid Targeting Agriculture

1980s	17%
2006-2008	5%

0% 5 10 15 20

Source: "World Development Report 2011: Conflict, Security and Development," World Bank, 2011, p. 230, http://wdr2011.worldbank.org/sites/default/files/pdfs/WDR2011_Full_Text.pdf

With so much riding on them, land disputes are increasingly combustible, says Lorenzo Cotula, a senior researcher on law and sustainable development at the London-based International Institute for Environment and Development. In Latin America, she says, the heat further intensifies "where there's growing pressure on land, driven by local processes, demographic growth, changes in socio-economic conditions and outside interest."

Land disputes have ignited some of the world's most intransigent conflicts — such as between Israel and the Palestinians, India and Pakistan and North and South Korea — plus countless others. Land disputes even play an underreported role in Afghanistan's insecurity, in post-genocide Bosnia-Herzegovina's fragility and in the hostility between former allies Ethiopia and Eritrea. And land is the underlying cause of violence — usually described as ethnic or tribal — in Sudan's Darfur region, in Kenya's post-election crisis in 2007 and in Rwanda's 1994 genocide. [4]

Contemporary examples of violent land disputes can be found around the globe, including in:

- India, where rebels have justified attacks on villages as protests against mining deals.
- China, where thousands of peasants have lost their land and homes to make way for highways, dams

and other infrastructure projects. A Chinese man ignited a bomb in front of a local government office, killing himself and two other people, after the government ignored his repeated pleas for better compensation after his home was razed to make way for a hydroelectric plant. [5]

- Hungary, where the government has forcibly migrated or deported its nomadic Roma — or "gypsies" — who have clashed with more settled communities. [6] In April, for instance, the government "evacuated" more than half the Roma population in the town of Gyöngyöspata, where Roma marches — harassed by right-wing agitators — recently ended in bloodshed. [7]

- East Timor, which emerged from a 24-year-long civil war in 1999 and where land disputes are among the most likely causes of future violence. [8]

- Guatemala, where land is the proverbial "third rail" of politics. Although the 1996 peace agreement ending a 36-year civil war included market-based land reforms, the measures did not supply enough land to meet the demand.

"There's a huge demand for land access still unsolved," says Annalisa Mauro, the International Land Coalition's Latin America analyst, yet the private sector exhibits no willingness to accept compromise. "In Guatemala, land is not something you can deal with in a solution-oriented manner. . . . These land issues are untouchable."

If land can create a political stalemate, as in Guatemala, it can also create intractable problems between individuals. "These conflicts become what people call 'total' — they pervade even mundane aspects of people's lives," says Peter Coleman, director of the International Center for Cooperation and Conflict Resolution at Columbia University, who is working on post-earthquake communal land issues in Haiti. "When they become that total, the land takes on a quality that transcends just property and becomes symbolically meaningful, tied to people's beliefs or vengeances or rights, to some fundamental sense of self."

In Latin America and Asia land conflicts often involve indigenous peoples' rights. After gaining independence from colonial masters, many Latin American countries introduced land reforms designed to break apart *latifundios*, industrial-sized property holdings usually established

by expropriating tribal lands. The reforms were supposed to result in the land being returned to indigenous communities and landless farmers for small-scale crop production. [9]

However, some of those deals have been reversed recently, either overtly or tacitly, making this year's U.N. Declaration of Indigenous Rights even more important for land rights advocates. They have cited the U.N. declaration to pressure governments to consult with them before land concessions are granted. Bolivia, where more than 60 percent of the population is indigenous, has literally reorganized its national substructures around these new U.N. principles, even changing its name to the Plurinational State of Bolivia.

In Africa, however, land rights often are not honored. The continent has recently attracted the attention of large-scale agro-investors, who buy up huge tracts of farmland. Roughly 70 percent of "land grabs" today occur in sub-Saharan Africa, according to the World Bank, where governments are weak and post-colonial property systems clash with traditional concepts of land ownership. That opens the door to countries needing food imports, such as China or Saudi Arabia, and to speculative investment firms, such as Goldman Sachs, which are betting that escalating food insecurity will boost land values.

Individual investors are getting into the game, too. In 2009 American banker Philippe Heilberg bought 400,000 hectares from a southern Sudanese warlord in sub-Saharan Africa's single biggest private land deal.* Heilberg said he had no problem dealing with warlords and rebels, even if it provided funds that armed rebels. "This is Africa," he told the *Financial Times*. "You have to go with the guns." [10]

Heilberg's thinking suggests why land and conflict will likely remain linked: Even conflict can be an investment strategy. Literature on the causes of conflict suggests that some goods, like diamonds or minerals, "seem to extend the length of conflict, while others" — like oil — "increase the incentive for having those conflicts," says Solomon Hsiang, a postdoctoral fellow in science, technology and enviromnental policy at the Woodrow

---

* One hectare is about 2.5 acres. Most international reports and studies on land reform measure land in hectares.

Wilson School of Public and International Affairs at Princeton University.

Heilberg put it another way. "If you bet right on the shifting of sovereignty, then you are [in] on the ground floor," he said. "I am constantly looking at the map and looking if there is any value." [11]

As landowners, land rights advocates and governments struggle to devise equitable land ownership rules and avoid conflicts, here are some of the questions being debated:

Will rising demand for resources trigger more land conflicts?

The global appetite for land acquisition seems increasingly insatiable. Since 2006, foreign investors have purchased up to 20 million hectares (about 50 million acres) of farmland — an area roughly five times the size of Belgium — in low-income countries. [12] In Africa alone, access and usage rights to another 50 million hectares already have been secured or are being negotiated by foreign investors, according to the World Bank. [13]

The growing demand for resources is not new, of course, and neither is the developed world's demand for developing countries' resources, at virtually any environmental or human cost. "All colonialism was exactly that, and today it continues in different varieties," says El-Sioufi of UN-HABITAT.

Developed-world interest in tropical timber increased dramatically after World War II, when vast amounts of raw materials were needed to rebuild devastated Europe and East Asia. [14] Today, as global interest in green energy grows — along with government subsidies to promote alternative fuels — European and American companies increasingly are investing in biofuel production. Fifty percent of recent major land acquisitions were made to produce biofuels, according Taylor at the International Land Coalition.

The developed world's appetite for foreign resources can also reflect shifting consumer tastes. For instance, much of the land-related conflict in the Democratic Republic of Congo is fueled by the rising worldwide demand for coltan, tin and other minerals used in cell phones, laptops and portable electronic devices. [15]

The legacy of indifference could spark new conflicts, at both local and national levels. Central India's Chhatisgarh state, for example, has been plagued by

more than five years of violence after the government sold more than $2 billion worth of land — with unclear title — to big steel and power corporations in 2005. The transactions sparked confrontations between opponents of the sales and local police, several of whom were kidnapped by Maoist rebels. The rebels, who had committed terrorist acts in the past against industrial interests in the region, claimed to be fighting for impoverished communities cheated by the big land deals. [16]

Chhatisgarh state then organized a local militia of about 4,000 youths, armed with guns, spears and bows and arrows. Confrontations between the militia and the rebels forced more than 50,000 people from their homes. The militia was accused of rape, robbery and murder, while the rebels attacked security forces and villages. In February, the state's top official disbanded the youth militia, saying, "Innocent people were being killed." [17]

The underlying grievances spurred by land sales, however, remain unaddressed. "States like Chhattisgarh are seething with anger over this issue," a tribal campaigner told *The Guardian*. While an individual may own land for farming or settlement, the newspaper added, the government owns the rights to all minerals below the surface. [18]

Some observers suggest that conflict could be avoided by allowing local communities to set the terms of land use or sales. The main issue surrounding resource investments, says Cotula of the International Institute for Environment and Development, "is who decides whether that piece of land should be given over to an outside investor."

In fact, the coastal Raigad district is a perfect counterpoint to the violence in central India. The district managed to peacefully rebuff interest from Reliance Industries, a part of Reliance Group, the largest company in India. The company withdrew its interest in the region after 95 percent of residents surveyed opposed rezoning to accommodate the company's plans. [19]

In East Africa, Mozambique and Tanzania similarly tried to decentralize decision-making for land sales in the 1990s, allowing local communities to negotiate the sale of nearby lands. "Now we're seeing in those countries governments trying to take back that decision-making from the local level," says Taylor. "When the value of these resources starts to rise, the governments have less incentive to let the benefits go to the communities.

Island Landowners Have That Sinking Feeling

Legal questions abound for those who lose land due to climate change.

Half a dozen island nations around the globe — home to nearly 1 million people — are sinking, or, more accurately, the ocean around them is rising due to global warming.

When the water gets high enough, their countries will cease to exist, presenting a host of legal challenges. Where will the residents go? Who — if anyone — will pay for their relocation? Without land, can they continue to be countries? Do citizens who lose their homes to rising oceans — due to carbon-emitting activities on the other side of the globe that are said to exacerbate global warming — have any legal recourse against the emitters? Climate experts say similar challenges will face landowners living on the coasts of low-lying developing countries like Bangladesh.

These are not idle questions, as Michael Gerrard, director of the Center for Climate Change Law at Columbia University, learned first-hand during a recent visit to the Marshall Islands, a former U.S. territory that gained its independence in 1986. The threatened nation's 30-mile-long, dog-leg shaped capital island of Majuro sits on the rim of an extinct volcano and is flanked by the Pacific Ocean on one side and a lagoon on the other.

"The distance between them is about the distance between Fifth and Sixth avenues in Manhattan," he says. "You feel fairly vulnerable just standing there." To such countries, already feeling the effects of rising global temperatures — in Papua New Guinea, for example, residents are already fleeing land made uninhabitable by rising sea levels — climate change is a "very urgent" problem, Gerrard says.

Some island communities have already had to relocate, and many of their governments are incorporating into their disaster preparedness policies measures to help adapt to climate change, such as preparing designated communities to receive those displaced by climate change. "An island becomes uninhabitable well before it is submerged, for several reasons," Gerrard explains. First, "drinking water supply is likely to become contaminated with salt water. Second, flooding becomes so frequent and extensive it becomes hard to live there. And third, a place becomes so vulnerable to large waves it becomes dangerous."

While the threat is environmental, the consequences are political. "For the first time in history, we are contemplating the disappearance of a [nation] state without the possibility of a successor," raising many legal questions, said Phillip Muller, ambassador of the Marshall Islands to the United Nations. [1] If the countries' land is submerged, who controls their fishing or mineral rights? Where will the residents go, and who will pay for their relocation? Are other countries obligated to admit them?

Legal scholars have offered a variety of responses. One option might be to artificially reinforce the islands so their land rises above the encroaching seas. [2] On the other hand, Gerrard points out, there are precedents to being a sovereign, but landless, country. The Holy See, the official jurisdiction of the Catholic Church, was recognized as a sovereign nation before it had secured the territory of the Vatican. The international system also recognizes the Sovereign Military Order of Malta, a religious lay order founded nearly 1,000 years ago that lost its territory to Napoleon.

Many scholars and diplomats expect other countries to "continue to recognize the statehood of these small nations for a long time, partly out of a sense of moral obligation, since the disappearance of the state was in no way their own fault," says Gerrard, who convened the first conference on the topic at Columbia this summer.

"At the root of these reversals is the increased value of land," he continues. "Just land — not necessarily even minerals or timber or anything on the land, but farmland itself — is becoming more valuable."

Can new laws resolve land conflicts?

When they work as intended, legal reforms can resolve or preempt a variety of land tensions, experts say. Central and Latin America's era of agrarian reform, in the early-to mid-20th century, is an oft-cited example.

Governments across the region tried to redress imbalances in land ownership by breaking up vast estates and redistributing property to landless peasants and farmers. But the outcome of these reform experiments was preempted by a series of civil wars, and in some cases, conflict not only halted but reversed the reforms, resulting

Then, whose fault is it? Scientifically, the answer to that question is simple: industrialized nations. But while no one can prove that one country's troubles were due to specific emissions from a given factory or country, "the science is extremely clear that the accumulation of greenhouse gases in the atmosphere from major emitting countries is the principal cause of sea level rise around the world," says Gerrard. (Greenhouse gases include carbon dioxide, nitrous oxide, methane and other gases produced from the burning of fossil fuels such as oil, natural gas and coal. They are dubbed greenhouse gases because they trap the Earth's heat, acting as a greenhouse.)

Legally, the question is murkier. For example, are major carbon-emitting nations culpable for climate-induced migration? That's what the Federated States of Micronesia contended in a recent legal paper. Micronesia wants to see carbon emitters held accountable under international law for the consequences of their environmental choices. [3] Although other island nations and some academics support the idea, no legal battles have been won yet.

In fact, legal precedents aren't particularly favorable for this line of thinking. One oft-cited precedent comes from the Marshall Islands, where the United States tested 67 nuclear weapons between 1946 and 1958. The islands sought financial reparations for the damages caused by the tests. The United States eventually agreed to set up a Nuclear Claims Tribunal to adjudicate those claims, and it was given $563 million to disperse for damages. But most of the money was never paid, and last year, the U.S. Supreme Court declined to hear the case, effectively blocking any legal recourse for reparations. [4]

Muller, however, thinks there may be new, more effective strategies yet to be tried. "The most vulnerable countries need to think hard, together, about how to use the law to make emitters responsible for their actions," he said. [5]

— *Jina Moore*

[1] "Nations prepare for climate change fight," *Marshall Islands Journal*, June 3, 2011, www.law.columbia.edu/null/download?&exclusive= filemgr.download&file_id=5758.

Indian farmer Srikanta Doloi fears he may lose his ancestral farmland on Ghoramara Island, some 60 miles south of Kolkata. Over the last 25 years, the island's land mass has been reduced by 50 percent by rising sea levels due to melting polar ice caps. Half a dozen island nations around the globe face the same dilemma, presenting a host of legal challenges.

[2] Jenny Grote Stoutenberg, conference, "Threatened Island Nations: Legal Implications of Rising Seas and a Changing Climate," Center for Climate Change Law, Columbia University, May 23-25, 2011, www .livestream.com/clsit/video?clipId=pla_a49e3b77-3399-44b9-8ca6- 6550e72a4f39&utm_source=lslibrary&utm_medium=ui-thumb.

[3] "Federated States of Micronesia have legal document blaming European carbon emitters," *O Globo*, May 23, 2011, www.law.columbia .edu/centers/climatechange/resources/threatened-island-nations/ background.

[4] Alexander Wong, "Comparative Relocation: Case Study and Analysis of Options for Threatened Island Nations," Working Paper, Columbia Law School Center for Climate Change Law, Aug. 9, 2011, pp. 14-16, www.law.columbia.edu/null/download?&exclusive=filemgr.download &file_id=601091.

[5] "The Way Forward," presentation, "Threatened Island Nations" conference, *op. cit.* Streaming video available at www.livestream.com/clsit/ video?clipId=pla_12d2341f-f8ef-408f-836a-52967491e9cf&utm_ source=lslibrary&utm_medium=ui-thumb.

in tensions that would later explode. In Guatemala, for example, a 1954 coup d'etat brought down the government that championed reform — and the newly installed government reversed it. Grievances about land ownership and equity fueled the country's civil war, from 1960 to 1996. Today, for a multitude of reasons — from the rise and fall of global commodity prices to the ebb and flow of civil war — many of those original reforms have

been reversed, and land ownership is again concentrated in the hands of the few. [20]

To deal with gender-related land issues, some countries recently have turned to corrective legislation. In many cultures, women are barred from owning land. That especially causes problems after armed conflicts, when widowed women become the heads of households. Many are left destitute after losing land battles with

"Land Grabs" Target Africa, Former Soviet Republics

Governments and private investors are purchasing vast tracts of arable land across the globe for future food or biofuels crops. In the last two years, large-scale acquisitions — dubbed "land grabs" — have increased more than 10-fold. Asian and the Middle Eastern governments have bought tracts in Africa, where weak land tenure laws often foster ownership disputes. European investors, meanwhile, have been land shopping in Russia, Ukraine and other former Soviet republics, predominantly for biofuels production.

Selected Government-to-Government Land Purchases, 2006-2009		
Target country	Investor country	Amount of land (in hectares*) and proposed land use
Democratic Rep. of Congo	China	2.8 million — biofuels production
Sudan	South Korea	690,000 — wheat production
Sudan	United Arab Emirates	378,000 — investment
Tanzania	Saudi Arabia	500,000 — for lease/use unknown
Zambia	China	2 million — biofuels production
Pakistan	United Arab Emirates	324,000 — purchased/use unknown
Selected Private Sector Land Investments, 2006-2009		
Target country	Investor company	Amount of land (in hectares*) and proposed land use
Mozambique	Skebab, biofuel producer (Sweden)	100,000 — biofuels production
Brazil	Mitsui, trading company (Japan)	100,000 — soybeans production
Ukraine	Landkom, agricultural producer (U.K.)	100,000 — leased/use unknown
Russia	Alpcot Agro (Sweden)	128,000 — use unknown
Russia	Trigon, commodities producer (Denmark)	100,000 — use unknown
Russia	Black Earth Farming (Sweden)	331,000 — use unknown

* A hectare is equivalent to about 2.5 acres.

Source: Joachim von Braun and Ruth Meinzen-Dick, " 'Land Grabbing' by Foreign Investors in Developing Countries: Risks and Opportunities," International Food Policy Research Institute, April 2009, www.ifpri.org/sites/default/files/publications/bp013all.pdf

mandated equal rights to land ownership by women but also returned confiscated property to women and female orphans. [23]

Sometimes legal reforms or judicial processes can clarify land status, such as in most of sub-Saharan Africa, where multiple ownership systems compete for primacy. In Liberia, Sierra Leone and Kenya, for instance, individual ownership didn't exist before British colonization; the land was held by the community, and local leaders established rules of access, such as how much land a family needed or what was to be grown where. Colonialism brought a new system of individual ownership, organized around titles and deeds. Today, many individuals and communities claim ownership rights to land but have no paperwork to prove it, creating chaos.

"There is a bunch of confusion about who owns what," acknowledges Cecil T. O. Brandy, chairman of Liberia's Land Commission. Some of that confusion results from competing systems of land ownership or because devious buyers cheated the original owners, marking off territory in units no one understood in order to acquire larger tracts. "No villager has an idea that one acre is a football field." And sometimes, he says, "When they sold the land to somebody, they sold their whole villages as well."

But depending on the law to resolve such problems is itself problematic, because of the overlapping legal systems. "Land is quite complex, because globally you have five or six legal systems — the Spanish, Roman, British, French and so on. Each country's legislation depends on the previous colonial administration," says UN-HABITAT's El-Sioufi. However, he says locally tailored legal reforms can work, and some practices "can be transposed from one conflict to another."

surviving male family members — including their dead husbands' male relatives or their own sons or brothers — who, as males, claim ownership to the land. [21]

In Latin America, Costa Rica, Nicaragua and Colombia have adopted joint titling schemes, which allow women to share the title to their homes with their husbands. [22] In Central Africa, Rwanda in 2005 not only

Community-based dialogue programs, for instance, can be replicated easily. In northern Uganda, villages handle land disputes themselves, using culturally familiar processes often led by women, according to Donald Steinberg, deputy administrator of the U.S. Agency for International Development and former deputy president for policy at the International Crisis Group. Indeed, according to one study, when local communities in neighboring Rwanda tried to resolve conflict themselves, attempts to inject national laws into the process made things worse. [24]

But even locally crafted solutions may not work, "if the relevant official documents do not exist, having been destroyed during the conflicts as happened deliberately in East Timor, Somaliland and Kosovo and as a haphazard consequence of conflict in Afghanistan," according to Patrick McAuslan, a legal consultant for the World Bank on land acquisition. [25] Clarifying land ownership also might not work where two people can produce titles — sometimes fraudulent — to the same piece of land, as often happens in Liberia. [26]

And neat solutions are unlikely in countries with weak central governments, where clarifying land ownership policies can sometimes mean redistributing land to communities disenfranchised by dishonest or unfair past sales practices. "To be able to take the land of people who are economically and politically very powerful and give it to poor land users, you've got to be very strong," says Taylor, of the International Land Coalition.

Countries with strong governments, on the other hand, don't attract foreign land investors. A World Bank study found a negative correlation between the strength of foreign governments and investor interest in foreign land, according to Taylor. "Investors wanted land where governance was weakened, because there was the perception that land could be picked up cheap and there would not be strong controls, no need for environment assessments, no social issues or labor issues," he says.

Even where strong laws exist, laws are only as good as a government's willingness to enforce them. "In most of the countries in Asia, they have fairly good policies on land," says Seema Gaikwad, a land analyst in the Philippines, working with the coalition. She cites Bangladesh as an example of a country with rules about compensating people displaced by economic

Maasai warriors approach a group of Kalenjin fighters during a bow-and-arrow battle in Western Kenya's Transmara District on March 1, 2008, during post-election violence in Kenya, which stoked land-related tribal grievances.

AFP/Getty Images/Yasuyoshi Chiba

Thousands of indigenous Colombians march toward the city of Cali on Oct. 23, 2008, demanding expanded land rights. Colombia is one of several countries that recently adopted joint titling schemes, which allow women to share the title to their homes with their husbands.

AP Photo/Christian Escobar Mora

development projects. "The biggest question is whether these policies are being effectively implemented. There's a policy in place, but there's a lack of political will."

Modern laws and deeds aside, many rural landowners believe their land is part of their identity. In Africa, for example, "most of the population has no documents. They believe they own the land as a group because they've been there for millennia, and their mythology about how they came into the world involves that specific location, so identity is often very much tied up in where groups want

Land Disputes Spark Conflicts in Africa

Controversies over land have played a role in many modern conflicts in Africa and threaten to cause violence in other long-simmering disputes. Here are eleven selected places in the eastern half of the continent in which land already has sparked — or threatens to spark — violence.

Land Disputes That Led to Conflict:

(1) Western Sudan (Darfur) — In the 1970s, the Sudanese government rejected traditional land rights, depriving Darfur's herders of access to grazing lands. When famine exacerbated land disputes in the 1980s, violence broke out. The grievances have never been resolved, and in 2003 disenfranchised landholders revolted against the Sudanese government, which retaliated by arming camel herders, known as janjaweed, to repress the rebellion. The janjaweed, who were promised large tracts of land, reportedly murdered or chased hundreds of Darfuris off their land, emptying out entire villages.

(2) Democratic Republic of Congo — Africa's deadliest conflict is as much about land rights as it is about the many minerals in the country's eastern region. Dictator Mobutu Sese Seko's land nationalization in the 1970s compounded grievances left lingering from colonial days. Rwanda's 1998 invasion of Congo reignited land disputes in the Kivu provinces in northeastern Congo, and disputes between farmers and herders often turned violent.

(3) Ethiopia and Eritrea — A 1998 dispute over the dusty border town of Badme turned into all-out war that killed 100,000 people in four years. Both sides wanted to control Badme because it contains the Red Sea port of Assab. The town also became the flashpoint for an older argument, still unresolved, over the border between the two countries.

(4) Kenya — Tribal land grievances inflamed violence after Kenya's 2007 presidential election, which resulted in the deaths of at least 1,000 people.

(5) Rwanda — The slaughter of 800,000 Tutsis during the 1994 genocide may have been triggered as much by land scarcity as by ethnic tension. Africa's most densely populated country found itself with barely enough land to allow farmers to support themselves.

(6) Zimbabwe — Land grievances helped fuel the war for independence in 1979, but the most recent violence resulted from land reform efforts by President Robert Mugabe, who seized white-owned farms and turned them over to blacks, often government officials who knew little about farming. Agricultural production has plummeted, food has become scarce and inflation has spiked.

Land disputes that led to conflict

Potentially combustible land disputes

Potentially Combustible Land Disputes:

(7) Burundi — More than 500,000 refugees who fled post-independence violence in the early 1960s have been returning home in the past decade, finding their homes occupied legally, since the law recognizes anyone who has peacefully occupied land for at least 30 years as the owner. Experts fear the grievance could spark renewed conflict.

(8) South Africa — As part of the transition to democracy, the government planned to redistribute about a third of white-owned farms to blacks within 20 years. Transfers are behind schedule, and more than half of the completed transfers have failed. Racial violence broke out in 2009, and some observers fear the situation is still combustible.

(9) Southern Sudan — Clashes between the north and the south over property ownership rules aggravated the country's civil war, which ended in 2005. When South Sudan became an independent country following a referendum earlier this year, violence erupted in the border regions of southern Kordofan, technically part of the north, and Abayei, whose status remains contested.

(10) Uganda — Disputes are erupting over who owns property as those who fled a 20-year conflict in the north return home. Roughly 80 percent of Ugandans have property claims based on traditional land ownership systems, but the authority of elders to resolve disputes or enforce land rules has been weakened. Although the government has stepped in to resolve disputes, experts fear a backlash.

(11) Zambia — White farmers forced off their land in neighboring countries initially were welcomed by the government. The tone changed as some immigrant farmers began putting down roots on traditional lands. New arrivals are closely scrutinized, and observers fear deepening tensions.

Source: Compiled by Jina Moore from news reports

access," says Jon Unruh, a land expert at McGill University in Montreal, Canada.

That deep and personal relationship with the land can obstruct efforts to use the law to resolve disputes.

Land can be an underlying cause of what Columbia University's Coleman calls "the 5 percent problem" — the small number of conflicts around the world that have become virtually impossible to resolve. Once land becomes symbolic — as in the conflict over Jerusalem between Israel and the Palestinians, legal compromise about ownership or usage rights is viewed by both sides as tantamount to surrender. [27]

"To give the land up, to negotiate parts of it, seems impossible," Coleman says. "Land becomes non-negotiable," and the parties lock themselves into further conflict.

Does development exacerbate land conflicts?

Attracting investment is a common way for low- and middle-income countries to advance economically. [28] But economic growth require resources — especially land.

Sometimes, as in the construction of a highway in India's Uttar Pradesh state, the government acquires the land through eminent domain. In other cases, the relationship between developer, government and residents is less clear, as in the Gulbarga district in southern India, where hundreds of homes were demolished without giving the owners any notice, residents say. The reason remains unclear; one resident suggested it was to build a road.

"I don't know if it is the government that has done this or if it was a private company," said villager Vishal Pawar. "When we asked why our homes were being demolished, the officials showed us the photocopy of what looked like a map, and they said it was a 'masterplan.' " [29]

Even when the reasons are clearer, development plans can divide communities by stoking "tensions between the rich, who want to develop, and the poor, who are occupying the land," says El-Sioufi of UN-HABITAT. What's needed, he says, is to set up systems "that are responsive and take into the account the people."

In Latin America that approach is known as "territorial development." It involves dialogue among community members about future development, ultimately devolving authority for final development decisions. [30] "People at the local level are making decisions . . . not just about the land that's next to their house, but the land across the community," says Taylor, of the International Land Coalition. "I think one can assume that with that kind of decision-making, conflicts will be decreased."

Brazil, the world's largest exporter of biofuels, has developed a regional innovation that amounts to what Taylor calls "affirmative action" for small-scale farmers. [31] In 2005, the country passed regulations requiring biodiesel producers to purchase as much as 50 percent of their raw materials (such as sugar cane) from local farmers (percentages vary by region). [32] "That gives a bit of space to small farmers," Taylor says, because they can't compete on a level playing field with big agribusinesses for a share of the market. It also helps Brazil avoid conflict, since small-scale farmers represent 85 percent of Brazil's agriculture sector.

But when foreign investment is needed to develop the agricultural sector, it can create a tradeoff between protecting agriculture and development. Most developing countries get their food from small-scale farming, but local practices often lack the sophisticated — and expensive — tools, seeds, fertilizers or techniques needed to boost output. The share of all official aid worldwide provided to agriculture declined from a high of 17 percent in the 1980s to 5 percent in 2006-2008, with only 18 percent of that (some $1.2 billion) going to fragile and conflict-affected states. [33]

"There are genuine concerns as to how you finance the agricultural sector in a context in which there are expectations that development aid will not increase, and will probably decrease," says Cotula, of the International Institute for Environment and Development.

That makes governments desperate for big investment. "Quite often, there's a perception that there's a strong push to attract as much investment as possible, and many countries set up contracts to reflect that," he continues. "They're sort of desperate to bring in [big] investment."

BACKGROUND
Customary vs. Statutory

Land disputes are rooted in the Age of Discovery, when Spanish, French and British explorers imposed their legal ideas about social organization on indigenous peoples. Among the alien notions they transplanted was private property. In most traditional societies, communities collectively owned land, and each group had rules for access and use, often managed by elders or other local authority figures. With the advent of private property, land title trumped tradition.

But today "only 30 to 50 percent of the land globally is actually registered, which means [ownership is] agreed upon," says UN-HABITAT's El-Sioufi. Thus, ownership of the rest of the world's territory is potentially

CHRONOLOGY

1945-1960s *Territorial disputes ignite violence across international boundaries.*

1945 Greece and Cyprus face off in one of the world's longest-running boundary/land disputes, which has been monitored by U.N. peacekeepers since 1964.

1947 War between newly independent India and Pakistan ends with the partition of Kashmir into contested regions — a division still disputed by the two countries.

1967 Six Day War between Israel and its Arab neighbors ends with Israel seizing the Gaza Strip, the West Bank, East Jerusalem and Syria's Golan Heights, exacerbating existing territorial tensions created by Israel's statehood in 1948.

1990s *Internal political strife and disputes over land trigger civil and regional conflicts, notably in Central and South America. . . . Yugoslav republics vote for independence after Soviet Union collapses, leading to civil war between Serbia, Croatia, Bosnia-Herzegovina and Kosovo.*

1990-1994 Rwandan refugees, who fled ethnic violence in 1959, attack their homeland and neighboring Uganda after failed negotiations over refugees' right to return to their land. The ensuing civil war ends with a 1993 peace accord, which includes new rules about land claims, but the peace fails and genocide breaks out in 1994.

1995 Turkish troops invade Iraqi Kurdistan, fearful that a growing Kurdish independence movement might spread to Turkey's large Kurdish population.

1996 Guatemala's 36-year civil war between the government and guerrilla groups, sparked by a land redistribution plan, ends with a peace agreement that tackles land reform, but implementation lags.

1998 Rwanda invades Democratic Republic of Congo, allegedly to clear out perpetrators of the 1994 genocide taking shelter in refugee camps. But international observers say Rwanda covets Congo's natural resources. . . . Ethiopia and Eritrea begin a fight over a border town that escalates into a four-year war with 100,000 deaths.

2000-Present *International awareness of land ownership issues grows as returning refugees seek their old homesteads, natural disasters proliferate and huge "land grabs" increase.*

2000 Peruvian economist Hernando de Soto's *The Mystery of Capital* urges policymakers worldwide to enable poor people to get clear title to their land so they can aquire capital.

2004 Earthquake in Indian Ocean sparks tsunami that overruns many coastal areas in South and Southeast Asia, including nearly 600 square miles in Banda Aceh, Indonesia.

2005 U.N. Office for the Coordination of Humanitarian Assistance calls land analysis a "critical gap" in the international community's responses to global crises.

2008-2009 Land disputes overwhelm local administrators after more than 100,000 Burundian refugees return home following nearly 40 years in exile in Tanzania.

2008 South Korea tries to lease half of Madagascar's arable land, prompting a coup d'etat.

2009 American banker Philippe Heilberg buys nearly 1 million acres in Sudan, an area five times the size of Belgium, from a local warlord — the single biggest "land grab" in African history.

2010 "Land grabs" follow a devastating 7.0 magnitude earthquake in Haiti that destroys nearly 200,000 homes. UN-HABITAT and the Food and Agriculture Organization release guidelines for nongovernmental organizations on how to deal with land ownership issues after natural disasters.

2011 As debates over "land grabs" intensify, World Bank holds a meeting at its Washington, D.C., headquarters where investors, government officials and diplomats discuss voluntary principles for more responsible land acquisitions.

Norwegians Help Liberians Untangle Land Ownership

One Million Signatures Campaign seeks major changes.

Miles down a dirt path, more than two hours from the nearest large town, about two dozen mud huts huddle together in a small clearing in rural Liberia. Roughly half of the village of Kolonta moved to these temporary shelters after their homes were burned down last year by residents of neighboring Dankpansue.

The two villages were at odds over land, a common point of conflict in Liberia. Often, such conflicts can escalate, sparked by the most unlikely of scenarios — as happened in Kolonta. The village is next to a 2,000-acre rubber plantation, and many Kolontans rent out rooms to the plantation workers. But when the plantation owner expanded his farm by usurping some of Dankpansue's land, the infuriated residents took out their anger on the Kolontans, who appeared to be giving shelter to the enemy by renting rooms to the laborers.

Mary Winnie, 29, who lost her home in the arson, at first dreamed of revenge. "I was planning to retaliate," she says. "I would organize my people to burn [Dankpansue]. It would have been a vicious conflict. . . . If somebody hits you, and you hit them, they will hit you more, and it will continue. The end result would be death, or long suffering."

Winnie changed her mind because of Franklin Gonlepa, who works with the Norwegian Refugee Council (NRC), a nongovernmental organization that has facilitated more than 1,600 land disputes in four rural Liberian counties. "If you speak to the elders and ask what might cause another war in Liberia, they're going to tell you it's going to be a war over land," says Laura Cunial, a former NRC project manager, "because land provides the major source of income for the majority of the population."

The risk is so great that Liberia last year established a land-reform commission to untangle confusion rooted in land policies half a century old. While many Liberians will argue that they own the land they farm, most don't have deeds, which are expensive to register and open owners up to yearly tax payments. But they may have tribal certificates — paperwork from elders attesting that the land has belonged to their families for generations.

But land deeds and tribal certificates often differ. As refugees who fled the country's civil war return to a stabilizing Liberia and expatriates come home from abroad, conflicts are brewing. "When the war came some people took advantage and tried to settle on people's land. They thought people . . . wouldn't return," says Jericho W. Dorwazin, chairman of the Special Presidential Land Dispute Mediation Commission for Nimba County.

The Tokpah family, whose three daughters process rice using an age-old mortar and pestle method, has been feuding for years with a neighboring family over a small plot of land abutting both their properties in northern Liberia. The Norwegian Refugee Council, a nongovernmental organization that has a land-dispute mediation project in Liberia, has helped the two families reach a tentative agreement.

Liberia's courts are bogged down and notoriously corrupt, making a legal solution difficult. But the NRC has 36 field personnel who travel by motorcycle to the most remote villages, interviewing angered parties and walking property boundaries. Their hands-on approach, which has successfully resolved more than 700 land conflicts since 2006, has two distinct advantages over the adversarial legal process: It doesn't involve the courts, and it preserves the village peace.

"Liberians especially in the rural areas feel that the judicial system is a system for the rich — at least that's what they tell us," says Cunial. In addition, when the NRC helps villagers reach a compromise "you don't completely destroy the relationship between the two parties. Don't forget that these are neighbors who are going back home, and the next day they're going to see one another. They're farming next door. They live next door."

In addition, there's more at stake than food, peace and community, says Cecil T. O. Brandy, chairman of the country's new Land Commission. "Land is the only thing I own, or my father owns. It borders on my nationality," he says. "It's a national identity."

— Jina Moore

Guidelines to Control "Land Grabs"

Four international organizations have drafted voluntary guidelines for the responsible, large-scale acquisition of land. The Food and Agriculture Organization, International Fund for Agricultural Development, U.N. Conference on Trade and Development and the World Bank suggest that purchases of large tracts be guided by the following principles:

- **Existing rights to land and associated natural resources are recognized and respected.**
- **Investments do not jeopardize food security but rather strengthen it.**
- **Processes for accessing land and making the investments are transparent, monitored and ensure accountability by all stakeholders, within a proper business, legal and regulatory environment.**
- **All those affected are consulted, and agreements stemming from those consultations are recorded and enforced.**
- **Projects respect the rule of law, reflect industry best practice, are economically viable and result in long-lasting shared value.**
- **Investments generate desirable social impacts and do not increase vulnerability.**
- **The environmental impacts from a project are quantified and measures are taken to encourage sustainable use of resources while minimizing and mitigating the risk/magnitude of negative impacts.**

Source: Food and Agriculture Organization, the International Fund for Agricultural Development, the U.N. Conference on Trade and Development and the World Bank

in dispute — and up for grabs. Land experts describe two different land tenure systems —"customary" and "statutory."

Customary systems are those in which land policies are matters of tradition, or local custom, and ownership is generally communal in nature. In statutory systems land policies are legally regulated, and ownership is proven through titles. Invariably, tensions have flared around the world over whether access to land is granted through tradition or title. Perhaps nowhere is the conflict as incendiary as in Africa, the last continent carved up by colonial powers.

Spain, Portugal, Britain and the other colonial overlords forever changed Africa, just as Central and Latin America had shifted under Spanish settlement and Asia under the British and French. The settler system transformed the land system, by taking large amounts of land

out of customary use and putting them in a new form, says Taylor of the International Land Coalition. "It more or less permanently alienated that land from the people who had used it for generations before that," he adds.

By the mid-20th century, Central and Latin America saw civil war and revolutions, even in countries that had made progress on land tenure. "The nature of conflict differs by region," writes Samir Elhawary, a research fellow at the Overseas Development Institute, a think tank in London. "In regions where property rights are defined, conflicts tend to revolve around wages and working conditions; where property rights are still disputed, conflicts tend to revolve around land ownership." [34]

African countries that have successfully addressed the dual land tenure system have accommodated both types of land rights. In Taylor's native Botswana, for example, rural communities can use customary systems, while urban land issues are regulated by statute.

However, the competing systems can create confusion. In Liberia, for example, one man may produce a deed to a piece of property, while the village elder may also hold a "customary title" to the same property — a kind of legal placeholder for those foregone traditional rights. So far, the country hasn't decided who wins when there are competing claims, and much of the work to manage them is being done by outside mediators.

Similarly, "ownership of many plots is unclear" in Thailand, which can spark conflicts, according to Sunee Chaiyarose, a former Thai human rights commissioner. The lack of clarity complicates a land redistribution scheme designed to alleviate the squeeze on small-scale farmers created by dwindling land availability. In 2008, the Thai government sought to turn over to farmers 1 million rai — about 160,000 hectares — to cultivate biofuel crops. But competing ownership claims made the plan untenable. "Allocating these problematic land plots will only worsen the conflicts," Chaiyarose said. [35]

Today, most countries see value in the statutory system, even if many indigenous peoples argue that it encroaches on their livelihoods or culture. The value is literal: Titled land is a commodity. It can be useful as collateral for borrowing money to grow a business and to attract foreign investment. By distilling access rights into a single document, land titles allow any buyer with enough cash to buy a plot from a willing seller.

"Hidden Architecture"

It was this system of financing, opened up by privatized land, that world-renown Peruvian economist Hernando de Soto had in mind when he called land the "hidden architecture" of economies. De Soto has led efforts to privatize land titles and strengthen the informal market economy in Peru. People on communal lands "need what the rest of us have — clear property rights over what they own, so that they can get credit and capital, and so that there's no discussion over who owns what," he has said. [36] De Soto's work with the Institute for Liberty and Democracy in Lima led Peru to issue 1.2 million land titles in the 1990s, a move heralded by the World Bank and others for improving people's access to capital.

But others dispute the meaning of the achievement. "The most important areas of Lima were developed because of land security and the availability of water, not because the people who lived there were given land titles," Gustavo Riofrio, a researcher at the Peruvian think tank Desco, told the BBC. [37]

In fact, some researchers think that this shift and its implied economic development plan — using newly titled land to secure a business loan, for example — may not be the wisest move, given the lessons of the global financial crisis. Those who push land reform "are asking people who really can't afford to use their land as collateral, who see their land in a completely different way — as their livelihood — to use their land as a source of capital," says Ambreena Manji, author of *The Politics of Land Reform in Africa: From Communal Tenure to Free Markets.*

In other places, land titling projects may only reinforce concentrations of power and wealth. The World Bank threatened to cut off loans to Cambodia over a development dispute that pitted a ruling party politician and his lakeside property against 4,000 of his neighbors, who were forced to move elsewhere because of plans to develop the lake. [38] Some observers in Thailand warned against the biofuel land reallocation, not just because of confusion over ownership but also for fear it would further consolidate concentrated land holdings among the wealthy. The Shinawatras, Thailand's most politically powerful family, rose to prominence in large part by confiscating the land of peasants who couldn't pay back loans to the family. [39]

Some argue that titling schemes bring the risk of manipulation by those with resources, to the detriment of those who rely on land for food security and livelihoods. "The minute you start [to] document land rights, the people who have the most power are going to have every reason to take rights from the people who have the least power," says lawyer Nielsen, of the Rural Development Institute. That, she warns, "is lighting the match, potentially, that causes the fire."

"Land Grabs"

Land rights may become even more combustible as so-called "land grabs" spread around the world. In the last five years, analysts say, governments and private companies have invested huge sums in the biggest land deals, by acre, in modern history. The global rise in food prices in 2008 and growing concerns about food security have only hastened the purchases. "Compared to an average annual expansion of global agricultural land of less than 4 million hectares before 2008, approximately 56 million hectares worth of large-scale farmland deals were announced even before the end of 2009," the World Bank noted in this year's much-awaited report on land grabs, "Rising Global Interest in Farmland." [40] Since 2009, the money behind large-scale acquisitions has increased more than 10-fold — to at least $25 billion worldwide. [41]

Such investments are often kept quiet, and media reports of formal deals are not always reliable, according to the Food and Agriculture Organization (FAO). Meanwhile, some countries informally have been offered investment in exchange for rights to more than half of their arable territory, FAO says.

More than 70 percent of the transactions have taken place in Africa, but investor interest appears universal. [42]

The Saudi government paid $100 million to lease land for wheat in Ethiopia, while Qatar purchased land in Kenya and the Philippines. [43] China bought 2 million hectares in Zambia to develop biofuels. Kuwait owns land in Sudan and Cambodia, while a Japanese company has acquired soybean farms in Brazil. The investment bank Goldman Sachs, meanwhile, recently invested $450 million in poultry and pig farms in China. [44] Indian companies have formed a consortium to invest in oilseeds in Uruguay and Paraguay. [45]

Determining the motives behind these deals can be difficult, but they are likely to be speculative investments. "Although a lot of land has been acquired, a minority of that has been put into production, which raises the issue of how much of this really was genuinely in the interest of production, and how much of it was aimed at securing access to an asset likely to increase in value in the future," says Cotula, of the International Institute for Environment and Development.

While land grabs in Africa involve governments with food security concerns, land grabs in Asia reinforce the trend toward consolidation of wealth. In Cambodia, UN-HABITAT has observed that those with power — the military and the wealthy — are the quickest to acquire land. [46] As a result, says Gaikwad, the land analyst in the Philippines, "large amounts of land are actually owned by a very small percentage of owners, while a small amount of land is owned by farmers."

The same pattern is reasserting itself in Latin America. After civil wars reversed earlier land-redistribution efforts, market-based land reforms became more fashionable, and Latin American governments shifted their land policies accordingly. The result, in many countries, has been a reappearance of the consolidation of land and wealth that earlier agrarian reforms tried to prevent. [47]

The World Bank, the FAO and others have recently partnered to create a set of voluntary guidelines for land acquisitions. Targeted especially at those eyeing massive "land grab" style investments, the principles call on investors to respect existing ownership, consider environmental sustainability and ensure their investments do not jeopardize food security. [48] Many land rights organizations have denounced the principles as an attempt to avoid the "social backlash" that land grabs often ignite. [49]

Most land grabs occur in rural areas, but urban land disputes also are on the rise as more and more people move to urban areas. [50] For the first time in history, more people live in urban areas, as of 2008, than in rural areas. [51] "Their arrival in the city leads to another dynamic of conflict . . . in this case over access to utilities and services," says UN-HABITAT's El-Sioufi.

But burgeoning urban communities quickly infringe on already scarce land. By 2025, it is projected that Nepal's fabled Kathmandu Valley won't have any high-grade agricultural land left, because the region is growing too fast, making land more valuable as real estate than as agricultural fields. The number of apartments in Kathmandu tripled just between 2007 and 2008, and the value of land has jumped 300 percent since 2003. [52]

Economic opportunity, however, goes both ways. In Kalimantan, the Indonesian portion of the island of Borneo, palm oil is a hugely profitable industry. Analysts expect the need for additional palm oil plantations to displace more and more indigenous people and "exacerbate land conflicts" with those who remain. [53]

CURRENT SITUATION
Landless Returnees

The international community is moving toward greater recognition of the challenges posed by conflicts over land as developing countries make economic progress. In a 2005 report on the state of global humanitarian assistance, the U.N.'s Office for Coordinated Humanitarian Response identified land and property issues as a "critical gap" in international response to conflict and natural disasters. [54] That spurred nongovernmental organizations to examine their methods of intervention.

A U.N. peacebuilding agency has allocated more than $1 million to adjudicate land disputes in Liberia and Burundi to help prevent a return to violence. [55] In Burundi, that support helped the local land commission resolve 3,000 land conflicts. In Liberia, the funding helped establish a Land Dispute Resolution Task Force, which uses both legal and alternative dispute-resolution methods to solve arguments over land.

But dealing with land disputes is about more than setting up commissions to adjudicate conflicting claims. Implicit in that process is a decision about history. As El-Sioufi, of UN-HABITAT, puts it, "To which era do you go back," especially if you have had multiple displacements?

In Afghanistan, up to 70 percent of the refugees who returned home in the early days after U.S. operations found themselves landless or homeless. [56] In Colombia, paramilitaries have pushed up to 4.5 million people off their land. [57] The dispute between India and Pakistan over Kashmir occasionally erupts into violence that has displaced at least 265,000 people since 1990. [58] After the Balkan wars and the genocide in Bosnia, many refugees feared that their land had been or would be appropriated by others and simply chose not to return. [59]

Displacement following Liberia's civil war, for instance, brought to light long-running land disputes between communities that believed they owned the land their grandfathers had farmed and entrepreneurs who said they had bought the land from elders before the wars. In addition, many refugees didn't return to their homesteads but moved to the capital, Monrovia, creating new post-war arguments over land ownership. The country's Land Commission is still debating how to untangle the many historical layers of ownership involved in the country's land disputes.

Sometimes, that debate comes down to a stark and difficult choice, between justice and peace. In post-genocide Rwanda, for instance, refugees on both sides of the country's genocide and civil war are returning home as stability takes root and the economy grows. For the sake of procedural clarity and peace, the government has chosen not to acknowledge any land claims older than 1983.

"That was seen by some activists in the [humanitarian] sector as infringement, not only on the right of restitution but also more generally on human rights. But it was a situation deemed necessary to make sure peace . . . is possible," says Sara Pantuliano, program leader of the Humanitarian Policy Group at the Overseas Development Institute in London.

Several principles are at stake when refugees return after war. The right to shelter is broadly recognized in Article 11 of the 1966 International Covenant on Economic, Social and Cultural Rights, which has been signed by 160 countries. [60] The right to restitution after human rights violations — common during war — is supported by the U.N. Commission on Human Rights and the International Criminal Court's founding Rome Statute, which authorizes the court to establish restitution principles. [61]

Sugar cane is harvested for ethanol production in Sertaozinho, Brazil — about 250 miles from São Paulo. Much of the nearly 4 million acres of Brazilian farmland recently acquired by big investors will be used for biofuels production. Rising food prices and surging demand for biofuels are leading big investors to buy up huge tracts of land in Brazil and other developing countries — some as an investment and some to grow food or biofuels.

Protesters gather outside parliament in Mbabane, the capital of Swaziland, on Aug. 3, 2011, to ask for improved property rights rules. Vast land purchases — many occurring in Africa — are taking property away from those without clear title, spurring more and more people to call for the government to beef up laws governing land rights.

Can regulations help prevent "land grabs"?

YES

Wendy Call
Author, No Word for Welcome: The Mexican Village Faces the Global Economy

Written for *CQ Global Researcher,* September 2011

Regulatory oversight, combined with fair land tenure policies — which govern both land ownership and access — can prevent illegal land grabs, such as occurred in the Mexican state of Oaxaca. Several years ago, a small group of private investors illegally bought several hundred hectares* of coastal land to build an industrial shrimp farm.

The land belonged to the town of Union Hidalgo, an indigenous Zapotec community that practices traditional land tenure (as do many Mexican villages). Under this system, the town's land is held in common trust, with individuals permitted to farm, fish, collect plants or build on particular plots. The process serves as a local regulatory system. In the Oaxaca case, a corrupt mayor orchestrated secret, illegal land sales, and the community learned of the sale only after villagers discovered stretches of coastal mangrove forest destroyed. Many villagers were outraged, knowing that the town assembly had not given permission for this deforestation.

So began a three-year battle against the illegal land seizure. The struggle didn't require a set of voluntary international guidelines — the focus of current discussions on regulating land use. It required something more basic and, possibly, more replicable: Local grassroots oversight combined with national regulatory authority to halt the illegal land grab.

The villagers alerted the media and national and international environmental organizations as well as the Mexican environmental protection agency. After much pressure from Union Hidalgo villagers, the environmental inspectors surveyed the damage to the mangrove stands and requested that the investors prepare an environmental impact statement. The agency later rejected the statement as inadequate, halting the building of the shrimp farm.

Such an approach to solving communal land tenure disputes gives everyone a stake and a voice in the conservation of local lands. Because their livelihoods depend on healthy land, villagers have a deeper interest in land conservation than transnational corporations, federal governments or even international agencies.

Unfortunately, this system is threatened. In the 1990s, constitutional changes required in order for Mexico to join the North American Free Trade Agreement forced Mexico to move toward a U.S.-style system of private land tenure. The Mexican government is pressuring villages and towns to discard communal land tenure systems. But in doing so, they may dismantle the local oversight that best protects against illegal land grabs and environmental destruction.

*A hectare is equivalent to about 2.5 acres.

NO

Olivier De Schutter
U.N. Special Rapporteur on the Right to Food

from an article prepared for the International Land Coalition, www.commercialpressuresonland.org/opinion-pieces/how-not-think-about-land-grabbing

In the international discussion surrounding the phenomenon referred to as "land-grabbing" — the acquisition or long-term lease of large areas of land by investors — the debate has focused on whether or not this development can be regulated at the regional or international level.

Large-scale investments in farmland have been criticized [primarily due to] questions about the capacity of the countries targeted by these land deals, many of which suffer from problems of governance, to effectively manage these investments to ensure that they contribute to rural development and poverty alleviation.

The real concern behind the development of large-scale investments in farmland is rather that giving land away to investors [with] better access to capital to "develop" it implies huge opportunity costs: It will result in a type of farming that will have much less powerful poverty-reducing impacts than if access to land and water were improved for the local farming communities.

There is clear tension between ceding land to investors for the creation of large plantations and the objective of redistributing land and ensuring more equitable access to land — something governments have repeatedly committed to, most recently at the 2006 International Conference on Agrarian Reform and Rural Development.

What we need now is not just investment in agriculture: It is a vision that goes beyond disciplining land deals and providing policymakers with a checklist of how to destroy global peasantry responsibly. If it is to be truly responsible, agricultural investment must benefit the poor in the South, rather than leading to a transfer of resources to the rich in the North. It must be investment that truly reduces hunger and malnutrition, rather than aggravating them.

It is my belief that we have been moving both too slowly and too fast: too slowly, because the increase of commercial pressures and speculation over land has been developing on a very broad scale without the international community acting in a truly coordinated way to guide this development; and too fast, because we have focused on how to promote responsible investment, when investment can only be seen as one small part of a much broader strategy. What we need is, in sum, to think beyond the debate about access to land as it is framed today.

But many countries are finding that restitution may be too high a standard, given the many challenges they face after war. In Burundi, more than 7,000 disputes remain unresolved, stretching back to 1972, when Hutus fled ethnic conflict for refugee camps in neighboring Tanzania. [62] Those camps closed in 2008, and more than 150,000 Hutus have returned home, triggering a spike in local land conflicts.

Both grassroots and international organizations are trying to solve those conflicts, largely through mediation and negotiation. But all parties acknowledge that in such a complicated situation — where land claims go back more than a generation, in a small country with a burgeoning population — restitution is too difficult a standard. Anderson Masabo, a Burundian involved in a land dispute, invokes a local proverb to describe how the situation will play out: "We will carry each other on our backs."

In fact, moments of collective tragedy, such as natural disasters, often become windows of opportunity, according to Coleman, the conflict resolution expert at Columbia University. It's "a time when something transcends the importance of a conflict," he says. "You see a de-escalation of conflict around natural disasters. A tsunami will occur, and you'll see warring ethnic groups put down their arms for a time and help stabilize the community, then pick up their arms again."

Post-Disaster Problems

Land issues are a growing concern in the aftermath of natural disasters, when illegal or stealthy land acquisitions frequently occur, experts say.

"In the aftermath of a crisis, this is the prime moment for land grabbing. It's when the 'elite capture' takes place," says the Overseas Development Institute's Pantuliano, referring to the process by which already wealthy or powerful individuals acquire, or "capture," large land holdings.

From Burma and Indonesia to Thailand and Pakistan, the chaos that follows storms, earthquakes or tsunamis affect land ownership and usage. Land grabs followed the devastating magnitude 7.0 earthquake in Haiti in 2010, for instance. [63] First responders, such as the United Nations and disaster relief organizations, are only beginning to deal with the phenomenon.

"The first thing everybody thinks of post-disaster is survival, food security, livelihoods and shelter," says Gaikwad, of the International Land Coalition in the

World-renowned Peruvian economist Hernando de Soto has argued that helping the poor obtain titles to their property gives them the economic power to get credit and raise capital. His work led Peru to issue 1.2 million land titles in the 1990s, a move heralded by the World Bank and others.

Philippines. "Access to land comes maybe in the fourth or fifth round of [thinking about] what's most needed."

UN-HABITAT last year released a set of guidelines on how to handle land issues after natural disasters. But in some cases, local residents have the best solutions. After the 2004 Indian Ocean tsunami flattened much of Banda Aceh, Indonesia's westernmost island, survivors from 25 coastal villages ignored a government relocation plan and moved back to their land, rebuilt their houses and erected buffers between their villages and the sea. [64] Their actions helped to end a generation of conflict in the province. [65]

In Haiti, the Center for International Earth Science Information Network (CIESIN) is taking a similar approach. The Columbia University-based initiative is holding community-level workshops in the capital, Port au Prince, about how to handle land redistribution after the earthquake.

Humanitarian organizations, however, can inadvertently exacerbate land conflicts by altering the power structure in communities long after the groups have left, points out Alex de Waal, a Sudan expert and a regional adviser to the Conflict and Peace Forum of the Brooklyn, N.Y.-based Social Science Research Council. The organizations often tap local people to help organize the internally displaced persons (IDPs) seeking help. [66] Those appointees, who organize such things as housing distribution, food rations and other necessities, are then "likely to become figures of authority, power and wealth," writes de Waal. Indeed, the very systems for "registering newcomers to IDP camps and exercising jurisdiction over where they live are likely to become systems of power over land." [67]

The solution, experts say, is to work with local elders or other recognized authority figures. When the government or outside organizations have taken this locally based approach, the results have been positive.

"It's hard sometimes because the experts come in with their view of what's right, and the locals have their view of what's right, and it may be difficult for them to reach mutual understanding," says Columbia University's Coleman. "But that's key, because that's what allows a locally sustainable solution."

OUTLOOK
Climate and Land Disputes

As if legal uncertainty and capital inequity weren't problems enough for rural land users, climate change is altering the landscapes where they earn their livelihoods.

Longer and more frequent droughts are complicating agriculture in some regions, and deserts are expanding, especially in Africa, leaving fewer places for roving pastoralists to graze their livestock. [68] China's first-ever comprehensive environmental survey found that its northwestern Kumtag desert is expanding in all directions, and even some of Latin America's most fertile territories have been experiencing puzzling droughts. [69]

In India, indebted farmers are being squeezed between creditors and changes in land ownership laws — a situation exacerbated by environmental disasters, says a regional analyst. "There is a very high percentage of farmer suicides in India due to the fact that people are not able to pay their dues on losses incurred because of flood or drought," says the International Land Coalition's Gaikwad. The Indian government estimates that 200,000 farmers have committed suicide in the last 13 years. [70]

Scientists acknowledge that in some cases, it may be too soon to blame ongoing weather aberrations on climate change. "Climate change cannot be characterized by one single event, but rather by a series [of events] over the long term," according to climatologist Vicente Barros, a professor emeritus at the University of Buenos Aires, in Argentina, and a member of the U.N. Intergovernmental Panel on Climate Change (IPCC). Nevertheless, the IPCC projects that 150 million people worldwide will be displaced by 2050 due to changes in climate. [71]

Even if climate change isn't the real culprit in all cases, analysts have found a relationship between the environment and conflict, according to Hsiang, at the Woodrow Wilson School's Program on Science, Technology and Environmental Policy. Scientists have found clear relationships between what happens in different societies as temperature and rainfall fluctuate.

In China, for example, temperature data from the last millennium show that cold periods were accompanied by more warfare and dynastic changes. [72] Likewise, an analysis of global rainfall levels suggests that below-average rainfall elevates the risk of high-intensity conflict. [73] In Africa, warmer periods correlate with more war, leading to projections that Africa will see a 54 percent increase in armed conflict by 2030. [74]

Hsiang recently published a study suggesting a close relationship between rainfall and conflict. "In the modern world, the global climate goes back and forth between something we call a La Niña phase and an El Niño phase; it happens all the time," he says. "Basically, in the El Niño phase, the tropics become a lot warmer and a lot drier." When that happens, he says, "civil conflicts in the tropics double." Hsiang's findings were published last month. [75]

The numbers look small — Hsiang estimates the risk of conflict at from 3 percent to 6 percent — but their effect is significant. "We go back in time and think about how many conflicts since 1950 could have been affected by El Niño," he says. "We estimate that about 20 percent of all conflicts we observe had some sort of influence by El Niño. It's a very big effect."

Unlike other researchers, Hsiang resists predicting how these relationships may affect future conflict. "There may be future impacts that we've never seen, in which case data from the past is not going to tell us anything," he says.

Coleman, of Columbia University, also resists pessimism about the future relationship between climate change and conflict. "This problem could be a uniting challenge," he says. After all, climate change is one factor that will affect everyone, universally. "As the water table rises, it's going to flood shores; it's going to flood rice fields; it's going to flood Manhattan."

If that happens, analysts fear the domino effects will be significant. A decrease in global land mass means less food and fewer natural resources — and, in all likelihood, greater competition for those resources, especially as the global population continues to grow.

NOTES

1. Liz Alden Wily, "The tragedy of public lands: The fate of the commons under global commercial pressure," International Land Coalition (2011), p. 30.

2. *Ibid.*

3. "Slow progress on land-grabbing regulation," Nov. 29, 2010, IRIN, www.irinnews.org/Report.aspx?Reportid=91223. Also see HighQuest Partners, "Private financial sector investment in farmland and agricultural infrastructure," Organisation for Economic Co-operation and Development, August 2010, http://farmland-grab.org/post/view/16060. See "Food Price Watch," World Bank, February 2011, www.worldbank.org/foodcrisis/food_price_watch_report_feb2011.html.

4. For background, see the following *CQ Global Researchers*: Karen Foerstel, "Crisis in Darfur," Sept. 1, 2008, pp. 243-270 and Jason McLure, "Sub-Saharan Democracy," Feb. 15, 2011, pp. 79-106.

5. Jina Moore, "Power Tools," *The Christian Science Monitor*, June 30, 2010, www.csmonitor.com/World/Global-Issues/2011/0630/Social-media-Did-Twitter-and-Facebook-really-build-a-global-revolution#disqus_thread.

6. For background, see Sarah Glazer, "EU Immigration Turmoil," *CQ Global Researcher*, Dec. 1, 2010, pp. 289-320.

7. "A New Wave of Anti-Roma Violence in Hungary," *Der Spiegel*, April 27, 2011, www.spiegel.de/international/europe/0,1518,759349,00.html.

8. "Land and Conflict: A Handbook for Humanitarians," UN-HABITAT, September 2009, p. 11, http://postconflict.unep.ch/humanitarianaction/documents/02_03-04_03-08.pdf.

9. Alain de Janvry and Elisabeth Sadoulet, "Land Reforms in Latin America: Ten Lessons Toward a Contemporary Agenda," World Bank Latin American Land Policy Workshop, June 14, 2002, http://are.berkeley.edu/~sadoulet/papers/Land_Reform_in_LA_10_lesson.pdf.

10. Javier Blas and William Wallis, "US investor buys Sudanese warlord's land," *Financial Times*, Jan. 9, 2009, www.ft.com/cms/s/0/a4cbe81e-de84-11dd-9464-000077b07658.html#axzz1TGhoXtAU.

11. *Ibid.*

12. Chris Huggins, "A history perspective on the 'global land rush,' " International Land Coalition, January 2011, p. 16, www.landcoalition.org/publications/historical-perspective-global-land-rush.

13. *Ibid.*

14. Richard P. Tucker, *Insatiable Appetite: The United States and the Ecological Degradation of the Tropical World, Concise Revised Edition* (2007), p. 202.

15. Kristi Esseck, "Guns Money and Cell Phones," *Industry Standard Magazine*, June 11, 2001, reprinted at www.globalissues.org/article/442/guns-money-and-cell-phones. For background, see Josh Kron, "Conflict in Congo," *CQ Global Researcher*, April 5, 2011, pp. 157-182.

16. Randeep Ramesh, "Inside India's Hidden War," *The Guardian*, May 9, 2006, www.guardian.co.uk/world/2006/may/09/india.randeepramesh.

17. Pradip Kumar Maitra, "CM: Salwa Judum now over," *Hindustan Times*, Feb. 7, 2011, www.hindustantimes.com/CM-Salwa-Judum-is-now-over/Article1-659693.aspx.

18. Ramesh, *op. cit.*

19. Roel R. Ravanera and Vanessa Gorra, "Commercial Pressures on Land in Asia: An overview," International Land Coalition, January 2011, p. 38.

20. "The Concentration of Land Ownership in Latin America: An approach to current problems," International Land Coalition, 2011, pp. 1-22, www.landcoalition.org/sites/default/files/publication/913/LA_Regional_ENG_web_11.03.11.pdf.

21. Jina Moore, "The African Divide," *The Christian Science Monitor*, Jan. 24, 2010, pp. 27-31.

22. Stephen Baranyi and Viviane Weitzner, "Transforming land-related conflict: Policy, practice and possibilities," North-South Institute, 2006, p. 9.

23. Ernest Uwayezu and Theodomir Mugiraneza, "Land Policy Reform in Rwanda and Land Tenure Security for all Citizens: Provision and Recognition of Women's Rights over Land," Gender Issues in Land Administration, Paper No. 4914, "Bridging the Gap Between Cultures" conference, Marrakesh, Morocco, May 18-22, 2011, pp. 2-3, http://77.243.131.160/pub/fig2011/papers/ts04g/ts04g_uwayezu_mugiraneza_4914.pdf.

24. John W. Bruce, "International Standards, improvisation and the role of international humanitarian organizations in the return of land in post-conflict Rwanda," in Sara Pantuliano, ed., *Uncharted Territory: Land, Conflict and Humanitarian Action* (2009), p. 112-115.

25. Patrick McAuslan, "Post-conflict land administration: A note," World Bank, June 11, 2007, p. 4.

26. Moore, *op. cit.*

27. For background, see Irwin Arieff, "Middle East Peace Prospects," *CQ Global Researcher*, May 1, 2009, pp. 119-148.

28. For analysis of individual countries across a spectrum of economic and development indicators, see data sets from the Human Development Report, United Nations Development Programme, 2010, http://hdr.undp.org/en/.

29. Manu Joseph, "Land, Power and Rural Rebellion," *The New York Times*, May 30, 2011, www.nytimes.com/2011/05/31/world/asia/31iht-letter31.html.

30. "Land access and participatory territorial development in South Africa and Brazil: A DFID supported policy research project 2004-2006," National Resources Institute, undated, www.nri.org/projects/reed/led.pdf.

31. "Background Note: Brazil," U.S. Department of State, March 8, 2011, www.state.gov/r/pa/ei/bgn/35640.htm.

32. Anna Mohr, "The national program for production and use of biodiesel and its social components," paper prepared for the 9th European IFSA Symposium, July 4-7, 2010, Vienna, http://ifsa.boku.ac.at/cms/fileadmin/Proceeding2010/2010_WS3.3_Mohr.pdf.

33. "World Development Report 2011: Conflict, Security and Development," World Bank, 2011, p. 230, http://wdr2011.worldbank.org/sites/default/files/pdfs/WDR2011_Full_Text.pdf.

34. Samir Elhawary, "Between war and peace: Land and humanitarian action in Colombia," in *Uncharted Territory, op. cit.*, p. 173.

35. "Thailand: NHRC warns land redistribution plan will lead to conflicts," *Bangkok Post*, Sept. 10, 2008, reprinted at www.asiapacificforum.net/news/thailand-nhrc-warns-land-redistribution-plan-will-lead-to-conflicts.

36. Linda Pressly, "Can free market economics harmonize Amazonian land rights?" BBC's "Crossing Continents," April 28, 2010, http://news.bbc.co.uk/2/hi/8648699.stm.

37. *Ibid.*

38. "World Bank halts new loans to Cambodia over evictions," Agence France-Presse, Aug. 8, 2011, www.google.com/hostednews/afp/article/ALeqM5gt2BxXar_0-pCRXSzfVb4MwDroqw?docId=CNG.b67300196a0d906b8819cbbadd1aeba1.11.

39. Thomas Fuller, "Shinawatras pull off another political magic act," *The New York Times*, July 4, 2011, www.nytimes.com/2011/07/05/world/asia/05iht-village05.html?pagewanted=all.

40. Klaus Deininger, *et al.*, "Rising Global Interest in Farmland: Can it yield sustainable and equitable benefits?" World Bank, 2011, p. xiv, http://siteresources.worldbank.org/INTARD/Resources/ESW_Sept7_final_final.pdf.

41. "Slow progress on land-grabbing regulation," Nov. 29, 2010, IRIN, www.irinnews.org/Report.aspx?Reportid=91223. Also see HighQuest Partners, *op. cit.*

42. *Ibid.*

43. "'Land Grabbing' by Foreign Investors in Developing Countries: Risks and Opportunities," IFPRI Policy Brief, International Food Policy Research Institute, April 13, 2009.

44. *Ibid.*

45. Alexandra Spieldoch, "Global Land Grabs," *Foreign Policy in Focus*, June 18, 2009, www.fpif.org/articles/global_land_grab.

46. "Land and Conflict: A Handbook for humanitarians," *op. cit.*, p. 25.

47. "The Concentration of Land Ownership in Latin America," *op. cit.*, pp. 1-22.

48. "Principles for Responsible Agricultural Investment that Respects Rights, Livelihoods and Resources," World Bank, Jan. 25, 2010, http://siteresources.worldbank.org/INTARD/214574-1111138388661/22453321/Principles_Extended.pdf.

49. "Stop Land Grabs Now!" Land Research Action Network, Aug. 18, 2011, www.landaction.org/spip.php?article553.

50. For background, see Jennifer Weeks, "Rapid Urbanization," *CQ Global Researcher*, April 1, 2009, pp. 91-118.

51. "Land and Conflict: A Handbook for humanitarians," *op. cit.*

52. Ravanera and Gorra, *op. cit.*, p. 24.

53. *Ibid.*, p. 36. For background, see Doug Struck, "Disappearing Forests," *CQ Global Researcher*, Jan. 18, 2011, pp. 27-52.

54. "Land and Conflict: A handbook for humanitarians," *op. cit.*, p. 3.

55. U.N. Peacebuilding Fund Factsheet, United Nations Multi-Donor Trust Fund, http://mdtf.undp.org/factsheet/fund/PB000. For background, see Jina Moore, "Peacebuilding," *CQ Global Researcher*, June 21, 2011, pp. 291-314.

56. Liz Alden Wily, "Land, Conflict and Peace in Afghanistan," prepared for the World Bank's, Afghanistan Research & Evaluation Unit, Kabul, March 4-5, 2004.

57. In Patuliano, *op. cit.*, p. 173.

58. "IDP Population Figures: Jammu and Kashmir," Internal Displacement and Monitoring Center, September 2010, www.internal-displacement.org/idmc/website/countries.nsf/(httpEnvelopes)/7C4ACF1BFD3AC477C125779000281FFC?OpenDocument.

59. Brad K. Blitz, "Balkan Returns: An overview of refugee returns and minority repatriation," United Sates Institute of Peace, December 2009, www.usip.org/publications/balkan-returns-overview-refugee-returns-and-minority-repatriation.

60. "International Covenant on Economic, Social and Cultural Rights," United Nations, Dec. 16, 1966, www2.ohchr.org/english/law/cescr.htm.

61. "The right to restitution, compensation and rehabilitation for victims of grave violations of human rights and fundamental freedoms," U.N. High Commission on Human Rights, April 23, 2003, www.unhchr.ch/huridocda/huridoca.nsf/(Symbol)/E.CN.4.RES.2003.34.En?Opendocument. Also see Article 75: "Reparations to Victims," Rome Statute of the International Criminal Court, 1998, accessible at http://untreaty.un.org/cod/icc/statute/99_corr/cstatute.htm.

62. "Burundi: A sharing approach to land disputes," IRIN, Aug. 1, 2011, www.irinnews.org/report.aspx?reportid=84272.

63. *Ibid.*

64. "World Disaster Report 2010: Focus on urban risk," International Federation of the Red Cross, 2010, www.ifrc.org/Global/Publications/disasters/WDR/wdr2010/WDR2010-full.pdf.

65. "Land and Conflict: A Handbook for humanitarians," *op. cit.*, p. 42.

66. For background, see John Felton, "Aiding Refugees," *CQ Global Researcher*, March 1, 2009, pp. 59-90.

67. "Why humanitarian organizations need to tackle land issues," in Patuliano, *op. cit.*, p. 20.

68. "More Frequent Droughts Likely in East Africa," U.S. Geological Survey, Jan. 28, 2011, www.usgs.gov/newsroom/article.asp?ID=2690.

69. "Desert Expansion Threatening China's Most Prestigious Grottoes," Xinhau, Oct. 8, 2007, reprinted at www.china.org.cn/english/environment/227153.htm. Also see Marcela Valente, "Tenacious Drought Puzzles Climate Experts," Inter Press Service News, Feb. 13, 2009, http://ipsnews.net/news.asp?idnews=45768.

70. George Lerner, "Activist: Farmer suicides in India linked to debt, globalization," CNN, Jan. 5, 2010,

http://articles.cnn.com/2010-01-05/world/india
.farmer.suicides_1_farmer-suicides-andhra-pradesh-
vandana-shiva?_s=PM:WORLD.

71. Azadeh Ansari, "Climate change forces Eskimos to Abandon Village," CNN, April 24, 2009, http://articles.cnn.com/2009-04-24/tech/climate.change.eskimos_1_climate-change-indigenous-communities-eskimos?_s=PM:TECH.

72. David D. Zhang, *et al.*, "Climatic Change, wars and dynastic cycles in China over the last millennium," *Climate Change*, Vol. 76, 2006, pp. 459-477.

73. Marc A. Levy, *et al.*, "Freshwater Availability Anomalies and Outbreak of Internal War: Results from a Global Spatial Time Series Analysis," paper presented at the "Human Security and Climate Change: An International Workshop," Asker, Norway, June 21-23, 2005, www.ciesin.columbia.edu/documents/waterconflict.pdf.

74. Marshall B. Burke, *et al.*, "Warming increases the risk of civil war in Africa," PNAS, Dec. 8, 2009, pp. 20670-20674, www.pnas.org/content/106/49/20670.full.

75. Quirin Schiermeier, "Climate cycles drive civil war: Tropical conflicts double during El Niño years," *NatureNews*, Aug. 24, 2011, www.nature.com/news/2011/110824/full/news.2011.501.html#B1.

BIBLIOGRAPHY

Selected Sources

Books

Autesserre, Severine, *The Trouble with Congo: Local violence and the failure of international peacebuilding*, Cambridge University Press, 2010.
A humanitarian aid worker turned political scientist dissects the role of land conflict in the ongoing unrest in the Democratic Republic of Congo.

Call, Wendy, *No Word for Welcome: The Mexican Village Faces the Global Economy*, University of Nebraska Press, 2011.
A journalist and activist who spent several years in Oaxaca, Mexico, documents the rifts between the Mexican government and its citizens as economic development encroaches on their land.

Diamond, Jared, *Collapse: How Societies Choose to Fail or Succeed*, Penguin, 2011 (revised edition).
The Pulitzer Prize-winning author of *Guns, Germs and Steel* examines why societies crumble, focusing on land scarcity and its impact on conflicts throughout history.

Manji, Ambreena S., *The Politics of Land Reform in Africa: From communal tenure to free markets*, Zed Books, 2006.
A political scientist at the London School of Economics analyzes the pros and cons of customary and statutory land ownership systems in modern Africa.

Pantuliano, Sara, ed., *Uncharted Territory: Land, Conflict and Humanitarian Action*, Practical Action, 2009.
An expert on humanitarian aid at Britain's Overseas Development Institute argues, based on several essays on land ownership and emergency response, that land must figure more prominently in humanitarian action in complex emergencies.

Articles

Moore, Jina, "Africa's Continental Divide," *The Christian Science Monitor*, Jan. 30, 2010.
The author examines the role of land disputes in conflict in Africa, with a focus on the clash between formal and informal land ownership systems.

Rice, Andrew, "Is There Such a Thing as Agro-Imperialism?" *The New York Times Magazine*, Nov. 22, 2009.
In an exposé on "land grabs" in Africa, the author reveals the impact on average Africans of the massive land deals occurring between African governments and foreign investors.

Reports and Studies

"World Disaster Report 2010: Focus on urban risk," International Federation of the Red Cross, 2010, www.ifrc.org/Global/Publications/disasters/WDR/wdr2010/WDR2010-full.pdf.
The global humanitarian organization analyzes how natural disasters affect urban land issues around the world.

Alden Wily, Liz, "Who Owns the Forest?" Sustainable Development Institute, 2007, www.fern.org/sites/fern.org/files/media/documents/document_4078_4079.pdf.
One of the world's foremost experts on land and conflict examines the ownership challenges arising from exploitation of forests for their timber. She puts special focus on Liberia's experiment in halting timber exports until land use and ownership policies are reformed.

Baranyi, Stephen, and Viviane Weitzner, "Transforming Land-Related Conflict: Policy, Practice and Possibilities," North-South Institute, May 2006.
Canadian researchers — political scientist Baranyi and natural resources specialist Weitzner — analyze the relationship between land and conflict, proposing policy prescriptions based on past failures and successes.

Deininger, Klaus, "Land Policies for Growth and Poverty Reduction," World Bank, 2003, http://siteresources.worldbank.org/EXTARD/Resources/336681-1295878311276/26384.pdf.
A leading analyst surveys the relationship between land issues and national economics in the bank's first comprehensive look at land issues since the 1970s.

Rice, Andrew, "State of the World 2011: Nourishing the Planet," Worldwatch Institute, 2011, www.worldwatch.org/sow11.
A journalist takes an academic approach to the relationship between land, food and agribusiness.

Videos

"Threatened Island Nations: Legal Implications of Rising Seas and a Changing Climate," Columbia University Law School, May 23-25, 2011, www.law.columbia.edu/centers/climatechange/resources/threatened-island-nations.
U.N. diplomats and legal scholars study the implications of climate change on land ownership and anticipated forced migrations in this video record of a conference.

For More Information

Asian NGO Coalition for Agrarian Reform and Rural Development, 73-K Dr. Lazcano St., Barangay Laging Handa, Quezon City, Philippines; (+63) (2) 351-0581; www.angoc.org. A network of grassroots activists campaigning for land reforms that will benefit the poor.

Association for Land Reform and Development, 10/11 Iqbal Road, Block-A Mohammadpur, Dhaka-1207, Bangladesh; (880) (2) 911-4660; www.alrd.org. An umbrella organization for nearly 300 NGOs that lobby on land, food and indigenous rights issues.

Center for Climate Change Law, Columbia University, Jerome Greene Hall, Room 517, 435 West 116th St., New York, NY 10027; (212) 854-3287; www.law.columbia.edu/centers/climatechange. Works with governments and nongovernmental organizations to develop responses to new legal and policy issues, such as land rights after climate-induced displacement.

Center for International Earth Science Information Network, 61 Route 9W, Palisades, NY 10964; (845) 365-8988; www.ciesin.columbia.edu. A project of Columbia University's Earth Institute that aims to integrate different types of data to find sustainable land solutions.

Fundacion Tierra, Calle Hermanos Manchego 2566, Sopocachi, La Paz, Murillo, Bolivia; (591) (2) 243-2263; www.ftierra.org. A think-tank focused on rural development strategies that focus on indigenous and peasant rights.

GRAIN, Girona 25 pral., Barcelona, Spain; (34) (93) 3011381; www.grain.org. An international nonprofit that monitors land grabs and advocates on behalf of small-scale farmers, environmental stewardship and community control.

International Institute for Environment and Development, 3 Endsleigh St., London, United Kingdom; (44) (0) 20 7388 2117; www.iied.org. An independent research organization working on sustainable development issues in Africa, Asia, the Americas, the Middle East and the Pacific.

International Land Coalition, Via Paolo di Dono 44, Rome, Italy; (39) 06 5459 2445; www.landcoalition.org. An international alliance of nongovernmental organizations focused on land access and security among the rural poor.

UN-HABITAT, P.O. Box 30030, GPO, Nairobi, Kenya; (254) (20) 762-3151; www.unhabitat.org. A United Nations agency that works to make human settlements socially and environmentally sustainable, particularly in urban areas.

World Resources Institute, 10 G St. N.E., Suite 800, Washington, DC; (202) 729-7600; www.wri.org. A think tank that investigates how the environment affects human needs, with a focus on disaster preparation and response.

Voices From Abroad:

GAVIN HALES

Lead Researcher, Yemen Armed Violence Assessment, Yemen

Pre-emptive measures

"Undoubtedly there are significant hurdles to be overcome, but it is hoped that land and water resources can be given the urgent attention they require, by the state and communities alike, to avoid even bigger problems in the future."

Yemen Times, October 2010

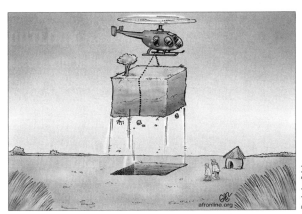

Dario La Crisis

GUGILE NKWINTI

Rural Development and Land Reform Minister, South Africa

Ensuring productivity

"We need to review the whole system of restitution so that when we give the land back it is land that is used productively."

Business Day (South Africa), December 2010

MANMOHAN SINGH

Prime Minister, India

An equitable process

"I do recognise that land acquisition has become a very sensitive issue and that the acquisition of prime land arouses valid concerns and they have to be addressed. . . . That process has to be equitable and one way to ensure it is so is to see that land acquisition does not become an instrument of depriving farmers of their livelihood."

The Hindu (India), May 2011

SUTHEP PORWARETWITTAYALAN

Director, Royal Forest Department, Thailand

Don't challenge the government

"If they (developers) cannot present any documents to prove their ownership of the land, we will strictly enforce the law against them, as they have challenged the government's power."

The Nation (Thailand), August 2011

PHILIP OCAYA

Resident, Lakang village Kenya

'It belongs to us'

"Land is life and no one will succeed in claiming ownership of this land, it belongs to us, the people of Lakang, and we are defending it without fear."

U.N. Integrated Regional Information Network, February 2011

SANTOSH KUMAR

Superintendent of Police, Nagapattinam, India

Not knowing the difference

"There is a world of difference between a civil dispute and land grab, and most cases that have arrived here were mostly civil disputes."

The Hindu (India), July 2011

NESTOR CUTI

Resident, Espinar, Peru

A bleak future

"In the future we know we will have less water. We cannot trust the rainy season any more. Every year the water levels are diminishing. Climate change and global warming indicate in the next years we will have even less. You don't need to be clever to see climate change is affecting everything here."

Guardian Unlimited (England), September 2010

KAEW WONGKRAI

Chairman, Alliance of Northeastern Villagers, Thailand

Skirting the issue

"Many communities in Isan (Thailand) have been holding talks with local authorities on the community land title deed issue, but they prefer to work with easy cases rather than those with serious problems, especially those facing bitter disputes with government agencies."

Bangkok Post, February 2011

LUNGISILE NTSEBEZA

Professor of Sociology, University of Cape Town, South Africa

A political matter

"The majority have been robbed of the means of production. In Africa, the majority are landless and land has been alienated from the indigenous. There are disagreements on land issues. The issue is not about land but bio-politics (land grabs for biofuels versus land needs for the poor). The land remains critical to the rural poor."

The Herald (Zimbabwe), December 2010

5

Weapons in Space

Konstantin Kakaes

The U.S. Air Force launched the X-37B, a reusable unmanned shuttle, into space for the second time on March 5. The vehicle can orbit for up to 270 days before gliding to a landing on Earth. The X-37B signals the increased role of the military in U.S. space policy, experts say.

From *CQ Researcher*, Aug. 16, 2011

O n March 5, the U.S. Air Force launched its new X-37B into space for its second voyage. The reusable, unmanned craft can orbit for up to 270 days before gliding back to Earth.

But that's about all that's known publicly about the X-37B. Its civilian predecessor, NASA's now-retired space shuttle, ferried crews and supplies to the International Space Station. But plans for the new shuttle are secret. The U.S. military will say only that the X-37B is a test platform, refusing to comment about its specific function.

Some military analysts speculate that it might be designed as a "space bomber," but Brian Weeden — a technical adviser to the Colorado-based Secure World Foundation, which advocates the peaceful use of outer space — suspects it's probably designed to test new military reconnaissance technologies.

Whatever its purpose, the secrecy surrounding the X-37B has renewed debate about the role of militaries in setting space policy. [1] The secrecy also raises concerns abroad.

China "has a deep concern and distrust toward the U.S. on the issue of the weaponization of space," says Arthur Ding, a research fellow in the Division of International Relations at Taiwan's National Chengchi University.

So-called space weapons can either attack targets in space or on Earth, or be ground-based and attack targets in space, such as satellites or incoming missiles. Whether space- or Earth-based, they can be either "kinetic" weapons — like those that hit a target with a bullet — or "directed energy" weapons, such as lasers. But most of these weapons still exist only in theory, and many analysts doubt

10 Countries Can Launch Satellites

Ten countries currently can launch satellites into Earth orbit. The Soviet Union, which disbanded in 1991, launched the first satellite — Sputnik I — in 1957. Iran, the newest member of the satellite club, launched its first satellite in 2009. The European Space Agency, which has 18 members,* also launches satellites. Countries that can launch satellites are most capable of creating space weapons and have the most to lose if such weapons were ever used.

Countries That Have Launched Satellites

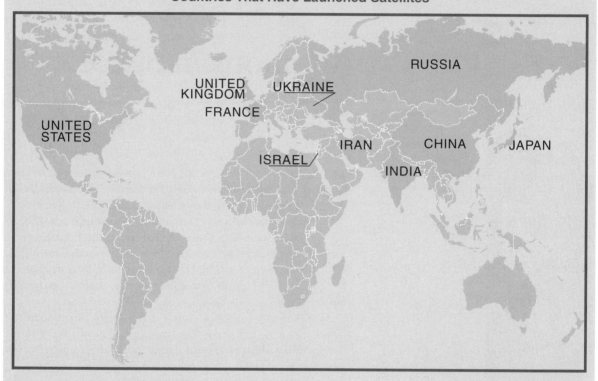

* European Space Agency members are Austria, Belgium, Czech Republic, Denmark, Finland, France, Germany, Greece, Ireland, Italy, Luxembourg, Netherlands, Norway, Portugal, Spain, Sweden, Switzerland and the United Kingdom.

Sources: Carl E. Behrens, "Space Launch Vehicles: Government Activities, Commercial Competition, and Satellite Exports," Congressional Research Service, March 2006, www.fas.org/sgp/crs/space/IB93062.pdf; "Iran: Satellite Launch Is 'Source of Pride,' " CNN, February 2009, articles.cnn.com/2009-02-03/world/iran.satellite_1_launch-iranian-technicians-rocket?_s=PM:WORLD. Map by Lewis Agrell

that a science-fiction-style laser can be developed that can destroy something in space.

"There's a lot of hyperbole going on about space-based weapons," says John Sheldon, professor of space and cyberspace strategic studies at the Air Force's School of Advanced Air and Space Studies in Montgomery, Ala.

Many tasks proposed for space weapons could be accomplished just as easily by a B-2 bomber, he says.

Weeden calls the laser idea a "dead man walking." A space-based laser program was canceled in 2002 as unfeasible; since then development of a chemical laser weapon mounted on a 747 remains in the federal budget, despite Pentagon efforts to mothball the project. Lower-power lasers that can disable — but not destroy — a satellite already exist.

The almost unlimited potential of space — for communication, observation and navigation — underscores its global importance. For instance, the now ubiquitous Global Positioning System (GPS) run by the Air Force enables civilians and military personnel alike to accurately pinpoint location by triangulating signals from several satellites.

The federal government has spent more than $1.5 trillion in space since 1959. [2] The military and NASA have spent the vast majority of that on Earth-orbit projects — satellites, the space shuttle and the International Space Station. Commercial communication satellites have become a major global industry, generating $168 billion in revenue in 2009 — almost double the amount in 2004. [3]

And while American companies once controlled 75 percent of the global satellite business, they now account for less than half, according to William Lynn, deputy secretary of Defense. [4] Russia, China and the European Space Agency account for the bulk of the rest.

But while more countries now use space, the United States is still the biggest user by far, with military forces around the world relying on vulnerable global reconnaissance and communications satellites. "Our space assets are exposed and fragile," Bruce MacDonald, a former National Security Council official, recently told Congress. "They can't run, they can't hide and today they can't defend themselves." [5]

Last January the Defense Department sparked debate when it released the unclassified part of the Obama administration's new, mostly secret National Security Space Strategy. [6] It is "not the least bit clear . . . whether this was really a change in the packaging or a change in the fundamental policy," says Nancy Gallagher, assistant director of the Center for International and Security Studies at the University of Maryland. "That is still an open question."

U.S. Leads in Space Spending

The United States spent nearly 70 percent of the nearly $58 billion spent worldwide in 2009 on civilian and military uses of space — including satellites. China, considered an emerging space power, spent only $2 billion during the same year, or 4 percent of the world's total. At least a quarter of the expenditures are made by the more than 50 countries that have satellites circling the globe.

Worldwide Global Space Expenditures, 2009

Rest of world 25% ($14.7 billion); Russia 2% ($1.3 billion); China 4% ($2.2 billion); United States 69% ($39.5 billion)

Source: Michael Krepon and Samuel Black, "Space Security or Anti-Satellite Weapons?" Henry L. Stimson Center, May 2009

The administration apparently plans to continue spending $8.5 billion a year on the Missile Defense Agency, which has been charged with developing a space-based "shield" against missile attacks, proposed in 1983 by President Ronald Reagan. The plan, often dubbed "Star Wars" by its critics, initially called for stationing defensive weapons both in space and on Earth, but after constant cost overruns and technical failures, it has never come to fruition. Nevertheless, politicians have been unwilling to let it go, and some limited tests of missile defense systems (which also can be used as anti-satellite weapons) have been successful. But technical experts generally believe the system as a whole is unworkable. [7]

To date, no country has ever deployed offensive weapons in space or attacked someone else's satellites. And only a handful of tests have been conducted in which a country destroyed its own satellites.

China shot down one of its weather satellites in 2007, in its first test of an anti-satellite weapon, and the United States destroyed a malfunctioning spy satellite in 2008 — the first time since 1985, when the United States destroyed an earlier satellite. The shoot-downs prompted some hawkish types in India to demand that New Delhi

Defining Space Weapons Can Be Tricky

Some are based in space and some on the ground.

To define space weapons, one must first define space. Technically, space begins about 62 miles up at a point known as the Kármán Line. Above that, a satellite can remain in orbit on its own.

In theory, there are three kinds of space weapons:

- Those placed in space to attack targets either in space or on Earth,
- Ground-based, or terrestrial, weapons designed to attack targets in space, and
- Ground-based missile defense systems that can attack targets in space but are not specifically designed to do so.

Some opponents of space weapons would include in the definition anything that is *capable* of attacking space targets, while proponents prefer to define them more narrowly, including only items that are physically in space.

There are two basic categories of space weapons:

- **Kinetic energy weapons** — those that attack their targets by hitting them, including explosives and objects that slam into their targets. These include "direct ascent" weapons and "co-orbital" anti-satellite (ASAT) weapons.
- **Directed energy weapons** — such as lasers or beams of particles like electrons that attack their targets by subjecting them to radiation.

Direct ascent kinetic-energy weapons include those used by China and the United States in 2007 and 2008, respectively, to shoot down their own satellites. Such weapons take about 15 minutes to reach their targets and are relatively easy to aim, because satellites usually travel in predictable paths. [1]

Satellite predictability is also key in the second kind of kinetic energy weapon — the co-orbital anti-satellite weapon. The Soviet Union tested and deployed such weapons in the 1960s and '70s. Unlike direct ascent weapons, co-orbital ASATs actually attain orbit, which requires much more powerful rockets, and then can either accelerate into and collide with the target or approach it and explode.

Directed energy weapons in their most powerful form could destroy their targets or, in the case of lower-power weapons, just blind the target.

conduct an anti-satellite (ASAT) test of its own, largely to show that India can, says Wing Commander Ajey Lele, a former Indian Air Force officer and research fellow at the Institute for Defence Studies and Analyses in New Delhi. Iran recently launched its second satellite, and North Korea has been trying to launch one for years.

Throughout the U.S.-Soviet space race of the 1950s-1990s, satellites were never targeted. Even at the height of the Cold War, military leaders on both sides realized satellites tended to defuse tensions because they aided communications and allowed each side to see what the other was doing. In fact, no one had tested anti-satellite weapons since 1985 — until China's 2007 test broke the taboo.

China's action provoked an outcry in the space policy community, not only because it was an aggressive act but also because it created a huge cloud of space debris — 2,317 pieces.

The Chinese test demonstrated what everyone knew: Satellites are very vulnerable, primarily because they are fragile and travel in fixed orbits.

"Current spacecraft have less freedom of movement than mammoth warships at sea," Wilson Wong and James Fergusson, of the Centre for Defence and Security Studies at the University of Manitoba, Canada, pointed out in their recent book, *Military Space Power: A Guide to the Issues.* [8] Though built to withstand rough vibrations during launch and dramatic heat variations, spacecraft are essentially fragile. And there is no easy way to "harden" satellites against attack, which would make them heavier, since it costs about $10,000 a pound to launch something into space. And satellites so far have not been made "stealthy" — difficult to spot either with radar or a telescope.

One of the biggest threats to satellites is space debris. A one-pound scrap of metal orbiting the earth at 17,000 miles per hour packs as much energy as a tank going 60 miles

However, defining such low-power weapons is difficult. Brian Weeden — a former Air Force officer and now a technical adviser to the Secure World Foundation in Superior, Colo., which advocates peaceful uses of outer space — points out, "Lasers are being fired into space all the time" to track satellites and as astronomical guide stars. But using lasers to destroy a target is "really difficult and really expensive," he adds, and it has never been done.

The widespread use of lasers highlights the difficulty of defining space weapons — the types of lasers routinely used for non-weapon purposes can also be used as weapons, much as a baseball bat can be thought of as a weapon, in a particular context.

As for space-based weapons designed to hit a target on Earth, they are much more technologically challenging. For starters, it is very difficult to put a satellite or weapon into geostationary orbit — in which a satellite remains over a fixed point on Earth. Geostationary orbit is more than 22,000 miles away, or 220 times farther away than low-Earth orbit, and requires more energy to reach.

Thus, for now, any space-based weapons would likely have to be in low-Earth orbit, but such objects circle the globe only once every 90 minutes or so. So, to be able to quickly attack a specific target, a whole constellation of satellites would be needed — a very expensive endeavor.

Besides the cost, placing weapons in space likely would be considered provocative. Though U.S. and Chinese tests have

A 2001 artist's rendering shows the proposed airborne laser system mounted on a Boeing 747 – an example of a so-called "directed energy" weapon and one of the early ideas for the U.S. Missile Defense System recommended by former President Ronald Reagan. The laser system is thought to have a limited future.

somewhat normalized the idea of terrestrially based anti-satellite weapons, no one yet has stationed weapons in space.

— *Konstantin Kakaes*

[1]Brian Weeden, "China's BX-1 Microsatellite: A litmus test for space weaponization," *The Space Review*, Oct. 20, 2008.

per hour — enough to easily punch through the thin walls of a satellite or spaceship. Space debris is created both by deliberate collisions, such as the Chinese anti-satellite test, and by accidental collisions, such as a 2009 crash between Russian and U.S. satellites.

Satellites' vulnerability makes them potentially attractive targets. If, for instance, China were to invade U.S. ally Taiwan, it would benefit tactically from destroying U.S. spy and communications satellites. The same would be true if North Korea were to attack South Korea. India and China eye each other's space programs warily. Pakistan, in turn, sees India's space program as potentially aggressive, while Israel regards both Iran's and Pakistan's programs with concern.

Today, nearly 60 countries have satellites in orbit, though only 10 can launch them. But more countries eventually will be able to access space, and potentially threaten adversaries.

No legal framework exists today banning or regulating space weapons. As the world grows increasingly dependent on satellites and concern grows about their vulnerability, here are some of the questions being debated:

Should weapons be allowed in space?

Often, the question posed is not if space should be weaponized but whether weaponization is inevitable.

As far back as 1981, advocates of space weapons were calling space the "ultimate high ground." [9] And in 1996, Gen. Joseph Ashy, then the commander of the Air Force Space Command, told *Aviation Week & Space Technology*: "It's politically sensitive, but it's going to happen. . . . [A]bsolutely, we're going to fight in space. We're going to fight from space, and we're going to fight into space." [10]

But Weeden of the Secure World Foundation says calling space "the ultimate high ground" betrays "an absence of understanding of the space domain."

A Japanese destroyer launches a missile on Oct. 29, 2010, during a joint Japan-U.S. exercise to test missile defense capabilities. The missile successfully intercepted a ballistic missile launched from the Navy's Pacific Missile Range Facility at Barking Sands, Kauai, Hawaii. The test showed that under controlled circumstances and against known targets, an Earth-based missile defense system can work.

Space is not an effective place for many weapons, he says. "From a military strategy standpoint, there are some huge deficiencies in space," he says. Because it's so expensive to launch something into space, he explains, payloads must be small and light compared to Earth-based weapons, which limits their capabilities.

In addition, surprise is lost in space. "It's really hard — if not impossible — to disguise what you are doing in space," he says. Finally, Weeden points out, satellites and spacecraft have limited fuel, so they have poor maneuverability. "They can maneuver, but only so much, and not very often, and it reduces fuel supply."

Often, advocates of weaponization compare space weapons to air and naval power. But, as Karl Mueller, an analyst with the RAND Corp. think tank, pointed out,

spacecraft are quite different from ocean-going vessels: "Ships primarily transport goods and people, while spacecraft carry information." [11]

The argument over weaponizing space goes back to the early days of the Space Age. In 1946 Gen. Curtis LeMay proposed a $300 million ($3.5 billion in today's dollars) Army Air Force research center for space weapons, but the plan never came to fruition. [12] Then, as NASA's lunar landing program got under way in the 1960s, discussion of space weapons faded until 1983, when President Reagan began pushing a missile defense system.

By the time a commission to assess U.S. national security in space said in 2001 that weaponizing space was inevitable, advocates of space weapons had become the dominant voice in the military establishment. "We know from history that every medium — air, land and sea — has seen conflict. Reality indicates that space will be no different," said the report by the panel, chaired by soon-to-be Defense Secretary Donald Rumsfeld. [13]

But Mueller of RAND calls the inevitability arguments "weak." [14] And Joan Johnson-Freese, a professor of national security at the Naval War College, says, "The 'space domination' rhetoric that dominated in the U.S. during the George W. Bush years has for the most part been overtaken by both politics and technology." In other words, the politics have shifted toward more international cooperation, while the technical challenges of space weapons have become ever more apparent.

Lele, at the Institute for Defence Studies and Analyses in New Delhi, says that while some in India oppose the development of anti-satellite weapons, others say "India should go ahead and develop an ASAT so that if a treaty grandfathers in countries that have already conducted anti-satellite tests (as the Nuclear Non-Proliferation Treaty did for nuclear weapons), then India would not be left out."

Advocates of space weapons note that orbiting weapons could potentially be used to attack missiles while they are in the "boost phase" — when they are still ascending into space and before they have deployed decoys.

"If the international community is truly worried about the debris-generating effects of ASAT weapons, then it ought to embrace, indeed demand, development and deployment of boost-phase missile defenses capable of intercepting ASAT missiles long before they reach their satellite targets," Jeff Kueter, president of the conservative George C. Marshall Institute in Arlington, Va., said in 2007. [15]

But Weeden points out that boost-phase defenses require a decision to launch a counter-attack within minutes. "If you start thinking about the command-and-control problem — you have to detect the launch, determine it is a threat, launch the interceptor — then you are looking at what has to be an automated system," Weeden says. "What is the cost if it goes wrong?"

Moreover, as Johnson-Freese points out, technical considerations are changed by the proliferation of technology. "The more countries have assets in space, the more they realize the damage done by ASATs through debris creation," she says.

"A lot of the things that people do to satellites or would like to do to protect satellites don't actually involve weapons in the traditional sense of blowing stuff up," said RAND's Mueller. "They involve jamming . . . or the use of things that don't really look like weapons."

"It is not clear exactly at what point you cross a line from space not being weaponized to space being weaponized." [16]

Would a binding treaty prevent attacks on satellites?

On Feb. 20, 2008, Defense Secretary Robert Gates ordered a malfunctioning American spy satellite destroyed. Nearly 10 hours later, a missile was fired from the *USS Lake Erie*, a guided missile cruiser steaming a few hundred miles northwest of Hawaii, which had been tracking the satellite for several days. The 15-foot-long USA-193 satellite had failed soon after launch and carried up to a ton of volatile fuel. The missile shot was dead-on.

Officially, the shoot-down was to prevent the fuel-laden satellite from crashing and causing death and damage. But many observers saw it as a show of force. It was, says the University of Maryland's Gallagher, a way to show that missile defenses were useful for something. The

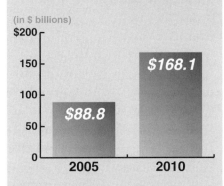

Satellite Revenues Have Rocketed

The worldwide satellite industry generated approximately $170 billion in revenue in 2010, nearly double the amount earned five years earlier.

World Satellite Industry Revenues, 2005 and 2010

(in $ billions)

2005: $88.8
2010: $168.1

Source: "State of the Satellite Industry Report," Satellite Industry Association, June 2011, www.sia.org/IndustryReport .htm

strike occurred just as the U.S. government was making a big decision about how much money to spend on missile defense.

"The decision to go forward was made by a very small number of people," says Gallagher, "some of whom thought very explicitly about the fact that if the U.S. did this, it's less likely that you'll be able to get constraints on ASAT weapons without getting into missile defense." In other words, using a missile defense system to shoot down a satellite deliberately blurred the boundaries between ASATs and missile defense weapons. [17] The United States adamantly opposes any treaties that would limit its abilities to deploy missile defenses, although it might consider an anti-satellite weapon ban of some sort.

A treaty to prevent weaponization of space could either ban the deployment of space weapons or ban terrestrial weapons that threaten space objects (such as anti-satellite weapons). Because they are technically much easier to deal with, international deliberations have focused on terrestrially based weapons.

Since 2008, China and Russia have been pushing a broader treaty, however, through the Conference on Disarmament (CD), a U.N. group in Geneva that has been trying to negotiate a space treaty since it was founded in 1979. [18] Ze Zhang, China's deputy director for arms control and disarmament, outlines his country's position clearly: "No weapon[s] placed in outer space; no use of force against outer space objects; no threat of use of force against outer space objects." [19]

But the United States has made it clear "in no uncertain terms that it will not negotiate on the basis of the Russian and Chinese proposals," says Theresa Hitchens, director of the U.N. Institute on Disarmament Research, also in Geneva, who was speaking in her personal capacity and not as a representative of a U.N. agency. The United States sees the Russian-Chinese effort as an attempt to limit its abilities to build a missile defense system.

A private American Iridium telecommunications satellite like this one collided on Feb. 10, 2009, with a defunct Russian Cosmos satellite orbiting nearly 500 miles above Earth. The first-ever collision between two satellites produced massive debris clouds, highlighting long-standing concerns about the need to track space debris.

The question of whether a binding treaty would work hinges on two things: whether it is technically feasible and whether the political will exists to adopt and enforce it.

Some have proposed just banning the testing or widespread deployment of weapons that can destroy a satellite, without banning them outright. Zhang said inspections at research laboratories and launching sites could provide adequate verification. [20]

But Gregory Kulacki, a Beijing-based American who is a senior analyst at the Union of Concerned Scientists, says although the Chinese are pushing for more substantive talks, "the U.S. doesn't want to negotiate any sort of binding agreements on its behavior in space. It doesn't want a treaty, doesn't see the need for one, doesn't want to be constrained by one."

"China wants to put constraints on the U.S., and the U.S. doesn't want to be constrained," he continues. "I don't know how you break that logjam."

Hitchens says just banning tests might work. "The U.S. is right to point that out. What do you do about a space tug to get rid of orbital debris?" she asks. Such a tug would have similar capabilities to a weapon. Of course, this begs the question of whether the shootdown of USA-193 would have been prohibited under an agreement banning anti-satellite tests, since it supposedly was done not as a test but as a matter of public safety.

Pessimists say even if a treaty were adopted, it might have all the force of the Hague Peace Conference of 1899, which "banned the use of aircraft, existing or projected, for combatant use in war," wrote Michael Sheehan, a professor of international relations at the University of Swansea in Wales, in a recent book. "Their use was restricted to passive employment such as reconnaissance." [21] But within a few years, aircraft were dropping bombs during World War I.

"I'm skeptical about the role of arms control in any domain," says Sheldon of the Air Force's School of Advanced Air and Space Studies. "It's never done what it said it would do."

And Bharath Gopalswamy, a visiting scholar at Cornell University's Institute for Peace Studies, says, "There are lots of grey areas. That's where we are, and where we will be."

Can satellites be protected from anti-satellite weapons?

The easy answer is no. As the Naval War College's Johnson-Freese says, "Space is a harsh environment, and offense is much easier than defense. Any country that has a ballistic [high altitude] missile capability can theoretically threaten satellites in orbit."

Satellites generally "are hardened to endure vibrations during launch and radiation in the atmosphere, but in general they are optimized to operate in a benign environment, not to deter or evade enemy attacks," said a recent article in *Jane's Defence Weekly*, a trade publication. [22]

Peter Marquez, vice president of strategy and planning at the Orbital Sciences Corp. in Dulles, Va., explains that for a long time, engineers asked, "How do I gold-plate this satellite?" But Marquez thinks "that was the wrong question." The real issue, he says, is "mission assurance" — protecting satellites in general (rather than just one in particular), or, failing that, finding a way to maintain the capabilities satellites provide.

Actively protecting satellites is not only technically difficult but can also be politically provocative. "The thing that makes you worry about the safety of your satellites is that ground-based laser in downtown Beijing interfering with your satellites during a crisis over Taiwan," wrote RAND's Mueller. [23]

There are two ways to protect satellites. They can be made smaller, which both makes them harder to hit and allows for a network of redundant smaller satellites, making a successful attack less likely, says Weeden of Secure World. The second is to make satellites easily and quickly replaceable, reducing the damage from a successful attack and thus the incentive to attack.

But Les Doggrell, a senior defense contractor with the Aerospace Corp., pointed out that quickly replacing satellites would be prohibitively expensive for the Air Force and NASA. [24]

Gregory Schulte, deputy assistant secretary of Defense for space policy, told Congress in May that "resilience" — creating a system that is less vulnerable — also can be achieved by relying on commercial satellites and foreign partners for backup and by finding non-space alternatives to replicate satellite functions. [25]

The United States military is "holding training exercises where we experience 'a day without space' [and] slowly learning how to 'fight through' the interference" that would be caused if support satellites were suddenly not available, Lynn, the deputy secretary of Defense, said in November. [26]

Other analysts worry that the physical threats to satellites — given their relative difficulty to implement and likely traceability — pale in comparison to the electronic threats. "Investing in back-end computing systems that prevent jamming and spoofing, undermining the integrity of data networks and downlinks — that's where a lot of the action is taking place," says Kueter of the Marshall Institute.

But Sheldon, of the Air Force's School of Advanced Air and Space Studies, says the U.S. military's electronic warfare capabilities have been, "in many ways, atrophying. In terms of how they are organized, they are almost forgotten."

Meanwhile Europeans have had "no discussion of deploying countermeasures against potential human threats in space, such as space weapons," according to *Space and Defense* author Michael Searway. Instead, Europe's efforts to protect satellites have been focused on diplomacy. [27]

China, meanwhile, has developed small "companion satellites" that could be useful in many contexts, such as making a system more resilient or as defensive or offensive weapons. [28] Russia, which maintains an important space presence but is doing little innovation, has not made much progress on protecting its space assets.

> "Any country with ballistic missile capability can theoretically threaten satellites in orbit. The question is, for what purpose?"
>
> — **Joan Johnson-Freese, professor of national security, Naval War College**

Active defenses, such as space-based lasers, might be useful against weapons that could be detected before they strike, "but they would provide no protection against attacks by ground-based lasers or covert mines already positioned near their targets, against electronic jamming or against attacks on the infrastructure that supports satellites," wrote Mueller. [29]

But while defense is technically difficult, offense is not. "Converting ballistic missiles into taking down satellites is . . . much easier than it is imagined to be. The Indians say they are within reach," Cornell's Gopalswamy points out.

Will Marshall, a research fellow at NASA's Ames Research Center in Moffett Field, Calif., designed a "constellation architecture" for micro-satellites (those weighing less than 220 pounds) that can be networked together, orbiting at different altitudes, to make them difficult to attack with anti-satellite weapons. [30] So far, however, the idea remains only on paper.

BACKGROUND
The Race Begins

Even before the space race began, some military leaders wanted to put weapons in space. But Gen. LeMay's 1946 proposal to build a $300 million research center for space weapons never came to fruition. [31]

At first, high-altitude intercontinental ballistic missiles (ICBMs) were considered "space weapons." In 1957, the Soviet Union launched *Sputnik 1*, the first artificial satellite to orbit the Earth. The historic achievement prompted Wernher Von Braun, a leading rocket scientist in Nazi Germany who came to the United States after World War II, to predict that, "Ten or 15 years from now, space superiority will have taken the place of today's air superiority." [32]

Space Junk Outnumbers Satellites

Of the nearly 16,000 manmade objects in Earth orbit, the vast majority comes from the Commonwealth of Independent States (10 former Soviet states) and the United States, including 2,500 satellites and nearly 8,500 pieces of space debris.

Satellites and Space Debris
(by country or organization, as of January 2011)

Country/organization	Satellites	Rocket bodies and debris	Total
China	100	3,388	3,488
Commonwealth of Independent States	1,406	4,646	6,052
European Space Agency	39	44	83
France	49	431	480
India	41	132	173
Japan	114	75	189
United States	1,142	3,691	4,833
Other	489	112	601
Total	**3,380**	**12,519**	**15,899**

Source: "Orbital Debris Quarterly News," National Aeronautics and Space Administration, January 2011, orbitaldebris.jsc.nasa.gov/newsletter/pdfs/ODQNv15i1.pdf

Sputnik galvanized the United States into accelerating efforts to explore space, launching the U.S.-Soviet space race. [33]

Just before Sputnik's launch, the United States had proposed that the U.N. enact a global ban on ICBMs. But *Sputnik* spurred the military and U.S. Congress to increase their pressure to develop the huge missiles, which became a mainstay of American defense policy. [34]

In 1958, then-Senate Majority Leader Lyndon B. Johnson, D-Texas, said "control of space means control of the world, far more totally than any control has ever been or ever could be achieved by weapons or by troops of occupation." [35]

More technically minded individuals recognized early on, however, the challenge of producing and operating space weapons. One major difficulty: Objects in Earth orbit move so fast they are hard to slow down enough to steer toward a specific target.

Consequently, the first practical military uses of space were reconnaissance and communications, which remain its major uses today. Initially, it was uncertain whether other countries would protest satellite overflights. But when *Sputnik* elicited no protests, the precedent was established.

Nonetheless, the United States tried to disguise early reconnaissance satellites, such as the supersecret Corona. The Air Force called it the *Discoverer*, to take "mice and monkeys into orbit as part of biomedical research." [36]

Soon afterward, the U.N. General Assembly adopted a resolution in 1961 declaring that "the exploration and use of outer space should only be for the betterment of mankind and to the benefit of States, irrespective of the stage of their economic and scientific development." The resolution also held that the U.N. charter would apply to outer space and celestial bodies, and countries couldn't claim celestial bodies (such as the Moon) as their territory. [37]

Nevertheless, the space race proceeded at full throttle. The Soviet Union developed missiles with nuclear warheads designed to shoot down incoming missiles. [38] The United States, for its part, detonated the first nuclear weapons in space, with two low-altitude tests in 1958. A high-altitude explosion in 1962, 250 miles over the Pacific Ocean, called "Starfish Prime," destroyed seven satellites, knocked out 300 streetlights in Hawaii and left radiation belts in space that survived for decades. [39] The Soviets also conducted four nuclear tests in space in the early 1960s.

Space Treaties

By the late 1960s, the United States was relying on nuclear-tipped Thor missiles as anti-satellite weapons. [40] The Soviets, meanwhile, had developed a "co-orbital" weapon that used radar, optical or infrared tracking to match orbits with a target satellite. It could then get close enough to the target to detonate and destroy it. [41]

In 1967, the two superpowers signed the Outer Space Treaty. Modeled after the Antarctic Treaty of 1959 banning all military activities on the icy continent, the space treaty banned nuclear weapons in space. [42]

Meanwhile, the Soviets conducted about 20 tests of their anti-satellite weapon until 1972, when they signed, along with the United States, the Anti-Ballistic Missile Treaty, which limited both ground-based missile defenses and space weapons that could counter ballistic missiles. The Russians stopped testing their anti-satellite weapon, even though the treaty did not specifically limit them.

However, they began testing them again in 1978 after the United States announced plans to develop the space shuttle, which the Soviets perceived as a threat. [43]

Indeed, the shuttle then was considered at least as important militarily as it was to the civilian space program. "The United States will have an active, manned military space program starting in 1983, when the Pentagon obtains a space shuttle," The Associated Press reported in 1978. Pentagon planners saw the shuttle "as a good reconnaissance tool and as a potential fighter plane or satellite destroyer in case of war." [44]

The two Cold War superpowers went through a period of détente in the mid-70s, particularly regarding space. The joint *Apollo-Soyuz* mission in July 1975 stood as a high-water mark of U.S.-Soviet cooperation until the mid-1990s, when the space shuttle docked with Russia's Mir space station.

Meanwhile, the European Space Agency (ESA) was established in 1975 to promote civilian uses of space, such as communications and weather satellites, exploration of the solar system and basic science. Some European countries — notably France — established military space programs, primarily for reconnaissance, but not until the early 21st century did the European Union begin to draft its own military space policy, according to Thomas Beer, the ESA's Paris-based policy coordinator for global monitoring and environmental security. [45] That still-undefined policy reflects a growing reluctance to be dependent on the United States for protection, according to *Space and Defense* journal. [46]

Despite the mood of détente in the 1970s, some in the United States continued to stoke fears of the Soviets. In 1977, Gen. George Keegan, Air Force assistant chief of staff for intelligence, claimed the Soviets had developed a directed-energy "death ray" that could "neutralize" all U.S. ballistic missiles — an allegation President Jimmy Carter, his Defense secretary and the CIA all publicly refuted. [47]

Just two days before Carter's 1977 inauguration, outgoing President Gerald R. Ford told the Air Force to

> *"The more people have assets on orbit, the more they have an incentive to protect those assets and not screw around. "*
>
> *— Victoria Samson, office director, Secure World Foundation, Washington, D.C.*

develop an anti-satellite weapon to counter the Soviets' co-orbital system. However, the Carter administration preferred that neither superpower deploy such weapons, "but rather negotiate an arms control regime that would constrain ASAT technologies," wrote author Michael Sheehan, in his 2007 book, *The International Politics of Space.*

The United States and the Soviets continued negotiating a ban on anti-satellite weapons, but the talks fell apart with the 1979 Soviet intervention in Afghanistan and the changeover from Carter to Reagan in 1981. [48]

"The first U.S. administration to openly advocate the weaponization of space was that of President Reagan," according to Sheehan. [49]

"Star Wars"

After taking office, Reagan revised the U.S. National Space Policy, renewing calls for an anti-satellite system in a March 23, 1983, speech. Although he did not mention weapons in space, the speech set in motion the creation of the Strategic Defense Initiative (SDI), his proposed space-based weapons system, dubbed by critics as "Star Wars." [50]

Domestic opposition to Reagan's proposal came swiftly but failed to stop him from aggressively pursuing SDI. "The Strategic Defense Initiative . . . is a dangerous hoax and a cruel and potentially expensive exercise in self-deception," William Burrows, a veteran reporter, wrote in *Foreign Affairs* in 1984. [51] If the United States built Reagan's anti-ballistic missile system, which Burrows doubted was possible, the logical Soviet response, he said, would be a renewed emphasis on advanced anti-satellite weapons.

Some of the stiffest resistance came from the president's own Republican Party. "The most desirable remedy to the space-weapons threat is a ban on space weaponry," wrote Sen. Larry Pressler of South Dakota, chairman of the Arms Control Subcommittee of the Senate Foreign Relations Committee." [52] Sen. Dan Quayle, R-Ind., called Reagan's SDI claims "political jargon." [53]

Reagan got pushback from abroad as well. In 1984, France proposed a renewable five-year moratorium on testing and deploying anti-ballistic missile systems and strict limits on anti-satellite systems able to reach high orbit satellites. [54]

A year later the United States fired an anti-satellite missile from an F-15 fighter jet. [55] Despite the test's success, the F-15 ASAT weapon program died, says historian Dwayne Day, of the National Academy of Sciences, because "the weapon had only limited utility and cost an incredible amount of money — and the Air Force never really wanted it." [56]

The Soviets continued to push for a ban on anti-satellite weapons through the mid-1980s, but the Reagan administration blocked it. [57] Meanwhile, neutral observers, including the Congressional Office of Technology Assessment, said SDI faced a "significant probability of catastrophic failure." [58]

In the final analysis, space weapons expert Michael Krepon, a co-founder of the nonpartisan Stimson Center for Global Security, wrote in 2001, although "both countries periodically tested ASATs, their efforts were half-hearted and episodic." [59]

Meanwhile, both countries were pushing forward with reconnaissance and communications satellites, as well as constellations of satellites that could provide worldwide "position and timing" signals — used by the U.S. Global Positioning System (GPS). The similar Soviet Glonass system is now operational, though its development lagged for years.

The 1991 Persian Gulf War saw the first widespread military use of the new technologies, including weather, communications and imagery satellites and the fledgling GPS. Five years before, in a colossally mistaken assessment, a former director of the Pentagon's Defense Advanced Research Projects Agency had confidently declared that satellite systems were "generally viewed by military field commanders as peacetime systems; nice to have, but not to be relied on in wartime." [60]

Space Race Ends

The space race ended and the push for missile defense slowed after the Berlin Wall fell in 1989 and the Soviet

Union began breaking apart. But evolving technology continued to make space an ever more essential part of military and civilian life. [61]

Satellites to guide munitions — so-called "smart bombs" — played a key role in NATO's 1998 bombing of Serbia. Although President Bill Clinton never enunciated a clear policy toward space weapons, the Air Force published a series of ambitious studies, culminating in the 2001 Rumsfeld committee report. [62]

Using a phrase coined in 1965 by the hawkish Sen. Barry Goldwater, R-Ariz., the report warned of a potential "Space Pearl Harbor." [63] Laying the foundation for George W. Bush's space weapons policy, the Rumsfeld report warned that unless the United States were to "maintain and ensure continuing superiority," China, India, Pakistan and states in the Middle East might attack U.S. space capabilities. [64]

Right-wing proponents of missile defense, such as Gary Bauer, then-president of the conservative Family Research Council, called missile defense a "moral imperative" akin to the defense of fetuses. [65]

"Space superiority," Sheldon of the School of Advanced Air and Space Studies said, "can be achieved." And then Air Force Secretary James Roche told the *Financial Times* the United States should be able to put weapons in space as "some form of deterrent." [66]

But Johnson-Freese of the Naval War College described the Rumsfeld report as "nearly histrionic." [67]

And the Stimson Center's Krepon wrote in *Foreign Affairs* that the "language and logic of the Rumsfeld space report evoke the worst periods of the Cold War," at a time when "Russia's underfunded space programs are but a pale shadow of Soviet efforts." [68]

Jeffrey Lewis, director of the East Asia Nonproliferation Program at the Center for Nonproliferation Studies at the Monterrey Institute, explains, "The Bush administration itself underwent a transformation. . . . By the end of it they weren't so nutty." Early in Bush's term, the administration had wanted to approach space unilaterally. By the end, it was more willing to cooperate with Europe and even to negotiate with Russia and China, he says.

Krepon observed that, given U.S. military strength, China and Russia would naturally want to develop ASATs; the hard thing would be dissuading them from doing so. [69] Indeed, during the past decade in the Iraq and

C H R O N O L O G Y

1940-1970 *The space race begins.*

1942 Germany launches first successful military missile.

1957 Soviet Union launches *Sputnik 1*, first manmade object to orbit Earth.

1962 United States conducts nuclear test 250 miles above Pacific Ocean.

1963 United States, U.K. and Soviet Union ratify treaty banning nuclear testing in outer space, the atmosphere and under the sea.

1966 U.S. military launches first global satellite communications system.

1967 Outer Space Treaty bans nuclear weapons in outer space and military activity from celestial bodies.

1968 Soviet Union conducts first anti-satellite test, blowing up Cosmos 249 near another of its own satellites, creating hundreds of debris bits.

1970 Japan and China launch their first satellites.

1970s-1980s *Ronald Reagan proposes Strategic Defense Initiative (SDI). Treaties constrain weapons in space.*

1972 Anti-Ballistic Missile (ABM) treaty between United States and Soviet Union limits space weapons.

1975 European Space Agency (ESA) is established with 10 founding members.

1980 India launches its first satellite.

1983 Soviet Union proposes a treaty prohibiting the use of force in outer space. . . . Ronald Reagan proposes SDI, a missile defense system involving placing weapons in space.

1985 United States launches an anti-satellite weapon from an F-15, destroying a malfunctioning U.S. scientific satellite.

1988 Israel launches its first satellite.

1990-2006 *Cold War ends. U.S. military strategists, seeing no peer opponents, craft a strategy of "space superiority" that is later toned down by the George W. Bush administration.*

1994 The U.S. military completes the Global Positioning System satellite constellation, which finds widespread civilian application. The space shuttle docks with Russia's Mir space station, initiating U.S.-Russian space cooperation.

1998 Construction begins on International Space Station, which will become counterpoint to growing military use of space.

1999 A U.N. resolution to prevent arms race in outer space passes with a vote of 162-0, with only the United States and Israel abstaining.

2001 In January a commission amplifies the Air Force's plan for space superiority. . . . President Bush withdraws from ABM treaty in December.

2005 United States launches a micro-satellite able to closely examine other satellites, viewed by the Russians and the Chinese as a threat.

2007-Present *China and other countries enter space. Diplomats continue negotiating limits on space weapons.*

2007 China tests anti-satellite weapon, destroying one of its own weather satellites and creating an enormous amount of space debris. International indignation ensues. . . . European Union proposes a code of conduct for countries in space.

2008 United States destroys one of its defunct satellites in a test, after announcing it in advance, and avoids creating debris. . . . China and Russia propose a draft treaty to prevent weapons in space or threats against space objects.

2009 U.S. commercial satellite is destroyed in an accidental collision with an abandoned Russian satellite, the first such collision. . . . Iran launches a satellite.

2010-2011 President Barack Obama proposes more conciliatory space strategy than Bush, but continues missile defense program.

Space Junk Poses Risk

Debris plays a significant role in the debate over space weapons.

Compared to the vastness of outer space, the band of space that makes up Earth orbit is tiny and becoming increasingly crowded with manmade objects.

More than 3,000 satellites and thousands of other manmade objects left behind by civilian and military space programs litter both geostationary orbit, about 22,000 miles up, and low-Earth orbit — located roughly between 60 and 200 miles above the Earth. The less-crowded medium orbit lies between the two.

Orbiting space debris includes, among other things, old satellites and abandoned rocket stages — sometimes with residual fuel that could explode, sending shrapnel into functioning satellites. Debris plays a major role in the debate over space weapons, because using a space weapon could create huge amounts of debris, and an accidental collision of debris could be misperceived as an attack.

"There are hundreds of thousands of potentially lethal objects in orbit, and millions of smaller objects that pose at least some risk," Bruce W. MacDonald, a former National Security Council staffer, told Congress in March 2009. The problem had been "dramatically illustrated" a month earlier, he said, when a U.S. Iridium satellite collided with an abandoned Russian Cosmos rocket body, the first time two manmade space objects of such large size ran into each other. [1]

Since then, attitudes on space debris have changed drastically, says Brian Weeden of the Secure World Foundation, which advocates the peaceful use of outer space. Before the collision, the Joint Space Operations Center (JSpOC) screened 100-150 essential, high-priority mostly American-owned objects daily — including the space shuttle, International Space Station and national security satellites — for potential collisions, he says. Now, the command screens every active satellite — about 1,000 — every day and warns satellite operators, including the Russian and Chinese governments. [2]

Over the past year, "JSpOC has provided Russia with 252 notifications and China with 147 notifications regarding close approaches between satellites," Frank Rose, a deputy assistant secretary of State, told the European Space Policy Institute recently in June. [3]

The biggest single debris-creating incident in history occurred in 2007, when China shot down one of its weather satellites to test its anti-satellite capabilities. The incident expanded by 10 percent the total number of trackable orbiting objects (those larger than about four inches in diameter). It will take a century for the effects to dissipate, scientists say. (Objects in low-Earth orbit travel through a very thin atmosphere in which satellites eventually burn up.) [4]

The Chinese test and the 2009 collision demonstrate the biggest worry regarding space debris: the risk of a chain reaction, in which colliding spacecraft generate massive amounts of space junk that in turn strikes other objects.

Afghanistan wars the United States has enjoyed technological pre-eminence. During the 2003 Iraq War, for instance, Iraqi forces tried unsuccessfully to jam U.S. satellites. [70]

China and India have been working on space programs for years. The Chinese first orbited a satellite in 1970, India in 1980. Two leading figures in the Chinese space program, Chien Wei-Chang and Chien Hsue-Shen, both worked at the California Institute of Technology in Pasadena before returning to China. [71]

China had been developing an anti-satellite program as far back as the 1980s. [72] But it did not attract widespread attention until Jan. 11, 2007, when a test missile launched from southwestern China destroyed the country's Fengyun 1-C weather satellite. The test created significant debris and provoked international outrage and is widely believed to have been a mistake.

"This is an enormous mess they [the Chinese] have created," the Monterrey Institute's Lewis told *Space News*. "There is no excuse for what is a reckless, stupid and self-defeating decision on their part." [73] The most popular explanation is that overeager elements of the Chinese army conducted the test without fully informing the political leadership.

Two NASA scientists predicted such collisions in the late 1970s. "According to their models, large pieces of space debris would get hit by smaller pieces of debris, creating hundreds or thousands of new pieces of small debris, which could then collide with other large pieces," Weeden said in a paper this year. The process, which they called "collisional cascading," would cause the amount of space debris to increase "at an exponential rate and significantly increase the risks and costs of operating in space." [5]

To prevent such chain reactions, engineers have suggested modifying the orbits of large pieces of debris — such as old rocket bodies and defunct satellites — so they either burn up in the atmosphere or are moved to less-congested orbits. Darren McKnight — a former Air Force officer who works for the defense contractor Integrity Applications — says developing and utilizing debris-removal technology, such as lasers or space tugs, should begin immediately. "Pay me now, or pay me more later," he told a 2010 conference. [6]

But so far no such technology exists. And Andrew Palowitch, director of the Pentagon's Space Protection Program, says some countries might consider such technology a weapon.

Nancy Gallagher, assistant director of the Center for International and Security Studies at the University of Maryland, says it's "infinitely more sensible to stop creating debris in the first place." Only 11 of 21 spacecraft in geostationary orbit that stopped functioning in 2009, she says, were disposed of properly — meaning they were either sent into the lower atmosphere to burn up or put into out-of-the-way "parking orbits."

— *Konstantin Kakaes*

An artist's rendering shows the thousands of pieces of manmade debris that circulate in low-Earth orbit. Debris created by the use of a space weapon could create huge additional amounts of space junk that could accidentally destroy satellites and possibly be misperceived as an attack.

[1] Bruce W. MacDonald, testimony before House Armed Services Committee, March 18, 2009, http://i.cfr.org/content/publications/attachments/MacDonald_Testimony_031809.pdf.

[2] "SATCAT Boxscore," CelesTrak, Aug. 4, 2011, www.celestrak.com/satcat/boxscore.asp.

[3] Frank Rose, "Defining Space Security for the 21st Century," speech to European Space Policy Institute, June 13, 2011, www.state.gov/t/avc/rls/165995.htm.

[4] Bruce W. MacDonald, "China, Space Weapons, and U.S. Security," Council on Foreign Relations Special Report, September 2008, http://i.cfr.org/content/publications/attachments/China_Space_CSR38.pdf.

[5] Brian Weeden, "Overview of the Legal and Policy Challenges of Orbital Debris Removal," *Space Policy* (2011), p. 38.

[6] Darren McKnight, "Active Debris Removal," Armed Forces Communications and Electronics Association, Space Symposium, November 2010, www.afcea.org/events/pastevents/documents/McKnight.ppt.

"Beijing's right hand may not have known what its left hand was doing," wrote Bates Gill, director of the Stockholm International Peace Institute in Sweden, and Martin Kleiber, a researcher at the Center for Strategic and International Studies in Washington. [74]

In 2008, the United States destroyed one of its own satellites, in what some claim was a response to the Chinese test. China's response mirrored the international indignation engendered by its own ASAT test.

"America's pledge that the test would not produce dangerous space debris is difficult to confirm. At present, the United States is the only country capable of monitoring space worldwide. . . . Neither the United States nor Russia makes data public," said a Chinese newspaper. [75] (The United States does, in fact, make some data public.)

But whether it's the United States, Russia or China, the same dynamic often comes into play: Military planners who favor aggressive technology development butt heads with diplomats and policymakers who point out that newer is not necessarily better.

As space historian Day noted, the Air Force's chief scientists end up "serving as a reality check for goofy proposals from Air Force Space Command, like using lasers to blow up tanks." [76]

Common Satellite Orbits Around Earth

Most satellites are found in one of three Earth orbits located within 22,000 miles above Earth: low-Earth orbit, medium-Earth orbit and geostationary orbit. Low-Earth orbit, which is located from 60 to 1,000 miles above the Earth's surface, is crowded with reconnaissance and weather satellites. Geostationary orbit is crowded with communications satellites, because at that altitude (22,000 miles) satellites can hover over one spot on the Earth's surface, so antennas on the ground can be pointed in a fixed direction at the satellite, allowing uninterrupted communication. Medium Earth orbit — which is less crowded than the others — is where the American and Russian satellite-based navigation systems are located. The U.S. system consists of a constellation of 32 satellites, and the Russian system has 21. Highly elliptical Earth orbit is useful for satellites providing communications coverage to vast countries like Russia, with large areas far from the equator, where it is difficult to use satellites in geostationary orbit.

Earth's Four Orbits

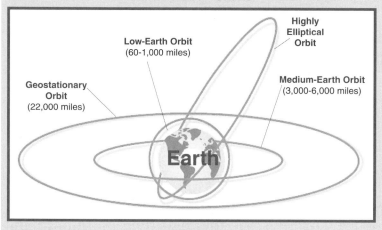

Source: Tech-Faq, www.tech-faq.com/medium-earth-orbit.html

CURRENT SITUATION

Code of Conduct

At 8 a.m. on June 28 the six crew members of the International Space Station took to emergency lifeboats — as a precaution. Soon after that, a piece of space debris moving at a potentially lethal 29,000 miles per hour passed within 1,100 feet of the station. Such dangerous close encounters will become increasingly common as the amount of space debris grows each year. Much of the problem stems from more and more countries launching their own satellites into space. Most eventually are abandoned after they run out of fuel, which could take anything from a few years to decades.

Iran — which launched its second satellite into Earth orbit on June 15 — became the newest member of the satellite club in 2009 when it launched the communications satellite Omid. [77] The central question about the future of space — Is war in space inevitable? — includes uncertainty about the role Iran and other rogue states like North Korea might play.

Scott Pace, director of The George Washington University's Space Policy Institute, told Congress that "new entrants such as Iran and possibly North Korea" raised the greatest concerns about sustainability in space, because they cannot "monitor and control space objects." In other words, they might be reckless with the space environment. [78]

Sheldon, of the School of Advanced Air and Space Studies, says other second- and third-tier powers are jumping into space. Turkey and Algeria, for instance, both have reconnaissance satellites.

"The United Arab Emirates is talking about Dubaisat 2, and the Saudis and Egyptians are talking about satellites, too," he points out. "The first space war will probably occur between adversaries" who have nothing to do with the United States.

For instance, Israel has expressed interest in developing anti-satellite weapons, according to S. Samuel C. Rajiv, an associate fellow at the Institute for Defence Studies and Analyses in New Delhi. Israel would be unlikely to target the United States. [79]

Frank Rose, a deputy assistant secretary of State who is the administration's top space diplomat, said in a June 2011 speech, "The United States considers the space systems of all nations to have the rights of passage through, and conduct of operations in, space without interference." [80]

America's attitude about behavior in space matters disproportionately, because it spends about 40 times as much as Europe on defense-related space activities. In 2009

U.S. military space spending was $43.5 billion — covering everything from spy and communications satellites to missile defense systems — compared to Europe's roughly $1 billion. [81]

China, meanwhile, also is making progress. "China is pursuing, in a sustained and systematic fashion, the development, testing and deployment of counter-space [anti-satellite] capabilities," said Beijing-based Kulacki, with the Union of Concerned Scientists. [82]

The Prevention of the Placement of Weapons in Outer Space Treaty (PPWT) advocated by China and Russia in the Conference on Disarmament in Geneva requires unanimity. [83]

But, the U.N.'s Hitchens says, the United States has made clear "in no uncertain terms" that it "will not negotiate on the basis of this text." For one thing, she says, the United States argues the treaty is too weak because it doesn't cover "ground-based testing, use or development of terrestrially based ASATs."

Kueter, of the George C. Marshall Institute, argues that Russian and Chinese efforts to advance a new treaty "provide cover for their self-serving attempts to constrain the United States while doing nothing to restrict their own clandestine anti-satellite programs." In the past several years, he continues, "the Chinese military successfully executed at least two anti-satellite tests, while their diplomatic corps raged against the supposed weaponization of space by the United States."

However, the United States also would object if anti-satellite prohibitions were inserted into a treaty, says Lewis of the Monterrey Institute, because it would block the development of a missile defense program. "Missile defense is not compatible with a prohibition on ASATs," and missile defense programs, which still receive about $8.5 billion a year from the U.S. Congress, are politically untouchable in the United States today. As a result, "there are just no rules," says Lewis.

"The United States has never wanted to talk about rules," he continues. "There's this misguided idea that having rules ties your hands, which is exactly the opposite lesson that should be drawn." Thus, the treaty is "going nowhere fast."

Other opportunities for international negotiation involve the Committee on the Peaceful Uses of Outer Space, which usually doesn't deal with military issues. But at a June meeting the Vienna-based panel agreed to create

NASA

Like other manmade satellites, the International Space Station is extremely vulnerable to a deliberate attack and has had to maneuver repeatedly to avoid potentially dangerous encounters with space debris. The station, which is near completion, is a collaboration between the United States, Russia, Japan, Canada and the European Space Agency.

a working group to deal with (among other issues) "international cooperation in peaceful uses of outer space as a means of enhancing the long-term sustainability of outer space activities and supporting sustainable development on Earth." [84] Such an agenda would allow the group to work on agreements limiting weapons in space.

The U.N. General Assembly, at Russia's urging, also has convened a group of experts to meet next summer to work out the details of a U.N.-backed Code of Conduct for space, another indication that negotiations for the PPWT are not progressing.

The European Union last October proposed a Code of Conduct for outer space, tentatively supported by the United States, which already takes some of the actions recommended by the code, such as giving advance notice when satellites will be moved to new orbits.

But in February, 37 Republican senators wrote Secretary of State Hillary Rodham Clinton warning the code had a "multitude of potential highly damaging implications" — both for sensitive military and intelligence programs and for "a tremendous amount of commercial activity." The code would preclude "the research and development, testing and deployment of a kinetic defensive system in outer space . . . capable of defeating an anti-satellite weapon, such as the one tested by the People's Republic of China in 2007," they claimed. [85]

Remnants of a Chinese Long March rocket lie in southern China's Guizhou Province after carrying a navigation satellite into orbit in April 2009. Thousands of similar pieces of debris proliferate in low-Earth orbit, creating potentially deadly projectiles capable of destroying a fragile satellite. A one-pound scrap of metal orbiting the Earth at 17,000 miles per hour packs as much energy as a tank going 60 miles per hour — enough to easily punch through the thin walls of a satellite, spaceship or the manned International Space Station.

In any case, advocates of the code point out that a kinetic defensive system would be very technically challenging — so no one is giving up much by promising not to develop what would be a costly and ineffective system. Defense is always harder than offense in space, because a defensive system would need to carry sufficient fuel to launch projectiles that could intercept all attackers, while anti-satellite weapons can be launched from the Earth.

The Chinese, meanwhile, worry about knocking the wind out of the formal treaty process, says Kulacki. "They don't want the Code of Conduct to serve as a substitute for a treaty," he says. "They especially don't want to be put in an environment where it's the United States and its allies on one side of the table, and China on the other."

However, some Russians see a Code of Conduct as a first step toward a formal treaty. "The greatest potential contribution of such a code of conduct in space would be to create the political conditions needed for negotiations on full-fledged and legally binding treaties to ban or limit space weapons," wrote Alexei Arbatov, head of the Center for International Security at the Russian Academy of Sciences, and Vladimir Dvorkin, a retired Soviet Navy major general. [86]

At a certain level, says Lele of India's Institute for Defence Studies and Analyses, "Everybody appears to be slightly happy with the [current] situation. The U.S. becomes a simple punching bag. In their heart of hearts, other countries are pretty happy [with the status quo], but they can blame the U.S."

Situational Awareness

On Feb. 10, 2009, the U.S. Iridium 33 satellite collided with the Russian Cosmos 2251 satellite nearly 500 miles above the Earth — the first collision in history between two satellites. [87] The impact created more than 1,000 pieces of trackable debris — and possibly hundreds of thousands of smaller pieces — highlighting experts' long-standing concern about the lack of "space situational awareness" (SSA).

SSA is important for two reasons: to avoid collisions, which cause troublesome debris, and to provide basic forensic ability to determine the source of a kinetic attack against a satellite. Knowing the source of an attack, some argue, could help serve as a deterrent.

Currently, only the U.S. military can track satellites and debris in space, and it relies on a ground-based detector network using a Cold War-era program designed to detect a Soviet nuclear attack. Recently, there has been some discussion of putting the detectors in space.

But an SSA system would require satellite owners to share information on the location and paths of their satellites. "You need the sensors — telescopes and radars — to track the debris," says Weeden, of the Secure World Foundation, "but you also need the owner-operator information on where satellites are, because it will be more accurate. They are the only ones who know when they are going to maneuver [or] where they are going."

Even skeptics about international cooperation see the need for situational awareness in space. The Air Force's Sheldon — who is dismissive of arms control agreements — says "space cooperation and collaboration will begin with SSA. It's something everybody has a mutual interest in developing, something friends and allies need as well. We need a global picture of SSA."

Commercial operators are generally happy to share data, as it makes their very expensive satellites safer. But the national security community is often hesitant about sharing.

This, says Hitchens, "is completely silly" because Pakistan and India both were able to test nukes without

Should space weapons be banned?

YES
Bharath Gopalaswamy
Visiting scholar, Institute for Peace Studies, Cornell University

Written for *CQ Global Researcher*, August 2011

As the space disarmament process has ground to a halt, missile defense programs have been thriving. The strategic environment could become even more competitive as missile defense research yields technologies for offensive space-based weapons. Thus, it is hardly a surprise that the prevention of an arms race in outer space is the subject of intense international debate and controversy.

Over the past 20 years, more and more states have been using space for military purposes — from communications to mapping to intelligence-gathering and weapons-targeting. Although the militarization of space has become inevitable, we should be careful not to adopt the same norm for the weaponization of space.

A space war — a mutual shooting down of other nations' satellites — would be devastating for all. The resulting debris would pose enormous risks to all satellites in orbit, as highlighted by the Chinese anti-satellite test in 2007.

The threat from uncontrolled military expansion into space was recognized very early in the space race. In 1962, the U.N.'s "Declaration of Legal Principles Governing the Activities of States in the Exploration and Use of Outer Space" became the basis of negotiations of a multilateral mechanism regulating the use of space. The resulting Outer Space Treaty — the first treaty governing access to space — entered into force in October 1967. It established the principle that outer space is not open to national appropriation but is a global commons free for the use of all states. It also codified the phrase "peaceful use of outer space," banning the placement of weapons of mass destruction in orbit and the establishment of military bases in space.

Why focus on developing an anti-satellite technology for a war that no nation can win in the foreseeable future? The lack of progress on a legally binding treaty for space assets needs to be dealt with. The debris issue, which has received far less attention than it warrants, needs more awareness.

In spite of this, there is currently no ban on attacking satellites in space. The 1967 Outer Space Treaty prohibits only the placement of nuclear weapons on celestial bodies. The lack of a legally binding treaty sends the message that there is no potential arms race in space. Although international treaties can involve extensive, time-consuming negotiations, they seem to be a much better path than other imaginable alternatives.

NO
Jeff Kueter
President George C. Marshall Institute

Written for *CQ Global Researcher*, February 2012

Few criticized the U.S. decision to destroy a disabled, fully fueled spy satellite before it crashed to Earth in February 2008. Using missile defense assets to further minimize the risk of harm is commendable, but some questioned our motives and claimed we were shooting at the satellite not to protect lives and property but to demonstrate an anti-satellite capability. They have called for an international treaty to ban weapons in space.

As it has for the past 50 years, the United States should resist calls for a new space treaty. Space is routinely used for military purposes, and the integration of space-based intelligence, reconnaissance and surveillance into tactical military operations offers clear incentives for others to attack U.S. spacecraft.

A ban is neither enforceable nor verifiable. Cold War-era space arms control efforts faltered when negotiators could not reach agreement on what constitutes a space weapon. The U.S. space shuttle was viewed as a space weapon by the Soviets.

The Chinese used a standard ballistic missile topped with a sophisticated warhead in their January 2007 anti-satellite test, but a treaty that would eliminate such a missile is improbable, as is verifying whether a warhead (or the capacity to reproduce it in the future) was destroyed pursuant to a disarmament agreement.

Electronic warfare — by blinding satellites with lasers or jamming information sent from space — presents a widespread and immediate challenge to the United States. But determining the source of such attacks would be technically difficult, and the capabilities draw upon technologies readily available for other nonaggressive purposes.

Russian and Chinese efforts to advance a new treaty provide cover for their self-serving attempts to constrain the United States while doing nothing to restrict their own clandestine anti-satellite programs. In the past several years, the Chinese military successfully executed at least two anti-satellite tests, while their diplomatic corps raged against the supposed weaponization of space by the United States.

Those who suggest that such an agreement would protect U.S. interests have yet to explain why others would abandon the capability to hold at risk the most vulnerable elements of American military power. A restraint on space weaponry — far from keeping the heavens safe — instead leaves them vulnerable to 9/11-style space terrorism.

Iranian President Mahmoud Ahmadinejad unveils a new satellite in Tehran on Feb. 3, 2010. Iran — which launched its second satellite into Earth orbit on June 15 — became the latest country to launch its own satellite in 2009, when it launched a communications satellite. Much of the concern about the possibility of war in space centers around the intentions of Iran, North Korea and other rogue states.

the United States knowing about it "because they knew when the satellites were passing over. I can see a reconnaissance satellite with an $88 telescope I bought from Target." It takes some political will, she says, to get militaries to share data for SSA, but their refusal to do so is "like a little kid putting his hands over his eyes saying, 'If I can't see you, you can't see me.'"

And although international negotiations can be drawn out or even hopelessly deadlocked, Hitchens says, "I'm more optimistic now that something is going to happen than I have been in 10 years of working on space."

OUTLOOK

Competition and New Technology

"Missile defense," says Sheldon, at the Air Force's School of Advanced Air and Space Studies, "is disseminating." India and Israel already have some capabilities, as do the Chinese. A successful missile defense test, however, is a long way from a working, real-world system. But if someone has missile defense capabilities, it means they also have anti-satellite abilities.

Johnson-Freese, of the Naval War College, notes that dissemination of technology alone is not enough. "Space is a harsh environment, and offense is much easier than

defense. Any country with ballistic missile capability can theoretically threaten satellites in orbit. The question is for what purpose?" she says.

U.S. dominance in space might also depend not so much on weapons, per se, but rather on what competition arises. Russia's Glonass system is already competing with America's GPS system, and both China and the European Union plan to build their own systems, despite the expense and technical difficulty.

"Not surprisingly, the United States military has been extremely critical of Galileo [the European system], calling it unnecessary and a potential security threat during wartime," wrote Harsh V. Pant, a lecturer at the India Institute of King's College in London, and Lele, of India's Institute for Defence Studies and Analyses. [88]

If China and the EU end up not building competitive systems, America's GPS could be perceived as a U.S.-controlled global public utility.

As new technologies emerge, space could become less useful militarily. Unmanned aerial vehicles (UAVs), which can hover in one location for days taking pictures over an area of interest, already are replacing satellites for some applications, says Weeden, of Secure World. They could even play a significant role in missile defense, because a UAV could be closer to a missile launch site than a satellite in low-Earth orbit. The United States could station a UAV just outside the territory of hostile countries like Iran or North Korea, deterring them with boost-phase anti-missile systems. [89]

Meanwhile, satellites are expected to become more maneuverable. Currently, active satellites can't refuel while orbiting, which severely limits their maneuverability. But Intelsat, a commercial communications satellite operator, announced in March that it expects to be able to refuel orbiting satellites within the next four years. [90]

As for evolving military technology, most of it is happening in secret. Lewis of the Monterrey Institute says it was embarrassing to the United States when amateur observers spotted two classified micro-satellites in geostationary orbit. "It caused concern," he says, "even if they're not being used as weapons."

Sheldon says, "black programs [do exist] out there, but they are onesies, twosies. Are there secret squadrons out there? The answer is absolutely not."

Secret or not, "Evolving technology guarantees both that we will depend even more on these assets in the future; and these vital assets will likely face greater threats than today," said Bruce MacDonald, senior director of the Nonproliferation and Arms Control Program at the United States Institute of Peace. [91]

However, Victoria Samson, Washington, D.C., office director of the Secure World Foundation, believes that the more people who use space, the better.

"Some people see space as a zero sum game — if China gets more powerful, we lose," she says. "But I say the more people have assets on orbit, the more they have an incentive to protect those assets and not screw around."

NOTES

1. Brian Weeden, "X-37B Orbital Test Vehicle Fact Sheet," Secure World Foundation, http://swfound.org/media/1791/x-37b_factsheet.pdf.

2. Michael Krepon and Samuel Black, "Space Security or Anti-satellite Weapons," Stimson Center, May 2009, www.isn.ethz.ch/isn/Digital-Library/Publications/Detail/?ots591=0c54e3b3-1e9c-be1e-2c24a6a8c7060233&lng=en&id= 103310. The report gives a partial breakdown of U.S. space expenditures: GPS: $26 billion, weather satellites: $450 million, spy satellites: $10 billion, Space Shuttle: $1.7 billion, Space Station: $25 billion, satellite launch costs: $10-150 million/satellite, Apollo Program: $125 billion.

3. "State of the Satellite Industry Report," Satellite Industry Association, June 2010, www.sia.org/SSIR%20Final/2010%20State%20of%20the%20Satellite%20Industry%20Report%20Presentation%20(August%20Employment%20Update)%202010_08.pdf.

4. William Lynn, "Remarks on Space Policy," *High Frontier: The Journal for Space and Cyberspace Professionals*, February 2011, p. 3, www.afspc.af.mil/shared/media/document/AFD-110224-052.pdf.

5. Bruce W. MacDonald, testimony to House Armed Services Committee, March 18, 2009, http://i.cfr.org/content/publications/attachments/MacDonald_Testimony_031809.pdf.

6. "National Security Space Strategy: Unclassified Summary," Department of Defense, January 2011, www.defense.gov/home/features/2011/0111_nsss/docsNationalSecuritySpaceStrategyUnclassified-Summary_Jan2011.pdf.

7. George Lewis and Theodore Postol, "A Technically Detailed Description of Flaws in the SM-3 and GMD Missile Defense Systems Revealed by the Defense Department's Ballistic Missile Test Data," *Arms Control Today*, May 2010, http://web.mit.edu/stgs/pdfs/White_Paper_Associated_With_May_2010_Arms_Control_Today_Article.pdf.

8. Wilson Wong and James G. Fergusson, *Military Space Power: A Guide to the Issues* (2010), p. 21.

9. Clarence Robinson, "Beam Weapons Technology Expanding," *Aviation Week & Space Technology*, May 25, 1981.

10. William Scott, "USSC Prepares for Future Combat Missions in Space," *Aviation Week & Space Technology*, Aug. 5, 1996.

11. Karl Mueller, "Is the Weaponization of Space Inevitable?" International Studies Association Annual Convention, March 27, 2002, http://isanet.ccit.arizona.edu/noarchive/mueller.html.

12. "Rocket Plans Raise Rivalry: Contest Of Army, Navy and Air Forces Suggested," *The Baltimore Sun*, May 12, 1946 (ProQuest Historical Newspapers: 1837-1986), p. 5.

13. "Report of the Commission to Assess United States National Security Space Management and Organization," Department of Defense, Jan. 11, 2001, p. 99, www.dod.gov/pubs/space20010111.html.

14. Mueller, *op. cit.*

15. Jeff Kueter, "Crossing the Rubicon in Space Again: Iacta Alea Est," George C. Marshall Institute, January 2007, www.marshall.org/pdf/materials/492.pdf.

16. Karl Mueller, "Toward a U.S. Grand Strategy in Space," conference in Arlington, VA., organized by the George C. Marshall Institute, 2006, www.marshall.org/pdf/materials/408.pdf.

17. Brian Weeden, "The Space Security Implications of Missile Defense," *The Space Review*, Sept. 28, 2009, www.thespacereview.com/article/1474/1.

18. Michael Searway, "European Approaches to Space and Security: Implications for Transatlantic Cooperation,"

Space and Defense, summer 2010, p. 28, www.unidir .ch/unidir-views/pdf/pdf-uv-30-33.pdf.

19. Ze Zhang, "China's Efforts in Pushing Forward the PPWT," Space Security Conference, 2011, United Nations Institute for Disarmament Research, www .unidir.ch/pdf/conferences/pdf-conf1039.pdf.

20. *Ibid.*

21. Michael Sheehan, *The International Politics of Space* (2007), p. 122.

22. Caitlin Harrington, "USAF seeks to harden satellite defenses," *Jane's Defence Weekly*, Jan. 30, 2008.

23. Mueller, "Toward a U.S. Grand Strategy in Space," *op. cit.*

24. Les Doggrell, "The Reconstitution Imperative," *Air and Space Power Journal*, winter 2008, www.air power.maxwell.af.mil/airchronicles/apj/apj08/ win08/doggrell.html.

25. Gregory Schulte, testimony before Senate Committee on Armed Services, May 11, 2011, http://armed-services.senate.gov/statemnt/2011/ 05%20May/Schulte%2005-11-11.pdf.

26. "William Lynn Remarks on Space Policy at US Strategic Command Symposium," Nov. 3, 2010, www.defense.gov/speeches/speech.aspx?speechid= 1515, www.afspc.af.mil/shared/media/document/ AFD-110224-052.pdf.

27. Searway, *op. cit.*

28. David Wright and Gregory Kulacki, "Chinese Shenzhow 7 'companion satellite,'" Union of Concerned Scientists, Oct. 21, 2008, www.ucsusa.org/assets/documents/ nwgs/UCS-Shenzhou7-CompanionSat-10-21-08 .pdf.

29. Mueller, "Is the Weaponization of Space Inevitable?" *op. cit.*

30. Will Marshall, "Reducing the Vulnerability of Space Assets: A Multitiered Microsatellite Constellation Architecture," *Astropolitics*, 2008, pp. 154-199.

31. "Rocket Plans Raise Rivalry," *op. cit.*

32. Wernher Von Braun, "Will Take Us Five Years To Equal Reds," *The Hartford Courant*, Nov. 10, 1957, p. 1A, ProQuest Historical Newspapers.

33. For background, see W. R. McIntyre, "National Space Policy," *Editorial Research Reports*, Dec. 9, 1959, available at *CQ Researcher Plus Archives*.

34. Patrick Skene Catling, "U.S. Proposes Missile Curb: Would Ban Outer Space Military Projects," *The Baltimore Sun*, April 26, 1957, p. 5, ProQuest Historical Newspapers.

35. James Lee, "Senate Maps Space Arms Race," *Daily Defender*, Jan. 8, 1958, p. 1, ProQuest Historical Newspapers.

36. Sheehan, *op. cit.*, p. 44.

37. *Ibid.*

38. *Ibid.*

39. Joan Johnson-Freese, *Heavenly Ambitions: America's Quest to Dominate Space* (2009), p. 18.

40. George Wilson, "U.S. Plans New Weapon Against Space Satellites," *Los Angeles Times*, Feb. 12, 1968, p. 1.

41. *Ibid.*

42. Karl Grossman, *Weapons in Space* (2001), p. 30.

43. *Ibid.*

44. "Space War on Drawing Boards," *Hartford Courant*, March 21, 1978.

45. Thomas Beer, "The Use of Outer Space for Security and Defence: The European Perspective," in *Space Security and Global Cooperation* (2009).

46. Searway, *op. cit.*

47. John Pike, "The Death-Beam Gap," Federation of American Scientists, 1992, www.fas.org/spp/eprint/ keegan.htm.

48. Robert Toh, "U.S., Soviets to Seek Ban on Satellite Killers," *Los Angeles Times*, Nov. 4, 1977.

49. Sheehan, *op. cit.*, p. 97.

50. Ronald Reagan, speech, March 23, 1983, www .reagan.utexas.edu/archives/speeches/1983/32383d .htm.

51. William Burrows, "The Star Wars Debate: Ballistic Missile Defense: The Illusion of Security," *Foreign Affairs*, spring, 1984.

52. Larry Pressler, "Avoiding a Crippling Space-Weapons Race" *Los Angeles Times*, Jan 6, 1983.

53. Johnson-Freese, *op. cit.*, p. 48.

54. Thierry de Montbrial, "The European Dimension," *Foreign Affairs*, 1985, p. 499.

55. Sheehan, *op. cit.*

56. Dwayne Day, "General Power vs. Chicken Little," *The Space Review*, May 23, 2005, www.thespace review.com/article/379/1.

57. William Dullforce, "Moscow Offers Separate Talks on Space Weapons," *The Financial Times*, June 25, 1986, p. 36.

58. Lionel Barber, "Study Warns of Race for Control of Outer Space," *The Financial Times*, June 9, 1988, p. 3.

59. Michael Krepon, "Lost in Space: The Misguided Drive Toward Anti-satellite Weapons," *Foreign Affairs*, May/June 2001.

60. Sheehan, *op. cit.*, p. 100.

61. Victoria Pope, "Soviet Republics Rebel," *CQ Researcher*, July 12, 1991, pp. 465-488.

62. "Report of the Commission to Assess United States National Security Space Management and Organization," *op. cit.*

63. Barry Goldwater, "U.S. Lag in Space Weapons Could Result in Another 'Pearl Harbor,'" *Los Angeles Times*, Aug. 1, 1965, p. L7, ProQuest Historical Newspapers.

64. "Report of the Commission to Assess United States National Security Space Management and Organization," *op. cit.*

65. Johnson-Freese, *op. cit.*, p. 54.

66. Demetri Sevastopulo, "White House Wraps Star Wars Weapons in Cloak of Darkness," *The Financial Times*, May 20, 2005.

67. Johnson-Freese, *op. cit.*, p. 53.

68. Krepon, *op. cit.*

69. *Ibid.*

70. Sheehan, *op. cit.*, p. 117.

71. *Ibid.*, p. 160.

72. Gregory Kulacki, "Potential for Cooperation with China," speech, "Moving Ahead on Space Security," Carnegie Endowment for International Peace, Dec.15, 2010, www.ucsusa.org/assets/documents/nwgs/cooperation-with-china-on-space-gkulacki.pdf.

73. Colin Clark and Jeremy Singer, "China's Anti-satellite test widely criticized," *Space News*, Jan. 26, 2007.

74. Bates Gill and Martin Kleiber, "China's Space Odyssey: What the Anti-satellite Test Reveals About Decision-Making in Beijing," *Foreign Affairs*, May/June 2007.

75. Wu Ganxiang, "The New Space Threat?" *Beijing Review*, March 21, 2008, www.bjreview.com/quotes/txt/2008-03/21/content_106134.htm.

76. Day, *op. cit.*

77. Charles Vick, "Iran's Second Satellite Launch after Two Year Major Delays," Globalsecurity.org, June 15, 2011, www.globalsecurity.org/space/world/iran/irans-second-satellite-launch.htm.

78. Scott Pace, "Keeping the Space Environment Safe for Civil and Commercial Users," testimony before House Committee on Science and Technology, April 28, 2009, http://gop.science.house.gov/Media/hearings/space09/april28/pace.pdf.

79. Samuel Rajiv, "Space and the Israeli Experience," *Space Security and Global Cooperation* (2009).

80. Frank Rose, "Defining Space Security for the 21st Century," speech to European Space Policy Institute, Prague, June 13, 2011, www.state.gov/t/avc/rls/165995.htm.

81. Searway, *op. cit.*

82. Kulacki, *op. cit.*

83. "China and Russia jointly submitted the draft Treaty on PPWT to the Conference on Disarmament," press release, Feb. 12, 2008, www.mfa.gov.cn/eng/wjb/zzjg/jks/jkxw/t408634.htm.

84. "Terms of Reference and Methods of Work of the Working Group on the Long-term Sustainability of Outer Space Activities of the Scientific and Technical Subcommittee," Annex II, United Nations Office of Outer Space Affairs, June 10, 2011.

85. Eli Lake, "Republicans wary of EU code for space activity," *The Washington Times*, Feb. 3, 2011, www.washingtontimes.com/news/2011/feb/3/republicans-wary-of-eu-code-for-space-activity/?page=all#page break.

86. Alexei Arbatov and Vladimir Dvorkin, *Outer Space: Weapons, Diplomacy, and Security* (2011), p. 108.

87. Theresa Hitchens, "Saving Space: Threat Proliferation and Mitigation," International Commission on Nuclear Non-Proliferation and Disarmament, 2009, www.icnnd.org/Documents/Hitchens_Saving_Space.doc.

88. Harsh V. Pant and Ajey Lele, "India in Space: Factors Shaping the Indian Trajectory," *Space and Defense*, summer 2010, http://web.mac.com/rharrison5/Eisenhower_Center_for_Space_and_Defense_Studies/Journal_Vol_4_No_2_files/Space_and_Defense_4_2.pdf.

89. Mike Corbett, "The Role of Airpower in Active Missile Defense," *Air & Space Power Journal*, June 1, 2010, www.airpower.au.af.mil/airchronicles/apj/apj10/sum10/09corbett-zarchan.html.

90. "Intelsat Picks MacDonald, Dettwiler and Associates Ltd. for Satellite Servicing," press release, March 15, 2011, www.intelsat.com/press/news-releases/2011/20110315-1.asp.

91. MacDonald, *op. cit.*

BIBLIOGRAPHY

Books

Chapman, Bert, *Space Warfare and Defense: A Historical Encyclopedia and Research Guide,* **ABC-CLIO, 2008.**
A professor of library science at Purdue University compiled this useful reference source.

Johnson-Freese, Joan, *Heavenly Ambitions: America's Quest to Dominate Space,* **University of Pennsylvania Press, 2009.**
A professor at the Naval War College provides a lucid, critical appraisal of America's military ambitions in space.

Klein, John J., *Space Warfare: Strategy, Principles, and Policy,* **Routledge, 2006.**
A U.S. Navy commander attacks the Air Force idea that space-based weapons confer superiority and applies maritime strategy to space.

Lele, Ajey, and Gunjan Singh, eds., *Space Security and Global Cooperation,* **Academic Foundation, in association with the Institute for Defence Studies and Analyses, 2009.**
A research fellow (Lele) and researcher (Singh) with the Institute for Defence Studies and Analyses in New Delhi edited these papers presented at a 2007 international conference.

Moltz, James Clay, *The Politics of Space Security: Strategic Restraint and the Pursuit of National Interest,* **Stanford University Press, 2011.**
A professor of national security affairs at the Naval Postgraduate School considers the lessons of the U.S.-Soviet relationship for the future of military space.

Sheehan, Michael, *The International Politics of Space,* **Routledge, 2007.**
A professor of international relations at Swansea University in Wales examines the political implications of space issues.

Wong, Wilson, and James G. Fergusson, *Military Space Power: A Guide to the Issues,* **Praeger, 2010.**
The director (Fergusson) of the Centre for Defence and Security Studies at the University of Manitoba, Winnipeg, and his researcher provide a good survey of the issues surrounding the military use of space.

Articles

Marshall, Will, "Reducing the Vulnerability of Space Assets: A Multitiered Microsatellite Constellation Architecture," *Astropolitics,* **2008, pp. 154-199.**
A researcher at NASA's Ames Research Center in California looks at how the United States (and others) can reduce the vulnerability of their satellites.

Pant, Harsh, and Ajay Lele, "India in Space: Factors Shaping the Indian Trajectory," *Space and Defense,* **Summer 2010.**
A research fellow (Lele) at the Institute for Defence Studies and Analyses in New Delhi and an affiliate (Pant) at the India Institute of King's College in London explain why India might pursue space weapons.

Weeden, Brian, "The Space Security Implications of Missile Defense," *The Space Review,* **Sept. 28, 2009, www.thespacereview.com/article/1474/1.**
A former U.S. Air Force officer currently with the Secure World Foundation examines how anti-ballistic missile technology affects the space environment.

Weston, Scott, "Examining Space Warfare: Scenarios, Risks, and U.S. Policy Implications," *Air & Space Power Journal,* March 1, 2009, www.airpower.maxwell.af.mil/airchronicles/apj/apj09/spr09/weston.html.
An Air Force major examines U.S. space vulnerabilities.

Reports and Studies

"Space Security 2010: From Foundations to Negotiations," United Nations Institute for Disarmament Research, 2010, www.unidir.org/pdf/ouvrages/pdf-1-92-9045-010-C-en.pdf.
Papers from a U.N.-sponsored conference on multilateral negotiations for space security provide a good overview of diplomatic efforts to regulate space weapons.

Arbatov, Alexei, and Vladimir Dvorkin, "Outer Space: Weapons, Diplomacy, and Security," Carnegie Endowment for International Peace, 2010, www.carnegieendowment.org/publications/?fa=view&id=41904.
The head of the Center for International Security of the Russian Academy of Sciences (Arbatov) and a retired major general in the Soviet Navy (Dvorkin) examine Russian attitudes toward space weapons.

Gates, Robert, and James Clapper, "National Security Space Strategy, Unclassified Summary," U.S. Department of Defense and U.S. Office of the Director of National Intelligence, 2011, www.defense.gov/home/features/2011/0111%5Fnsss/docs/NationalSecuritySpaceStrategyUnclassifiedSummary_Jan2011.pdf.
The Obama administration outlines its plans for military space, which stresses international cooperation.

Krepon, Michael, and Samuel Black, "Space Security or Anti-satellite Weapons," The Henry L. Stimson Center, May 2009.
A co-founder (Krepon) of the Stimson Center, a Washington, D.C., national security think tank, and a research associate (Black) outline why anti-satellite weapons are destabilizing.

For More Information

Air University, School of Advanced Air and Space Studies, 600 Chennault Circle, Maxwell AFB, Montgomery, AL 36112; (334) 953-7537; www.au.af.mil/au/saass/. The U.S. Air Force's premier school for air, space and cyberspace strategists.

Center for Nonproliferation Studies, Monterey Institute, 460 Pierce St., Monterey, CA 93940; (831) 647-4154; http://cns.miis.edu. An institute for the study of proliferation issues.

George C. Marshall Institute, 1601 N. Kent St., Suite 802, Arlington, VA 22209; (571) 970-3180; www.marshall.org. A right-of-center think tank that holds discussions on the military uses of space.

Institute for Defence Studies and Analyses, 1, Development Enclave, Rao Tula Ram Marg, New Delhi 110 010, India; (91) 11 2671 7983; www.idsa.in. A nonpartisan think tank that deals with space.

Nonproliferation Program, Carnegie Moscow Center, Moscow, Russia; (7) 495 935 8900; http://carnegie.ru/?lang=en. One of the premier independent research institutes in Moscow; established in 1994 as part of the U.S.-based Carnegie Endowment for International Peace.

Secure World Foundation, 314 W. Charles St., Superior, CO 80027; (303) 554-1560; http://swfound.org. Think tank that studies space weaponization.

Stockholm International Peace Research Institute, Signalistgatan 9, SE-169 70 Solna, Sweden; (46) 8-655 97 00; www.sipri.org. An independent think tank, established by the Swedish government, that has done extensive work on space security.

U.N. Committee on the Peaceful Uses of Outer Space, Office for Outer Space Affairs, Vienna International Centre, Wagramerstrasse 5, A-1220 Vienna, Austria; (43) 1 260 60 4950; www.oosa.unvienna.org/oosa/es/COPUOS/copuos.html. Deals with nonmilitary uses of space and is beginning to fashion a code of conduct in space.

U.N. Institute for Disarmament Research, Palais des nations, 1211 Geneva 10, Switzerland; (44) 22 917 31 86; www.unidir.org. A think tank within the United Nations for the study of disarmament.

Union of Concerned Scientists, Two Brattle Sq., Cambridge, MA 02138-3780; (617) 547-5552; www.ucsusa.org. A lobbying group that originated at MIT; an excellent resource for the study of China's space program.

Voices From Abroad:

HUANG HUIKANG

Director, Department of Treaty and Law, Ministry of Foreign Affairs, China

Proper guidance

"All treaties, principles, and declarations established by the COPUOS (U.N. Committee on the Peaceful Uses of Outer Space) have played an important role in regulating space activities, maintaining space order and promoting space cooperation, and they should guide all countries' outer space activities."

Xinhua news agency (China), June 2011

The Ottowa Citizen/Caglecartoons.com

SERGEI LAVROV

Foreign Minister, Russia

Time is of the essence

"If we do not get down to it without delay, we may lose time. We are confident that preventing the appearance of weapons in space is extremely necessary for the predictability of the strategic situation on the Earth. Let's not forget that the chimera of the nuclear monopoly led to the arms race, whose inertia we're only beginning to overcome."

Press Trust of India, March 2011

V.K. SARASWAT

Scientific Advisor, Defence Ministry, India

No space wars

"Our country does not have a policy to attack anybody in space. We don't believe in it. But as part of the Ballistic Missile Defence Programme, we have all the technology elements which are required to integrate a system through which we can defend our satellites or take care of future requirements. . . . we do not believe in space wars."

Press Trust of India, February 2011

LINDA JAKOBSON

Director of China and Global Security Programme, Stockholm International Peace Research Institute, Sweden

No longer timid

"The PLA (People's Liberation Army) certainly no longer shies away from displaying its power as is evident from numerous incidents and also the 2007 anti-satellite test. And these were actions that the Chinese knew quite well would antagonize both the United States and its neighbors."

Thai Press Reports, October 2010

IGOR MARININ

Editor, Space News magazine, Russia

A safer orbit

"The orbit used by the [International Space Station] is no longer being littered. The incidents we might see in the future could be extreme, but they will not be fatal."

Kuwait Times, June 2011

WANG QUN

Chinese Ambassador to the United Nations

The 'common wealth'

"Outer space is the common wealth of mankind, and the peaceful use and exploration of outer space is in the interest of the whole human [race]."

States News Service, October 2010

MAZLAN OTHMAN

Director, U.N. Office for Outer Space Affairs

Greater risks involved

"Any space debris is very dangerous not only to satellites but also to human life because of the International Space Station."

UzReport.com (Uzbekistan), October 2010

LI HONG

Secretary-General, China Arms Control and Disarmament Association, China

Fair talks needed

"That Washington wants to establish dialogue with Beijing on space shows that the U.S. is concerned about the direction and intention of China's space strategy. China should understand the U.S.' concern and respond openly and confidently. China has always wanted dialogue and opposed confrontation, so it will never reject an offer of dialogue. But the dialogue should be based on equality and mutual respect."

Chinadaily.com.cn, August 2011

VLADIMIR DVORKIN

Chief Scientist Russian Academy of Sciences, Russia

Holding out hope

"There is some reason to hope that under President Obama the U.S. position will change in a constructive direction and non-arming of space will become a task for negotiations."

Interfax (Russia), October 2010

6

U.S.-Pakistan Relations

Marcia Clemmitt

A poster from the Muslim Pakistani political party Jamaat-e-Islami protests against the release of Raymond Davis, an American CIA contractor who last January shot and killed two civilians in Lahore who he said had tried to rob him. Davis, who was in Pakistan to monitor international terror groups, was allowed by Pakistan to leave the country without standing trial.

From *CQ Researcher*,
Aug. 5, 2011

W hen U.S. Navy Seals killed Osama bin Laden May 2 in a raid on his house in Abbottabad, Pakistan, the death sparked a mixture of glee, relief and satisfaction in the West. After a decade-long manhunt, the mastermind of the September 2001 terror attacks was no longer a threat, and the murders of nearly 3,000 innocent people had been avenged.

Bin Laden's demise marked "the most significant achievement to date in our nation's effort to defeat Al Qaeda," President Barack Obama declared. [1]

But the U.S. assault on bin Laden's lair also inflamed longstanding tensions between the United States and Pakistan, sparking charges and counter-charges of deceit and betrayal and further shaking the long, rocky alliance between the two countries in the fight against Islamic extremism.

After the raid, reports quickly surfaced that bin Laden may have hidden in the Abbottabad house — a conspicuously upscale compound a stone's throw from Pakistan's top military academy — for as long as five years, increasing suspicion that Pakistani authorities knew of his whereabouts and kept silent. [2] Many Pakistanis, meanwhile, charged that the raid — swift, violent and stealthy — was tantamount to an illegal invasion.

All "peace-loving people" should be happy that bin Laden is dead, but "no country will accept such a violation by the U.S., which undermines Pakistan's sovereignty, army and intelligence," declared Pervez Musharraf, the former army chief who ruled Pakistan as a dictator from 1999 until 2008, when he stepped down amid calls for his impeachment. [3]

Global Hotspot

Sandwiched between Afghanistan and India — and bordering China to the north — Pakistan exists in one of the world's most tumultuous regions. Hindu-dominated India has had a long-running territorial dispute with Muslim Pakistan over Kashmir, and both countries maintain robust nuclear arsenals. Afghan insurgents and terrorist groups take refuge in Pakistan's lawless northwestern territories. The United States has maintained close ties with Pakistan when the U.S. needed help elsewhere in the region, such as in the early 1970s in establishing relations with China, in the 1980s in driving the Soviets from Afghanistan and today in fighting the war against terrorism.

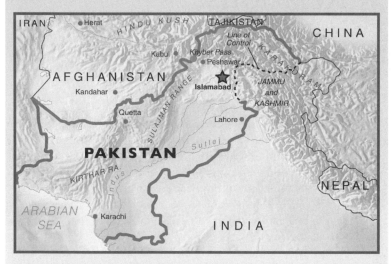

Sources: Political Handbook of the World 2008, *CQ Press, 2008;* The World Factbook, *Central Intelligence Agency*

While bin Laden's presence on Pakistani soil stoked American anger, many experts say that because the United States needs Pakistan to fight terrorism, it must encourage the country's development into a stable, civilian-led state. Otherwise, they say, Pakistan could skid further into chaos, ally itself with extremist regimes and grow as a terrorist haven.

Heightening concern over Pakistan's stability are its possession of nuclear weapons and a bitter, decades-long struggle it has carried on with its cross-border nemesis, India, also nuclear-armed.

With such high stakes, many analysts say the United States must maintain a strategic alliance with the nation.

In recent years, that alliance has paid big dividends, experts note: Pakistani military authorities have tacitly approved U.S. drone strikes in western tribal regions adjacent to Afghanistan and allowed CIA operatives to search for terrorists inside Pakistani cities — all despite bitter recriminations from some who claim such operations violate the country's sovereignty.

To underscore the importance of the alliance, C. Christine Fair, an assistant professor at Georgetown University's Center for Peace and Security Studies, points to an incident last January in which CIA contractor Raymond Davis shot dead two Pakistani nationals in Lahore who he said had tried to rob him, then was allowed by the Pakistani government to leave the country without standing trial. Davis was in Pakistan to keep tabs on international terror groups such as Lashkar-e-Taiba (LeT), suspected of numerous attacks, including one in Mumbai, India, in November 2008, that killed 174 people.

To keep its agents protected and intelligence flowing, Fair says, the United States must even maintain a relationship with Pakistan's ruthless Inter-Services Intelligence (ISI) agency, without whose cooperation U.S. agents couldn't operate in the country. "Sometimes you have to deal with the fireman even if the fireman is an arsonist," Fair says.

Other analysts, however, question whether the alliance between Pakistan and the United States already is beyond repair. They point to increasing anti-Americanism inside Pakistan, the proliferation of militant groups whose aims are increasingly unclear and suspicion that Pakistan continues to provide cover for terrorists like bin Laden.

Indeed, some in Congress are calling for a sharp reduction or complete end to U.S. economic and military aid to Pakistan, arguing it has been exploiting its ties with the United States. The United States provided nearly $4.5 billion in aid to Pakistan in fiscal 2010 — about $2.7 billion for military and anti-drug uses and $1.7 billion in economic and food aid.

"Pakistan has a lot of explaining to do," said Rep. Ted Poe, R-Texas, who introduced the Pakistan Foreign Aid Accountability Act, aimed at halting all aid to Pakistan unless it's proven that Pakistani leaders had no knowledge of bin Laden's whereabouts. "We need to re-evaluate the foreign aid that we send to countries that do not have America's best interest in mind," said Poe. [4]

Concerns over Pakistan's stability and trustworthiness extend beyond the anti-terrorism realm and include questions about Pakistan's internal governance and economic structure.

Pakistan's "federal and provincial governments appear helpless in the face of strong economic mafias that manipulate supplies to markets and increase prices of essential commodities," wrote Hasan-Askari Rizvi, an independent political and defense analyst in Pakistan. The resulting poverty and injustice "increases the threat of anarchy, if not total collapse, in many parts of Pakistan." [5]

In recent years, Pakistan has consistently ranked near the top of an annual "Failed States Index" compiled by the Fund for Peace, an independent, Washington-based research and advocacy group. This year, Pakistan ranks as the 12th most risky nation; last year it ranked 10th. [6]

But some foreign-policy experts caution that U.S. concerns over Pakistan may be somewhat overstated. "Americans get into despair easily" about Pakistan, says Stephen P. Cohen, a senior fellow at the Brookings Institution, a centrist think tank in Washington. But, while the current situation is grim, "Pakistan has a huge number of competent people" and has navigated rough shoals in the past, he says, pointing, for example, to the fact that the nation has returned from military dictatorship to democratic rule several times during its history and moved on intact after the assassinations and untimely deaths of several of its top leaders.

Key Facts on Pakistan
Area: 307,374 sq. mi.
Population: 187.3 million; world's sixth-largest nation (36 percent urban, 64 percent rural)
Median age: 21.6 years
Literacy rate: 49.9 percent (63 percent males, 36 percent females)
Infant mortality rate: 63.26 deaths per 1,000 births
Annual per capita GDP: $2,500
No access to modern sewage systems: 28 percent of urban dwellers; 71 percent of rural population

Source: *The World Factbook*, U.S. Central Intelligence Agency, https://www.cia.gov/library/publications/the-world-factbook/geos/pk.html

As Congress and the Obama administration wonder how — and whether — to salvage the Pakistan alliance, here are some questions that are being asked:

Are Pakistan and the United States allies?

After the Abbottabad raid, some Pakistanis complained that the United States routinely violates Pakistan's sovereignty, while some in Congress argued the incident proves Pakistan can't be trusted. However, many South Asia analysts argue that, despite conflicts, the countries do often support each other's interests.

"It is undeniable that our relationship with Pakistan has helped us pursue our security goals," said Senate Foreign Relations Committee Chairman John Kerry, D-Mass. [7]

"Pakistan has been a critical partner in capturing Al Qaeda leadership in Pakistan," wrote Georgetown's Fair. Without Pakistan's prior "cooperation, the United States would not have even been in a position to kill bin Laden." [8]

Since the 2001 terrorist attacks on the United States, Pakistan has "given us bases and over-flight rights, and we, in turn gave them aid and debt relief," notes Dennis Kux, a senior policy scholar at the nonpartisan Washington-based Woodrow Wilson International Center for Scholars and a retired State Department South Asia expert.

Furthermore, despite the Pakistani military's continued conviction that India, to Pakistan's east, is its primary enemy, the army has "moved a number of divisions to the western front," bordering Afghanistan, at the behest of the United States, says William Milam, a senior policy scholar at the Wilson center and a former U.S. ambassador to Pakistan.

"The help of the Pakistani intelligence services to Britain," which has a large Pakistani population, "has been absolutely vital to identifying the links" of potential Pakistani militants now living in the United Kingdom to militant "groups in Pakistan, and to preventing more attacks on Britain, the USA and Europe," wrote Anatol Lieven, a professor of war studies at King's College, in London, and a senior research fellow at the New America Foundation, a centrist think tank in Washington. [9]

The United States has greatly increased aid to Pakistan in the past decade, from $36.76 million in 2001 to $4.46 billion 2010, a 2,273 percent increase, according to the nonpartisan Congressional Research Service. [10]

Nevertheless, the alliance has long been troubled.

For example, the United States has provided and withdrawn economic aid to Pakistan repeatedly over the decades, depending on Pakistan's cooperation with U.S. strategic aims and the level of interest in South Asian affairs shown by various congressional leaders and presidents. In fiscal 2000, Pakistan didn't even rank in the top 15 nations in the amount of U.S. economic aid received (No. 15 Nigeria received $68 million.) But in fiscal 2010, Pakistan leapfrogged to third as the United States sought its cooperation with drone strikes and other targeting of Islamic militants in the region. [11]

The ups and downs of U.S. aid have exacerbated Pakistan's difficulties in developing economically and greatly contributed to Pakistanis' distrust of the United States, many scholars say.

In 1965, the United States walked away from the alliance altogether, says Kux. Pakistan was one of the first countries to recognize the communist government of the People's Republic of China, on its northeast border, and President Lyndon Johnson "was mad over that" as well as generally "sick of South Asia," where Pakistan and India had squabbled for years, Kux says. Johnson cut off both military and civilian aid, although "he regretted it later, I was told," Kux says. "To me, that was the turning point for Pakistan. The relationship was all downhill from there."

"Until recently our South Asia policy has been made because of our anti-Soviet policy," says Brookings' Cohen. As a result, the U.S. policy "has been, 'Let's let them solve their own problems, unless there's a crisis' " or specific U.S interests are at stake, says Cohen.

Because the United States has viewed the alliance as a way to achieve defense goals, it has allied itself primarily with Pakistan's military and "reinforced a message that we're only interested in working with dictators," not in supporting Pakistan's development into a democracy, says Marvin Weinbaum, a scholar in residence at the Middle East Institute, a nonpartisan research center in Washington. Both countries "gloss over the fact that their interests are often inconsistent."

In recent years, the United States has stoked Pakistani resentment by building America's relationship with rival India with acts that, many Pakistanis charge, symbolize neglect of the longstanding U.S.-Pakistan alliance.

In 2000, on a South Asia visit, President Bill Clinton "spent five glorious days in India and five cold hours in Pakistan," observes Kux.

Throughout the Cold War, India was a Soviet ally and Pakistan a friend of the United States, but when the Soviet Union collapsed in 1991, "the United States said, 'Oh, look, India's the bigger country! Let's get involved with them,' " says Barry Blechman, cofounder of the Stimson Center, a nonpartisan think tank in Washington that researches security issues. In 2008, for example, President George W. Bush "made that terrible nuclear deal" — allowing India to engage in nuclear-technology trade although it hadn't signed the Nuclear Nonproliferation Treaty —"which was a slap in the face to everyone we had hectored over the years" about nuclear nonproliferation, including Pakistan, he says. [12]

"We care about a geographical location, not about a country," says Paula Newberg, director of Georgetown University's Institute for the Study of Diplomacy. Talk in the United States of helping Pakistan "reform" is "worse than useless," since it's accompanied by "actions that do the opposite," such as channeling aid "to people who shouldn't be in power in the first place."

Partly because the countries exaggerate the extent to which their interests align, "there's this long story line of desertion" on both sides, says Adil Najam, vice chancellor at Pakistan's Lahore University of Management Sciences. This is exacerbated in Pakistan by "tribal notions of what it means to be a friend — that a friend stands by you even when you're wrong."

Anti-Americanism is increasing throughout Pakistan, says Aqil Shah, a post-doctoral fellow at Harvard University. "Many people feel the United States has let them down, talking about how they support democracy but not protecting them against dictators," and periodically "washing their hands of us and walking away." Now, with the United States winding down the Afghan war, Shah says, "it looks to people as if the United States is planning another exit" from its alliance with Pakistan, as it did when the Soviet Union withdrew in defeat from Afghanistan around 1990. Just as occurred then, Shah says, Pakistanis fear that Washington will leave them with another bad situation on their doorstep, this time in the form of an Afghanistan permanently aligned with Pakistan's nemesis, India.

Complicating matters is the fact that Pakistan's military and intelligence agency continue to tell the public that India is the country's chief enemy and that they will defend Pakistan's borders against all foreign encroachments, including U.S. strikes on terrorist targets, says Milam. In fact, they "have played a double game with the public," acting "in complicity with the United States in the drone program since 2004, but not telling that truth to Pakistanis, who remain largely unaware that the government has been in favor" of many of the drone attacks, he says.

The alliance is like a marriage disintegrating, says Najam. "When things start falling apart, you start promising more than you can deliver" as a misguided way to patch things up, he observes. That's what Pakistan has done by telling the United States that "we will be with you completely in the fight against terror." Public opinion inside Pakistan makes that politically impossible, but when Pakistan doesn't fully deliver, the United States sees betrayal.

Both countries "need to be smarter about what they really want" and more honest about what they can give, says Najam. "I wish Pakistan told the United States 'No' more often," because it would be better "to promise less but deliver better."

Is Pakistan on the verge of collapse?

Pakistan faces many challenges, from growing political violence to looming water shortages. Furthermore, "a weak Pakistan now could mean a radicalized Pakistan, increasingly dominated by extremist groups," says the Middle East Institute's Weinbaum. Nevertheless, Pakistanis have persisted through many troubles and may do so again, some South Asia experts say.

Pakistan's top internal threats include:

- a huge population of refugees, displaced by war in Afghanistan, violence at home and natural disasters;
- escalating ethnic, regional and religious violence;
- highly uneven economic development;
- government corruption;
- military and security agencies divided against themselves and infiltrated by terrorist sympathizers; and
- government institutions that can't deliver services. [13]

Pakistan is "a state in perpetual crisis," says retired Brig. Gen. Feroz Khan, a 32-year veteran of Pakistan's army and a lecturer at the U.S. Naval Postgraduate School in Monterey, Calif.

Pakistan's political system "is corrupt, with only 400 families" largely monopolizing the voter support needed to win elections or govern once in office, says Blechman of the Stimson Center. Furthermore, the central government "has only limited say in large parts of the country and is currently losing control completely" in many areas.

The terrorism that increasingly threatens Pakistanis is fueled partly by public discontent and thus can't be controlled "without introducing a system based on justice," said Shahbaz Sharif, chief minister of Pakistan's Punjab province. But justice eludes the nation because the elites continue to hold the lion's share of wealth, he said. [14]

Pakistan's government "can be accused of not doing enough to stop" violence; however, "their ability to do so is very limited," given the central government's traditionally limited role in many regions, wrote the New America Foundation's Lieven. "The overwhelming majority of human rights abuses . . . stem from a mixture of freelance brutality and exploitation by policemen, working either for themselves or for local elites; actions by local landlords and bosses; and punishments by local communities of real or perceived infringements of their moral code." [15]

Worse problems loom, says Bruce Riedel, a senior fellow at the Brookings Institution and former CIA officer who oversaw a 2009 review of U.S. Pakistan and Afghanistan policy for the Obama administration. [16] "Their demographics are terrible, with a terrific youth bulge and not enough water for them all to drink," he says. Massive floods that occurred in 2010 "were a severe climate-change disruption" that will eventually

Terror Groups Have Varied Goals

The United States has designated the Pakistan-based groups below as foreign terrorist organizations. But Pakistan takes a more pragmatic view of militancy. Groups with domestic targets are hunted down; those with international goals are sometimes tolerated; and groups with some strategic value, especially those active in the disputed region of Kashmir, may even enjoy the covert support of Pakistan's powerful Inter-Services Intelligence (ISI) agency. Even officially banned groups may operate with some impunity throughout Pakistan, exacerbating Pakistan's already troubled relationship with the United States.

Jaish-e-Mohammed (Army of the Prophet, JeM)

Objectives: Free Jammu & Kashmir from India
Pakistani designation: **Banned**
— Linked to 2001 attack on Indian Parliament
— Linked to the 2002 death of American journalist Daniel Pearl
— Linked to Al Qaeda, Afghan Taliban, Inter-Services Intelligence (ISI)

Lashkar-e-Taiba (Army of the Pure, LeT)

Objectives: Free Jammu & Kashmir from India, establish Islamic rule in South Asia
Pakistani designation: **Banned**
— Implicated in 2001 attack on Indian Parliament
— Implicated in 2008 attack on Mumbai
— Tied to charity organization Jamaat-ud-Dawa
— Linked to Al Qaeda, ISI

Lashkar-e-Jhangvi (Army of Jhangvi, LeJ)

Objectives: Establish a Sunni state in Pakistan
Pakistani designation: **Banned**
— Has funding ties to Al Qaeda, Afghan Taliban

Sipah-e-Muhammed Pakistan (SMP)

Objectives: Protect and promote Shiites in Pakistan
Pakistani designation: **Banned**
— Shiite group devoted to countering anti-Shiite violence
— May have ties to Iranian government

Tehrik-e-Taliban Pakistan (Pakistani Taliban, TTP)

Objectives: Establish a global Islamic state
Pakistani designation: **Banned, military target**
— Biggest domestic terrorist organization in Pakistan
— Not a part of Afghan Taliban
— Extremely close to Al Qaeda
— Target of large Pakistani military operations, but still active

Sources: Institute for Conflict Management; National Counterterrorism Center, Belfer Center for Science and International Affairs, Harverd University; Federation of American Scientists

lead to long-term drought, and no drought-amelioration measures are in place.

However, Pakistan is home to many capable people and has demonstrated the ability to rebound from difficulties in the past, some analysts say.

In the 1950s, the U.S. Agency for International Development "actually used to send Koreans to Pakistan" to see an example of American aid well used, observes Kux of the Woodrow Wilson Center.

Furthermore, "almost all the [Pakistani] military governments have ended with uprisings" of citizens, including tradesmen, lawyers and students, who sought democracy, says Shah of Harvard.

"Contrary to much instinctive belief in the West," Pakistan "has actually worked according to its own imperfect but functional patterns," wrote Lieven. All South Asian countries face regional unrest, he notes. Sri Lanka and Burma have experienced worse insurrections, and even India "has faced repeated rebellions" in various regions, some "lasting for generations." [17]

Pakistan's proliferating broadcast media, especially, spread lies and pernicious conspiracy theories, which "could show a system falling apart," says Lahore University's Najam. "But it could also be a symptom of a system improving," demonstrating "that people are paying attention" and ultimately giving a corrupt elite less "room to misuse the system." Similarly, the fact that President Asif Ali Zardari is "totally embattled " might also be a blessing in disguise, he says. "For the first time in my memory people seem to be demanding accountability."

In a 2010 poll, "less than a fifth of Pakistanis viewed the Taliban favorably," and "the masses do not want Islamist revolution," wrote Lieven. Furthermore, while extremists have infiltrated the military, "the Taliban could gain a meaningful political foothold . . . only after a large-scale military mutiny" that is unlikely to occur, he argues. [18]

"I would like to believe that at the end of the day logic" will keep the military from throwing in its lot with terrorist groups rather than the United States, says Shah. "They need their F-16s, they don't want to be [a state in chaos such as] Sudan."

Should the United States cut off aid to Pakistan?

Since the Abbottabad raid on bin Laden's hideout, debate has raged over whether U.S. aid should be discontinued.

"We've been providing billions of dollars . . . while they've been committing hostile acts behind our back," said Rep. Dana Rohrabacher, R-Calif., who introduced legislation (H.R. 1790) to cut off aid entirely, without giving Pakistan a chance to prove it merits such help, as some other lawmakers recommend. [19] Recent U.S. moves to redirect aid to civilian rather than military purposes is useless, wrote Nitin Pai, editor of *Pragati — The Indian National Interest Review*. "As long as the military establishment is in effective control of the administrative spigots, it can divert" cash, he said. Cutting off aid altogether, on the other hand, could induce Pakistanis "to force the army to change course." [20]

But cutting off aid, military or civilian, means "you've lost all your leverage," says the Stimson Center's Blechman.

"Economic sanctions are not really a credible threat, because the economic collapse of Pakistan would play straight into the hands" of terrorist groups the United States opposes, said Lieven. [21]

"Unless the U.S. military presence in Afghanistan is meant to be permanent . . . Pakistan's support for a peaceful and viable settlement in Afghanistan is a must,"

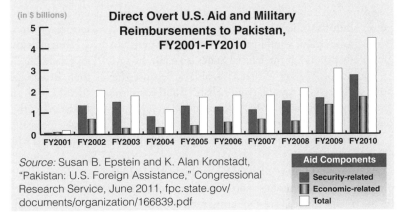

Pakistan Aid Tied to Anti-Terror Fight

U.S. military and economic aid to Pakistan rose sharply after the Sept. 11, 2001, terror attacks as the United States sought Pakistan's help in fighting Al Qaeda in neighboring Afghanistan. Aid totaled about $4.5 billion in fiscal 2010, about 50 percent more than the previous fiscal year alone as the newly elected Obama administration successfully sought increased economic and military aid.

Source: Susan B. Epstein and K. Alan Kronstadt, "Pakistan: U.S. Foreign Assistance," Congressional Research Service, June 2011, fpc.state.gov/documents/organization/166839.pdf

making the alliance necessary, wrote Hassan Abbas, a senior adviser at Harvard University's Belfer Center for Science and International Affairs. And, in fact, Pakistan has "paid a heavy price for supporting the U.S.-led 'war on terror' . . . [,] facing a brutal backlash from . . . militant and terrorist groups as well as a negative impact on its economy," he said. [22]

Many analysts argue for reshaping aid policies to focus on long-term economic development.

"Military assistance should be dramatically reduced," wrote Parag Khanna, a senior research fellow at the New American Foundation. [23]

Congress should make it clear that it will continue aid only if Pakistan makes changes the United States has sought, such as ditching propagandizing school textbooks that stoke antipathy toward Hindus, says Danielle Pletka, vice president for foreign and defense policy studies at the conservative American Enterprise Institute think tank. [24]

The Obama administration has recently indicated "that we're going to try to do a few big things that are important" with currently authorized aid, a welcome change, says the Middle East Institute's Weinbaum. In the past "We've disrupted the effectiveness of our aid by spreading money across too many projects," thus diluting its visibility and effectiveness, he says.

A single big project, such as building more electric-power capacity, would provide bang for the buck, says Najam. Pakistan's inadequate electricity system leaves residents to cope with five to 10 hours daily of "load shedding," or "rolling blackouts" — intentional localized power shutoffs undertaken to keep the system running. A new power plant would provide ordinary citizens tangible daily proof that the United States is an ally, he says.

Today, "people say, 'What U.S. aid?'" because they don't see its results, says Harvard's Shah. "Solid economic development that would reach down to local communities" would pay dividends, he says.

Others suggest looking beyond aid to improve the alliance.

"The biggest failure of the U.S. is the lack of public diplomacy" to counter false anti-American claims spread by the media, argues Pakistani army veteran Khan.

"Trade, not aid," should be the rallying cry, says Brookings' Riedel. Pakistan faces "a higher U.S. tariff on its products than India or China do," largely because "there is no effective Pakistan lobby in Congress," he says. If tariffs for Pakistani goods — mostly textiles — were lowered, "it could do a lot to help the economy and the entrepreneurial class over time," which would strengthen the push for democracy, he says.

Substituting favorable trade policies for aid would also limit the extent to which mostly U.S.-based contractors, rather than Pakistanis, end up with much of the aid cash, Riedel says.

"It would also help if the United States said clearly that 'we will deal with the military when it comes to Al Qaeda, but we'll regularly talk with the civilian government, too,'" on all topics, says Shah.

BACKGROUND

Birth of a Nation

When the United States and Pakistan first declared themselves allies in the 1950s, the United States was a superpower, locked in competition with the other reigning superpower, the Soviet Union. Pakistan, meanwhile, was emerging from

an independence struggle that left India as a bitter rival on its doorstep and regional disputes within. [25]

From the early 1800s through the mid-20th century, the dominant power in the Indian subcontinent was Great Britain. Despite its imperial reach, Britain held only loose sway over much of its empire, including territories in the north and west that, in 1947, became Pakistan. Today, the northwestern frontier areas, which border Afghanistan, are among the world's most prominent safe havens for terrorist groups.

British colonial rulers egged on religious communities, especially Hindus and Muslims, to view each other, rather than Britain, as their chief enemies, in an example of "divide and rule" thinking, wrote Hussain Haqqani, Pakistan's current ambassador to the United States. That legacy persists in the grudge match between Pakistan, formed as a Muslim nation, and India, a primarily Hindu one, he argued. [26]

Revolts against Britain erupted periodically in the 19th century, and, in 1885 the Indian National Congress Party was established, initially seeking more clout for locals in the colonial government but soon switching to a quest for independence. Hindus in the region outnumbered Muslims two to one, however, and in 1906, some Muslim politicians founded the All-India Muslim League to look after Muslim interests on the road to independence.

In 1936 and 1937, under Britain's aegis, provincial elections took place as a preparation for local rule. The Indian National Congress — led by Mohandas Gandhi — racked up big victories, but the Muslim League won few seats, even in Muslim-majority areas.

Following the losses, Muslim League President Muhammud Ali Jinnah "focused on religious differences" as a way to draw voters' support for the party, despite being a "quintessentially secular, rather than a religious, man himself," says Sumit Ganguly, a professor of political science at Indiana University in Bloomington. The strategy consolidated many Muslims into a voting bloc and ultimately led to formation of two separate nations, one Muslim, one mainly Hindu. Historians don't agree about whether this was Jinnah's intent, Ganguly says.

"River of Blood"

In 1946, hoping to keep the region a single state, the British suggested establishing a decentralized government that would allow localities substantial power. Both Jinnah and Congress Party chief Jawaharlal Nehru rejected the plan, and in July 1947 the area was "partitioned" into two nations: India occupied a large central area and Pakistan had two areas, West Pakistan, in the northwest, and the province of East Bengal — later East Pakistan and now Bangladesh — nearly 1,000 miles away, across India, to the east.

As a result, when independence came, 12 million panicking Muslims and Hindus rushed to relocate. "The border . . . became a river of blood, as the exodus erupted into rioting," said the BBC. [27] As many as a million people may have died.

In 1948, Jinnah died, leaving no blueprint for how the new state should develop.

Partly as a result, "the state got into a crisis within the first two years of its existence," says retired Brig. Gen. Khan.

Confusion about religion's role and traditions of tribal rather than central rule complicated Pakistan's development.

Pakistan "was created as a modern Muslim nation rather than a theological state," intended "to be neutral" in defending the rights of all residents to practice religion as they saw fit, "as Jinnah stated in unambiguous terms," says Khan. Pakistan's ideal should be that status as a citizen does not depend on belonging "to any religion or caste or creed," Jinnah declared in a 1947 address. [28]

Nevertheless, Pakistanis' views about religious tolerance varied, says Milam, of the Wilson Center. Pakistan's Constitution, for example — which aroused so much contention that it took nine years to complete — even defines one Muslim sect, the Ahmadis, as "non-Muslim," he notes. [29]

The new nation inherited a traditionally "clannish society" in which established elites hold power by passing out patronage spoils to a network of friends and relatives who then support them, says the Middle East Institute's Weinbaum. This tradition repeatedly dooms attempts to establish merit-based, democratic government, he says. Military leadership is also clan-based, "when you look at who they recruit from."

The clan system's strength is demonstrated by "the phenomenon of a woman such as Benazir Bhutto" — twice elected prime minister — "rising to the top of the political system in an extremely conservative male-dominated society," wrote the New America Foundation's

Minutes before she was assassinated, former Pakistani Prime Minister Benazir Bhutto addresses supporters in Rawalpindi on Dec. 27, 2007. Bhutto and her family were relatively progressive national leaders with close ties to the United States. U.S. intelligence officials suspect she was killed by Islamist military who viewed her as too friendly with the West.

Lieven. "This was power by inheritance," and no more a sign of advancing women's rights than was Queen Elizabeth I's inheritance of her throne from her father, Henry VIII, in 16th-century England, he said. [30]

"This is still a country run by a feudal elite," where wealth exists side by side with grinding poverty and powerlessness, says the Brookings Institution's Cohen.

Bhutto's father, Zulfikar Ali Bhutto, served as president and, later, prime minister in the 1970s, and her widower, Asif Ali Zardari, is Pakistan's current president. But while Bhutto family members have been relatively progressive national leaders, "they owned a massive spread" in Sindh province that exhibits Pakistan's underlying feudalism, says Milam. "You'll find no school there. They've done nothing to improve or develop" the region into a modern economy, he says.

Pakistan's founders "had little or no idea how to accommodate difference," with the consequence that "they hardly have an iota of democracy, even today" says Ganguly. This sets the stage for the civil service and military to run the country, he says.

India and the Bomb

By contrast, neighboring India "had a quite methodical" beginning, agreeing on a constitution by 1950 and holding its first elections in 1952, says the Wilson center's Kux.

India was also luckier in the partition, holding more territory that Britain had brought under centralized rule, says Ganguly. "Many parts of Pakistan had never been properly administered" and were difficult to govern, he says. Because of its location, India also inherited Britain's infrastructure, including government buildings, while Pakistan built from scratch.

"The Indians were rather niggardly when it came to handing over the spoils" from the departure of colonial governors, including money and supplies owed to Pakistan, Ganguly says. "There are stories about bureaucrats sitting on crates" because Indians refused to hand over office furniture.

Disputes over borders were not fully settled when independence came. They involved, for example, water rights to the Indus River that flows into Pakistan through India, as well as territories, mainly Kashmir, at Pakistan's and India's northern edges.

Before independence, Kashmir was a majority-Muslim region, ruled by a small Hindu elite. Both countries expected to receive it in the partition, but its Hindu maharajah signed a treaty granting it to India. Pakistan launched attacks, but India retaliated, winning control of more than half the territory. Called to mediate, the United Nations ordered a popular vote that India blocked. A ceasefire in 1948 ended the initial fighting, and treaties officially divided Kashmir. But conflict simmered, breaking into full-fledged wars in 1965 and 1999.

As part of the dispute, India and Pakistan have, since 1984, maintained military outposts on the "world's highest battlefield," the vast Siachen Glacier in disputed territory three miles above sea level in the Himalayan Mountains. Thousands have died there, where avalanches, altitude sickness and frostbite are soldiers' ruthless enemies. "It's totally insane to be fighting a war at these altitudes," said Rifaat Hussain, a professor of strategic studies at Quaid-i-Azam University in Islamabad. [31]

Each country blames the other for the continued hostilities.

"Pakistan has existed under the threat of invasion throughout its existence," and "since the mid-1980s six major military crises of varying degrees of intensity have forced Pakistan to consider physical invasion from India an existential threat in perpetuity," wrote Khan, in an expression of the Pakistani military's long-held view. [32]

India, meanwhile, "does not want to acknowledge that it has played any negative role," denying "any abuse of Kashmir," for instance, says Georgetown's Fair.

"The Pakistani state has evolved as a garrison, under threat," an idea that's "permeated textbooks that speak to the glory of the Islamic nation and the insidiousness of the Hindu state," says Harvard's Shah. Pakistanis are conditioned by a lifetime of such rhetoric, although "there's a growing recognition that this demonization has held Pakistan back, while [India's economy] has grown by nearly 10 percent a year," he says.

Widespread belief in an implacable Indian military threat has allowed Pakistan's military to force elected officials to do its bidding, says Shah. That's true even though the Pakistan People's Party, the country's largest, "has a radically different view," favoring establishing India as a trading partner, he says.

Nuclear arsenals back the longstanding enmity.

Neither India nor Pakistan has signed the 1968 Nuclear Nonproliferation Treaty to limit the spread of nuclear weapons, and both have substantial nuclear arsenals, with Pakistan's the larger. At least one Pakistani nuclear expert, A. Q. Khan, helped spread nuclear-arms technology to countries including Libya, Iran and North Korea in the 1990s. [33]

"If we're lucky the nukes will cancel each other out," says the Middle East Institute's Weinbaum.

"When the U.S. pulls out of Afghanistan in 2014 or 2015, we'll have a Pakistan with 115 [nuclear] weapons, more than England or France," says Zia Mian, director of Princeton University's Program on Science and Global Security.

In the case of a relatively weak country with nuclear arms, the old principle that such weapons deter conventional warfare doesn't hold, and more conventional fighting takes place than there would be otherwise, contends S. Paul Kapur, an associate professor of national security at the Naval Postgraduate School.

"A weak power like Pakistan uses the nuke as a backstop that allows it to behave more aggressively toward its

CHRONOLOGY

1940s *British rule ends in India; partition creates Pakistan.*

1947 Pakistan is created by combining regions in India widely separated geographically and culturally.

1948 Pakistan's legendary first governor general, Muhammad Ali Jinnah, dies. . . . First war with India over disputed territory of Kashmir.

1950s-1970s *United States enlists Pakistan as ally in Cold War.*

1956 Constitution adopted, establishing Pakistan as Islamic republic.

1965 Second war with India over Kashmir; Pakistan outraged over absence of U.S. assistance.

1971 East Pakistan secedes, becoming new nation of Bangladesh.

1979 Pakistani student group burns U.S. Embassy in Islamabad, killing two Americans. . . . United States suspends all aid except flood assistance over human-rights violations. . . . Soviet Union invades Afghanistan.

1980s *United States increases aid to Pakistan as it becomes staging ground for militant groups fighting the Soviets.*

1990s *Soviets depart Afghanistan in defeat.*

1990 United States suspends aid, declaring that Pakistan has secretly advanced its nuclear weapons program.

1999 United States reduces aid after Gen. Pervez Musharraf overthrows democratically elected Nawaz Sharif.

2000s *United States seeks Pakistan's help fighting Islamic terror groups.*

2001 Musharraf promises support for anti-terror fight.

2003 United States forgives $1 billion of Pakistan debt as reward for anti-terror assistance.

2004 Pakistani nuclear scientist Abdul Qadeer Khan admits leaking nuclear-weapons information, possibly to Libya, North Korea and Iran. . . . Pakistan attacks Al Qaeda militants near Afghan border.

2007 Public outcry follows Musharraf's suspension of Supreme Court Chief Justice Iftikhar Chaudry. . . . Musharraf secretly discusses sharing power with ex-prime minister Benazir Bhutto. . . . Pakistani army fights militants in North Waziristan, a stronghold of pro-Al Qaeda groups. . . . Bhutto, recently returned from exile, assassinated.

2008 U.S. airstrike on Afghan-Pakistan border kills 10 members of Pakistan's Frontier Corps. . . . After terrorist attacks kill 174 people in Mumbai, India says attackers have Pakistani ties.

2009 President Barack Obama vows United States will take long-term view of the U.S.-Pakistan alliance, focusing on economic and political development rather than short-term military goals. . . . Militants kill 40 in attack on Pakistani police academy in Lahore. . . . U.S. drone attack in South Waziristan kills powerful Pakistan Taliban leader Baitullah Mehsud.

2010 Joint raid by U.S. and Pakistani intelligence forces captures Afghan Taliban's second in command, Abdul Ghani Baradar. . . . Worst floods in 80 years inundate one-fifth of Pakistan, with economic damages exceeding $40 billion; government assistance fails to reach many; United States provides about $600 million in aid.

2011 CIA contractor Raymond Davis kills two Pakistani men he said tried to rob him; Pakistani officials allow Davis to leave without a trial. . . . Pakistan Taliban claims responsibility for the apparently religiously motivated assassination of Minorities Minister Shahbaz Bhatti, the only Christian in Pakistan's cabinet. . . . U.S. Navy Seals raid a house in Abbottabad, Pakistan, and kill Al Qaeda leader Osama bin Laden; some U.S. lawmakers vow to cut off aid, charging Pakistan protected bin Laden. . . . Obama administration withholds more than a third of military aid ($800 million) to pressure Pakistan to cooperate on anti-terrorism; U.S. civilian aid continues. . . . Indian Prime Minister Manmohan Singh opens talks with Pakistan on improving relations.

Pakistanis Hold Mixed Views of Terror Groups

Government supports some militants for political reasons.

Ever since the Al Qaeda attacks on New York City and the Pentagon in 2001, the United States has sought Pakistan's help in eliminating militant Islamic groups, many of which operate in Pakistan's outlying northern and western areas.

But Pakistan has its own way of viewing the militants. It feverishly fights some extremist groups while turning a blind eye to others for political reasons.

Since the United States went to war in Afghanistan after the 9/11 attacks, pledging to stop Al Qaeda, Pakistan has become a haven for "an ever more lethal stew" of Al Qaeda operatives, Uzbek militants, Afghani and Pakistani Taliban and local tribal militants, wrote Zahid Hussain, senior editor of the Karachi-based online newsmagazine *Newsline* and a scholar at the Woodrow Wilson International Center in Washington. An estimated 10,000 to 15,000 militants now operate from within Pakistan, mostly in its loosely governed, far-western territories, said Hussain. [1]

The militants, a growing number of whom are now migrating into Pakistani cities, fall into five general categories, according to C. Christine Fair, an assistant professor of security studies at Georgetown University. Pakistan actively opposes the first two groups, which it views as enemies of the state:

• Al Qaeda operatives based in Pakistan but generally not native Pakistanis. They "work with and through

networks of supportive Pakistani militant groups," planning international attacks and, increasingly, carrying out attacks in Pakistan alongside other groups that oppose the Pakistani government, Fair told the Senate Foreign Relations Committee in May. [2]

• The Pakistan Taliban, also called the Tehreek-e-Taliban-e-Pakistan (TTP), which emerged around 2004 inside Pakistan and has since conducted an increasingly violent insurgency against the government.

The three other categories of militant groups cited by Fair are viewed by Pakistan as much less likely to oppose the government, which in some cases has seen them as supporters of Pakistan's geopolitical goals. As a result, Pakistan generally has not fought these groups, although recently some have attacked targets in Pakistan itself, according to Fair. The three categories are:

• The Afghan Taliban, conservative Islamists who fight mainly to control Afghanistan's government after the United States departs. These extremists frequently take sanctuary in Pakistan. But Pakistan doesn't fight them because it sees them as potential allies in its struggle to keep India from seizing power in Afghanistan.

• Groups representing either Islam's Sunni or Shia sect. Members of one sect attack those in the other in a rivalry carried on for decades throughout the Muslim world.

stronger enemy," Kapur argues. Because "India realizes that full-blown war" could expose it to a nuclear blast, it holds back its firepower when Pakistan attacks, he says. That dynamic has helped lead to nearly constant low-level conflict over the decades, Kapur says.

Troubled Alliances

Pakistan's on-again, off-again alliance with the United States began in the early 1950s, when the United States sought support to fight communism's spread, says Kux of the Wilson center. Located just south of the Soviet Union, Pakistan was a handy U.S. listening post and air base for U-2 spy planes. Pakistan, meanwhile, hoped the alliance could strengthen its hand against India.

While Pakistan initially sought the alliance, "the Democrats kept putting them off and wouldn't commit to a military relationship," says Kux. But when President Dwight D. Eisenhower took office in 1953, "Republicans saw it differently." Secretary of State John Foster Dulles "thought neutrality [in the Cold War, which India maintained] was immoral" and, partly on those grounds, entered a military alliance with India's chief rival, he says.

"Dulles never committed the United States to come to Pakistan's military aid against India," but only agreed to protect Pakistan against communist attack, in keeping with overall U.S. Cold War strategy, says Kux. Pakistan, however, didn't really register the caveat and felt betrayed on several occasions when the United States failed to send

• Islamist groups such as the Jamaat-e-Islami and Lashkar-e-Taiba (LeT) that declare that their goal is to force India to leave Kashmir, which Pakistan and India have fought over since they became independent nations in 1947. Fair calls the LeT "the most lethal terrorist group operating in and from South Asia."

Some groups in this last category sprang up on their own, but "most came into being as surrogates of Pakistan's intelligence agency" and thus are not treated as enemies by the Pakistani military, said Fair. While the groups claim to focus on Kashmir, however, their operations are expanding, with some carrying out terror attacks in India and fighting U.S. forces in Afghanistan.

Fair said some of the Kashmir-focused groups also now work against Pakistan itself, in apparent retaliation against its "participation in the U.S.-led global war on terrorism."[3] That does not include the dangerous LeT, however, which Fair says has "tight linkages" with Pakistan's own security forces.

Like their government, the Pakistani public has a far more complicated attitude toward militant groups than Americans generally realize. Few support militancy generally, as some in the United States fear. However, many do "support small militant organizations when those organizations use violence to achieve political goals the individual cares about," wrote Fair and Jacob N. Shapiro, an assistant professor of politics at Princeton University.[4]

The nuanced views aren't surprising, Shapiro and Fair wrote. "Someone who supports a group operating in Kashmir because they believe that Kashmiris living under Indian control are grievously abused . . . need not have any strong feelings toward the Afghan Taliban," for example, they argued.[5]

That being the case, there's no simple way to dissuade average Pakistanis from supporting some militant groups, as U.S. lawmakers, among others, might hope, Shapiro and Fair said. "Much can be done, however, to address political factors that drive support for militancy, such as corruption, human rights abuses, lack of security, limited access to the rule of law and longstanding geopolitical disputes," such as the standoff between India and Pakistan over Kashmir, they argued.[6]

— *Marcia Clemmitt*

[1]Zahid Hussain, *The Scorpion's Tail: The Relentless Rise of Islamic Militants in Pakistan — and How it Threatens America* (2010), p. 3.

[2]C. Christine Fair, testimony before U.S. Senate Foreign Relations Committee, May 24, 2011, www.humansecuritygateway.com/documents/US-Senate-Foreign-Relations-Fair-Testimony-Lashkar-e-Taiba-Region-International-Community.pdf.

[3]*Ibid.*

[4]Jacob N. Shapiro and C. Christine Fair, "Why Pakistanis Support Islamist Militancy," Harvard University Belfer Center Website, Feb. 10, 2010, http://belfercenter.ksg.harvard.edu/publication/19922/why_pakistanis_support_islamist_militancy.html.

[5]Jacob N. Shapiro and C. Christine Fair, "Why Support Islamist Militancy? Evidence from Pakistan," May 18, 2009, www.princeton.edu/~jns/papers/Shapiro_Fair_2009_Why_Support_Islamist_Militancy.pdf.

[6]Shapiro and Fair, *op. cit.*, Feb. 10, 2010.

help, Kux says. That fact has contributed to the long, downward spiral of the alliance over the decades, he says. The relationship has repeatedly waxed and waned. In the early 1970s, President Richard Nixon strengthened the tie to gain Pakistan's help in opening relations with communist China, on Pakistan's northeast border. The relationship soured in 1977 when President Jimmy Carter's foreign policy stressed democratic institutions, human rights and nonproliferation of nuclear weapons. "Pakistan struck out on all three," Kux says.

Beginning in 1979, the Soviet Union deployed troops in Afghanistan, Pakistan's western neighbor, to help a fledgling socialist government squelch rebellion. In response, the CIA secretly began to fund and train Muslim groups — the so-called Afghan mujahedeen — for guerrilla warfare against the Soviets. Much of the training took place in Pakistan, where many Afghan refugees had fled.

Soon the United States was giving Pakistan $600 million in aid annually, half to the military and half designated as economic, says Kux.

In 1989, a battered Soviet army retreated, and the United States once again lost interest in South Asia. Meanwhile, a decade of guerrilla warfare, with Pakistan as the staging area, had seen numerous militant groups spring up in Pakistan's northwestern territories. Many of the groups were jihadists, engaged in a struggle to defend Islam, while some focused on regional or ethnic grievances.

Bloody Regional Conflicts Color Pakistan's History

Ethnic factionalism has been biggest obstacle to peace and stability.

Ever since Pakistan's 1947 independence, its status as a functioning nation has been threatened less by foreign enemies or militant Islamists than by internal strife.

Cobbled together from territories in India with Muslim-majority populations that were differently managed by the British colonial government and that harbored a range of ethnic and tribal grievances, Pakistan has struggled to make a functioning whole out of a geographic and ethnic hodgepodge. [1]

At independence, the new nation consisted of two areas widely separated by not only geography but also ethnic prejudice. West Pakistan was located in the northwest Indian subcontinent, while the densely populated province of East Bengal — later East Pakistan and now Bangladesh — lay far to the east, separated from the rest of the country by nearly 1,000 miles of territory belonging to Pakistan's chief rival, India.

Ostensibly bound by a shared Muslim tradition, East and West Pakistan in fact were light years apart culturally.

West Pakistan consisted of many ethnic groups, of which Punjabis and Pathans were the most numerous, with Kashmiris and Sindhis also in the mix. Most Punjabis and Pathans "never really thought of the East Bengalis as fellow countrymen or even true Muslims," wrote Anatol Lieven, a professor of war studies at King's College, in London, and a senior research fellow at the New America Foundation, a centrist think tank in Washington. The Punjabis and Pathans also "shared much British racial contempt for" the Bengalis "and contrasted their alleged passivity with the supposedly virile qualities of the ethnicities dubbed by the British as 'martial,' the Punjabis and Pathans," Lieven wrote. [2]

From the bifurcated nation's inception, contempt for Bengalis led to mistreatment by the central government, located in West Pakistan.

"East Pakistan pays most of Pakistan's taxes, provides most of the sterling and dollar earnings, but gets the short end of revenues," *Time* magazine reported in 1954. "Even in his own area, the East Pakistani feels like a second-class citizen, exploited by carpetbagger" West Pakistanis, "who hold most of the top government posts and most of the top police jobs. [3]

"Last week the news seeped through tight censorship that East Pakistan's hatred had flared into appalling bloodshed," when "the owners of the world's newest, biggest jute mill at Narayanganj, East Pakistan, pampered their imported West Pakistan workers, gave them better jobs and a higher wage scale than the East Pakistan Bengalis," *Time* continued. When frustrated Bengalis responded with violence, the West Pakistanis in charge answered with greater violence.

Soon "two Bengali villages were in ashes, the water in two hyacinth-covered ponds was red from the blood of floating bodies," as many as 1,000 Bengalis were dead, and newspapers in West Pakistan "thundered for punitive martial law in the east." [4]

The conflict between the young country's two halves seethed for another 17 years, with occasional violent outbreaks and ongoing economic exploitation of East Pakistan by the central government in the West. In December 1971, the situation flamed into war in the east after India intervened in favor of rebelling Bengalis. West Pakistan's army, far from its base and surrounded by enemies, soon lost the fight, and West Pakistan lost the province, which became the independent nation of Bangladesh.

West Pakistan's harsh treatment of Bengal casts doubt on the whole effort to unify the nation around Islam, argues Sumit Ganguly, a professor of political science at Indiana University in Bloomington. "If you're so concerned about Muslims," Ganguly asks, "why did the Bengalis leave you" in 1971 amid international cries of a "Bengali genocide"?

The Bengali east is not the only region where Pakistan's fractures are exposed.

Before the British extended colonial rule throughout the Indian subcontinent in the 18th and 19th centuries, the sparsely populated tribal areas along the northern and western border of what is now Pakistan "had jirgas — councils — that met to make decisions" with input from the local clans, says Kimberly Marten, a professor of political science at Barnard College, Columbia University, in New York. "Nobody was set up as a particularly permanent leader" or was able to completely consolidate power in most of the region now known as the FATA, or Federally Administered Tribal Areas, Marten says. But the British colonial government essentially replaced the more deliberative, jirga-based governance system and consolidated power under hereditary tribal leaders, Marten says.

The British sought to govern remote regions while dealing with as few locals as possible, she says. To that end, they analyzed each locality to determine which family most often came out on top in disputes. They then established a system of inherited power in which colonial officials would deal only with these handpicked leaders and reward them — and their descendants — with arms and other resources to help them hold power securely. Thus was the system of all-powerful local tribal warlords born, Marten says.

"If somebody created a problem for the British," the local British-approved "malik" — or chieftain — would impose a remedy for which the accused "had no appeal," she says. The central colonial government "didn't penetrate there. It was the official maliks who alone decided what the law said."

At Pakistan's independence, the tradition continued, at least partly because it "proved effective for Pakistan when they wanted to fight off foreign powers," says Marten. For example, in 1948 "Pakistan got the maliks to send troops to fight" in the disputed territory of Kashmir.

But there's a price to pay, says Marten. With power in the hands of wealthy, hereditary mini-monarchies, "there has been no penetration of state institutions" such as schools or courts into many areas and thus little chance for those areas to develop into modern societies. The system creates "extreme resentment," says Marten. "People know what the rest of the world is like" and know they haven't gained any benefits of modernity, she says.

Meanwhile, another western border region, the vast province of Balochistan, has waged an independence battle that dates back to Pakistan's own independence and has recently grown bloodier, according to the human rights organization Amnesty International.

Every month between October 2010 and February 2011, there was "an increase in the cases of alleged disappearances and unlawful killings" of Baloch residents, whose

A Bengali woman performs a traditional dance during the spring festival in Dhaka, capital of Bangladesh, on Feb. 13, 2010. Hostility between the Punjabis and Pathans of West Pakistan and the Bengalis of East Pakistan (now Bangladesh) led to war in 1971.

bodies often turn up later showing signs of torture, said Sam Zarifi, Amnesty's Asia-Pacific director. [5]

Baloch groups blame the killings on Pakistani security forces, which deny the allegations. Nevertheless, "many of the victims were abducted by [the] uniformed Frontier Corps " — a paramilitary group from Pakistan's outlying territories that was founded by the British colonial government in 1907 and is currently supported by both the Pakistani and U.S. governments — "in front of multiple witnesses," Amnesty reports. Meanwhile, "armed Baloch groups have also been implicated in a surge in targeted killings of non-Baloch civilians and government employees, including teachers. . . . bringing the education system to [a] breaking point," says the group. [6]

— Marcia Clemmitt

[1] For background, see Iftikhar Malik, *The History of Pakistan* (2008).

[2] Anatol Lieven, *Pakistan: A Hard Country* (2011), Kindle Edition, Location 275.

[3] "Pakistan: Butchery in Bengal," *Time*, May 31, 1954, www.time.com/time/magazine/article/0,9171,819913,00.html.

[4] *Ibid.*

[5] "Pakistan Must Provide Accountability for Rising Atrocities in Balochistan," press statement, Amnesty International, Feb. 23, 2011, www.amnesty.org/en/news-and-updates/pakistan-must-provide-accountability-rising-atrocities-balochistan-2011-02-23.

[6] *Ibid.*

AFP/Getty Images/Aamir Qureshi

U.S. Navy Seal commandos killed Al Qaeda leader Osama bin Laden in a raid on this house in Abbottabad, Pakistan, on May 2. Conducted without the Pakistani Army's knowledge, the raid inflamed longstanding tensions between the United States and Pakistan and weakened the shaky alliance between the two countries in the fight against Islamic extremism.

Pakistan's military and the ISI have covertly used such groups to pursue geopolitical goals as far back as 1947, when the new government inherited from Britain vast areas that were home to warring clans. [34] Over the years, many such groups have been useful to Pakistan in pursuing border disputes with India and Afghanistan and squelching uprisings in the territories, leading the government to aim at "containing rather than destroying them," says the Middle East Institute's Weinbaum.

In 2001, the United States declared a "war on terror" and sought Pakistan's cooperation in eliminating all militant groups in the region. But, while promising — and providing — cooperation, Pakistan fought some groups while tolerating and supporting others that it believed would act in, not against, Pakistan's interest.

Pakistan has not fought the Afghan Taliban, for example, which arose in the 1990s to oppose a socialist-leaning Afghan government left by the Soviets. Because the other major Afghan rebel group, the Northern Alliance, is allied with India, Pakistan has regarded the Afghan Taliban as its sole hedge against Afghanistan becoming a permanent Indian ally after the United States departs.

Some members of Pakistan's military and intelligence services apparently have allied themselves with the Lashkar-e-Taiba, which formed around 1990 with the stated

mission of forcing India to cede Kashmir to Pakistan's control. The group is suspected of having connections to numerous violent acts, including the devastating November 2008 attacks on India's largest city, Mumbai. [35]

"All this creates a problem with us, because we're against terrorism," says the Wilson center's Kux. Nevertheless, it's "also partly our fault. When we were leaning on the Pakistanis" to push the Soviets from Afghanistan, "they were leaning on the Taliban" to actually do the job.

CURRENT SITUATION

Trouble at Home

Pakistan's attempt to handle various militant groups in different ways has led to complications.

Some groups considered friendly to Pakistan now mount attacks against national institutions. And some declare their intent to push ultra-conservative Islamic rule into the Pakistani mainstream, attacking girls' schools, for example. Meanwhile, many see the U.S.-Pakistan alliance crumbling as many Americans condemn Pakistan for harboring bin Laden. [36]

On May 23, three weeks after the Abbottabad raid that killed bin Laden, militants attacked Pakistan's heavily guarded Mehran naval air base near Karachi, destroying two aircraft and killing several members of the armed forces.

The attackers belonged to the Taliban's Pakistan wing, an Al Qaeda-affiliated group that Pakistan has fought, not to the Afghan Taliban, which Pakistan has tolerated if not encouraged. Both Taliban groups draw their members from the same ethnic tribe, the Pashtuns, whose traditional lands span the Pakistan-Afghan border. The attack by the Pakistan Taliban "was the revenge of martyrdom of Osama bin Laden" and "proof that we are still united and powerful," a spokesman for the group told Reuters. [37]

The naval-base attack alarmed Pakistanis. Early press reports suggested that India was involved, while subsequent reports raised the likelihood that the attackers had help from military insiders. "Did the Taliban raiders have information inside the naval base? Such a possibility cannot be ruled out, because the involvement of serving personnel in several previous attacks has been well established," wrote the English-language paper *Dawn.* [38]

Should the United States cut off aid to Pakistan?

YES
Rep. Dana Rohrabacher, R-Calif.
Chairman, House Foreign Relations Oversight and Investigations Subcommittee

Written for *CQ Researcher*, July 2011

Pakistan is not a friend of the United States. It has very different strategic interests. Over the past decade we have given Pakistan $18 billion to buy their help in the War on Terrorism, and it has become increasingly clear that strategy has failed. In the aftermath of the Navy Seal raid on Osama bin Laden's hideout, Islamabad demanded the U.S. reduce the number of our personnel in Pakistan. They arrested informants who helped us locate Bin Laden, after Pakistan gave him safe harbor for years. Mike Rodgers, R-Mich., chairman of the House Permanent Select Committee on Intelligence, said he believes "there are elements of both the [Pakistani] military and intelligence service who in some way, both before and maybe even currently, provided some assistance to bin Laden." That is putting it mildly; the Pakistan's intelligence service is the Taliban.

Joint Chiefs of Staff Chairman Adm. Michael Mullen said in a newspaper interview, "It's fairly well known that the ISI [Directorate of Inter-Services Intelligence] has a longstanding relationship with the Haqqani network. . . . Haqqani is supporting, funding and training fighters that are killing Americans and . . . coalition partners." It is suspected that Pakistan tips off insurgent groups about raids U.S., Afghan and coalition forces are planning. *The Wall Street Journal* reported the Pakistani prime minister traveled to Kabul and told Afghan President Hamid Karzai not to cooperate with America and to move towards their friends the Chinese.

Another example of Pakistan's divergent interests is its alignment with Communist China, against their common enemy India. Recently the Pakistani ambassador in Beijing said the relationship with China "is higher than the mountains, deeper than the oceans, stronger than steel, dearer than eyesight, sweeter than honey and so on." In contrast, the Pakistani prime minister has reportedly denounced America's "imperial designs."

The China-Pakistan alliance has included intelligence sharing, nuclear weapons development, infrastructure expansion, military training, arms sales and defense industrial cooperation. Their imperial design is to control Afghanistan (the reason Pakistan created the Taliban), drive out Western influence and contain India. Building the Gwadar naval base is part of China's "String of Pearls" strategy that includes bases in Burma, Sri Lanka, Bangladesh and elsewhere to contain India. American aid has not pulled Pakistan away from this alliance; it has only served to subsidize it and China's hegemonic designs.

Recognizing that our strategic interests are no longer in Pakistan is long overdue, which is why I have introduced House Resolution 1790 to cut off all financial aid.

NO
Lisa Curtis
Senior Research Fellow for South Asia, Heritage Foundation

Written for *CQ Researcher*, July 2011

Cutting off all U.S. aid to Pakistan would spell disaster for U.S. interests in the region. But sticking with the status quo — providing generous assistance to a country with an increasingly defiant posture toward the United States — also makes little sense.

The Obama administration's announcement earlier this month that it planned to withhold $800 million in military aid to Pakistan sends a signal that the current state of affairs between the two countries is no longer sustainable. U.S. security assistance to Pakistan is legally conditioned on it meeting counterterrorism benchmarks, and we ought to hold firmly to the letter of the law.

The recent reduction in security assistance makes sense, especially in light of Pakistan's expulsion of 150 U.S. and British military trainers from the country and reports about Pakistani officials alerting terrorists to U.S. information on bomb-making facilities in the tribal border areas.

But the United States must balance the need to demonstrate dissatisfaction with Pakistani actions with the goal of encouraging Pakistan to develop into a stable, moderate and economically vibrant country at peace with its neighbors. Strengthening Pakistan's democratic institutions and civilian authorities offers the best chance to create a functional, mutually beneficial relationship. And the U.S. diminishes the chances of pushing the relationship in this direction if it only pursues punitive measures.

Abruptly stopping all aid would also come at a steep price. Pakistan could react by cutting off NATO supply lines that run through Pakistan to coalition troops in Afghanistan. In addition, it may expel U.S. intelligence officials, thus denying the United States access to valuable information that helps the CIA track terrorists.

The U.S. has a broader interest in maintaining steady relations with Pakistan and encouraging stability in the nuclear-armed nation of 180 million. If the U.S. were to cut all aid to Pakistan and prevail on the International Monetary Fund and World Bank to do the same, the Pakistani economy would teeter on the brink of collapse. The chances of Pakistan's nuclear arsenal falling into terrorist hands, while currently remote, would increase.

The United States must carefully calibrate its large-scale aid programs to Pakistan in a way that helps shape their policies toward terrorism and at the same time assures them of U.S. goodwill and interest in maintaining close ties over the long term. The strategy may not succeed, but it is worth a try.

Eight days after the attack, Syed Saleem Shahzad, Pakistan bureau chief for the newspaper *Asia Times Online*, turned up dead and tortured in a canal 90 miles from Pakistan's capital, Islamabad. Shahzad had reported on alleged links between terrorists and the military and told friends that intelligence agents had threatened him. [39]

The "deeper underlying motive" behind the attack on the naval air base "was a reaction to massive internal crackdowns" by the navy on Al Qaeda sympathizers in its ranks, Shahzad had written on May 27, two days before he disappeared. Navy insiders affiliated with terror groups provided information that helped militants enter and seize the base, he wrote. [40]

Some groups in Pakistan also signal their intention to institute conservative Islamic law and squelch religious tolerance. In January, Salman Taseer, liberal governor of Pakistan's most economically developed and populous province, Punjab, was assassinated by his bodyguard, apparently as retribution for his having supported a Christian woman whom clerics accused of heresy, which is punishable by death. [41]

The bodyguard "had gone through the same security program that the people guarding Pakistan's nuclear weapons have gone through," evidence of the dire possibilities inherent in the rising Pakistani-on-Pakistani violence, observes the Stimson Center's Blechman.

Acts of violence and religious intolerance once confined to remote border regions are creeping closer to urban areas, says Weinbaum, of the Middle East Institute. In the past, he says, Pakistanis "could more easily dismiss these things, saying, 'Well, everybody's crazy out there.'" But in 2009, when video surfaced of Taliban men publicly flogging a 17-year-old girl accused of sexual immorality a mere 60 miles from Islamabad, the "video turned many people against them" for the first time, he says.

Increasingly, it becomes clear "that if you let these people continue to share influence, eventually you'll have to share power with them," says Weinbaum. At least one militant group has declared that "we're coming to Islamabad to change the constitution," he says. Pakistan's leaders have likely "created a monster that eventually will turn on them."

It's unclear how the public will respond to militant groups' changing goals and strategies.

Nearly two-thirds of Pakistan's population is under age 25, and many "are unemployed. They're very angry. Many don't have the education they need" to succeed in a technological world, says retired Brig. Gen. Khan. Such conditions can fuel anti-establishment views, including sympathy for militant groups, he says.

While some Pakistanis blame India or the United States for rising troubles, "most of Pakistan's problems are home-grown," including the long tradition of cronyism that stints public investment and rewards a favored few, says the Brookings Institution's Riedel. Because of what's essentially mass tax evasion on the part of Pakistan's elite, "only 2 percent of the population pays taxes," a dangerous situation that is one of the largest threats to stability, he says.

U.S. Aid

In the wake of bin Laden's death, some members of Congress called for ending aid to Pakistan. In July the Obama administration suspended, at least temporarily, $800 million in military aid. [42]

"I don't think our military assistance is serving the interests we are intending it to serve," said Rep. Howard Berman, D-Calif. "What I'm asking the administration to do is focus on getting Pakistan to . . . go after extremist groups. If they're not successful, we should reconsider giving this money." [43]

Ironically, the calls to cut off aid come just as many South Asia experts say U.S. policy is improving, after many past blunders.

Previous U.S. policy "encouraged the dysfunctional civilian-military relationship," but "the Obama administration is making efforts, though it hasn't made a breakthrough, to change the pattern," says Riedel.

"[Secretary of State] Hillary Clinton has said some spectacular things and means them," such as reiterating that "while there is a war on terror, we also want to make Pakistan's governance better" and seek a long-term relationship, says Najam of Lahore University of Management Sciences.

"There's a growing realization in D.C. that Washington's method of engagement has boosted the military's credibility" in Pakistan, giving it "leeway to do whatever it wants to do domestically," says Harvard's Shah. That approach, he says, has curtailed development of Pakistan's democracy and its economy.

The Enhanced Partnership with Pakistan Act, which authorizes $1.5 billion in annual nonmilitary aid from

2010 through 2014, is a step in the right direction, some analysts say. [44]

The legislation "took all the things that people like me had been saying should be done," such as focusing on civilian development aid, says Najam.

The legislation attempts to set up mechanisms to ensure that aid goes where it's supposed to, a step that many say they'll welcome, if it works. "When you look at the other post-2001 aid, there was $750 million a year in nonmilitary aid, and nobody ever saw it," says Weinbaum. "How much even got into the country, since so much was siphoned off into contractors? Maybe a third?"

The aid law's reception in Pakistan has been anything but warm, however, especially from the Pakistani military and some political parties, which have complained that the accountability provisions smack of colonialism. "This is less an assistance program than a treaty of surrender," wrote Ayaz Amir, a journalist and member of Pakistan's Parliament. [45]

The negative reaction "surprised everyone," says Najam. "Instead of sending a thank you note, there were new critics." He blames the skepticism partly on the country's weak democracy. "When people don't believe that anyone will give them a fair deal, it lowers trust in everything," such as by "causing people to assume that the United States is always doing the worst things they can possibly do" to Pakistanis, he says.

In response to critics, two of the law's chief architects, Sen. Kerry, D-Mass., and Rep. Berman, issued a statement declaring that the "legislation does not seek in any way to compromise Pakistan's sovereignty . . . or micromanage any aspect of Pakistani military or civilian operations." [46]

Harvard's Shah calls the backpedaling a "huge mistake, reinforcing the idea that the military can get away with murder" simply by raising a ruckus about U.S. policies it doesn't like.

It will take time for Pakistanis to adjust to the troubling notion that the growing violence they face comes from Muslim groups, not from the United States or Hindu India, says Shah. "The media play a nasty, jingoistic theme," blaring conspiracy theories such as that "the U.S. is coming after our nukes," and those messages reinforce what "people were taught to believe since they were children — that Muslims don't kill Muslims," while non-Muslims do, he says. "The Iraq War, the things that have happened to Palestinians" have bolstered such

thinking as well, says Shah. "It's simply easier to believe that somebody else is doing it — easier to believe that it cannot be our guys."

OUTLOOK

Accord with India

Unless relations between Pakistan and India improve, Pakistan's future, and peace in the region, will continue to be at risk.

How India and Pakistan negotiate water rights for the Indus River will have a huge effect on both nations, especially Pakistan, which faces devastating water shortages as its population swells, says Brookings' Cohen. The two countries "operate one of the largest irrigation systems in the world, but there is no cooperation" currently on a management plan to sustain it, he says.

Pakistan's military is likely to continue to cooperate with some violent groups as long as the military remains fixated on India as the nations' chief enemy, many analysts say.

"The army has brainwashed themselves on India," says the Wilson center's Kux.

Persuading the public that India is a frightening, close-by enemy has solidified the military's hold on power, many analysts say.

"The military is the largest property holder and the largest highway builder, and the officer corps has the only health insurance" in the country. So it's "no wonder they like the status quo," says Brookings' Riedel.

Meanwhile, "India is very concerned that Pakistan will continue to wage asymmetric warfare" on it by surreptitiously supporting militant groups, says Kapur, of the U.S. Naval Postgraduate School. Leaders of the 2008 Mumbai attacks, for example, are believed to have significant Pakistani connections, although Pakistani military and intelligence officials largely deny the links. [47]

Opinions vary on what role the United States should play in resolving the Pakistan-India conflict. "Leaving India and Pakistan alone to do it on their own, as has been done, is counterproductive to the U.S.," says the Postgraduate School's Khan.

The United States should "become more active" in discussion but should not take an official mediating role, says Riedel. The U.S. should focus on coming up with "creative ideas for dealing with Kashmir" and "being a cheerleader for bilateral actions by Pakistan and India" to overcome differences, he says.

"We have a window of opportunity" because Indian Prime Minister Manmohan Singh, a Sikh who is the first non-Hindu to hold the office, "re-engaged Pakistan this spring," says Riedel. "We have to encourage Singh and [Pakistan President] Zardari to reach deals that they can present to the Indian and Pakistani people, starting with easy stuff like transportation — creating more crossing routes over the border, for example — and trade," he says.

Facilitating development of more commercial air routes would be a small step that would improve the reputation of both governments, says Riedel. "It's easier to fly from the United States to any country in Europe or Latin American than it is to fly between India and Pakistan," he says. "You have to fly to Doha" in Qatar or elsewhere in the Middle East or Asia, then double back.

Others dismiss the possibility of peace. "The enmity has gotten worse" in recent years, says Ganguly, of Indiana University. Singh "is on a fool's errand, thinking he can bring about rapprochement. I don't think that's going to happen."

Pakistanis' growing mistrust of the United States, exacerbated by a warming U.S.-India relationship, also presents problems.

American policymakers are "largely unaware that, because of our new wonderful relationship with India, Pakistan perceives us as having sided with them," says Brookings' Cohen. "We must talk with both."

"I'm not optimistic" that the trust issue can be overcome, "given how policy is made, particularly at the congressional level," says Georgetown's Fair. India has a large lobbying presence, recently "tutored by the [highly effective] Israeli lobby," while Pakistan has little Washington clout, "so the policy process is skewed toward India." Furthermore, "we have pretty much signaled that we have no problem with India being a regional hegemon" — the dominant South Asian state — "but we get annoyed when Pakistan makes childlike overtures to China."

India, meanwhile, "believes that it's a global power with Pakistan as an albatross around its neck. So, rather than looking at the outstanding issues, it hopes they'll simply go away and puts off negotiating with Pakistan because tomorrow Pakistan will be weaker," Fair says.

NOTES

1. Remarks by the President on Osama Bin Laden, The White House Blog, May 2, 2011, www.whitehouse.gov/blog/2011/05/02/osama-bin-laden-dead.

2. Peter Walker, "Osama bin Laden Lived in Two Rooms for Five Years, Wife Says," *The Guardian* [United Kingdom], May 6, 2011, www.guardian.co.uk/world/2011/may/06/osama-bin-laden-lived-two-rooms.

3. "Musharraf Slams U.S. Over bin Laden Raid," Dawn.com, May 7, 2011, www.dawn.com/2011/05/07/musharraf-slams-us-over-bin-laden-raid.html; for background, see Kamran Haider, "Pakistan Coalition to Move for Musharraf Impeachment," Reuters, Aug. 7, 2008, www.reuters.com/article/2008/08/07/us-pakistan-politics-idUSISL15267920080807.

4. "Congressman Poe to Introduce Pakistan Foreign Aid Accountability Act," press release, office of Rep. Ted Poe, May 3, 2011, http://poe.house.gov/News/DocumentSingle.aspx?DocumentID=239188.

5. Hasan-Askari Rizvi, "Analysis: Uncertain Future?" *Daily Times* [Pakistan], Feb. 14, 2010, www.dailytimes.com.pk/default.asp?page=2010\02\14\story_14-2-2010_pg3_2.

6. *The Failed States Index 2011*, The Fund for Peace, www.foreignpolicy.com/articles/2011/06/17/2011_failed_states_index_interactive_map_and_rankings.

7. Quoted in Aqil Shah, "Time to Get Serious With Pakistan," *Foreign Affairs*, May 6, 2011, www.foreignaffairs.com/articles/67836/aqil-shah/time-to-get-serious-with-pakistan.

8. C. Christine Fair, "The Road from Abbottabad Leads to Lame Analysis," *Huffington Post*, June 21, 2011, www.huffingtonpost.com/c-christine-fair/the-road-from-abbottabad-_b_881256.html.

9. Anatol Lieven, *Pakistan: A Hard Country* (2011), Kindle Edition, Location 275.

10. Susan B. Epstein and K. Alan Kronstadt, "Pakistan: U.S. Foreign Assistance," Congressional Research Services, June 7, 2011, p. 5, www.fas.org/sgp/crs/row/R41856.pdf.

11. Curt Tarnoff and Marian Leonardo Lawson, "Foreign Aid: An Introduction to U.S. Programs

and Policy," Congressional Research Service, Feb. 10, 2011, www.fas.org/sgp/crs/row/R40213.pdf, p. 14.

12. For background, see Jayshree Bajoria, "The U.S.-India Nuclear Deal," Council on Foreign Relations website, Nov. 5, 2010, www.cfr.org/india/us-india-nuclear-deal/p9663.

13. *The Failed States Index 2011*, *op. cit.*, www.foreign-policy.com/articles/2011/06/17/2011_failed_states_index_interactive_map_and_rankings.

14. Quoted in "System Based on Justice Needed to Stem Terror: Shahbaz," *PakTribune*, June 13, 2011, www.paktribune.com/news/index.shtml?240307.

15. Lieven, *op. cit.*, Kindle Location 610.

16. For background, see Thomas J. Billitteri, "Afghanistan Dilemma," *CQ Researcher*, Aug. 7, 2009, updated May 25, 2011.

17. Lieven, *op. cit.*, Kindle Location 503.

18. Anatol Lieven, "5 Myths About Pakistan," *The Washington Post*, June 5, 2011, p. B2, www.washingtonpost.com/opinions/five-myths-about-pakistan/2011/05/24/AGkPs4HH_story.html.

19. Quoted in Pete Kasperowicz, "Rohrabacher Dismisses GOP Leadership Position on Aid to Pakistan," *The Hill Floor Action Blog*, May 6, 2011, http://thehill.com/blogs/floor-action/house/159733-rohrabacher-dismisses-gop-leadership-position-on-aid-to-pakistan.

20. Nitin Pai, "Cut Pakistan Loose," *The Wall Street Journal online*, June 9, 2011, http://online.wsj.com/article/SB10001424052702304259304576373073934473728.html.

21. Lieven, *op. cit.*, *Pakistan: A Hard Country*, Kindle Location 282.

22. Quoted in "Should U.S. Continue Aid to Pakistan," Council on Foreign Relations website, May 17, 2011, www.cfr.org/pakistan/should-us-continue-aid-pakistan/p25015.

23. Parag Khanna, "Cut Military Aid Now," *The New York Times Room for Debate Blog*, May 10, 2011, www.nytimes.com/roomfordebate/2011/05/09/should-the-us-cut-off-aid-to-pakistan/cut-military-aid-now.

24. For background, see "U.S. Report Ties Militancy to Pakistan School Woes," Reuters, Inform Education website, http://informeducationnetwork.com/education/report-ties-militancy-pakistan-school-woes-969901a.

25. For background, see Robert Kiener, "Crisis in Pakistan," *CQ Global Researcher*, December 2008; Iftikhar Malik, *The History of Pakistan* (2008).

26. Hussain Haqqani, *Pakistan: Between Mosque and Military* (2005), p. 20.

27. "In Pictures: India's Partition," BBC News, http://news.bbc.co.uk/2/shared/spl/hi/pop_ups/06/south_asia_india0s_partition/html/1.stm.

28. "Mr. Jinnah's Address to the Constituent Assembly of Pakistan," Aug. 11, 1947, www.pakistani.org/pakistan/legislation/constituent_address_11aug1947.html.

29. "The Constitution of Pakistan," Part XII, Section 260, www.pakistani.org/pakistan/constitution/part12.ch5.html.

30. Lieven, *op. cit.*, *Pakistan: A Hard Country*, Kindle Location 420.

31. Quoted in Tim McGirk and Aravind Adiva, "War at the Top of the World," *TimeAsia*, May 4, 2005, www.time.com/time/asia/covers/501050711/story.html.

32. Feroz Hassan Khan, "Nuclear Security in Pakistan: Separating Myth from Reality," *Arms Control Today*, July/August 2009, www.armscontrol.org/act/2009_07-08/khan.

33. For background, see Douglas Frantz and Catherine Collins, *The Nuclear Jihadist: The True Story of the Man Who Sold the World's Most Dangerous Secrets . . . and How We Could Have Stopped Him* (2007).

34. For background, see C. Christine Fair, "The Militant Challenge in Pakistan," *Asia Policy*, National Bureau of Asian Research, January 2011, pp. 105-137, www.nbr.org/publications/asia_policy/AP11/AP11_F_MilitantPakistan.pdf, and C. Christine Fair, "The U.S. Strategy in Afghanistan: Impacts Upon U.S. Interests in Pakistan," testimony before the House Armed Services Subcommittee on Oversight and Investigations, Nov. 5, 2009, http://home.comcast.net/~christine_fair/pubs/Fair_Pakistan_Afghanistan_11_5_09.pdf.

35. For background, see Mark Magnier and Subhash Sharma, "Terror Attacks Ravage Mumbai," *Los*

Angeles Times, Nov. 27, 2008, http://articles.latimes.com/print/2008/nov/27/world/fg-mumbai27.

36. For background, see Thomas J. Billitteri, "Drone Warfare," *CQ Researcher*, Aug. 6, 2010, pp. 653-676.

37. Faisal Aziz and Michael Georgy, "Pakistan Retakes Naval Base After Attack," Reuters, May 23, 2011, www.reuters.com/article/2011/05/23/us-pakistan-blast-idUSTRE74L2I320110523.

38. "PNS Mehran Attack," *Dawn online*, May 24, 2011, www.dawn.com/2011/05/24/pns-mehran-attack.html.

39. For background, see "Saleem Shahzad," Committee to Protect Journalists website, http://cpj.org/killed/2011/saleem-shahzad.php, and Amir Mir, "Who Killed Syed Saleem Shahzad," *Asia Times Online*, June 4, 2011, www.atimes.com/atimes/South_Asia/MF04Df03.html.

40. Syed Saleem Shahzad, "Al-Qaeda Had Warned of Pakistan Strike," *Asia Times Online*, May 27, 2011, www.atimes.com/atimes/South_Asia/ME27Df06.html.

41. For background, see Ed Husain, "Explaining the Salman Taseer Murder," Council on Foreign Relations website, Jan. 7, 2011, www.cfr.org/pakistan/explaining-salman-taseer-murder/p23755.

42. Jawayria Malik, "Suspension of U.S. Aid to Pakistan," *The News International* [Pakistan], July 29, 2011, www.thenews.com.pk/TodaysPrintDetail.aspx?ID=60067&Cat=6&dt=7/29/2011.

43. Quoted in Josh Rogin, The Cable blog, *Foreign Policy*, May 5, 2011, http://thecable.foreignpolicy.com/posts/2011/05/05/congress_preparing_options_to_cut_pakistani_aid.

44. For background, see Mahanth Joishy, "The Enhanced Partnership With Pakistan Act of 2009: Challenges Along the Money Trail," *Foreign Policy Digest*, May 1, 2010, www.foreignpolicydigest.org/2010/05/01/the-enhanced-partnership-with-pakistan-act-of-2009-challenges-along-the-money-trail.

45. Quoted in *ibid.*

46. "Chairman Kerry and Chairman Berman Release Joint Explanatory Statement to Accompany Enhanced Partnership With Pakistan Act of 2009,"

press release, Office of Sen. John Kerry, Oct. 14, 2009, http://kerry.senate.gov/press/release/?id=34cf9b3a-2791-4dec-bc23-8611417466ed.

47. For background, see Sebastian Rotella, "Pakistan and the Mumbai Attacks: The Untold Story," *ProPublica*, Jan. 26, 2011, www.propublica.org/article/pakistan-and-the-mumbai-attacks-the-untold-story/single.

BIBLIOGRAPHY
Selected Sources
Books
Ali, Tariq, *The Duel: Pakistan on the Flight Path of American Power*, Scribner, 2009.
A veteran Pakistani journalist describes his encounters with many key figures in Pakistan's political past and argues that both longstanding Pakistani government corruption and faulty U.S. policy have played pernicious roles in creating the unstable state that exists today.

Lieven, Anatol, *Pakistan: A Hard Country*, PublicAffairs, 2011.
A professor of war studies at King's College, London, describes how Pakistan's complex society and difficult history have led to a militarized state with ineffective civilian institutions.

Articles
Brown, Vahid, "The Façade of Allegiance: Bin Ladin's Dubious Pledge to Mullah Omar," *CTC Sentinel*, Jan. 13, 2010, www.ctc.usma.edu/posts/the-facade-of-allegiance-bin-ladin%E2%80%99s-dubious-pledge-to-mullah-omar.
A research fellow at West Point's Combating Terrorism Center describes the complicated relationship between Al Qaeda and the Afghan Taliban, arguing that, contrary to claims that they are strongly allied, the two groups currently pursue conflicting objectives.

Schaffer, Teresita C., "The U.S. and Pakistan: The Third Divorce?" *South Asia Hand blog*, May 17, 2011, http://southasiahand.com/pakistan/the-u-s-and-pakistan-the-third-divorce.
A Brookings Institution senior fellow and retired State Department South Asia expert argues the United States

and Pakistan must openly discuss how their objectives and constraints differ and then rebuild more limited but more achievable agreements about intelligence sharing and drone strikes.

Reports and Studies

Beyond Bullets and Bombs: Fixing the U.S. Approach to Development in Pakistan, **Study Group on a U.S. Development Strategy in Pakistan, Center for Global Development, June 2011, www.cgdev.org/content/ publications/detail/1425136.**
Analysts for a Washington-based think tank concerned with inequality and poverty argue that U.S. Pakistan policy should be refocused on economy-building measures such as removing U.S. trade barriers to Pakistani goods and providing incentives such as risk insurance for investment in the country's economy.

Abbas, Hassan, *Militancy in Pakistan's Borderlands: Implications for the Nation and for Afghan Policy*, **The Century Foundation, 2010, http://tcf.org/publications/ 2010/10/militancy-in-pakistan2019s-borderlands- implications-for-the-nation-and-for-afghan-policy/pdf.**
A senior advisor at Harvard University's Belfer Center on Science and International Affairs chronicles the rise of many militant leaders and groups in Pakistan's remotest regions, beginning in the 19th century under British colonial rule. He argues that Pakistan must institute long-term political reforms in those regions or risk increasing violence and chaos.

Cohen, Stephen P., *The Future of Pakistan*, **Brookings Institution,** January 2011, www.humansecuritygateway. com/documents/BROOKINGS_TheFutureofPakistan .pdf.
A senior foreign policy fellow at the center-left think tank argues that a future for Pakistan as a moderate, mainly secular, economically strong country may be slipping out of reach, which could leave the country's large nuclear arsenal up for grabs in a splintered state. If the United States and India, together with other nations, can work with Pakistan's elite and its democracy-hungry middle class to strengthen civilian institutions and convince the military to loosen its grip on power, the country may pull itself back from the brink, Cohen argues.

Fair, C. Christine, "The Militant Challenge in Pakistan," *Asia Policy*, **January 2011, pp. 105-137, www.isn.ethz .ch/isn/Digital-Library/Publications/Detail/?ots591= 0c54e3b3-1e9c-be1e-2c24-a6a8c7060233&lng=en&id= 126157.**
An assistant professor in Georgetown University's School of Foreign Service recounts the long history of Pakistan's use of small militant groups to pursue both foreign and domestic objectives.

Fair, C. Christine, *et al.*, *Pakistan: Can the United States Secure an Insecure State?* **RAND Corporation, 2010, www.rand.org/pubs/monographs/MG910.html.** Political instability and anti-Americanism in Pakistan have both increased since the country committed itself a decade ago to helping the United States fight Islamic terrorism. If Pakistani elites worked together to create a stronger civilian government to control the military and respond to public needs, the country might yet pull out of its downward spiral, RAND analysts write. The United States could help by providing assistance for development of civilian institutions and avoiding "the temptation to support a 'strong man' to pursue U.S. interests," they advise.

Kronstadt, K. Alan, *Pakistan-U.S. Relations*, **Congressional Research Service, Feb. 6, 2009, www.fas.org/ sgp/crs/row/RL33498.pdf.**
An analyst at Congress' nonpartisan research arm chronicles U.S.-Pakistan relations since the late 1990s, when the United States first became focused on Islamic terrorism in the Middle East and South Asia.

For More Information

All Things Pakistan, http://pakistaniat.com. Five-year archive (2006-2011) of the now-closed blog of Adil Najam, vice chancellor at Pakistan's Lahore University of Management Sciences; posts news, essays and a lively comment section.

Belfer Center for Science and International Affairs, John F. Kennedy School of Government, Harvard University, 79 JFK St., Cambridge, MA 02138; (617) 495-1400; www.belfercenter.org. Research group of international-security scholars, including nuclear-arms experts.

Center for Strategic and International Studies, 1800 K St., N.W., # 400, Washington, DC 20006-2230; (202) 887-0200; http://csis.org. Nonpartisan think tank pursuing research and policy recommendations in international affairs.

Council on Foreign Relations, 1777 F St., N.W., Washington, DC 20006; (202) 509-8400; www.cfr.org. Washington- and New York City-based membership organization of international-relations experts providing research and commentary.

Dawn.com, www.dawn.com. Pakistan-based English-language newspaper.

Middle East Institute, 1761 N St., N.W., Washington, DC 20036-2882; (202) 785-1141; www.mei.edu. Research group providing analysis and information on Middle Eastern and South Asian affairs.

New America Foundation, 1899 L St., N.W., Suite 400, Washington, DC 20036; (202) 986-2700; www.newamerica.net. Centrist think tank providing analysis of international issues, including terrorism.

South Asia Hand, http://southasiahand.com. The blog of two retired State Department South Asia experts who post reports and commentary.

Woodrow Wilson International Center for Scholars, Ronald Reagan Building and International Trade Center, One Woodrow Wilson Plaza, 1300 Pennsylvania Ave., N.W., Washington, DC 20004-3027; (202) 691-4000; www.wilsoncenter.org. International group of scholars providing commentary on world issues.

7

Foreign Aid and National Security

Nellie Bristol

Workers in Rwanda learn to install solar panels at health clinics under a project funded by the U.S. Agency for International Development. Defense Secretary Robert Gates has endorsed efforts by President Obama to increase U.S. foreign assistance, but congressional Republicans are calling for reductions.

From *CQ Researcher*,
June 17, 2011

F ormer Marine Capt. Rye Barcott is no stranger to suffering. When he was a University of North Carolina undergraduate, even before he joined the Marines, he and two Kenyans founded a leadership-building youth center and health clinic in the infamous Kibera slum in Nairobi.

But it was while he was serving in Iraq, as he watched kids playing soccer on a dusty field at Abu Ghraib prison, that he fully grasped the potential of economic and social development assistance in struggling countries.

As Barcott watched an 11-year-old accused killer kick a goal, he realized the connection between the boy and his 15-year-old accomplice and many of the youths he knew in Kenya. "As troubled as I was by the [Iraqi] boys' situation, I had still viewed them as the enemy," he wrote in his just-published memoir, *It Happened on the Way to War: A Marine's Path to Peace.* "Now, they had confessed and were playing soccer, and I was seeing them again for who they were. Kids. They were just boys."

It dawned on him with particular clarity that separating his two callings — soldier and humanitarian worker — wasn't possible. "They were different means toward the same goal: peace and stability in a violent world," he wrote. "Surely we would always need a strong military, though there had to be a better way toward peace than this: our detention at Abu Ghraib of two kids almost half my age."

Barcott is now out of the military and working with U.S. groups pushing to give a larger role to U.S. foreign aid, for both humanitarian and national security reasons. The boys in Iraq, Barcott learned, had been coerced into murdering an Iraqi leader, caught up in forces far beyond their control. And that, he says today,

Afghanistan Now Receives Most U.S. Aid

Afghanistan received more U.S. aid in 2010 than any other country, and nearly twice as much as Israel. A decade ago, Israel by far was the biggest aid recipient, and Afghanistan was not even on the list.

Top Recipients of U.S. Foreign Assistance

Fiscal 2000

Country	Amount
Israel	$4,069
Egypt	$2,053
Colombia	$899
West Bank/Gaza	$485
Jordan	$429
Russia	$195
Bolivia	$194
Ukraine	$183
Kosovo	$165
Peru	$120
Georgia	$112
Armenia	$104
Bosnia	$101
Indonesia	$94
Nigeria	$68

(U.S. aid in $ billions, in constant 2011 dollars)

Fiscal 2010

Country	Amount
Afghanistan	$4,102
Israel	$2,220
Pakistan	$1,807
Egypt	$1,296
Haiti	$1,271
Iraq	$1,117
Jordan	$693
Kenya	$688
Nigeria	$614
South Africa	$578
Ethiopia	$533
Colombia	$507
West Bank/Gaza	$496
Tanzania	$464
Uganda	$457

(U.S. aid in $ billions, in constant 2011 dollars)

Source: Curt Tarnoff and Marian Leonardo Lawson, "Foreign Aid: An Introduction to U.S. Programs and Policy," Congressional Research Service, February 2011, assets.opencrs.com/rpts/R40213_20110210.pdf

improve living conditions, rather than deal with the consequences after the situation has deteriorated. Poverty and poor governance can spur violence and instability anywhere in the world, the argument goes, spawning terrorism, desperation and disease that may come to haunt the United States or need to be addressed through a larger military investment.

After the terrorist attacks on the United States on Sept. 11, 2001, the George W. Bush administration pushed the connection between long-term economic and social development assistance and national security, a link the Obama administration has continued.

"We need an integrated civilian-military national security budget," said Secretary of State Hillary Rodham Clinton. "[I]t's now so important to have diplomats and development experts working side by side [with the military]." Clinton said civilian efforts led by the State Department and the U.S. Agency for International Development (USAID) were especially crucial in the "front-line states" of Pakistan, Iraq and Afghanistan as the U.S. military reduces its forces.

U.S. foreign aid is designed to help increase government stability and develop reliable services, including water and schools, making citizens less dissatisfied with their government and less apt to seek or be susceptible to alternatives. "Too many people on Capitol Hill and throughout the country say, 'Okay, so the military's gone, we don't need to spend any money,' which would be a terrible mistake," Clinton said. "It would make Iraq even more vulnerable to outside interference from Iran." [1]

But House Republicans are pushing for sharp cuts in foreign aid as they seek to slash federal spending and reduce the size of the government. To many of them,

"shows me there are just clearly dramatic limitations to what the military can do, and at that particular moment it wasn't going to be any type of positive force in these kids' lives."

Barcott is not alone in his belief that U.S. foreign policy would be more effective by putting greater emphasis on the civilian tools of diplomacy and development, rather than military force. It is far preferable, he says, to work proactively with faltering countries to and others, the bigger threat to national security is out-of-control government spending and the massive federal debt. The projected $9.7 trillion national debt over the next decade not only will make the United States more dependent on foreign creditors and international financial markets but also could force cuts to the defense budget that could weaken the military. [2]

Although he also supports a greater role for development aid and diplomacy, Joint Chiefs of Staff Chairman Adm. Mike Mullen said, "The more significant threat to our national security is our debt." He added, "That's why it's so important the economy move in the right direction, because the strength and the support and resources that our military uses are directly related to the health of our economy over time." [3] The defense spending reauthorization bill in the House this year calls for a study of the security risks associated with the U.S. debt held by China. [4]

Complicating the argument is aid's uneven past. Advocates of international assistance point to numerous successes over the years — increased agricultural yields for millions of hungry people, reduced disease worldwide and improved childbirth safety for vulnerable women. But even advocates of aid acknowledge its shortcomings. The United States devoted more than $50 billion to projects in Iraq, for example, including construction of police stations, government buildings and health facilities. [5] Yet poor management, corruption and security problems resulted in billions in cost overruns, and many projects may never be finished. [6]

Afghanistan is another example. While remarkable aid-driven improvements have been made in the country in the last several years, the Senate Foreign Relations Committee released a report on June 8 showing that efforts to push money toward short-term development projects in volatile areas have been counterproductive and may result in an economic crisis in the country when the United States withdraws. It suggests the Obama administration overhaul its approach to ensure projects are "necessary, achievable and sustainable before funding is allocated." The report is sure to play into continuing debates both on the value of foreign aid and the U.S. role in Afghanistan. [7]

In addition, foreign aid may be the most misunderstood piece of the federal budget. According to a 2010 poll, Americans think 25 percent of the federal budget goes to foreign aid and that a more appropriate percentage would be 10 percent. [8] In reality, foreign aid constitutes only around 1.1 percent of the budget.

Another complicating factor is the confusing nature of aid, which is used for a variety of purposes. Slightly more than half of the 2010 foreign aid budget was directed at humanitarian and development projects. [9] The remainder was intended for strategic purposes or to bolster civilian law enforcement or militaries and never intended to improve economic growth in a country. Still, in the eyes of the public, the accounts often are lumped together.

"If we give money to a friendly dictator, 10 years later not much development comes of it, and people say 'Oh, well foreign aid doesn't work,' " says David Beckmann, president of the anti-hunger group Bread for the World. "But the point was to buy an air force base, it wasn't to help people, so we shouldn't be surprised later that it doesn't help people."

As lawmakers on Capitol Hill debate the size of the federal budget, USAID Administrator Rajiv Shah, widely viewed as a dynamic, progressive leader, is trying to convince members of Congress of the value of aid in an era of tight budgets. Shah is making the agency and its aid recipients more accountable, working more closely with developing countries and better tracking effectiveness.

"Like an enterprise, we're focused on delivering the highest possible value for our shareholders — in this case, the American people and the congressional leaders who represent them," Shah said. "We will deliver that value by scaling back our footprint to shift resources to critical regions, rationalizing our operations and vigilantly fighting fraud, waste and abuse." [10]

As the debate over foreign aid and the federal deficit heats up, here are some of the questions being asked:

Is foreign aid necessary for national security?

The importance of the connection between non-military foreign aid and national security is being supported strongly by what may be a surprising group: former and active members of the U.S. military. And the message is coming from the top: Secretary of Defense Robert Gates. "It has become clear that America's civilian institutions of diplomacy and development have been chronically undermanned and underfunded for far too

Foreign Aid Is Tiny Part of U.S. Budget

Foreign assistance accounted for 1.1 percent of U.S. federal budget outlays in fiscal 2010. Foreign aid spending has represented, on average, just over 1 percent of total budget authority annually since 1977.

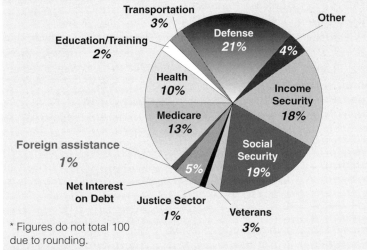

Transportation 3%
Education/Training 2%
Defense 21%
Other 4%
Health 10%
Income Security 18%
Medicare 13%
Foreign assistance 1%
Social Security 19%
Net Interest on Debt 5%
Justice Sector 1%
Veterans 3%

* Figures do not total 100 due to rounding.

Source: Curt Tarnoff and Marian Leonardo Lawson, "Foreign Aid: An Introduction to U.S. Programs and Policy," Congressional Research Service, February 2011, assets.opencrs.com/rpts/R40213_20110210.pdf

long relative to what we spend on the military, and more important, relative to the responsibilities and challenges our nation has around the world," Gates said in 2008. [11]

Gates sees civilian tools of "persuasion and inspiration" as indispensable to a stable world. "We cannot kill or capture our way to victory," he said. "What the Pentagon calls 'kinetic' operations should be subordinate to measures to promote participation in government, economic programs to spur development and efforts to address grievances that often lie at the heart of insurgencies and among the discontented from which the terrorists recruit."

Retired Adm. James M. Loy, former deputy secretary of Homeland Security and Coast Guard commandant, traces the shift in approach to September 11. Since the attacks, he says, "the very definition of national security is much broader in scope." While pre-9/11 security operations might have involved the White House, the National Security Council and the State and Defense departments, they now include participants ranging from the Treasury and Justice departments to the Agriculture Department and Environmental Protection Agency.

"Who would have thought we'd ever pine for the good old days of the Cold War, with the simplistic notion of a couple of superpowers keeping client states under their wing and in order, all fostered by the notion of mutually assured destruction?" says Loy, now co-chair of the National Security Advisory Council at the U.S. Global Leadership Coalition, a network of business and nongovernmental leaders that advocates increased use of civilian power. In today's more complicated world, he adds, "We're still trying to understand it."

Investment in civilian operations is considered a "best buy" by J. Stephen Morrison, senior vice president at the Center for Strategic and International Studies (CSIS). It is much cheaper to send specialists in health or elections to a country than to fund a military intervention, not to mention saving the lives and limbs of soldiers, he notes. Supporters of development as a national security tool acknowledge that definitive results for the approach are hard to find, mostly because it's difficult to measure what would have happened absent the aid. But, Morrison argues, "there's the kind of presumptive, wise, forward investment in creating a form of human security, accountability and transparency that will make for a better-functioning world."

Afghanistan is frequently cited as an example of how aid would have protected the United States. When the Russians left in 1989, after nearly 10 years of war and occupation, the United States didn't follow through in rebuilding. Such actions can have serious consequences, comments Adm. Loy, who says, "Often when we've watched [foreign aid] fall, we've paid the price shortly thereafter."

But not everyone agrees. James Roberts, a research fellow for economic freedom and growth at the Heritage Foundation, a conservative think tank, warned that "out of control federal spending" leads to a national security threat and that traditional development assistance "does not work, at least not if the goal is to foster sustainable development in poor countries." [12] He said development is better accomplished through private organizations. He did, however, laud humanitarian aid delivered under U.S. global HIV/AIDS programs.

Justin Logan, associate director of foreign policy studies at the Cato Institute, a libertarian think tank, says strategic aid is unnecessary and counterproductive. "I think we're secure, independent of these efforts to try to tinker with the balance of power in other regions," he says. He calls a lot of aid, especially to problematic allies such as Egypt and Pakistan, "bribery." "I don't buy the Rube Goldberg theory that regional instability everywhere will always come back to bite us, [a view] I think is quite prevalent in Washington," he adds.

U.S. willingness to engage throughout the world has made other countries less motivated to provide services for their citizens or even shore up their own defenses, Logan says. The U.S. tendency to pick and choose when and how to get involved in conflicts internationally "taints the image of America as a beacon of liberalism and democracy to the rest of the world and in some cases causes actual animosity and terrorism against the United States," he adds.

Significantly, among those not fully convinced by the development aid-as-national security argument are lawmakers influential in budget matters. House Budget Committee Chairman Paul Ryan, R-Wis., developed a 2012 budget plan that would have cut international affairs funding, which includes foreign aid, by as much as 28 percent. [13]

And Rep. Kay Granger, R-Texas, chair of the House Appropriations Committee's State, Foreign Operations and Related Programs Subcommittee, said that given the country's constrained economic circumstances, foreign aid needs to be focused on "direct national security." [14]

While she acknowledged the connection between foreign aid and national security in long-term U.S. commitments to Israel, Iraq, Afghanistan, Pakistan and Mexico, she suggested other, less pressing development investments would be a lower priority in the current climate. "We have to look at our national security, particularly in foreign aid, and say, What is in our national security interest?" she said.

Sen. Rand Paul, R-Ky., makes the most extreme case against foreign aid, saying all aid should be cut, even to longtime ally Israel. Citing a Reuter's poll, Paul said, "71 percent of the American people agree with me that when we're short of money, when we can't do the things we need to do in our country, we certainly shouldn't be shipping the money overseas." In making his case, Paul said that while he's sympathetic to challenges faced by developing countries, aid money too often goes to unscrupulous leaders. "You don't want to just keep throwing money to corrupt leaders who steal it from their people," he argued.

Moreover, Paul said, U.S. aid to Israel is matched by aid to Islamic countries, possibly contributing to an arms race in the region. "I don't think that funding both sides of an arms race, particularly when we have to borrow the money from China to send it to someone else — we just can't do it anymore. The debt is all-consuming, and it threatens our well-being as a country." [15]

Does the U.S. benefit from foreign aid spending?

Foreign aid has always been a hard sell, but in the current political and economic climate, it's harder still. While much of official Washington considers aid vital, the value is often lost on everyday Americans, many of whom are struggling to hold on to their houses, find new jobs and educate their kids.

"It's really important that you all know this committee is extremely supportive of programs that really will save the lives and positively impact the developing world," Rep. Jerry Lewis, R-Calif., a member of the Foreign Operations Subcommittee, told USAID and State Department officials March 31. "In turn, our public just plain doesn't believe it, and they wonder why, for God's sake, we're spending this money when we don't actually sense there's any positive result for the American taxpayer." [16]

Calculating the ultimate value of aid to the donor is difficult to begin with. Further, examples of misspent, ineffective and even harmful aid are plentiful. Several prominent economists, including William Easterly of New York University, author of *The White Man's Burden: Why The West's Efforts to Aid the Rest Have Done So Much Ill and So Little Good*, and Dambisa Moyo, author of *Dead Aid: Why Aid Is Not Working and How There Is a Better Way for Africa*, have harshly criticized Western

The ABC's of Foreign Assistance

U.S. foreign assistance totaled $39.4 billion, or 1.1% of the federal budget in fiscal 2010, the highest amount since 1985. Aid has three primary rationales: enhancing national security, bolstering commercial interests and addressing humanitarian concerns. U.S. aid falls into several categories based on the goal and form of the aid:

- **Bilateral Development Assistance** totaled $12.3 billion in 2010, or 34 percent of foreign aid appropriations, and is largely administered by USAID. It is used for long-term projects supporting economic reform, private-sector development, democracy promotion, environmental protection and human health.

- **Multilateral Development Assistance** made up 7 percent of the 2010 budget, totaling $2.6 billion. It is combined with contributions from other donor nations and implemented by international organizations such as the United Nations.

- **Humanitarian assistance** was allotted $5.1 billion in 2010, or 13.5 percent of the assistance budget. Funding is used to help victims of earthquakes, floods and other crises. A large portion addresses issues related to refugees and internally displaced persons.

- **Assistance serving both development and special political/strategic purposes** includes the Economic Support Fund, which now largely goes to countries key to the war on terrorism. Several other programs in this category are aimed at Europe and Asia. These funds totaled $9.6 billion in 2010, or 25 percent of total assistance.

- **Civilian Security Assistance** focuses on terrorism, illicit narcotics, crimes and weapons proliferation and totaled 9 percent of the foreign aid budget in 2010.

- **Military Assistance** is provided to U.S. friends and allies to help them purchase U.S. military equipment and training. In 2010, Congress appropriated $4.7 billion for this account, or 12.5% of total foreign aid.

Note: Totals do not add to 100 due to rounding.

Source: Curt Tarnoff and Marian Leonardo Lawson, "Foreign Aid: An Introduction to US Programs and Policy," Congressional Research Service, Feb. 10, 2011, www. fas.org/sgp/crs/row/R40213.pdf.

steadily, particularly in the last decade, to document program effectiveness.[17] For example, the *Oportunidades* program in Mexico was proven to successfully alleviate poverty and ill health by providing payments to families to keep their kids in school and take them to health clinics.[18] Similar programs have been established in Brazil and Nicaragua.[19] Other successful interventions include deworming, immunization, vitamin supplements and oral rehydration solutions to treat diarrhea in areas in the developing world with high child mortality rates.

But when it comes to specific programs, determining value is "a little bit tricky," says Christopher J. L. Murray, director of the Institute for Health Metrics and Evaluation at the University of Washington in Seattle. The health arena boasts several obvious winners, Murray says, including programs providing insecticide-treated bed nets to prevent mosquito-borne malaria in Africa and HIV/AIDS treatments to millions of sufferers, also particularly in Africa. "Pretty much anyone would say there's been a real benefit, and the U.S. has played an important role in both," Murray says. But with other programs, he says, "evaluating value for money is much harder."

It's not that aid isn't having an effect, Murray adds, but that it's harder to pinpoint exactly what is creating the positive result. For example, while there has been marked progress recently in reducing child morality in the poorest countries, it's hard to prove with certainty which factors are most responsible. "So many things contribute to reductions in child mortality . . . rising incomes contribute at the household and community level, better housing, better water, etc. Probably half of

attempts at poverty alleviation. Some experts urge a move toward expanded trade opportunities with developing countries rather than continued direct assistance.

To counter theories that aid is akin to pouring money down a rat hole, development professionals have worked the decline in child mortality is related to improvements in educating young girls. So the challenge here is teasing out the effect of, let's say, vaccination programs versus these broader development trends," Murray notes. "I think it's likely that development assistance has contributed to that. Can I prove that in a rigorous, scientific way like we can for bed nets or [HIV/AIDS therapies]? Much harder to do," he says.

Dean Karlan, a professor of economics at Yale University and president and founder of Innovations for Poverty Action, a consulting firm that evaluates poverty programs, thinks at least partial evaluation of programs is possible. When asked if the U.S. gets value for its foreign aid dollars, Karlan says, "The answer is, sort of. Some things work, and some things don't."

Both Karlan and Murray see the development sector as much more motivated and able now to examine specific programs, largely because more tools have become available to collect and analyze data, and more development organizations, including governments, the U.N. and private donors, are demanding transparency and accountability of both funding and data.

But objectivity has its limitations. Karlan favors randomized evaluations to rigorously examine intervention effectiveness. The method works for discrete programs, including health services, and is being adopted vigorously by USAID and other U.S. government programs. However, Karlan says, the method doesn't work for everything. Efforts such as judicial reform, democracy building or even road construction are more difficult to evaluate for their impact on local citizens.

Whether projects result in goodwill and enhanced security for Americans is even more difficult to measure.

U.S. Contributes Most Aid

The United States contributed nearly $29 billion in official development assistance (ODA) in 2009, the most in the world and more than twice the amount of France, which ranked second (top graph). As a percentage of gross national income (GNI), however, the U.S. contributed only 0.2 percent to such assistance, ranking far behind Nordic countries such as Sweden and Norway, each of which gave more than 1 percent (bottom graph).

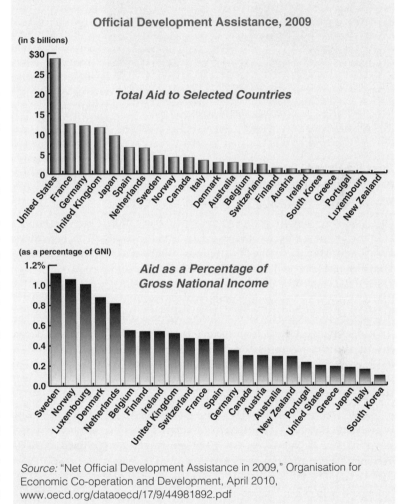

Source: "Net Official Development Assistance in 2009," Organisation for Economic Co-operation and Development, April 2010, www.oecd.org/dataoecd/17/9/44981892.pdf

"There are some areas of aid that still elude us in terms of establishing good, clear, rigorous evaluation," Karlan says. Without clear evidence, "all we can do is fire rhetoric and bad data at each other, but no one's ever going to convince the other side on it."

A U.S. military helicopter delivers cement to Pakistan's flooded Swat Valley last October. Slightly more than half of the U.S. foreign aid budget for 2010 supported humanitarian and development projects. The remainder was allocated for strategic purposes, including military aid.

Does the United States give too much aid to authoritarian governments?

America has long bestowed aid to win friends and influence people — and not always to the most savory individuals. Despots who have received U.S. aid include Ferdinand Marcos in the Philippines, "Baby Doc" Duvalier in Haiti, and even Saddam Hussein in Iraq. During the Cold War, the practice of supporting harsh, non-democratic governments, while roundly criticized, was viewed as a necessary evil in ensuring regional stability and keeping countries from turning to communism. But the doctrine has come under renewed scrutiny during the recent "Arab Spring" unrest, when the United States was criticized for being on the wrong side of several democratic uprisings, most notably in Egypt.

Egypt is a top recipient of U.S. aid — more than $70 billion since 1948 — mostly for weapons. [20] The Egyptian-Israeli Peace Treaty of 1979 cemented U.S. backing. [21] From America's perspective, the aid increases Egypt's stability, raises regional support for the United States and helps Egypt stay at peace with Israel. But the recent protests in Cairo's Tahrir Square against the now-ended regime of Hosni Mubarak put the United States in the difficult position of having to denounce a government it had financially helped for many years, and the administration's lukewarm initial reaction to the uprisings generated widespread criticism.

"The Obama administration now appears to be wavering on whether America really backs the demands of the Egyptian people, or just wants to return to stability with a façade of change," Rep. Gary Ackerman, D-N.Y., said in February. [22]

The Obama administration's experiences with the Egyptian upheaval and others in the Middle East may prompt a re-evaluation of its strategies toward countries with autocratic leaders, such as Yemen and Bahrain. [23]

Anthony Kim, a policy analyst at the Heritage Foundation, says it's about time. "In the name of stability the United States has been giving out a lot of taxpayers' money to a lot of authoritarian regimes, and as we know now better than before, in countries like Egypt and Pakistan political freedom is very limited," Kim says. "We blindly, without thinking through the true effect of foreign aid, have been wasting our money on those countries."

Referring largely to the billions of dollars of non-military aid to Egypt over the years, Kim said the funding did little for economic development. "Year after year, the data show economic development has been at best cosmetic" and has not reached citizens," he says. "So basically we end up empowering and enriching those corrupt powers in the government" and perhaps contributing to the longevity of non-democratic regimes. "The money we paid hasn't paid off for the United States," he says.

An even more complicated situation is occurring in Pakistan, according to Molly Kinder, a senior policy analyst at the Center for Global Development, a development think tank in Washington. The United States has aided the country for many years, but it stepped up funding after 9/11 to enlist Pakistan's anti-terrorism help. The assistance started out heavily weighted toward military aid, but Congress forced a more balanced approach in 2009, tripling the amount designated for economic development. [24]

Overall, U.S. aid for Pakistan has been largely based on U.S. strategic needs rather than the needs of the people of Pakistan, says Kinder. "The ebbs and flows of foreign aid are contingent on what's going on in the world," she says. "So when Pakistan is needed as an ally in the war on terror or the Cold War, our aid to Pakistan spikes, often corresponding with military regimes [there]. So I think it's a very fair criticism to say Pakistanis view the United States as putting money disproportionately to non-democratic regimes" in Pakistan, Kinder says.

While such a policy may endear the United States to ruling authoritarian powers and give it at least the illusion of an ally, the U.S. ends up looking bad to the citizenry, Kinder says. "There's a real ethical conundrum and a real foreign policy challenge because it certainly can breed resentment toward the United States, which we're seeing now in Pakistan," she says. A recent poll by the Pew Research Center showed that only 11 percent of Pakistanis have favorable views of the United States, one of the lowest levels in Muslim countries surveyed. [25]

"My big question about aid to countries we're not quite comfortable with is whether we are just keeping a lid on things and hoping that the governments stay in power to do the things we want them to do?" Kinder asks. "Is the aid just blunting pressure for reform or pressure for change, giving the government resources to just kind of survive against the will of the people? That's something that I think requires a lot of soul-searching from the U.S. perspective."

But Roberts of the Heritage Foundation said that while development aid is ineffective in Egypt and many other places, military aid paid big dividends for the United States during the Egyptian revolt. He cited the U.S.-supported Egyptian military as having succeeded in "holding the line against virulently anti-U.S. elements." [26] That view is echoed by Secretary of State Hillary Rodham Clinton, who said U.S. support of the Egyptian military "was one of the best investments America made" because the relationship facilitated communication between the United States and the Egyptian military during the protests. [27]

Joint Chiefs Chairman Mullen made a similar argument, noting military aid to Egypt has been of "incalculable value" in transforming the country's army into a capable force. "Changes to those relationships — in either

U.S. Aid Tracks Events, Presidential Initiatives

Foreign aid funding in recent decades can be attributed to specific foreign policy events and presidential initiatives. Since the Sept. 11, 2001, terrorist attacks, funding has been closely tied to U.S. strategy in Iraq and Afghanistan. Global health initiatives by the Bush and Obama administrations, including the Global Health Initiative, the Millennium Challenge Corp., and the PEPFAR HIV/AIDS program, also drove increases. Aid to the Middle East also rose, especially in nations viewed as vital partners in America's War on Terror.

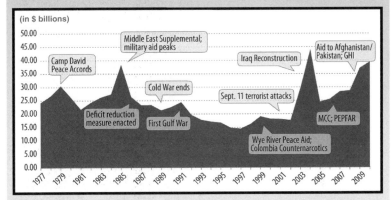

Source: Curt Tarnoff and Marian Leonardo Lawson, "Foreign Aid: An Introduction to U.S. Programs and Policy," Congressional Research Service, Feb. 10, 2011

aid or assistance — ought to be considered only with an abundance of caution and a thorough appreciation for the long view, rather than in the flush of public passion and the urgency to save a buck," he added. [28]

BACKGROUND
Rise of Modern Aid

Foreign assistance became a key component of U.S. foreign policy during and after World War II. The United States began providing support for war-devastated European countries in 1945. Those diffuse efforts were centralized when Secretary of State George C. Marshall and other officials called for a massive, coordinated effort to rebuild Europe's infrastructure. The European Recovery Program, known as the Marshall Plan, pumped $12.5 billion into Western Europe over a three-year period beginning in 1948. The aid was designed to advance U.S. interests as well as help Europe.

CHRONOLOGY

1940s-1960s *United States begins a tradition of foreign assistance.*

June 5, 1947 Economic assistance for postwar Europe proposed by Secretary of State George C. Marshall. "Marshall Plan" plays key role in stimulating Western Europe's economic revival.

Jan. 30, 1961 Citing concerns about the spread of communism, President John F. Kennedy announces plans for a new aid program: "Our role is essential and unavoidable in the construction of a sound and expanding economy for the entire noncommunist world, helping other nations build the strength to meet their own problems, to satisfy their own aspirations — to surmount their own dangers."

Sept. 4, 1961 Congress passes Foreign Assistance Act, separating military and non-military aid.

Nov. 3, 1961 Kennedy establishes U.S. Agency for International Development as the first foreign-assistance organization focused primarily on long-range economic and social development.

1970s *U.S. foreign aid focuses on Middle East, begins to decline.*

1970 U.N. calls for "economically advanced countries" to progressively increase their development assistance to 0.7 percent of gross national product.

1971 Senate rejects foreign-assistance funding for fiscal 1972 and 1973.

1973 Congress passes amendments to the Foreign Assistance Act that break aid into targeted sectors including food and nutrition, population planning and health and education and human resources.

1979 Camp David Accords boost U.S. aid to Israel and Egypt to encourage the peace process. Most of the aid is military assistance to buy U.S. weapons.

1990s *U.S. foreign aid continues to decline.*

1990 U.S. spending on foreign aid peaks at $65.5 billion and begins a 20 percent decline to $53.1 billion by 2000.

1997 Sen. Jesse Helms, R-N.C., makes unsuccessful attempt to downsize USAID and place it fully in the State Department.

2000s *Terrorist attacks on Sept. 11, 2001, renew U.S. interest in stabilizing "failing states"; U.S. becomes a leader in global health funding.*

Sept. 8, 2000 World's nations adopt U.N. Millennium Declaration vowing to reduce extreme poverty by half and address other inequities by 2015.

March 14, 2002 President George W. Bush creates a new aid mechanism, the Millennium Challenge Account, which offers assistance only to countries that adopt reforms and effective policies. He pledges $5 billion a year for the effort.

Jan. 28, 2003 President Bush announces the $15 billion, five-year President's Emergency Plan for AIDS Relief (PEPFAR), which becomes the largest international commitment by any country dedicated to a single disease.

Jan. 18, 2006 Secretary of State Condoleezza Rice announces move toward transformational diplomacy, or elevating the role of diplomacy and development in U.S. foreign policy.

2008 Democratic presidential candidate Barack Obama pledges to double U.S. foreign assistance to $50 billion by 2012, a promise that runs headfirst into the global economic collapse.

Dec. 8, 2010 Incoming House Foreign Affairs Committee Chairwoman Ileana Ros-Lehtinen, R-Fla., pledges to "restore fiscal discipline to foreign affairs."

Dec. 16, 2010 Secretary of State Hillary Rodham Clinton releases long-awaited Quadrennial Diplomacy and Development Review, a blueprint for making U.S. foreign policy more coherent and calling for greater engagement of "civilian power" in advancing national interests.

April 15, 2011 House passes budget resolution that would cut international affairs budgets by as much as 28 percent in 2012.

A primary driver of the efforts was concern that a Europe on its knees would allow westward expansion of the Soviet Union and the spread of communism. The plan also advanced U.S. economic interests by requiring the purchase of U.S. goods.

The Marshall Plan was considered by most to be a success, although some would argue other factors contributed to the recovery, notably a 32 percent increase in Western Europe's gross national product, spurred by an 11 percent rise in agricultural production and a 40 percent increase in industrial output over pre-war levels. [29]

Inspired by the success in Europe, President Harry S Truman proposed aid to developing countries. Nonetheless, foreign aid spending was stagnant during the costly Korean War (1950-53) and the Eisenhower administration (1953-61).

Much of the modern architecture of foreign aid was developed during the foreshortened presidency of John F. Kennedy (1961-1963). On Nov. 3, 1961 Kennedy consolidated assistance programs into the United States Agency for International Development (USAID). Its creation was mandated by the Foreign Assistance Act of 1961, which for the first time separated military and non-military aid. It was the first U.S. assistance organization to focus on long-range economic and social development and to offer direct support to developing countries. Even then, the threat of global economic disparity weighed heavily in arguments for foreign aid.

"[W]idespread poverty and chaos lead to a collapse of existing political and social structures which would inevitably invite the advance of totalitarianism into every weak and unstable area," Kennedy said in 1961. "Thus our own security would be endangered and our prosperity imperiled. A program of assistance to the underdeveloped nations must continue because the nation's interest and the cause of political freedom require it." [30]

Although the stated goal of foreign aid was development, during the Vietnam War era, concerns arose that it was too focused on short-term military goals. In 1971, as the conflict was nearing its end, the Senate defeated foreign assistance funding for 1972 and 1973; it was the first time since the start of the Marshall Plan that either chamber of Congress had rejected aid funding. In 1973, Congress amended the Foreign Assistance Act to steer funds into specific, functional categories including education, agriculture and family planning. The aid structure developed by the amendments remains largely intact today.

Controversies have cropped up since the United States began handing out foreign assistance. One of the most contentious occurred during Ronald Reagan's presidency (1981-1989), when anti-abortion groups complained that taxpayer money was supporting abortion in foreign countries, particularly in China. That prompted Reagan, through a 1984 executive order, to bar government funding for family planning to any foreign, non-governmental organizations that "perform or actively promote" abortions or conduct research to improve abortion methods. [31]

Known by opponents as the "global gag rule," it targeted groups providing "abortion as a method of family planning." The ban applied to groups even using their own funds for abortion-related activities. Reaction to the rule reflected the politics of the abortion debate: Democratic President Bill Clinton rescinded the policy, Republican George W. Bush reinstated it and Democrat Obama again rescinded it.

Organizational dysfunction and lack of clear successes also plagued foreign aid. Programs were criticized as being too dispersed and U.S. bureaucracies too hidebound to be effective. The intermingling of aid used to curry friends — mostly in the form of military and strategic accounts — and aid aimed at long-term development made it difficult to determine whether the aid was achieving the goal of poverty alleviation.

Congressional requirements for the use of U.S. commodities, goods and services also kept aid administrators from pursuing the most effective interventions. Dissatisfaction with the program both among the public and in Congress led to a decline in USAID funding. Foreign Service permanent staffing declined from a high of about 4,500 in 1970 to a low of 1,000 in 2000. The level is projected to be around 2,000 in 2012. [32]

Moreover, several unsuccessful efforts were made to reform the Foreign Assistance Act, including a move to abolish USAID. In 1991, President George H. W. Bush proposed a comprehensive rewriting of the act, but Congress did not seriously consider it. President Clinton also tried his hand at reform through the 1994 Peace, Prosperity and Democracy Act, but it too failed to gain traction in Congress.

New Approach

The 9/11 terrorist attacks put foreign aid back in the spotlight. While little evidence suggested that poverty in

China's Growing Aid to Africa

Does it undermine U.S. influence?

With U.S. foreign aid budgets threatened on Capitol Hill, the Obama administration is warning that decreasing American influence abroad could lead to greater influence for China. "Let's put aside the moral, humanitarian, do-good side of what we believe in, and let's just talk, you know, straight realpolitik," Secretary of State Hillary Rodham Clinton told the Senate Foreign Relations Committee on March 2. "We are in competition with China." [1]

China has increased its foreign aid significantly over the past few years, particularly in Africa, where it grew from $300 million in 2001 to $2.1 billion in 2009. [2] Most of the aid is in the form of loans. The rise has caused alarm from some who say China is baldly seeking influence in developing countries by, among other things, constructing high-profile buildings such as hotels, conference centers and soccer stadiums. [3]

"These highly visible investments, seemingly unavoidable across Africa, are designed to buy influence with governments," writes *Washington Post* columnist Michael Gerson. [4] The move seems to be working, at least among the public. In a recent poll, developing nations had more positive than negative views of China, especially Nigeria (82 percent) and Kenya (77 percent). [5] China has been active in both countries for several years. [6]

China's growing aid budget raises concerns about:

- The general threat of another power seeking influence in the developing world;
- A lack of transparency associated with Chinese aid;
- Extraction of natural resources without much return for the host country, and
- Aid without regard to a country's governance record that will weaken attempts to encourage countries to reform.

But China expert Deborah Brautigam, a professor of international relations at American University in Washington, sees the situation differently. "There are a lot of myths out there about China's aid program," she says, pointing out that China focuses more on export credits, which foster exports and business, while the United States emphasizes outright aid. China's focus on exports stems from the affordability of its goods in Africa, unlike those from the United States, she explains.

As for China locking up all Africa's natural resources, "that's really unrealistic," she says. She acknowledges Chinese aid programs lack transparency but says that's not unusual for countries relatively new to the foreign-assistance arena. Nonetheless, she notes, China recently released a white paper outlining some of its activities. [7] While it was not the detailed, country-by-country data that would have been expected from a more experienced donor country, Brautigam says, "I thought for them this was a very big step. Expecting this kind of transparency to happen immediately, people are bound to be disappointed."

Meanwhile, critics complain that despite China's deep pockets, reflected in both its growing aid efforts

the Arab world had motivated the terrorists, U.S. officials noted that al-Qaida, the group behind the attacks, was based in Afghanistan, one of the world's poorest countries.

Concern about the link between poverty and terrorism led to a focus on stabilizing other fragile and "failing states" to minimize the number of places where terrorist groups could flourish as well as to attract allies in the war against Islamic extremists. A reshuffling of U.S. foreign aid followed. While Israel and Egypt had been the top aid recipients in fiscal 2000, Afghanistan was in the No. 1 spot in 2010, and Pakistan, Haiti, Iraq and Kenya had become major recipients as well. [33]

The attacks also fostered a new approach to foreign policy, which Secretary of State Condoleezza Rice termed "transformational diplomacy." The goal, Rice said in 2006, was "to work with our many partners around the world to build and sustain democratic, well-governed states that will respond to the needs of their people and conduct themselves responsibly in the international system." [34]

The effort included a new post: director of foreign assistance, who served concurrently as USAID administrator.

and ability to put on costly events like the 2008 Olympics, it continues to receive aid from the Global Fund to Fight AIDS, Tuberculosis and Malaria — $539 million since 2003.

"China's aggregate award from the fund is nearly three times larger than that of South Africa, one of the most affected countries from these three diseases," wrote Jack Chow, a former assistant director general of the World Health Organization, now a professor at Carnegie Mellon University. [8] A fund spokesman said China isn't usurping money from other needy countries because the fund so far has been able to approve all applications "of quality." [9]

The question may soon be moot. The fund recently froze its grants to China over a dispute about management of the money and funding of community organizations, a move likely to intensify the debate over whether China should be receiving grants at all. [10]

— *Nellie Bristol*

Masai tribesmen perform a traditional dance as a Chinese hospital ship departs Mombasa, Kenya, after providing residents with free medical help.

[1]Transcript of Senate Foreign Relations Committee hearing on the Proposed Fiscal 2012 Budget for the State Department, March 2, 2011, http://micevhill.com/attachments/immigration_documents/hosted_documents/112th_congress/TranscriptOfSenateForeignRelationsCommitteeHearingOnTheProposedFiscal2012ForeignAffairsBudget.pdf.

[2]Benedicte Vibe Christensen, "China in Africa: A Macroeconomic Perspective," The Center for Global Development, Dec. 22, 2010.

[3]Michael Gerson, "China's African Investments: Who Benefits?" *The Washington Post*, March 28, 2011, www.washingtonpost.com/opinions/chinas-african-investments-who-benefits/2011/03/28/AF8G7mqB_story.html.

[4]*Ibid.*

[5]Andrew Walker, "China's New Economic Power Fans Fear, BBC Poll Finds," BBC, March 27, 2011, www.bbc.co.uk/news/business-12867892.

[6]"China's Hu boosts Kenyan Business," BBC, April 28, 2006, http://news.bbc.co.uk/2/hi/africa/4953588.stm, and "Chinese Engagement in Nigeria Would Aid the Industrialization of the Country," Pan-African News Wire, May 30, 2009.

[7]Sven Grimm, "China's Aid Policy White Paper: Transparency Now?" *Devex*, May 20, 2011, www.devex.com/en/blogs/full-disclosure/chinas-aid-policy-white-paper-transparency-now.

[8]Jack C. Chow, "China's Billion-Dollar Aid Appetite: Why is Beijing Winning Health Grants at the Expense of African Countries," *Foreign Policy*, July 2010, www.foreignpolicy.com/articles/2010/07/19/chinas_billion_dollar_aid_appetite.

[9]Gillian Wong, "China Rises and Rises, Yet Still Gets Foreign Aid," *The Daily Journal*, Oct. 1, 2010, www.smdailyjournal.com/article_preview.php?id=142573&title=China%20rises%20and%20rises,%20yet%20still%20gets%20foreign%20aid.

[10]Sharon LaFraniere, "AIDS Funds Frozen for China in Grant Dispute," *The New York Times*, May 20, 2011, www.nytimes.com/2011/05/21/world/asia/21china.html.

The goal was to better coordinate foreign assistance programs, which spanned more than 20 government agencies, and better align foreign assistance with national security goals.

The effort also was aimed at increasing America's civilian capability to address instability and crisis abroad. Over time, responsibility for foreign operations increasingly had fallen to the military, and it began to ask for help. Secretary of Defense Gates in 2007 called for "a dramatic increase in spending on the civilian instruments of national security — diplomacy, strategic communications, foreign assistance, civic action and economic reconstruction and development." [35]

While the development and humanitarian communities applauded the increased focus on civilian efforts, they also had a fundamental concern. Many worried that folding USAID more tightly into the State Department linked foreign assistance too closely with short-term policy goals, leaving little room for sustainable development and poverty alleviation. The USAID administrator post was appointed as a separate position in the Obama administration.

More Aid Sought for Women and Girls

Secretary Clinton: "They represent potential that goes unfulfilled."

A majority of the planet's poor, jobless, illiterate, hungry and uneducated people are females. [1] They are subject to domestic violence, child marriage and poor reproductive health services that result in unwanted pregnancies and pregnancy-related death and disability. Yet, women and girls receive only 2 cents of every development dollar, according to some estimates, despite evidence that investing in females creates broad social gains. [2]

For example, an extra year of secondary school increases wages by 15-25 percent; girls who stay in school longer than seven years marry later and have fewer children, and women are more likely than men to reinvest their incomes in their families. [3]

Special attention to the needs of women and their connection to broader development progress was underscored at a 1994 United Nations Conference on Population and Development in Cairo, Egypt. [4] Then-first lady Hillary Rodham Clinton was a prominent leader of the U.S. delegation. While goals for achieving better health care for women became mired in anti-abortion politics during the Bush years, the issue has become popular again now that Clinton is secretary of State.

"When a girl becomes a mother before she becomes literate, when a women gives birth alone and is left with a permanent disability, when a mother toils daily to feed her large family but cannot convince her husband to agree to contraception, these struggles represent suffering that can and should be avoided," Clinton said on the 15th anniversary of the Cairo conference. "They represent potential that goes unfulfilled. And they also represent an opportunity to send critical help to women worldwide and the children who depend on them." [5]

Opportunities and health care for woman and girls are centerpieces of several Obama administration assistance programs, including the secretary's International Fund for Women and Girls and the Global Health Initiative (GHI). The fund, a public-private effort started by Clinton, invests in organizations with innovative ideas to combat violence and create economic and political opportunities for women and girls. A focus on women, girls and gender equality is one of the first principles of the GHI, which proposes a $63-billion, six-year expansion of U.S. programs addressing infectious disease, nutrition, maternal and child health, neglected tropical disease and other issues.

In addition, as HIV/AIDS began to affect more women than men in high prevalence regions, the United States global HIV/AIDS program PEPFAR began to shift resources to address mother-to-child transmission of the disease and develop female-controlled prevention strategies.

Bush's Initiatives

But Bush also instituted programs to benefit countries that were not key to U.S. political strategy. Calling the fight against poverty a moral imperative, Bush in a speech to the Inter-American Development Bank in Monterrey, Mexico, in 2002 pledged increases in core development assistance by 50 percent over three years. [36] The funds would be administered through a newly developed Millennium Challenge Account, separate from USAID. The approach was approved by Congress in 2004 and is administered by a State Department arm, the Millennium Challenge Corporation (MCC).

Before doling out funds, the MCC requires countries to prove they are well-governed and have the administrative capacity to effectively use them. In addition, countries have to show progress in fighting corruption, educating girls, building democracy and other actions. Instead of deciding in Washington which projects would be funded, MCC sponsors programs suggested by the countries themselves. But sluggish appropriations from Congress and difficulties in getting projects off the ground have slowed MCC's progress. Bush originally envisioned the agency receiving $5 billion per year, but MCC has approved only $7.4 billion in development programs in the seven years since its inception. [37]

Some aid experts worried that the MCC's strict approach would result in further suffering by poor people in countries with ineffective or corrupt leaders. Meanwhile, some U.S. beneficiaries, including Afghanistan and Pakistan, were not meeting many of the MCC criteria.

Obama is pushing combining HIV treatment with family planning and other health services.

The shift responds to recent research showing that supporting the development of women and girls has a multiplier effect. Ensuring a basic education for girls, for example, helps them control their fertility better, allows them more opportunities in the workplace and gives them the knowledge they need to keep their families healthier, according to Nandini Oomman, a senior program associate at the Center for Global Development in Washington. "If development and foreign assistance that's supposed to support development doesn't address gender differentials, then you're not going to make a lot of progress in human development no matter how much economic development you have," she says.

Reaching women with aid is difficult in many places, especially rural areas. Women tend to be mostly at home, out of the public sphere, and bear a disproportionate share of the family burden. Girls, for example, are more likely than boys to carry out household chores rather than go to school. "When you don't think specifically about how you can bring services to women, then they can't avail themselves of those services," said Oomman. In other words, she says, aid for women can only be effective when it focuses on their circumstances.

"If you start with a man as a norm, you leave off women," agrees Serra Sippel, president of the Center for Health and Gender Equity in Washington.

But raising the issue of gender is difficult in countries where discrimination is firmly entrenched. USAID recently stripped several gender-equity provisions from large projects in Afghanistan. [6] When asked at a congressional hearing about the change, Clinton acknowledged that promoting opportunities for women in the country "is really hard. And there are deep cultural challenges to doing this work." Nonetheless, Clinton reaffirmed America's commitment to gender equality. "We believe strongly that supporting women and girls is essential to building democracy and security," she told the panel. [7]

— *Nellie Bristol*

[1] Ritu Sharma, "Written Testimony: House Subcommittee on State Foreign Operations, and Related Programs," April 14, 2011, http://appropriations.house.gov/_files/041411WomenThriveWorldwideTestimony.pdf.

[2] Nancy Gibbs, "To Fight Poverty, Invest in Girls," *Time*, Feb. 14, 2011, www.time.com/time/magazine/article/0,9171,2046045,00.html.

[3] *Ibid.*

[4] Lori S. Ashford, "What Was Cairo? The Promise and Reality of ICPD," Population Reference Bureau, September 2004, www.prb.org/Articles/2004/WhatWasCairoThePromiseandRealityofICPD.aspx.

[5] Hillary Rodham Clinton, "Remarks on the 15th Anniversary of the International Conference on Population and Development," Jan. 8, 2010, www.state.gov/secretary/rm/2010/01/135001.htm.

[6] Rajiv Chandrasekaran, "In Afghanistan, US Shifts Strategy on Women's Rights as it Eyes Wider Priorities," *The Washington Post*, March 14, 2011, www.washingtonpost.com/wp-dyn/content/article/2011/03/05/AR2011030503668.html?nav=emailpage.

[7] Rajiv Chandrasekaran, "Clinton: US Will Keep Helping Afghan Women," *The Washington Post*, March 11, 2011, www.washingtonpost.com/wp-dyn/content/article/2011/03/10/AR2011031005181.html.

The biggest aid effort of the George W. Bush administration was the President's Emergency Plan for AIDS Relief (PEPFAR). After an initially slow response to the burgeoning global HIV/AIDS epidemic, Bush proposed the plan in his 2003 State of the Union address, promising $15 billion over five years. Congress enthusiastically approved the U.S. Leadership Against HIV/AIDS, Tuberculosis and Malaria Act with the goal of providing HIV/AIDS care, treatment and prevention to specific hard-hit countries. PEPFAR is the largest single disease program ever supported by one nation. It has provided antiretroviral drugs to millions of HIV sufferers in poor countries, helped develop key prevention programs and prevent the transmission of the disease from mothers to newborns. [38] The U.S Office of the Global AIDS coordinator, housed at the State Department, oversees the program. The act was reauthorized in 2008, allowing funding of up to $39 billion for the program over five years. Bush also developed the freestanding President's Malaria Initiative.

In addition, Bush authorized major U.S. contributions to multilateral efforts to improve global health. In 2001, the U.S. appropriated $100 million for the fledging Global Fund to Fight AIDS, tuberculosis and Malaria, which helps low- and middle-income countries. As of late last year, donors have pledged $30 billion to the fund, which has approved nearly $20 billion in grants to more than 140 countries. [39] The United States has pledged $9.7 billion and had contributed 28 percent of the fund's total contributions as of October 2010. But the fund is facing

An Israeli tank guards the border with the Gaza Strip. U.S. military aid to Israel dropped to $2.2 billion last year from $4 billion in 2000. According to a 2010 poll, most Americans think 25 percent of the federal budget goes to foreign aid. In reality, foreign aid constitutes only about 1.1 percent of the budget.

criticism and potential budget cuts in Congress as it works through a fraud investigation of some of its grants. [40]

Through PEPFAR and other efforts, Bush established the United States as a leader in foreign assistance through global health programs, a tradition that President Obama continued but may now be threatened by concerns over the budget deficit.

As foreign aid increased in the United States in the last decade, other countries were embracing it as well. In 2001, the United Nations adopted the Millennium Development Goals (MDGs), eight measures for reducing poverty in the developing world by 2015. The MDGs offered concrete targets in areas including poverty and hunger reduction, universal education, gender equality and improved health. The purpose was to galvanize nations and development experts toward meeting specific goals with a set timeline. While solid progress is being made on some of the goals, others are proving more difficult. Many regions have improved access to primary school for girls, for example, while there is less progress in the areas of women's paid employment and reductions in deaths related to childbirth.[41]

Also during this heady time for international assistance, the developed country members of the Organisation for Economic Co-operation and Development (OECD) began increasing their funding for foreign aid. While amounts for development, known as Official Development Assistance (ODA), rose steadily from 1960 to 1992, they faltered

through the mid-1990s. Then they started to climb again and rose from $67.9 billion in 1997 to $127 billion by 2010. [42] The United States is by far the largest donor in dollar terms, contributing $28 billion in 2009, followed by France, Germany, the United Kingdom and Japan. Nonetheless, the United States contributes only 0.2 percent of its gross national income to development assistance while Denmark, Luxembourg, the Netherlands, Norway and Sweden each exceeded the United Nations target of 0.7 percent in 2009. [43] Many are concerned that the global economic downturn will diminish foreign assistance.

While governmental foreign aid boomed in the 2000s, private aid rose as well. The leader in funding for global health and development was the Bill & Melinda Gates Foundation. Since 1994, the foundation has donated $3.3 billion to global development and another $14.5 billion to global health activities. [44] InterAction, an umbrella group for non-government organizations, estimates that aid provided by foundations, corporations, NGOs, universities and religious organizations totaled $49 billion worldwide in 2007, almost half the amount of aid provided by governments that year. In the United States, InterAction says, private aid to developing countries exceeded U.S. government assistance that year, totaling $33.4 billion compared with $21.8 billion. [45]

Obama's Initiatives

Global health and development were key features of the presidential campaigns of both Obama and Hillary Clinton. Both followed the Bush administration in advocating development as one of the three pillars of United States foreign policy along with defense and diplomacy. Obama, whose father was Kenyan, was considered to have a personal interest in the welfare of developing countries, especially those in Africa. In August 2006, Obama and his wife Michelle were both publicly tested for HIV/AIDS in an attempt to reduce stigmas associated with the procedure. Obama called for increased funding for PEPFAR, creation of stronger health systems globally to help combat AIDS and other diseases and increased funding for multilateral organizations involved with global health.

Obama came into office determined to double yearly foreign aid funding to $50 billion by 2012. But the global economic crisis, followed by a battle in Congress over health care reform, and foreign assistance fell down the priority list. Development experts and supporters in Congress saw

Does foreign aid help governments and their societies?

YES Samuel A. Worthington
President and CEO, InterAction

NO Anthony B. Kim
Policy Analyst, Center for International Trade and Economics, The Heritage Foundation

Written for *CQ Researcher*, June 13, 2011

Written for *CQ Researcher*, June 13, 2011

Robust foreign assistance helps governments in developing nations build more stable, prosperous societies and can be a catalyst in pulling a country out of poverty. Such an investment by the United States, in turn, makes our nation more secure and may create new economic partners, as was the case with former aid recipient South Korea.

Cash-strapped governments in developing nations often leverage foreign assistance to supplement their own health, education, infrastructure and other programs that enable a society to grow and prosper. This assistance — which for the United States amounts to less than 1 percent of the federal budget — saves lives.

Programs like USAID's Feed the Future initiative, for example, help boost agricultural capacity and enable a family to get nutritious food. The President's Emergency Plan for AIDS Relief (PEPFAR) has provided help to tens of millions of people suffering from HIV and AIDS, via the delivery of retroviral drugs and counseling.

In many countries, disaster risk-reduction programs funded by USAID build on existing preparedness efforts. Experts estimate that for every dollar invested in such programs, $7 is saved in disaster-response costs later on. Often implemented in partnership with nongovernmental organizations (NGOs), this assistance strengthens local and national governments and better prepares them to deal with future disasters.

The best U.S. foreign-assistance programs involve a range of stakeholders, including civil society groups and the private sector, who should work together to achieve measurable goals. Some Millennium Challenge Corporation (MCC) programs reward good governance and encourage civil society involvement as well as that of the private sector.

The debate over U.S. foreign aid and how it helps developing governments and their people takes place amid efforts to make this assistance more effective and better aligned with the priorities of the societies we are trying to help.

Aid given to governments without active citizen engagement serves only to create dependency, particularly if a government views aid solely as a way to develop the state instead of improving the lives of its people. That is why assistance should be aligned with a country's broader development strategies that have been developed in consultation with citizens and their communities.

There will always be those who argue that foreign assistance is a luxury, particularly as we are trying to balance our own budget. But for economic, moral and security reasons, the opposite is true. We can't afford not to do it.

President Obama recently unveiled a new foreign aid package for the Middle East and North Africa. The announcement has conveyed a "feel-good" public diplomacy message that the United States is willing to help the region. But can foreign aid, in general, effectively deliver much-needed economic vitality and development?

Real-world cases strongly indicate that development assistance has a dismal record in catalyzing economic growth. Indeed, recipients of large amounts of aid tend to become dependent on it — and more likely to founder than to prosper.

All too often over the decades, U.S. foreign aid has wound up enriching corrupt and anti-democratic governments that have severely undermined economic development for ordinary people in their countries. Perhaps it's not surprising, then, that U.S. foreign aid has come under more intensive scrutiny in recent months.

Instead of following an approach that has repeatedly failed, the United States, as well as aid-recipient nations, would benefit from a re-evaluation of their foreign assistance agendas, which should be focused on real reforms and advancing economic freedom.

Numerous studies indicate that policy changes that create a more conducive environment for economic transactions are far more important to development than the amount of aid a country receives. Such changes, in turn, bolster a free and fair legal system while strengthening government accountability and responsiveness.

In other words, entrepreneurship encouraged by greater economic freedom leads to innovation, economic expansion and overall human development. A fresh case in point is Rwanda, now undergoing an entrepreneurial revolution. According to The Heritage Foundation's 2011 *Index of Economic Freedom*, Rwanda had notable improvements in half of the 10 indicators of economic freedom, achieving the largest score gain among 179 economies examined.

It's no coincidence that Rwanda's gross domestic product per capita increased to more than $1,000 in 2009, from less than $350 in 1994. Along with solid economic growth backed by sound economic policies, social indicators are rising fast, too. For example, primary-school enrollment has risen 50 percent.

As the index noted, "in pursuing sustainable prosperity, both the direction of policy and commitment to economic freedom are important." Indeed, over the last decade, the countries with greater improvements in economic freedom have achieved much higher reductions in poverty.

To successfully revamp foreign aid programs to provide more effective development assistance, we need to employ the principles of economic freedom.

their best opportunity for reform in decades fade away as the United States grappled with enormous debt and a sluggish economy. While many thought a foreign assistance reform bill could pass the Democratic-controlled House and Senate and be signed by Obama, the November 2010 elections brought in a large class of conservatives to the House and turned control of the chamber to the Republicans. The shift not only put reform efforts suddenly out of reach, but also resulted in foreign assistance coming under attack in a way it hadn't been for many years.

Nonetheless, Obama thrilled global development advocates when he brought the issue front and center in a speech at the United Nations in September 2010. He announced a Presidential Policy Directive that officially made global development a part of national security and realigned its goals.

"My national security strategy recognizes development as not only a moral imperative, but a strategic and economic imperative," Obama said. [46]

He proposed revitalizing USAID, and after years of having its mission outsourced to other parts of the government, ensured the agency was the lead development focus for the United States. Obama followed the directive in December 2010 with release of the first ever Quadrennial Diplomacy and Development Review (QDDR), a State Department document aimed at giving civilian leadership a greater role in advancing national interests and working with the military. "The QDDR is a blueprint for how we can make the State Department and USAID more nimble, more effective and more accountable," Secretary of State Clinton said in announcing the plan. [47] A key goal of the effort is to bolster the use of "soft power," encompassing a non-military approach to improve global stability. "Leading through civilian power means directing and coordinating the resources of all America's civilian agencies to prevent and resolve conflicts; help countries lift themselves out of poverty into prosperous, stable and democratic states; and build global coalitions to address global problems," State Department documents explain. [48]

CURRENT SITUATION

Modest Reforms

While wholesale reform of America's foreign assistance apparatus is seen as unlikely in the foreseeable future, development nonetheless remains a key goal of the Obama administration, which is pushing modest changes on several fronts.

First and foremost, USAID is transforming itself to become more businesslike and efficient, largely to improve its functional status, but also in an effort to stave off conservative efforts to trim it. Administrator Shah has embarked on a number of efforts to transform the agency it into what he called a "modern development enterprise." [49] The effort includes the "USAID Forward" initiative, which Shah hopes will allow countries to eventually graduate from needing U.S. aid. The reforms include changing the way USAID works with contractors, increasing and improving the technical capability of local staff and recreating USAID policy and budget bureaus. In addition, technology and innovation will be emphasized, and monitoring and evaluation of aid's effectiveness will be made more rigorous.

The Obama administration is also championing two global development programs in particular, one promoting sustainable agriculture in the developing world and the other addressing health issues. Obama is seeking $3.5 billion from Congress to be spent over three years for Feed the Future, a new program aimed at increasing agricultural productivity, expanding markets and trade and bolstering economic resilience in poor, rural areas. [50]

He also proposed $63 billion over six years for the Global Health Initiative (GHI), which broadens and builds on President George W. Bush's PEPFAR program. While continuing its primary focus on combating AIDS, tuberculosis and malaria, the initiative also targets neglected tropical diseases; maternal, newborn and child health; and nutrition and health systems improvement. [51] The program is led by USAID, the Centers for Disease Control and Prevention and the U.S. Global AIDS coordinator and seeks to ensure fairness and effectiveness by focusing on:

- Gender equality;
- Allowing countries to choose which projects the United States will invest in;
- Increased integration and coordination in providing aid; and
- Improved monitoring and evaluation.

Even with efforts to improve efficiency and accountability, foreign aid faces a tough battle for funding in the new Congress. Several key House Republicans began indicating as early as last year that foreign assistance would be a prime target in future deficit-reduction talks. "I have identified and will propose a number of cuts to the State Department and foreign aid budgets," House Foreign Affairs Committee Chairwoman Ileana Ros-Lehtinen, R-Fla., said last December. "There is much fat in these budgets, which makes some cuts obvious. Others will be more difficult, but necessary, to improve the efficiency of U.S. efforts and accomplish more with less." [52]

In January, the conservative Republican Study Committee, a group of more than 175 House Republicans, proposed a spending reduction act that gutted USAID funding. [53] In a continuing resolution proposed by Republicans in February, foreign aid received the third-largest percentage of cuts out of the 12 appropriations subcommittees, according to State and Foreign Operations Subcommittee Chairwoman Kay Granger, R-Texas. [54] Cuts proposed by the House mainly target international development, not assistance to conflict zones.

Ros-Lehtinen is also using her leadership post to blast another traditional target of conservatives: the United Nations. Some in Congress are dismayed with the international organization over allegations of sexual abuse committed by U.N. peacekeepers in Africa and reports of abuse of the oil for food program in Iraq in 2004. The U.N.'s Human Rights Council regularly has been accused of anti-Semitism and being comprised of member countries with spotty human rights records. [55] However, initial efforts to cut funding to the organization failed in February to gain the two-thirds House majority needed to pass under an expedited consideration process. [56]

Senators, particularly Democrats, are more supportive of foreign assistance funding. The Senate Appropriations Committee, chaired by Hawaii Democrat Daniel K. Inouye, preserved funding for foreign aid, echoing the Obama administration position that aid is vital in supporting national security. Still, Senate Democrats proposed a $6.5 billion reduction to the State Department and foreign operations budget compared to the amount requested by the Obama administration. This compares to an $11.7 billion reduction outlined by the House.

OUTLOOK

Budget Battle

The inevitable all-out war on the federal budget means lawmakers on Capitol Hill and administration officials can expect an especially long and hot summer this year in Washington.

House Republicans have shown willingness to take on even the most popular programs, including Medicare, in the name of government and deficit reduction. While the international-affairs funding cuts outlined by the House Appropriations Committee are not as drastic as those suggested in the Republican's budget resolution, they are worrisome to economic development advocates.

"The core programs (non-war-related funding) are certainly being reduced with serious long-term funding implications," said the U.S. Global Leadership Coalition, a broadbased group of business leaders and NGOs that advocates increased foreign aid. [57] The group estimates the allocations would cut some programs by 12-16 percent. The House Appropriations Committee also is considering cuts to international agriculture programs. [58]

The Senate appears to be taking a different course, having rejected the House-passed budget proposal as well as the president's fiscal 2012 budget request. It also overwhelmingly rejected, 90-7, the budget cuts proposed by Sen. Paul. [59]

Indeed, foreign assistance as a means of enhancing national security has strong bipartisan support in the Senate, notably from South Carolina's Lindsey Graham, the ranking Republican on the State, Foreign Operations and Related Programs Subcommittee.

"If you don't want to use military force any more than you have to, count me in," said Graham. "State Department, USAID, all of these programs, in their own way, help win this struggle against radical Islam. The unsung heroes of this war are the State Department officials, the [Department of Justice] officials and the agricultural people who are going out there."

Graham added: "To those members [of Congress] who do not see the value of the civilian partnership in the war on terror, I think they are making a very dangerous decision." [60]

Aid supporters are lining up to make their case. Seventy top military leaders signed a recent letter to Congress stressing the importance of foreign assistance. [61] Global health advocates are particularly concerned about future funding for flagship programs like PEPFAR and other global health initiatives and are hitting the Hill with their support.

While acknowledging that the current budget environment is "very, very tough," Nora O'Connell, senior director of policy development and advocacy for the international welfare-advocacy group Save the Children, says she sees important support for foreign assistance.

"If you talk to congressional leaders and particularly those that are charged with oversight of foreign affairs, the Foreign Relations Committee and the Appropriations Committee, there's actually very strong bipartisan support for foreign affairs, and it comes from this fundamental belief that this is critical for our national security," she says. "What we're hoping for is that members of Congress can sort of stay strong to what the facts show . . . that this is a tiny percent of our budget, that the U.S. gets a lot out of this money and that some of these programs are serving some of the poorest and most vulnerable people in the world."

But the pressure from Republicans is fierce, especially for other Republicans who stray from the party line. Newly elected Florida Republican Sen. Marco Rubio got a taste of that intensity when he made some positive comments about foreign aid: "Foreign aid serves our national interests, and by the way, foreign aid is not the reason why we're running trillions of dollars of debt." [62] He was soon attacked for the comment on a political website. "This man ran under the Tea Party bandwagon just to get elected. He puts other countries [sic] interest before our own. Why would a supposed Tea Party candidate do this?" [63]

NOTES

1. "Hillary Clinton on Foreign Aid, Secretary of State insists on a link between foreign assistance and national security," ABC News Extra, Feb. 2, 2011, http://abcnews.go.com/ThisWeek/video/web-extra-hillary-clinton-foreign-aid-12959689.

2. Gerald F. Seib, "Deficit Balloons into National Security Threat," *The Wall Street Journal*, Feb. 2, 2010, http://online.wsj.com/article/SB1000142405 2748703422904575039173633482894.html.

3. "Mullen: Debt is Top National Security Threat," CNN, Aug. 27, 2010, http://articles.cnn.com/2010-08-27/us/debt.security.mullen_1_pentagon-budget-national-debt-michael-mullen?_s=PM:US.

4. Pete Kasperowicz, "GOP Bill Would Study Security Threat Posed by Chinese-Held Debt," *The Hill*, May 10, 2011, http://thehill.com/blogs/floor-action/house/160163-house-defense-bill-treats-us-debt-held-by-china-as-possible-security-risk.

5. Kim Gamel, "US wasted billions in rebuilding Iraq: Hundreds of Infrastructure projects are incomplete or abandoned," The Associated Press, Aug. 8, 2010, www.msnbc.msn.com/id/38903955/ns/world_news-mideastn_africa/.

6. *Ibid.*

7. Majority Staff Report, "Evaluating U.S. Foreign Assistance to Afghanistan," Prepared for the Committee on Foreign Relations, United States Senate, June 8, 2011.

8. "American Public Opinion on Foreign Aid," WorldPublicOpinion.org, Nov. 30, 2010, www.worldpublicopinion.org/pipa/pdf/nov10/ForeignAid_Nov10_quaire.pdf.

9. Curt Tarnoff and Marian Leonardo Lawson, "Foreign Aid: An Introduction to US Programs and Policy," Congressional Research Service, Feb. 10, 2011, www.fas.org/sgp/crs/row/R40213.pdf.

10. Dr. Rajiv Shah, "The Modern Development Enterprise," Center for Global Development, Jan. 19, 2011, www.usaid.gov/press/speeches/2011/sp110119.html.

11. Robert Gates, speech to the U.S. Global Leadership Campaign, July 15, 2008, Washington, D.C., www.defense.gov/speeches/speech.aspx?speechid=1262.

12. James Roberts, "Not All Foreign Aid is Equal," Backgrounder, The Heritage Foundation, March 1, 2011.

13. "The Path to Prosperity: Restoring America's Promise, Fiscal Year 2012 Budget Resolution," House Committee on Budget, http://budget.house.gov/UploadedFiles/PathToProsperityFY2012.pdf.

14. Kay Granger, "PBS NewsHour," March 10, 2011, www.pbs.org/newshour/bb/world/jan-june11/foreignaid_03-10.html.

15. Matt Schneider, "Sen. Paul Rand: We Should End all Foreign Aid to Countries, Including Israel," *Medialite*, Jan. 30, 2011, www.mediaite.com/tv/rand-paul-we-should-end-all-foreign-aid-to-countries-including-israel/.

16. "House Appropriations Subcommittee on State, Foreign Operations and Related Programs Holds Hearing on Proposed Fiscal Year 2012 Appropriations

for Global Health and HIV/AIDS Programs, March 31, 2001.

17. Steven Radelet, "Bush and Foreign Aid," *Foreign Affairs*, September/October 2003, www.cgdev.org/doc/commentary/Bush_and_Foreign_Aid.pdf.

18. Theresa Braine, "Reaching Mexico's Poorest," *Bulletin of the World Health Organization*, 2002, www.scielosp.org/scielo.php?script=sci_arttext&pid=S0042-96862006000800004&lng=pt&nrm=iso&tlng=en.

19. Hyun H. Son, "Conditional Cash Transfer Programs: An Effective Tool for Poverty Alleviation?" Asian Development Bank, July 2008, www.adb.org/Documents/EDRC/Policy_Briefs/PB051.pdf.

20. Jeremy M. Sharp, "Egypt in Transition," Congressional Research Service, March 29, 2011, www.fas.org/sgp/crs/mideast/RL33003.pdf.

21. "Background Note: Egypt," Department of State, Nov. 10, 2010, www.state.gov/r/pa/ei/bgn/5309.htm.

22. Ashish Kumar, Sen., "Lawmakers Criticize Obama's Response to Egypt Crisis," *The Washington Times*, Feb. 9, 2011, www.washingtontimes.com/news/2011/feb/9/republican-and-democratic-lawmakers-criticized-the/.

23. David Francis, "Foreign Aid Dilemma: Dictators on Our Dole," *The Fiscal Times*, March 16, 2011, www.thefiscaltimes.com/Articles/2011/03/16/Foreign-Aid-Dilemma-Dictators-on-our-Dole.aspx?p=1.

24. "Aid to Pakistan by the Numbers," Center for Global Development, www.cgdev.org/section/initiatives/_active/pakistan/numbers.

25. "Obama's Challenge in the Muslim World: Arab Spring Fails to Improve US Image" Pew Research Center, May 17, 2011, http://pewglobal.org/files/2011/05/Pew-Global-Attitudes-Arab-Spring-FINAL-May-17-2011.pdf.

26. James Roberts, "Not all Foreign Aid is Equal," Backgrounder, The Heritage Foundation, March 1, 2011, www.heritage.org/Research/Reports/2011/03/Not-All-Foreign-Aid-Is-Equal.

27. "ABC News Extra," *op. cit.*

28. "US Military: Aid to Egypt has 'Incalculable Value,'" Reuters, Feb. 16, 2011, www.reuters.com/article/2011/02/16/us-usa-budget-egypt-idUSTRE71F4CO20110216.

29. Diane B. Kunz, "The Marshall Plan Reconsidered, A Complex of Motives," *Foreign Affairs*, May/June 1997.

30. "About USAID, USAID History," USAID, www.usaid.gov/about_usaid/usaidhist.html.

31. Richard P. Cincotta and Barbara B. Crane, "The Mexico City Policy and US Family Planning Assistance," *Science*, Oct. 19, 2002.

32. "USAID Foreign Service Permanent Workforce & USAID Managed Program Dollars," USAID, www.usaid.gov/press/speeches/2011/ty110330b.pdf.

33. Tarnoff and Lawson, *op. cit.*

34. Condoleezza Rice, remarks at Georgetown School of Foreign Service, Jan. 18, 2006, www.unc.edu/depts/diplomat/item/2006/0103/rice/rice_georgetown.html.

35. Thom Shanker, "Defense Secretary Urges More Spending for US Diplomacy," *The New York Times*, Nov. 27, 2007, www.nytimes.com/2007/11/27/washington/27gates.html?_r=1.

36. Radelet, *op. cit.*

37. "About MCC," Millennium Challenge Corporation, www.mcc.gov/pages/about.

38. The President's Emergency Plan for AIDS Relief, "Latest Results," www.pepfar.gov/results/index.htm.

39. "The US & The Global Fund to Fight AIDS, Tuberculosis and Malaria," Kaiser Family Foundation, November 2010, www.kff.org/global-health/upload/8003-02.pdf.

40. John Heilprin, "AP Enterprise: Fraud Plagues Global Health Fund," The Associated Press, Jan. 23, 2011, http://news.yahoo.com/s/ap/20110123/ap_on_re_eu/eu_aids_fund_corruption.

41. *Ibid.*

42. "Net ODA Disbursements, Total DAC Countries," Organisation for Economic Co-operation and Development, http://webnet.oecd.org/dcdgraphs/ODAhistory/.

43. *Ibid.*

44. "Foundation Fact Sheet," Bill & Melinda Gates Foundation, www.gatesfoundation.org/about/Pages/foundation-fact-sheet.aspx.

45. "Private Aid Flows," *InterAction*, www.interaction.org/private-aid-flows.

46. Barack Obama, "Statement by the President at the Millennium Development Goal Summit in New York, New York," Sept. 22, 2010, www.whitehouse.gov/the-press-office/2010/09/22/remarks-president-millennium-development-goals-summit-new-york-new-york.

47. "Leading Through Civilian Power: Quadrennial Diplomacy and Development Review," *DipNote*, Dec. 15, 2010, http://blogs.state.gov/index.php/site/entry/civilian_power_qddr.

48. *Ibid.*

49. Shah, *op. cit.*

50. Angela Rucker, "$3.5B US Hunger Plan to Feed 40 Million People," "Frontlines," USAID June 2010, www.usaid.gov/press/frontlines/fl_jun10/p01_hunger100601.html.

51. The US Global Health Initiative, www.ghi.gov/.

52. Nicole Gaouette, "Ros-Lehtinen To Seek Cuts in Diplomatic, Foreign Aid Funding," Bloomberg, Dec. 9, 2010, www.bloomberg.com/news/2010-12-09/ros-lehtinen-to-seek-cuts-in-diplomatic-foreign-aid-funding.html.

53. Emily Cadei, "Proposed Cuts Thrust Foreign Aid Into Center of Spending Debate," *CQ Today*, Jan. 21, 2011.

54. Emily Cadei, "In Fiscal 2011 Bill, Senate Democrats Take a Broader view of Security Spending," *CQ Today*, March 4, 2011.

55. Emily Cadei, "Key Post Gives Ros-Lehtinen a Platform to Hammer U.N." *CQ Today*, Jan. 7, 2011.

56. Frances Symes, "Effort to Cut U.N. Funding Over Tax Payments Falls Short on House Floor," *CQ Today*, Feb. 9, 2011.

57. Stuart B. Baimel, "International Affairs Budget Update, 5-12-11," US Global Leadership Coalition, May 24, 2011, www.usglc.org/2011/05/24/international-affairs-budget-update-5-12-2011-2/.

58. Stuart B. Baimel, "International Affairs Budget Update, 5-27-11," US Global Leadership Coalition, May 27, 2010, www.usglc.org/2011/05/27/international-affairs-budget-update-5-27-11/.

59. "Senate Rejects Rand Paul Budget Plan," Kentucky Politics, May 25, 2011, http://cincinnati.com/blogs/nkypolitics/2011/05/25/senate-rejects-rand-paul-budget-plan/.

60. Josh Rogin, "Lindsey Graham to the Rescue for State and USAID," *The Cable*, Feb. 1, 2011, http://thecable.foreignpolicy.com/posts/2011/02/01/lindsey_graham_to_the_rescue_for_state_and_usaid.

61. "Military Leaders Letter to Congress," US Global Leadership Coalition, March 30, 2011, www.usglc.org/wp-content/uploads/2011/03/NSAC-letter-2011.pdf.

62. "Sen. Marco Rubio: 'Foreign Aid Serves Our National Interest," YouTube, "Your World with Neil Cavuto," March 30, 2011, www.youtube.com/watch?v=KAcfaXEDem8.

63. "Tea Party Has Been Swindled by Marco Rubio," The Truth Stings, April 8, 2011, http://truthstings.com/tea-party-has-been-swindled-by-marco-rubio/.

BIBLIOGRAPHY

Selected Sources
Books

Brautigam, Deborah, *The Dragon's Gift: The Real Story of China in Africa,* **Oxford, 2009.**
A noted China expert at American University in Washington explains China's African aid strategy.

Easterly, William, *The White Man's Burden: Why the West's Efforts to Aid the Rest Have Done So Much Ill and So Little Good,* **Penguin Books, 2006.**
A New York University economics professor argues that Western attempts to alleviate poverty have been futile.

Moyo, Dambisa, *Dead Aid: Why Aid is Not working and How There is a Better Way for Africa, Farrar, Straus and Giroux, 2009.**
An African economist argues that African countries are worse off as a result of foreign aid.

Sachs, Jeffrey, *The End of Poverty: Economic Possibilities for Our Time,* **Penguin, 2005.**
A Columbia University economist contends that extreme global poverty can be eliminated through development aid by 2025.

Karlan, Dean, *More than Good Intentions: How a New Economics is Helping to Solve Global Poverty*, Penguin, 2011.
A Yale University economics professor discusses behavioral economics and worldwide field research to explore what works in development aid.

Calderisi, Robert, *The Trouble with Africa: Why Foreign Aid Isn't Working, Palgrave,* Macmillan, 2006.
A former World Bank international spokesman on Africa discusses the shortcomings of foreign aid.

Articles

Ali, Ambreen, "Tea Party: Unimpressed — and Angry as Ever," *CQ Weekly*, March 7, 2011.
Ali examines the Tea Party's insistence on smaller government.

Cadei, Emily, "Proposed Cuts Thrust Foreign Aid Agency into Center of Spending Debate," *CQ Today Online News*, Jan. 21, 2011.
Cadei outlines House Republican criticism of the U.S. Agency for International Development.

Kunz, Diane B., "The Marshall Plan Reconsidered: A Complex of Motives," *Foreign Affairs*, May/June 1997.
Kunz argues that the posts-World War II aid effort paid huge dividends for the United States and that similar efforts can be justified today.

McKenzie, A. D., "Parliamentarian ask G8 to focus on Women," *Guardian Development Network*, May 19, 2011.
Countries at the G8 conference in France call for an increased focus on the role of women and girls in development.

Norris, John, "Five Myths about Foreign Aid," *The Washington Post*, April 28, 2011.
The executive director of the sustainable security program at the Center for American Progress discusses foreign aid budget cuts proposed by Republicans and misconceptions about economic development.

Pennington, Matthew, "Clinton Says US in Direct Competition With China," *The Associated Press*, March 2, 2011.
Pennington recounts Secretary of State Hillary Rodham Clinton's comments to the Senate Foreign Relations Committee.

Reports and Studies

"A Woman-Centered Approach to the US Global Health Initiative," *Center for Health and Gender Equity*, February 2010.
Explains and supports "woman-centered" approach in the US global health policy.

Epstein, Susan, "Foreign Aid Reform, National Strategy, and the Quadrennial Review," *Congressional Research Service*, Feb. 15, 2011.
An analyst for the nonpartisan agency details congressional and administration efforts to reform foreign-assistance programs.

Levine, Ruth, Cynthia B. Lloyd, Margaret Greene and Caren Grown, "Girls Count: A Global Investment and Action Agenda," *Center for Global Development*, December 2009.
The authors detail the disadvantages faced by girls in developing countries and make a case for gender equality.

Sharp, Jeremy M., "Egypt in Transition," *Congressional Research Service*, March 29, 2011.
Sharp gives an overview of the transition occurring in Egypt and outlines U.S. foreign aid to the country.

Tarnoff, Curt, and Marian Leonardo Lawson, "Foreign Aid: an Introductory Overview of US Programs and Policy," *Congressional Research Service*, Feb. 10, 2011.
CRS analysts present an overview of the types and goals of U.S. foreign assistance.

Williams-Bridgers, Jacquelyn, "Foreign Operations, Key Issues or Congressional Oversight," *Government Accountability Office*, March 3, 2011.
The author reviews a GAO study of weaknesses in U.S. foreign assistance programs.

For More Information

Bread for the World, 425 Third St., S.W., Suite 1200, Washington, DC 20024; (800) 822-7323; www.bread.org. Christian citizens' movement dedicated to ending hunger domestically and abroad.

Cato Institute, 1000 Massachusetts Ave., N.W., Washington, DC 20001; (202) 842-0200; www.cato.org. Libertarian think tank opposing strategic foreign aid and promoting economic freedom as a solution to problems overseas.

Center for Global Development, 1800 Massachusetts Ave., N.W., Third Floor, Washington, DC 20036; (202) 416-4000; www.cgdev.org. Independent and non-partisan research institute working to reduce global poverty.

Heritage Foundation, 214 Massachusetts Ave., N.E., Washington, DC 20002; (202) 546-4400; www.heritage.org. Conservative think tank advocating for policies that oppose traditional development assistance.

InterAction, 1400 16th St., N.W., Suite 210, Washington, DC 20036; (202) 667-8227; www.interaction.org. Alliance of U.S.-based nongovernmental organizations focusing on disaster relief and sustainable development.

Millennium Challenge Corporation, 875 15th St., N.W., Washington, DC 20005; (202) 521-3850; www.mcc.gov. Bilateral U.S. foreign aid agency distributing funds through a process of competitive selection.

Modernizing Foreign Assistance Network, 425 Third St., S.W., Suite 1200, Washington, DC 20024; (202) 688-1087; www.modernizeaid.net. Coalition of foreign policy practitioners advocating for a larger U.S. leadership role in reducing poverty and suffering around the world.

U.S. Agency for International Development, 1300 Pennsylvania Ave., N.W., Washington, DC 20523; (202) 712-0000; www.usaid.gov. U.S. federal agency primarily responsible for administering civilian foreign aid.

U.S. Global Leadership Coalition, 1129 20th St., N.W., Suite 600, Washington, DC 20036; (202) 833-5555; www.usglc.org. Coalition of American businesses and NGOs promoting greater U.S. diplomatic and development efforts.

8

Russia in Turmoil

Jason McLure

Vladimir Putin has led Russia as either prime minister or president for 12 years and is considered the overwhelming front-runner in the March 4 presidential election. His tenure was built on an implicit deal with voters: In exchange for a rising standard of living fueled by surging energy exports, citizens' legal and political rights have been curtailed.

From *CQ Researcher*,
Feb. 21, 2012

W hen Vladimir Putin stepped into the ring at a Moscow stadium to congratulate the winner of an "anything goes" mixed martial arts bout on Nov. 20, he couldn't have been more at home.

During his 12 years at the head of Russia's government — first as president and then as prime minister — the 59-year-old former KGB agent has cultivated a macho image: allowing himself to be photographed shirtless on horseback in Siberia, practicing judo and shooting a tiger with a tranquilizer dart. And Putin's harsh regime has exiled and imprisoned dozens of opposition supporters, journalists and human rights activists, while others have died in suspicious circumstances.

So it came as a surprise that the popular Putin was lustily booed by the fight fans, angered, like many other Russians, by the announcement in September that he would run for president again in 2012 to replace Dmitry Medvedev, the man he had handpicked to succeed him in 2008. [1]

The discontent erupted into the streets in three major protests in December, after Putin's United Russia Party retained control of the Duma, Russia's lower house, after what was seen as rigged parliamentary elections.

Protesters hit the streets of cities across Russia again on Feb. 4, despite sub-zero temperatures, just a month before the presidential elections. Their anger indicates that Putin's grip on power has weakened and raises questions about the viability of the political and economic system he has built. Putin's 12 years in power reflected an implicit deal with voters: In exchange for a rising standard of living fueled by surging energy exports, citizens would have fewer legal and political rights.

A Giant on the World Stage

The world's largest country, Russia stretches across Asia from the Pacific Ocean to Europe. In recent years it has battled Islamic insurgents in the outlying republics of Ingushetia, Dagestan and Chechnya, situated in the southwestern Caucasus region. One of the world's largest oil producers, Russia recently completed a new oil pipeline to China and supplies much of Europe's natural gas. Many of Russia's neighbors — including Kazakhstan, Ukraine, Belarus and Estonia — were under Moscow's control during the Soviet era.

Russia and Surrounding Countries

Source: map by Lewis Agrell

Already the world's largest source of natural gas, Russia under Putin expanded its oil production and now rivals Saudi Arabia as the world's largest oil producer. Increased production, combined with rising oil prices, has dramatically improved living standards, at least in Moscow and St. Petersburg — and oil and gas now provide about half of Russia's revenues. [2]

Yet authoritarian rule and record energy revenues have proven a recipe for corruption, which both reinforces Putin's control by providing a source of patronage while undermining his legitimacy. The spread of corruption into all facets of life — from hospital surgeries to kindergarten admissions — and the recent global economic turmoil have led to deep doubts about Russia's long-term survival as a one-party petro-state.

Meanwhile, the growing popularity of social media websites has enabled urban, middle-class Russians to circumvent state-censored media and share information about everything from corrupt local officials and ballot-box stuffing to protest plans.

Public frustration with Putin gained momentum on Dec. 24, when some 80,000 people gathered in the streets of Moscow to call for an end to his tenure. "Putin should stand aside, he looks out of touch with reality," Alexei Frolov, a 26-year-old clothing shop manager, said, explaining that he decided to join the protests after he saw that the demonstrators were "normal, happy people who just wanted to defend their rights." [3]

They were joined by protesters in dozens of other cities, shocking many analysts with the scale of popular unrest. "No one really expected the middle class to protest so long as they had a solid, secure income," says Tamirlan Kurbanov, a Russian legal scholar researching Russian youth activism at the National Endowment for Democracy, a private, Washington-based, nonprofit foundation that supports democratic institutions around the world. "They came to protest not potential threats to their income but stolen votes — a purely political issue. This is a big shift in mentality."

Along with a Feb. 5 protest in which tens of thousands braved sub-zero temperatures, the demonstrations recalled the throngs who took to Moscow's streets in March 1991, demanding the resignation of the last Soviet premier, Mikhail Gorbachev. [4] Gorbachev, who resigned nine months after those protests and is now 80, has joined the current calls for Putin to leave, telling a Moscow radio station: "He has had three terms: two as president and one as prime minister. Three terms — that is enough." [5]

The Internet and the social media sites LiveJournal, Twitter and Facebook have been key tools for the protesters. Even though state television removed the audio of Putin being booed in the martial arts ring, one version of the unedited video has been viewed more than 449,000 times on YouTube. [6] Bypassing Russia's quiescent opposition parties, the largely leaderless movement has been shaped by up-and-coming activists, such as lawyer and anti-corruption blogger Alexei Navalny, who has more than 190,000 followers on Twitter and whose blog has more than 60,000 daily readers. [7]

Despite the protests, analysts say Putin is still the heavy favorite to win another term, largely because the government has divided the opposition. Some so-called

Russia at a Glance

Russia is nearly twice as big as the United States but has less than half the population. Its per capita income of $16,700 is about the same as Argentina's. Vladimir Putin, who has been in a leadership role for nearly 12 years, is expected to be elected president again in March.

Area: 6.3 million sq. miles (nearly twice as large as the U.S.)

Population: 138.7 million (July 2011 est.; slightly less than half the U.S. population)

Chief of state: President Dmitry Medvedev (since May 2008)

Head of government: Prime Minister Vladimir Putin (since May 2008; he served as president from 2000 to 2008.

Government type: Federation; president elected by popular vote for up to two four-year terms, but terms will increase to six years starting with 2012 election; legislative branch consists of the Federation Council (upper house) with members appointed for four-year terms by the top executives in the federal administrative units; members of the State Duma (lower house) are elected to four-year terms by popular vote.

Ethnic groups: Russian 79.8%, Tatar 3.8%, Ukrainian 2%, Bashkir 1.2%, Chuvash 1.1%, other or unspecified 12.1% (2002 census)

Religion: Russian Orthodox 15-20%, Muslim 10-15%, other Christian denominations 2%, other/agnostic 53-73% (2006 est.)

Infant mortality rate: 10.08 deaths/1,000 live births (147th in the world)

GDP: $2.373 trillion* (7th in the world, about the same as Brazil)

GDP per capita: $16,700* (similar to Argentina and a third of the United States)

Unemployment rate: 6.8%* (71st in the world, about the same as Indonesia)

Primary industries: complete range of mining and extractive industries producing coal, oil, gas, chemicals and metals; defense industries including radar, missile production and advanced electronic components, shipbuilding; road and rail transportation equipment; communications equipment; electric power generating and transmitting equipment

* 2011 estimate

Source: The World Factbook, Central Intelligence Agency, 2012, https://www.cia.gov/library/publications/the-world-factbook/geos/rs.html

opposition parties are in league with the Kremlin, says Stephen Sestanovich, a fellow at the Council on Foreign Relations think tank in New York City. However, Putin may not win the 50 percent needed to prevent a run-off. "That will put a lot of pressure on Putin," says Sestanovich. "It will be seen as a tremendous humiliation" for Putin if the election goes to a second round.

Real Spies *Do* Use Invisible Ink and "Sleeper Cells"

East-West espionage apparently is alive and well.

Messages written in invisible ink. Money buried in a field in upstate New York. Identical bags surreptitiously exchanged at a train station.

They sound like the makings of a good Cold War spy novel, but in fact such techniques were in the bag of tricks used by an alleged Russian spy ring broken up in the United States in 2010 — nearly 20 years after the breakup of the Soviet Union.

Nor did these alleged spies use typical cover stories, such as claiming to be diplomats or representatives of vague-sounding Russian think tanks. In an effort to become culturally American, these so-called sleeper agents had come to the United States to live and work as ordinary middle-class people in suburban Boston, New York and Washington, where they spent years developing American identities. [1] One worked for an accounting firm; another was a real estate agent; a third worked at a travel agency. All reportedly were part of a bizarre scheme that apparently gathered little information of value.

Moscow and the West may no longer fear nuclear war with each other, but the shadowy "spy vs. spy" dance between Russia and its Western counterparts has never slackened. Prime Minister Vladimir Putin, a former KGB agent and director of its successor agency, the Federal Security Service (FSB), has ensured that Russia's intelligence agencies have played a large role in his government. [2] But at times, the nonstop spying has complicated post-Cold War diplomatic relations.

Indeed, the FBI uncovered the sleeper ring just as Presidents Barack Obama and Russian President Dmitry Medvedev were discussing how to "reset" U.S.-Russia relations on more friendly terms. Instead of being prosecuted, 10 of the agents were sent back to Russia in exchange for four men accused of spying for Britain and the United States in Russia (the 11th slipped away after a court in Cyprus released him on bail). [3]

Not all alleged Russian intelligence operations have been so benign or inept. Three Chechen militants — two of them linked to a 2011 suicide bombing at Moscow's Domodedovo airport — were gunned down in the Turkish capital Istanbul last September. All were executed in daylight by an assailant who fired 11 shots in less than 30 seconds from a silenced pistol. The pistol, a night-vision camera, binoculars and a Russian passport were later found in a Turkish hotel room. The Russian government officially denied any involvement in the killings. [4]

Russian operatives also are active in other Western countries. Former Russian agent turned dissident Alexander Litvinenko died a slow and excruciating death in London in 2006, after being poisoned with radioactive polonium shortly after meeting with Andrei Lugovoy, a former KGB bodyguard. Litvinenko blamed the Kremlin for his poisoning, and British police sought Lugovoy's extradition from Russia to face charges. The Kremlin has denied the extradition request, and Lugovoy is now a senior member of the Russian parliament representing the ultra-nationalist LDPR party. [5] Lugovoy denies the murder and has variously suggested that it was perpetrated by a dissident Russian oligarch, British security services, the Russian mafia and unnamed people with links to Georgia. [6]

More recently, four Russian diplomats in Canada abruptly left their embassy in Ottawa after a Canadian

The upheaval comes on the heels of the 2011 Arab Spring — popular revolts that unseated dictators in Egypt, Tunisia, Libya and Yemen, and it is difficult not to see parallels between those movements and Russia's current unrest. [8] As U.S. Sen. John McCain, R-Ariz., tweeted in December "Dear Vlad, The Arab Spring is coming to a neighborhood near you."

When asked about McCain's comment during a televised call-in show, Putin responded sharply. "Mr. McCain fought in Vietnam," said Putin. "I think that he has enough blood of peaceful citizens on his hands. It must be impossible for him to live without these disgusting scenes anymore." [9]

But McCain wasn't the only American to draw Putin's wrath. Shortly after the protests erupted in December, naval intelligence officer was charged with passing secrets to a foreign entity. [7] However, a British court in November rejected efforts to deport a 26-year-old Russian woman who had an affair with a member of Parliament and was charged with being a Russian agent. The court said British intelligence officials had failed to prove she was an agent. [8]

But espionage is a two-way street. In January Jonathan Powell, former British Prime Minister Tony Blair's chief of staff, admitted that in 2006 British agents had been caught using a fake rock in a Moscow park to transmit and receive electronic signals. The embarrassing revelation led to Russian accusations that Britain was funding groups opposed to Putin. [9]

Still, the break-up of the alleged American sleeper cell last year was arguably even more embarrassing to Russia. State media gave heavy coverage to the 10 "suburban spies" being awarded medals by Medvedev upon their return home. But in a humiliating twist, it turns out the Moscow-based spymaster who operated the ring had been passing information to the Central Intelligence Agency since 1999. He was whisked out of Russia on the eve of the U.S. crackdown. [10]

"The activity of both intelligence services will not stop and never will," said Boris Solomatin, a retired KGB general, who spent two decades supervising Russian spy operations in the United States. "But the end of the Cold War gives us an opportunity to put an end to uncivilized methods." [11]

— *Jason McLure*

A courtroom drawing shows five members of an alleged Russian spy ring after their arrest in the United States in 2010 — nearly 20 years after end of the Cold War

[1]Scott Shane and Charlie Savage, "In Ordinary Lives, U.S. Sees the Work of Russian Agents," *The New York Times*, June 28, 2010, www.nytimes.com/2010/06/29/world/europe/29spy.html?pagewanted=all.

[2]Steven Eke, "KGB Influence 'Soars Under Putin,'" BBC News, Dec. 13, 2006, http://news.bbc.co.uk/2/hi/6177531.stm.

[3]Helena Smith, "Russian Spy Ring Suspect Jumps Bail in Cyprus," *The Guardian*, June 30, 2010.

[4]Lee Ferran and Rym Momtaz, "Payback? Istanbul Assassination Victims Linked to Moscow Bombing," ABCNews.com, Sept. 22, 2011, http://abcnews.go.com/Blotter/payback-istanbul-assassination-victims-linked-moscow-bombing/story?id=14581977.

[5]"Zhirinovsky's New Sideman: Lugovoy," U.S. State Department Cable, Sept. 18, 2007. Released by Wikileaks and available at www.guardian.co.uk/world/us-embassy-cables-documents/122689.

[6]"Lugovoy Points to Possible Killers of Litvinenko," *RT*, Oct. 23, 2011, http://rt.com/news/lugovoy-litvinenko-court-hearing-509/.

[7]Steven Chase, Oliver Moore and Tamara Baluja, "Ottawa expels Russian diplomats in wake of charges against Canadian," *The Globe and Mail*, Jan. 19, 2012, www.theglobeandmail.com/news/politics/ottawa-expels-russian-diplomats-in-wake-of-charges-against-canadian/article2308879/.

[8]John Fahey, "MI5 'Unfairly' Pursued Spy Accused Katia Zatuliveter," *The Independent*, Nov. 29, 2011, www.independent.co.uk/news/uk/home-news/mi5-unfairly-pursued-spy-accused-katia-zatuliveter-6269410.html.

[9]"UK Admits Spying With Fake Rock," BBC News, Jan. 18, 2012, www.bbc.co.uk/news/world-europe-16619623.

[10]Tom Parfitt, "Russian double agent sentenced in absentia to 25 years in prison," *The Guardian*, June 27, 2011, www.guardian.co.uk/world/2011/jun/27/russian-double-agent-tried-absence.

[11]Pete Earley, "Boris Solomatin Interview," truTV Crime Library, undated, www.trutv.com/library/crime/terrorists_spies/spies/solomatin/1.html.

Putin blamed U.S. Secretary of State Hillary Rodham Clinton for prompting the Russian protests by calling the parliamentary vote "neither free nor fair." Clinton's comment, he said, "sent a signal" to "some of our public figures inside the country. They heard this signal and launched active work with the U.S. State Department's support." [10]

The upheaval may be aggravating tensions between Russia and the West, but analysts debate whether it poses a threat to the underlying relationship, which warmed during a "reset" in 2010 between presidents Obama and Medvedev.

"There is a very different agenda for inside Russia and outside of Russia," says Fatima Tlisova, a Russian journalist who has worked for the Russian newspaper *Novaya Gazeta* and The Associated Press. "Inside Russia he can play very anti-American populist games, and outside Russia he can be very sensitive. He tries to create a special image of Russia as being democratic."

The protests, however, reveal a Russian political and economic system more fragile than many analysts believed before the demonstrations. As policy experts gauge the recent upheaval on the streets of Moscow, here are some of the questions they are asking:

Will an Arab Spring-style revolt topple Putin?

Russia's recent uprising shares several similarities with the popular revolts that toppled autocratic regimes in the Arab world last spring. In both instances, protesters objected to political stagnation, pervasive corruption and the absence of democracy. And, as in the Arab world, the Russians are organizing online, because television and radio are state-controlled.

But analysts differ strongly on whether the death knell is sounding for Putin's regime. Some say the system Putin build is near collapse, while others say it's hardly the end of a regime that has run the world's largest country for the last 12 years.

"Putin still enjoys the support of a large number of the population and is still the most popular leader," says Andranik Migranyam, an adviser to former President Boris Yeltsin and now director of the pro-Kremlin Institute for Democracy and Cooperation in New York. "It's not going to be something like what happened in Egypt or some other places."

"People who came out to rally don't want revolution, they want evolution," says Kurbanov, at the National Endowment for Democracy. "I don't think they were inspired by the Arab Spring."

Because many of the protesters are middle-class city-dwellers, their demands are different from other revolutionaries' demands. "They are mostly educated enough about the past to fear blood in the streets," Esther Dyson, a Swiss-born columnist, wrote recently in the *Prague Post.* [11] "They want Putin gone, not punished (mostly); they realize it is the system that produced Putin, who then reinforced the system. They want to reverse that cycle, putting an end to corruption, official impunity and being treated like cattle."

Putin and his inner circle likely will resist surrendering power until the bitter end in order to avoid

prosecution for corruption or other criminal behavior by a future Russian government, according to Michael Bohm, opinion page editor of the English-language *Moscow Times.* "The best, and perhaps only, guarantee of securing immunity for Putin — and dozens of his friends and colleagues who have become millionaires and billionaires over the past 10 years . . . is to remain in power," Bohm wrote recently. [12]

Others say the protests will continue to grow in size and passion, potentially toppling the regime. "My guess is that it's going to continue and radicalize," says Leon Aron, director of Russian studies at the American Enterprise Institute (AEI), a conservative think tank in Washington. "The first demonstrations were calling for new [parliamentary] elections. Then they were saying 'Putin is a thief, Putin is a dictator,' and it started to move into a critique of the regime itself."

With some form of protest taking place in more than 100 cities, the movement has reached critical mass, and Putin's government is close to collapse, says Anders Aslund, a Swedish fellow at the Peterson Institute for International Economics in Washington. "I think it will disappear quickly because Putin's magic is broken now," he says. "A dictator needs to be feared to be respected. Now Putin is just seen as a joke."

Aslund says many of the police that watched the most recent demonstrations were high-ranking officers, indicating that Putin's government can no longer be sure of the loyalty of the rank-and-file security forces, he says. "I don't think anybody will shoot for Putin now," he adds. "I don't think anybody will be killed. That moment has passed."

However, many Russians now say the system can't evolve, says Stephen Blank, a Russia researcher at the U.S. Army War College. "Putin's gang, they basically tell people: 'You count for nothing; we're going to take power,' " says Blank. "It's a system that can't reform itself. It has to be transformed."

Will Putin's new government tackle corruption?

The scale of corruption in Russia is widely seen as staggering. Transparency International ranked Russia 143rd out of 182 countries in its 2011 corruption perceptions index, on par with Nigeria and more corrupt than international pariahs such as Syria, Iran and Eritrea. [13]

Corruption costs Russia as much as $318 billion annually, or one-third of its total economic output, according to the Moscow-based InDem Foundation, a nongovernmental organization that researches corruption and governance. [14] The average commercial bribe paid to a government or corporate official in the first half of 2011 was 293,000 rubles ($10,573). "Everyday" bribes to get children into kindergarten, avoid the military draft or fix traffic tickets were 5,285 rubles ($191), according to Russian government figures. [15]

Although corruption has been a fixture under Putin's rule, some say he could still tackle the problem. Bribery already was rife before Putin came to power; in 2000 Transparency International ranked Russia 82nd out of 90 countries surveyed. [16]

By some measures corruption has declined in recent years. A survey by the PriceWaterhouseCoopers accounting firm found that 40 percent of businesses reported being victims of bribery and corruption in 2011, down from 48 percent in 2009. "There is reason to be hopeful that some effect is being felt from both the increased publicity and legal activities promoted by the Russian government," the report said. [17]

Putin launched his 2012 presidential campaign by addressing the need to crack down on corruption. [18] And after the Dec. 24 protests he ordered managers at state-owned companies to declare their income and property and disclose the owners of all companies with which they do business. [19]

"To defeat systemic corruption, a line should be drawn to separate not only authority and property but

Russia Ranks High on Corruption Scale

Russia is among the world's most corrupt nations, according to the corruption watchdog group Transparency International. Russia's corruption perception index score of 2.4 in 2011 was the same as Nigeria's, known worldwide for its rampant corruption. And Russia's corruption problem is more serious than countries with similar economic conditions such as China and India.

Corruption Perceptions Index Scores for Select Countries, 2001 and 2011
(on a scale from 0 to 10, with 10 being the least corrupt)

Country	2001	2011
Russia	2.3	2.4
Poland	4.1	5.5
Turkey	3.6	4.2
Indonesia	1.9	3.0
Nigeria	1.0	2.4
Estonia	5.6	6.4
India	2.7	3.1
China	3.5	3.6
Brazil	4.0	3.8
Mexico	3.7	3.0

Source: "Corruption Perceptions Index 2001," Transparency International, June 2001, www.transparency.org/policy_research/surveys_indices/cpi/2001; "Corruption Perceptions Index 2011," Transparency International, 2011, cpi.transparency.org/cpi2011/results/

also executive power and control over it," Putin wrote in *Kommersant*, a Russian business daily, in February. In the same article, Putin promised a new system of administrative courts for corruption as well as online broadcasts and public transcripts of court hearings. [20]

"Authorities have adopted a number of steps indicating that they . . . are ready to act decisively," Migranyan, of the Institute for Democracy and Cooperation, wrote recently. "Both the prime minister and the president have spoken about important steps taken to combat corruption." [21]

Others say Putin cannot tackle corruption because he and his closest allies are heavily implicated. "Putin himself is one of the biggest thieves," says Aslund, of the Peterson Institute. "He has organized a set-up where he taps a number of government sources, and the money goes to his reliable friends."

Though such allegations are unconfirmed, anecdotal evidence abounds. In 2011, just hours after a Russian website patterned after Wikileaks published photos of a massive new mansion on the Black Sea reportedly owned by Putin, it suffered a cyber-attack that shut down the site. [22] And Vladimir Litvinenko, an economics professor who oversaw Putin's doctoral thesis, is now one of Russia's richest men and chairman of a phosphate mining company worth at least $350 million. [23]

"The fortune is raising eyebrows because Litvinenko, who has headed the state mining institute since 1994, was not previously known as a businessman," wrote Nikolaus von Twickel, a reporter for the *Moscow Times*.

Russia Leads World in Gas Reserves

With more than 1.5 quadrillion cubic feet of proven natural gas reserves, Russia has the world's largest gas deposits — about 50 percent more than Iran, which ranks second. Since Vladimir Putin came to power in 2000, Russia has increased its crude oil production by 50 percent, boosting the value of its oil exports more than fivefold. Critics say that by increasing Russia's dependence on lucrative energy exports, Putin has made the economy vulnerable to fluctuating world energy prices and fueled rampant corruption.

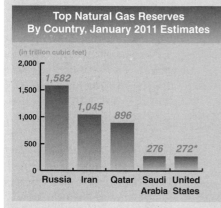

Top Natural Gas Reserves By Country, January 2011 Estimates
(in trillion cubic feet)

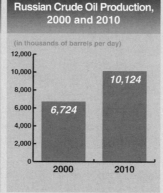

Russian Crude Oil Production, 2000 and 2010
(in thousands of barrels per day)

* January 2009 estimate

Source: "Natural Gas — Proved Reserves," The World Factbook, Central Intelligence Agency, 2012, https://www.cia.gov/library/publications/the-world-factbook/rankorder/2179rank.html; "Russia Country Analysis Brief," U.S. Energy Information Administration, November 2010, www.eia.gov/countries/cab.cfm?fips=RS; Bank of Russia

"Litvinenko's apparently rapid rise to riches speaks volumes in a country where who you know can be as important as what you know, if not more so." [24]

Some regime critics say Putin is worth up to $40 billion and controls hidden stakes in natural gas giant Gazprom, oil explorer-Surgutneftegaz and oil-trader Gunvor. [25] Putin and the companies involved have denied this repeatedly, but the lack of transparency in Russian corporations makes verifying such assertions impossible.

Corruption also has become a core function of the Russian state itself, according to U.S. State Department cables released by Wikileaks. Intelligence agencies use the Russian mafia to carry out arms trafficking, according to the cables, and police, prosecutors and spy agencies operate a de facto protection racket. Bribery is so common, said the cables, it comprises a parallel tax

system for the enrichment of security services. [26]

In a February 2010 cable released by Wikileaks, former U.S. ambassador to Russia John Beyrle wrote about the problem in Moscow's government. "The Moscow city government's direct links to criminality have led some to call it 'dysfunctional,' and to assert that the government operates more as a kleptocracy than a government," he wrote. [27] "Criminal elements enjoy a 'krysha' (a term from the criminal/mafia world literally meaning 'roof' or 'protection') that runs through the police, the Federal Security Service (FSB), the Ministry of Internal Affairs (MVD) and the prosecutor's office, as well as throughout the Moscow city government bureaucracy."

Reports of the links between criminal gangs and government security services are not exaggerated, says journalist Tlisova. Putin, who led the FSB before entering politics, restored the intelligence agency's pre-eminent role in the country after it had been greatly weakened in the decade following the fall of the Soviet Union. "When he came in, it grew and took over the whole country," she says. "If you're in with FSB, you can get rich all over the country."

Are Russia's relations with the West worsening?

Putin's accusation that Secretary Clinton and the American government were behind the protests was not the only dent in U.S.-Russia relations during Russia's current election season. There was also a nasty dispute over U.S. and European Union funding for Golos, the only independent Russian election-monitoring group to oversee the elections.

Putin accused the group of interfering in the elections on behalf of foreign powers. "Representatives of some states are organizing meetings with those who receive money from them, the so-called grant recipients, briefing them on how to 'work' in order to influence the course of the election campaign in our country," Putin said. [28]

During the parliamentary elections the group documented 5,300 complaints of fraud and hosted an interactive map online for the public to post video and other evidence of irregularities. [29] In the run-up to the March presidential election, state television labeled the group a U.S. lackey, and it was ordered evicted from its Moscow offices.

Putin's criticism of the United States comes at a time when he may have determined that it's more useful for Russians to see America as a rival than as a friend. "There have been efforts to resurrect the image of an external enemy to unite the people," says Kurbanov, the legal scholar. "It distracts attention from the true and real problems."

The crackdown on Golos came as Russia increasingly was critical of U.S. plans to build a missile defense system in Eastern Europe. While the U.S. says the system, designed to shoot down enemy missiles, is being built to protect European allies from Iran, Russia views it as a threat to its own ballistic missiles.

The Russian military announced it would move missiles to within striking distance of European Union nations, and Putin's United Russia lambasted the new U.S. ambassador, Michael McFaul, for meeting with opposition groups. Meanwhile, Putin was ratcheting up opposition to Western efforts to isolate Syria over its crackdown on democracy protesters and Iran for its efforts to enrich uranium. [30]

"You can see that Putin is trying to pursue an anti-American campaign with his vicious attacks on McFaul and Clinton," says Aslund, of the Peterson Institute. "Putin is trying to mobilize his people. He's doing what it takes to win the presidential election."

U.S. presidential politics also have raised tensions. Republican presidential front-runner Mitt Romney said in December that Putin "endangers the stability and peacefulness of the globe." [31] Earlier in the year, Russia's ambassador to NATO, Dmitry Rogozin, met with two GOP U.S. senators and said the election of a Republican to replace Obama would harm U.S.-Russia relations.

"It was a very productive meeting because it showed that the alternative to Barack Obama is [the] folding of all cooperation programs between Russia and the United States," he said. [32]

That means a difficult future for relations. "The sides have exhausted the positive agenda, and the election-related political fervor in both countries will only emphasize areas of dissonance," said Fyodor Lukyanov, a foreign affairs columnist for Moscow-based Ria Novosti, a government-run news agency. [33]

Others see the harsh words as simply campaign rhetoric that is unlikely to either sway large numbers of voters or do lasting damage to the relationship between Russia and the West. "Typically, in moments like this, foreign policy issues disappear and the rhetoric and internal debate are focused on questions of power and the issues of legitimacy of the different political forces," says Sestanovich, of the Council on Foreign Relations. "I would be surprised if relations with the U.S. mattered a lot."

Indeed, some say the underlying relationship between Russia and the West is still strong, at least by historical standards. For instance, Russia has been a key ally in the NATO operation in Afghanistan, primarily by providing an important corridor for shipment of supplies to the United States and its allies in Kabul, especially as U.S. relations with Pakistan have worsened. By the end of 2011, about 52 percent of cargo to allied forces in Afghanistan was shipped through Russia — a reflection of the fact that Russia wants NATO to succeed against the Taliban. Moscow fears the growth of radical Islam in Afghanistan and its neighbors. [34]

Other indications of a successful reset in U.S.-Russia relations in recent years include: the START nuclear arms reduction treaty signed by Medvedev and Obama in 2010; Russia's decision not to veto the U.N. Security Council vote allowing NATO missions against Libyan strongman Moammar Gadhafi; and cooperation in other areas ranging from cyber-security to the International Space Station. [35]

Indeed, though the warming of U.S.-Russia relations occurred under the presidencies of Obama and Medvedev, Putin's return to the presidency is not likely to herald a rolling back of previous agreements, some analysts say.

"Putin was involved with the reset from the very beginning," said Dmitry Suslov, of the Moscow-based Council on Foreign and Defense Policies. [36] "In fact, it would be weird to think that any major policy could have been developed in Moscow over the past four years without his leadership."

BACKGROUND

Revolutionary Dictatorship

From the 17th century to the early 20th century Russia was ruled as a feudal state by emperors known as tsars. Russia's entry into World War I and the massive suffering that ensued — with 4 million casualties in the first year-and-a-half alone — helped to trigger a communist revolution led by Vladimir Lenin, the iron-willed son of an education official. [37] With the country exhausted by six years of war and revolution, Lenin set about consolidating the Communist Party's control over what by then was called the Union of Soviet Socialist Republics (U.S.S.R.) and establishing a "dictatorship of the proletariat" led by factory workers and peasants.

However, by 1921, it was clear that all major decisions would be made solely by the party's leadership. Those opposed to centralized control were purged ruthlessly by Josef Stalin, a Georgia-born revolutionary who had become secretary of the party. [38]

After Lenin died following a series of strokes in 1924, Stalin used his power over the secret police and the party's bureaucracy to seize absolute control by 1929.

Leading a "revolution from above," he turned the Soviet Union into a totalitarian state infested with secret police in which citizens could not criticize the government and had few property rights. Millions of peasants starved as Stalin forced them from their land to join collective farms and systematically killed, starved and imprisoned the wealthiest farmers, known as *kulaks*. [39]

Internationally, Stalin tried to protect his empire from a resurgent Germany by signing a nonaggression pact with Hitler in 1939. But when Hitler abrogated the pact and invaded the Soviet Union in 1941, Stalin joined Great Britain and the United States against Hitler. The Soviets suffered catastrophically during the war: Cities and vast swathes of the countryside were destroyed, and

Per Capita GDP Soars

Russia's per capita gross domestic product (GDP) increased eightfold over the past decade, as production and export revenues at state-owned oil and gas companies skyrocketed along with rising energy prices. By comparison, per capita GDP in the United States is $48,100.

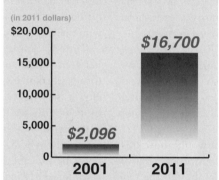

Russian Per Capita GDP 2001 and 2011

Source: The World Factbook, Central Intelligence Agency, 2012, https://www.cia.gov/library/publications/the-world-factbook/*geos/rs.html*

an estimated 27 million soldiers and civilians died — about 14 percent of the population. [40]

After Hitler's defeat, Stalin sought to regain territory lost to Germany in World War I. He installed satellite regimes in Eastern European countries occupied by the Red Army — a plan formalized by Stalin, British Prime Minister Winston Churchill and U.S. President Franklin D. Roosevelt at the 1945 Yalta summit. By the time he died in 1953, Stalin had lowered what Churchill called an Iron Curtain over Eastern Europe and had turned the Soviet Union into a nuclear superpower and foe of its former allies. [41]

Fraying Empire

After Stalin's death, a power struggle ensued in the Soviet politburo over who would succeed him. His top deputies were determined that no one would amass as much power as Stalin had during his three decades in power. In 1953, after a two-year internal struggle, Nikita Khruschev, a former coal miner and the son of peasants, emerged as the victor. [42]

Khruschev repudiated Stalin's "cult of personality" in a 1956 speech, but mixed reforms with hardline measures in the Soviet bloc, such as sending Soviet tanks to Hungary in 1956 to quell an anti-communist uprising. He was ousted in 1964 in a bloodless coup from within the party. In 1968, his successor, Leonid Brezhnev, sent Warsaw Pact troops into Czechoslovakia to halt reforms proposed by Premier Alexander Dubcek. [43]

By the 1970s Western capitalist economies clearly were far more prosperous than centrally planned communist countries. Fortunately for Brezhnev, the Soviet Union had become an oil exporter, and high oil prices in the 1970s had brought a large inflow of foreign cash. From 1973 to 1985, energy exports accounted for 80 percent of the country's hard-currency exports,

CHRONOLOGY

1910s-1940s *Communist era begins after Russian Revolution ends Romanov dynasty and establishes Union of Soviet Socialist Republics (U.S.S.R).*

October 1917 Communist regime takes over Russia; Marxist Vladimir Lenin becomes first Soviet leader. . . . Czar Nicholas II and his wife and children are assassinated in July 1918.

1924 Lenin dies and within a few years is replaced by Josef Stalin, who will cause the deaths of tens of millions of peasants and potential dissidents.

1941 Soviet Union joins the Allies to help defeat Nazi Germany in World War II. After the war, Stalin negotiates with United States and Great Britain for control of Eastern Europe.

1950s-1980s *United States and Soviet Union vie for nuclear dominance and reach a Cold War standoff.*

1985 Mikhail Gorbachev becomes general secretary of the Communist Party and, as the Soviet Union's last leader, initiates political reforms.

1990s *Soviet Union disintegrates. Relations with the West warm.*

1991 Communist hard-liners fail to overthrow Gorbachev in August coup attempt, but he steps down four months later. . . . U.S.S.R. officially dissolves on Dec. 25. . . . Soviet Union eventually fragments into 15 republics.

1992 President Boris Yeltsin launches economic reforms. U.S. commits $24 billion in aid to Russia. Yeltsin and President George H. W. Bush sign Strategic Arms Reduction Treaty.

1994 Yeltsin starts war against separatist Chechen republic.

1997 Russia and NATO agree to cooperate on defense issues.

1999 Yeltsin resigns, designates Prime Minister Vladimir Putin as acting president. Putin restarts suspended

Chechen offensive. . . . Former satellite states Poland, Hungary and Czech Republic join NATO, despite Russian objections.

2000-Present *Economy benefits from high world prices for oil and gas exports; Putin rolls back democratic freedoms as he and a protégé trade leadership positions.*

2000 Newly elected Putin moves against oligarchs and independent media.

2001 After Sept. 11 terrorist attacks on New York and the Pentagon, Putin allows U.S. to use bases in Central Asia to launch Afghan war.

2004 Putin re-elected. . . . Freedom House downgrades Russia's rating to "not free."

2005 Yukos oil company founder and Putin critic Mikhail Khodorkovsky is convicted of financial crimes and sent to prison in Siberia.

2008 Putin is ousted by term limits; Dmitry Medvedev is elected president, vowing to crack down on corruption. Putin becomes prime minister. Duma extends presidential terms from four years to six.

2010 Medvedev and U.S. President Barack Obama sign a nuclear arms reduction treaty, as the two sides seek to reset relations that deteriorated under Putin and Bush. Russia decides not to veto U.N. decision to send NATO missions against Libyan strongman Moammar Gadhafi.

2011 Medvedev announces in September that he won't run for president in 2012, but Putin will. . . . Putin's party wins 49 percent of the vote — down from 64 percent in 2007 — in December parliamentary elections roundly condemned as fraudulent, triggering weeks of anti-Putin demonstrations across Russia.

2012 Largest-yet anti-Putin demonstrations are held in Moscow in early February, despite frigid weather and the near-certainty that Putin will be re-elected on March 4. Russia and China block Western efforts at United Nations to condemn Syria's president, Bashar Assad, whose security forces have killed several thousand citizens in ongoing unrest.

In Frigid Siberia, Warming Friendship With China

Cross-border trade and immigration are on the rise.

After the collapse of the Soviet Union, the military outpost of Mirnaya, along the border between Siberia and China, lost its garrison. To make enough money to survive, the Russian townspeople began selling what was left to buyers across the border in China.

First, villagers sold the garrison's prefabricated buildings and windows. Then the radiators and pipes went to scrap dealers. Finally even the stones that made up the outpost walls were sold.

The future of the tiny village, population 713, looked grim. More than two dozen people died in 2010, but not a single baby was born. [1]

The dismantling of the Soviet Union meant an end to subsidies that once encouraged people to settle in Siberia. Now China's huge population, combined with its booming economy's thirst for the raw materials found in abundance in Siberia, means the region is slowly drifting out of Moscow's orbit and into Beijing's.

The Far Eastern Federal District where Mirnaya is located stretches from the Pacific in the east to Lake Baikal in central Siberia. About 13 times the size of France, the area has only 6.3 million people — about the same as the Dallas-Fort Worth metropolitan area. And the region's population is declining: Its current census shows 21 percent fewer people than in 1992. [2] In contrast, the three Chinese provinces just across the border — Liaoning, Jilin and Heilong — together have a total of about 110 million people. [3]

In cities like Novosibirsk, Siberia's largest, workers ride to work on Chinese buses, and Russian housewives use Chinese words to buy vegetables from Chinese traders. "Everything we have comes from China — our dishes, leather goods, even the meat we eat is from China," Vyacheslav Ilyukhin, head of the Building Department at Novosobirsk city hall, said. [4] "Siberia is becoming Chinese."

Once a feared destination for exiled political prisoners under the tsars and communists, Siberia boasts vast forests that stand atop massive reserves of minerals and petroleum needed by Chinese factories. China's demand for Siberian raw materials has made it Russia's largest trading partner.

allowing the Soviets to try to maintain near military parity with the United States. [44]

In the 1980s oil prices ebbed, as did the economy. The Soviet Union's "outer empire" in Eastern Europe also was fraying — most notably in Poland, where the Solidarity trade union movement had begun to challenge communist rule. Gorbachev, who had risen through the ranks of provincial Soviet officialdom to become general secretary in 1985, understood the decline of Soviet power and the weakness of the oil-based economy.

His *perestroika* (restructuring) and *glasnost* (opening) policies were designed to reduce the role of central planners in the economy and to check corruption by increasing freedom of speech and press. Better relations with the United States were meant to allow the Soviet Union to reduce its military budget and improve living standards. But greater openness only served to undermine Soviet authority, and resistance to Moscow's dominance grew in republics from Estonia to Uzbekistan. [45]

The Soviet empire began crumbling in June 1989, when Solidarity swept Polish elections that were considered free and fair. Hungary already had begun removing the fence along its border with non-communist Austria. By November thousands of German civilians, unmolested by authorities, were tearing down the infamous Berlin Wall between the communist East and capitalist West Berlin. Peaceful revolutions would follow in Czechoslovakia and Bulgaria, along with the bloody toppling of Romania's communists.

The dissolution of the Soviet Union's "outer empire" had immediate ramifications for satellites in its "inner empire," such as Ukraine, Belarus and Kazakhstan, which

Massive infrastructure projects abound in the region, often financed by Chinese banks. They include:

- The Kimkan open pit mine on the Russia-China border, thought to have enough iron ore to build hundreds of millions of cars. [5]
- The East Siberia Pacific Ocean Pipeline, a $25 billion project that opened last year to bring oil from eastern Siberia to the northeastern Chinese city of Daqing. [6]
- A 750-megawatt electricity transmission project, part of a Russian plan to export 60 billion kilowatt hours of electricity to China by 2020 — an amount equivalent to Minnesota's annual electricity consumption. [7]

Besides stimulating trade and resource development, the Chinese investments also have been accompanied by some migration, but not the tens of millions of Chinese immigrants that Russians feared would pour across the border when it was opened in 1989. In fact, while there was some migration from China to Russia over the past two decades, much of the immigrant traffic has been from north to south. With China's economy vastly outperforming Russia's and Chinese urban professionals earning more than their Russian counterparts, many Russian businessmen have set up shop in border cities on the Chinese side.

Stanislav Bystritski, a Russian television producer living in the Chinese border city of Suifenhe, explained, "Many Russian businessmen say it's easier to work here. There is so much less corruption and bureaucracy."

— *Jason McLure*

[1] Matthias Schepp, "China's Growing Interests in Siberia," *Der Spiegel*, May 6, 2011, www.spiegel.de/international/world/0,1518,761033,00.html.

[2] Kataryzna Jarzynska, "The Results of the 2010 Census — A Deepening Demographic Crisis in Russia," Eastweek, Centre for Eastern Studies (Poland), Dec. 21, 2011, www.osw.waw.pl/en/publikacje/eastweek/2011-12-21/results-2010-census-a-deepening-demographic-crisis-russia. See also Vladimir Borisov, "Demographic Situation in Russia: The Role of Mortality in the Reproduction of Population," *Demographia*, 2005, http://demographia.ru/eng/articles/index.html?idR=68&idArt=1363.

[3] "Communiqué of the National Bureau of Statistics of People's Republic of China on Major Figures of the 2010 Population Census," National Bureau of Statistics of China, April 29, 2011, www.stats.gov.cn/english/newsandcomingevents/t20110429_402722516.htm.

[4] Anna Nemtsova and Owen Matthews, "Fear and Loathing in Siberia," *Newsweek*, March 26, 2006, www.thedailybeast.com/newsweek/2006/03/26/fear-and-loathing-in-siberia.html.

[5] Andrew E. Kramer, "China's Hunger Fuels Exports in Remote Russia," *The New York Times*, June 9, 2010, www.nytimes.com/2010/06/10/business/global/10ruble.html?pagewanted=all.

[6] "Russia-China Oil Pipeline Opens," BBC News, Jan. 1, 2011, www.bbc.co.uk/news/world-asia-pacific-12103865.

[7] "China Completes Power Transmission Project With Russia," Xinhua, Jan. 2, 2012, www.china.org.cn/china/2012-01/02/content_24309649.htm. Also see "Electricity Consumption by State, 2009," University of Kansas Institute for Policy and Social Research, www.ipsr.ku.edu/ksdata/ksah/energy/18ener7.pdf.

were governed directly by Moscow. By March 1990, the Communist Party in Lithuania had split from the Soviet Union, and within two years the nuclear superpower had fragmented into 15 independent republics.

Yeltsin and Putin

Like Gorbachev, Boris Yeltsin also had risen through the ranks of provincial Soviet officialdom. In 1985, when Gorbachev took power, Yeltsin quickly became a force for greater democracy within the party — so great that the KGB, the Soviet spy agency, conducted a public smear campaign against him.

As Gorbachev struggled to preserve Russia's links with its surrounding republics in 1991, Yeltsin resoundingly won a campaign for the newly created position of president of Russia — leaving two leaders in Moscow. In August Gorbachev agreed to devolve many government functions to individual republics. Yeltsin claimed that Soviet assets such as the oil and gas fields were now the property of the Russian republic, triggering an attempted coup by hardliners seeking to preserve Soviet power. [46]

Most of the members of the security services failed to back the coup, but four months later Gorbachev formally resigned. The red flag of the Soviet Union, with its iconic hammer and sickle, was lowered from the Kremlin and replaced with the red, white and blue tricolor of Russia. [47]

As president, Yeltsin did not object when Ukraine and Belarus left the union, but when Chechnya, a Muslim region in the Caucasus Mountains, tried to break away in the early 1990s, he repeatedly sent in troops to try to quell the uprising, which has survived in varying forms to this day.

Meanwhile, Yeltsin had begun privatizing state assets. Often, former communist officials ended up owning state

Famed investigative journalist Anna Politkovskaya, who wrote about atrocities by Russian troops in Chechnya and about Russians' loss of civil liberties under Vladimir Putin, was shot to death in the elevator of her apartment building in 2006. She is one of several key anti-Putin dissidents to die of unnatural causes or in mysterious circumstances in recent years. Three men were tried for the murder, but they were aquitted in 2009.

companies they previously had run, or state assets were bought up on the cheap by businessmen who had made their fortunes importing smuggled goods or changing money on the black market during Soviet times. The fire sale bred lawlessness: In 1994 alone, 600 businessmen, politicians and journalists who were covering the scramble for assets were killed. [48]

A new class of so-called oligarchs emerged in the 1990s — businessmen who had excelled at buying up state assets cheaply. For instance, Mikhail Khodorkovsky, a former communist youth league official who operated an import-export business but had never seen an oilfield, was able to buy the vast assets that would become Yukos Oil for $350 million.

Though the chaotic breakup of the Soviet Union resulted in massive profits for some, the vast majority of Russians saw the government social safety net crumble and secure jobs in state-run factories vaporize. The resulting hyperinflation meant that an item that cost 100 rubles in 1990 cost 1.6 million rubles in 1999. By 1998, after a financial crisis and falling oil prices, gross domestic product had fallen 40 percent below 1991 levels. [49]

Yeltsin, weakened by alcoholism and illness, stepped down in late 1999, naming his last prime minister, former KGB director Putin, as his successor. The ascendance of Putin, who spoke nostalgically of the Soviet Union and was dismissive of press freedoms and other human rights, was greeted warily in the West. [50]

After several months as acting president, Putin won a lackluster presidential election that featured no presidential debates, fawning coverage of his campaign by progovernment television and little discussion of the ongoing war in Chechnya. [51] The Kremlin soon began extinguishing the nation's few independent television channels and stepped up attacks on oligarchs who threatened to use their wealth to challenge Putin politically. [52]

Perhaps most notably, Yukos tycoon Khodorkovsky was arrested in 2003 and later convicted of tax evasion and embezzlement and sentenced to nine years in prison. His supporters said he was prosecuted for financing pro-Western opposition parties. [53] Even more worryingly, several critics of Putin have been killed or died under suspicious circumstances, including:

- Yuri Shchekochikhin, a journalist who had long campaigned against the Chechen war and who had investigated corruption in Moscow city government and in the military. His death in 2003 was described as an allergy attack; his family said he was poisoned. [54]
- Paul Klebnikov, founding editor of the Russian edition of *Forbes* and known for investigating corruption among business tycoons, was shot as he left his office in 2004. [55]
- Investigative journalist Anna Politkovskaya, who wrote about atrocities by Russian troops in Chechnya, was shot in the elevator of her apartment building in 2006. [56]
- Stanislav Markelov, a lawyer for the family of a Chechen woman murdered by a Russian army officer, was killed in 2009 after speaking out at a news conference in Moscow. [57]

Relations with the United States, which had warmed under Yeltsin, grew chillier as President George W. Bush announced plans to build an anti-missile system in Europe viewed by Russia as a threat. Meanwhile, Putin remained popular within Russia. By the end of his second term in 2007, Putin's popularity had been bolstered by rising living standards fueled by high oil prices, obsequious domestic television coverage and his success at casting the liberal opposition as Western pawns. [58]

Constitutionally barred from seeking a third consecutive term in 2008, Putin anointed Medvedev, a lawyer and former Putin campaign manager, to succeed him. Backed by Putin's United Russia Party, the little-known Medvedev won the election with 70 percent of the votes, while Putin became prime minister.

Medvedev took office vowing to fight corruption and to make the economy less dependent on oil and gas revenues. [59] He accomplished neither, and Russia's fragile, energy-dependent growth was shaken by the 2008 global financial crisis. Soon it became apparent that Medvedev was subservient to Putin, a fact most starkly illuminated when he announced that Putin would run for president to replace him in 2012. [60]

CURRENT SITUATION

Protesters and Polls

Most of the anti-Putin protesters are young, urban and middle class. Many have traveled abroad and have seen how other political systems work.

"They realize there is a connection between politics and public life as a whole," says Kurbanov, of the National Endowment for Democracy. "If you don't participate in political life, then you cannot control many other things."

Putin's Opponents for the Presidency

When Russians go to the polls on March 4, Prime Minister Vladimir Putin will face these four opponents:

Gennady Zyuganov, 67
Chief, Communist Party
Has called for the "re-Stalinisation" of Russian society and has placed a distant second in presidential polls over the years.

Vladimir Zhirinovsky, 65
Liberal Democratic Party of Russia
A lawyer and ultra-nationalist who has run in four previous elections and finished third in 2008, with 9 percent of the vote.

Sergei Mironov, 58
Former head, A Just Russia Party
A Putin ally who famously said during the 2004 campaign that he would vote for Putin, even though he was a candidate; has become more critical of Putin since being ousted from his position as speaker of the upper house of parliament in May.

Mikhail Prokhorov, 46
Owner, Polyus Gold and New Jersey Nets
Made his fortune by buying Norilsk Nickel. Has denied reports that he is running at the Kremlin's request to attract votes from the disaffected middle class. Has suggested he might appoint Putin as his prime minister if he wins.

Source: "Profiles of Russia's 2012 Presidential Election Candidates," BBC News, Jan. 30, 2012, www.bbc.co.uk/news/world-europe-16750990

Many fear that Russia is beginning to resemble a Central Asian dictatorship, says Aron of the American Enterprise Institute. [61] With Russia's Duma extending presidential terms to six years and the constitution allowing two consecutive terms, Russians now face the prospect of Putin being in power for a total of 24 years.

Protest leader Navalny, 35, a former leader of the liberal Yabloko party, runs a small, corporate law firm in Moscow. Now enjoying a huge online following about government corruption, he has been a thorn in Putin's side since 2007, when he bought $40,000 worth of shares in Kremlin-owned Gazprom, the Rosneft oil company and the pipeline company Transneft. As a shareholder, he began filing lawsuits seeking information about how the companies were run and where their profits were going. [62]

He soon found that Transneft had donated $300 million — the equivalent of 10 percent of its profits — to "charity" in 2007, but the company wouldn't reveal where it went and no major Russian charities had received any of the money. He later found that Gazprom had been buying gas from a supplier through a mysterious intermediary at a 70 percent markup and that the state-owned bank V.T.B. had purchased 30 oil rigs from China at a 50 percent markup, paid to a little-known intermediary registered in Cyprus. [63]

Navalny's website now posts government procurement orders and invites readers to contribute evidence of corruption, which has led to dozens of canceled contracts. More importantly, he has helped to galvanize a grassroots movement, one of the few civic organizations that provides young people with an alternative to their authoritarian government.

"If the swindlers and thieves continue robbing us and lying to us, we will ourselves get back what belongs to us," Navalny told the crowd during the Moscow protest on Dec. 24. "We don't want to scare anyone, but we believe that next year there will be a peaceful change of power, and power will belong to . . . the people." [64]

By focusing on corruption, Navalny has found an issue that unites both the right and the left in opposition to Putin's government — the right out of fear that their wealth can be stripped in a system without the rule of law, and the left out of anger at government officials who have enriched themselves while allowing social services for the elderly and poor to wither away.

"The new middle class is concerned they don't have enough legal security, and the left is concerned about justice," says Aslund of the Peterson Institute. "What you have now is the two sides . . . acting against the establishment."

Despite Navalny's popularity and apparent political ambitions, he is not on the March 4 presidential ballot, a process that requires 2 million signatures. Instead Putin faces four other candidates — none of them formidable.

How Putin fares against the official candidates is less important than whether he can succeed through a mixture of coercion and repression in stopping the protest movement, says Aslund. "The opposition lives in one country, which is free and they have already won; and the

government lives in another country, where they are still in power and the opposition has only let out steam," he says. "Time will show what is real."

Economic Prospects

Russia's upheaval comes as its short-term economic prospects remain bright. Higher oil prices helped the economy grow 4.1 percent in 2011, and growth is predicted to slow to a still-healthy 3.3 percent this year, according to the International Monetary Fund. [65]

In December, Russia joined the World Trade Organization (WTO) after 18 years of negotiations, ending its status as the only major economy not in the global commerce treaty. [66] A customs union with Belarus and Kazakhstan that began in January enlarged the market for Russian goods. [67] Domestic car sales rose 39 percent in 2011, unemployment stood at just 6.1 percent at the end of 2011 and there are plans to build a Disneyland-style theme park outside Moscow. [68]

The economy's longer-term outlook is decidedly darker, however, largely because of the nation's overreliance on energy production. Oil and gas shipments comprise nearly two-thirds of Russia's exports and about 40 percent of government revenues. [69] A deepening crisis in the European Union, Russia's largest trading partner, could darken the picture even further.

"Oil and gas are making Russia very dependent on foreign markets and external factors, which is not good for any country," says Migranyan of the Institute for Democracy and Cooperation. "When the price of oil goes down, the country is in a mess."

Russia has few globally successful nonextractive companies, and the World Economic Forum ranks it 66th — behind Vietnam and Iran — in its 2011 Global Competitiveness rankings, down three spots from 2010. [70] "Under Putin Russia has become almost a half petro-state," says Aron. "It needs to regain a semblance of technological prowess. Problems are not solved just by money anymore."

"The intellectual people are running away from Russia if they can," says journalist Tlisova. Four of the last five Russian-born Nobel Prize winners finished their careers at universities abroad. "You need to belong with the Kremlin. Otherwise you have two options: exile or jail."

That was the case for Yevgeny Chichvarkin, a flamboyant billionaire known for his mullet hairstyle and flashy clothes. Chichvarkin was 22 when he founded the

Should the West give more support to Russia's protesters?

YES
Tamirlan Kurbanov
Fellow, National Endowment for Democracy, Washington, D.C.

Written for *CQ Global Researcher*, February 2012

The protests that erupted in December in Russia have surprised the government, the official opposition in the Duma and smaller opposition groups. It became clear that the protesters represented a broad group of citizens unhappy not only about fraud in the Dec. 4 parliamentary elections but also about Russia's political system in general.

The international community should support Russia's people in their aspirations to improve institutions such as the judiciary, the media and civil society. People from across Russia took to the streets because they realized that the Putin regime cannot reform itself and Russians must seize their rights. To do that, the democracy movement must reach critical mass.

For the last decade the executive branch has subsumed legislative and judicial powers, while silencing dissent. Checks and balances have disappeared. Without real competition between political parties and oversight of government institutions, corruption has flourished.

International support for Russia's grassroots democracy movement should occur at the diplomatic level, through official support for pro-democracy institutions and international nongovernmental human-rights and democracy organizations. The aid should include not only political and moral support but economic pressure to help Russia's citizens effect change. Russian officials may not be afraid of their own people's cries for democracy, but they crave the international community's respect.

Obviously, such aid is meaningless — even counterproductive — without the Russian people's genuine demand for change. Such indigenous support for new governance has been clearly established, given Russia's current environment. The government's effort to paint the protesters as U.S. pawns has failed, because much of the Russian public sees it as just another attempt to blame Russia's problems on an external force.

When the government abrogates human rights guaranteed by both the Russian constitution and international treaties, citizens have the right to exercise nonviolent resistance and public pressure against that government. International support for efforts to peacefully rebuild a democratic Russia should be strengthened, not weakened.

Ultimately, the world is interconnected, and a democratic Russia will provide greater opportunities for all of its citizens — at least all except those who have enriched themselves under the current corrupt system. The West must choose which side it will support.

NO
Andranik Migranyan
Director, Institute for Democracy and Cooperation, New York; Former Member, Russian Presidential Council

Written for *CQ Global Researcher*, February 2012

The answer lies in the recent history of Russian-American relations. They were tainted in the 1990s, when the economy and foreign policy were conducted by young reformers, such as Yegor Gaidar, Anatoly Chubais, Andrey Kozyrev. The perception was widespread that all important decisions regarding personnel and key domestic and foreign policy matters were made with Washington's input and approval.

During that period, many Russians felt deeply humiliated by their de facto loss of sovereignty as the former superpower was undergoing an economic, social and psychological catastrophe. Since the 1990s, therefore, many Russians have harbored an aversion toward U.S. meddling in Russian affairs — either directly or through American political and economic advisers.

Putin's presidency is widely seen as having restored Russian self-sufficiency domestically, resurrected Russian sovereignty and reconstituted Russia as a strong partner of the West in foreign affairs.

Now Russia has entered a new phase in its domestic political development, which coincides with the start of a new electoral cycle. Putin, who will run for president again in March as a member of the party in power, retains a high level of trust among many Russians. But against this backdrop, there have been major societal divisions, mass protests and demands for more responsiveness and dialogue from the authorities.

In this context, the recent meeting of American diplomats, including Ambassador Michael McFaul, with representatives of the radical opposition appears to authorities in Moscow as an attempt by Washington to meddle in sovereign matters in order to push for regime change.

Now, throw in the fact that the record of both the United States and Ambassador McFaul provides a basis for such assumptions. McFaul is famous in both the United States and Russia as a supporter of the American policy of promoting democracy worldwide and is known to be close to those circles in Russia calling for regime overhaul.

Nobody is arguing the right of U.S. diplomats to meet with the opposition, but they should take into consideration the format, time and venue for such meetings, as well as overall political context and possible reaction of Russian officials and the public at large. Otherwise such actions can harm Russian-American relations.

Masked demonstrators, including one impersonating Russian Prime Minister Vladimir Putin with blood on his hands, protest at the United Nations on Jan. 24, 2012, against Russia's support for Syrian President Bashar Assad and his violent suppression of citizens. The demonstrators said they had delivered a petition to the U.N. containing signatures from 600,000 people demanding that the Security Council refer the Assad regime to the International Criminal Court for war-crimes prosecution.

mobile phone retailer Yevroset in 1997 with less than $5,000 in capital. By 2010 the company was valued at about $2.5 billion. [71]

But Chichvarkin was forced to sell his company and flee to London in 2008 after one of his employees was arrested and charged with kidnapping and extortion. Corrupt members of the Interior Ministry also were pursuing him, he said, although the charges against him were dropped this year.

The politicians "were the ones demanding bribes," Chichvarkin said in 2010. "If I'd paid off the people I was supposed to, I wouldn't be sitting here with you. I'd be sitting in Cantinetta Antinori on Denezhny Lane in Moscow." [72]

Putin has promised that — under the competitive framework of the WTO — Russia will become a leader in pharmaceuticals, composites and aviation. In addition, he says, government control of the energy sector will continue, as will public financing of key sectors like technology.

Putin acknowledges the corruption problem. "The main problem is insufficient transparency and accountability on the part of state officials," Putin wrote in a recent editorial. "We are talking about systemic corruption." Yet he offered few specifics on how he will fix the problem. "Clearing the way for business that is ready to win in fair competition is a fundamental, systemic task. . . . We need to change the state itself — executive and judicial power." [73]

Few of his critics take such promises seriously. Meanwhile, the business climate for those without connections to the security forces or key government officials continues to be tenuous, says Kurbanov. "Smart people flee," he says.

OUTLOOK

Bleak Future?

The confluence of long-term problems — rampant corruption, a shrinking population, the brain drain, overdependance on oil exports, authoritarianism and continuing conflict in the North Caucasus — prompts many analysts to paint a gloomy portrait of the country's future should Putin continue to lead the country.

"The country is facing huge problems: economic, social, demographic," says Aron of the American Enterprise Institute. "If Putin survives, 10 years from now you'll see a Russia totally dependent on oil revenue, declining across the board in social indicators and losing its best and brightest. It will be a basket case."

If that happens, Putin would have to exercise even harsher repression in order to maintain control. "I hope we will be able to have a government that will meet the people half way, but I don't know how it will happen," says Kurbanov, of the National Endowment for Democracy. "The current group knows if they do one compromise, they won't be able to stop it, and they'll have to leave the country to avoid prosecution."

Regardless of who becomes president, Russia's population will continue to shrink, experts say. The population declined for 14 straight years before growing slightly in 2009, based largely on higher immigration numbers. [74]

Poor health contributes to Russia's demographic problems. Russian men can expect to live only to age 62 (compared to 78 in Germany), in part because of high rates of alcoholism. [75] The average 18-year-old Russian man has a 50 percent chance of living to retirement age, against a 90 percent probability in the West. [76]

The demographic challenges mean that Russia needs up to 1 million immigrants per year in order to maintain economic growth, says Migranyan, of the Institute for Democracy and Cooperation. But due to "the failure of multiculturalism" in Russia, he says, newcomers are not integrated into society and, in fact, face anti-immigrant hostility. In April 2011, an immigration service spokes-man was fired after cautioning about "mixing bloods" of immigrants with Russian blood and warning that the "survival of the white race is at stake." [77]

Ethnic minorities and immigrants "don't feel like Russians, because there is such a strong message coming from the Kremlin and all these Russian nationalists," says journalist Tlisova, who herself is Circassian, a minority that is referred to as "blacks" in Russia. "The message is very clear: There is a black Russia and a white Russia, and black Russia does not have any rights."

Some of the ethnic tension stems from Russia's ongo-ing conflicts with separatist rebels in the North Caucasus, including Chechnya, Ingushetia and Dagestan. Although the war in Chechnya officially ended in 2009, attacks by both Islamist rebels and Russian security forces have con-tinued. Some fear the attacks will spike in the run-up to the 2014 Winter Olympics in Sochi, a southern city less than 250 miles from the hometown of an Ingushetian suicide bomber who killed 37 people at Moscow's airport last January. [78]

If Putin is ousted, the country's prospects improve, ana-lysts say. "If the protesters do spark a political crisis that leads to a change of regime, then Russia goes back to around 2002 or 2003," says Aron. "It will be far less dependent on oil exports, it will be less corrupt, the courts will regain their independence, the political parties will be competing freely and television will be uncensored."

Aslund, however, of the Peterson Institute and the author of 12 books about Russia and Eastern Europe, sees a better future ahead.

"No country that has been even half as wealthy as Russia has returned to authoritarianism after a democratic breakthrough," he says. "We will see a new democratic breakthrough this year. It will be peaceful, and new elec-tions will be held for parliament and president, and Russia will start cleaning out corruption."

NOTES

1. David Remnick, "The Civil Archipelago," *The New Yorker*, Dec. 19, 2011, www.newyorker.com/reporting/2011/12/19/111219fa_fact_remnick.

2. Gleb Bryanski, "Russia's Putin Promises Change, Warns of New Crisis," Reuters, Jan. 16, 2012, www.reuters.com/article/2012/01/16/us-russia-putin-idUSTRE80F12O20120116.

3. Miriam Elder and Tom Parfitt, "Russian Anti-Putin Protests Draw Thousands to Moscow Again," *The Guardian*, Dec. 24, 2011, www.guardian.co.uk/world/2011/dec/24/russia-europe-news.

4. Timothy Heritage, "Anti-Putin Protesters Show Staying Power in Russia," Reuters, Feb. 5, 2012, www.reuters.com/article/2012/02/05/us-russia-protests-idUSTRE8140D220120205. Also see Serge Schmemann, "100,000 Join Moscow Rally, Defying Ban by Gorbachev to Show Support for Rival," *The New York Times*, March 29, 1991, www.nytimes.com/1991/03/29/world/100000-join-moscow-rally-defying-ban-by-gorbachev-to-show-support-for-rival.html?pagewanted=all&src=pm.

5. Amanda Walker, "Mass Anti-Vladimir Putin Protest in Moscow Over Disputed Elections," Sky News, Dec. 24, 2011, http://news.sky.com/home/world-news/article/16136696.

6. "Putin Was Booed, Full Record From Sports Complex," YouTube, www.youtube.com/watch?v=ZxQslFifQBw.

7. Stephen Ennis, "Profile: Russian Blogger Alexei Navalney," BBC News, Dec. 20, 2011, www.bbc.co.uk/news/world-europe-16057045.

8. For background, see Roland Flamini, "Turmoil in the Arab World," *CQ Global Researcher*, May 3, 2011, pp. 209-236.

9. Alex Spillins, "Vladimir Putin Calls John McCain 'Nuts' in Outspoken Attack," *The Daily Telegraph*, Dec. 15, 2011, www.telegraph.co.uk/news/worldnews/europe/russia/8958294/Vladimir-Putin-calls-John-McCain-nuts-in-outspoken-attack.html.

10. Kathy Lally, "Putin Lashes Back at Clinton Criticism," *The Washington Post*, Dec. 8, 2011, www.washingtonpost.com/world/putin-lashes-back-at-clinton-criticism/2011/12/08/gIQAQ5lYgO_story.html.

11. Esther Dyson, "Russia Protests Include a Broad Swath of Society," *Prague Post*, Feb. 1, 2012, www.praguepost.com/opinion/11928-russia-protests-include-a-broad-swath-of-society.html.

12. Michael Bohm, "Why Putin Will Never, Ever Give Up Power," *The Moscow Times*, Jan. 20, 2012, www

.themoscowtimes.com/opinion/article/why-putin-will-never-ever-give-up-power/451332.html.

13. "Corruption Perceptions Index 2011," Transparency International, http://cpi.transparency.org/cpi2011/results/.

14. Fred Weir, "Russia Corruption Costs $318 Billion — One-third of GDP," *The Christian Science Monitor*, Nov. 23, 2009, www.csmonitor.com/World/Global-News/2009/1123/russia-corruption-costs-318-billion-one-third-of-gdp.

15. Scott Rose, "Russia's Average Bribe Was $10,573 in First Half, Ministry Says," Bloomberg News, July 22, 2011, www.bloomberg.com/news/2011-07-22/russias-average-bribe-was-10-573-in-first-half-ministry-says.html.

16. "Corruption Perceptions Index 2000," Transparency International, www.transparency.org/policy_research/surveys_indices/cpi/previous_cpi/2000.

17. "Russia: The Global Economic Crime Survey," PriceWaterhouseCoopers, November 2011, www.pwc.ru/en/forensic-services/crime-survey-2011.jhtml.

18. Lyubov Pronina, "Putin Orders Graft Probe at Utilities to Increase Transparency," Bloomberg News, Dec. 19, 2011, www.bloomberg.com/news/2011-12-19/putin-orders-graft-probes-at-utilities-to-increase-transparency.html.

19. "State Corporations Resist Putin Order," Vedemosti (reprinted in English by the *Moscow Times*), Jan. 17, 2012, www.themoscowtimes.com/business/article/state-corporations-resist-putin-order/451133.html.

20. "Putin Ponders Corruption, Internet Democracy in New Article," *Ria Novosti*, Feb. 6, 2012, http://en.rian.ru/russia/20120206/171165740.html.

21. Andranik Migranyan, "Russian Protests Won't Stop Putin," *The National Interest*, Dec. 28, 2011, http://nationalinterest.org/commentary/russian-protests-wont-stop-putin-6312.

22. Olga Razumovskaya, "Russia's Own WikiLeaks Takes Off," *The Moscow Times*, Jan. 21, 2011, www.themoscowtimes.com/news/article/russias-own-wikileaks-takes-off/429370.html.

23. Nikolaus von Twickel, "Putin's Old Teacher Mines a Fortune," *The Moscow Times*, April 5, 2011, www.themoscowtimes.com/news/article/putins-old-teacher-mines-a-fortune/434471.html.

24. Von Twickel, *op. cit.*

25. Luke Harding, "Putin, the Kremlin Power Struggle and the $40 Billion Fortune," *The Guardian*, Dec. 20, 2007, www.guardian.co.uk/world/2007/dec/21/russia.topstories3.

26. U.S. Ambassador John Beyrle, "The Luzkhov Dilemma," U.S. Department of State cable, Feb. 12, 2010, released by Wikileaks, http://wikileaks.org/cable/2010/02/10MOSCOW317.html.

27. *Ibid.*

28. Kathy Lally, "Russia Targets U.S. Linked Election Group," *The Washington Post*, Nov. 20, 2011, www.washingtonpost.com/world/russia-targets-us-linked-election-monitor/2011/11/30/gIQAlqzcDO_story.html.

29. "Russian PM Vladimir Putin Accuses U.S. Over Poll Protests," BBC News, Dec. 8, 2011, www.bbc.co.uk/news/world-europe-16084743. See also: "Russians Vote in Duma Poll Seen as Referendum on Putin," BBC News, Dec. 4, 2011, www.bbc.co.uk/news/world-europe-16020632.

30. Daniel McLaughlin, "Putin Ratchets Up Anti-Western Rhetoric Before Presidential Poll," *Irish Times*, Jan. 27, 2012, www.irishtimes.com/newspaper/world/2012/0127/1224310807528.html.

31. Steve Holland and Jim Gaines, "Iraq Pullout a Signature Failure for Obama: Romney," Reuters, Dec. 22, 2011, www.reuters.com/article/2011/12/22/us-usa-campaign-romney-idUSTRE7BJ15R20111222.

32. "Hawkish Republicans May Harm Future Russia-U.S. Relations: Rogozin," *RIA Novosti*, July 27, 2011, http://en.rian.ru/russia/20110727/165407874.html.

33. Fyodor Lukyanov, "Uncertain World: Russia-United States — minimizing the damage," *RIA Novosti*, Dec. 29, 2011, http://en.rian.ru/columnists/20111229/170547384.html?id=170549753.

34. John Vandiver and Martin Kuz, "Military Looks at Supply Routes Away From Pakistan," *Stars and Stripes*, Nov. 28, 2011, www.stripes.com/news/military-looks-at-supply-routes-away-from-pakistan-1.161855.

35. Jim Wolf, "U.S. Russia Work to Expand Cyberspace Cooperation," Reuters, Dec. 9, 2011, www.reuters.com/article/2011/12/10/us-russia-usa-cyber-idUSTRE7B901N20111210.

36. Fred Weir, "As Putin Rises Again, Will the U.S.-Russia 'Reset' of Ties Hold?" *The Christian Science Monitor*, Oct. 26, 2011, www.csmonitor.com/World/Europe/2011/1026/As-Putin-rises-again-will-the-US-Russia-reset-of-ties-hold.

37. John Lawrence, *A History of Russia* (1960), pp. 240-241.

38. Lawrence, *op. cit.*, pp. 266-270.

39. Michael Kort, *The Soviet Colossus: A History of the USSR* (1985), pp. 171-177.

40. Kenneth Jost, "Russia and the Former Soviet Republics," *CQ Researcher*, June 17, 2005, pp. 541-564. See also Michael Ellman and S. Maksudov, "Soviet Deaths in the Great Patriotic War: A Note," *Europe-Asia Studies*, Vol. 46, Nov. 4, 1994, pp. 671-680, http://sovietinfo.tripod.com/ELM-War_Deaths.pdf.

41. Roland Flamini, "Dealing with the New Russia," *CQ Researcher*, June 6, 2008, pp. 481-504.

42. Kort, *op. cit.*, pp. 235-242.

43. Jan Velinger "The Soviet Invasion of Czechoslovakia and the Crushing of the Prague Spring," Radio Prague, Aug. 20, 2003, www.radio.cz/en/section/czechs/the-soviet-invasion-of-czechoslovakia-and-the-crushing-of-the-prague-spring.

44. Stephen Kotkin, *Armageddon Averted: The Soviet Collapse 1970-2000* (2008), pp. 15-16.

45. Helene Carrere d'Encausse, *The End of the Soviet Empire: The Triumph of Nations* (1993).

46. Kotkin, *op. cit.*, pp. 92-99.

47. *Ibid.*, pp. 100-111.

48. *Ibid.*, p. 127.

49. Marshall Goldman, *Petrostate: Putin, Power and the New Russia* (2008), pp. 73-74.

50. Michael Specter, "Kremlin, Inc.: Why Are Vladimir Putin's Opponents Dying," *The New Yorker*, Jan. 29, 2007, www.newyorker.com/reporting/2007/01/29/070129fa_fact_specter. See also: "What Next, President Putin?" *The Economist*, March 30, 2000, www.economist.com/node/297415.

51. "A Russian Coronation," *The Economist*, March 23, 2000, www.economist.com/node/295952.

52. Michael Wines, "Russian Court Orders Dissolution of Independent TV Network," *The New York Times*, Jan. 12, 2002, www.nytimes.com/2002/01/12/world/russian-court-orders-dissolution-of-independent-tv-network.html?pagewanted=all&src=pm.

53. "Yukos Ex-Chief Jailed for Nine Years," BBC News, May 31, 2005, http://news.bbc.co.uk/2/hi/business/4595289.stm.

54. Felix Corley, "Yuri Shchekochikhin," *The Guardian*, July 9, 2003, www.guardian.co.uk/news/2003/jul/09/guardianobituaries.russia.

55. Otto Pohl, "The Assassination of a Dream," *New York*, May 21, 2005, http://nymag.com/nymetro/news/people/features/10193/.

56. Anna Politkovskaya, "Her Own Death, Foretold," *The Washington Post*, Oct. 15, 2006, www.washingtonpost.com/wp-dyn/content/article/2006/10/14/AR2006101400805.html.

57. "Prominent Russian Lawyer Killed," BBC News, Jan. 19, 2009, http://news.bbc.co.uk/2/hi/europe/7838328.stm.

58. "Putin's Phoney Election," *The Economist*, Nov. 29, 2007, www.economist.com/node/10217312.

59. Owen Matthews, "The Medvedev Doctrine," *Newsweek*, Nov. 21, 2008, www.thedailybeast.com/newsweek/2008/11/21/the-medvedev-doctrine.html.

60. Christian Neef and Matthias Schepp, "The Puppet President: Medvedev's Betrayal of Russian Democracy," *Der Spiegel*, Oct. 4, 2011, www.spiegel.de/international/world/0,1518,789767,00.html.

61. For background, see Brian Beary, "Emerging Central Asia," *CQ Global Researcher*, Jan. 17, 2012, pp. 29-56.

62. Julia Ioffe, "Net Impact: One Man's Cybercrusade Against Russian Corruption," *The New Yorker*, April 4, 2011, www.newyorker.com/reporting/2011/04/04/110404fa_fact_ioffe.

63. *Ibid.*

64. Sergei Loiko, "Tens of Thousands of Russian Protesters Want Vladimir Putin Out," *Los Angeles Times*, Dec. 24, 2011, http://articles.latimes.com/2011/dec/24/world/la-fg-russia-protest-putin-20111225.

65. "World Economic Outlook Update," International Monetary Fund, January 2012, www.imf.org/external/pubs/ft/weo/2012/update/01/index.htm.

66. David Jolly, "W.T.O. Grants Russia Membership," *The New York Times*, Dec. 16, 2011, www.nytimes.com/2011/12/17/business/global/wto-accepts-russia-bid-to-join.html?pagewanted=all.

67. Ilya Arkhipov and Lyubov Pronina, "Russia, Kazakhstan, Belarus Sign Accord on Economic Union," Bloomberg News, Nov. 18, 2011, www.bloomberg.com/news/2011-11-18/russia-kazakhstan-belarus-sign-accord-on-economic-union-1-.html.

68. "Russian Automotive Market is to Maintain a Consistent Growth in 2012," globalautoindustry.com, Jan. 12, 2012, www.globalautoindustry.com/article.php?id=7739&jaar=2012&maand=2&target=Euro. Also see "Site in Northwest Moscow Could Host 'Russian Disneyland' — Deputy Mayor," *RIA Novosti*, Oct. 14, 2011, http://en.rian.ru/business/20111014/167680991.html.

69. "Key Economic Indicators in 2011," Bank of Russia, www.cbr.ru/eng/statistics. Also see James Brooke, "Russia Gets Giant Boost From Rising Oil Prices," Voice of America, March 11, 2011, www.voanews.com/english/news/europe/Russia-Gets-Giant-Boost-from-Rising-Oil-Prices-118258659.html.

70. "Global Competitiveness Index 2011-2012 Rankings," World Economic Forum, www3.weforum.org/docs/WEF_GCR_CompetitivenessIndexRanking_2011-12.pdf.

71. Anastasia Golisyna, Igor Tsukanov and Tatyana Romanova, "Yevroset Planning for IPO Next Year," *Vedemosti* (reprinted in English by the *Moscow Times*), Nov. 12, 2010, www.themoscowtimes.com/business/article/yevroset-planning-for-ipo-next-year/422383.html.

72. Shaun Walker, "The Whiz Kid Billionaire Who Says He Can't Go Home," *The Independent*, July 29, 2010, www.independent.co.uk/news/people/news/the-whiz-kid-billionaire-who-says-he-cant-go-home-2038006.html.

73. Douglas Busvine, "Putin Puts State Capitalism First for Russia," Reuters, Jan. 30, 2012, www.reuters.com/article/2012/01/30/us-russia-putin-economy-idUSTRE80T0PC20120130.

74. "Resident Population," Russian Federation Federal Statistical Service, 2011, www.gks.ru/wps/wcm/connect/rosstat/rosstatsite.eng/figures/population.

75. "Global Health Observatory," World Health Organization, 2009 statistics, www.who.int/countries/en/.

76. Grace Wong, "Russia's Bleak Picture of Health," CNN, May 19, 2009, http://edition.cnn.com/2009/HEALTH/05/19/russia.health/index.html.

77. Alissa de Carbonnel, "Russia Migration Official Fired in Racism Row," Reuters, April 2011, http://uk.reuters.com/article/2011/04/20/uk-russia-race-idUKTRE73J5CW20110420.

78. C. J. Chivers, "Author Q&A: The Insurgency in Chechnya and the North Caucasus," At War blog, *NYTimes.com*, Jan. 20, 2012, atwar.blogs.nytimes.com/2012/01/20/author-qa-the-insurgency-in-chechnya-and-the-north-caucasus/. Also see Clifford Levy, "Russia Faces 3-Year Race to Secure Site of Olympics," *The New York Times*, March 7, 2011. URL= www.nytimes.com/2011/03/08/world/europe/08sochi.html.

BIBLIOGRAPHY

Selected Sources

Books

Goldman, Marshall, *Petrostate: Putin, Power and the New Russia,* **Oxford University Press, 2010.**
Russia's expanding energy resources have been key to its recovery from the 1998 financial crisis, even as they've fueled corruption and harmed other parts of the economy.

Politkovskaya, Anna, *Putin's Russia: Life in a Failing Democracy,* **Metropolitan Books, 2005.**
Before the muckraking Russian journalist was assassinated in 2006, she authored this critical portrait of Putin's rule and the death of democracy in Russia.

Putin, Vladimir, Nataliya Gevorkyan, and Andrei Kolesnikov, *First Person: An Astonishingly Frank Self-Portrait by Russia's President,* **Public Affairs, 2000.**

The product of six interviews between Putin and Russian correspondents, the book may not be "astonishingly frank," but it does provide illuminating detail of the Russian politician's life and thinking when he first began to rule.

Satter, David, *Darkness at Dawn: the Rise of the Russian Criminal State*, Yale University Press, 2003.
A former Moscow correspondent for the *Financial Times* chronicles Russia's transformation from a communist state to a playground for organized criminal gangs.

Shevtsova, Lilia, and Andrew Wood, *Change or Decay: Russia's Dilemma and the West's Response*, Carnegie Endowment for International Peace, 2011.
Two decades after the fall of the Soviet Union, the West's relationship with Russia is still fraught, as revealed in a series of exchanges between a Russian scholar and a former British ambassador to Russia.

Articles

Anderson, Scott, "Vladimir Putin's Dark Rise to Power," *GQ*, September 2009.
Rare is a feature article so sensitive that a mainstream magazine refuses to post it on the Internet. But that was the case with this investigation challenging the provenance of a series of bombings in Moscow in 1999, officially blamed on Chechen separatists.

Eberstadt, Nicholas, "The Dying Bear," *Foreign Affairs*, November/December 2011.
Eberstadt examines the human, economic and social costs of Russia's baby drought.

Freeland, Chrystia, "The Next Russian Revolution," *The Atlantic Monthly*, October 2011.
A Reuters editor describes Russia's efforts to create a Silicon Valley on the Volga, providing a glimpse of the country's peculiar form of capitalism.

Ioffe, Julia, "Net Impact: One Man's Cyber-Crusade Against Russian Corruption," *The New Yorker*, April 4, 2011.
Anti-corruption blogger Alexei Navalny is profiled, eight months before protests against Putin's government made him a democracy icon in Russia.

Knight, Amy, "The Concealed Battle to Run Russia," *New York Review of Books*, Jan. 13, 2011.
In reviewing a new book on the KGB's impact on Russian society, Knight's own reporting adds insight to a society dominated by security service strong-men.

Passell, Peter, "Why Putinomics Isn't Worth Emulating," *Foreign Policy*, Jan. 27, 2012.
Despite the glittering new buildings in Moscow and St. Petersburg, Russia's economy "is still a Potemkin façade" that runs on oil and weapons sales, the author argues.

Reports and Studies

"Georgia-Russia: Learn to Live Like Neighbors," International Crisis Group, Aug. 8, 2011.
Three years after Russia's war with Georgia over South Ossetia, the two sides are still preoccupied with bitter aspects of their relationship.

"2010 Human Rights Report: Russia," U.S. Department of State, April 8, 2011.
The U.S. government's annual list of human rights abuses in Russia — including the beating of a defense lawyer, an attack on a human rights activist and the killing of seven journalists — makes for grim reading.

"Who Will Tell Me What Happened to My Son?" Human Rights Watch, Sept. 27, 2009.
The New York-based human rights group researched 33 cases of extrajudicial killings in Chechnya by Russian security forces or their allies. No one has been prosecuted, even though the alleged perpetrators have been named in European Court judgments.

Trenin, Dmitri, and Pavel Baev, "The Arctic: A View From Moscow," Carnegie Endowment for International Peace, September 2010.
As the Arctic ice cap melts, northern Russia — which might have twice the oil reserves of Saudi Arabia — may be transformed by oil exploration.

For More Information

Brookings Institution, 1775 Massachusetts Ave., N.W., Washington, DC 20036; 202-797-6999; www.brookings .edu. A nonprofit, centrist think tank providing research designed to "create a more open, safe, prosperous and cooperative international system."

Carnegie Moscow Center, Carnegie Institute for International Peace, 16/2 Tverskaya, Moscow, 1250009, Russia; +7 495 935-8904; www.carnegie.ru. Russian branch of a Washington think tank that includes Russian and foreign researchers analyzing a range of policy issues.

Center for Russian and East European Studies, University Center of International Politics, 4400 Wesley W. Posvar Hall, University of Pittsburgh, Pittsburgh, PA 115260; 412-648-7404; www.ucis.pitt.edu/crees/. A clearinghouse for studies on Russia and its environs, with access to 400,000 volumes on Russia and Eastern Europe.

Center for Strategic and International Studies, 1800 K St., N.W., Washington, D.C. 20006; 202-887-0200; www.csis.org. Foreign policy think tank, founded in 1962, with experts that include academics, former politicians and diplomats.

Institute for U.S. and Canadian Studies, 2/3 Khlebny per., Moscow 123995, Russia; +7 (0) 95 290-5875; www.iskran .ru/engl/index-en.html. Military and strategic research center offering research on U.S. and Canadian relations with Russia — from a Russian perspective.

Peterson Institute for International Economics, 1750 Massachusetts Ave., N.W., Washington, DC 20036; 202-328-9000; www.petersoninstitute.org. Think tank focused on international economic policy, with more than two dozen fellows focused on international economics, trade and the international financial system.

Russia and Eurasia Program, Royal Institute of International Affairs, Chatham House, 10 St. James's Square, London SW1Y 4LE, England; +44 207 7957-5700; www.chatham house.org. Provides foreign and domestic policy analysis of Russia and other former Soviet states.

Voices From Abroad:

YELENA PANFILOVA

Director, Transparency International, Russia

A different corruption

"Unfortunately, in Russia we are dealing not with the traditional kind of corruption, which is observed all over the world at all times. Our corruption has acquired the features of forced corruption. That is when people in public offices treat their positions as sources of constant illegal [personal] enrichment."

RIA Novosti News Agency, (Russia), December 2011

VLADIMIR PUTIN

Prime Minister, Russia

Losing ground

"If you are saying that our elections were objective and fair, in my opinion, I have already said publicly that, beyond any doubt, the results of these elections reflect the actual line-up of forces in the country, as well as the fact that the ruling force — United Russia — has lost certain positions."

Philippine News Agency, December 2011

SERGEY PRIKHODKO

Presidential aide, Russia

Obstructionists

"The idea of a precipitous deterioration in Russo-American relations is being imposed by those that do not want to see real results of the work and do not want an improvement in relations."

Gazeta.ru (Russia), October 2011

DMITRY MEDVEDEV

President, Russia

Making progress

"We are prepared to develop full strategic relations with the United States. Our economic relations [still] trail the political relations considerably."

Rossiyskaya Gazeta (Russia), March 2011

SERGEI GURIEV

Rector, New Economic School, Russia

New demands

"Now, it seems, sufficient prosperity has arrived, calling forth a middle class solid enough to demand government accountability, the rule of law and a genuine fight against corruption. . . . The political mobilization of the middle class will eventually lead to democratization."

Korea Times (South Korea), January 2012

GENNADIY GUDKOV

Deputy Chairman, State Duma Security Committee, Russia

A future at stake
"We are launching an anti-corruption march that will continue until corruption has been eradicated in Russia. Because of corruption, we may lose our future, our children and our country."

Interfax News Agency (Russia), April 2011

ALEKSEY CHESNAKOV

Chairman, United Russia General Council Presidium, Russia

No Arabs in Russia
"Such a scenario [Arab Spring revolution] is impossible in Russia, since we do not have enough Arabs for this."

Gazeta.ru (Russia), March 2011

ALESKO NEVLENI

Political opposition leader, Russia

"There is no sense in leading a life like mice, frogs and animals in stability and economic development. We have the voice and the votes and the strength to utilize them."

Jagran Post (India), December 2011

SERGEY MARKOV

Political analyst, Russia

Collapse leads to corruption
"The Soviet companies were the least corrupt. . . . Large-scale corruption appeared with the collapse of the Soviet Union, [its] system of social relations and work ethic and [the] transition to rabid individualism."

RIA Novosti (Russia), November 2011

TATYANA YAKOVLEVA

First Deputy, One Russia party, Russia

Civil society's role
"The effectiveness of the fight against corruption depends not only on the political will of the head of the state, not only on correct legislative work . . . but, to a large extent, on an active stance of civil society."

Interfax News Agency (Russia), February 2011

9

Sharia Controversy

Sarah Glazer

Afghan men perform ritual ablutions before attending Friday prayers in Kabul. Sharia, which means "the way," deals not only with legal issues and punishments but also instructs how Muslims should live a devout life — including washing before praying, what to eat and how much to donate to charity. Many Western legal systems borrow from Sharia concepts in areas such as contract law.

From *CQ Researcher*,
Jan. 3, 2012

I n a desperate bid to escape her marriage after repeated beatings and a death threat from her husband, Jameela, a Muslim woman in England, turned last year to her local Sharia council — a panel of religious scholars operating out of her local Birmingham mosque.*

Sitting across a desk from a handful of Muslim scholars, including one woman, Jameela described how her husband spent most of his time with his second wife but became abusive when he returned home. Islamic law allows men to have up to four wives but polygamy is illegal in Britain. [1]

The scholars granted Jameela a religious divorce, but not before lecturing her on the importance of maintaining a peaceful relationship with her husband. "For the sake of the children, you must keep up the façade of cordial relations," Mohammed Naseem, chairman of the council, told the mother of three. "The worst thing that can happen to a child is to see the father and mother quarrelling." [2]

They advised her that if she wanted to remarry she should get a civil marriage, recognized by English law. Jameela is one of hundreds of Muslim women living in Britain, many from Pakistani and

---

* Sharia councils are informal panels set up by clerics and religious scholars at mosques to resolve family disputes using Quranic teachings. England's five largest and most widely recognized councils — in London, Birmingham, Bradford, Coventry and Manchester — mostly issue religious divorces. The London think tank Civitas says there are up to 85 Sharia councils operating in the United Kingdom, but University of Reading researcher Samia Bano estimates 30 to 50, based on her ongoing research.

Islamic Law Guides 35 Nations

Islamic or Sharia law is the world's most widely used religious legal system, with 35 countries adhering to it either strictly or within a hybrid system that incorporates Sharia with civil, common or customary law. Iran, Saudi Arabia and 12 states in northern Nigeria apply fundamentalist interpretations of Sharia, which call for stoning and amputations for adultery and theft, but they are rarely used. Hybrid systems are used in most other Muslim countries.

Countries Following Sharia Law

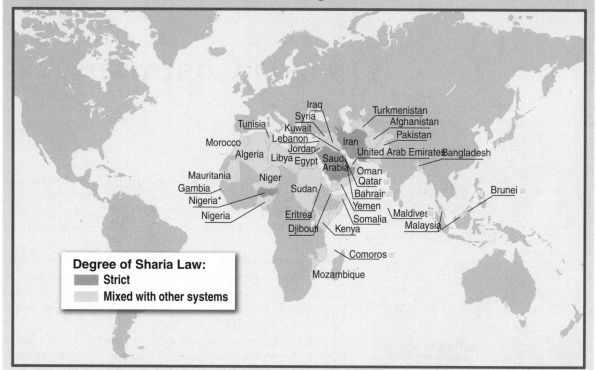

* Twelve states in northern Nigeria adhere to strict Sharia law: Zamfara, Kano, Sokoto, Katsina, Bauchi, Borno, Jigawa, Kebbi, Yobe, Kaduna, Niger and Gombe.

Source: "Legal System," The World Factbook, Central Intelligence Agency, 2011, https://www.cia.gov/library/publications/the-world-factbook/fields/2100.html; map by Lewis Agrell

Bangladeshi communities, who turn to such informal councils each year seeking a religious divorce. Many have never had their marriages registered under English law, depriving them of the right to a divorce in civil court and leaving them defenseless in settling financial matters.

Such councils have proliferated in Britain since the 1980s, raising concerns that England is developing a parallel legal system that does not provide the same rights to women that they enjoy under English law. [3] Some think Britain has gone too far in allowing such a system to

develop — believed to be the most extensive among Western countries. The political sensitivity of the question was highlighted in 2008 when the Archbishop of Canterbury, the chief religious figure of the Church of England, triggered a storm of protest after saying it was "unavoidable" that some form of Sharia law eventually would be accepted in England. [4]

Not if Baroness Caroline Cox, a member of the House of Lords, has anything to say about it. She has introduced a bill that would make it a criminal offense for any Sharia council judge to present his decision as legally valid in matters of family or criminal law.

"Many [Muslim] women I've spoken to say they came here to get away from Sharia law, and [that] it's worse here than in the countries they came from," she says. Women are frequently told by Sharia councils to return to their physically abusive husbands to reconcile, she claims.

"We have one set of family-law rules for Muslims and one set for everybody else," says Anne Marie Waters, spokesperson for One Law for All, a secular, London-based group campaigning against religious tribunals in Britain. "And the family-law rules for Muslims are extremely hard on women."

But researchers who have studied the councils say they provide a useful service — a divorce that frees a woman to remarry in the eyes of her community. If women don't like a council's decision, they can try a different Sharia council, and most are aware of their rights under English law, says Samia Bano, a lecturer in law at England's University of Reading, who has studied the councils. "There *is* one law for all; we don't have parallel legal systems in the U.K.," she says. "What we have is privatized forms of dispute resolution; those mechanisms have always been there, whether in secular communities or in Jewish, Hindu or Catholic communities."

For instance, a study at Cardiff Law School in Wales found that the Birmingham Sharia council was similar to Jewish and Catholic religious courts that have existed in England for many years. [5]

But the spotlight on Muslim religious councils reflects a wider anxiety in the West — that such informal judicial forums sustain the most horrifying aspects of Sharia, such as stoning for adultery (although this is rare even in Muslim countries and non-existent in the Western context) and unequal treatment of women in divorce and inheritance cases.

Stoning, Amputation Are Rarely Used

A handful of predominantly Muslim countries — such as Saudi Arabia, Iran and Pakistan — allow hadd punishments (such as stoning or amputation) for serious crimes, but such punishments are rarely carried out.

Hadd Punishments in 12 Muslim Countries

Country	Allowed by law	Are used today
Egypt	No	n/a
Morocco	No	n/a
Saudi Arabia	Yes	No recent stonings, but amputations continue
Sudan	Yes	Has declined significantly
Turkey	No	n/a
Afghanistan	Yes, but with disputed legality	No
Iran	Yes	Irregularly
Pakistan	Yes	No
Indonesia	No	n/a
Malaysia	No, except in certain states	No
Mali	No	No
Nigeria	Yes, in northern states	No stoning; amputations have declined significantly

Source: Jan Michiel Otto, Sharia Incorporated, Amsterdam University Press, p. 633

Extremists help fan such fears. In July, hate preacher Anjem Choudary, whose organization has been banned by the British government for inciting violence, posted fliers in the heavily Muslim neighborhood of Tower Hamlets in London and in Muslim areas of other English cities, declaring them "Sharia controlled zones," proclaiming bans on music, gambling and prostitution. [6]

Anxieties haven't been helped by comments from conservative Muslims like Suhaib Hasan, secretary general of the Islamic Sharia Council in London, who has said that if Sharia law were implemented in Britain, "you can turn this country into a haven of peace, because once a thief's hand is cut off nobody is going to steal." [7]

In Switzerland, the right-wing anti-Islamic Swiss Peoples Party (SVP) promoted the slogan "Maria instead of Sharia," used in posters showing a pretty blond girl next to a veiled Muslim woman with bars over her eyes. The phrase became a rallying cry in the party's 2009

Are British Sharia Councils out of Touch?

"I felt like I'd gone to a rural court in a village in Pakistan."

Three years ago, Nazia, a British Muslim woman of Pakistani descent, wrote to the Islamic Sharia Council in London, a panel of religious scholars and clerics, asking for a religious divorce. She already had obtained a civil divorce in an English court, which had granted her custody of her two children and child support from her ex-husband. [1]

But having been raised as a traditional Muslim, Nazia says she could not be at peace with her conscience until she also had a religious divorce. For starters, if she remarried, it would be considered unlawful in the eyes of her religion. Secondly, her husband refused to recognize the civil divorce and bullied her, insisting he still had "rights" over her, according to Nazia.

"For my peace of mind and sanity I wanted the Islamic divorce so I was not in limbo anymore," she says.

As Nazia tells it, she "naively assumed" a religious divorce would be as efficient as her civil divorce. She filled out the council's divorce request form, paid a fee and heard back from a council imam that she had valid grounds for a divorce under Islamic law. Then she waited — and waited.

Months later, the council summoned her to a meeting with one of its religious judges, instructing her to bring along a male family member. At the meeting, she was shocked when the *shaykh* (religious leader) ignored her, speaking only to her brother in Urdu.

"I felt like I'd gone to a rural court in a village in Pakistan, that I was a woman behind some kind of a partition and I can't speak my mind," she recalls. "I was aghast. I'm independent, I'm an educated woman, I feel I can represent myself," says Nazia, who teaches physics at a secondary school.

But she was equally shocked — and distraught — when the scholar recommended she try to reconcile with her ex-husband. She had already lived apart from him for more than two years after several failed reconciliation efforts. "I felt I'd hit a brick wall," she says. In desperation, she asked her divorce lawyer to intervene.

After several weeks, the lawyer did obtain the Islamic divorce certificate. Nazia blames the delay on the council's all-volunteer staff, but she also is critical of the all-male tribunal: The older imams from Pakistan "can't relate to life here," she says.

At 31, Nazia is one of a new generation of Muslim feminists who can cite the Prophet Muhammad's utterances in support of women's rights. "Islam offers options," she says, "and it's about time the shroud of secrecy and bureaucracy was lifted, so women can access those options."

According to Aina Khan, a London attorney specializing in both English and Islamic family law, complaints like Nazia's are more common today, a phenomenon Khan blames partly on the growing demand for such divorces.

Some secular British groups, such as One Law for All, have called for abolishing such councils, saying they constitute a parallel legal system that is inherently discriminatory toward women. But Khan says the councils, which have no legal authority, fill "a natural demand" among women like Nazia, who believe a religious divorce is required by their faith.

Ideally, she suggests, English law should recognize Muslim religious marriages on an equal plane with civil marriages. Muslim women who have not obtained a civil wedding in addition to their religious marriage are often shocked to discover that they can't seek financial awards in English courts when the marriage breaks up, according to Khan.

However, Muslim hardliners in England do not want legal recognition of their marriages, she says, because that would end the underground, polygamous unions of Muslim men who regularize their relations with girlfriends

referendum campaigns to limit immigration and ban minarets in Switzerland. With support from 57 percent of voters, Switzerland banned minarets later that year — even though the country has only four minarets and 400,000 Muslims. [8] In Germany, Chancellor Angela Merkel responded to fears about the lack of Muslim integration by assuring the public that Muslims in Germany must obey German law, and that the German constitution —not Sharia — is the law of the land. [9]

In the United States, more than two dozen states are considering bills to ban Sharia law, which have passed in one form or another in Tennessee, Arizona, Louisiana through religious marriages. The Quran allows Muslim men to have up to four wives, but because polygamy is illegal in Britain, those marriages are not recognized by English courts.

Khan favors some reforms — short of legal recognition — in the operation of Sharia councils. "It's unhealthy for anybody to be able to set up an organization and dispense justice in their front room," she says. "We need to regularize it."

Those sentiments were echoed at a recent seminar for family-law experts in London after a lecture by Kahn. Over the past two decades, British family courts have encouraged all couples to use out-of-court mediation to resolve the terms of their divorces before going to court. To do that, said one judge, more Muslim mediators are needed to work with Muslim couples. Divorce mediators need special training, said a representative of a government-funded mediation service, who asked if Sharia councils should be required to have similar training — and auditing. [2]

Cardiff Law School Professor Gillian Douglas calls concern about training "a red herring" if the mediation is voluntary and the mediator receives no public funding. Also, studies find that most women are granted the divorces they seek from Sharia councils. In a recent study, Douglas found that out of 27 divorces requested from the Birmingham Central Mosque's Shariah Council, about three-quarters were granted. [3]

A speedier religious divorce — taking three-and-a-half months instead of a year — is offered by the four-year-old Muslim Arbitration Tribunal. Originally founded to handle commercial arbitration cases, the tribunal now handles about 600 divorces a year, partly due to dissatisfaction with the mosque councils, according to Shaykh Faiz Siddiqi, an attorney and founder of the tribunal.

He contrasts the councils' lack of consistent, publicized procedures and standards with the tribunal panel, which consists of one lawyer and a religious authority and publishes its procedures on its website. "I hope we can make the councils obsolete," he says.

Although little is known about the informal settings in which Muslim clerics settle disputes or hand out religious

Anti-Sharia demonstrators in London's Hyde Park on Nov. 21, 2009, contend that religion-based courts discriminate against women and children.

AFP/Getty Images/Leon Neal

divorces in continental Europe, many experts view Britain as having the most extensive network of such councils in Europe.

As for the British media's jitters about the specter of Sharia courts replacing English law, Siddiqi says groups like his allow Muslims to be "good citizens and not think they have to go back to Bangladesh" to get a decision aligned with their faith. Citing long-standing Jewish religious courts in Britain, he says, "The Jews have done this for hundreds of years, and it helped them to integrate."

— *Sarah Glazer*

[1]Nazia's name has been changed to protect her privacy. The Islamic Sharia Council is the largest such council in England.

[2]Aina Khan, "Islamic Family Law in Legal Practice," Institute of Advanced Legal Studies, University of London, Oct. 27, 2011, http://events.sas.ac.uk/events/view/9854.

[3]See Gillian Douglas, *et al.*, "Social Cohesion and Civil Law: Marriage, Divorce and Religious Courts," Cardiff University, June 2011, www.law.cf.ac.uk/clr/research/cohesion. An unpublished study of 200 cases at the London Islamic Sharia Council by John Bowen of Washington University found most divorces requested by women were granted.

and Oklahoma. The Oklahoma law is being challenged on constitutional grounds.

Much like Jewish law, which is based on thousands of years of elaboration and interpretation of the Torah, Sharia is the body of Islamic sacred laws derived from the Quran and the ensuing written interpretations and rulings that

have evolved over centuries. Its interpretations may vary significantly from country to country and community to community.

Broadly, Sharia means "the way" and encompasses all prescriptions about how Muslims should live a devout life — from how they should pray to what they should eat and how much they should donate to charity. Although many of its religious rules would never be included in a secular legal code, Sharia also encompasses rules that, depending on the country, can become part of national statues on issues such as child custody, inheritance and criminal penalties.

While these laws derive originally from the Quran and the teachings of the Prophet Muhammad, they have been interpreted in a multitude of ways in scholarly tomes over hundreds of years. That process and the resultant body of interpretation, known as the *fiqh*, continues to evolve today, as various Muslim scholars and Sharia judges revisit specific issues. For example, the website of the Islamic Sharia Council in London spells out four different sets of divorce custody rules about the age at which a boy must be turned over to his father, each following one of the four leading Sharia schools of thought. [10]

Today Sharia is implemented in many Muslim countries, ranging from ultra-conservative Saudi Arabia and theocratic Iran — where harsh punishments such as amputations have been implemented — to countries with progressive family laws, such as Tunisia and Morocco.

According to Jan Michiel Otto, a professor of law and governance in developing countries at the Netherlands' University of Leiden, lawmaking in much of the Muslim world is now in the hands of state and secular courts, marginalizing religious courts. "The emancipation of women all over the world and enrollment in secondary and university education is changing the whole picture and making it impossible for patriarchal systems such as Sharia . . . to keep their dominant position," he says. Otto, who edited a recent study of 12 major Muslim countries, says about half of the countries his team studied had nothing in their legal codes about stoning or amputation. In Pakistan and Nigeria, for instance, those punishments are on the books but are not being implemented. [11]

"Virtually all Muslim countries today are governed by modern legal systems, and some elements in the statute may draw inspiration from the Quran or *fiqh*, just like Christian thinking made its way into the legal system of France or the U.S.," says John R. Bowen, an anthropologist at Washington University in St. Louis, who has studied Islamic practices in Indonesia, France and England.

Increasingly in the Middle East — and in Nigeria, where Sharia is on the books in the Muslim north of the country — women's groups are arguing for equal rights based on a reinterpretation of Sharia. Even for some secular women in Muslim countries such as Iran, "the fault lines are very clear that the problem is not with Sharia or Islam — but with patriarchy and despotism," says Ziba Mir-Hosseini, a research associate at the Centre for Middle Eastern and Islamic Law at the School of Oriental and African Studies in London.

Until the 19th century, Islamic legal traditions offered more rights for women than Western laws did, particularly in such areas as inheritance and economic independence for married women. Property rights for married women weren't recognized in England until 1887.

Many aspects of U.S. and English law derived from Islamic law, particularly in contract law, says Raj Bhala, a professor of law at the University of Kansas and author of the textbook *Understanding Islamic Law.*

Despite those shared roots, the recent Arab Spring upheaval in the Muslim world has raised fresh uncertainties — both in the West and in the Arab world — about which direction the newly constituted governments will take in regard to Sharia and secular law. While some experts say the popular uprisings reflect a desire for more democracy and women's rights, others warn about the rising influence of puritanical Islamist parties.

As governments, academia and voters around the world debate the role of Sharia law, these are some of the questions being debated:

Is Sharia law incompatible with Western values?

The debate over Sharia law's lack of compatibility with Western values has become especially heated in recent years, particularly in Western countries that have considered incorporating some version of Sharia into their legal systems.

In Canada, the province of Ontario in 2005 banned Sharia-based arbitration on Muslim family matters, which since 1991 had been legally binding for several religious groups. The decision followed a campaign by women's groups, including Muslims, who charged that such arbitration discriminated against women. [12]

Critics of Sharia say its traditionally patriarchal approach to solving disputes recognizes fewer rights for women than for men. For example, under a classic tenet of Islamic law, only a Muslim man has a unilateral right to divorce without the consent of his wife. Traditionally, he need only utter the phrase, "I divorce you," three times. A wife, however, must seek the consent of her husband or, failing that, of a religious authority. [13]

Diana Nammi, an Iranian who directs the London-based Iranian and Kurdish Women's Rights Organization, cites other examples as well in which classical Sharia discriminates against women: Women inherit half as much property as men, domestic violence is not an automatic justification for a woman to get a divorce, and children must be returned to their father's custody at a pre-set age.

Nammi says such rules are used in Britain's Sharia councils when they issue religious divorces. And while their decisions are not legally binding, many women think they are, she says. "Having Sharia law is holding the community in the Dark Ages," she says. "It will bring backward practices to the community and to people like us, who came to England to have a safer life." The result, she says, is a system in which women "are not counted as a human being at all."

Baroness Cox says many of Sharia's precepts violate basic human rights, including women's equality. "There are aspects of Sharia law that are inherently discriminatory against women, and, therefore, it is fundamentally incompatible with values of a liberal democracy and with our commitments to eradicating gender discrimination in Britain."

But experts in Sharia law say many of its precepts have been evolving and modernizing over time, depending on the specific country or school of thought.

"People seem to think Sharia is one single uniform system of laws. It's not; it's an ocean of legal principles," says Ian Edge, director of the Centre of Islamic and Middle Eastern Law at the School of Oriental and African Studies (SOAS) in London. "You can find a legal principle for almost anything — which is helpful for modern reformers."

Most of the Muslim world has modernized its laws on issues such as child custody, he says. In the United Arab

Some Muslim Constitutions Based on Sharia

In a study of the constitutions of 12 Muslim countries, half specify Sharia as a primary source of law. Except for Saudi Arabia, which severely restricts women's rights, all of the constitutions guarantee equality between the sexes, but two — Egypt and Iran — include some limits on gender equality to accommodate Sharia principles. For instance, Egypt's constitution says a woman's work outside of the home should not conflict with her family duties, as outlined in Sharia.

Sharia and Gender Equality in 12 Muslim Constitutions

Country	Constitution lists Sharia as a main source of law	Constitution specifies gender equality	Gender equality is limited, based on Sharia
Egypt	Yes	Yes	Yes
Morocco	No	Yes	No
Saudi Arabia	Yes	No	n/a
Sudan	Yes	Yes	No
Turkey	No	Yes	No
Afghanistan	Yes	Yes	No
Iran	Yes	Yes	Yes
Pakistan	Yes	Yes	No
Indonesia	No	Yes	No
Malaysia	No	Yes	No
Mali	No	Yes	No
Nigeria	No	Yes	No

Source: Jan Michiel Otto, Sharia Incorporated, Amsterdam University Press, p. 657

Emirates, for example, the ages that children of divorced parents must return to the custody of the father have been extended for a boy from the traditional 7 to age 11 and for a girl to age 13. They can be extended further, on application to a judge, to as late as 15 for a boy and marriage for girls, in keeping with contemporary notions that consistency in living arrangements is best for children.

"I've seen quite a number of cases where this has been done, and they've done away with the automatic losing of custody by a mother if she remarries. Most of these [Arab Muslim] countries have adopted the United Nations Convention on the Rights of the Child and focus on the welfare of the child," Edge says.

Ultimately, much like Christianity, Islam is divided between "puritans," who claim to abide by a literal interpretation of the Quran, and moderates, who believe that Sharia should be interpreted in light of a

Crowds in Banda Aceh, Indonesia, watch the caning of a woman on Jan. 12, 2007. Caning is prescribed in Sharia for violations of the Islamic code of conduct, such as gambling or drinking alcohol. It is carried out in only a handful of Islamic countries. Aceh province adopted caning as a form of punishment when it instituted Islamic law as part of a peace agreement after a 29-year separatist war. It exists parallel to state laws and applies only to the Muslim population.

changing modern life, writes Khaled Abou El Fadl, a professor of law at the University of California-Los Angeles, in his 2007 book about Muslim extremism, *The Great Theft*.

The University of Leiden's Otto concurs. "What Sharia means to a puritan is completely different than what it means to a moderate," he says.

While Sharia interpretations have been evolving over hundreds of years, strict traditionalists abide only by interpretations written before A.D. 1000. Other schools of thought employ more recent interpretations.

Experts like Asifa Quraishi, who teaches comparative Islamic and U.S. constitutional law at the University of Wisconsin-Madison, notes that historically, "*fiqh* always facilitated variety," a tradition that continues today.

"All kinds of people are saying, 'Maybe there shouldn't be unilateral divorce for a husband; that's not actually in the Quran,'" she says. "So people are interacting in a very sophisticated way with the scripture and coming up with new *fiqh* rules for today," she says. Moreover, she says, "If you look at the [U.S.] Bill of Rights, a lot of that is consistent with or already in classical *fiqh*: private property rights, innocence of the accused, freedom of religion."

Sharia textbook author Bhala says most Westerners don't realize how much of the English and American legal systems evolved from Islamic law, which in turn borrowed from Roman and Babylonian precedents. "Sharia is not inconsistent with Western values, because Islam itself is in the Judeo-Christian-Islamic tradition and part of our Western civilization. But the manifestations of the values sometimes are different and misperceived as incompatible," he says. For example, "It's not authentic Sharia to systematically discriminate against women or abuse children."

In the Quran, many rulings concerning the rights of women were considered reforms in their day, and some continue to provide protection for women from exploitation. For example, the tradition of the *mahr*, or the "dower," a substantial gift from the groom to the bride that is written into their marriage contract, was intended to provide women with financial security in the event that the wife outlived her husband, Fadl writes. [14] Today it can provide a "nest egg" for women upon divorce, Quraishi says.

Notably, women's groups in several Muslim countries, including Nigeria and Iran, argue that equality for women is consistent with the fundamental values prescribed in Sharia, rather than the often tribal and patriarchal forms it has taken over the centuries.

Musawah, a Malaysia-based international women's group campaigning for non-discriminatory family laws, was founded in 2009 to bring together an Islamic and human-rights framework that both religious and secular women could agree upon. According to Ziba Mir-Hosseini, one of the founders of Musawah ("equality" in Arabic), the group believes that "Muslim family laws are neither divine nor immutable" and that traditional family rulings "are no longer in line with the justice that is the spirit of the Sharia." [15]

Muslims in the West who try to follow Islamic laws have values that "are pretty adaptable to conditions of life in Britain or America," says Washington University

Major Muslim Countries Sign Human-Rights Treaties

Among 12 of the world's biggest Muslim countries, most support treaties that ban the use of torture and protect gender equality and civil and political rights. Some legal experts see a convergence between Sharia principles and human-rights standards in the signing of these treaties, but governments don't always follow them when it comes to women's equality.

Status of Human-Rights Treaties in 12 Muslim Countries

Country	International Covenant on Civil and Political Rights		Conv. on the Elimination of Discrimination Against Women		Convention Against Torture	
	Signed	Ratification (R), accession (A), signing (S)	Signed	Ratification (R), accession (A), signing year (S)	Signed	Ratification (R), accession (A), signing year (S)
Egypt	Yes	1982 (R)	Yes*	1981 (R)	Yes	1986 (A)
Morocco	Yes	1979 (R)	Yes*	1993 (R)	Yes	1993 (R)
Saudi Arabia	No	n/a	Yes*	2000 (R)	Yes	1997 (A)
Sudan	Yes	1986 (A)	No	n/a	Yes	1986 (S)
Turkey	Yes	2003 (R)	Yes	1986 (R)	Yes	1998 (R)
Afghanistan	Yes	1983 (A)	Yes	2003 (R)	Yes	1987 (R)
Iran	Yes	1975 (R)	No	n/a	No	n/a
Pakistan	Yes	2008 (S)	Yes	1996 (R)	Yes	2008 (A)
Indonesia	Yes	2006 (A)	Yes	1984 (R)	Yes	1998 (R)
Malaysia	No	n/a	Yes*	1995 (A)	No	n/a
Mali	Yes	1974 (A)	Yes	1985 (R)	Yes	1999 (A)
Nigeria	Yes	1993 (A)	Yes	1985 (R)	Yes	2001 (R)

* With reservations, related to Sharia

Source: Jan Michiel Otto, Sharia Incorporated, Amsterdam University Press, p. 634

anthropologist Bowen, who is writing a book about Britain's Sharia councils. And Muslim countries' modern statutes, which may get their inspiration from the Quran, don't always follow it literally, just as Western laws may draw in part upon the Ten Commandments.

He suggests that Westerners' fears about the use of Sharia law has more to do with their discomfort over the large numbers of Muslim immigrants in the West rather than substantive differences on issues such as marriage and divorce.

Has England been too accommodating to Sharia councils?

According to its website, London's Islamic Sharia Council, England's largest, has handled 1,000 religious divorces since 2006, and according to researchers almost all these divorces are sought by women. The council now gets about 50 inquiries per week, according to London attorney Aina Khan. [16]

With an estimated 30-50 such tribunals based in British mosques, experts generally agree that England is unique among Western countries in having developed such an extensive system. "This is a singular British development," says Mathias Rohe, director of the Erlangen Center for Islam and Law in Europe, at the University of Erlangen, Germany.

Although the British press describes the councils as "Sharia courts," their religious divorces and decisions about custody and finances are not recognized under English law. Yet several British women's groups, think tanks and politicians charge that a parallel legal system is developing that discriminates against women and is fundamentally at odds with the English legal system's values. And, critics argue, many of the women who

A rare copy of the Quran, Islam's most holy text, is displayed during an exhibition in Dubai on Nov. 9, 2009. Muslims believe the Quran (also spelled Koran) is the literal word of God as revealed to the Prophet Muhammad. Besides containing the rules for living a devout Muslim life, the Quran is the basis for Sharia. Since the 7th century, Islamic scholars have interpreted the Prophet's teachings in a variety of ways, contributing to divergent interpretations of Sharia.

consult the councils do not realize that their decisions are not binding.

"Many of these women don't know these are so-called voluntary tribunals. Many don't speak English, have no idea of their rights and are being told it's the law when it's not," says Waters of One Law for All.

"Should we allow Sharia law to exist alongside British law?" asked the London think tank Civitas. "Most British people would answer this question with a resounding 'no!' " The group, which claims there are 85 Sharia councils in England — far more than most experts estimate, partly because Civitas counts online advice services — warns that the councils are "a recipe" for a legal system "that holds Muslims and non-Muslims to different standards." [17]

Baroness Cox has introduced a bill in Parliament that would make it a criminal offense, punishable by up to five years in prison, for an imam or Sharia council scholar to falsely claim legal jurisdiction in family or criminal-law matters. "At the moment" she says, many women who go to the councils "haven't got a clue how to access their rights" under English civil law.

Sharia councils often tell women to go back and reconcile with husbands who beat them, critics claim. "It's very dangerous for many women," says Nammi, of the Iranian and Kurdish Women's Rights Organization. In 2007, researcher Bano reported that among 10 cases she observed at British Sharia councils, four women already had obtained civil injunctions against their husbands for threatening or violent behavior, and several of those agreed reluctantly to attend reconciliation meetings at the bidding of the Sharia council. [18]

Yet critics of Cox's bill, such as Prakash Shah, a senior law lecturer at the University of London-Queen Mary, say it's "overkill." It's already illegal for Sharia councils to make legally binding decisions in divorce, custody or related family matters, they point out.

"You can make this a criminal offense but it's an offense anyway," says Bano.

Under England's Arbitration Act, two parties in commercial disputes can voluntarily agree to a binding arbitration conducted under Sharia principles. But an English court can enforce the agreement — such as requiring one party to pay an agreed-upon amount — only if the agreement follows standard requirements for an English contract, such as voluntary participation by both parties. Cox's bill would explicitly ban sex discrimination in the procedures used in such arbitration, but some lawyers say English courts already could not enforce a contract under procedures that discriminate against women.

Most Sharia-based arbitration in England occurs under the supervision of the Muslim Arbitration Tribunal, headed by a trained English barrister and Sufi spiritual leader, Shayk Faiz Siddiqi.* Some critics, including Cox, cite the tribunal's website, which also offers mediation in family disputes, as proof that the tribunal portrays its domestic violence and divorce decisions as legally binding in a "quasi-judicial parallel system," Cox says.

But anthropologist Bowen, who has observed the tribunal and Sharia councils for three years, says Cox's criticism "comes from a reading of the website" and is not borne out by his observations.

Calling Cox's charges "unfair," Siddiqi insists the tribunal only carries out legally binding arbitration in commercial matters, which only occurs if both parties come voluntarily. In its four years, the tribunal has never had

---

* Sufism is a mystical strand of Islam that emphasizes spirituality. Shaykh Siddiqi is the son of a British Sufi leader who was devoted to establishing moderate mainstream Islam and promoting both classical Muslim and secular education.

an unhappy party contest the arbitration or try to get it enforced in an English court, he says. The tribunal also offers religious divorces and counseling to couples wishing to reconcile after domestic violence, he says, but if a criminal assault is involved tribunal staff members encourage the victim to report it to police or do so themselves.

"Where child custody or assets are involved we hold mediation, not arbitration" in a legally "nonbinding forum," he stresses. "We are like hundreds of other mediation agencies offering mediation to young couples to reduce the acrimony in that relationship, which is not assisted by aggressive litigation."

As for Cox's charge that a woman's testimony is worth half of a man's, Shaykh derides that as an anachronistic rule that is not even considered in any of the tribunal's proceedings.

Like Bowen, other researchers who have observed the tribunal and Sharia councils have found no evidence that they are portraying their decisions in family matters as judicially valid. For example, Cardiff Law School's Douglas, who recently completed a study of the Birmingham Sharia council, says it was made very clear to people who came to the proceedings "that if they wanted recognition in the eyes of the law, they would have to use the family courts."

As for Cox's assertion that the women are clueless, University of Reading researcher Bano, who interviewed 25 Pakistani-British Muslim women, says she found the women "very sophisticated in using councils for their particular purposes" — including taking their case to another council if they didn't like a decision.

"They knew about civil law but wanted to be divorced Islamically, because it was part of their religious identity," she says. Although the predominantly male panels can be patriarchal in their attitude, she adds, the women she interviewed "weren't ignorant and being misled by conservative Muslim men."

"I've had hundreds of cases involving women seeking divorces from Sharia councils," says London solicitor Aina Khan, who specializes in Islamic family law, "and all of them know the legal system. It's a tiny minority who are so isolated they don't know their rights."

Even the most housebound Muslim woman in England has access to ethnic TV channels informing women of their rights, Khan says.

Sharia Stirs Strong Sentiments

Women in Mogadishu, Somalia, celebrate the news on April 19, 2009, that the U.N.-backed government had unanimously agreed to implement a moderate version of Islamic law in the war-torn Horn of Africa country (top). The move was aimed at defusing support for al-Shabaab Islamist insurgents, who have been fighting for control of the country in order to impose a stricter interpretation of Sharia. In contrast, Canadian women express their strong disapproval of the use of Sharia tribunals to a Muslim supporter of such religious panels in Toronto (bottom). After an Ontario Muslim announced in 2005 that he intended to set up a Sharia-based arbitration council that all "good Muslims" should consult on legal matters, the government banned binding arbitration by religious tribunals in marriage and divorce cases.

In addition, she says, rather than being told to go back to violent husbands, in her experience "if you provide a crime report involving violence by a husband, they give you a divorce."

Hardline Islamist militiamen patrol Somalia's lower Shabelle region in 2009. Radical Islamic factions such as the al Qaeda-supported al-Shabaab are fighting for control of Somalia, where a deadly struggle to impose strict Sharia law, including punishments such as stoning and amputations, has been going on for years.

Anthropologist Bowen recently analyzed 200 divorce cases that came before the London-based Islamic Sharia council. In every case where women followed the case through, they got the divorce, he says.

Are Muslim countries taking increasingly fundamentalist approaches to Sharia?

Horrifying reports of hand amputations for theft in northern Nigeria or stonings of women in Iran give Westerners the impression that those are widespread practices in the Muslim countries that are governed according to Sharia.

"We do have a move in the last decade in some countries to introduce punishments that were abolished decades before," says Erlangen law professor Rohe. Such moves, he continues, are being used "as a political tool" to demonstrate "the Islamicness of the government in Nigeria, Iran, Somalia."

But while governments often say they are incorporating Sharia in order to win political support, many are implementing more secular laws in practice, says the University of Leiden's Otto, who edited a recent study of 12 major Muslim countries. In most Muslim countries, he says, "the religious establishment has been marginalized. Of course, the clerics try to win back their lost position, but by and large they are not very successful."

Iran, which has a theocratic government, and Saudi Arabia, which is governed under the conservative Wahhabi interpretation of Sharia, are notable exceptions.

Pakistan has had a law on its books since 1979 prescribing stoning for adultery, but so far judges in both secular and Sharia courts have refused to issue such sentences, according to Otto's study. Although stonings have occurred as a form of mob lynching in Pakistani villages, Otto notes, it "has nothing to do with courts and no relation to law."

In northern Nigeria, predominantly Muslim states adopted a harsh version of Sharia starting in 1999, but after the first few amputations and stonings spurred a huge world outcry, popular support for them withered away, and there have been no such sentences in recent years. [19] In two death-by-stoning sentences for women convicted of *zina* (sex outside marriage), Sharia courts of appeal overturned the sentences and issued a reinterpretation of the Sharia penalty, saying the sentence could only be carried out if the guilty party submitted herself voluntarily to the court.

After the first convicted thief had his hand amputated in 2000, international agencies threatened sanctions against the Nigerian states that had introduced Sharia penal codes. "It wasn't in the interest of these states to keep it up," notes Philip Ostien, a former member of the law faculty at the University of Jos, Nigeria, and author of the chapter on Nigeria in Otto's study.

"In my opinion," says Ostien, "there was little sentiment among Muslims even in Sharia states to keep it up." Although at first many Nigerian Muslims "really did believe Sharia would cure social ills," he says, disillusion set in when it became clear punishments were falling mainly on the poorest members of society.

Brutal penalties like amputation and stoning have occurred in a small handful of other countries — including Iran, Saudi Arabia, Somalia and Sudan, but not in most of the other 52 countries that make up the 57-nation Organisation of Islamic Cooperation, encompassing most countries with a Muslim-identified government. [20]

When it comes to family law, over the last 20 years Muslim countries previously under colonial rule have transformed their systems, to varying degrees, to create more equal legal situations for men and women in marriage and divorce cases, notes Bowen, an expert on Islam in Indonesia. He cites the forward-looking family codes in both Indonesia and Morocco, which allow either a man or a woman to request divorce on grounds of irreconcilable differences — a departure from classical Sharia, where only a husband can divorce his wife at will.

"There's been parallel movement [in Muslim and non-Muslim countries] toward giving women greater powers in effecting a divorce," Bowen says.

Women's groups have pushed for reforms in countries such as Tunisia — which banned polygamy and claimed the prohibition was based on the Quran — and Morocco, inspiring women's rights movements in other Muslim countries.

But there also have been backlashes. Since the 1990s, fundamentalists in Malaysia have repealed legal reforms on polygamy, divorce and inheritance — "a steady regression in the legal status of Muslim women," according to Zainah Anwar, director of the Malaysian women's group Sisters in Islam.

In Iran, "theocratic forces are becoming more despotic," reports Mir-Hosseini, an expert on Iran. Since 2009, she says, nearly all of the prominent leaders of women's groups who campaigned for equality have been imprisoned in Iran or were forced to leave the country, though they continue their organizing efforts using Facebook and other websites.

Yet, even in a theocracy like Iran, Islamic scholars disagree on whether Sharia requires stoning for adultery. "Many clerics are coming out saying stoning is not in the Quran and needs to be suspended," Mir-Hosseini reports. "There haven't been any stoning cases issued by penal courts in big cities; it's done in small cities by judges not well trained in Islam or modern law."

Most Muslim countries have ratified the Convention on the Elimination of All Forms of Discrimination Against Women (CEDAW), adopted by the U.N. General Assembly in 1979, but many have not reformed their domestic family laws to conform to it, according to a recent report by the Malaysia-based women's group Musawah. Those governments contend the convention conflicts with Sharia.

Syria and Egypt, for example, say they can't abolish inheritance laws discriminating against women because Sharia law is fixed on that matter. Other countries cite Sharia as the reason they do not reform their laws on polygamy, child marriage and marital rape to bring them in line with the convention. [21]

Judging from the Musawah report, women still have a long way to go in persuading some governments that classical Islamic *fiqh* is not a fixed code and that Islam supports gender equality. But the launch of Musawah in 2009 with 250 women from 47 countries also shows support for the group's view that "the huge disconnect" between discriminatory family laws and women's lives today is "no longer tolerable," in the words of Anwar.

BACKGROUND
Revelations

In Islam, Sharia — literally the "way" of truth and justice that exists in God's mind — is said to be based on God's revelation of his plan for mankind, as revealed to the Prophet Muhammad in the Quran and in later written accounts of his deeds. Muslims believe the Quran is the literal word of God.

Most Muslims view the *Sunna* — accounts compiled starting in the 9th century about the religious deeds of Muhammad two centuries earlier — as the second-most authoritative text. The compiled *Hadith*, reports of what the Prophet said in his lifetime, also contribute to Sharia. Based on legend and hearsay and reflecting the mores of desert society at the time, the *Hadith* came to overshadow the importance of the Quran in Sharia, and represented an ideology designed to limit rational analysis, according to some scholars.

Islamic law consists of both Sharia and the *fiqh*, the human interpretations of Sharia contained in an amorphous body of rulings and opinions that have accumulated over the centuries. By its very nature, the *fiqh* is considered — at least to moderates — as subject to human error, alterable and dependent on human understanding at a certain point in history.

Unlike moderate Muslims, conservative Saudi Arabian Wahhabis and other so-called Muslim puritans rely almost entirely on the Quran and the *Sunna*, contending that 90 percent of revealed law is not subject to discussion or later human interpretation. The *fiqh*, they say, applies to the other 10 percent. In the small number of instances where they rely on later interpretations, according to UCLA's Abou El Fadl, puritanical Muslims specifically select jurists who are the most hostile to women in their *fiqh* opinions. [22]

The most fundamentalist puritans ignore interpretations in the *fiqh* made after A.D. 900, insisting that scholars had already answered all the great questions definitively by that time, notes Bhala, the author of *Understanding Islamic Law*.

CHRONOLOGY

600s-1800 *"Golden era" of Muslim rule under Sharia (Islamic law), when Islam was ruled first by Prophet Muhammad and later by secular leaders (caliphs), who actually operated a parallel secular judicial system.*

632 Prophet Muhammad dies. Muslims believe he received divine words from God, recorded in the Quran and in later reports, called the *Sunna.*

900 Fundamentalist Muslims believe all great questions of Sharia were answered by this date; they reject all interpretations, or *fiqh.*

1500 Three powerful Muslim empires expand: the Ottoman in the Middle East and Europe, the Mughal in India and the Safavid in Persia.

1792 Ad al-Wahhab, founder of conservative branch of Islam later adopted by rulers of modern Saudi Arabia, dies.

19th Century *British colonial rulers allow religious communities throughout British Empire to govern their own marital affairs, establishing precedent for today's Sharia councils in Britain. . . . English law catches up to Islam on married women's economic independence.*

1887 England passes Married Women's Property Act, allowing married women to own property — a right already recognized in Sharia.

20th Century *First World War leads to end of Ottoman Empire, rise of independent Muslim countries, Arab nationalism and secularism, followed by Islamists' call for Sharia. Sharia councils emerge in England.*

1923 Treaty of Lausanne between British-French allies and Turks partitions Ottoman Empire into new Arab countries — including Saudi Arabia and Yemen.

1952 Gamal Abdel Nasser, Egyptian nationalist, leads revolution in Egypt.

1956 Tunisia bans polygamy.

1964 Ayatollah Khomeini, spiritual leader of Iranian revolution, is exiled.

1967 Iran's Shah Reza Pahlevi puts men and women on equal footing in custody and divorce.

1979 Shah is overthrown and an Islamic Republic is installed in Iran. . . . U.N. General Assembly passes Convention to Eliminate Discrimination Against Women.

2000s *Some Muslim countries pass progressive laws on women's rights, but fundamentalists roll back progress in others. Bans on Sharia are introduced in some U.S. states. . . . Revolutions raise questions about return of strict form of Sharia in some Arab countries.*

2000 As northern Nigerian states adopt Sharia law, the first hand amputation for thievery raises international uproar.

2004 Muslim women win egalitarian family law reforms in Morocco, inspiring women's movements elsewhere.

2005 Ontario, Canada, bars legally binding religious arbitration after uproar over a proposed Sharia court.

2007 German judge is removed after her decision to excuse a Muslim husband's domestic violence on grounds it's allowed by the Quran.

2009 Iran's Green Movement protests re-election of Islamist hardliner President Mahmoud Ahmadinejad.

2010 Oklahoma passes referendum banning Sharia from state courts; constitutional challenge blocks it; Tennessee, Louisiana pass similar bills but don't mention Sharia.

2011 Arab Spring protests overturn governments in Tunisia, Egypt, Libya and, eventually, Yemen. . . . Sharia ban passes in Arizona. . . . British hate preacher Anjem Choudhary announces "Sharia Zones" in London's Muslim neighborhoods. . . . Interim Libyan leader Mustafa Abdel-Jalil says polygamy should be restored in Libya. . . . Islamist parties — Muslim Brotherhood and fundamentalist Salafis — capture a majority in first-round parliamentary elections. Final results due in February 2012.

From the outset, many differences of opinion cropped up among writers of the *fiqh* books during the first two centuries after Mohammad's death. Some of the most influential authors gave their names to four different *fiqh* schools within the Sunni sect, which came to represent the dominant opinions of classical Sharia — Hanafi, Maliki, Shafi'i and Hanbali. Of these, the Hanbali school is generally considered the strictest and most conservative, especially in the form embraced by the fundamentalist Wahhabis. Hanafi, the oldest, is considered the most liberal school, with a focus on rationalism. Hanafi Muslims predominate in Turkey, Syria, Jordan, Lebanon, Pakistan, Afghanistan and India. (There are also two surviving schools of thought among the Shiites: Ja'fari in Iran and Iraq and Zaydi in Yemen.) [23]

Sharia's Golden Age

Fundamentalist Muslims often portray Islam's first 1,000 years, when the Prophet and subsequent Muslim leaders ruled Medina, as an ideal age of justice and fairness. That was when one law — Sharia — ruled the Muslim people. Puritans limit this "golden age" to the first 50 years of Islam, starting with the *hijrah* (migration) of Mohammad in A.D. 622 to Medina, where he established his seat of power, through the reign of the succeeding four "Rightly Guided Caliphs," close companions and supporters of the Prophet. That Golden Age ended in A.D. 661 — or in some views, with the reign of the fifth Caliph ending in A.D. 720. [24]

But, in reality, a parallel secular system was established by the Caliphs — the secular rulers — who issued decrees and administered justice in their own courts, particularly in criminal and trade cases. The scope of Sharia courts eventually was reduced to family, inheritance and contract law.

Starting in 1500, three powerful Muslim empires expanded: the Ottoman Empire in the Middle East and southeast Europe, India's Mughal Empire and Persia's Safavid Empire. While Sharia was the official law in all three, the rulers' edicts sometimes conflicted with Sharia. In the 15th century, the Ottoman sultan ordered that the strict Quranic punishments known as *hadd*, such as amputation for theft, not be used under his rule. [25]

In 1680, after viewing the stoning death of an adulterous woman, Ottoman Sultan Mehmet IV put an end to such punishments, saying, "From now on, I do not want such disgrace in the Ottoman lands." [26]

Contrary to popular opinion, the Quran does not specify stoning to death as the punishment for *zina* (extra-marital sex), according to Sharia expert Bhala. It prescribes 100 lashes. The punishment of stoning for adultery developed based on a *Hadith* (a separate written account of a deed of the Prophet), which involved a woman who became pregnant through adultery and was sentenced to stoning with the approval of Muhammad. [27]

In the 18th century, the Saudi evangelist Muhammad bin Abd al-Wahhab sought to rid Islam of what he considered modern corruptions such as rationalism, spawning the Wahhabi sect. Wahhabis treated the Quran and the *Sunna* as the only valid legal instruction manual and viewed later jurisprudence as heresy. They rejected the long-established practice of accepting several *fiqh* schools of thought.

Later, Wahhabism would be adopted as the official state religion of the Saudi Kingdom, starting in the late 18th century when the Al Saud family allied with the Wahhabis to rebel against Ottoman rule in the Arabian peninsula. In the 20th century, extremists like Osama bin Laden adopted the same Islamic precedents as al-Wahhab to justify the killing of innocents on the grounds they were "heretics."

Ironically, the "pure" form of Islam espoused by Wahhabi himself drew more from Bedouin tribal tradition than from a faithful reading of the Quran, according to El Fadl.

Colonialism and Modernity

Starting in the 1800s, modern law and governance were introduced in the Ottoman Empire and Europe's Asian colonies. In India, British rulers decided to let religious communities govern marital affairs according to their own traditions. South Asian Muslims would bring these ideas and practices with them to England, helping to explain their formation of Sharia councils for divorce and family issues.

By contrast, marriage and divorce in France and its colonies were governed by uniform civil law, an assumption about "the supremacy of state law" that North Africans from Algeria and Tunisia carried with them when they migrated to France, writes anthropologist Bowen. [28]

Britain also allowed Anglicans, Quakers and Jews to regulate marriage in their own communities in Britain

Sharia Bans in U.S. Stir Constitutional Debates

States run into legal roadblocks.

More than two dozen states have considered laws aimed at barring American courts from considering Sharia law in their deliberations, and four have approved such measures. But the threat of constitutional challenges, starting with Oklahoma, has watered down the most recent bills moving through state legislatures — rendering them practically toothless.

The movement to ban Sharia law in U.S. courtrooms has won support from some Tea Party supporters and from Republican presidential contender Newt Gingrich, who claims that "stealth jihadists" want to impose Sharia based on principles "abhorrent to the Western world." [1]

Tennessee Republican state Rep. Rick Womick has argued that Sharia is a political and legal system that seeks world domination. [2]

Gingrich and supporters of state bans point to a New Jersey case in which a judge cited Islamic law in turning down the request of a woman of Moroccan descent for a restraining order against her husband. Although the husband repeatedly assaulted and raped her, the judge claimed the husband lacked criminal intent because under Islamic law the wife was required to satisfy his desire for sex.

The case was overturned on appeal on the grounds that the husband's religious beliefs did not excuse him from New Jersey's criminal code. A person's religious beliefs cannot trump American law, the appellate court said. Among other cases, it cited the landmark 1878 Supreme Court decision in the case of a Mormon who was practicing polygamy. It ruled that freedom of religion was not a defense against the Morrill Anti-Bigamy Act of 1862, a federal statute prohibiting bigamy in territories of the United States, which was aimed at the Mormon practice in Utah. [3]

The New Jersey case is one of 50 state appellate cases over the last three decades cited by supporters of the anti-Sharia movement as evidence of the extent to which Sharia "is being insinuated into the fabric of American society." [4]

"Oklahoma does not have that problem yet," said Oklahoma state Sen. Rex Conrad, as he introduced legislation to prohibit state courts from considering Sharia. "But why wait until it's in the courts?" [5]

But in many of these cases, as in New Jersey, judges have given primacy to constitutional rights over foreign or religious laws. The frequency of such cases is unknown, according to a recent investigative report by *The New York Times.* [6]

According to the U.S. Constitution's Supremacy Clause, which proclaims the Constitution and laws of the United States the supreme law of the land, U.S. law generally takes precedence over conflicting foreign laws, especially where they would violate fundamental American public policies in areas such as polygamy or discrimination. Matthew Duss, a policy analyst at the liberal Center for American Progress think tank in Washington, says the clause, familiar to most 9th-grade civic students, essentially makes the Constitution "Sharia-proof" — and the state laws unnecessary. [7]

Nonetheless, 70 percent of Oklahoma voters in 2010 approved a state constitutional amendment to prohibit state courts from considering Sharia and foreign laws in their decisions. Just a few weeks later, however, a federal district court in Oklahoma City temporarily blocked the law from taking effect, saying that there was a high probability the amendment would be found unconstitutional in an ongoing lawsuit.

In the lawsuit filed by the Council on American-Islamic Relations (CAIR), its Oklahoma chapter director, Muneer Awad, claimed that Oklahoma's anti-Sharia amendment violates his constitutional right to religious freedom.

Judge Vicki Miles-LaGrange said the state constitutional amendment could be viewed "as specifically singling out Shariah law, conveying a message of disapproval of plaintiff's faith." The federal courts have long held that such a message violates the U.S. Constitution's First Amendment prohibiting the establishment of a state religion. [8]

The state of Oklahoma appealed the decision, and the 10th U.S. Circuit Court of Appeals heard arguments on

Sept. 12. Many legal experts expect the law to be ruled unconstitutional. [9]

Three other states — Arizona, Louisiana and Tennessee — have passed similar laws with an important difference: They have removed any reference to Sharia, although they still refer to foreign laws. One early version of the Arizona bill even mentioned "karma" in an effort to widen its religious scope beyond Islam. [10]

Although the statutes appear religiously neutral, they apparently are based on a draft aimed at avoiding Oklahoma's constitutional problem, crafted by the author of the anti-Sharia model legislation — New York lawyer David Yerushalmi, founder of the think tank, the Society of Americans for National Existence, which first proposed criminalizing adherence to Sharia in 2007 and continues to push for state bans. The group's e-newsletter describes Yerushalmi as "at the forefront of the fight against Shariah and its doctrine of jihad to establish a worldwide political order." [11] The Anti-Defamation League has criticized Yerushalmi for a record of "anti-Muslim, anti-immigrant and anti-black bigotry," including acting as general counsel for a right-wing group that lobbied to close a New York City public school that taught Arabic. [12]

Despite the seemingly grassroots nature of the movement, the prime originators of the legislative campaign, according to the *Times* investigation, are Yerushalmi and Frank J. Gaffney, Jr., a former Reagan Pentagon official and founder of the hawkish Washington, D.C., think tank the Center for Security Policy. Gaffney has been a vocal opponent of mosque construction near Ground Zero and was quoted in 2009 as saying there's mounting evidence that President Obama "not only identifies with Muslims but actually may still be one himself." [13]

Gaffney's center has contributed "unspecified" amounts to Yerushalmi's efforts, specifically a controversial study finding that 82 percent of American mosques' imams promote violent texts. Gaffney also contacted his network of Christian and Tea Party Groups — including ACT for America, a group opposed to "radical Islam" — which raised $60,000 to promote the Oklahoma initiative. [14]

The other states that passed Yerushalmi's revised bill removing all references to Sharia "have reduced it so it does nothing at all," says CAIR's attorney Gadeir Abbas.

But some business and legal experts remain concerned that the prohibitions on considering foreign or international laws could stymie standard business contracts, and

Knoxville businessman Nadeem Siddiqi tells a press conference on March 1, 2011, that his religious beliefs would be outlawed under a proposed Tennessee bill. It eventually passed after all references to Sharia were removed.

several states have exempted corporations from these bills. Some experts also fear Oklahoma's law could hamper courts' consideration of foreign adoptions and marriages. Muslims fear it could prevent courts from enforcing Muslim marriage contracts or wills.

Tennessee originally had considered another bill, similar to federal anti-terrorist legislation and drafted by Yerushalmi, who argued that Muslim terrorists were the main target of his legislative campaign. Under the original Tennessee bill, the state attorney general could identify Islamic groups suspected of terrorist activity as "Sharia organizations." Support of such organizations would have been a crime punishable by 15 years in prison.

"There are so many different arms of Shariah, and depending on how people interpret and follow those laws, some become extremists. That's what this bill addresses," said Tennessee Republican state Sen. Bill Ketron, who introduced the bill. [15]

Comparing the law to the anti-Semitic Nuremburg laws of Nazi Germany, Abbas says the bill could "criminalize an imam organizing prayers, and if you brought a prayer rug to that [prayer session], it would be a crime."

Under threat of a CAIR lawsuit, the bill Tennessee eventually passed removed all references to Sharia. Now it merely allows state prosecutors to bring charges for federal crimes against groups identified by the U.S. Department of State as terrorist organizations. [16]

"Everything objectionable came out of the bill," says Abbas.

Tennessee is the only state to introduce a bill aimed at criminalizing support to designated terrorist groups. But in the current political climate Abbas predicts, "we'll see more of those types of bills this year."

Although Abbas acknowledges the state bills have been defanged, the political movement to promote them is primarily about "stigmatizing Muslims," he says.

"Hate crimes against the Muslim community and fear about Muslims is up," says Faiz Shakir, vice president for research at the Center for American Progress. "These kinds of measures stoke it."

— *Sarah Glazer*

[1] Speech to American Enterprise Institute, Washington, D.C., July 29, 2010, www.youtube.com/watch?v=oMvQ95ftvYI.

[2] Andrea Elliott, "The Man Behind the Anti-Shariah Movement," *The New York Times*, July 30, 2011, www.nytimes.com/2011/07/31/us/31shariah.html?_r=1&ref=andreaelliott.

[3] "Sharia the Threat to America," Center for Security Policy, 2010, www.worldsecuritynetwork.com/documents/Shariah_The_Threat_to_America_(Team_B_II_Report)_9-14-10.pdf. Also see "Sharia in American Courts," June 21, 2011. http://shariahinamericancourts.com/ and http://scholar.google.com/scholar_case?case=17690081954141610726. The case is *S.D. v. M.J.R.*, 2A.3d 412 (N.J. Superior Court, Appellate Division, July 23, 2010).

[4] "Shariah: the Threat to America," *op. cit.* Also see "Sharia in American Courts," *op. cit.*

[5] "Sharia law outlawed in Oklahoma state courts, ignites movement," ABC News, Nov. 11, 2010, http://abcnews.go.com/Politics/shariah-law-ban-oklahoma-renews-debate-draws-legal/story?id=12112985#.Tt4DO3Gs0sE.

[6] Elliott, *op. cit.*

during the 19th century and did not recognize civil marriage until 1837.

Until the 19th century, women enjoyed broader rights under the Islamic legal tradition than under its Western counterparts, writes Musawah co-founder Mir-Hosseini. For instance, Muslim women always retained their legal and economic autonomy in marriage, while in England women did not have the right to own property after marriage until 1882, when the Married Women's Property Act was passed.

The current debate over classical *fiqh* provisions governing marriage and women's rights began in the late 19th century. For Muslims, writes Mir-Hosseini, their encounter with modernity coincided painfully with their humiliating takeover by colonial forces. At that point the traditional role of women and Sharia took on special symbolism as carriers of their cultural tradition —"a battleground between the forces of traditionalism and modernity" that continues to this day, she writes. [29]

The First World War helped to end the Ottoman Empire, paving the way for the independence of most Middle Eastern countries. During the subsequent period of nationalism and modernization in the 1950s and '60s, interpreters of Sharia would confront new political ideas, including liberalism and socialism.

With the emergence of Muslim nation states in the first part of the 20th century, governments modernized their legal systems. Unfortunately for women, in most countries *fiqh* was shoved aside in all areas of law except family and marriage, where the classical *fiqh* rules remained "more or less unchanged," according to Mir-Hosseini. [30] Saudi Arabia went further than most countries, declaring the Quran and the *Sunna* to be its constitution. Although educated political elites pushed for a more secular, modern vision for their societies, they encountered public resistance to modernization. The notable liberal exceptions were Tunisia, which banned polygamy in 1956, and Turkey, which replaced *fiqh* with Western-inspired statutes.

The secular nationalism movement began to decline in the mid-1960s. By then, the age of nationalist leaders — such as former Egyptian President Gamal Abdel Nasser, who led the 1952 revolution in Egypt, and former Indonesian President Sukarno, who led his country's struggle for independence from the Netherlands — was coming to an end.

"Disappointed by broken promises of development and the failures of governments, several countries experienced ideological and power vacuums," writes the University of Leiden's Otto. Coups in Iran, Pakistan and Sudan brought back Islamic law and government under the slogan "Return to Sharia." [31]

Pushing for Equality

The 1980s saw the introduction of regressive policies for women in many parts of the Muslim world: In Iran and Egypt, family law reforms introduced earlier in the

[7]"Islamic Law in America?" WAMU Interfaith Radio, Aug. 11, 2011, http://interfaithradio.org/taxonomy/term/15. Article VI, Section 2, of the U.S. Constitution is known as the Supremacy Clause because it provides that the "Constitution, and the Laws of the United States . . . shall be the supreme Law of the Land." It means that the federal government, in exercising any of the powers enumerated in the Constitution, must prevail over any conflicting or inconsistent state exercise of power.

[8]James C. McKinley, Jr., "Judge Blocks Oklahoma's Ban on Using Shariah Law in Court," *The New York Times*, Nov. 29, 2010, www .nytimes.com/2010/11/30/us/30oklahoma.html.

[9]See American Civil Liberties Union, www.aclu.org/religion-belief/ muneer-awad-v-paul-ziriax-oklahoma-state-board-elections-et-al and www.aclu.org/blog/human-rights-religion-belief/oklahoma-seeks-save-itself-requirements-us-constitution. The appeal is on the preliminary injunction. The lawsuit will proceed in Judge Miles-LaGrange's court following the appellate court's decision.

[10]Elliott, *op. cit.*

[11]"SANE Special Update: Material Support of Jihad Statute in Tennessee," Society of Americans for National Existence, March 1, 2011, www.saneworks.us/indexnew.php.

[12]"David Yerushalmi: A Driving Force Behind Anti-Sharia Legislation in the U.S.," Anti-Defamation League, March 25, 2011. www.adl.org/ main_Interfaith/david_yerushalmi.html. Also see, ThinkProgress, "David Yerushalmi," Aug. 25, 2011, http://thinkprogress.org/david-yerushalmi-founder-society-of-americans-for-national-existence/.

[13]Anti-Defamation League, *op. cit.*

[14]Elliott, *op. cit.*

[15]Joshua Rhett Miller, "Tennessee Lawmaker Renews Fight to Make Following Shariah a Felony," Fox News, March 2, 2011, www.foxnews .com/politics/2011/03/02/tennessee-lawmaker-continue-push-make-following-shariah-felony/.

[16]Giving state prosecutors this power could raise constitutional questions, however.

century were dismantled; in Iran and Sudan, gender segregation and dress codes for women became compulsory; in Pakistan, harsh Quranic punishments against women were enforced. [32]

But the 1980s also saw the rise of the international women's movement, the expansion of human-rights legislation and the rise of many women's-rights groups in Muslim countries. The U.N. General Assembly in 1979 had given gender equality a clear international mandate when it adopted the Convention on the Elimination of All Forms of Discrimination Against Women (CEDAW).

However, 1979 was also the year that conservative clerics led a popular revolution in Iran and established an Islamic republic, a theocratic regime, despite the democratic hopes of some of the revolutionaries — reversing the trend toward secularizing Islamic laws. Iran had experienced perhaps the most dramatic reversals in its struggle to find its Islamic identity. From 1926 to 1941, Sharia laws were replaced by European-inspired codes. In 1967, legal reform introduced by the Shah, Mohammad Reza Pahlavi, put men and women on the same footing with regard to divorce and child custody.

Three years earlier, however, the Muslim religious leader Ayatollah Khomeini had been exiled from Iran, marking the start of the revolutionary movement against the Shah's regime.

The fervor to reinstate Sharia would spread to other countries. In 1999, the newly elected governor of the predominantly Muslim Zamfara state in northern Nigeria announced he was instituting Sharia; 11 neighboring states with majority Muslim populations followed suit. But harsh punishments ceased after the first few amputations and stoning sentences in 2000 spurred an international outcry.

Meanwhile, Muslim countries in North Africa were liberalizing their laws affecting women. In 2004 Morocco adopted a liberal family code, following a campaign in which progressive and women's groups used the language of Islam to argue for the reforms. A series of shocking terrorist attacks in Casablanca the previous year had helped turn public and government opinion against radical Islam. [33]

Another important turning point occurred in 2009, when the Green Movement emerged in Iran as a protest against questionable presidential election results, triggering what the Arabic-language news network Al-Jazeera called the "biggest unrest since the 1979 revolution." Using the language of democracy, protesters demanded the resignation of hard-line President Mahmoud Ahmadinejad, who they claimed had stolen the election and who was backed by Supreme leader Ayatollah Ali Khamenei. [34]

The global Islamic women's movement Musawah ("Equality") also was launched that year to help bring religious and secular women together to argue for women's rights in Muslim countries.

In addition, many Muslim governments in recent decades abandoned their previously dismissive attitudes toward human rights and signed off on international conventions upholding them. A study of 12 Muslim countries representing two-thirds of the world's Muslims found that all but two of them — Iran and Malaysia — had signed the U.N. Convention Against Torture and Other Cruel, Inhuman or Degrading Treatment or Punishment, adopted in 1984 and ratified by more than 100 countries. And only two — Iran and Sudan — have not signed CEDAW. [35]

Nigeria has also ratified the U.N. Convention on the Rights of the Child, which sets the minimum age for a girl to be married at 18. Yet girls in Nigeria's Muslim north often are married off as early as 9 or 10. [36]

Although Muslim countries are often cited for human-rights violations by groups such as Human Rights Watch, the abuses often have nothing to do with Sharia. In some cases, the violations may result from tribal customs or regional customary law. In Nigeria, for example, women's groups have targeted customary and tribal law in their campaigns against discrimination, arguing that Islamic law, as they interpret it, should grant them greater equality. [37]

Meanwhile in the West, South Asians migrating to England in the 1980s began establishing Sharia councils in London and Birmingham to satisfy the growing need for religious divorces and mediation in family disputes.

In 2005, the government of Ontario, Canada, announced that binding arbitration by religious tribunals in marriage and divorce cases would no longer be allowed. The decision followed the announcement by an Ontario Muslim that he intended to set up a Muslim arbitration council and that any Muslim who did not subject himself or herself to it would not be a "good Muslim."

But Ontario's premier, Dalton McGuinty, said Muslims would feel pressured to give up their legal rights and access to civil courts. His decision also ended the long-standing tradition of allowing other religious courts, such as the Jewish Beth-Din, to offer legally binding arbitration to community members. Significantly, his decision was described in the press as making sure Ontario did not become the first Western government to accept Sharia law as valid. [38]

CURRENT SITUATION

Draconian Penalties

Today, the best Muslim countries for women are Tunisia, Morocco and Indonesia, where progressive family laws

have been instituted, in Mir-Hosseini's opinion. The worst, she says, are Iran, with its theocratic government, and Saudi Arabia, where women aren't even allowed to drive.

However, the Muslim world is changing. Even in Saudi Arabia, King Abdullah recently decreed that women would be able to vote and run for office — though he delayed that right until the 2015 municipal elections, partly to avoid conflict with conservative clerics.

Still, the easiest Muslim countries in which to be a female or a homosexual in the view of the late British writer Christopher Hitchens — a committed atheist and author of the 2009 book *God is not Great* — are two that don't even mention Sharia in their constitutions, Bosnia-Herzegovina and Kosovo. They are "culturally Muslim, democratic open societies saved from obliteration by the United States . . . a secular country with a godless constitution — the last best hope of humanity." [39]

At least five Sharia-guided Muslim countries — out of 12 studied by researchers at the University of Leiden — still have statutes calling for the most draconian Quranic penalties for aberrant behavior, such as adultery and theft. Although the five still have *hadd* punishments on their books, only Saudi Arabia is still conducting amputations today, and stonings are rare to nonexistent in the other four countries. [40]

Iran in 2002, under pressure from the European Union, had imposed an unofficial moratorium on stonings, but both amputations and stonings resumed after Ahmadinejad took power in 2005. In May 2006, the stoning execution of a woman convicted of adultery led to a campaign by the Iranian Network of Volunteer Lawyers to remove the punishment of stoning from Iran's criminal code. Since then, many stoning convictions have been reversed and others frozen. [41] New legislation authorizes judges to substitute another punishment for stoning.

"Authorities realized these cases are bad publicity," says Iranian expert Mir-Hosseini. But no one knows how many stonings are still being carried out today in Iran, she says, because government statistics are not released.

For the crime of apostasy, or converting from Islam to another religion, the Quran specifies heavy penalties, including death. But only four of the 12 countries in the Leiden study — Saudi Arabia, Sudan, Iran and Malaysia — still have the crime on the books, and none has punished anyone for it recently. [42]

AT ISSUE

Do Sharia councils threaten English legal values?

YES
Baroness Caroline Cox
Member, House of Lords United Kingdom

Written for *CQ Global Researcher*, December 2011

The United Kingdom has a tradition of commitment to the fundamental freedoms enshrined in the Universal Declaration of Human Rights, equality of access to the law and the eradication of gender-based discrimination. However, we have seen the growth of a quasi-legal system based on principles fundamentally incompatible with the tenets of liberal democracy.

More than 80 Sharia courts now exist in the U.K. Some function as an inherently discriminatory, quasi-legal system to the point that many Muslim women claim their plight here is worse than in the Muslim countries they left.

Examples of discriminatory Sharia tenets include:

- A husband can divorce his wife, often by simply declaring divorce three times. A wife must obtain her husband's permission, apply to a Sharia "court" for a ruling and may have to pay money, which she may need to request from her husband.
- A man can have four wives; many Muslim men in the U.K. have polygamous marriages, even though they are illegal under U.K. law.
- Custody of a divorced woman's children transfers to the father, starting from age 7.
- A husband may beat his wife, subject to certain limitations.
- Evidence presented by a woman in a Sharia court is counted as having half the value of a man's.

Many British women today suffer abuse and humiliation associated with Sharia law. Some women are so badly beaten by their husbands they are hospitalized and then are pressured by the community not to prosecute the husbands or are told by their imams to give their abusive husbands "another chance." Then the violence is repeated. A widow in her late 40s, wanting to remarry in the U.K., was required to obtain permission from her only male relative — her 11-year-old son living in Jordan.

I have introduced a private member's bill in the House of Lords designed to prevent this quasi-legal system from harming women, protect women from domestic violence and to require authorities, such as social workers, to inform women of their rights under the U.K. legal system.

Whether or not the bill becomes law, I hope it will generate responsible, sensitive discussion to address practices fundamentally incompatible with liberal democracy and gender equality, which are causing great suffering among Muslim women in Britain today.

NO
Gillian Douglas
Professor of Law, Cardiff University Cardiff, Wales

Written for *CQ Global Researcher*, December 2011

A sense of religious identity encompasses both one's belief in the tenets of the faith and acceptance by the religious community of one's membership within it. For observant Muslims, Sharia councils provide an essential means of validating their status within the faith.

There is a general dearth of really robust research into the workings of Sharia councils in the U.K. This gap in hard knowledge is too often filled by anecdotes or scare-mongering, leading to calls for a general ban on their activities, particularly if it is felt that they are seeking to "take over" the state's authority.

But the limited research that has been undertaken (including my own, which focused on the attitudes of those working in one such council and compared these with a Catholic marriage tribunal and Jewish Beth Din), suggests the need for a more nuanced response.

My research reveals that the fundamental rationale for the grant of a religious divorce is to declare that the religious marriage is over and to enable the parties to remarry within their faith. Regardless of the view that civil law may take of a person's marital status, those who believe that they must be married — and divorced — in the eyes of their faith will want to have that status recognized by their religion.

The Sharia council in my study was clearly influenced in the interpretation and application of Islamic law by the social norms of the wider society and recognized that litigants must live their lives within that wider context.

Far from seeking to take over the function of determining marital status from the state, there was a clear understanding of the primacy of the civil law and acceptance that a religious tribunal cannot give binding rulings on matters relating to child custody or allocation of property.

Sharia councils currently operate alongside rather than superseding the civil legal system. Were they to be banned, they would continue to provide the religious validation their believers seek, but they would do so underground and become cut off from, rather than engaged with, the values of the state. They could then indeed pose a threat to English legal values.

The way to protect those who are vulnerable to pressure from their religious communities is not to ban religious tribunals, but to increase the visibility — and hence accountability — of such bodies, both to their adherents and to the state.

Anti-government protesters in post-revolution Cairo, Egypt, carry an injured man in Tahrir Square after clashes with the army on Dec. 16. Disagreement over the future role of Sharia is among the issues sparking continued protests. New Islamist governments have formed in Tunisia and Morocco, while the ultraconservative Salafi al-Nour party in Egypt won a quarter of the votes in a November election. The party has vowed to introduce traditional Islamic corporal punishments like stoning for adultery, along with censorship of music and "equality restricted by Sharia."

Human-rights conditions have worsened considerably in Iran since the government crackdown on protests after the disputed June 2009 presidential election, according to Human Rights Watch. Over the past year, Iranian authorities continued a "brutal campaign to crush dissent," using lethal force against peaceful protesters, arresting hundreds and killing dozens, according to the organization. [43]

A series of Christmas Day church bombings in Nigeria that killed dozens, attributed to the Islamist group Boko Haram (which means "Western education is forbidden"), was a harsh reminder that militants like Boko Haram want to see an even stricter form of Sharia than is currently practiced in their country and may be expanding their terrorist attacks of the past two years to exploit the already tense relations between Muslims and Christians in Nigeria.

Western Fears

In Europe, Sharia has become one of the most controversial terms in public political debate. In addition to Chancellor Merkel's recent assurance that Sharia would not become law in Germany, the word has become a flashpoint for resentment over Muslim immigration and anxiety about Islamic terrorism, oppression of women and brutal punishments.

According to 2010 polls, nearly half the population in many European countries believes there are too many Muslims in the country — including Germany, Britain, Hungary, Italy and Poland. [44] Right-wing, anti-Islamic parties have gained representation in the parliaments of Norway, Denmark, the Netherlands, Belgium, France, Switzerland and Austria. In Switzerland, a right-wing party is campaigning against the construction of any new mosques. And anti-mosque legislation already has been passed in the Austrian state of Kaernten.

As in the United States, European secular states must treat all religions equally and neutrally. Most European lawyers think that a minaret ban passed in Switzerland in 2009, for example, violates the European Convention on Human Rights, which guarantees freedom of religion.

Meanwhile, extremist Muslim groups such as Muslims Against Crusades, which was recently banned by the British government for glorifying terrorism, insist that Sharia is the only law Muslims should follow. [45]

Greece is the only European country that officially recognizes Sharia, but only for Muslims in western Greece — a vestige of the 1923 Treaty of Lausanne, which split up the Ottoman Empire after World War I. [46]

Some secular groups worry, however, that Sharia law is creeping into European courtrooms. They cite a 2007 decision by a German family court judge, who rejected an expedited divorce request from a German woman of Moroccan origin. She had complained that her Moroccan husband beat her and had threatened to kill her, despite having been ordered by authorities to stay away from her. In rejecting the request, the judge quoted the Quran, which, she wrote, contains "both the husband's right to use corporal punishment against a disobedient wife and the establishment of the husband's superiority over the wife." The judge argued that the woman should have "expected" that her husband, who had grown up in an Islamic country, would exercise his religious "right to use corporal punishment." [47]

The case spurred outrage in the German press, prompting the German weekly newsmagazine *Der Spiegel* to ask "Does Germany already have Sharia law?" [48]

However, German law expert Rohe says the decision — which was quickly overturned — was an isolated case, and no other such case has been reported. The judge was wrong on several counts, he points out: Beating one's wife is illegal in Morocco, and the Quran is not "a valid legal book in Germany or in Morocco." Furthermore, even if Moroccan law had permitted a husband to beat his wife, "This would have been a gross violation of German public policy, so in this case we wouldn't have applied Moroccan law at all."

Critics of what they call "creeping Sharia" also cite lower-court decisions in Germany that have excused violence against women on the grounds that so-called honor killings and beatings are part of Muslim culture. [49] In 2003 the Frankfurt District Court handed down a mild sentence against a Turkish-born man who had stabbed his German-born wife to death. She had disobeyed him and demanded a divorce, leading the court to suggest the husband's reaction was in line with his "foreign socio-cultural moral concepts." [50] But Germany's supreme court overturned that decision in 2004, making clear that all such violence must be judged by a single criminal standard.

"There is no such thing as a cultural exemption under German penal law," Rohe says. "Very rarely, you find a case in one lower court, which is immediately changed if it comes to a court of appeal. This danger is very much exaggerated," he maintains. Sharia has become in the public debate the "enemy" of human rights, which he sees as "a very narrow and prejudiced idea of what Sharia is about."

Parallel Systems?

Compared to other European countries and the United States, Britain appears to have the most extensive network of Sharia councils for issuing religious divorces and settling family disputes.

The Archbishop of Canterbury sparked a debate about whether Sharia councils should be given a formal legal role, but, surprisingly, the councils themselves have not pushed for such powers, and British Muslims have shown little enthusiasm for such a move, say Bano and others.

Political observers predict that Baroness Cox's proposed bill to make it a jailable crime for a Sharia council to claim legal jurisdiction is unlikely to become law. But it has raised the debate over whether Sharia councils should exist or be regulated in some way.

Some critics of the councils say they should be abolished altogether, but that would probably just force them underground, says Cardiff Law Professor Douglas. People would still want their marital status reaffirmed within their faith, just as Jews and Catholics do in similar religious courts across England.

No one knows how many informal Sharia courts are springing up in other European countries, according to University of London law expert Shah, since much of this activity comes in the form of individual imams providing religious guidance in private consultations.

"In France there are no such councils, though sometimes an imam will give a religious divorce," says anthropologist Bowen, author of the 2008 book *Why the French Don't Like Headscarves.* "If you ask in the Netherlands, there's no such development. In the U.S. there are [councils] here and there, but there's not a whole lot of communication among them, and they're nothing like the network you see in England."

Extremist groups recently claimed to have established a "Sharia court" in Antwerp, but Belgian authorities shut down the website of the organizer, Sharia4Belgium. [51] So-called Sharia Zones have been declared in some heavily Muslim neighborhoods in England — but so far the effort seems limited to plastering neighborhoods with posters forbidding pornography and drinking.

The British jihadist hate preacher Anjem Choudhary is behind both efforts, but the British government bans each new organization he establishes on grounds that they incite terrorism. Experts like Shah say it's hard to take these kinds of "nutters" seriously. [52]

In Germany, a recent book gaining public attention — *Judges without Laws*, by journalist Joachim Wagner — says some imams are settling violent acts with threats and intimidation of victims or witnesses. Some criminal cases have thus fallen apart once they reach court, leading Wagner to declare: "The Islamic parallel justice system is becoming a threat to the constitutional legal system." [53]

Rohe says Wagner's claims are based on 16 cases. "These are not very typical cases for the Muslim community as such," he says, but appear limited to traditional clan justice among Kurdish extended families from northern Iraq or Turkey. "I am far from sure whether this is the application of Sharia law rather than the application of customary law from these parts of the world," he says.

Meanwhile, the Canadian government's response to a proposed Sharia court — Ontario's Family Statue Law Amendment Act of 2005 — removed legal power from religious courts. As a result, Muslim arbitrations continue to operate under the radar, "invisible" to official law, experts say. [54]

OUTLOOK

Fear and Hope

The Arab Spring revolutions have raised questions about the future role of Sharia in the Middle East, especially with new Islamist governments recently formed in Tunisia and Morocco and Islamist parties poised to take control in Egypt. Some women activists were still hoping before the Egyptian elections in November that these popular movements would fulfill their promises for democracy and equality. [55]

But after Egypt's first round of voting for a new parliament in late November, the ultraconservative Salafi al-Nour party surprised experts by winning a 25 percent share of the vote with its vows to introduce traditional Islamic corporal punishments like stoning for adultery, along with censorship of music and "equality restricted by Sharia."

Together with the 40 percent share of the vote won by the Muslim Brotherhood's Freedom and Justice Party, which came in first, Islamists could control a majority of the seats in parliament once elections are completed for the lower house of Parliament in January and for the upper house in February. [56] Shortly after the election, however, Freedom and Justice, which is expected to remain the dominant party, denied it would form a coalition with the Salafis, insisting it would seek a broad-based coalition, presumably with reformers. Although the party's position on Sharia is hard to pin down on details, some experts see hope for a more liberal vision of Islamic law in the party's platform, which promises to guarantee equal rights for Christians and Muslims and to retain a role for secular institutions such as Egypt's supreme court in interpreting Sharia. "That's a new political development . . . a really new interpretation," says German Sharia expert Rohe.

"We don't hold stagnant positions," said Dina Zakaria, a party spokeswoman, stressing that unlike the Salafis, who bar women from political leadership roles, her party has an evolving understanding of Islam that allows women to define their roles. [57]

The call for Sharia has cropped up in other countries that overthrew governments during the Arab Spring, raising fears about how these new governments will approach gender equality. Following the fall of Libya's longtime dictator Moammar Gadhafi in October, interim leader Mustafa Abdel-Jalil stated, "Sharia allows polygamy," apparently paving the way for polygamy's return to Libya.

A Gadhafi-era law had made polygamy conditional on the consent of the first wife, making it rare in Libya. That same week, men demonstrated in Benghazi in support of Abdel-Jalil and demanded the return of Sharia. [58]

In the West, continuing nervousness about the role of Sharia is evident in the bills in U.S. state legislatures to ban Sharia from U.S. courts, the ongoing controversy over Sharia councils in England and anti-Muslim sentiment in Europe. But even if Sharia bans are enacted, informal religious advice-givers likely will continue operating in private, as they have in Ontario.

According to Harvey Simmons, a professor emeritus of political science at Canada's York University, "Ironically, because religious arbitration now takes place mainly outside the scrutiny of the Ontario courts, there is no way to tell whether women are being treated well or badly in informal religious arbitrations conducted by imams, rabbis or, indeed, any other arbitrator chosen by the parties involved." [59]

At a Dec. 16 panel discussion in London hosted by the BBC, female activists who had participated in Arab Spring demonstrations in Libya and Bahrain expressed confidence that women would continue to play a leading role once new governments take over. Mervat Mhani, a founder of The Free Generation Movement, a protest group that grew out of the Libyan uprising, dismissed audience concerns that Abdel-Jalil's recent speech favoring polygamy signaled a turn toward repressive legislation against women.

"We're not going to stand back and let it happen," said the mother of two, wearing a bright pink headscarf. "I think women will affirm their role in society. Women played a huge role in the revolution," she said, stressing that Libya's women demonstrators had been arrested and beaten just like the men.

But Sussan Tahmasebi, an Iranian-American who has campaigned in Iran to reverse the country's discriminatory laws against women, warned that revolutionary leaders historically have bought women activists' silence during revolutions with false promises of gender equality later — as occurred during the 1979 Iranian revolution.

Once the revolution is successful, "women are told to go back home and take care of the family," Tahmasebi reminded the crowd.

Women need to ask specific questions of the Islamist parties now gaining power in countries like Egypt, Tahmasebi cautioned. When these parties advocate Sharia law, she said, "Whose interpretation of Sharia law do they mean? Cutting off hands? Giving women different rights?"

The Arab Spring countries have a golden opportunity to write constitutions that reflect Muslim feminists' view of a Sharia that upholds gender equality, Tahmasebi said, a view she said is widely shared by women in these countries.

"Human dignity is not a Western concept," she said, adding, "It's no democracy if the laws discriminate against 50 percent of the population."

NOTES

1. Polygamy is illegal in England. However, some Muslim men get around this prohibition by marrying a second or third wife overseas in a country where it is legal or by marrying multiple wives in England in a Muslim religious marriage, which is not recognized by English courts.

2. Jonathan Wynne-Jones, "Sharia: a law unto itself?" *The Telegraph*, Aug. 7, 2011, www.telegraph.co.uk/news/uknews/law-and-order/8686504/Sharia-a-law-unto-itself.html.

3. For purposes of this article, comparisons are to the law of England and Wales; Scotland's law is different.

4. "UK Law Needs to Find Accommodation with Religious Law Codes," BBC, Radio 4, 2008, www.archbishopofcanterbury.org/articles.php/707/archbishop-on-radio-4-uk-law-needs-to-find-accommodation-with-religious-law-codes.

5. Gillian Douglas, *et al.*, "Social Cohesion and Civil Law: Marriage, Divorce and Religious Courts," Cardiff University, June 2011, www.law.cf.ac.uk/clr/research/cohesion.

6. Rebecca Camber, " 'No Porn or Prostitution,' " *Mail Online*, July 28, 2011, www.dailymail.co.uk/news/article-2019547/Anjem-Choudary-Islamic-extremists-set-Sharia-law-zones-UK-cities.html.

7. "Sharia Law in Britain," One Law for All, June 2010, p. 5, www.onelawforall.org.uk/new-report-sharia-law-in-britain-a-threat-to-one-law-for-all-and-equal-rights/.

8. "Swiss Voters Back Ban on Minarets," BBC, Nov. 29, 2009, http://news.bbc.co.uk/1/hi/8385069.stm.

9. "Constitution, not sharia, is supreme law in Germany — Merkel," Reuters, Oct. 7, 2010, http://blogs.reuters.com/faithworld/2010/10/07/constitution-not-sharia-is-supreme-law-in-germany-merkel/.

10. Islamic Sharia Council, London, www.islamic-sharia.org. The four major Sunni schools are Hanafi, Maliki, Shafi'i and Hanbali. (Sunnis account for about 85 percent of all Muslims). A Muslim is free to adopt the teachings of any one of the four schools even if he or she lives in a jurisdiction in which that school is not predominant. See Raj Bhala, *Understanding Islamic Law (Shari'a)* (2011), p. 391.

11. Jan Michiel Otto, ed., *Sharia Incorporated* (2010).

12. Harvey Simmons, "One Law for all Ontarians," *The Star*, Nov. 14, 2011, www.thestar.com/opinion/editorialopinion/article/860513--one-law-for-all-ontarians.

13. Bhala, *op. cit.*, pp. 879-880. Unilateral divorce by a Muslim husband is known as a *talak*.

14. Abou El Fadl, *The Great Theft: Wrestling Islam from the Extremists* (2007), p. 271.

15. Ziba Mir-Hosseini, "Women in Search of Common Ground Between Islamic and International Human Rights Law," in Anver Emon, ed., *Islamic and International Human Rights Law: Searching for Common Ground?* (forthcoming 2012).

16. Islamic Sharia Council, www.islamic-sharia.org/about-us/about-us-9.html.

17. "Sharia Law or 'One Law for All'?" Civitas, 2009, www.civitas.org.uk/pdf/ShariaLawOrOneLawForAll.pdf.

18. Samia Bano, "Islamic Family Arbitration, Justice and Human Rights in Britain," *Law, Social Justice & Global Development Journal*, 2007, www.go.warwick.ac.uk/elj/lgd/2007_1/bano.

19. Otto, *op. cit.* There have been no amputations since three hand amputations were carried out in the early 2000s.

20. Bhala, *op. cit.*, p. 1168.

21. "CEDAW and Family Laws," Musawah, January 2011, pp. 7-9, www.musawah.org.

22. Abou El Fadl, *op. cit.*, pp. 150-152.

23. *Ibid.*, pp. 147-153.

24. *Ibid.*, p. 163.

25. Otto, *op. cit.*, p. 43. The *hadd* are punishments fixed in the Quran for crimes considered as violations of God's limits: theft, extramarital sex, armed robbery, wrongful/unproven accusation of extramarital sex, consumption of alcohol — and according to some schools of thought, apostasy.

26. *Ibid.*, p. 234.

27. Bhala, *op. cit.*, pp. 1209-1210.

28. John R. Bowen, "How Could English Courts Recognize Shariah?" *University of St. Thomas Law Journal*, vol. 7, issue 3, 2010, p. 417.

29. Mir-Hosseini, *op. cit.*, p. 5

30. *Ibid.*, p. 6.

31. Otto, *op. cit.*, p. 42.

32. Mir-Hosseini, *op. cit.*, p. 8.

33. Otto, *op. cit.*, pp. 108-109.

34. "Poll Results Prompt Iranian Protests," *AlJazeera*, June 14, 2009, www.aljazeera.com/news/middleeast/2009/06/2009613172130303995.html.

35. Otto, *op. cit.*, p. 634. For background, see Seth Stern, "Torture Debate," *CQ Global Researcher*, Sept. 1, 2007, pp. 211-236.

36. Otto, *op. cit.*, p. 600.

37. Otto, *op. cit.*

38. "Faith Special," CTV News, Sept. 12, 2005, www.ctv.ca/CTVNews/PromoNewsletter/20050912/faith_special_050912/#ixzz1dhcdY2Rv.

39. Christopher Hitchens, speaking at 92nd Street YMCA, Oct. 5, 2010, www.youtube.com/watch?v=PyID7E1SjjY.

40. Otto, *op. cit.*, p. 633.

41. *Ibid.*, p. 359.

42. *Ibid.*, p. 659.

43. "UN: Expose Iran's Appalling Human Rights Record," Human Rights Watch, Sept. 21, 2011, www.hrw.org/news/2011/09/21/un-expose-iran-s-appalling-rights-record.

44. Andreas Zick, *et al.*, "Intolerance, Prejudice and Discrimination: A European Report," Friedrich-Ebert-Stiftung Forum Berlin, 2011, pp. 60-62, www.library.fes.de/pdf-files/do/07908-20110311.pdf.

45. Richard Ford, "Muslim Group that Planned to Burn Poppies Is Banned," *The Times* (London), Nov. 11, 2011, p. 27.

46. Prakash Shah, "A Reflection on the Sharia Debate in Britain," Queen Mary University of London, *School of Law Legal Studies Research Paper No. 71*, 2010, http://ssrn.com/abstract=1733529, p. 2.

47. "Paving the Way for a Muslim Parallel Society," *Der Spiegel*, March 29, 2007, www.spiegel.de/international/germany/0,1518,474629,00.html. The request was for legal aid to obtain a divorce without waiting the standard one-year separation required for German divorces, unless there are exceptional circumstances, according to Rohe.

48. *Ibid.*

49. For background, see Robert Kiener, "Honor Killings," *CQ Global Researcher*, April 19, 2011, pp. 183-208.

50. "Paving the Way for a Muslim Parallel Society," *op. cit.*

51. Soeren Kern, "Islamic Sharia Law Court Opens in Belgium," *Hudson New York*, Hudson Institute, Sept. 15, 2011, www.hudson-ny.org/2425/belgium-islamic-sharia-law-court.

52. *Ibid.*

53. "Islamic Arbitrators Shadow German Law," *Der Spiegel*, Sept. 1, 2011, www.spiegel.de/international/germany/0,1518,783361,00.html.

54. Shah, *op. cit.*, p. 11.

55. For background, see Roland Flamini, "Turmoil in the Arab World," *CQ Global Researcher*, May 3, 2011, pp. 209-236.

56. David D. Kirkpatrick, "Egypt's Vote Puts Emphasis on Split over Religious Rule," *The New York Times*, Dec. 3, 2011, www.nytimes.com/2011/12/04/world/middleeast/egypts-vote-propels-islamic-law-into-spotlight.html?_r=1&ref=todayspaper.

57. *Ibid.*

58. Adam Nossiter, "Hinting at End to a Curb on Polygamy," *The New York Times*, Oct. 29, 2011, www.nytimes.com/2011/10/30/world/africa/libyan-leaders-remark-favoring-polygamy-stirs-anger.html?pagewanted=all.

59. Harvey Simmons, "One Law for all Ontarians," *The Star*, Nov. 14, 2011, www.thestar.com/opinion/editorialopinion/article/860513--one-law-for-all-ontarians.

BIBLIOGRAPHY

Selected Sources
Books

Abou El Fadl, Khaled, *The Great Theft: Wrestling Islam from the Extremists*, HarperOne, 2007.
A University of California-Los Angeles law professor explains the history of fundamentalist "puritan" Muslims, who supply Muslim ideology for extremists.

Bhala, Raj, *Understanding Islamic Law (Shari'a)*, LexisNexis, 2011.
A University of Kansas law professor compares Sharia to Christian thought in this 1,455-page tome — the first textbook on Sharia by a non-Muslim — written in a clear, engaging style.

Otto, Jan Michiel, *Sharia Incorporated*, Leiden University Press, 2010.
This study of 12 major Muslim countries led by a professor of law and governance in developing countries at the Netherlands' University of Leiden finds harsh Sharia legal systems are not as prevalent as many people believe.

Articles

Bano, Samia, "Islamic Family Arbitration, Justice and Human Rights in Britain," *Law, Social Justice & Global Development Journal*, 2007, www.go.warwick.ac.uk/elj/lgd/2007_1/bano.
A study finds that most Pakistani women who consulted Sharia councils in England were sophisticated users who went to a different council if they didn't like the first ruling, but doing so may have put them in danger.

Bowen, John, "Private Arrangements: 'Recognizing Sharia' in England," *Boston Review*, March/April 2009, http://bostonreview.net/BR34.2/bowen.php.
A Washington University anthropologist explains the Sharia debate that has engulfed England and how London's Islamic Sharia Council works.

Brulliard, Karin, "In Nigeria, Sharia Fails to Deliver," *The Washington Post,* Aug. 12, 2009.
Nigerians are disillusioned with Sharia, established 10 years ago in 12 mostly Muslim northern states.

McVeigh, Karen, and Amelia Hill, "Bill Limiting Sharia Law is Motivated by 'Concern for Muslim Women,'" *The Guardian*, June 8, 2011, www.guardian.co.uk/law/2011/jun/08/sharia-bill-lords-muslim-women.
A proposed bill by House of Lords member Baroness Caroline Cox would make it a jailable crime for a Sharia council to falsely claim legal jurisdiction in family or criminal matters.

Popp, Maximilian, "Parallel Justice: Islamic 'Arbitrators' Shadow German Law," *Der Spiegel*, Sept. 1, 2011, www.spiegel.de/international/germany/0,1518,783361,00.html.
Imams who arbitrate disputes among Muslims in Germany reportedly are inserting a form of rough, home-grown justice into criminal cases.

Shah, Prakash, "A Reflection on the Sharia Debate in Britain," Queen Mary University of London, *School of Law Legal Studies Research Paper No. 71*, 2010, http://ssrn.com/abstract=1733529.
A senior lecturer in law at the University of London examines the pros and cons of recognizing Sharia law in Britain and other Western countries.

Wynne-Jones, Jonathan, "Sharia: A Law Unto Itself?" *Telegraph*, Aug. 7, 2011, www.telegraph.co.uk/news/uknews/law-and-order/8686504/Sharia-a-law-unto-itself.html.
A reporter describes visiting the Birmingham Sharia Council and the debate over Sharia councils in Britain.

Reports and Studies

"CEDAW and Muslim Family Laws: In Search of Common Ground," Musawah, 2011, http://musawah.org/docs/pubs/CEDAW%20&%20Muslim%20Family%20Laws.pdf.
An international Muslim women's group based in Malaysia says Muslim countries frequently fail to amend their laws in keeping with the U.N. Convention on the Elimination of All Forms of Discrimination Against Women because governments say it conflicts with Sharia law.

"Sharia Law in Britain: A Threat to One Law for All & Equal Rights," One Law for All, 2010, www.onelaw forall.org.uk/wp-content/uploads/New-Report-Sharia-Law-in-Britain.pdf.
Sharia councils in Britain should be abolished because they discriminate against women and constitute a parallel legal system that conflicts with England's laws and values, says the One Law for All advocacy group.

"Sharia Law or 'One Law for All'?" Civitas, 2009, www.civitas.org.uk/pdf/ShariaLawOrOneLawForAll. pdf.

A London think tank lays out its argument against Sharia councils in Britain.

Douglas, Gillian, et al., "Social Cohesion and Civil Law: Marriage, Divorce and Religious Courts," Cardiff University, June 2011, www.law.cf.ac.uk/clr/research/cohesion.
A Cardiff University team concludes that England's Jewish Beth Din Court, Wales' Cardiff Catholic Tribunal and the Sharia Council in Birmingham provide an important service for Jews, Muslims and Catholics.

For More Information

Civitas, First Floor, 55 Tufton St., Westminster, London SW1P 3QL, U.K.; +44 20 7799 6677; www.civitas.org.uk. Research and educational group that has been critical of Sharia councils in England and Wales.

Council on Foreign Relations, The Harold Pratt House, 58 East 68th St., New York, NY 10065; 212-434-9400; www.cfr.org/religion. Nonpartisan think tank that sponsors a religion website that tracks Islam and Sharia.

Fiqh Council of North America, www.fiqhcouncil.org. Advises and educates on matters related to the application of Sharia in Muslims' individual and collective lives in the North American environment.

Human Rights Watch, 350 Fifth Ave., 34th Floor, New York, NY 10118-3299; 212-290-4700; www.hrw.org. Monitors human rights around the world.

Islamic Sharia Council, 34 Francis Road, Leyton, London E10 6PW, United Kingdom; +44 20 8558 0581; www.islamic-sharia.org. England's largest Sharia council.

Musawah, No. 7, Jalan 6/10, 46000 Petaling Jaya, Selangor, Malaysia; +603 7785 6121; www.musawah.org. Global movement of Muslim women seeking equality and justice in the Muslim family.

One Law for All, BM Box 2387, London WC1N 3XX, UK; +44 7719966731; www.onelawforall.org.uk. Campaigns to abolish all religious courts, including Sharia councils, in Britain.

Organisation of Islamic Cooperation, P.O. Box 178, Jeddah-21411, Kingdom of Saudi Arabia; + 966 2 65 15 222; www.oic-oci.org. Intergovernmental organization of 57 states in four continents representing the collective voice of the Muslim world.

U.N. Committee on the Elimination of Discrimination Against Women; www.un.org/womenwatch/daw/cedaw/committee.htm. Monitors progress for women in countries that adopted the 1979 anti-discrimination convention.

Voices From Abroad:

MICHAEL NAZIR-ALI

Former Bishop of Rochester, England

Compromising traditions

"The problem with Sharia law being used in tribunals is that it compromises the tradition of equality for all under the law. It threatens the fundamental values that underpin our society."

Sunday Telegraph (England), August 2011

JOSEPH WAKIM

Founder, Australian Arabic Council, Australia

More perspective needed

"For centuries, Islamic scholars and imams have had diverse interpretations of sharia, with many cultural customs. . . . The extreme interpretations of sharia criminal codes [involving] abhorrent punishments have attracted most attention and need most perspective."

Canberra (Australia), Times July 2011

USAMA HASAN

Senior Lecturer, Middlesex University, England

Many agree

"A lot of people will say Sharia law should only apply in Muslim countries, and Britain isn't one. But press them further and they will admit that they actually agree with the principle of Sharia law in its most fundamentalist form. They just defer their answer. And if you try and put another view, they call you a heretic."

The Express (England), January 2011

YOUSSERI HAMAD

Spokesman, Salafi al-Nour Party, Egypt

God's decision

"In the land of Islam, I can't let people decide what is permissible or what is prohibited. It's God who gives the

Bulgaria/Christo Komarnitski

answers as to what is right and what is wrong. If God tells me you can drink whatever you want except for alcohol, you don't leave the million things permitted and ask about the prohibited."

The Guardian (England), December 2011

MARYAM NAMAZIE

Spokeswoman, One Law for All Campaign

Same rights for all

"Human rights are non-negotiable and religious tribunals put religion before people's rights and their freedoms. Law based on any religion — whether the Bible, Torah or the Quran — is completely antithetical to rights woman have in this day and age. Many of the rights women have now in the U.K. [are] the result of a hard fight to wrestle control out of church hands."

Guardian Unlimited (England), March 2010

FATHI BUZAKHAR

Leader, Amazigh Congress, Libya

No Sharia in politics

"Separation between politics and religion is essential to build a democratic state, but the new Libyan interim government seems to have completely forgotten about that."

Newstime Africa (England), November 2011

TAF HAIKAL

Democratic Activist, Indonesia

Secular enforcement necessary

"It's a waste of money. We're not even sure why the sharia police was established in the first place. If the [provincial] administration is serious about implementing Islamic law, they should let the [secular] police do the monitoring."

Jakarta Post (Indonesia), January 2010

GERHARD HOFFSTAEDTER

Co-founder, Melbourne Free University Project, Australia

Judgment Day can't wait

"In sharia law, it is ultimately God who judges. This would be fine if we could wait for Judgement Day, but sharia dictates earthly punishments for crimes against God and nature."

Canberra (Australia), Times October 2010

10

Peacebuilding

Jina Moore

Tigie Koroma, a weaver in Makeni, Sierra Leone, is one of many small entrepreneurs who receive support through a microenterprise grant from the U.N. Peacebuilding Fund. The agency has budgeted $45 million for peacebuilding activities in Sierra Leone — more than in any other country — since a brutal civil war ended there in 2002.

CQ Press/Jina Moore

From *CQ Researcher*,
June 21, 2011

Michael von der Schulenburg, the United Nations' top representative in Sierra Leone, remembers driving into a riot in 2009, surrounded by a crowd of about 5,000 people. Although the country's brutal civil war had ended seven years before, a provincial election had stirred controversy — and violence — between the two main political parties.

The conflict, which many feared would reignite hostilities across the country, had spread to the coastal capital of Freetown, where a mob of angry ruling party members had gathered outside the opposition's headquarters. Twenty-two men were trapped on the headquarters roof. Below them, von der Schulenburg remembers, rioters shouted, "Hand them over! Hand them over!"

He tried to contain the situation by talking with the leaders of the angry mob and with police standing nearby. Eventually, he was able to get the men off the roof, and the police dispelled the crowd. A few weeks later, the feuding political parties agreed to rules for future political interactions, including elections.

Thanks to von der Schulenburg's intervention — and the subsequent agreement — violence was averted. The agreement, von der Schulenburg says, was possible because of a process called peacebuilding — a new international approach to the age-old problem of putting an end to war. Unlike peace-*making*, in which politicians negotiate an agreement to end ongoing conflict, and peace*keeping*, which sends foreign soldiers to monitor peace agreements and protect civilians in conflict zones, peace*building* involves stabilizing states and strengthening institutions to build lasting peace in post-conflict societies.

Africa Has Most U.N. Peacebuilding Projects

Fourteen of the 19 countries with peacebuilding projects financed by the U.N. Peacebuilding Commission in 2010 were in Africa. Peacebuilding tries to stabilize societies, strengthen institutions and reinforce post-conflict governments to build lasting peace. Besides the United Nations and numerous individual countries, many international organizations fund peacebuilding projects, such as the Quakers' American Friends Service Committee and Geneva-based Interpeace.

Recipients of U.N. Peacebuilding Funds in 2010

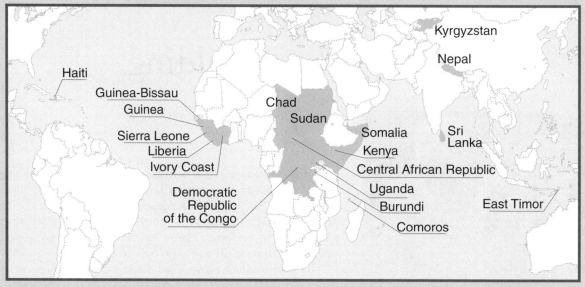

Source: "Trust Fund Factsheet," Multi-Donor Trust Fund Office, United National Development Programme, www.mdtf.undp.org/factsheet/fund/PB000; map by Lewis Agrell

"Everybody understands peacemaking . . . and peacekeeping," says Judy Cheng-Hopkins, U.N. assistant secretary-general for peacebuilding support. "Peacebuilding goes beyond either."

Peacebuilding is the slow, difficult task of rebuilding post-conflict states and societies. "Peacebuilding helps put in place all the pieces that would do that," says Edward Luck, senior vice president of the International Peace Institute, a think tank in New York.

After a decade of intense global conflict in the 1990s, peacebuilding specialists now believe they understand many of the measures needed to move a country toward stability. The laundry list of needs grew out of wrenching conflicts in Bosnia and Rwanda in the 1990s, and in West Africa and Southeast Asia in the early 21st century. [1]

Peacebuilding includes a variety of activities, such as:

- Disarming ex-combatants; unless former soldiers feel productive and engaged as civilians, they might cause trouble;
- Establishing truth and reconciliation commissions;
- Creating a legal process to help returning refugees deal with people living on their old homesteads;
- Jump-starting economies; building roads and generating electricity;
- Training competent judges and lawyers;
- Building functioning army barracks and jails.

A generation ago, the international community dealt with each of those needs individually. That changed in 2005, when the United Nations established its

Peacebuilding Commission (PBC), the first global entity to focus exclusively on the new approach to ending conflict. The U.N. is rapidly defining the peacebuilding terrain, although other well-known organizations — from religious groups such as the Quakers' American Friends Service Committee to large international organizations like the International Rescue Committee — also have incorporated peacebuilding concepts into their work.

The U.N.'s peacebuilding budget — $389 million spent since 2007 on projects in 19 countries — pales in comparison to the $7.3 billion spent each year on peacekeeping operations. The peacebuilding funds are donated by 47 U.N. members. [2]

The PBC advises governments both on how to better stabilize their societies and maintain peace after the guns have gone silent. While the U.N. Peacebuilding Fund supports projects in 19 countries, the Peacebuilding Commission itself works with only six African countries that have requested help: Guinea, Guinea-Bissau, Liberia and Sierra Leone (in West Africa) and the Central African Republic and Burundi in central Africa.

The diplomatic challenges alone are daunting. Heads of state don't look very kindly on the U.N. telling them how to run their governments. But when the General Assembly voted to create the PBC, it gave the commission a "political mandate" — permission to engage foreign governments on political questions. Many observers think the PBC's mandate gives it the best shot at making a real difference.

"The mandate is to work with leaders, to look them in the eyes and say, 'Look, thank you for your coffee, but I think you need to be doing something different,' " says Michael Massaquoi, Sierra Leone's liaison to the PBC.

Others suggest privately that the PBC's permission to be so direct and political

African Nations Receive Most Peacebuilding Funds

Since its creation in 2005, the U.N. Peacebuilding Fund has budgeted $250 million for projects in 19 post-conflict countries — 14 of them in Africa. Of the 182 projects undertaken so far, only 12 were not in Africa.

Countries Receiving Peacebuilding Funds		
Country	Approved PBF budget	Number of projects
Sierra Leone	$45,008,170	33
Burundi	$39,623,868	21
Central African Republic	$31,001,975	26
Liberia	$20,047,444	28
Sudan	$18,726,228	6
Democratic Republic of Congo	$17,174,751	11
Uganda	$13,999,756	4
Guinea	$12,850,829	11
Nepal	$10,000,000	7
Comoros	$9,400,000	13
Côte d'Ivoire (Ivory Coast)	$8,527,750	3
Guinea-Bissau	$6,268,653	7
Haiti	$3,800,000	2
Somalia	$3,000,000	5
Sri Lanka	$3,000,000	1
Kyrgyzstan	$2,999,948	1
Chad	$2,728,500	1
Kenya	$1,000,000	1
East Timor	$993,625	1
Total	**$250,151,497**	**182**

U.N. Peacebuilding Accomplishments

The four biggest recipients of U.N.-funded peacebuilding projects are in West and Central Africa, where 108 projects have been undertaken. Here are some examples of those projects:

Sierra Leone
Transitional justice — 20,000 war victims were paid reparations after a four-year delay
Justice/courts — More than 70 percent of backlogged cases cleared

Liberia
Demobilization/reintegration — 800 ex-combatants trained in farming, growing rubber, raising livestock
Youth employment — More than 5,000 young people trained in community mediation, leadership, political participation
Social welfare — 40 social workers trained; addressed more than 600 referrals in two years

Central African Republic
Peace deals — Rebellions ended by political dialogue
Child soldiers — More than 600 former child soldiers disarmed, reintegrated into their villages
Media — Two rural radio stations built; two teams of journalists trained to cover local issues
Elections — Peaceful presidential elections held

Burundi
Land — 3,000 land disputes settled peacefully
Justice/courts — 17 local tribunals set up
Corruption — $400,000 returned to public treasury after corruption investigations
Barracks — 23,000 soldiers housed
Transitional justice — 17 provinces consulted on a truth commission

Source: "Trust Fund Factsheet," Multi-Donor Trust Fund Office, United National Development Programme, www.mdtf.undp.org/factsheet/fund/PB000; research by CQ Global Researcher

Peacebuilding Begins with Disarming Ex-Combatants

The process also involves demobilization and reintegration.

The top priority of most peacebuilding programs is transforming rebels into civilians: getting them to give up their guns and rejoin civilian life.

The process — called "DDR," for disarmament, demobilization and reintegration — usually is led by the United Nations, which has worked on DDR in 20 countries since its first such project in 1990, in Nicaragua. [1] Today, the U.N. maintains 13 active DDR programs, most of them in Africa. [2]

The process reflects a shift in rebel groups' missions: from violently pursuing their grievances against governments to pursuing those grievances nonviolently as civilians — and sometimes as statesmen — through politics and civil society. "The incentive of DDR is political will: 'We will go toward disarmament because we have decided within our organization that's how we want to grab power, to share it by integrating into the government,' " says a U.N. staffer, who asked not to be named because he was not an official spokesperson.

The process requires militants to renounce armed rebellion. "In order to be part of the political process, they need to disarm — to become political, and not military, actors," says Tino Kreutzer, who worked with the U.N. on DDR in the Central African Republic (CAR), where dissatisfaction over a 2005 election sparked rebellions in much of the country.

The former insurgents — or their leaders — often hope to exchange military power for political power. But not all members of an ex-rebel group are likely to get an equal share of the post-conflict political spoils. While leaders of former rebellions may make presidential bids or receive high political appointments, the foot soldiers frequently are left to return to civilian life with little or no income and few prospects for a good livelihood.

Rebel groups often raise funds by extorting "taxes" — essentially, bribes — from civilians. "The way in which rebel groups fund themselves is largely by preying on the population — 'taxing' roads, 'taxing' . . . traders or villagers on their way to the market," notes Ned Dalby, a Nairobi-based researcher for the International Crisis Group, a nongovernmental organization dedicated to resolving conflicts. In the CAR and in neighboring Democratic Republic of Congo, rebel groups extort taxes from local, independent miners. [3]

For such groups, disarmament is against their interest because ongoing conflict assures an income. Thus, whatever agreement rebel leaders may make at a negotiating table can provide cover for other groups, especially nongovernmental organizations (NGOs), which typically have to be less confrontational when working with government officials.

Grassroots efforts are also crucial to peacebuilding. If U.N. efforts can support community-level work and target large-scale needs — such as building army barracks, prisons, roads or courts — local groups can work at the grassroots level more effectively, some argue. Sierra Leone's *Fambul Tok* (Krio for "family talk") program brings ordinary people together, village by village, to talk about the 11-year civil war that ended in 2002. By the time local human-rights activist John Caulker founded the community-based reconciliation program in 2007, the country had already been through a peace process, a truth and reconciliation commission and national elections. But many villagers say those activities hadn't brought the kind of communal peace they needed to help heal from the atrocities of a war in which children were kidnapped into armies and drugged, women were raped and resisters mutilated.

"We feared one another. We were not even allowing the people to get near us. . . . The perpetrator would not allow his own children or family to mix with mine," says George Sambayo, who lives in a small village in northeastern Sierra Leone. "If the person is coming your way, you change direction. If you have malaria, or if you have a naming ceremony — nothing, he doesn't even go there."

may not be followed by their subordinates — at least not without some kind of supplement for their lost income.

That's where reintegration comes in. Once combatants hand over their weapons, they usually are offered food assistance, skills training or even cash when they return to their villages. "The idea is that they don't depend on the movement to feed their family," says Kreutzer. Reintegration support "helps them reestablish households and provide for their family [until they can] find a job."

That support can take several forms. Former combatants may be given pots and pans, blankets and cooking oil. Sometimes they are given food directly; sometimes they are offered seeds to plant. Occasionally, they may be given money for transport or other immediate needs.

Cash, though, can complicate the picture. For instance, peacebuilders have learned that buying back guns — an early approach to disarmament — is usually counterproductive. More often than not, it just drives up the local price of weapons. And sometimes the money is spent on new weapons. [4]

Peacebuilders also have learned that post-conflict economic development and nation-building go hand-in-hand with DDR. After all, says Laurent Banal, the DDR operations chief in the CAR, "These armed movements are, in fact, rebellion against poverty, mainly, and lack of presence of the state."

— *Jina Moore*

AFP/Getty Images/Sia Kambou

Militiamen loyal to Ivory Coast's former President Laurent Gbagbo — who gave up power after a deadly months-long post-election conflict — gather for a disarmament ceremony on April 29, 2011, in the country's commercial capital, Abidjan. Troops loyal to the new president, Alassane Ouattara, and U.N. peacekeepers also attended. Disarmament is a peacebuilding priority.

[1]"DDR in peace operations: a retrospective," U.N. Department of Peacekeeping, undated, p. 3, http://unddr.org/docs/DDR_retrospective .pdf.

[2]"Country Programmes," United Nations Disarmament, Demobilization and Reintegration Resource Center, www.unddr.org/country programmes.php.

[3]For background, see Josh Kron, "Conflict in Congo," *CQ Global Researcher*, April 5, 2011, pp. 157-182.

[4]"Operational Guide to the Integrated Disarmament, Demobilization and Reintegration Standards," United Nations Inter-Agency Working Group on Disarmament, Demobilization and Reintegration, 2010, p. 142.

Peacebuilding is also about issues that don't usually come up in formal peace negotiations, such as poverty, national histories and management of natural resources.

The infamously chronic conflict in Congo, Africa's second-largest country, also would benefit from micro-level attention, says Séverine Autesserre, an assistant professor of political science at Barnard College in New York City and author of *The Trouble With Congo*. [3] Most international efforts to end the conflict in Congo have focused on imposing settlements at the national and international level, she says. "There has been a lot of money spent on organizing big international conferences and general elections . . . but there has really been barely any support to the local actors who were trying to resolve the conflict

at the local level," she writes. As a result, "local conflicts festered, [and] they eventually escalated and jeopardized the national and international settlements." [4]

As the United Nations, NGOs and governments strive to implement effective peacebuilding programs, here are some of the questions being asked:

Does peacebuilding work?

Although the word itself has been in use for some 20 years, the diplomatic consensus and political will needed to implement peacebuilding agendas in failing states did not develop until the U.N. General Assembly voted to establish the Peacebuilding Commission at its 2005 annual meeting.

U.N. Projects Foster Peaceful Coexistence

More than 40 percent of the 162 U.N. peacebuilding projects in 2010 promoted peaceful coexistence and conflict resolution. About one-third supported peace agreements and political dialogue.

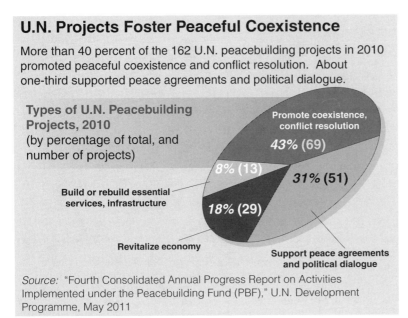

Types of U.N. Peacebuilding Projects, 2010 (by percentage of total, and number of projects)

Promote coexistence, conflict resolution
43% (69)

31% (51)

8% (13)
Build or rebuild essential services, infrastructure

18% (29)
Revitalize economy

Support peace agreements and political dialogue

Source: "Fourth Consolidated Annual Progress Report on Activities Implemented under the Peacebuilding Fund (PBF)," U.N. Development Programme, May 2011

Trying to help failing states is hardly a new enterprise, and the success record of such programs has been mixed. In Somalia, efforts at creating a stable, working government infamously failed in the early 1990s, and hostilities continue today, as African Union peacekeepers try to help the U.N.-supported transitional government prevent Islamic extremists from taking over the country. [5] In Iraq and Afghanistan, U.S.-led efforts at stabilizing the two countries continue to face obstacles, including insurgencies. Meanwhile, the Central African Republic, despite international interventions, still does not control its eastern territory, which borders war-torn Darfur, Sudan, and has become a refuge from which Uganda's Lord's Resistance Army rebels terrorize the region.

On the other hand, Bosnia-Herzegovina has stabilized since the civil war and genocide in the 1990s. And East Timor, which the U.N. administered from 1999 to 2002, is making significant progress toward post-conflict stability. [6]

Peacebuilding philosophy and practice are based on a mix of lessons learned over a generation — sometimes from failure, sometimes from success. "They're based on a lot of experience but not a lot of [scientific] evidence about things that we know can help support peace," says Vanessa Wyeth, co-editor of the book, *Building States to Build Peace.*

The list of countries targeted by the U.N. for peacebuilding is daunting, including Liberia, Côte d'Ivoire

(Ivory Coast), Nepal, Chad, Sri Lanka and Haiti. "Success is too high a hurdle in some of these places," says the International Peace Institute's Luck. Still, he remains optimistic that, "on balance, chances of [peacebuilding] being a moderate success over time are relatively good."

Getting donors to support peacebuilding efforts is another major goal, but measuring success is difficult. The United Nations attributes any increase in donor giving to peacebuilding activities, although it does not ask donors what motivated the higher level of giving, according to U.N. officials.

In other instances, successful peacebuilding efforts are clearly visible. In Sierra Leone roads are being built, sanitation trucks regularly cart away residential and commercial trash in the capital and newly trained lawyers and paralegals are helping to reduce by more than 70 percent the backlog of unresolved cases in the program's first year. [7]

Elsewhere, success depends on the work being done behind the scenes. Carolyn McAskie, the first U.N. assistant secretary-general of peacebuilding, remembers how crucial quiet diplomacy was between Burundi's U.N. ambassador and the Peacebuilding Commission. "In subtle ways, without fanfare and without headlines or public statements, the very fact that Burundi was on the PBC agenda helped to bring it back from the brink," she says. "We changed behaviors in Burundi in [some] instances."

But changing day-to-day behavior can be difficult in societies suffering from cyclical violence. For generations, violence has defined power in Guinea-Bissau — first during the country's long and bloody war for independence from the Portuguese in the 1960s and '70s and thereafter in frequent military coups. Though more recent political violence has been confined to the capital and often the halls of power, the instability affects all Bissau-Guineans.

"There's a kind of inversion of values," says Fafali Koudawo, director of *Voz di Paz*, a civil society organization in Bissau, the capital. "Before, he who steals was a bad guy. Now, he who steals a huge amount of money is great. Because the state is weak, violence has overturned all the values."

In most of the troubled countries, however, successes and failures unfold simultaneously, and incrementally. In the Central African Republic (CAR), for example, peacebuilding efforts helped advance a political dialogue that ultimately resulted in a major rebel group signing a ceasefire and agreeing to give up its guns. [8] But most observers consider the agreement fragile. "We're not talking about real peace," says Frederick Cook, then-U.S. ambassador to the CAR. "We're just talking about not fighting."

The decision whether to use, or continue to use, violence doesn't necessarily respond to outside pressure, according to Ned Dalby, a Nairobi-based researcher on the CAR for the International Crisis Group, a nongovernmental group that works to resolve conflicts. One must "think carefully about the multiple factors behind violence and whose interest it would serve," he warns. The answer varies across different conflicts.

The sheer number of programs and interventions also makes it difficult to evaluate peacebuilding, partly because it is difficult to balance successes against failures and determine a net effect. For example, the CAR's point man for disarmament and demobilization was fired after allegedly embezzling more than half a million dollars in donations earmarked for reintegrating former combatants. But the same peacebuilding operation succeeded in demobilizing 600 child soldiers, at a cost of $2 million, according to local U.N. staff. Even in a perfect world, where programs run efficiently and corruption is minimal, it would be hard to prove that peacebuilding succeeds at preventing war. "Prevention obviously is a difficult thing to prove. It's counterfactual," says Luck. "It [is about what] didn't happen."

All of which begs the question: What does peace look like to those outside the international decision-making process? In the CAR, international organizations and local politicians talk about peace from their desks in the capital, Bangui, but some Central African citizens think such talk is premature.

"We have peace in the town, but not in the provinces," says Arlette Ngarina, who lives in the capital. "Our families live in the provinces. If they are not in peace, we cannot be in peace, either."

Does peacebuilding require democracy?

Telling new governments what kind of governing bodies to establish is tricky. And, officially, peacebuilding is agnostic about which kind of government is needed to build a stable state.

"If you look at the U.N. charter," says Philip Dive, head of strategic planning with the U.N.'s Sierra Leone mission, "I don't see the word 'democracy' in the preamble." Instead, he points out, the charter focuses only on general goals, such as peace, security, justice and respect for human rights. "We're not lobbyists," Dive says. The purpose of the U.N. is not to achieve a specific type of government, he argues, but to achieve the values set out in the charter. "There are many ways to do that."

Nevertheless, international donors "increasingly make democratization a central tenet of the post-conflict reconstruction plan," writes Irfan Nooruddin, a political scientist at Ohio State University. "Holding elections is thought to signal a move to peace and to provide an avenue for former combatants to enter peaceful discussions with one another about the future of their countries." [9]

Political scientists Dawn Brancati of Washington University in St. Louis and Jack L. Snyder of Columbia University in New York City say elections are more fashionable these days. For example, after analyzing 136 civil wars ending after World War II, they found that:

- Wars that ended after the Cold War were more likely to involve elections;
- U.N. interventions increased a country's likelihood of having post-conflict elections;
- U.N. peacekeeping missions increased the likelihood of early elections, and
- Elections were more likely to follow a rebel victory than a government victory. [10]

The authors think elections are more popular today because of a combination of international pressure and the interests of the formerly warring parties.

But, if neither side is a clear-cut winner and the fighting ended only through negotiation, the result can be disastrous. "[T]he increasingly common combination of early elections and inconclusive civil war outcomes creates exactly the conditions that make elections especially dangerous," they write. "International pressures in favor of negotiated settlements, together with quick elections, have contributed to this trend over the past two decades." [11]

Yet a country's ability to organize and hold a successful national election is itself seen by the international

Paulino Rodrigues Santim, a blacksmith in Bissau, the capital of Guinea-Bissau, will buy a generator using a microloan financed by the U.N. Peacebuilding Fund. Helping young people establish small businesses is seen as an effective way to maintain peace in post-conflict countries.

community as an indicator of stability. Though the U.N. peacebuilding staff insists elections are not a prerequisite for their work, the history of U.N. peacebuilding suggests otherwise. The West African nation of Guinea — where government soldiers killed 157 pro-democracy protesters and raped at least 109 women in the capital in 2009 [12] — joined the U.N.'s peacebuilding body earlier this year, only after holding elections in December 2010 deemed fair by international observers. [13]

Guinea's neighbor, Côte d'Ivoire, on the other hand, was refused PBC membership because elections there were delayed for five years. And when a vote finally was held in November 2010, the country erupted into violence that was worse than anything since the end of the 2005 civil war. [14]

Meanwhile, the PBC has advocated elections elsewhere. In the CAR, for instance, elections were a key part of the 2008 agreement between a major rebel group and the government, which peacebuilders facilitated. In Burundi, the U.N. established a political dialogue to pave the way for last year's bizarre presidential election. While it unfolded without the violence many feared, the only candidate was the incumbent president. [15]

In such "democratic" elections, the results are often less important to the U.N. than the peacefulness of the process, and true democracy is not always the outcome, some observers acknowledge. "It really depends more on [whether] that country is stable enough to have the trust of the international community to advance the cause of peacebuilding," says Frank Jarasch, a former adviser to PBC Chairman Peter Wittig, Germany's permanent U.N. representative. "If the impression to the member states at the U.N. is that [the government] has this kind of ownership of the coming peacebuilding process, then . . . it doesn't have to be 100 percent democratic elections."

Running a successful election is not always the same as practicing democracy. "[F]rom the point of view of a self-interested political leader," other options are "superior . . . to the tough and unreliable option of trying to be a good government," writes Paul Collier, a professor of economics at Oxford University and a leading thinker on the causes of conflict. They include taking bribes, intimidating voters and intentionally miscounting votes, which may explain why incumbents win re-election 60 percent more often in developing countries than in developed countries. [16] "Electoral competition creates a Darwinian struggle for political survival in which the winner is the one who adopts the most cost-effective means of attracting votes," Collier continues. [17]

Burundi's 2010 presidential election — the first direct presidential poll since the end of the civil war in 2000 — was a case in point. Although the rhetoric focused on "free and fair" elections, the national electoral commission was accused of bias and fraud, and ruling party cabinet ministers interfered in the opposition campaign. Ultimately, all of the opposition candidates pulled out of the election, leaving the incumbent president as the only contender. Despite the controversy and suspicion that swirled within the country, the United Nations and the European Union's Election Observation Mission stood by the process.

The Burundi debacle, and peacebuilders' hesitation about promoting democracy, may be less about peacebuilding than about old-fashioned diplomacy. Says the U.N.'s McAskie: "It's not so much that they're agnostic on what kind of government there should be; most of them know. But they're not prepared to pronounce [it], . . . partly because governments don't tell governments off often enough."

Is peacebuilding replicable?

Proponents of peacebuilding hope that countries can copy each other's ways of maintaining peace. "Whether in Africa, Asia, Europe — anywhere, almost always one has to focus on" the same objectives, says Cheng-Hopkins, the U.N.'s chief peacebuilding official. Those goals include improving access to justice, reforming the military and police and jump-starting the economy.

McAskie, Cheng-Hopkins' predecessor, says replicability is equally about flexibility. "There are certain traditional ideas we have of what peacebuilding is — sorting out the corrections system, getting the justice system up and running . . ., classic interventions that are generic and applied to all situations," she says. "Then you also maintain a second track [of peacebuilding], which is flexible to the local situation."

In Sierra Leone in 2008, that meant funding something that seemed to have almost nothing to do with conflict: repairing the country's only power plant. Traditionally, this would be considered a long-term development project and not a U.N. peacebuilding activity, which usually involves short-term interventions to help maintain a stable peace during a fragile time.

"We had a very useful and quite heated debate about whether support for getting the electricity up and running in Sierra Leone was peacebuilding," McAskie remembers. The Sierra Leonean speakers "all made a very convincing argument that if the lights are out in Freetown, you're not going to have peace — you're going to have riots in the street, crime at night, rape." The commission gave $9 million to avert a break in power services in the capital and to supplement the supply in two rural districts. [18]

Another approach to peacebuilding focuses on analyzing the history of conflict to understand "incentives or motives for violence." This process involves identifying "root causes of conflict" — what the U.S. Agency for

Relatives of those killed during Kyrgyzstan's violent 2010 political crisis commemorate the one-year anniversary of their deaths with prayers near their graves at a cemetery outside of the capital Bishkek on April 7, 2011.Peacebuilding efforts in the country have focused on improving the livelihoods of youths and empowering women to participate in peace, security and reconstruction efforts.

International Development (USAID) calls the "the raw material" of conflict. [19] The causes differ from country to country and, perhaps more importantly, from one political circumstance to another.

Addressing root causes is a common and replicable approach, but agreeing on the causes is not always easy. Some people in Sierra Leone say the root cause of the war was frustration among unemployed youth; others say it was a breakdown in traditional power structures that prevented local conflicts from being resolved easily. Still others blame the war on a desire by some to control the country's diamond trade.

Sometimes the interpretation of a root cause transforms into a peacebuilding solution. The U.N. gave $4 million in peacebuilding funds to develop a youth empowerment and employment program in Sierra Leone, for instance, citing youth unemployment as a root cause of the conflict. Another $4 million was earmarked to clear backlogged legal complaints, with the same justification. [20]

While "root cause" has become a bit of a buzzword in peace operations, many observers agree there's no guarantee that using financial or programmatic interventions to target what some believe caused a conflict 15 years ago will necessarily stop current conflicts or prevent future ones.

Furthermore, there are limits to identifying and addressing root causes. In Guinea-Bissau, for example, most international organizations acknowledge that the army's frequent coups promote instability. But engaging the military directly is too sensitive for most nongovernmental organizations, which instead focus on socioeconomic programming.

Such political engagement has been a major strength of U.N. efforts in Sierra Leone, however. "If those issues are not dealt with, no matter how much the [U.N.] gives in additional resources, no matter how much government commits itself, no matter how glossy you present it to [diplomats in] New York, things will never work," says Massaquoi, Sierra Leone's peacebuilding liaison to the PBC.

Von der Schulenburg, the U.N. special representative in Sierra Leone, says some elements of the mission's approach can be replicated elsewhere: closely reading the political landscape, engaging key figures, gaining the trust of the country's political elite. But those are diplomatic tools that existed long before peacebuilding became an international priority.

Get more specific than that, others say, and peacebuilding becomes more and more difficult to replicate. "In reality, you cannot compare Burundi at all to the Central African Republic or Guinea Bissau," says Jarasch, of the German mission to the U.N. "That doesn't mean there shouldn't be any lessons learned, but certainly you'd need [lessons] from lots of different countries [on which] to base future involvement."

BACKGROUND

Prior Peace Paths

Since 1648, when the Treaty of Westphalia ended the Thirty Years' War in Europe, peace has been the byproduct of agreements between modern nation states. Interstate wars ended with treaties, signed by officials from all sides. Civil wars were crushed or occasionally crushed the government the insurgents rose up against.

Since 1945, at least 260 wars and 357 successful military coups have erupted. [21] And civil wars in particular are prone to reignite; nearly 60 percent of countries that have experienced civil wars since 1945 have seen a return to violence. [22]

A vast body of research suggests several factors influence post-conflict peace, including whether the conflict ended with a "total win" by one side or whether parties negotiated the peace. Which terms they negotiated — and

which they ignored — also influence the peace, along with other factors.

In the Westphalian model, peace talks and peace accords are a sign that a conflict has ended. Peacebuilding, on the other hand, looks at what's happening outside the halls of power. For instance, peacebuilders scrutinize what's happening in the fields, where men who once fought each other now farm side-by-side; in the schools, where children once forced to serve as child soldiers are learning trades; and in the courtrooms and legislative chambers, where problems once solved with weapons are addressed through tedious democratic processes.

The word peacebuilding was introduced in 1992, when U.N. Secretary-General Boutros Boutros-Ghali outlined a post-Cold War vision for the world body in his "Agenda for Peace." It would take another decade, however, for serious movement on that agenda. Yet, even in Boutros-Ghali's early sketch, peacebuilding was a way of seeing the economic and social dimensions to conflict as well as the political aspects. Today, peacebuilding crafts interventions designed to address them all.

"We're talking about a specific set of challenges in a specific set of circumstances," says Wyeth, of the International Peace Institute.

Wyeth and other observers recognize the same needs from country to country: restoring law and order; providing for minimal livelihoods; rebuilding infrastructure and jumpstarting the economy.

For generations, the international community has taken a patchwork approach to these challenges, dividing its work into three main areas, according to Dive at the U.N. office in Sierra Leone. Peace and security experts focused on peacekeeping patrols and ceasefire agreements; humanitarian-affairs officers focused on food and medical aid; and development experts focused on preparing countries for long-term, post-conflict economic growth — usually in that order.

Over time, says Dive, it became clear this "silo" approach didn't work. "The peace and security people can't go up on the hill, and the humanitarian people can't go off by the river and the development people can't have their bunker under the hill. It has to come together," he says.

Roots of Peacemaking

That lesson came into clear focus in central Africa after the 1994 Rwandan genocide, in which nearly 800,000

Tutsis and moderate Hutus were murdered over a three-month period. [23] Following the genocide, approximately 2 million Rwandan refugees crossed the border into Zaire (modern Democratic Republic of Congo). Among the refugees were many perpetrators of the genocide, some of whom — operating from inside refugee camps run by international aid agencies — bought weapons and tried to reorganize militias to return to Rwanda and continue the slaughter. [24]

But because the aid workers viewed themselves as neutral and the aid was seen as emergency help, the humanitarian agencies did little to halt the activity. The Rwandan government later used their inaction to justify a war against Congo, which lasted until 2002. [25]

Peacebuilding has its roots in both the U.N. failure in Rwanda and later in Bosnia. U.N. peacekeepers were on the ground when the genocide began in Rwanda in 1994 but were not allowed to intervene to stop the massacre they saw unfolding. A year later, in Bosnia-Herzegovina, Dutch peacekeepers abandoned the "safe haven" they had established in Srebrenica, leaving 8,000 Muslim men and boys to be murdered by Serb soldiers. [26] In both instances, peacekeepers were following rules against the use of force in conflict zones — rules designed to protect their "neutrality."

Each tragedy spurred U.N. "lessons learned" documents. In a 2004 report, Secretary-General Kofi Annan acknowledged, "[P]eace agreements by Governments or rebels that engage in or encourage mass human-rights abuses have no value and cannot be implemented. These contexts are not appropriate for consent-based peacekeeping; rather, they must be met with concerted action." [27] Though articulated in tame, diplomatic prose, this idea marked a radical departure from the principle of neutrality, and the admonition against peacekeepers using force that had led to the atrocities in Srebrenica and Rwanda.

Power to Be Political

The move away from a posture of neutrality paved the way for U.N. peacebuilding's greatest strength: its freedom to tackle politics. In most cases, international organizations — including some U.N. agencies — are barred, directly or tacitly, from overt political engagement. Few heads of state want to be told how to run their countries.

Providing Clean Water and Shelter

Haitian medical workers wash their hands using a portable water supply at St. Nicolas Hospital in St. Marc, north of Port-au-Prince, on Oct. 24, 2010 (top). The country has suffered from several cholera outbreaks since the massive January 2010 earthquake, primarily because of a lack of clean water. Peacebuilding aid for Haiti has focused on providing clean water and improving sanitation. In Sri Lanka, peacebuilding funds have been used to aid internally displaced persons (IDPs) like these members of the Tamil minority group, waiting to leave an IDP camp in Vavuniya on Dec. 23, 2009 (bottom). Hostilities ended in Sri Lanka in May 2009, when government troops defeated a long-running insurgency by the Tamil Tigers.

But the Peacebuilding Commission was specifically authorized — by the General Assembly and the Security Council — to engage heads of state, ministers and other officials on political issues. In U.N. jargon, having such a "political mandate" is key: Every U.N. mission is deployed to a country under Security Council rules. Unless the council gives a mission a political mandate, it can't get involved in politics.

U.N. missions have political mandates in countries where the PBC operates. Many observers say the combination of the mandate and the PBC's rationale give peacebuilding the power to make a real difference — as when U.N.'s von der Schulenburg helped defuse the tense election situation in Sierra Leone in 2009. As the mob gathered around the men trapped on the roof of the minority party's headquarters, he literally stepped in, negotiated with the riot leaders, engaged the police and facilitated meetings that led to a truce between the two parties.

"I could do that because I have a political mandate," he explains.

But some experts say the PBC often lacks the courage or organizational structure to use its mandate effectively.

Limits of Intervention

Regardless of an organization's mandate, peacebuilding can be only as effective as its country partners.

In the Central African Republic, for instance, money and partnerships could not overcome government inertia to establish a local radio station in Paoua, a town near the northern border with Chad — a 12-hour drive on terrible roads from the capital of Bangui. With no local news available that far north, the U.N. offered to pay for training and equipment to build a radio station — if the community could find a building and the government would pay for the antenna.

The mayor donated her own property, and a local committee collected funds and donated labor to refurbish it. But the government dawdled on the $2,000 antenna, holding up the radio station for more than a year before providing the antenna. The journalists trained by the U.N., meanwhile, had begun looking for other work.

Meanwhile, Burundi's demobilization of former combatants is a good example of how an unwilling or uncooperative local partner can limit the success of peacebuilding. Some of the ex-combatants from the 12-year civil war were integrated into the Burundian army after the war ended in 2005. But many still are waiting to be officially discharged. Although demobilization is part of most peacebuilding operations, many of Burundi's former rebels feel they have been misled by empty political promises. For example, many received seed money to start small businesses, but the enterprises couldn't be sustained after initial funding ran out.

"There were lots of promises for ex-soldiers from different institutions," says Jean-Marie Nindorera, who leads an association of nearly 150 former combatants near Gitega, Burundi's second-largest city. "When they didn't come true . . . [the ex-soldiers] were not satisfied." In 2006, an ex-combatant briefly commandeered the local outpost of the demobilization office. "He destroyed windows," Nindorera says, "but they could . . . kill people or steal."

The former combatants' frustration is palpable — and dangerous, says Oscar Ndiswarugira, with the Ministry for Peace and Reconciliation Under the Cross (Mi-PAREC), a grassroots Lutheran-sponsored Burundian organization in Gitega. "I can see they're just waiting, waiting. They're very angry. . . . Some of them are very powerful. . . . The issue is how long they are going to be patient."

In the Democratic Republic of Congo, where the U.N. is conducting peacekeeping and peacebuilding simultaneously, the problems are decidedly local, says political scientist Autesserre of Barnard College. "We're talking about conflict over political, social and economic agendas . . . at the level of the individual, the family, the clan," she said. Yet, she noted, "Most of the international peacebuilders are based in the capital, Kinshasa." [28]

Some post-conflict countries have decided to go it alone, in part because of the gap between what people in the hinterlands say they need and what foreign civil servants based in capitals perceive is needed. For instance, Mozambique — often labeled a post-war success — has seen relative peace and a growing economy since its civil war ended in 1992 after more than a decade of fighting. But its success can be attributed in large part to patient peace negotiations between Mozambicans themselves, according to Lucia van den Bergh, a former liaison between Mozambique and the European Parliament. The talks were facilitated, she notes, by the Catholic Church, supported by a U.N. envoy and driven

CHRONOLOGY

1940s *United Nations is created to "prevent the scourge of war."*

1942 Twenty-six countries sign the United Nations Declaration, paving the way for creation of the international organization.

1945 Forty-five nations — all former World War II Allies — gather in San Francisco to write the U.N. charter, which formally establishes the United Nations.

1948 U.N. launches first peacekeeping mission, along Arab-Israeli border.

1960s-1980s *The Cold War polarizes world politics and diplomacy, marginalizing the United Nations as a global player.*

1960 U.N. sends its first peacekeepers into Congo.

1964 U.N. launches peacekeeping mission on the island of Cyprus; mission is still operating today.

1989 Berlin Wall falls, symbolizing the collapse of communism and ushering in a new era of activity at the United Nations.

1990s *Ethnic conflict becomes the predominant form of warfare; the U.N.'s image is tarnished by genocides in Europe and Africa.*

1990 Rwanda civil war begins when the Tutsi-led Rwandan Patriotic Front invades Rwanda from Uganda.

1992 U.N. Secretary-General Boutros Boutros-Ghali introduces the word "peacebuilding" in his "Agenda for Peace" document, which lays out the U.N.'s post-Cold War vision.

1993 U.N. Mission in Rwanda deploys to Kigali, the capital, to monitor a peace agreement ending the country's three-year civil war.

April 1994 Rwandan president dies in a plane crash, sparking a three-month genocide that unfolds as U.N. peacekeepers stand by.

July 1995 More than 8,000 men and boys are massacred at Srebrenica, in Bosnia-Herzegovina, after Dutch peacekeepers abandon a U.N. "safe haven."

1999 In a speech to the U.N. General Assembly, Secretary-General Kofi Annan, who had refused to permit U.N. peacekeepers to stop the Rwandan slaughter, argues for stronger U.N. interventions to protect civilians in conflict zones.

2000s *In an attempt to address the previous decade's peacekeeping failures, the U.N. adopts peacebuilding as a focus.*

2002 Kofi Annan outlines the U.N.'s vision for peacebuilding.

2005 Security Council and General Assembly create U.N. Peacebuilding Commission (PBC).

2007 PBC activities begin in Burundi and Sierra Leone. . . . Sierra Leone holds its first presidential election since the end of a brutal civil war in 2002.

2008 PBC begins to work with Central African Republic and Guinea-Bissau.

2009 Local elections spark political violence in Sierra Leone for the first time since the end of the country's civil war. Political parties sign a dialogue protocol, facilitated by U.N. peacebuilders.

2010 In advance of presidential elections in October 2011, PBC begins to work with Liberia on political issues. . . . Guinea-Bissau military leaders seize the prime minister, prompting the European Union and United States to withdraw military aid. . . . Burundi holds single-candidate presidential election after the country's opposition parties allege fraud and pull out of the race. . . . Burundian president releases independent survey on truth and reconciliation commission, after seven months' delay.

2011 After a successful national election, Guinea joins the list of countries working with the PBC. . . . Central African Republic holds peaceful elections after a delay of nearly one year.

Success and Failure on the Road to Peacebuilding

The process worked in Sierra Leone, but not in Burundi.

Peacebuilding began at roughly the same time in Sierra Leone and Burundi. Both countries received attention from a steering committee at U.N. headquarters, and both received $35 million in peacebuilding funds.

Four years later, Sierra Leone has become a poster child for what peacebuilding can achieve, while Burundi is an experiment some peacebuilders would rather forget.

In Sierra Leone, the peacebuilding mission has trained paralegals, helped catalyze sustained attention and funding for youth programs and literally kept the lights on in Freetown, the capital. But U.N. staff on the ground and people who work for the government say the most meaningful achievement was streamlining myriad development strategies into a single agenda, designed to support the government's goals. While it sounds to outsiders like nothing more than an example of improved efficiency, it is difficult to imagine how much time mid- and senior-level civil servants spend filling out forms and documents related to international aid efforts. The streamlining has made that process faster and more effective, say U.N. and government staff in Freetown.

Meanwhile, U.N. peacebuilders — using their crucial authorization to engage the Sierra Leone government on political issues — helped to defuse an election-related dispute that most observers worried might reignite conflict nationwide. After a standoff was averted, the two political parties negotiated a Joint Communiqué — outlining new rules for political discourse and action — that will provide the foundation for the 2012 presidential elections.

But in Burundi, peacebuilding has stalled. The 2010 presidential election — rather than showcasing Burundi as a stable, post-conflict country — only heightened political tensions.

Opposition parties accused the ruling party of fraud and the election commission of bias, and neither group would meet with opposition candidates to discuss the issues — even though opposition politicians, ruling party members and the election commission president all had participated in a $3 million, peacebuilding "political dialogue" program.

primarily by the actors involved, not by international or regional concerns.

Van den Bergh also attributes Mozambique's success to its lack of a truth-telling mechanism. "There was no punishment, not even systematic identification and documentation of war crimes," she writes. Although that leaves the victims of wartime atrocities neglected, she acknowledges, state stability has resulted from the willingness of most Mozambicans to move on. [29]

Likewise, Rwanda — another paragon of post-conflict success — recently has taken a staunchly defiant attitude toward outside assistance. Less than 20 years after the 1994 genocide, Rwanda boasts universal health care, free education and one of Africa's most rapidly growing economies. In 2009 it was the first sub-Saharan African country to top the World Bank's list of business reformers. [30] And last year the bank named Rwanda one of the world's 10 most-improved economies. [31]

When he was inaugurated for a second term last September, Rwanda's president, Paul Kagame, railed against international organizations "who are not accountable to anyone themselves [and] think they have the right to dictate the conduct of legitimate state actors." He insisted such "external actors" lack legitimacy and "do not relate to the majority of the people and deserve nothing more than to be ignored."

He claimed the country's progress has been self-made, saying, "For more than a decade and a half now, the people of this country have increasingly come together as one to determine and share their destiny." [32]

An independent evaluator had called the dialogue program one of Burundi's most successful peacebuilding efforts, but the fact that participants refused to hold a dialogue after the electoral controversy suggests the program was a failure.

Meanwhile, human-rights advocates reported killings of opposition politicians, the murder of an anti-corruption investigator and the arbitrary arrest of journalists and perceived political opponents. [1]

The peace accords that ended Burundi's civil war called for a truth and reconciliation commission, the promotion of which became a centerpiece of the U.N.'s peacebuilding strategy in the country. [2] Using peacebuilding funds, a joint committee representing government, civil society and the United Nations filed a report outlining the need for such a commission and how it might operate. The president, however, delayed the release of the report until December 2010, undermining its findings. No action has been taken so far. [3]

The political situation in each country, of course, is different, and not every peacebuilding intervention in Sierra Leone has been a success. While the U.N. mission in Burundi operates in a rather constricted political context, the mission also lacks the tough leadership that many credit for Sierra Leone's success. The U.N. mission has had four different leaders in the last six years — each removed at the request, directly or tacitly, of the Burundian government.

— *Jina Moore*

A woman in Burundi's capital, Bujumbura, votes during the 2010 presidential election — the first direct presidential poll since the civil war ended in 2000. The vote that re-elected incumbent President Pierre Nkurunziza indicated that a $3 million peacebuilding "political dialogue" program did not work as intended, since opposition parties pulled out of the election after accusing the ruling party of fraud and the election commission of bias.

[1]"Closing Doors? The narrowing of democratic space in Burundi," Human Rights Watch, November 2010, p. 14, www.hrw.org/node/94300.

[2]For background, see Jina Moore, "Truth Commissions," *CQ Global Researcher*, Jan. 1, 2010, pp. 1-24.

[3]*Une commission doit enquêter sur le comportement des forces de sécurité*, Amnesty International *declaration publique*, May 10, 2011, www.amnesty.org/en/library/asset/AFR16/004/2011/en/29ff9871-5d37-46d2-aa06-70cc36c663b7/afr160042011fr.html.

Critics say that's a whitewashed view. Rwanda's state-building may have been led by a domestic vision, but more than half of Rwanda's budget comes from outside aid. [33] And the support has been growing. [34]

Rwanda's go-it-alone attitude led it in 1998 to launch a four-year war against neighboring Congo, where former perpetrators of the genocide were reorganizing and rearming from refugee camps overseen by U.N. agencies. Kagame saw the U.N.'s inaction in stopping the activity as an echo of the U.N.'s failure to prevent the genocide in 1994. In 1997, Kagame — then vice president of Rwanda — told South Africa's *Weekly Mail and Guardian* newspaper that in August 1996 he had delivered "a veiled warning" to the international community: If they failed to take action against the Hutu refugees rearming in Congo, then "Rwanda would take action."

But the world's response, he said, "was really no response at all." [35]

Unlike in Mozambique, however, Rwanda did not sacrifice truth-telling, which peacebuilders often prescribed. Nor did it want a quasi-international process, like the truth and reconciliation commissions in Sierra Leone and Liberia. Instead, the country implemented *gacaca*, a grassroots system of justice in which alleged genocide perpetrators were tried by their village peers. Though the process has attracted criticism from Western human-rights observers for not providing adequate due process, the *gacaca* courts have tried approximately 1 million perpetrators over roughly four years. [36] Their proceedings, currently being archived, are expected to serve as a valuable historical record of what happened in the genocide.

Andreson Masabo, left, fled ethnic conflict in Burundi in 1972. When he returned 36 years later, he found Terrance Sabukiza, right, living on part of his property in the rural southwestern district of Rumonge. The two mediated their land dispute with help from the local land commission, supported by the U.N. Peacebuilding Fund. Land disputes are often a cause of hostilities.

CURRENT SITUATION

Looking for Donors

Many post-conflict countries still face serious obstacles to stability. But in Sierra Leone, after the combustible years immediately following the civil war, some people are finally beginning to feel optimistic.

Inside a Freetown branch of a major African bank, tellers Joseph Sam and Tejan Sesay stack fat turquoise bricks of Sierra Leone's currency, the leone. After they run the bills through a counting machine, Sam and Sesay pass towering stacks of cash to patiently waiting customers. A 10,000 leone note, the country's largest, is worth about $3.

"In Sierra Leone," jokes Sam, "everyone can be a millionaire."

The two young men, 28, would have been teenagers during the civil war that tore Sierra Leone apart for 11 years, when child soldiers were infamously forced into militias and drugged into committing atrocities. It's a history they don't know, about a country they wouldn't recognize. For them, the war is over — and the word "peacebuilding" inspires disinterest.

"Nobody needs to tell me not to go to the bush and take up arms. We are here at 7 in the morning and we leave at 7 at night. It takes an hour to get to and from home. We don't have time for fighting," says Sam. "We already have peace," Sam adds. "What we need is investment. . . . So-called donors need to push money into industry."

Others share Sam's sentiments. While Sierra Leone is still far from developed, or even from securing long-term stability, many Sierra Leoneans agree with the common Krio phrase: "The war *don don*" — "The war is past."

Thus, in Freetown, peacebuilding is beginning to look more like development. But elsewhere, things aren't so rosy. In the Central African Republic, for example, after interminable delays, the focus is on disarmament and demobilization. In Burundi, a new U.N. mission chief — the country's fourth in less than a decade — has said and done very little since arriving in early 2011.

And in Guinea-Bissau — where the country seems unlikely to steer away from the cycle of coups that landed it on the commission's agenda in the first place — peacebuilding seems irrelevant. President João Bernardo Vieira was killed by a military faction in 2009. In April 2010, a high-level military officer kidnapped the army chief and the prime minister. The prime minister was released, and the leader of the April mutiny was appointed the new army chief in June. The European Union and the United States then suspended aid for military reform. The EU said the effort seemed "hopeless," while the United States cited the military's alleged involvement in drug trafficking. [37] The deposed army chief was released in December 2010, after seven months. [38]

Peacebuilding officials say they will complete the projects they are funding — new army barracks, prisons and micro-loan assistance to small entrepreneurs. But concerns persist about the country's stability and the government's intentions about democracy in a place notorious for corruption, even before it became a drug-trafficking hub. Looking back, Jarasch, the former adviser to the German mission to the U.N., says "Guinea-Bissau was maybe, in a way, a wrong evaluation [by] the PBC."

Recently, the PBC has added Liberia and Guinea to its peacebuilding agenda, which make an interesting study in contrasts as the commission tries to catalyze donor interest. Though neighbors, the two countries have vastly different post-conflict stories, especially when it comes to donors.

Liberia is already a "donor darling," taking in more than 10 times the amount of development assistance

Can outsiders build lasting peace?

YES
Vanessa Wyeth
Research Fellow, Peacebuilding and State Fragility
International Peace Institute

Written for *CQ Global Researcher*, June 2011

NO
John Caulker
Founder, Fambul Tok*
Sierra Leone

Written for *CQ Global Researcher*, June 2011

Since Liberia's civil war ended in 2003, the country has benefited from strong domestic leadership, billions of dollars in international support and the presence of 15,000 U.N. peacekeepers. As Liberia prepares for elections later this year, it is widely hailed as a peacebuilding success story.

Other countries have not been so lucky. In the Democratic Republic of Congo and Haiti, years of peacekeeping and billions of aid dollars have not led to peace and stability. Even cases once hailed as successes warrant a closer look. Recently, international observers warned that Bosnia faces a political crisis that threatens to undo the peace that has lasted there since 1995. The murder rate in Guatemala is now higher than it was at the height of the civil war in the 1980s.

Peacebuilding is a high-stakes political enterprise: It is complex and messy and requires tough compromises. And it takes a long time: The World Bank estimates that it takes at least a generation to move a country from where war-torn Liberia was in 2003 to where peaceful Malawi is today.

That requires domestic political leadership, the restoration of trust between citizens and their institutions and the slow work of transforming political processes so societal conflict can be managed without violence. Peace cannot be imposed from the outside, as the United States has learned in Afghanistan and Iraq. Lasting peace can be built only from within.

But resources matter. How can a country establish the rule of law if it can't pay its judges, let alone its police and prison guards? How can a government win the confidence of citizens who can't feed their families? International aid alone is not enough, but it can be essential, especially in the short- and medium-term. In 2008, for example, international aid to Liberia was worth 180 percent of the country's gross national income. International actors also provide crucial political support, technical assistance, training and security in the form of peacekeeping. Without international support for mediation efforts, there often would be no peace to build.

We still have much to learn about the impact — good and bad, intended and unintended — of international peacebuilding assistance and the complex political dynamics of war and peace. At the end of the day, peacebuilding contains a catch-22: Peace cannot be built from the outside. But it also might not survive without outside support.

Ultimately, peace is sustainable when it is internalized by those who experienced the conflict. They are in a better position to identify lasting solutions to the post-conflict problems of rebuilding state and society. As the saying goes: "He who wears it feels it." Within communities, local people know who can credibly lead a process, for example, and who instills confidence. This is only achieved when those people lead the peacebuilding process. The process and methodology must be designed, owned, led and contextualized by the people.

Effective peacebuilding involves constructive dialogue between all relevant stakeholders with the aim of finding a lasting solution to the underlying problems. Trust and respect are prerequisites for such open dialogue. These values can only be built by the parties themselves, not by outsiders.

Externally designed and led mechanisms can include, for example, truth and reconciliation commissions, special tribunals and support for the police and military in various forms. But these will not likely be sufficient to develop a lasting peace. Looking at Sierra Leone and Liberia as case studies, the ongoing threats to the fragile peace are clear, because people at the grassroots were not consulted in designing transitional justice institutions suitable for their contexts. The ownership then becomes questionable. Consequently, even with all the resources put into these countries there is little to show as a result of outside contributions toward lasting peace.

But by understanding the importance of the kind of dialogue I have described, and by providing the support needed to make it happen, outsiders can play a valuable facilitative role, if they work alongside local leadership.

In three-and-a-half years running *Fambul Tok* in Sierra Leone, I've seen ordinary people come up with creative approaches and follow their own route toward lasting peace — a process that comes when both victim and perpetrator acknowledge what went wrong, the dignity of victims is restored and the offenders seize the opportunity to apologize and to explain why they committed atrocities.

A process that allows this to happen can play an important role in reknitting the fabric of community that is torn by war. My hope is that *Fambul Tok*'s example will open the way for others to work in similar ways.

---

* Krio for "family talk"

> *"The mandate is to work with leaders, to look them in the eyes and say, 'Look, thank you for your coffee, but I think you need to be doing something different.' "*
>
> — *Michael Massaquoi, Sierra Leone's liason to the Peacebuilding Commission*

Guinea received in 2008. [39] Liberia's popular president, Ellen Johnson Sirleaf, a former World Bank economist, is expected to be re-elected in October in the country's second presidential poll since the end of its civil war. Guinea, by contrast, hosted elections only after its military massacred 157 pro-democracy protesters in 2009.

Observers often suggest Liberia's special relationship with the United States — freed American slaves founded the capital of Monrovia in 1822 — generates special interest. In 2010, Liberia received $230 million in U.S. aid, while Guinea received less than 10 percent of that. [40] (As a former French colony, Guinea has closer political and financial ties with France.)

After the Revolutions

A new wave of events in Arab countries has captivated the world's attention — and raised new questions about the role of peacebuilding beyond catalyzing outside cash.

"Let's be honest. There's a kind of stigmatization, but I think it's ill-placed," says Cheng-Hopkins, head of U.N. peacebuilding support. The PBC is "not a poverty commission," she says, even though the countries that receive aid from the panel "belong to the very poorest in the world." But the value of U.N. peacebuilding is to focus on "conflict drivers."

The U.N. is now funding a national reconciliation project in Lebanon, Cheng-Hopkins points out, and conflict analysts are focused on other countries in the Middle East and North Africa. This spring, the leaders of some of North Africa's notoriously autocratic countries — Egypt, Libya and Tunisia — faced off against citizens angered by rising fuel and food costs, unemployment and corruption. The popular uprisings triggered similar upheavals in Syria, Yemen and other Middle Eastern countries. [41]

Zine al-Abidine Ben Ali, who had ruled Tunisia as president for 23 years, fled the country in January, after nearly a month of public protests. [42] In February, Egypt's leader of 30 years, Hosni Mubarak, resigned following three weeks of mass protests. [43] In Libya, Col. Moammar Gadhafi, famous for lavishing money on pet projects across Africa, continues to battle rebels in an uprising that began in February and has been supported by NATO.

These are not classic peacebuilding scenarios. "If you look at Egypt or Tunisia, they are a very different category of country" from those in which U.N. peacebuilding operations usually work, says Wyeth, of the International Peace Institute. To begin with, in Egypt and Tunisia, the power transitions were largely peaceful. "There wasn't an armed group challenging the government, like there is in Libya — or there was in Burundi or Sierra Leone."

But there's another critical difference. Except for Yemen, "These are middle-income countries with very, very strong institutions in certain areas," she says. That changes how the international community might engage the transitions there, Wyeth says. "The sense I have from what, for example, donors are thinking about in Tunisia, is 'Let's support elections and make sure they go well; let's give them support in drafting new constitutions — but we don't see a long-term, big conflict-prevention or aid package,' " she says.

Wyeth and others acknowledge that, despite the size of their economies, income disparities in places like Egypt and Tunisia have been a serious, longstanding problem. [44] British economist and best-selling author Niall Ferguson argues that the economic consequences of these revolts — contracting economies and capital flight — will have debilitating effects on the coming transitions.

"Egyptian businessmen complain of soaring crime in the cities, the difficulty of carrying out normal transactions and, above all, nerve-wracking political uncertainty," he said. [45]

OUTLOOK
Power of Technology

Technology is rapidly changing what peacebuilding can do and how effective it might be — in part by providing more, and often better, information about the violence that precedes it.

For instance, during the violence following Kenya's 2008 presidential election, Harvard Law School graduate and popular Kenyan blogger Ory Okolloh subverted a government ban on live reporting by blogging in real-time about what was happening, based on reports readers sent her on violence in their neighborhoods.

"I got overwhelmed by the amount of information coming in," she remembers. With the help of some technically savvy volunteers, Okolloh invented Ushahidi, an open-source mapping software.

A Harvard study found that during the crisis Ushahidi generated more information, more quickly and with more geographical details than local mainstream media. [46]

After the violence subsided, a Kenyan NGO used Ushahidi to map "peace heroes," using reports about people who intervened during the crisis or otherwise helped neighbors or strangers. The idea was to strengthen post-conflict peacebuilding — in part by creating a "map of peace" as visually impressive and arresting as the map generated by reports of violence. [47]

Ushahidi also has been adapted to map the availability of medicine in Uganda, violence in eastern Congo and earthquake response in Haiti.

But not everyone agrees that this process of collecting user-generated information, called "crowdsourcing," always gives a clearer or more accurate picture of reality.

Jim Fruchterman, the founder and CEO of the technology-for-human-rights company Benetech, argues that crowdsourcing is sometimes an expensive distraction from less fancy tools that may provide information just as readily. "Misunderstanding relationships in data . . . can lead to choosing less effective, more expensive data instead of choosing obvious, more accurate starting points," he writes. [48] Benetech statisticians have warned against using crowdsourced data to understand any kind of patterns — of violence, of need, of aid — because of inherent limitations in data generated by users.

Technology is also changing the use of individual stories from the ground. The explosion of video over the last 20 years has also improved peacebuilding efforts. WITNESS, a New York-based video advocacy organization co-founded by popular British musician Peter Gabriel, trains human-rights activists around the world in videography and coaches activists on how to use video footage in compelling and appropriate ways.

In eastern Congo, WITNESS-trained advocates made a film for parents of children who want to join militia groups, composed predominantly of testimony from young boys who had made the choice and regretted it. Their second film, intended for the international community, highlighted underreported crimes in eastern Congo, especially sexual violence against female recruits. Their third production, broadcast in Congo, summarized International Criminal Court proceedings against an accused Congolese war criminal.

The United Nations, too, is getting into the technology game. Some peacekeeping missions are using mobile geographic information systems to collect data on conflict, allowing users to more easily recognize patterns in attacks. [49] Other U.N. agencies are developing mobile-based tools to improve food delivery, refugee services and human-rights monitoring. [50]

While tech enthusiasts can make them sound downright utopian, the new tools are more than just fancy bells and whistles. They help to repair the imbalance between elite-level conversations among international actors and the local people. "What you have now is a much more symmetrical relationship in which people who are recipients of the message can also become part of the conversation," says Nathaniel Whittemore, founder of the Center for Global Engagement at Northwestern University.

Travel and reporting for this issue of CQ Global Researcher *was supported in part by the Pulitzer Center on Crisis Reporting.*

NOTES

1. For background, see Jina Moore, "Truth Commissions," *CQ Global Researcher*, Jan. 1, 2010, pp. 1-24.

2. "Trust Fund Factsheet," Multi-Donor Trust Fund Office, U.N. Development Programme, www.mdtf.undp.org/factsheet/fund/PB000.

3. For background, see Josh Kron, "Conflict in Congo," *CQ Global Researcher*, April 5, 2011, pp. 157-182.

4. "How We Got Here: The Trouble with Congo," Public Radio International's "The World" podcast, Nov. 22, 2010, www.theworld.org/2010/11/the-trouble-with-the-congo/.

5. For background, see Jason McLure, "Troubled Horn of Africa," *CQ Global Researcher*, June 1, 2009, pp. 149-176.

6. Michael W. Doyle and Nicholas Sambanis, *Making War and Building Peace* (2006), pp. 230-256.

7. "Update on the Implementation of PBF Projects," Government of Sierra Leone, 2008, www.unpbf.org/docs/Sierra_Leone_PBF_Updates_SC_October_2008.pdf.

8. "Central African Republic: Keeping the dialogue alive," International Crisis Group, Africa Briefing No. 69, Jan. 12, 2010, pp. 2-4, http://reliefweb.int/sites/reliefweb.int/files/reliefweb_pdf/node-339891.pdf.

9. Irfan Nooruddin, "Voting for Peace? Do elections help or hinder recovery?" Paper prepared for presentation in Yale University's International Relations Seminar Series, 2008, p. 1, www.psweb.sbs.ohio-state.edu/faculty/nooruddin/research/15nooruddin_voting_for_peace.pdf.

10. "Rushing to the polls: The causes of premature post-conflict elections," *Journal of Conflict Resolution* (forthcoming), pp. 7, 19-23. Draft paper, http://brancati.wustl.edu/Rush2Polls.pdf.

11. *Ibid.*, p. 23.

12. For background, see Jina Moore, "Confronting Rape as a War Crime," *CQ Global Researcher*, May 1, 2010, pp. 105-130.

13. "Final Statement on Run-off Election in Guinea and the Post-Election Period," The Carter Center, Dec. 2, 2010, www.cartercenter.org/news/pr/guinea-120210.html.

14. "Ivory Coast Timeline," BBC, April 12, 2011, http://news.bbc.co.uk/2/hi/africa/country_profiles/1043106.stm. For background, see Jason McLure, "Sub-Saharan Democracy," *CQ Global Researcher*, Feb. 15, 2011, pp. 79-106.

15. "Review of the United Nations Peacebuilding Architecture," U.N. General Assembly and Security Council, July 21, 2010, p. 12, www.un.org/ga/president/64/issues/pbc/PBCReport.pdf.

16. Paul Collier, *Wars, Guns and Votes: Democracy in Dangerous Places* (2009), pp. 30-32.

17. *Ibid.*

18. "Sierra Leone Peacebuilding Fund Project Summary," U.N. Development Program, July 15, 2008, PBF/SLE/I-1, http://mdtf.undp.org/factsheet/project/00066695.

19. "Conducting a Conflict Assessment: A framework for strategy and program development," U.S. Agency for International Development, April 2005, p. 15, www.usaid.gov/our_work/cross-cutting_programs/conflict/publications/docs/CMM_ConflAssessFrmwrk_May_05.pdf.

20. "Peacebuilding Fund in Sierra Leone, Project Summaries," United Nations Peacebuilding Fund, 2007, www.unpbf.org/sierraleone/sierraleone-progress.shtml.

21. "PRIO Armed Conflict Database, Uppsala Conflict Data Program," www.prio.no/CSCW/Datasets/Armed-Conflict/UCDP-PRIO/; Collier, *op. cit.*

22. Barbara F. Walter, "Conflict Relapse and the Sustainability of Post-Conflict Peace," World Bank, Sept. 13, 2010, p. 1, http://wdr2011.worldbank.org/conflict-relapse-and-sustainability-of-post-conflict-peace.

23. For background, see Sarah Glazer, "Stopping Genocied," *CQ Researcher*, Aug. 27, 2004, pp. 685-708.

24. Linda Polman, "Crisis Caravan: What's wrong with humanitarian aid," Metropolitan Books, 2010, pp. 33-35.

25. Gérard Prunier, *Africa's World War* (2008) [electronic edition].

26. Abi Daruvalla, "Anatomy of a Massacre," *Time*, April 21, 2002, www.time.com/time/magazine/article/0,9171,232505,00.html.

27. "A More Secure World: Our shared responsibility: Report on the High-level Panel on Threats, Challenges and Change," U.N. General Assembly, Dec. 2, 2004, www.un.org/secureworld/report.pdf.

28. In "How We Got Here: The Trouble with Congo," PRI's The World podcast, Nov. 22, 2010, www.theworld.org/2010/11/the-trouble-with-the-congo/.

29. Lucia van den Bergh, "Why Peace Worked: Mozambicans look back," Association of European Parliamentarians with Africa, 2009, pp. 127-130, www.antenna.nl/images/mozambique.pdf.

30. "Doing Business: Reforming through difficult times," press release, World Bank, 2009, www.doingbusiness.org/reports/global-reports/~/media/FPDKM/

Doing%20Business/Documents/Press-Releases/2010/DB10-PR-Global.doc.

31. "Doing Business 2011: Making a Difference for Entrepreneurs," press release, World Bank, 2010, www.doingbusiness.org/reports/global-reports/~/media/FPDKM/Doing%20Business/Documents/Press-Releases/2010/DB11-PR-Global.pdf.

32. Paul Kagame, Second Inaugural Address, Amahoro Stadium, Kigali, Rwanda, Sept. 6, 2010, www.youtube.com/watch?v=-j1FyczU0pk.

33. Mailan Chiche, "Putting Aid on a Budget," Case Studies for the Collaborative Africa Budget Reform Initiative and the Strategic Partnership with Africa, Mokoro Ltd., 2008, p. 25.

34. *Ibid.* See also "Rwanda budget aid to rise 66 percent," *New Vision*, May 10, 2010, www.newvision.co.ug/D/8/220/720181.

35. Interview with Mahmood Mamdani, W*eekly Mail and Guardian*, Aug. 8, 1997, quoted in Prunier, *op. cit.*, accessed electronically.

36. Telephone Interview with Professor Timothy Longman, then at Vassar College, April 2009. Today he runs the African Studies program at Boston University.

37. Marco Vernaschi, "The Cocaine Coast," Virginia Quarterly Review, Winter 2010; "Timeline: Guinea Bissau," BBC News, December 2010, http://news.bbc.co.uk/2/hi/africa/1043376.stm.

38. "G Bissau bars military leaders from leaving," Radio Netherlands, Dec. 30, 2010, www.rnw.nl/africa/bulletin/gbissau-bars-military-leaders-leaving.

39. "HDR 2010 Statistical Tables, 15: Enabling environment, financial flows and commitments," *Human Development Index 2010*, http://hdr.undp.org/en/statistics/data/.

40. U.S. Agency for International Development Fact Sheets on Liberia and Guinea, www.usaid.gov/locations/sub-saharan_africa/countries/liberia/liberia_fs.pdf and www.usaid.gov/locations/sub-saharan_africa/countries/guinea/guinea_fs.pdf.

41. For background, see Roland Flamini, "Turmoil in the Arab World," *CQ Global Researcher*, May 3, 2011, pp. 209-236.

42. "Tunisia: Ex-president Ben Ali flees to Saudi Arabia," BBC News, Jan. 15, 2011, www.bbc.co.uk/news/world-africa-12198106.

43. "Egypt Unrest: Crowds celebrate Mubarak's departure, BBC News, Feb. 12, 2011, www.bbc.co.uk/news/world-middle-east-12438355.

44. "HDR 2010 Statistical Tables: Inequality-adjusted HDI," Human Development Index 2010, http://hdr.undp.org/en/statistics/data/.

45. "The Revolution Blows Up," *Newsweek*, June 6, 2011, www.thedailybeast.com/blogs-and-stories/2011-06-06/niall-ferguson-on-egypts-stock-market-plunge-the-revolution-blows-up/.

46. "Crisis Mapping Kenya's Election Violence: Comparing Mainstream News, Citizen Journalism and Ushahidi," Harvard Humanitarian Initiative, 2008, http://irevolution.wordpress.com/2008/10/23/mapping-kenyas-election-violence.

47. "Peace Initiative Uses the Ushahidi Platform," *Ushahidi blog*, April 13, 2010, http://blog.ushahidi.com/index.php/2010/04/13/peace-initiative-uses-the-ushahidi-platform-building-bridges/.

48. "Issues with Crowdsourced Data Part 2," *Benetech Blog*, April 21, 2011, http://benetech.blogspot.com/2011/03/issues-with-crowsourced-data-part-2.html.

49. Nicholas C. Martin, Charles Martin-Shields and Walter Dorn, "Without the most advanced technology, the UN isn't reaching its full potential in danger zones," *The Mark*, June 2, 2011, www.themarknews.com/articles/5470-smartphones-for-smart-peacekeeping?page=1.

50. "New Technologies in Emergencies and Conflict: The role of social information," UN Foundation-Vodafone Foundation Partnership, 2009, pp. 39-42, www.unfoundation.org/press-center/publications/new-technologies-emergencies-conflicts.html.

BIBLIOGRAPHY

Selected Sources
Books

Autesserre, **Séverine**, *The Trouble with Congo: Local violence and the failure of international peacebuilding*, **Cambridge University Press**, **2010**.

An assistant professor of political science at Barnard College at Columbia University analyzes the causes of local violence and criticizes international engagement for failing to address — or for exacerbating — them.

Call, Charles T., and Vanessa Wyeth, eds., *Building States to Build Peace*, Lynne Rienner Publishing, 2008.
Academics and specialists examine the relationship between peacebuilding and state-building, including case studies of successes and failures.

Collier, Paul, *Wars, Guns and Votes: Democracy in Dangerous Places*, Harper, 2009.
Using engaging prose written for nonspecialists, the director of the Centre for the Study of African Economics at Oxford University examines the relationship between holding elections and preventing — or renewing — violence.

Cortright, David, *Peace: A History of Movements and Ideas*, Cambridge University Press, 2008.
A professor of peace studies at the University of Notre Dame puts peacebuilding in its historical context, from the Vietnam War through the nonproliferation movement to today's conflicts.

Doyle, Michael W., and Nicholas Sambanis, *Making War and Building Peace*, Princeton University Press, 2006.
A professor of international affairs, law and political science at Columbia Law School (Doyle) and a professor of political science at Yale University examine the history of U.N. peace operations.

Kamara-Umunna, Agnes Fallah, and Emily Holland, *And Still Peace Did Not Come: A Memoir of Reconciliation*, Hyperion, 2011.
A woman who survived Liberia's civil war tells the stories of hundreds of victims and perpetrators, from child soldiers to "bush wives" — girls and women forced to marry soldiers in wartime — based on post-war interviews.

Lederach, John Paul, *Building Peace: Sustainable Reconciliation in Divided Societies*, United States Institute of Peace, 1998.
A professor at the Kroc Institute for International Peace Studies at the University of Notre Dame draws lessons from working with local communities in 25 countries on five continents.

Reports

"Review of the United Nations Peacebuilding Architecture," U.N. General Assembly and Security Council, A/64/868-S/2010/393, July 21, 2010.

The U.N.'s assessment of five years of peacebuilding efforts recommends a greater focus on youth employment, better coordination with other international organizations and a reduced administrative burden.

Bascuti, Dawn, and Jack Snyder, "Rushing to the polls: The causes of premature post-conflict elections," *Journal of Conflict Resolution* (forthcoming).
A statistical analysis of the relationship between elections and conflict suggests that the preference for polls can destabilize as much as develop states and societies after conflict.

Futamura, Madoka, Edward Newman and Shahrbanou Tadjbakhsh, "Research Brief: Toward a Human Security Approach to Peacebuilding," United Nations University, 2010.
The authors argue that peacebuilders should give priority to the needs of ordinary people in post-conflict countries.

Futamura, Madoka, and Mark Notaras, "Local perspectives on international peacebuilding," United Nations University, June 2011.
A workshop on peacebuilding focused on improving the balance between domestic and international voices.

Milner, James, "Refugees and the Regional Dynamics of Peacebuilding," *Refugee Survey Quarterly*, Vol. 28, Issue 1, 2009.
A Carlton University professor argues that peacebuilding takes too simple an approach to refugee problems, which can ultimately scuttle peacebuilding efforts after mass repatriations.

Documentaries

"Pray the Devil Back to Hell," Fork Films, 2008.
The film tells the story of female Liberian activists who tried to end the country's civil war — by literally standing between the belligerents.

"Acting Together on the World Stage," Brandeis University, 2010.
The documentary examines the work of peacebuilders around the world.

"Degrees of Separation," Al Jazeera, 2010.
Journalists talk with ordinary Sudanese on the eve of their historic referendum on whether to split Africa's largest country.

For More Information

Alliance for Peacebuilding, 1320 19 St., N.W., Suite 410, Washington, DC 20036; (202) 822-2047; www.alliance forpeacebuilding.org. A network of peacebuilders and advocates devoted to fostering new peacebuilding collaborations.

American Friends Service Committee, 777 United Nations Plaza #5, New York, NY 10017-3521; (212) 682-2745; http://afsc.org/office/quaker-united-nations-office. The U.N. branch of the pacifist Quaker organization, which works with peacebuilding partners around the world.

Fambul Tok, 47 Robert St., Freetown, Sierra Leone; (232) 78-500500; www.fambultok.org. A grassroots reconciliation group that takes a village-by-village approach to peacebuilding.

Interpeace, 7-9 Chemin de Balexert, 1219 Châtelaine, Geneva, Switzerland; (41) (0) 22 917 8593; www.interpeace .org. Nongovernmental organization that works with 300 local peacebuilders around the world to strengthen civil society.

Mi-PAREC, Ministry for Peace and Reconciliation Under the Cross, Musinzira Ave., Gitega, Burundi; (257) 22 40 3837; www.miparec.org. A local organization sponsored by the Lutheran church, devoted to nonviolent, community-based peacebuilding interventions.

Pulitzer Center on Crisis Reporting, 1779 Massachusetts Ave., N.W., Suite #615, Washington, DC 20036; (202) 332-0982; http://pulitzercenter.org. A nonprofit journalism organization that funds coverage of under-reported topics, including a three-month investigation into U.N. peacebuilding.

Timap for Justice, 4E Mudge Farm, Freetown, Sierra Leone; (232) 22-229-911; www.timapforjustice.org. A hybrid local-international nonprofit focused on training paralegals to provide free legal services for Sierra Leoneans.

Voices From Abroad:

ELLEN JOHNSON SIRLEAF

President, Liberia

It's about human needs, too

"Peacebuilding in the context of Liberia, while addressing the root causes and building institutions to manage and prevent conflict, is also about meeting basic human needs. This, together with the creation of jobs and other livelihood opportunities for our young people, remains a major challenge to our Administration. I am, nevertheless, convinced that with concerted effort, with commitment and dedication, the tasks ahead are surmountable."

The Analyst (Liberia), November 2010

Cartoon Movement/Giacomo Cardelli

MICHAEL VON DER SCHULENBURG

Executive Representative, U.N. Integrated Peacebuilding Office, Sierra Leone

No rush to judgment

"Nation-building in all of our countries has been an extremely long, bloody affair. . . . [Sierra Leone] is a country which still tries to create a nation that people feel like they belong to, together. They're trying to bring democracy and to do it peacefully. That's not been done in history. So let's not be arrogant about the whole thing. Let's see how we can help to speed it up."

The Christian Science Monitor, April 2011

PETER WITTIG

German Ambassador to U.N.

More commitment needed

"By linking the Peacebuilding Commission's work to that of peacekeeping, development and political actors in the field, the Commission has added considerable value. The challenge facing the Commission in demonstrating its full potentials, however, is to ensure that its work

is backed by a higher level of political commitment from Member States and the Senior United Nations leadership."

U.N. News Service, March 2011

BAN KI-MOON

Secretary-General, United Nations

Women play a key role

"Enabling women to contribute to recovery and reconstruction is integral to strengthening a country's ability to sustain peacebuilding efforts. . . . [P]eacebuilding strategies cannot be fully 'owned' if half the nation is not actively involved in their design and implementation."

Philippines News Agency, October 2010

SERGEY LAVROV

Minister of Foreign Affairs, Russia

Don't impose assistance

"The success of [Russia's] peacekeeping and peacebuilding efforts in the Middle East, Afghanistan, Africa, Haiti and

East Timor lies in the ability to consider the interests and priorities of the receiving side. Any assistance from the international community should not be imposed."

Statement before U.N. Security Council, September 2010

MAM-SAMBA JOOF

Executive Director, Agency for the Development of Women and Children, Gambia

Recovery takes time
"Wars and other conflicts leave societies destroyed, and post-conflict recovery takes [a] much longer time and requires a lot of financial resources to attain. The high human, financial, social and material costs of conflict are well documented, and . . . nearly 60 countries around the world — many of which are in sub-Saharan Africa — are in conflict or have recently come out of conflict."

Daily Observer (The Gambia), September 2010

DUMISANI NKOMO

CEO, Habakkuk Trust, Zimbabwe

African Union ineffective
"The multiplicity of internal contradictions and conflicting interests within leading member states makes the [African Union] ineffective as an instrument of promoting peace on the continent. The AU appears to be enmeshed in internal conflict on which of its objectives it should prioritise."

Zimbabwe Independent, April 2011

JOSE SOLER

E.U. Deputy Ambassador to Uganda

Reintegration is a challenge
"Uganda is now starting to recover from two decades of conflict. However, the impact of that conflict on women and girls and their particular needs in the process of demobilisation and reintegration is a very real challenge."

The Monitor (Uganda), November 2010

11

Gendercide Crisis

Robert Kiener

Far more boys than girls are born in China, creating a massive shortage of females. Abortions of female fetuses have skyrocketed since 1980, when prenatal gender-detection technology came into widespread use just as China was instituting its one-child population-control policy. The resulting shortage of females means that by 2030, when these two young boys from Shanghai will be looking for brides, one in five Chinese men — up to 50 million — won't be able to find a wife.

From *CQ Researcher*,
Oct. 4, 2011

As attendants in a morgue in Karachi, Pakistan, tenderly washed the bodies of two tiny lifeless infants — both girls — volunteer Mohammed Saleem explained that they had been found dead in a garbage dump.

"They can only have been one or two days old" when they were left to die, he said. [1]

In another Karachi morgue a visitor was shown a walk-in freezer containing five linen pouches, each about the size of a loaf of bread. Inside each was the tiny corpse of a newborn, also abandoned at birth.

Such gruesome scenes are common in Pakistan, where last year more than 1,200 newborns were killed and abandoned — about 100 a month. [2] About nine out of 10 of the victims were girls. [3]

"Sometimes they hang them, and sometimes they kill by the knife, and sometimes we find bodies which have been burned," said Anwar Kazmi, a manager of the Edhi Foundation, Pakistan's largest private social service agency. [4] The number of such murders in Pakistan was up 20 percent in 2010 over 2009, and many officials say hundreds of other bodies are never found. [5]

Why is this horrific slaughter of infants happening? In Pakistan, as in several other countries, girls are often killed at birth or aborted because they are viewed as economic liabilities for whom an expensive dowry could be required. Boys are preferred because in such cultures males traditionally care for their aging parents, while daughters leave home to care for their husband and his family. Many other girls die soon after birth from neglect or starvation — part of what some experts call "a global war on baby girls." [6]

Indeed, over the last 30 years at least 160 million baby girls have been aborted or killed because of their sex in South and East Asia

China and India Have the Most Male Births

Far more boys than girls are born in China, India and a handful of other countries with traditional preferences for boys. According to demographers, at least 160 million baby girls have been aborted or killed after birth because of their sex in South and East Asia alone over the last 30 years — more than the entire female population of the United States. Experts say the increases are the result of easy access to inexpensive sonograms (to determine fetal sex) and gender-selective abortions. China's one-child policy is also blamed for part of the country's gender imbalance: 113 boys are born for every 100 girls (a 1.13 ratio of male-to-female births).

Comparing Global Sex Ratios

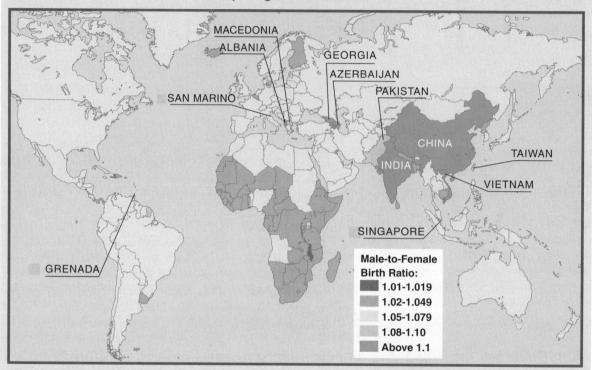

Source: "Sex Ratio," *The World Factbook,* Central Intelligence Agency, 2011, https://www.cia.gov/library/publications/the-world-factbook/fields/ 2018.html; and "Pakistan Demographic Survey," 2007. Map by Lewis Agrell

alone, according to demographers such as Christophe Guilmoto, at the Paris-based Research Institute for Development (IRD). [7]

"The number of these 'missing girls' is more than the entire female population of the United States," says award-winning journalist Mara Hvistendahl, a Beijing-based correspondent for *Science* magazine and author of the 2011 book *Unnatural Selection: Choosing Boys Over Girls and the Consequences of a World Full of Men.* [8]

In addition to China and India, "sex-selective abortions," or pregnancies terminated solely because of the gender of the fetus, have claimed thousands of female lives in Taiwan, the Balkans, Armenia, Georgia and even among some immigrant populations in the United States and other industrialized nations.

And the toll is rising, as modern ultrasound and abortion facilities have become increasingly widespread in recent decades. Up to 12 million girls were aborted in

India alone over the past 30 years, according to a recent *Lancet* study. While about 2 million girls' deaths were attributed to gender-selective abortions during the 1980s, the toll in India increased to 6 million during the 2000s — or about 600,000 per year. [9]

Although abortion statistics are not generally released in China, the state-run media reported in 2009 that more than 13 million abortions were performed that year alone. [10] While no one really knows how many of those were female, a Chinese researcher in 1996 found that 85 percent of all aborted fetuses in rural Zhejiang Province, on the southeastern coast, were females. [11] And demographers point to China's heavily skewed ratio of male-to-female births to further confirm that the vast majority of abortions must have been females.

Worldwide, between 102 and 106 males normally are born for every 100 females — a ratio that has held constant for as long as populations have been measured. In China, however, that ratio jumped to around 108 males per 100 females in the late 1980s, and to a significantly skewed 124 males by the early 2000s. Today, according to the United Nations Population Fund, 113 boys are born for every 100 girls in China; the ratio is 112 to 100 in India and 110 per 100 females in Pakistan. [12]

Population experts say such high sex ratios are biologically impossible without outside intervention. "These sex ratios have become completely unhinged," wrote Nicholas Eberstadt, a demographer with the conservative American Enterprise Institute (AEI). "This is a phenomenon utterly without natural precedent in human history." [13]

"Girls are seen as a burden, as a property which belongs to somebody else, so people see that as a waste of money and the wasting of an education of a girl," explained Bhagyashri Dengle, executive director of Plan India, a children's advocacy group in New Delhi. "Then, when the girl gets married, the families have a big, heavy dowry." [14]

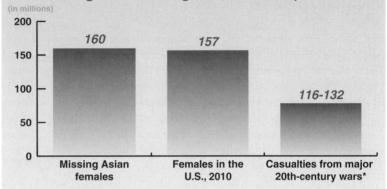

The Scope of Asia's "Missing" Female Problem

Asia is "missing" 160 million females who were either aborted or killed at birth over the last 30 years. The total exceeds the 2010 female population of the United States as well as the total number of casualties from all of the major wars of the 20th century.

Putting Asia's Missing Females in Perspective

(in millions)

	Missing Asian females	Females in the U.S., 2010	Casualties from major 20th-century wars*
	160	157	116-132

* Korean War (2 million); Vietnam War (350,000); Soviet Revolution (7 million); Stalin's Great Purge (10 million); World War I (35 million); World War II (including Holocaust and Chinese Revolutions) (62-78 million).

Sources: Christophe Z. Guilmoto, "Sex-ratio imbalance in Asia: Trends, consequences and policy responses," UNFPA; U.S. Census Bureau; Digital History; Spartacus Educational; BBC News; PBS; Telegraph, October 2008

In a handful of Asian cultures, tradition obligates brides' families to pay cash or goods to a groom's family. Although banned in India since 1961, the practice is still widespread, especially in rural areas, where a dowry can cost a family several times its annual income.

As a World Health Organization (WHO) report notes, "Female infanticide is still practiced in many parts of the world, sometimes through direct violence but also by intentional neglect or starvation. This is particularly the case where male children are considered more valuable than females. This attitude may also be manifested in traditions such as costly dowry obligations placed on the families of prospective brides." [15]

Many refer to the prejudice for males as "son preference," and it is reflected in ancient traditions. A Chinese poem from the first millennium B.C. proclaims: "When a son is born/Let him sleep on the bed/Clothe him with fine clothes/And give him jade to play . . ./When a daughter is born,/Let her sleep on the ground,/Wrap her in common wrappings,/And give broken tiles to play." [16]

In India, the well-known saying, "raising a daughter is like watering your neighbor's garden," reflects the belief that sons are typically seen as breadwinners who will eventually care for their aging parents, while daughters will leave to take care of their husband's family. An Indian proverb bluntly notes, "Eighteen goddess-like daughters are not equal to one son with a hump."

Although cultural preferences for sons go back for millennia, the number of female abortions has skyrocketed since 1980, when China instituted its one-child policy, aimed at controlling runaway population growth. That's also the year when the General Electric Co. (GE) began selling ultrasound machines in Asia, allowing a fetus' gender to be determined safely and cheaply.

Use of the machines spread rapidly in India and China. A clinic ad in India, for instance, reminds customers of the huge economic costs of bearing a female child: "Better 5,000 rupees [about $100] now than 500,000 later." [17]

Sex-selective abortions boomed as patients who wanted a son, but could never bring themselves to kill a baby daughter, chose abortion. So many females were aborted that China and India eventually made it illegal for ultrasound operators to disclose the sex of the fetus to parents. Today 36,000 registered sonography centers operate in India — and countless others illegally. [18]

Falling birth rates also contributed to the rise in sex-selective abortions. As education and income levels rise, women have fewer babies. In the late 1960s, for instance, the average Asian woman had 5.7 children, one of them likely a boy. By 2006 family size had dropped to 2.3 children, and the chances of having a boy had fallen to 24 percent. [19] In China, meanwhile, the government decreed that couples should have only one child. To get a son, couples would often sacrifice their unborn daughter.

"It's a combination of factors," says demographer Eberstadt. "There is the longstanding and widespread preference for boys, rapidly spreading prenatal sex-determination technology and declining fertility rates." *

Population-control programs funded by Western organizations, such as the World Bank and the International Planned Parenthood Federation, further contributed to the problem, claims Hvistendahl. Many of the programs, which advocated abortion and family planning, influenced strict population targets in China, India and elsewhere, she says.

Due to China and India's massive populations, their sex-ratio imbalances are affecting the global ratio of men to women. "The world is undergoing a demographic shift that is tilting our population in favor of men," Hvistendahl explains, predicting massive repercussions in the future.

"For example," she notes, "by 2030 one in five Chinese men will not be able to find a wife." Already there are reports of Chinese men having to import foreign brides, and human trafficking, kidnapping, forced marriages and prostitution are on the rise — all attributed at least in part to the gender imbalance.

As demographers, human rights experts and policy-makers confront what some have called a rising tide of gendercide, here are some of the questions they are asking:

Should China rescind its one-child policy?

When China introduced its one-child policy in September 1980, the government said it was a temporary measure to offset high unemployment and food shortages. "In 30 years, when our current extreme population growth eases, we can then adopt a different population policy," the Communist Party Central Committee said. [20]

Since then, however, the policy has become a cornerstone of China's economic and social planning, and last year, on its 30th anniversary, the government showed no signs of scrapping it.

Li Bin, head of China's National Population and Family Planning Commission, confirmed there were no immediate plans to change the policy. "Historical change doesn't come easily, and I . . . extend profound gratitude to all, to the people in particular, for their support of the national course," Li said. "So, we will stick to the family planning policy in the coming decades." [21]

According to its backers, the one-child policy has played a key role in China's stunning economic progress by:

- Reducing the nation's population growth by as much as 400 million people;
- Helping China conserve food and energy;
- Allowing children to be better educated and receive better health care; and,
- Allowing parents to save more money, which in turn has enabled banks to fund huge infrastructure expansion projects.

---

* The fertility rate is the average number of children a woman has over her lifetime.

Furthermore, say one-child proponents, a smaller population helps boost personal income, improves the environment and guarantees a better quality of life. "People who oppose the family-planning policy should consider some pressing problems we are already facing: depleting water sources, receding underground water tables, pollution of rivers and lakes, desertification, accelerating extinction of species, rising emission of greenhouse gases and fast-disappearing natural resources," said Li Xiaoping, a researcher with the Institute of Population and Labor Economy at the Chinese Academy of Social Sciences. "All these are obstacles to economic development and environmental protection. The government is already finding it difficult to control the birthrate because of the huge population. Even if we follow the existing family-planning policy, the population will grow by more than 10 million a year." [22]

But critics say it is time to abolish the policy. Many, especially anti-abortion advocates, claim it violates reproductive rights. Reggie Littlejohn, an American attorney who founded Women's Rights Without Frontiers, an international coalition that opposes forced abortion and sexual slavery in China, says, "For the Chinese Communist Party to function as 'womb police,' wielding the very power of life and death over the people of China is a terrible violation of both women's rights and human rights. After 30 years of such a legacy, it is time for the international community to pressure China to revoke the one-child policy."

When U.S. Vice President Joe Biden visited China recently and told his hosts, "Your policy has been one which I fully understand — I'm not second-guessing — of one child per family," he was immediately attacked for appearing to sanction the policy. House Speaker John Boehner, R-Pa., like Biden, a Roman Catholic, echoed many Western critics of the policy: "No government on Earth has the authority to place quotas on the value of innocent human life, or treat life as an economic commodity that can be regulated and taken away on a whim by the state." [23]

Critics say the policy not only has resulted in the deaths of millions of girls but also has skewed China's sex ratios to the point that today millions of Chinese men cannot find wives. "The one-child limit is too extreme," said Ye Tingfang, a historian at the Chinese Academy of Social Sciences. "It violates nature's law, and in the long run will lead to Mother Nature's revenge." [24]

Other observers note that the drop in China's fertility rate, from 5.8 children per woman, on average, in 1950 to an estimated 1.4 children today, reduces the need for the policy. [25] "The one-child policy was unnecessary," says Steven W. Mosher, president of the Population Research Institute, a self-described "pro-life" group in Virginia. "Birth rates were already falling in the 1970s and would probably have continued to fall to today's rates because of China's urbanization, industrialization and rising levels of education."

Many observers say Mother Nature's "revenge" already can be seen in the rapid aging of China's population, the result of the one-child policy, lower fertility rates and increased longevity. Eventually, experts say, each child from a one-child family will have to care for two parents and four grandparents. By 2040, according to some estimates, China will have 400 million people over 65, a quarter of the population. Chinese companies are already reporting shortages of young workers. [26]

As *The Economist* noted recently, 13.3 percent of China's population is over age 60 — up from 10.3 percent in 2000, while those under 14 dropped from 23 percent of the population to 17 percent. "A continuation of these trends will place ever-greater burdens on the working young who must support their elderly kin, as well as on government-run pension and health-care systems," the magazine said. "China's great 'demographic dividend' (a rising share of working-age adults) is almost over." [27]

Seniors' pensions and health-care expenses will become a "very severe burden" on China's budget, said Chen Wei, a professor at Renmin University's Population and Development Research Institute. And there will be fewer working-age citizens to support this aging population, he added. [28]

Despite the mounting criticism of its one-child policy and the resultant jump in sex-selective abortions, China shows little evidence that it plans to abolish the policy. "The momentum of fast growth in our population has been controlled effectively, thanks to the family-planning policy," explained Ma Jiantang, head of the National Bureau of Statistics. [29] China has, however, attempted to stave off female abortions by allowing rural families, where son preference is strongest, to have a second child if their first is a girl.

Some experts say the jump in sex-selective abortions and skewed sex ratios should convince the government

Banned Dowry System Perpetuates Infanticide

Families kill or abort baby girls to avoid — or get — the illegal payments.

In Sagarpur, a lower-middle-class area in New Delhi, Kulwant wept as she described how her husband and his family — desperate for a male heir — beat her regularly and forced her to have abortions until she bore a son.

After she had three daughters, she said, the family became enraged and once even tried to set her on fire. "They were angry. They didn't want girls in the family," she recalled. "They wanted boys so they could get fat dowries" from the brides' families. [1]

The mother-in-law told Kulwant that her husband would divorce her "if I didn't bear a son," Kulwant recalled. Whenever she got pregnant again, the family forced her to have a sonogram to determine the sex of the fetus and then ordered her to abort female fetuses three times until she finally produced a boy.

Such stories are commonplace in India and other countries where a preference for sons is driven in part by the dowry system, a traditional marriage custom that India outlawed 40 years ago. Dowries — once observed in much of the ancient world — have disappeared in most cultures but still hold sway in India, Pakistan, Bangladesh and parts of China.

Dowries typically are cash or goods, such as expensive television sets and appliances, that a bride's family must give the groom and his family at marriage. The amount demanded today often can be the equivalent of several years of income, which can ruin a poor family. Moreover, dissatisfaction with the amount of the dowry often results in violence, such as "bride burning," torture, murder or the forced suicide of a young wife. Dowry-related crimes are difficult to prosecute, however, because they often are disguised as accidents or suicides.

To avoid having to pay a dowry, many poor parents who cannot afford prenatal gender testing or an abortion will kill their infant girls instead. In Pakistan last year, about 100 newborns a month (most of them girls) were killed and left in garbage dumps or by the side of the road.

Families also are driven to abort or kill baby girls by the Asian tradition that a son supports his elderly parents while married daughters care for their husbands and aging inlaws. Sons "are the equivalent of an Indian 401(k) retirement plan," writes Prabhat Jha, director of the Centre for Global Health Research at the University of Toronto.

"The parents feel that the boy is a help for the future, where the girls are a liability," said Kailash Satyarethi, a

to change its stance. Mu Guangzong, a professor of demography at Beijing University, noted, "Having a balanced population is more important and challenging than curbing the size of the population." [30]

Activist Littlejohn is more critical: "China's one-child policy causes more violence against women and girls than any other policy on Earth, than any official policy in the history of the world."

Should abortions be more restricted, in order to prevent sex-selective abortions?

The shocking reality of Asia's 160 million "missing girls" has intensified the debate over the morality of — and justification for — abortion.

Abortion foes — especially those in the West — call the region's hundreds of thousands of sex-selective abortions "murders," and describe the aborted female fetuses as "victims." For abortion opponents, voluntarily terminating a pregnancy is not a right, and is never acceptable. *New York Times* columnist Ross Douthat says the debate over sex-selective abortions should not be about the morality of sex selection but about abortion itself: "The tragedy of the 160 million missing girls isn't that they're 'missing,' " he wrote recently. "The tragedy is that they're dead." [31]

But women's-rights activists argue that banning or drastically restricting abortions takes away a woman's right to choose whether to have an abortion. Legal abortions are founder of the India-based human rights group Global March. "If we spend money on her, then we have to spend money on her marriage, dowry probably, and then if something goes wrong, then we are always sufferers. So better that that girl is not born." [2]

Dowry abuses led to the 1961 Dowry Prohibition Act, which prohibits the request, payment or acceptance of a dowry. Violations are punishable by fines and up to six months in jail, but enforcement is lax. More than 8,300 dowry-related deaths were reported in India in 2009; only one-third resulted in convictions. [3]

Ironically, with up to 160 million Asian women "missing" due to sex-selective abortions and the murder of newborn girls, a critical shortage of marriageable women has developed in countries such as India and China. As a result, experts say, some families will be able to demand a higher "bride price" for their daughters — money or goods paid by a groom's family to a bride's family. Much less common than dowries, the paying of a bride price is another ancient marriage tradition still practiced in some rural areas of India, China, Thailand and parts of Africa.

Already, many men in India who cannot afford a bride price are becoming resigned to the fact that they may never marry. Babulal Yadav, a 50-year-old farmer from the Indian state of Haryana, where men far outnumber women, said, "I'm used to being alone. But I want a son." [4]

— *Robert Kiener*

New appliances — part of her initial dowry — surround Indian bride Nisha Sharma as she displays her wedding invitation. Sharma balked when her fiancée's family made additional dowry demands. She called off their wedding just hours before the ceremony in New Delhi. Fear of someday facing ruinous dowry demands prompts many Indian parents to abort female fetuses.

[1]Geeta Pandey, "India's unwanted girls," BBC, May 22, 2011, www.bbc.co.uk/news/world-south-asia-13264301.

[2]Corey Flintoff, "Selective abortions blamed for girl shortage in India," NPR, April 14, 2011, www.npr.org/2011/04/14/135417647/in-india-number-of-female-children-drops.

[3]See National Crimes Records Bureau, "Figures at a Glance, 2009," http://ncrb.nic.in/CII%202009/cii-2009/figure%20at%20a%20glance.pdf.

[4]"Haryana's lonely bachelors," *The Economist*, March 4, 2010, www.economist.com/node/15604465.

relatively new to Asia, they note, and outlawing them would curtail women's rights. "No one in Asia who is combating sex selection is arguing that the appropriate reaction to decades of violating women's rights is to swing in the opposite direction and violate them further," says author Hvistendahl. "Just as a woman should not be forced to abort a wanted pregnancy, she should not be forced to carry an unwanted pregnancy to term."

And prohibiting all abortions will force women to "seek out back-street, unsafe abortionists," warns University of Toronto professor of public health Prabhat Jha, founder of Toronto's Centre for Global Health Research.

Carmen Barroso, regional director of the International Planned Parenthood Federation (IPPF), noted, "Sex-selective abortion will not be eliminated by restricting access to abortion. In fact, it will only increase the already high risk of death or injury due to unsafe abortion. The solution to skewed sex ratios is simple: invest in the health and rights of girls and women." [32]

New Delhi obstetrician Puneet Bedi believes India should do more to clamp down on the illegal sex-selective abortions. "There are medical justifications for some abortions, and I am not in favor of banning those," he explains. "But there is no excuse for a sex-selective abortion, which is simply female feticide. You can choose whether you want to be a parent, but once you do, you cannot choose whether it's a boy or a girl, tall or short, black or white."

Asian Countries Have Most Males

Seven of the 10 countries with the world's highest male-to-female birth ratios are in Asia, led by China with 113 males born for every 100 females (a sex ratio of 1.13).

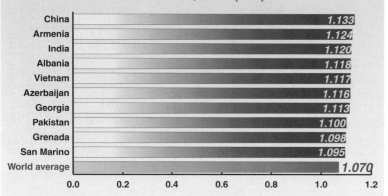

Countries with Highest Male-to-Female Birth Ratios, 2011 (est.)

China	1.133
Armenia	1.124
India	1.120
Albania	1.118
Vietnam	1.117
Azerbaijan	1.116
Georgia	1.113
Pakistan	1.100
Grenada	1.098
San Marino	1.095
World average	1.070

Source: "Sex Ratio," *The World Factbook,* Central Intelligence Agency, 2011, https://www.cia.gov/library/publications/the-world-factbook/fields/2018.html; "Pakistan Demographic Survey," 2007

Bedi explains that in India there is often little guilt connected with having an abortion. "We call them 'coffee-bar abortions,' " he explained, "She comes in for an abortion and relaxes at a coffee bar afterwards. By the early 1990s, no one who didn't want a daughter needed to have one." [33]

For anti-abortionists the argument against sex-selective abortion is clear-cut: Abortion is wrong under any circumstances. Period.

But organizations that support abortion or family planning face a tricky dilemma: After years of campaigning for a woman's right to decide whether to keep or end a pregnancy, it's hard now to attack women for abusing that right. Thus, many are reluctant to condemn sex-selective abortions outright. The U.S.-based National Organization for Women (NOW), for example, has been largely silent on the issue. And its reticence leads many to believe NOW is reluctant to be seen opposing an indefensible type of abortion.

"Where are the feminists on the issue of sex-selective abortion?" asks Mosher, of the Population Research Institute. "I challenge the National Organization for Women and other feminist groups to join us in the battle to ban this terrible form of sex discrimination that is killing so many unborn baby girls. Their continued silence only facilitates the killing."

When asked to explain the organization's position on sex-selective abortion, NOW president Terry O'Neill never replied to *CQ Global Researcher*'s repeated requests for an interview.

Some abortion advocates claim that anti-abortionists are using the sex-selective abortion issue to advance their own agenda. "Anti-abortion groups and pundits have proven all too eager to take on the issue, though they seem far more interested in driving home restrictions on abortion than they do in increasing the number of women in the world and protecting the rights of women at risk," writes Hvistendahl. [34]

With many countries already banning sex-selective abortions, few activists think they can get nations to ban or further restrict abortions. Activists do, however, hope they can get governments to enforce existing laws banning sex-selective abortions and abuses of ultrasound.

Often criticized by both pro- and anti-abortionists, international agencies such as the United Nations Population Fund (UNFPA) must walk a fine line when addressing the issue of abortions. "These are human rights issues," explains Aminata Toure, chief of the UNFPA's Gender, Human Rights and Culture Branch. "We are not about to go into a country and begin dictating on such sensitive issues. Our main aim is to solve this problem by raising the status of women."

In June, the UNFPA and four other U.N. agencies issued a joint statement on sex-selective abortions for the first time. Although it referred to "gender-biased sex selection" rather than using the term "sex-selective abortion," the statement warned against banning abortions outright.

"States have an obligation to ensure that these injustices are addressed without exposing women to the risk of death or serious injury by denying them access to needed services, such as safe abortion to the full extent of the law,"

> *"There is no excuse for a sex-selective abortion, which is simply female feticide. You can choose whether you want to be a parent, but once you do, you cannot choose whether it's a boy or a girl, tall or short, black or white."*
>
> **— Puneet Bedi, New Delhi obstetrician**

Women's-rights activists in New Delhi in May 2006 protest the continued use of sex-selective abortion to eliminate female fetuses. Because of a cultural preference for sons, pregnant women in India are often coerced by their husband's families to abort a fetus if it is determined to be a girl, even though it is illegal to perform an ultrasound or an abortion for gender-preference purposes.

the statement said. "Such an outcome would represent a further violation of their rights to life and health as guaranteed in international human rights treaties and committed to in international development agreements." [35]

Eberstadt, the American Enterprise Institute demographer, has called for a global war on abortion. "To eradicate sex-selective abortion, we must convince the world that destroying female fetuses is horribly wrong," he wrote. "We need something akin to the abolitionist movement: a moral campaign waged globally, with the victories declared one conscience at a time." [36]

Did the West cause Asia's epidemic of sex-selective abortions?

When journalist Hvistendahl began researching sex-selective abortion several years ago, she didn't know it may have been exported to developing countries by Western nations such as the United States.

"It wasn't until I went to India and met activists who told me to investigate the history of American population organizations that I found the link," she explains.

Concern about uncontrolled global population growth was intense in the West during the 1960s, with many scholars predicting an imminent population explosion, including Stanford University professor of population studies Paul Ehrlich, author of the 1968 bestseller *The Population Bomb.*

If "a simple method could be found to guarantee that first-born children were males, then population-control problems in many areas would be somewhat eased," he wrote, pointing out that in many countries "couples with only female children keep trying, in hope of a son." [37]

Ehrlich was not the only one to suggest that approach to curbing population growth. "Before long, sex selection emerged as a favored solution for the world's growing population, especially in the developing world," says Hvistendahl.

Birth-control programs, some advocating abortions, were supported by a wide range of organizations. Indeed, even President Nixon's Secretary of State, Henry Kissinger, in 1974 signed a classified U.S. government memo that stated, "Abortion is vital to the solution" of world population growth." [38]

Efforts to study sex-selective abortion were extensive. For example:

- In 1975, with funding from the Rockefeller Foundation, doctors at a government hospital in India began sex-selective abortion trials, offering free amniocentesis* for poor women and then helping them, if they so chose, to abort the fetus on the basis of sex. An estimated 1,000 women carrying female fetuses underwent abortions. The doctors touted the study as a population-control experiment, and sex-selective abortion spread throughout India. [39]

---

* Amniocentesis involves removing some amniotic fluid from a pregnant woman's uterus to diagnose generic disorders but was also used to determine the sex of the fetus before sonograms were introduced.

India's Gender Gap Is Growing

Gender-selective abortions have spread across India, resulting in up to 12 million fewer Indian girls being born over the past 30 years, according to a new study. Boys are more valued in Indian culture, and inexpensive sonograms are now widely available, making sex-selective abortions popular. Over the last decade, the percentage of the Indian population living in states with a very low ratio of fewer than 915 girls per 1,000 boys has more than doubled (bar graph).

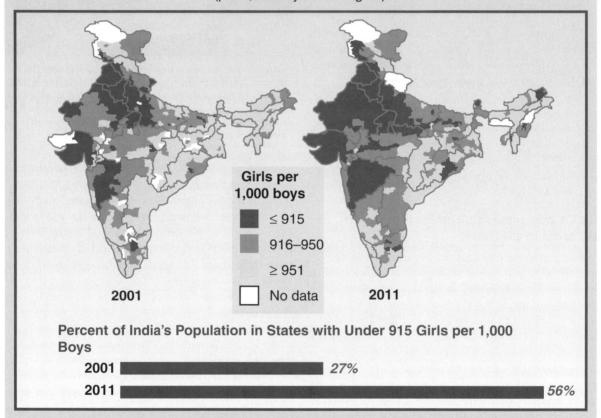

Ratio of Girls to Boys, 2001 and 2011
(per 1,000 boys under age 6)

Girls per 1,000 boys

- ≤ 915
- 916–950
- ≥ 951
- No data

2001   2011

Percent of India's Population in States with Under 915 Girls per 1,000 Boys

2001 — 27%
2011 — 56%

Source: "Selective Abortion May Account for Up to 12 Million Missing Girls in India," Centre for Global Health Research, University of Toronto, May 24, 2011,www.cghr.org/index.php/2011/05/selective-abortion-may-account -for -up-to-12-million-missing-girls-in-india-new-lancet-study/. Map by Lewis Agrell

- In 1976 International Planned Parenthood Federation (IPPF) medical director Malcolm Potts wrote, "Early abortion is safe, effective, cheap and potentially the easiest method to administer." [40] Others supported sex selection in academic papers and government-sponsored seminars.

- Although many reports described coerced and sex-selective abortions in China after the one-child policy was instituted, agencies such as the UNPFA and the IPPF nonetheless increased funding of China's population-control program. "For example, notes Hvistendahl, "as late as

1983 IPPF requested increased funding for China."

- Also in 1983, the UNFPA praised one-child policies, noting, "We must record our deep appreciation for the way in which their governments have marshaled the resources necessary to implement population policies on a massive scale." [41]

Bedi, the Delhi-based obstetrician and anti-sex-selection activist, says that both before and after abortion was legalized in India in 1971, "huge amounts of Western money flowed into this country to fund population control. Many of India's elite doctors were trained by the West, and they were encouraged to see sex-selective abortion . . . as a medical procedure."

Early sex-selective abortions in India were performed openly at government hospitals. [42] "The West had a lot of influence in making abortion acceptable here," says Bedi. "Eventually, with the coming of amniocentesis and the ready availability of ultrasound technology, sex-selective abortions proliferated. They were actually marketed here in India." Bedi now describes ultrasound machines as "weapons of mass destruction."

Others strongly disagree that the West is responsible "for the proliferation of ultrasound machines and their use in India and China," explains the University of Toronto's Jha. "They are a medical innovation and would have been adopted regardless of who was funding or promoting them. This is simply a worldwide diffusion of technology that was inevitable."

Likewise, evolutionary biologist Richard Dawkins at Oxford University said, "The ability to know the sex of a fetus is an inevitable byproduct of medical benefits such as amniocentesis, ultrasound scanning and other techniques for the diagnosis of serious problems. Should scientists have refrained from developing useful techniques, for fear of how they might be misused by others?" [43]

Others argue that it's "demeaning" to think that the West could have so much influence abroad on such a sensitive issue. "Do you really believe that China or India could be that influenced by the United States?" asks Paris-based demographer Guilmoto. "It's ridiculous."

China was essentially closed to the West at the time, and there is little evidence that it was influenced by the West, said a reviewer of Hvistendahl's book: "China's coercive population-control policies were developed in the late 1970s, at the end of the Cultural Revolution and the early reforms of Deng Xiaoping. This was a period of isolation and modest opening-up, when China was not much interested in Western advice." [44]

Others note that while the West may have influenced and funded earlier population programs in developing countries, sex-selective abortions have steadily increased without Western support. "The American establishment helped create the problem, but now it's metastasizing on its own," explained *New York Times* columnist Douthat. "The population-control movement is a shadow of its former self, yet sex selection has spread inexorably with access to abortion." [45]

Stung by criticism of its earlier role in funding such programs, the United Nations Population Fund no longer supports population-control programs. But critics like Hvistendahl and others believe the UNFPA is not doing enough to directly combat sex selection, partly because it is afraid of getting tangled up in abortion politics. "The agency's legacy in the developing world continues to haunt its leaders, to the detriment of women worldwide," she says. "It is reluctant to address sex selection directly."

The UNFPA's Toure disagrees, saying the agency "has been raising alarms about this odious practice for more than 20 years. We called attention to China's skewed sex ratio when it first became apparent in the 1990 census, and our advocacy helped persuade the government to outlaw sex selection in 1994." Since then, the fund has sponsored forums and studies on the causes and likely consequences of sex selection in China and elsewhere. "UNFPA has been a prominent leader in advocating against sex selection and other practices that discriminate against girls and women," she adds.

Rather than the West and other outside influences, many believe the true blame lies with "the cultural and religious practices that despise and discriminate against women in the first place," said biologist Dawkins. [46]

BACKGROUND

An Ancient Practice

Anthropologists believe that infanticide has been practiced throughout history. Some historians claim that infanticide rates ranged from 15-50 percent of children born during prehistoric times. [47] Finding enough food was a persistent problem, and killing offspring was seen as a way to prevent starvation.

As famed British biologist Charles Darwin noted in his landmark 1871 book, *The Descent of Man*, "[Thomas] Malthus has discussed these several checks, but he does not lay stress enough on what is probably the most important of all, namely infanticide, especially of female infants, and the habit of procuring abortion. These practices now prevail in many quarters of the world; and infanticide seems formerly to have prevailed." [48]

Prejudice against daughters — or a preference for sons — was another common reason for female infanticide. In ancient Greece and Rome, infants who were handicapped or the "wrong" sex sometimes were left "exposed" after birth — typically placed inside a pot left beside a road. A letter written by a first century B.C. Roman husband to his pregnant wife warned, "if it is a male, let it live; if it is a female, expose it." [49]

Because girls required expensive dowries in Roman times, they were considered of less value than males. In addition, sons could become wage earners and contribute to the family's upkeep. A Roman maxim observed, "Everyone raises a son, including a poor man, but even a rich man will abandon a daughter." [50]

In male-dominated ancient Persia, females also were seen as an economic burden to a family with limited resources, and infant girls were sometimes buried alive immediately after birth. [51]

In the seventh century A.D., the Muslim Prophet Muhammad expressly forbade female infanticide. According to the Koran, "buried girls" will rise out of their graves on Judgment Day and ask why they were killed. [52] "And do not kill your children for fear of poverty," the Koran also warns, "we give them sustenance and yourselves too; surely to kill them is a great wrong." [53]

In China, instances of female infanticide are recorded as early as the sixth century B.C. Because girls would leave home when married, they were seen an "expendable luxury," historian Stephen Milner wrote. According to an ancient Chinese proverb: "As to children, a father and mother when they produce a boy congratulate one another, but when they produce a girl, they put it to death." [54]

Female infanticide continued throughout Chinese history. In the late 19th century, a missionary in China interviewed 40 women, who reported having given birth to 183 sons and 175 daughters. But only 53 of the girls had survived to age 10, compared with 126 of the boys. The missionary noted, "by their own account the women had destroyed 78 of their daughters." [55]

According to American historian and anthropologist Sarah Blaffer Hrdy, "In large cities like Beijing, wagons made scheduled rounds in the early morning to collect corpses of unwanted daughters that had been soundlessly drowned in a bucket of milk while the mother looked away." One mother, Hrdy writes, reported killing 11 newborn daughters. [56]

While girls are much less valued than boys in India today, that was not always the case. From 1500 to 800 B.C., Indian women enjoyed equal status with men. They could become priests, had an equal say in choosing a partner and were heads of their households. Under Mogul rule, however, restrictions were placed on women, and their social status declined. By 600 B.C. women had become subservient to men, were largely confined to their homes and could marry only if their families paid big dowries. [57]

"It is clear that the onerous costs involved with the raising of a girl, and eventually providing her an appropriate marriage dowry, was the single most important factor in allowing social acceptance of the murder at birth in India," explained Milner. [58]

The cultural preference for sons, who traditionally take care of their elderly parents, also helped lower the status of women. The murder of baby girls is so common in India that it has its own term: *kuzhippa*, or "baby intended for the burial pit." [59]

Nineteenth-century British colonial overlords in India were so shocked by female infanticide that they tried to quantify the problem. After a special 1868 census showed that only 22 percent of the people in communities suspected of committing infanticide were females, they passed the Female Infanticide Act, which punished infanticide with a jail term of up to six months and allowed undernourished girls to be taken from their parents. [60]

By the 1901 census the situation had improved markedly to an overall male-to-female sex ratio of 102.9 boys per 100 females. Within a century, however, India's sex ratio imbalance would climb to alarming heights.

CHRONOLOGY

1950s-1970s *Abortion as population-control method spreads throughout Asia, with help of Western funding.*

1953 Abortion becomes widely accessible in China.

1960 Vietnam legalizes abortion.

1962 Concerns about burgeoning population prompts South Korea to institute a national family-planning campaign.

1968 Stanford professor of population studies Paul Ehrlich warns in *The Population Bomb* of impending disaster if world population growth continues unchecked.

1971 Law legalizing abortion goes into effect in India.

1973 South Korea legalizes abortions.

1975 Rockefeller Foundation funds sex-selective abortion trials at a government hospital in India.

1976 Alarmed at India's growing population, Prime Minister Indira Gandhi establishes a program that sterilizes more than 7.8 million men between in 1976-1977.

1980s-1990s *China's one-child policy and drooping fertility rates lead to skewed birth ratios.*

1980 China's "temporary" one-child policy begins nationwide.

1987 Bombay (now Mmbai) has 248 ultrasound clinics offering sex-determination services, up from fewer than 10 in 1982.

1983 U.N. Fund for Population Activities — predecessor of today's U.N. Population Fund (UNFPA) — praises China's one-child policy.

1985-1989 China allows couples in rural areas and those with daughters to have a second child.

1987 South Korea bans prenatal sex determination. . . . Indian society of obstetricians and gynecologists finds that out of 8,000 abortions, 7,999 occurred after tests showed a female fetus.

1989 China bans prenatal sex determination and pre-implantation sex selection.

1990 *New York Review of Books* publishes Nobel-Prize winning economist Amartya Sen's essay on Asia's 100 million missing females. . . . More than 116 Korean boys are born for every 100 girls.

1991 UNFPA raises the issue of China's gender imbalance — the first international agency to speak out about the problem.

1994 China, with more than 100,000 ultrasound machines, bans sex-selective abortion. . . . India bans prenatal sex determination. . . . South Korea raises penalties for physicians who provide prenatal sex determination.

1995 U.N.'s Fourth World Conference on Women, in Beijing, classifies female infanticide and prenatal sex selection as acts of violence against women.

2000s-Present *As sex ratios at birth become increasingly skewed, nations try to alter the gender misbalance.*

2002 Nepal legalizes abortion but bans prenatal sex determination and sex-selective abortion. . . . China's census indicates the sex ratio of newborns is 116 boys to 100 girls.

2003 Vietnam bans sex-selective abortion and all forms of sex determination.

2006 The average number of children an Asian woman will have (her fertility rate) drops to 2.3 children — from 5.7 in the late 1960s.

2010 India's fertility rate drops to 2.7 children per woman — from 5.7 in the mid-1960s.

2011 Publication of book *Unnatural Selection* re-ignites the global debate on sex-selective abortion when it claims that 160 million females are "missing" from Asia. . . . China announces a crackdown on anyone using ultrasound to determine fetal gender or performing sex-selective abortions.

How South Korea Reversed Anti-Female Bias

Within a generation, women's roles changed dramatically.

In South Korea, long one of Asia's most patriarchal societies, having a son was the dream of almost every young couple. "One son is worth 10 daughters," goes a once-common saying.

So when amniocentesis and ultrasound enabled couples to discover the sex of their unborn child, more and more couples began aborting female fetuses. By 1990, so many were opting for sex-selective abortions that more than 117 Korean boys were born for every 100 girls — one of the highest birth sex ratios in the world. [1]

The heavily skewed ratios prompted the government to ban prenatal gender selection. To underscore its concern, officials launched media campaigns designed to raise the status of females. For instance, the Love Your Daughter campaign featured the slogan, "One daughter raised well is worth 10 sons!" [2]

Because of the country's closely controlled health system, the ban on sex selection and other factors, the sex ratio gradually improved. By 2007 it had dropped to a much less alarming 107. [3] Today it is around 106. [4]

"Enforcement and media campaigns were only part of the solution," says Paris-based demographer Christophe Guilmoto. "You also have to take into account South Korea's changing society." Two decades of dramatic economic growth had transformed the nation's agrarian society into an industrialized one, he points out, resulting in fundamental changes.

Rapid urbanization and a growing desire for smaller families also helped lower the ratio. Strengthening of the nation's social safety net also helped to undercut the necessity of having a male child who, tradition dictated, would support his parents in their old age. Parents also began making and saving more money, having to depend less on their grown children for economic support in their later years.

"The changing role of women has also made a major difference," explains Guilmoto. "They are working more and in better jobs, have more rights and have become more valuable. Their status and respect have vastly improved." In 1981 fewer than one in 10 Korean women attended college, now it's more than six out of 10. [5]

A 2010 survey reflects the startling change in preference for sons. Thirty-eight percent of expectant Korean mothers wanted a daughter, compared to 31 percent who wanted a

Population Worries

In the middle of the 20th century, when Mao Zedong's Communist Party took control, China boasted that its half-billion population — more than triple the size of the United States – gave China an economic advantage over other countries.

"Even if China's population multiplies many times, she is fully capable of finding a solution; the solution is production. . . . Of all things in the world, people are the most precious," said Mao, outlawing birth control and contraceptives. [61]

China's population exploded, and birth control was introduced in 1958, only to be banned under the ruinous Great Leap Forward, Mao's attempt to modernize the economy. By 1962 the population had outstripped

food supply, and a massive famine claimed more than 30 million lives. [62] A propaganda campaign and a government-sponsored population-control program saw China's population drop by half between 1970 and 1976. Overpopulation was still a concern, however, and the one-child policy was introduced in 1980.

Meanwhile, birth control was introduced in Indian hospitals in the 1950s, but the government did not institute family-planning programs until the late 1960s. In 1971, the Medical Termination of Pregnancy Act legalized abortion for several reasons, including "the failure of a contraceptive device." [63]

By 1977 the population had reached 620 million, and Prime Minister Indira Gandhi pushed through a harsh program that called for mandatory sterilization of son. Among fathers-to-be, 37 percent wanted a daughter and 29 percent a son. [6]

The diminished concern about sex-selective abortions led the government recently to remove the ban on learning the gender of a fetus.

But Korea's population problems are not completely solved. There are 190,000 more men ages 29-33 than women ages 26-30. By 2013 male 29-33-year-olds in Korea will outnumber women by 360,000. [7] A large group of marriageable Korean men will soon find it difficult to find a wife. And because the nation's birth rate has dropped dramatically, the government is urging couples to have children — boys or girls.

Newspaper executive Park He-ran, now in her 60s, remembers how in an earlier era, when other women learned that she had three sons and no daughters, they would enviously ask what her secret was. Today, "They say they are sorry for my misfortune," she said. "Within a generation I have turned from the luckiest woman possible to a pitiful mother." [8]

— *Robert Kiener*

Daughters are now treasured in South Korea thanks to a massive government campaign to reverse patriarchal, anti-female attitudes that by 1990 had severely skewed gender ratios. Above, a girl plays happily in a fountain in downtown Seoul on June 20, 2011.

AFP/Getty Images/Jung Yeon-Je

[1]"Gendercide: the worldwide war on baby girls," *The Economist*, March 4, 2010, www.economist.com/node/15636231.

[2]Choe Sang-hun, "Where boys were king, a shift toward baby girls," *The New York Times*, Dec. 23, 2007, www.nytimes.com/2007/12/23/world/asia/23skorea.html?pagewanted=all.

[3]*Ibid.*

[4]CIA *World Factbook.*

[5]Sang-hun, *op. cit.*

[6]Lim Yung Suk, "S Korean parents now prefer daughters over sons," *Channel News Asia*, Feb. 18, 2010, www.channelnewsasia.com/stories/eastasia/view/1038190/1/.html.

[7]"The gender ratio gets worse for marriageable Korean men," *Chosun Ilbo*, June 14, 2011, http://english.chosun.com/site/data/html_dir/2011/06/14/2011061400321.html.

[8]Sang-hun, *op. cit.*

males who had already fathered two children. Between April 1976 and January 1977, more than 7.8 million sterilizations were performed. The government untruthfully claimed the sterilizations were voluntarily accepted, and the controversial program contributed to Gandhi's failed re-election bid. [64]

In 1962, South Korea, then one of the world's poorest countries, instituted a family-planning campaign after the government of Park Chung-hee became concerned that the nation's rapidly growing population was undermining economic growth. The fertility rate fell from 6.1 in 1960 to 4.2 in 1970. [65]

With Asia adding millions of citizens to the global population, Western observers were growing increasingly concerned. Ehrlich's 1968 book painted a grim picture:

"The battle to feed all of humanity is over," he wrote. "In the 1970s hundreds of millions of people will starve to death in spite of any crash programs embarked upon now. At this late date, nothing can prevent a substantial increase in the world death rate." [66]

During the 1960s and '70s the Rockefeller Foundation, World Bank and other organizations widely promoted — and funded — birth control and population-control programs in the developing world. The efforts led to claims the programs reflected the West's view that Asia's growing population posed a threat.

"Many in Washington were more concerned with the effect population growth was having on geopolitics as opposed to the environment or the economy,"

East Asia Has Highest Gender Imbalance

The East Asia-Pacific region has the world's highest number of baby boys — 113 per 100 girls — and South Asia has the second-highest number. Sub-Saharan Africa has the lowest number of boys born per 100 females. Blamed largely on the use of sex-selective abortion, high gender disparities at birth in China and India — which together account for more than a third of the world's population — have significantly skewed the average global birth ratio, which is now 1.07.

Male Births by Region, 2010
(per 100 females)

East Asia and Pacific	113
Excluding China	105
South Asia	107
Excluding India	105
Central, Eastern Europe and former Soviet republics	106
Middle East and North Africa	105
Latin America and Caribbean	105
Sub-Saharan Africa	104
Developing countries (including India and China)	107
World	**107**

Source: "Boys and Girls in the Life Cycle," UNICEF, 2011, www.childinfo.org /files/Gender_lo_res.pdf

wrote journalist Hvistendahl. They believed that larger populations resulted in more poverty, which was a fertile ground for the spread of communism.

The introduction of amniocentesis to Asia in the mid-1970s gave prospective parents an expensive and risky way to discover the sex of their coming children. By the early 1980s, the procedure was so common in India that it was known as the "sex test." [67] In fact, in a study of 11,000 couples who had undergone the procedure, nearly all admitted to using it "for the purpose of aborting unborn female fetuses." [68]

The arrival of far less expensive ultrasound technology in the 1980s brought the sex test to the masses. In the late 1970s China imported ultrasound machines from the United States, most made by General Electric, and in the 1980s began manufacturing them; by 1994 the country had more than 100,000. [69] The machines also proliferated in South Korea, Singapore, Taiwan and especially in India, where they appeared in the remotest villages.

Clinics offering ultrasound services popped up throughout India. In Bombay alone, the number

jumped from less than 10 in 1982 to 248 by 1987. [70]

There are between 70,000 and 100,000 ultrasound machines in India today, but fewer than half are registered with the government, even though it is required by the 1994 Prenatal Diagnostics Technique Act.

The widespread availability of ultrasound testing had a dramatic effect on sex-selective abortions. According to a 1987 study of 8,000 abortions, 7,999 occurred after tests showed a female fetus. In another large study, 97 percent of the fetuses were female; the rest were of undetermined sex. [71]

"Momentous Problem"

After demographers, other experts and journalists began publicizing the fate of Asia's "missing" girls," governments began to take action. Many cited Nobel-Prize winning Indian economist Amartya Sen's 1990 essay in the *New York Review of Books*, "More Than 100 Million Women Are Missing," as a wakeup call. Missing females, Sen wrote, are "clearly one of the more momentous, and neglected, problems facing the world today." [72]

By the late 1980s governments realized that sex-selective abortions were producing skewed sex ratios and instituted strict controls on prenatal sex selection. South Korea led the way in 1987, followed by China in 1989, India in 1994, Nepal in 2002 and Vietnam in 2003. Restrictions included limiting ultrasound use to authorized clinics and making it illegal to reveal the sex of the fetus (except on medical grounds). [73] Sex-selective abortions were also banned in most countries. At the Fourth World Conference on Women in Beijing in 1995, the United Nations listed both female infanticide and prenatal gender selection as acts of violence against women.

Despite the bans, ultrasound usage has steadily increased and, based on sex ratios, so have sex-selective abortions. Enforcement has been spotty, and there have been few prosecutions. It is hard to prove that an ultrasound operator has revealed the sex of a fetus; they may use verbal clues or nonverbal gestures (such as a "thumbs up" if it is a boy). And while there are frequent government crackdowns, few violators are caught.

Proving an abortion is sex selective is equally difficult. Because ultrasounds and abortions are often done at separate facilities, it is hard to prove a link.

Few believe laws or prohibitions will do much to change the skewed sex ratios that have resulted from the widespread killing of unborn females unless societies stop valuing boys over girls. "Laws are good because they may act as a deterrent," but sex-selective abortions continue underground because "people find more devious ways," said Ravinder Kaur, a professor of sociology at New Delhi's Indian Institute of Technology. [74]

CURRENT SITUATION

"Bare Branches"

The alarming shortage of females caused by sex-selective abortions and female infanticide is changing the fabric of Asian societies.

In Banzhushan, a village perched high in the mountains of China's central Hunan Province, 35-year old farmer Duan Biansheng confesses sadly that his chance of finding a wife is "almost zero." Like tens of millions of other single men in China, known as "bare branches," he is the victim of the nation's skewed sex ratios.

Male residents of dirt-poor rural settlements like Banzhushan — dubbed "bachelor villages" — have annual incomes of less than $100, and the very few marriageable women born in the village usually are lured away by more prosperous suitors from other villages. [75] Duan's problem is common throughout China, and it will get worse over time. During the next two decades, according to Li Shuzhuo, a professor of population studies at Xi'an Jiaotong University in Xian, 30-50 million men will be unable to find wives. [76]

India is also suffering from a shortage of women. In the remote farming village of Siyani in Gujarat, Girish Rathod has been looking for a wife for 15 years — since he was 20. "I am not alone in my search for a wife," he said. "Seventy percent of men in this village are unmarried because we have very few women to choose from." [77]

The shortage of women has begun changing Indian society in alarming ways. Brides' families often ask for

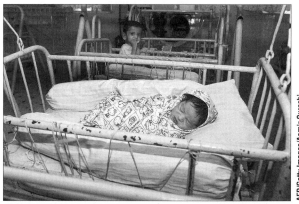

An abandoned baby girl sleeps safely at the Edhi Foundation, Pakistan's largest charity. To battle the nation's rampant gendercide, the foundation provides rows of empty cradles outside its offices, with signs urging: "Do not murder. Lay them here." In 2010, about 100 newborns — mostly girls — were killed and dumped in Pakistan each month, up 20 percent over 2009.

AFP/Getty Images/Aamir Qureshi

exorbitant "bride prices" – or money from a prospective groom — a reversal of the traditional dowry system.

There are also reports of instances in which brides abscond with bride prices worth several years' of income. "This women shortage is destabilizing our community," said Mohabbat Singh Chauhan, a community leader in Siyani. [78]

If the present birth ratio continues, by 2021 India will have 20 percent more men than women. [79]

Trafficking, Kidnapping and Crime

The scarcity of women in Asia means girls are now seen as valuable commodities on the black market, fueling a burgeoning sex trade in the region.

"The lack of women contributes to greater demand for prostituted women and girls . . . fueling the demand for victims of trafficking," said Mark Lagon, who oversaw human rights issues at the U.S. State Department during the George W. Bush administration. [80] "The impact is obvious. It's creating a 'Wild West' sex industry in China." [81]

The situation in China is leading to "a new tsunami of demand" for sex traffickers, according to Laura J. Lederer, a former U.S. Department of State senior adviser on trafficking and founder of The Protection Project, an anti-trafficking legal research institute at Johns Hopkins University. The State Department's 2009

"Trafficking in Persons" report describes China as a "source, transit and destination country for men, women and children trafficked for the purposes of forced labor and sexual exploitation." [82]

Many young girls are "bought" by farmers to guarantee wives for their young sons when they come of age. Others who desire a bride but don't want to pay a high bride price resort to kidnapping. In July, police rescued 179 babies, most of them girls, from kidnappers. According to China's state media, 39,194 cases of human trafficking have been reported since April 2009. [83]

While spikes in trafficking, kidnapping and prostitution can easily be traced to shortages of women, some experts also say the rising population of frustrated single men accounts for rising crime rates. Indeed, a study in China found that a 1 percent increase in the sex ratio (at birth) resulted in a 5- to 6-point increase in the crime rate.

"The increasing maleness of the young adult population in China may account for as much as a third of the overall rise in crime," said the report's author. [84] China's crime rate has nearly doubled over the last two decades. [85] And between 2003 and 2007, rape cases in India jumped by more than 30 percent and abductions by 50 percent. [86]

Officials fear that the country's "bare branches" are becoming even more aggressive. "Cross-cultural evidence shows that the overwhelming majority of violent crime is perpetrated by young, unmarried, low-status males," said a recent study. "Because they may lack a stake in the existing social order, it is feared that they will become bound together in an outcast culture, turning to antisocial behaviour and organized crime, thereby threatening societal stability and security."

G. D. Bakshi, a senior fellow at the New Delhi-based security think tank Vivekananda International Foundation, warns that the large numbers of unmarried men could lead to "the criminalisation of society." Shortages of females "will aggravate aggressive tendencies — whether they manifest in internal conflict, armed rebellions or you try and externalize conflict," he said.

Although China, India, Vietnam and other nations have outlawed sex-selective abortion and prenatal gender-testing, the laws have generally not been strictly enforced. However, stung by increasingly skewed birth ratios and international criticism, officials have recently pledged to renew efforts to crack down on such abuses:

- In April, Indian Prime Minister Manmohan Singh described the killing of girls as a "national shame" and ordered policy planners to increase efforts to stop sex-selective abortion. "The falling child sex ratio is an indictment of our social values," he said. [87] In a one-month campaign the government seized 32 illegal ultrasound machines. [88]

- In May the Taiwanese Health Ministry said it would impose fines on doctors who perform sex-selective abortions and revoke their licenses under the new Physicians Act, which forbids sex-selective abortions. Officials also are considering revising the law to allow offenders to face criminal charges. [89]

- In an effort to achieve "a significant rebalancing" of the sex ratio at birth by 2015, China recently announced an eight-month, multi-ministry crackdown on anyone using ultrasound to determine the sex of a fetus or performing sex-selective abortions. Penalties range from loss of medical licenses to criminal charges. [90]

Given the difficulty of proving that an abortion was performed for sex-selection purposes, most activists do not hold out much hope for major success. "China, for example, has shown little interest in prosecuting offenders," says activist Littlejohn, of Women's Rights Without Frontiers. "If it was really interested in saving lives, it would drop its one-child policy."

Others applaud the countries for at least acknowledging the problem, publicizing it and raising penalties. However, many experts believe that awareness and education are better "carrots" than the "stick" of prosecution.

Valuing Girls

The best way to solve the "missing girls" problem, says UNFPA's Toure, is for communities to be educated as to "how necessary and valuable females are to society." It's a long process, she admits, calling for "patience, planning and creativity." Simply put, all countries need to raise the value of girls and women.

Are sex-selective abortions really "elective"?

YES
Prabhat Jha, MD, D.Phil.
Director, Centre for Global Health Research,
University of Toronto

Written for *CQ Global Researcher*, October 2011

Up to 12 million females were aborted selectively before birth in India between 1980 and 2010 — about half just in the last decade. But four factors indicate that selective abortion is mostly an elective choice used by Indian parents to control their family composition.

First, over the past 20 years Indian girl-to-boy ratios fell for second births if the first child was a girl — but not if it was a boy. Thus, Indian families appear to be allowing nature to decide the gender of their first child. But to ensure that they have at least one boy, more parents are aborting their second child if ultrasound shows it to be a girl.

Second, unlike China, India does not enforce a one-child policy, so selective abortion of first births is not occurring, according to the data. Third, declines in girl-to-boy ratios for second or later births were larger in better-educated and wealthier households than in illiterate and poorer households, and declines did not differ between Hindus and Muslims. Coercion of female fertility choices would not be expected to show such patterns.

Finally, while large in absolute numbers, selective abortion accounts for only a small minority (about 2-4 percent in 2010) of all pregnancies carrying a girl.

While fertility has fallen substantially, Indians' preference for sons has not changed. (Sons traditionally care for their elderly parents in India, so they are the equivalent of an Indian 401K retirement plan.) As income and education levels rise, more Indian households can act on their son preference, and sex-selective abortion has spread widely. Today most Indians live in communities where selective abortion of girls is common.

The road back to gender balance in India will be long and difficult, but correct decisions can help make it possible. Restricting ultrasound or abortions may do more harm than good. Routine ultrasound improves prenatal health, and restricting abortions could increase maternal deaths from unsafe abortions. India already loses more mothers in childbirth than any other country.

And unlike China, India can take advantage of its rich tradition of public debate. The 2011 census can provide local data to enable community debates. In response to publicity, selective abortions appear already to have slowed somewhat in North India since 2006. Finally, India's government must do a better job of shutting down the small number of physicians who profit from unlawful testing and abortion.

NO
Reggie Littlejohn
President, Women's Rights
Without Frontiers

Written for *CQ Global Researcher*, October 2011

Some say sex-selective abortion is protected by a woman's right to choose to terminate a pregnancy for any reason. This view ignores the crushing social, economic, political and personal pressures that trample pregnant women carrying girls in cultures with a strong son preference. All too often, women in these cultures do not "select" their daughters for abortion. They are forced.

In China, for example, the birth ratio of girls to boys is the most skewed in the world: only 100 girls are born for every 120 boys in some places. Sons traditionally carry on the family name, work the fields and take care of their parents in old age. A daughter joins her husband's family at marriage. There is an Asian proverb: "Raising a girl is like watering someone else's garden." China's one-child policy exacerbates the underlying son preference. When couples are restricted to one child, women often become the focus of intense pressure to ensure a boy.

A woman need not be dragged out of her home and strapped down to a table to be a victim of forced abortion. Persistent emotional pressure, estrangement from the extended family, threat of abandonment or divorce, verbal abuse and domestic violence often overpower women who otherwise would choose to keep their daughters.

Systematic, sex-selective abortion constitutes gendercide, which has resulted in an estimated 37 million more men than women in China today. The presence of these "excess males" is the driving force behind human trafficking and sexual slavery, not only within China but from surrounding nations as well. Finally, China has the highest female suicide rate in the world. According to the World Health Organization, 500 women a day end their lives in China — further depleting the numbers of women.

A U.N. expert has estimated that the world is missing up to 200 million women — more than the total casualties of all the wars of the 20th century. And like war casualties, these women are not "missing." They are dead.

It is a woman's right to choose to give birth to her daughters. Together, China and India comprise one third of the world's population. The fact that one-third of the world's women are being deprived of their right to bear girls is the biggest women's rights abuse on Earth. It deserves a passionate response from groups that stand for women's rights. Forced abortion is not a choice.

> *"Where are the feminists on the issue of sex-selective abortion? . . . Their continued silence only facilitates the killing."*
>
> — *Steven W. Mosher, President, Population Research Institute*

French demographer Guilmoto says that once daughters are offered better educational opportunities, they will be seen as less of an economic burden to families and will be more valued. One way to do that, among other things, is to change "laws and customs that prevent women from inheriting property," he adds.

Programs are being established to encourage parents to value their daughters and eschew sex-selective abortions. For instance, India offers a stipend of about $3,000 to parents who raise and educate a girl until she is 18. Under the Care for Girls program in parts of rural China, parents who have two girls get about a $150 annual lifetime pension, plus educational benefits. [91] Posters that once warned couples it was illegal to have more than one child have been replaced by signs extolling the virtues of having a daughter. Signs such as "You can abort it. But you cannot give birth to it!" have been replaced in some areas by signs saying, "It is forbidden to discriminate against, mistreat or abandon baby girls," and, "Our current family planning policy is this, 'Pay attention to the issue of gender imbalance,' " and "Boy or Girl? Let Nature decide." [92]

In India, doctors known as "girl child champions" are working to convince their colleagues not to abort female fetuses. [93] Nongovernmental organizations support publicity campaigns promoting the value of women and organize sting operations to help document clinics that offer illegal sex-selective abortions. [94]

Plan India in New Delhi launched an awareness program this year, Let Girls Be Born. "I think we really need to reach out to young people [to] create an awareness, to change attitudes and dispel the notion that having a boy is better than a girl," said executive director Dengle. "Girls aren't a sect; they are as good as boys." [95] Even Indian soap operas are dramatizing the harm India's skewed birth ratio is causing. The Indian movie, "Matrubhoomi: A Nation Without Women," depicts a village in the future that is populated by men only.

Changing long-held beliefs and traditions will be a challenge, but a noble one, notes Mosher, of the Population Research Institute: "Human beings are the ultimate resource — the one resource you cannot do without."

In Karachi, the Edhi Foundation's Kazmi says change will come slowly. In the meantime, his organization keeps more than 300 cradles in front of its offices throughout Pakistan so families can drop off unwanted newborns (mostly girls).

"It's for awareness — please don't kill your innocent babies," he said. [96]

OUTLOOK

Cultural Shifts?

"Which scenario do you want, the good one or the bad one?" says the UNFPA's Toure when asked what the gender-imbalance problem will look like in the future.

"Some people see this crisis widening, but I don't agree. I think we are making progress," she explains. "I am an optimist, and I believe that in time the status of women around the world, especially in nations where sex selection is skewing the birth ratios, will rise enough so there will no longer be a preference for boys over girls. But we have a long way to go to help make that happen."

She and others hope raising women's status via educational and awareness programs will offset the long-held cultural and traditional customs of son preference.

"There is hope," says Paris-based demographer Guilmoto. "We are already seeing some small signs of improvement in parts of India. As more people become aware of the problem, more are taking action to combat it." Many point to South Korea where skewed birth ratios have returned to more normal rates as a model to follow.

But some experts, like Toronto University's Jha, believe the problem will get worse before it gets better. "We need to see real changes on the supply side, such as governments cracking down on illegal services, and societal shifts, such as governments instituting social security programs, before we will see numbers drop," says Jha. Already, he says, there is evidence of some slight cultural shifts, such as married women taking care of both their aging parents and their in-laws. "But until all these changes take hold, which will take decades," he admits, "the problem will get worse before getting better."

Guilmoto and other demographers admit that it is too late to help most of the millions of "bare branches" — the men in India, China and elsewhere who will not be able to find wives. "We need to ask: How will society change to accommodate these guys?" he says. "Will they be forced to migrate? Will they be husbands of the same wife? Will societies need to have new marriage rules? There are so many things we can't imagine now." In 20 years, he explains, governments won't be as worried about sex-selective abortions continuing to occur, but they'll still be dealing with the effects of today's skewed birth rates.

By 2020 China will have more than 20 million excess men of marriageable age. India, Pakistan and Taiwan will also have men who won't be able to find wives. Author Hvistendahl says, "In both China and India, nationalism is taking hold among these restless young men, and the governments are uneasy about them." A surplus of males in China in the 19th century contributed to a series of rebellions that ultimately toppled the emperor, she points out.

"Leaders in Beijing and New Delhi will be hard-pressed to address the potentially grave social instability that their countries' ever-increasing numbers of bare branches may produce in the next few decades," noted one study. To counter that threat, governments "may be inclined to move in a more authoritarian direction." [97]

For at least the next 20 years, observers believe trafficking, prostitution, kidnapping and rising crime rates — all problems linked to the sex ratio imbalance — are likely to soar in affected countries.

And some experts say the problem could be exacerbated by new advances in fetal DNA testing, which allow the fetal sex to be determined only seven weeks after conception, eliminating the need for ultrasound. [98] And other new technologies, such as preimplantation genetic diagnosis and sperm sorting, allow parents to choose the sex of their offspring. Both have spread throughout the world, including China and India, and will make sex selection easier but harder to police, especially as the new technologies become cheaper and more accessible.

Until a society values females as much as males, girls' lives will continue to be threatened by cultural and societal prejudices. And millions of girls will continue to be murdered each year, 40 years after Mao declared: "Times have changed, and today men and women are equal. . . . Women hold up half the sky." [99]

NOTES

1. "Newborn baby killings on the increase in Pakistan," Undhimmi, Jan. 17, 2011, http://undhimmi .com/2011/01/17/newborn-baby-killings-on-the-increase-in-pakistan/.

2. "Infanticide on the rise: 1210 babies found dead in 2010 says Edhi," *Express Tribune*, Jan. 18, 2011, http://tribune.com.pk/story/105019/infanticide-on-the-rise-in-pakistan-statistics/.

3. Reza Sayah, "Killing of infants on the rise in Pakistan," CNN.com, July 20, 2011, http://articles.cnn .com/2011-07-20/world/pakistan.infanticide_1_ edhi-foundation-abdul-sattar-edhi-karachi?_ s=PM:WORLD.

4. *Ibid.*

5. "Newborn baby killings on the increase in Pakistan," *op. cit.*

6. Nicholas Eberstadt, "The Global War Against Baby Girls," American Enterprise Institute, 2007, www .aei.org/docLib/20070105_eberstadtspeech.pdf.

7. Christophe Z. Guilmoto, "Sex-ratio imbalance in Asia: Trends, consequences and policy responses," United Nations Population Fund, www.unfpa.org/ gender/docs/studies/summaries/regional_analysis.pdf.

8. Mara Hvistendahl, "Unnatural Selection," *Psychology Today*, July 5, 2011, www.psychologytoday.com/ articles/201107/unnatural-selection.

9. Prabhat Jha, *et al.*, "Trends in selective abortions of girls in India: analysis of nationally representative birth histories from 1990 to 2005 and census data from 1991 to 2011," *Lancet*, May 24, 2011, www .thelancet.com/journals/lancet/article/PIIS0140-6736(11)60649-1/abstract.

10. "China has more than 13 million abortions a year," CNN, July 30, 2009, http://articles.cnn.com/2009-07-30/world/china.abortions.millions_1_abortions-family-planning-policy-birth-control-method?_ s=PM:WORLD.

11. Yaqiang Yi and William M Mason, "Prenatal Sex-Selective Abortion and High Sex Ratio at Birth in Rural China: A Case Study in Henan Province," California Center for Population Research, 2005, p. 3, http://escholarship.org/uc/item/8j01443f.

12. "UNFPA guidance note on prenatal sex selection," United Nations Population Fund, UNFPA, p. 3, www.unfpa.org/webdav/site/global/shared/documents/publications/2010/guidenote_prenatal_sexselection.pdf.

13. Eberstadt, *op. cit.*

14. Sayah, *op. cit.*

15. "Addressing violence against women and achieving the Millennium Development Goals," World Health Organization, www.who.int/gender/documents/women_MDGs_report/en/index6.html.

16. Eric Baculinao, "China grapples with legacy of its missing girls," MSNBC, Sept. 14, 2004, www.msnbc.msn.com/id/5953508/ns/world_news/t/china-grapples-legacy-its-missing-girls/.

17. Tina Rosenberg, "The daughter deficit," *The New York Times*, Aug. 19, 2009, www.nytimes.com/2009/08/23/magazine/23FOB-idealab-t.html?pagewanted=all.

18. Savita Verma, "Law against sex selection fails to save girl children," *India Today*, April 1, 2011, http://indiatoday.intoday.in/story/law-against-sex-selection-fails-to-save-girl-children/1/133999.html.

19. Mara Hvistendahl, *Unnatural Selection: Choosing Boys Over Girls, and the Consequences of a World Full of Men* (2011), p. 10.

20. Malcolm Moore, "Thirty years of China's one-child policy," *Daily Telegraph*, Sept. 25, 2010, www.telegraph.co.uk/news/worldnews/asia/china/8024862/Thirty-years-of-Chinas-one-child-policy.html.

21. Alexa Olesen, "One-child policy in China will not be relaxed," *The Christian Science Monitor*, Sept. 28, 2010, www.csmonitor.com/World/Latest-News-Wires/2010/0928/One-child-policy-in-China-will-not-be-relaxed.

22. Li Xiaoping, "We need to reduce, not increase, population," *China Daily*, Feb. 1, 2010, www.chinadaily.com.cn/cndy/2010-02/01/content_9404650.htm.

23. Michael A. Memoli, "Biden dismisses criticism of comment on China's one-child policy," *Los Angeles Times*, Aug. 26, 2011, http://articles.latimes.com/2011/aug/26/news/la-pn-biden-one-child-20110826.

24. "Consultative conference: 'The government must end the one-child rule,'" AsiaNews.it, March 16, 2007, www.asianews.it/index.php?l=en&art=8757.

25. "China's Population: The most surprising demographic crisis," *The Economist*, May 5, 2011, www.economist.com/node/18651512.

26. Malcolm Moore, "China's workforce 'dries up,'" *Telegraph*, March 27, 2011, www.telegraph.co.uk/news/worldnews/asia/china/8409513/Chinas-workforce-dries-up.html. For background, see Alan Greenblatt, "The Graying Planet," *CQ Global Researcher*, March 15, 2011, pp. 133-156.

27. "China's Population: The most surprising demographic crisis," *op. cit.*

28. Peter Ford, "Will China ease its one-child policy?" *The Christian Science Monitor*, Dec. 17, 2009, www.csmonitor.com/World/Global-Issues/2009/1231/Will-China-ease-its-one-child-policy.

29. "China's Population: The most surprising demographic crisis," *op. cit.*

30. Mu Guangzong, "A change is needed immediately," *China Daily*, March 21, 2011, www.chinadaily.com.cn/opinion/2011-03-21/content_12200002.htm.

31. Ross Douthat, "160 million and counting," *The New York Times*, June 26, 2011, www.nytimes.com/2011/06/27/opinion/27douthat.html.

32. Carmen Barroso, letter in response to Mara Hvistendahl, "Where Have All the Girls Gone?" *Foreign Policy*, June 27, 2011, www.foreignpolicy.com/articles/2011/06/27/where_have_all_the_girls_gone.

33. "Brides bound by traditions," *The Washington Times*, Feb. 26, 2007, www.washingtontimes.com/news/2007/feb/26/20070226-115011-6073r/.

34. *Ibid.*

35. "Preventing gender biased sex selection," World Health Organization, June 2011, p. v, http://whqlibdoc.who.int/publications/2011/9789241501460_eng.pdf. The four other organizations were the World Health Organization, the Office of the High Commissioner for Human Rights, UNICEF and U.N. Women (the United Nations Entity for Gender Equality and the Empowerment of Women).

36. Nicholas Eberstadt, "Should sex selective abortions be outlawed, American Enterprise Institute, May 23, 2008, www.aei.org/article/28040.

37. Hvistendahl, *Unnatural Selection*, op. cit., p. 96.

38. *Ibid.*, p. 127.

39. Mara Hvistendahl, "Where Have All the Girls Gone?" *Foreign Policy*, June 27, 2011, www.foreignpolicy.com/articles/2011/06/27/where_have_all_the_girls_gone?page=full.

40. *Ibid.*, p. 135.

41. *Ibid.*, p. 145.

42. Soutik Biswas, "Sex selection: The forgotten story," BBC News, July 22, 2011, www.bbc.co.uk/news/14213136.

43. Richard Dawkins, "Sex selection and the shortage of women: Is science to blame?" The Richard Dawkins Foundation, June 18, 2011, http://richarddawkins.net/articles/639930-sex-selection-and-the-shortage-of-women-is-science-to-blame.

44. "Cat got your tongue?" *The Economist*, Aug. 6, 2011, www.economist.com/node/21525348.

45. Ross Douthat, *op. cit.*

46. Dawkins, *op. cit.*

47. See, for example, Joseph, B. Birdsell, "Some predictions for the Pleistocene based on equilibrium systems among recent hunter gatherers," in Richard Lee and Irven DeVore, *Man the Hunter* (1968), p. 239; and Laila Williamson, "Infanticide: an anthropological analysis," in Marvin Kohl, *Infanticide and the Value of Life* (1978), pp. 61-75.

48. Carles Darwin, *The Descent of Man* (1872), p. 129, http://darwinsaid.wordpress.com/tag/infanticide/.

49. Mary R. Lefkowitz and Maureen B. Fant, *Women's Life in Greece and Rome* (2005), www.stoa.org/diotima/anthology/wlgr/wlgr-privatelife249.shtml.

50. John Boswell, *The Kindness of Strangers: The abandonment of children in Western Europe from Late Antiquity to the Renaissance* (1998), p. 102.

51. Larry Stephen Milner, *Hardness of Heart/Hardness of Life: The Stain of Human Infanticide* (2000), p. 227.

52. "Muhammad: Legacy of a Prophet," PBS, 2002, www.pbs.org/muhammad/ma_women.shtml.

53. "Introducing Islam," (no date), www.introducingislam.org/info/moralsquran/page1.php.

54. Milner, *op. cit.*, p. 86.

55. "Harmful practices to the female body; Part IV female infanticide," *Telegraph*, Aug. 20, 2011, http://my.telegraph.co.uk/hatefsvoiceofpeace/hatefsvoice/381/harmful-practices-to-the-female-body-part-4-female-infanticide/.

56. Sarah Blaffer Hrdy, *Mother Nature: A History of Mothers, Infants and Natural Selection* (1999), p. 320.

57. See Valerie M. Hudson, and Andrea M. den Boer, *Bare Branches* (2004), p. 72.

58. Larry Milner, "A brief history of infanticide," The Society for the Prevention of Infanticide, http://infanticide.org/history.htm.

59. Milner, *op. cit.*, p. 176.

60. Hudson and den Boer, *op. cit.*, p. 86.

61. Laursa Fitzpatrick, "A brief history of China's one-child policy," *Time*, July 27, 2009, www.time.com/time/world/article/0,8599,1912861,00.html.

62. Amartya Sen, "The quality of life: India versus China," *The New York Review of Books*, May 12, 2011, www.nybooks.com/articles/archives/2011/may/12/quality-life-india-vs-china/?pagination=false.

63. Hudson and den Boer, *op. cit.*, p. 108.

64. "The issue that inflamed India," *Time*, April 4, 1977, www.time.com/time/magazine/article/0,9171,947859-1,00.html.

65. "South Korea: The Society," www.mongabay.com/reference/country_studies/south-korea/SOCIETY.html.

66. Quoted in Ed Regis, "The Doomslayer," *Wired*, May, 2002, www.wired.com/wired/archive/5.02/ffsimon_pr.html.

67. Hvistendahl, *Unnatural Selection*, op. cit., p. 48.

68. Simon Johnson Williams, Lynda I. A. Birke and Gillian Bendelow, *Debating Biology: Sociological reflections on health, medicine, and society* (2003), p. 187.

69. Hudson and den Boer, *op. cit.*, p. 171.

70. Rita Patel, "The Practice of Sex Selective Abortion in India: May You Be the Mother of a Hundred Sons,"

http://cgi.unc.edu/uploads/media_items/the-practice-of-sex-selective-abortion-in-india-may-you-be-the-mother-of-a-hundred-sons.original.pdf.

71. "GE machines used to break laws," *The Washington Times*, Feb. 28, 1997, www.washingtontimes.com/news/2007/feb/28/20070228-113751-7882r/?page=all#pagebreak.

72. Sen, *op. cit.*

73. Bela Ganatra, "Maintaining access to safe abortion and reducing sex imbalances in Asia," 2008, www.ipas.org/Library/Other/Maintaining_access_to_safe_abortion_reducing_sex_ratio_imbalances_in_Asia.pdf.

74. "The aborting and starving of girls in India," *World*, May 4, 2011, http://online.worldmag.com/2011/05/04/the-aborting-and-starving-of-girls-in-india/.

75. Tania Branigan, "China's village of bachelors: no wives in sight in remote settlement," *Guardian*, Sept. 2, 2011, www.guardian.co.uk/world/2011/sep/02/china-village-of-bachelors/print.

76. *Ibid.*

77. Nanama Keita and Sanjay Pandey, "A village of eternal bachelors," *Trustlaw*, April 6, 2011, www.trust.org/trustlaw/news/a-village-of-eternal-bachelors.

78. *Ibid.*

79. "Gendercide leaves Indian men without partners," *RT*, April 6, 2011, http://rt.com/news/men-boys-child-family/.

80. Hvistendahl, *Unnatural Selection*, p. 185.

81. Cheryl Weztstein, "With 1-child policy, China missing girls," *The Washington Times*, Jan. 27, 2010, www.washingtontimes.com/news/2010/jan/27/with-1-child-policy-china-missing-girls/?page=1.

82. *Ibid.*

83. "China rescues dozens of infants from human traffickers," Reuters, July, 27, 2011, http://uk.reuters.com/article/2011/07/27/uk-china-trafficking-idUKTRE76Q0VA20110727.

84. Quoted in Hvistendahl, *Unnatural Selection, op. cit.*, p. 222.

85. *Ibid.*, p. 221.

86. *Ibid.*

87. "Indian PM dubs foeticide a 'national shame,'" *Straits Times*, Agence France-Presse, April 21, 2011, www.straitstimes.com/BreakingNews/Asia/Story/STIStory_659520.html.

88. Malathy Iyer, "Registration of many seized scanners may be suspended," *Times of India*, July 31, 2011, http://articles.timesofindia.indiatimes.com/2011-07-31/mumbai/29835523_1_ultrasound-machines-pcpndt-act-sting-operations.

89. "Taiwan warning over selective abortions," Hc2d.co.uk, May 18, 2011, www.hc2d.co.uk/content.php?contentId=18508.

90. Zhuang Ping, "Crackdown on sex selective abortions," *South China Morning Post*, Aug. 17, 2011, http://topics.scmp.com/news/china-news-watch/article/Crackdown-on-sex-selective-.

91. Beth Loyd, "China fears lopsided sex ratio could spark crisis," ABC News, Jan. 12, 2007, http://abcnews.go.com/International/story?id=2790469&page=1.

92. Peter Hitchens, "Gendercide: China's shameful massacre of unborn girls means there will soon be 30m more men than women," *Daily Mail*, April 10, 2010, www.dailymail.co.uk/news/article-1265068/China-The-worlds-new-superpower-beginning-century-supremacy-alarming-surplus-males.html.

93. "A killing obsession," *Deccan Herald*, www.deccanherald.com/content/171270/a-killing-obsession.html.

94. Samanth Subramanian, "Lawyer fights female foeticide in one of India's affluent states," *The National*, April 27, 2011, www.thenational.ae/news/worldwide/south-asia/lawyer-fights-female-foeticide-in-one-of-indias-affluent-states.

95. Reza Sayah, "Killing of infants on the rise in Pakistan," CNN, July 20, 2011, http://articles.cnn.com/2011-07-20/world/pakistan.infanticide_1_edhi-foundation-abdul-sattar-edhi-karachi?_s=PM:WORLD.

96. *Ibid.*

97. Hudson and den Boer, *op. cit.*, p. 263.

98. Arthur Caplan, "Fetal genetic testing: a troubling technology," MSNBC, Aug. 9, 2011, www.msnbc.msn.com/id/44078722/ns/health-health_care/t/fetal-genetic-testing-troubling-technology/.

99. Malik, Rashid, *Chinese Entrepreneurs in the Economic Development of China* (1997), p. 116.

BIBLIOGRAPHY

Selected Sources

Books

Connelly, Matthew, *Fatal Misconception: The Struggle to Control World Population*, Belknap Press, 2010.
A Columbia University historian examines 20th-century population-control programs and shows how they evolved into an oppressive international movement intent on suppressing population numbers in the developing world.

Hrdy, Sarah Blaffer, *Mother Nature: A History of Mothers, Infants, and Natural Selection*, Pantheon, 1999.
An anthropologist shows how female strategies as both mothers and wives have shaped the process of evolution. Includes a chapter that explores how son preference has led to a shortage of women in Asia.

Hudson, Valerie M., and Andrea M. den Boer, *Bare Branches: The Security Implications of Asia's Surplus Male Population*, MIT Press, 2004.
Focusing largely on China and India, two academics explore the causes of Asia's skewed sex ratios. The resulting surplus of male population in the two countries poses a threat to both domestic and international security, they argue.

Hvistendahl, Mara, *Unnatural Selection: Choosing Boys Over Girls, and the Consequences of a World Full of Men*, Public Affairs, 2011.
A China-based journalist examines how sex-selective abortions have resulted in 160 million girls being "missing" from Asia. She also looks into whether the West's population-control programs exacerbated the problem.

Articles

"The worldwide war on baby girls," *The Economist*, March 4, 2010.
This wide-ranging report examines how declining fertility, son preferences and new technologies are combining to produce skewed sex ratios in Asia and elsewhere.

Hitchens, Peter, "Gendercide: China's shameful massacre of unborn girls means there will soon be 30m more men than women," *Daily Mail*, April 10, 2010.
A British journalist travels through China to examine the nation's one-child policy and its relationship to an ever-growing preference for sons instead of daughters.

Hvistendahl, Mara, "Where Have All the Girls Gone?" *Foreign Policy*, June 27, 2011.
The author of *Unnatural Selection* summarizes the issue of sex-selective abortion and claims that Western proponents of population control influenced Asian nations to institute birth control measures such as gender-based abortions.

Kazmin, Amy, Pati Waldmeir and Girija Shivakumar, "Asia: heirs and spares," *Financial Times*, July 10, 2011.
This well-reported article examines the political, economic and social consequences caused by sex-selective abortion in India and China.

Sayah, Reza, "Killing of infants on the rise in Pakistan," *CNN*, July 20, 2010, http://articles.cnn.com/2011-07-20/world/pakistan.infanticide_1_edhi-foundation-abdul-sattar-edhi-karachi?_s=PM:WORLD.
This Pakistan-based account explains how one charity is dealing with the more than 1,200 newborn infants, mostly girls, abandoned or killed at birth in Pakistan last year.

Sen, Amartya, "More Than 100 Million Women Are Missing," *New York Review of Books*, Dec. 20, 1990.
A Nobel Prize-winning economist writes a landmark article on Asia's gender imbalance, cited by many as a "wakeup call" to the world about the skewed sex ratios in the region.

Reports and Studies

"Preventing gender-biased sex selection," World Health Organization, 2011, www.unhcr.org/refworld/docid/4df751442.html.
This interagency statement explores the background, causes and effects of sex-selection throughout the world. It includes a discussion on how patrilineal inheritance and a reliance on males for economic support have resulted in son preference in Asia.

Bhalotra, Sonia, and Tom Cochrane, "Where have all the young girls gone? Identification of sex selection in India," Centre for Market and Public Organisation,

December 2010, www.bristol.ac.uk/cmpo/publications/papers/2010/wp254.pdf.
This paper examines how having access to prenatal gender testing has affected India's sex ratio at birth.

Guilmoto, Christophe Z., "Sex ratio imbalance in Asia: Trends, consequences and policy responses," United Nations Population Fund, 2007.
A noted French demographer presents a regional overview of the mechanisms and consequences of Asia's growing gender imbalances — and potential policy responses.

Zhu, Wei Xing, and Therese Hesketh, "China's excess males, sex selective abortion, and one child policy: analysis of data from 2005 national intercensus survey," *BMJ* (*British Medical Journal*), 2009.
An academic investigation examines how sex-selective abortion and China's one-child policy have affected current trends and geographical patterns in birth sex ratios.

For More Information

Centre for Global Health Research, Li Ka Shing Knowledge Institute, St. Michael's Hospital, 30 Bond St., Toronto, Ontario, M5B 1W8, Canada; (416) 864-6042; www.CGHR.org. Nonprofit organization affiliated with the University of Toronto; conducts research that advances global health, with particular attention to the world's poorest populations.

Center for Reproductive Rights, 120 Wall St., 14th Floor, New York, NY 10005; (917) 637-3600; www.reproductiverights.org. Legal organization dedicated to advancing women's rights to reproductive health, self-determination and dignity around the world.

Edhi Foundation, Sarafa Bazar, Boulton Market, Mithadar, Karachi, Pakistan; 92 (21) 2413232; www.edhifoundation.com. Nonprofit that provides medical and welfare services across Pakistan and offers free burials to unclaimed bodies.

Human Rights Watch, 350 Fifth Ave., New York, NY 10118; (212) 290-4700; www.hrw.org. The largest U.S. human rights organization investigates abuses around the world, including those against children.

Population Research Institute, 1190 Progress Dr., Suite 2D, P.O. Box 1559, Front Royal, VA 22630; (540) 622-5240; www.pop.org. International nonprofit that aims to publicize and end coercive population control.

United Nations Population Fund (UNFPA), 605 Third Ave., New York, NY 10158; (212) 297-5000; www.unfpa.org/public/home/news/pid/6727. www.unfpa.org. International development agency that promotes reproductive health, gender equality and development strategies.

Women's Rights Without Frontiers, P.O. Box 54401, San Jose, CA; (310) 592-5722; www.womensrightswithoutfrontiers.org. International coalition opposed to forced abortion and sterilization in China; seeks to raise awareness on the coercive nature of China's one-child policy.

World Population Program, International Institute for Applied Systems Analysis, Schlossplatz 1, A-2361 Laxenburg, Austria; 43 2236 807 0; www.iiasa.ac.at. Studies how population trends influence society, the economy and the natural environment.

Voices From Abroad:

PRABHAT JHA

Epidemiologist and demographer, University of Toronto, Canada

Nature vs. technology

"It appears that families are saying, 'Nature will decide the first child, but we are going to let technology decide the second child if the first is a girl.'"

The Washington Post, May 2011

LI BIN

Minister, Family Planning Commission, China

Problems in favoritism

"Illegal fetal sex testing and sex-selective abortions are the direct causes of the long-term problem of a serious skewing in the sex ratio in the mainland, which arises from a deeply rooted tradition that favors boys."

Chinadaily.com.cn, August 2011

MARA HVISTENDAHL

Asia Correspondent, *Science Magazine,* China

U.S. is complicit

"It took millions of dollars in funding from U.S. organizations, along with thousands of fieldworkers and a good number of mobile clinics, for sex determination and abortion to catch on in the developing world."

Unnatural Selection (book), June 2011

K. S. JACOB

Professor, Christian Medical College, India

There's more to it

"Female foeticide and infanticide are just the tip of the iceberg; there is a whole set of subtle and blatant discriminatory practices against girls and women under

various pretexts. It is this large base of discrimination against women that supports the declining sex ratio."

The Hindu (India), April 2011

LIU QIAN

Vice Health Minister, China

Explaining the imbalance

"The gender ratio imbalance [in China] can be attributed to multiple causes, including a traditional preference for sons, the practice of arranging for sons to take care of elderly parents, illegal sex-selective abortions and other factors."

Xinhua news agency (China), August 2011

BHAGYASHRI DENGLE

Executive Director, Plan India

'Seen as a burden'

"Girls are seen as a burden [in India], seen as a property which belongs to somebody else, so people see that as a waste of money and the wasting of an education of a girl."

CNN, July 2011

JAMIR ARALIKAR

Son of infanticide survivor, India

Paying it forward

"I am proud of my mother. After surviving the attempted infanticide, she now helps others fight social injustices like dowry, eve-teasing [sexual harassment] and casteism."

Times of India, March 2011

SANJAY GUPTE

President, Federation of Obstetrics and Gynaecological Society of India

Identifying the perpetrators

"Although the Preconception and Prenatal Diagnostic Techniques Act is in place, which deters doctors and patients from sex determination tests, there is no action plan to bring about coordination and cooperation among doctors and the government. Doctors should voluntarily disclose information about medical practitioners who resort to sex determination tests and the heinous practice of sex selective abortions. . . . There are very few cases where doctors are actually punished for carrying out sex determination tests. The action plan that we are demanding should focus on such errant doctors. . . ."

Times of India, December 2010

12

Saving Indigenous Peoples

Brian Beary

A Mapuche girl sports traditional garb and plays with the group's national flag during festivities in Temucuicui, Chile, on Nov. 13, 2009. Argentina and Chile have deprived the indigenous Mapuche of control over their ancestral lands, according to the forest-dwelling group, in violation of international conventions. Mapuche activists have used violence and hunger strikes to press their case.

From *CQ Researcher*,
Sept. 20, 2011

This is what Jenny Macklin, Australia's minister for indigenous affairs, saw on a recent visit to an Aboriginal community in the Outback town of Alice Springs:

"Women and children slept on mattresses in the open air, exposed to the elements. Children roamed the streets at all hours of the day and night, with no regard to going to school or getting home safely at night. Alcohol visibly ravaged the communities, resulting in terrible health, terrible violence and terrible tragedy." [1]

Few in indigenous societies — native peoples who were conquered and are still dominated by white Europeans — face such dire living conditions, but the situation is nevertheless alarming. In the Americas, Australia, New Zealand and the Arctic, indigenous peoples have chronically high poverty rates, disproportionate shares of the prison population and life expectancies 10 years shorter than the general population. [2]

In recent years, however, some indigenous groups have made progress in bolstering their legal and political rights. Several Latin American nations, for example, now recognize the rights of indigenous peoples, according to the Copenhagen-based International Work Group for Indigenous Affairs (IWGIA). But a huge gap remains between those legal rights and how they are implemented in practice. [3] For instance, states and multinational corporations are exploiting many of the natural resources found on indigenous lands in Latin America, notes the IWGIA, while the residents typically share little in the profits and see few improvements in their economic status.

In Europe, the term "indigenous peoples" generally applies to the Sami of northern Scandinavia (formerly known as Laplanders),

Indigenous Peoples Are Sliver of Most Populations

More than 42 million indigenous people live in the 25 countries settled and still run by descendants of European colonizers,* but they represent less than 5 percent of the population in most of their homelands. In Bolivia, Guatemala and Greenland, however, 60 percent or more of the inhabitants are indigenous.

Indigenous Populations in Selected Countries
(by number and percentage of population)

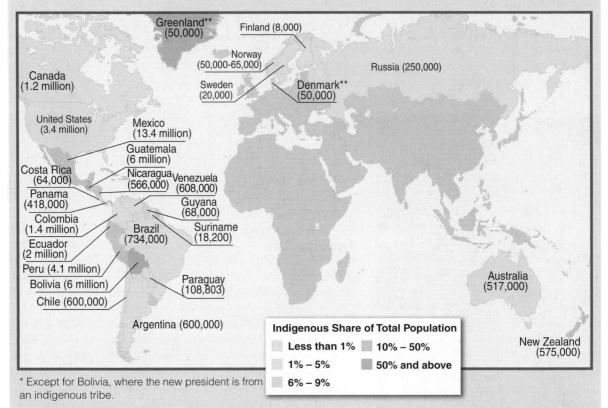

* Except for Bolivia, where the new president is from an indigenous tribe.

** Greenland is under Danish sovereignty but is largely autonomous. Greenlandic Inuit represent only 1% of all Danes, but 90% of Greenlanders

Sources: "State of the World's Minorities and Indigenous Peoples," Minority Rights Group International, July 6, 2011; Kathrin Wessendorf, "The Indigenous World 2011," The International Work Group for Indigenous Affairs, May 2011; Brian Beary, Separatist Movements, CQ Press, 2011; U.S. Census; James Anaya, "The situation of the Maori People in New Zealand, Report of the United Nations Special Rapporteur on the Rights of Indigenous Peoples," Feb. 17, 2011; "Closing the Gap — Prime Ministers Report 2011," Government of Australia, February 2011. Map by Lewis Agrell

the Inuit of Greenland and dozens of tiny enclaves in northern Russia. The Inuit — or Eskimos — also live in Canada, Russia and Alaska. In the United States the term applies to Native Americans. In Latin America, determining who is "indigenous" is more difficult.

"The [Spanish] Conquistadores intermarried more than other colonialists did with the native peoples, so it is harder to say who is an Indian and who is white," says Eduardo Gonzalez, a Peruvian who monitors indigenous rights issues for the International Center for Transitional

Justice (ICTJ). The New York-based group helps countries recovering from mass atrocities and repression to establish institutions to help provide accountability and redress for past abuses.

In his native Peru, Gonzalez notes, the 40 native Amazonian groups who make up less than 5 percent of the population self-identify as indigenous, while Quechua-speaking descendants of the Incas do not. By contrast, he says, the Mayans in Mexico and Guatemala call themselves "Indians." Meanwhile, in Hawaii, where most residents have mixed ancestry, some native Hawaiians want to create an electoral roll of so-called purebloods who would be granted a special form of autonomy.

Indigenous peoples in Latin America fare differently compared to those in the Anglophone New World countries of Australia, Canada, New Zealand and the United States. For example, while indigenous peoples usually comprise a minority of the overall population (with the notable exceptions of Bolivia, Guatemala and Greenland), they form even smaller percentages of the population in populous English-speaking countries, such as the United States, Australia and Canada. And while many indigenous groups live in remote settlements or reservations, in the United States fewer than half live on reservations, and in New Zealand, a majority of the Maori live in cities. [4]

Indigenous peoples share common political goals. Since the late 1960s, most have been demanding some form of autonomy or self-determination but have been struggling with their national governments over how those terms are defined. Shayna Plaut, who is studying Sami self-determination at Sami University College in Norway, says "self-determination can mean so many things — from control over cigarette taxes on Indian reservations to the right to devise your own education system, to running your own police force or having media in your native language."

Many Indigenous Groups Live in Cities

Many indigenous groups enjoy sovereignty and live on remote, rural reservations — such as in Guyana and Canada. In other countries, such as the United States and New Zealand, more than half of indigenous groups live in cities, including the Maori in Auckland and the Lakota Indians in Rapid City, S.D.

Where Select Indigenous Groups Live

- **United States** — More than 50 percent live off-reservation, mostly in large cities.
- **Colombia** — Reservations for indigenous peoples occupy one-third of the territory.
- **Chile** — Up to half of the Mapuche, the country's most populous indigenous group, live in urban areas. Most of the rest live on reservations.
- **New Zealand** — 80 percent of the Maori live in cities, 25 percent of them in the greater Auckland area.
- **Guyana** — 90 percent of the Amerindians live in vast, remote savannah or rainforest areas.
- **Australia** — 32 percent of the Aboriginals and Torres Strait Islanders live in major cities, 43 percent in regional areas, 25 percent in remote areas.
- **Canada** — 56 percent of indigenous Canadians live in urban areas.

Source: The International Work Group for Indigenous Affairs, www.iwgia.org/iwgia_files_publications_files/0454_THE_INDIGENOUS_ ORLD-2011_eb.pdf; Minority Rights Group International, www.minorityrights.org/10848/state-of-the-worlds-minorities /state-of-the-worlds-minorities-and-indigenous-peoples-2011.html; U.S. Census Bureau, www.census.gov/population/www/socdemo/race/censr-28.pdf

Historically, governments often have applied a double standard to the issue of self-determination, according to an article in *Human Rights Quarterly*. "In the process of decolonization, the right of self-determination was extended or forcibly exercised (through 'wars of independence') by the 'settlers' from the colonizing group, while the indigenous population remained subjugated, excluded and marginalized," two academics wrote. Modern states have "vociferously resisted" extending the right to self-determination to indigenous peoples, they added, because they feared it would be tantamount to admitting an "effective right of secession." [5]

Governments usually firmly oppose secession rights and are keen to control how natural resources in indigenous homelands are exploited, especially in fast-developing Latin America. According to Maria Railaf Zuniga, an

Latin America's First Indigenous Leader Makes Waves

Bolivia's Evo Morales remains a popular yet polarizing leader.

Chewing on an illicit coca leaf he brought in to a U.N. meeting on drug policy in Vienna, Bolivia's President Evo Morales, made the case for legalization of coca to a somewhat bemused audience: "This is a coca leaf. This is not cocaine. This represents the culture of indigenous people of the Andean region," he said. [1]

Morales, a former coca farmer, may be best known in the United States for his publicity stunts, colorful native clothing and close alliance with outspoken anti-American Venezuelan leader Hugo Chávez. But as an Aymara Indian who was elected president in December 2005, Morales is also widely recognized as Latin America's first indigenous leader.

Although he was re-elected four years later with an impressive 64.2 percent of the vote, many Bolivians have mixed feelings about him. Critics say his socialist government has pushed through constitutional amendments that have dangerously centralized power, particularly a provision allowing the government to seize lands and re-designate them as native community lands.

"The government is trying to control all the branches of government," said Javier Comboni, who was Bolivian finance minister under the previous administration and is now a professor of political economy at Wheaton College in Wheaton, Ill. "They have been successful but with absolute power comes absolute corruption," he continued, citing harassment of the judiciary and the takeover of private property in the natural gas-rich eastern lowlands as evidence. [2]

Bolivia's ambassador to the Netherlands, Roberto Calzadilla, who is of mixed ethnic background, firmly rejects such criticisms. The 2009 constitution, approved in a referendum, "recognizes the rights of indigenous peoples, which previously were denied and repressed for so long," he says. It establishes an "equal rank and hierarchy" among various tiers of government and formally recognizes that Bolivia's "36 indigenous communities and groups have the right to territory, language and their own communitarian justice."

Bolivia's wealthy class opposes the new constitution, largely because it bans private ownership of more than 5,000 hectares (12,400 acres) of land.

About 60 percent of Bolivia's 10 million people are indigenous, but until Morales' victory they had never reached the highest echelons of power. Previous Bolivian leaders came from among the country's "mestizo," or people of mixed European-indigenous descent, who today live mostly in the eastern lowlands.

The languages used by the two largest indigenous groups, the Aymara and Quechua, were not officially recognized until 1977. The two groups live mostly in the western highlands, while smaller indigenous groups, such as the Guarani, Arawak and Chiquitano live in the eastern lowlands.

Calzadilla says the situation for indigenous peoples in Bolivia has greatly improved since the 1950s, when the elite populations of largely European ancestry viewed the natives as slaves, or "pongos," and did not allow them to enter the main square of the capital, La Paz. Today, he says, indigenous people are represented in the executive and legislative branches of government and at all levels of the army. The Morales government also has adopted anti-racism laws, and many indigenous Bolivians credit Morales' policies with helping them to finally reach equality after centuries of discrimination.

activist with the Mapuche Foundation Folil, a human rights advocacy group founded in the Netherlands by Mapuche Indians for their countrymen who remained in Chile, "Chile and Argentina nowadays can be called ultra-liberal economies — economies where literally everything is for sale." Ancestral lands have been sold to forestry companies to plant environmentally damaging eucalyptus trees, she notes, and multinational corporations like Benetton have bought lands in southern Argentina's Patagonia to raise sheep.

Regardless of where they live, nearly all indigenous groups struggle with many of the same social problems, including serious domestic violence. Indigenous women in Australia are 35 times as likely to be hospitalized as a result of family violence-related assaults as nonindigenous females. [6] In the United States, two of every five

But the 40 percent of the population with European or mestizo ancestry who still control most of Bolivia's mineral and petroleum resources fear Morales will redistribute their wealth to poorer regions. The lowlands' economic dominance has emerged only in the past few decades. During colonial times, Bolivia's wealth was concentrated in the silver- and tin-rich highlands.

Eduardo Gamarra — a comparative politics professor at Florida International University in Miami and a Bolivian national — notes that lowlanders are worried because the Morales government "has been sending waves of indigenous people into the lowlands of Santa Cruz." That could erode the political power of the mestizo elite and make them more intolerant of indigenous groups. He adds that "Venezuela is financing Morales," and points out that Morales and Chavez "are both anti-U.S. and view the white elites as racist."

Calzadilla admits that in the early years of Morales' rule "strong resistance came from the nonindigenous population, mostly descendents of the Spanish colonizers" who live in the lowlands, some of whom in 2007 and 2008 even threatened to organize a secessionist movement. Such talk seems to have quieted down in the past couple of years. [3]

Although most indigenous Bolivians support Morales, some also criticize him. For example, the indigenous communities living in sprawling Madidi National Park worry about government plans to authorize oil and gas drilling and construction of a hydro-electric dam and highway in the park.

Mirna Fernández, coordinator of the Save The Madidi Campaign, says President Morales is guilty of "reprehensible incoherence" by invoking Pachamama — or Mother Earth, the Andean deity of indigenous peoples — while moving to exploit nonrenewable resources in protected areas. [4]

Calzadilla says the government's relations with indigenous groups in the lowlands are "very good" but admits that native communities take a more "ecological" view of government infrastructure projects in the area.

— *Brian Beary*

AFP/Getty Images/Aizar Raldes

Bolivian President Evo Morales — Latin America's first indigenous leader — greets Andean natives during a collective marriage ceremony for 355 couples in a coliseum in La Paz, on May 7, 2011. The ceremony was designed to honor ancient Andean rituals.

[1] "Bolivian President Chews Coca During Speech At UN," *The Huffington Post*, March 11, 2009, www.huffingtonpost.com/2009/03/11/bolivian-president-chews_n_174075.html.

[2] Comments made during conference entitled, "Bolivia: A Country Divided," at the Hudson Institute, Washington, D.C., April 1, 2009.

[3] For background, see Roland Flamini, "The New Latin America," *CQ Global Researcher*, March 1, 2008, pp. 57-84.

[4] Frank Chavez, "Madidi National Park and the Curse of Petroleum in Bolivia," IPS, Dec. 13, 2010, www.galdu.org/web/index.php?odas=5001&giella1=eng.

Native American women will suffer domestic violence during her lifetime, and one in three will be sexually abused. [7] Donald Rodgers, chief of South Carolina's Catawba Indian Nation, said violence against women "has been an issue for hundreds of years for Indians," largely due to alcohol abuse.

"There are so many vicious-cycle issues" involving violence, suicide, sexual abuse and drug and alcohol abuse among Native Americans, U.S. Sen. Al Franken, D-Minn., a member of the Senate Indian Affairs Committee, said in July. "We owe Indians a special debt for our own negligence in not fully funding Indian health care, education and law enforcement, which we are supposed to do by treaty." [8]

In New Zealand, the Maori comprise only 14 percent of the general population but 51 percent of prison

Problems Proliferate Among Indigenous Groups

The socioeconomic situation for indigenous societies around the globe is often significantly disparate from the general populations in their home countries. Life expectancy, for example, is much lower for indigenous individuals in Canada, Australia and New Zealand than for the overall population. Suicide rates among Native Americans and the Canadian Inuit are higher than in the nonindigenous populations, and Guatemala's indigenous peoples are less educated and poorer than other Guatemalans.

Socioeconomic Indicators for Select Indigenous Groups

- **Life expectancy:** Canadian Inuit die 15 years younger than other Canadians. New Zealand Maori die more than eight years earlier than non-Maori. Aboriginal Australian men die 12 years younger than non-Aboriginal men and Aboriginal women 10 years earlier than non-Aboriginal women.
- **Alcoholism:** Liver disease among Native Americans is four times greater than the U.S. national average.
- **Obesity:** Maori have nearly twice the national rate of obesity compared to the rest of New Zealand.
- **Suicide:** The suicide rate among Native Americans is 70 percent higher than among the general population. Canadian Inuit are 11 times more likely to commit suicide than the general population.
- **Poverty:** 80 percent of the indigenous population in Guatemala is poor, compared to 40 percent of the nonindigenous population.
- **Crime:** 51 percent of the prison population in New Zealand is Maori despite being only 14 percent of the overall population. 34 percent of Canadian male and 41 percent of female young offenders are members of the First Nations, despite being only 4 percent of the country's total population.
- **Education:** Only 5 percent of university students in Guatemala are indigenous, despite comprising more than half of the population.
- **Domestic violence:** Aboriginal Australian women are 35 times more likely to be hospitalized as a result of family violence-related assaults than nonindigenous females.

Sources: Peter Katel, "American Indians," *CQ Researcher,* April 28, 2006 (updated July 2010); Inuit Tapiriit Kanatami; Joanna Hoare, "State of World's Minorities and Indigenous People 2011," Minority Rights Group International, July 6 2011, pp. 113, 174

inmates. [9] The insecurity and violence prevalent in Mexico today are "particularly notable in states with significant numbers of indigenous peoples and/or African-descendant populations," according to the London-based Minority Rights Group International, which supports indigenous peoples in 60 countries worldwide. [10] In Canada, "the living conditions of First Nations are still

shocking," * says Shawn Atleo, national chief of the Assembly for First Nations, which represents Canada's Indians. "Some in my community have no running water. The gap is widening, and we need to close it."

Some governments have acknowledged that their past actions toward indigenous groups have caused or contributed to these problems. In February 2008 Australian Prime Minister Kevin Rudd delivered a heartfelt apology for government policies from 1900 to 1970 that led to some 50,000 Aboriginal children being forcibly taken from their parents and placed in white foster homes, creating the so-called Stolen Generation. [11] Later that year, the Canadian government apologized for its treatment of indigenous Canadians, notably the forced relocation of Inuit families to the High Arctic in 1953. *

While the overall picture seems bleak for indigenous peoples, some pockets of home-grown economic development provide some grounds for optimism. Since 1988, when the U.S. Congress gave Native Americans special rights to establish gaming casinos on their reservations, Indians have developed a lucrative gaming industry, with $26 billion in revenue in 2010. [12]

Donald Laverdure, U.S. deputy assistant secretary for Indian Affairs, says gambling has helped tribes provide better education and health care, but critics say the revenues are concentrated in a small number of tribes and aren't always used to promote Indians' social and economic development.

---

* First Nations refers to the Canada's more than 600 indigenous peoples, except for the Inuit and those of mixed European-First Nations ancestry, who are called Métis.

As indigenous societies struggle to make progress, here are some of the key questions being raised:

Should indigenous peoples control their natural resources?

Most governments resist the idea of ceding control over natural resources to indigenous peoples, notes Sheryl Lightfoot, a Canadian Anishinabe Indian and assistant professor in First Nations studies and political science at the University of British Columbia.

"Many countries accept that indigenous peoples should have their rights to language, culture and religion recognized and respected," she says. "What most countries in the world object to — whether they admit it or not — are indigenous rights to land and resources, as well as self-determination."

Governments often claim to consult systematically with indigenous peoples over the use of natural resources, but skeptics say they only give the semblance of doing so. Even in Bolivia — which has an indigenous president and claims to protect indigenous rights — large-scale government development projects have faced resistance from some indigenous groups. For example, groups from the Madidi National Park area are protesting plans by President Evo Morales to allow oil and gas drilling there and construction of a hydroelectric dam and highway.

In Argentina and Chile, according to Chilean human rights activist Zuniga, "The main problem of the Mapuche can be put in one word: land, more specific, ancestral land. . . . Not for nothing the word Mapuche means: 'People of the Earth.' " [13]

Zuniga lambasted Argentina and Chile for policies that effectively deprive indigenous communities of control over their lands, in violation of the two countries' legal obligations under the International Labour Organization's Convention 169. [14] The treaty gives indigenous peoples "certain collective rights," she says, "especially regarding foreigners entering the area for economic exploration and exploitation." Zuniga welcomed a recent court ruling in Argentina that supported the Mapuche, who argued a major land purchase by the Piedra del Aguila oil company would have pushed the Mapuche off their land. [15]

The Arctic's Inuit also are keen to avoid a resource grab by outsiders. International interest in their region is

Aboriginal elder Dick Brown, 58, partially paralyzed from a stroke, lives in a rough camp in the Australian Outback town of Alice Springs. Aboriginals are one of the world's poorest indigenous communities. While many countries have bolstered indigenous groups' legal and political rights in recent years, they continue to have chronically high poverty rates, disproportionate shares of the prison population and life expectancies 10 years shorter than the general population.

AFP/Getty Images/Anoek de Groot

growing due to the abundance of oil and other natural resources, which are becoming more accessible as the polar ice caps melt.

"We have lived here for thousands and thousands of years," said Patricia Cochran, former chairperson of the Inuit Circumpolar Council (ICC) and an Alaskan Inuit. "You must talk to us and respect our rights." [16]

Cochran's ICC colleague, Aqqaluk Lynge, is equally forceful. "This is Inuit territory. While we are very loyal to our respective governments, they must assist us in helping to build Inuit unity and helping Inuit use the resources in a sustainable manner," says Lynge, chairperson of the ICC, who is Greenlandic Inuit. Indigenous peoples historically have managed resources more sustainably than foreigners, he said, citing the 1600s, "when the first foreign whaling ship came to hunt our big whales and decimated our stocks, from which they have never recovered." [17]

Canada — with an abundance of oil sands, much of it on indigenous homelands — has adopted the First Nations Land Management Act, under which 30 participating nations manage their lands and resources. In 2009, First Nation companies performed $810 million in contract work for oil sands companies, and more than

1,600 native peoples were directly employed in oil sands operations. [18] According to Chief Atleo of the Assembly of First Nations, "more and more industries realize they need to consult indigenous peoples — it makes commercial sense." But he admits there remains some disagreement with the Canadian government over the precise meaning of "consultation" and "consent."

In New Zealand, the Maori's right to control their natural resources is enshrined in the 1840 Treaty of Waitangi. Article 2 of the treaty guarantees the Maori would have "full and exclusive possession of their fisheries," notes Valmaine Toki, a member of the U.N. Permanent Forum on Indigenous Issues and a law lecturer at the University of Auckland. When the government introduced a private property-based quota system for fish catches, the Maori sued to get their traditional community fishing rights recognized, and won. "This is an example of Maori exercising a form of self-determination," says Toki.

Brazil, however, lacks "an effective mechanism for consultation with indigenous peoples on the planning of major development projects, such as large-scale mining, and highway and dam construction," laments James Anaya, U.N. Special Rapporteur on the Rights of Indigenous Peoples. [19] In Guyana, a 2006 law earmarked 20 percent of the royalties from mining activities for Amerindians. But indigenous leaders have complained about not being consulted in the country's anti-deforestation campaign, including how to spend $250 million that Norway has donated to fight climate change. [20]

Should indigenous peoples have more autonomy?

The degree of autonomy enjoyed by indigenous peoples varies significantly from region to region.

In the Arctic, for instance, Sami parliaments exist in Norway, Finland and even Sweden, which traditionally has been among the most conservative Nordic states in recognizing Sami rights, according to Lars-Anders Baer, chairman of the Sami cultural organization Gáldu. In the last five to six years, he said, there has been "a dramatic shift in the Swedish position in favor of [the] Sami right to self-determination." [21]

In New Zealand, according to Margaret Mutu, head of the Maori Studies Department at the University of Auckland, "the Maori don't accept that the Pakeha [white settlers] are the legitimate colonizers, but rather are

immigrant settlers invited by the Maori to stay there." In Chile, the Mapuche see themselves as a separate nation culturally and ethnically, says César Millahueique, a Mapuche poet and language activist. The Mapuche want to reconstruct their territory, which the Chilean government confiscated in the 1880s and exploited, leaving them impoverished and marginalized, he says.

"Our government has programs today promoting bilingual education and better health services," Millahueique says. "But these are not enough. The Mapuche want political autonomy."

Some indigenous communities are split over what form their autonomy should take. For instance, a debate is raging among Hawaiians over whether everyone should have a special autonomous status or only those designated as "pure-blood" Hawaiians. About 400,000 of Hawaii's 1.3 million residents claim Hawaiian ancestry. [22] Mililani Trask, a pro-autonomy activist, supports extending self-government to all Hawaiians but acknowledges that the state government, two U.S. senators and the Council for Native Hawaiians "favor autonomy only for the pure-bloods."

In some cases, granting autonomy to a regional indigenous community can create resentment among the group it was intended to satisfy. For example, in Nicaragua the indigenous Miskito, who live on the Atlantic Coast, were granted regional autonomy in the 1980s, but that apparently did not satisfy all group members. According to Danish conservationist Claus Kjaerby at the International Work Group for Indigenous Affairs, high abstention rates in recent regional elections indicate that the Miskito reject the political party model of regional autonomy that has been imposed on them, saying it has not met their political aspirations. [23]

Elsewhere, the level of autonomy granted to a group can end up being insufficient in practice. For example, Native Americans are responsible for their own policing and judiciary, but their judicial system faces major obstacles because they cannot prosecute non-Indians, according to U.S. Assistant Attorney General Tom Perrelli. Yet four out of five people who commit sex crimes or battery against Indians are non-Indians, he said. [24]

To fix the problem, Aaron Running Hawk, a member of the Black Hill Sioux Treaty Council, a pro-independence Lakota Indian group, says the council wants "to set up a traditional form of government based on treaties from 1851 and 1868, which the U.S. Supreme Court ruled in

1978 were still valid." U.S. Deputy Assistant Secretary of the Interior Laverdure says the Obama administration would be amenable to reviewing the current model of autonomy. "If they want to re-do their framework, that is okay with us," he says. "Some of them are thinking about this, and we want to assist them."

Autonomy discussions are not as far advanced in some other countries. Indigenous peoples in Colombia have been caught in the crossfire of a vicious, decades-long civil war. The Regional Indigenous Council of Cauca, an advocacy group founded in 1971 in southwestern Colombia's Cauca Department, has launched a protest movement to try to get the Colombian army and the rebel militia to dismantle the bases and camps they operate in Cauca homelands. "We don't want to give either side a military advantage," the group has said. "What we want is to defend the lives and the autonomy of our communities." [25]

Some Latin American indigenous groups have focused on the judicial dimension of autonomy. In Ecuador, groups increasingly use communal justice to combat violent crime, triggering a nationwide debate. [26] For example, some nonindigenous critics demanded limits on the practice of indigenous justice after a man who confessed to murder was sentenced to receive corporal punishment and make financial payments to the victim's mother.

But researchers and sociologists countered that communal justice, such as a public flogging or a dousing in cold water, "are more effective than sending a young man away for a four-year prison sentence that is devoid of social context and lacks rehabilitation measures," noted Maurice Bryan, information officer for the Minority Rights Group International. [27] Similarly, in Guatemala the Mayans seem more interested in judicial and cultural autonomy, according to Arturo Arias, the Guatemalan novelist and critic. "They want to be judged under Mayan law. This was written into the 1996 peace treaty that ended the civil war, but implementation has been slow."

Should indigenous peoples be integrated into mainstream society?

When indigenous peoples become more socially integrated with the general population — for example through intermarriage or by living in closer proximity — it sometimes leads to a dilution or loss of indigenous culture. However, the recent experience of native Hawaiians shows how an indigenous people can integrate and function in mainstream society while keeping one of their main cultural carriers, their native language.

In the 1970s, incredibly, fewer than 50 children under age 18 were fluent in the Hawaiian language. Since then, the number of fluent children has skyrocketed, according to language activist Namaka Rawlins. [28] The Hawaiian Language College, where she teaches, offers 57 undergraduate- through doctorate-level courses in Hawaiian and operates a school for pre-K through grade 12. The graduating students are fluent in English as well as Hawaiian.

But Hawaii's positive experience hasn't been replicated in many other native U.S. communities. For instance, a settlement of Meskwaki Indians in Iowa has only a "dwindling number of fluent Meskwaki speakers," according to resident Larry C. Lasley, Sr. Specifically, only 16 percent of tribal members are fluent in Meskwaki, while 63 percent understand only a few or no words. He attributes the decline, which has accelerated since the 1960s, to the need to learn English to deal with local authorities to gain water, food, sanitation and housing. [29]

In Canada, Chief Atleo of the Assembly of First Nations says only three of the assembly's 52 indigenous languages are expected to survive: Inuit, Cree and Ojibwe. His own Nuu-chah-nulth language has only 24 fluent speakers left, most in their 60s or older, he notes.

Plaut, the researcher studying Sami culture in Norway, regrets that a corollary question — Should mainstream society become more fluent in indigenous languages? — is never asked. "This is a more interesting question," she says. "I have never met a mono-lingual Sami person in my time here."

Plaut likes the Sami model of self-determination. They have preserved their language and culture, but they still function in their home country societies. They also benefit from various privileges. For example, reindeer husbandry is reserved for the Sami, all laws in Norway must be translated into Sami and the Sami language can be used in communicating with public officials and the judiciary. [30]

Governments have learned that coercive integration policies can damage indigenous societies, as occurred among Aboriginal Australians in the 1900s. In an effort to integrate indigenous children — primarily those with lighter skin color — into mainstream society, the Australian government forcibly took many of them from

Leading one of their iconic reindeer, Sami people march through Stockholm on Nov. 23, 2007, to demand protection of their herding rights. Formerly called Laplanders, the Sami live above the Arctic Circle and enjoy a relatively high degree of autonomy, with their own parliaments in Norway, Finland and Sweden.

their parents and placed them in institutions or with white foster families.

The program was a dismal failure. The Aboriginals remained marginalized and suffered from discrimination. A 1997 report cataloged the pain inflicted on Aboriginal society by the coercive practices, spurring the Australian government, 11 years later, to issue its 2008 apology. [31]

Yet, others contest the notion that Aboriginals are better off being separated from the rest of society. Helen Hughes, a senior fellow at the libertarian Centre for Independent Studies, a think tank with offices in Australia and New Zealand, argues that "communal property rights have prevented development" among the 80,000 Aboriginals living on remote reservations, characterized by "dismal shops and public housing . . . reminiscent of communist Russia." Furthermore, Hughes writes with her son Mark, an independent researcher, "Aboriginal curriculums and poor teaching have denied indigenous children basic schooling, [and] so-called bilingual education has been an excuse for no education at all." [32]

Integration often occurs when indigenous and nonindigenous people intermarry, but the frequency of intermarriage differs from country to country — and sometimes from region to region inside a country. For example, Nicaragua's three main ethnic groups are the indigenous Miskito, the Ladinos (people of mixed Spanish-indigenous ancestry) and the Afro-Caribbean community. According

to the Rev. Norman Bent, a minister of the Moravian Church who is of mixed Miskito/Afro-Caribbean ancestry, although "there is a lot of intermarriage and not much conflict between the Miskito and Afro-Caribbean peoples, . . . there is more of a cultural conflict with the Ladinos."

The University of British Columbia's Lightfoot says intermarriage between indigenous and nonindigenous people, which has always been common, should not be used to deny indigenous peoples their right to nationhood. "No other group or nation faces this very unreasonable expectation that they should somehow retain 'purity of the blood' in order to be entitled to the same rights that all other peoples on Earth already possess," she says.

"For indigenous peoples, intermarriage is often read as a forfeiture of nationhood," she adds, calling the concept a "strangely colonial and racialized way of thinking."

BACKGROUND

Conquest and Settlement

Indigenous peoples lived in the Americas, Australasia and the Arctic for millennia before European settlers showed up.

Aboriginal Australians are thought to have arrived on the continent up to 60,000 years ago. The earliest residents of the North American Arctic probably arrived about 14,000 years ago. Scandinavia's Sami culture is around 5,000 years old, while the Inuit first arrived in Greenland from modern-day Canada some 4,500 years ago. The Mayan civilization flourished in Central America, roughly from 1000 B.C. to A.D. 900. The Maori first arrived in New Zealand around A.D. 800. [33]

European conquest began with the arrival of Viking leader Erik the Red, who set up a Norse colony in Greenland in A.D. 986. The Europeans left in 1450, but a permanent Scandinavian presence was re-established by Danish-Norwegian priest Hans Egede in 1721.

After Christopher Columbus landed in the Caribbean in 1492 on behalf of Spain's King Ferdinand and Queen Isabella, the Spanish went on to conquer and colonize much of Central and South America in the 1500s.

Over the next three centuries the French, English, Portuguese and Dutch competed with the Spanish to control

Reuters/Scanpix/Bertil Ericson

the Americas, and their policies toward the indigenous peoples differed considerably. The Northern Europeans — the French, British and Dutch — tended to negotiate treaties with aboriginal peoples rather than conquering them militarily. [34] The Southern Europeans — the Spanish and Portuguese — relied more on papal bulls (orders from the Roman Catholic pope) to claim indigenous lands and forcibly convert natives to Christianity. [35]

European whalers began exploring the Inuit's Arctic homelands in the 1700s, while Russians explored the western Arctic around Alaska, converting some of the Aleut and Inuit peoples to Orthodox Christianity. Australia and New Zealand came under European influence starting in the late 1760s, after the discoveries of English explorer Capt. James Cook. Many of Australia's earliest immigrants were convicted criminals, sent over to do hard labor in penal colonies.

Post-Colonial Assimilation

From the late 1700s, indigenous peoples increasingly found themselves living in newly independent countries established by descendents of European settlers. One of the first was the United States, which won its independence from Britain after the eight-year Revolutionary War. As the new nation expanded westward in the 1800s, whites began hunting and settling on Indian lands, fomenting bitter and bloody conflict.

In 1830, Congress adopted the Indian Removal Act, which led five large Southern Indian tribes — the Cherokee, Chickasaw, Creek, Seminole and Chocktaw — to be forcibly moved to Indian Territory west of the Mississippi River.

Forty years later, the U.S. government essentially replaced its policy of treaty-making with Indian nations with a policy of assimilation. The process was accelerated by the Dawes Act of 1887, which led to parcels of Indian land being sold off to private individuals, badly fragmenting the Indian tribes. [36] By 1900, the Indians had lost 95 percent of the land they had held in 1800, when they controlled 80 percent of the land in today's continental United States west of the Eastern Seaboard.

Meanwhile, the United States continued to expand its dominion over indigenous peoples, notably by buying Alaska from Russia in 1867 and invading and occupying Hawaii in 1893, when U.S. forces and business interests forced Queen Lili'uokalani to abdicate.

From 1871 to 1921, Canada signed 11 treaties with its aboriginal nations — the Inuit, Cree, Métis and others.

A key piece of Canadian legislation was the 1876 Indian Act, whose ultimate goal was to assimilate Canada's indigenous community. [37] In Latin America, indigenous peoples saw ever-increasing incursions onto their homelands — such as the Chilean government's seizure of Mapuche lands in the 1880s.

Meanwhile, the conversion of indigenous peoples to Christianity was proceeding apace. The Roman Catholic Church sent many missionaries to Central and South America in the 1500s. In the mid-1800s, Moravians from Germany, England and Sweden converted many of Nicaragua's indigenous Miskito. Christians also converted a large share of North America's Inuit.

A pivotal moment in Maori history occurred in 1840, when tribal leaders established their future political relationship with the English settlers by signing the Treaty of Waitangi. In 1867, four seats in the New Zealand parliament were designated for the Maori. The introduction of guns into Maori society, acquired from British settlers, exacerbated intertribal warfare. The Maori also lost much of their best land to white settlers in a war that lasted from 1860 to 1872. The Maori population declined dramatically, hitting a low of around 45,000 in 1901. (It is 575,000 today.) [38]

At the same time, in Scandinavia, the Sami also faced challenges: As Sweden, Finland, Norway and Russia consolidated their borders, they cut through Sami homelands, making travel and reindeer herding more difficult.

In the early 1900s, some governments adopted assimilation policies, encouraging — or coercing — indigenous peoples into shedding their distinct identity. In Australia, for instance, between 10 and 30 percent of Aboriginal children were removed from their families and placed in institutional or foster care, a policy that lasted until 1970. Moreover, the movement of Aboriginals who were not removed and assimilated was tightly circumscribed.

"In the name of protection, Indigenous peoples were subject to near-total control," a 1997 government investigation said. "Their entry and exit from reserves was regulated, as was their everyday life on the reserves, their right to marry and their employment." Partly to convert them to Christianity, "children were housed in dormitories and contact with their families strictly limited." [39]

The United States also embraced an assimilation policy. In 1906, for example, Congress ordered food rations withheld from Indians unless they agreed to cut their hair, traditionally worn long. Indian children in the West were taken into towns and forced to attend schools where they were prohibited from speaking their native languages. [40]

In 1953, Congress passed Concurrent Resolution 108, marking the beginning of the so-called termination policy, which revoked the recognition and support the government had given to many Indian nations via the reservations system. [41] The change led to the displacement of more than 10,000 Indians, many of whom moved from their reservations into large cities; the San Francisco Bay area was a popular destination.

Also in 1953, Denmark made largely Inuit Greenland an integral part of the country. Similarly, six years later, Alaska and Hawaii became U.S. states.

In Norway, the government tried from 1905, when Norway became independent from Sweden, until the 1960s to assimilate the Sami. As part of the new nation's "Norwegianization" policy, citizens wanting to buy land had to be able to read and write in Norwegian. The policy triggered a decline in the use of the Sami language until the government ended the policy in 1959. [42]

Self-Determination

As the 1900s progressed, indigenous peoples slowly began to find their political voice and to win some recognition and concessions from the governments ruling their homelands. In the United States, for instance, the government's initial move toward self-government for Native Americans was the Indian Reorganization Act of 1934, which created a system of tribal government on certain Indian reservations.

In the 1960s, however, the Civil Rights movement provoked a political awakening among American Indians. In 1969 several dozen Indians occupied Alcatraz Island in San Francisco Bay, site of an abandoned maximum-security prison. The Alcatraz occupation, which lasted until 1971, attracted public attention — and some sympathy — to Indian demands for genuine autonomy. In the end, the government in the 1970s adopted a policy of self-determination for Indians and a raft of legislation aimed at promoting their autonomy, land rights, economic development and cultural preservation. [43]

In New Zealand, Maori sovereignty claims over their land and natural resources got a boost in 1975 when the

Waitangi Tribunal was established to examine such claims. But the Maori suffered a setback in 2004 when the parliament passed the Foreshore and Seabed Act denying Maoris sovereignty over coastal areas. Maori anger over the edict forged a new sense of political unity and sparked the creation of the Maori Party in 2008.

Aboriginal Australians' scored a major legal victory in 1992 when the High Court rejected a notion espoused by successive Australian governments, known as "terra nullius," which held that no one owned the land until white Australians settled it. The case had been filed by Eddie Mabo, an Aboriginal from the Torres Strait Islands, which separate Australia from Papua New Guinea. The ruling led to the 1993 passage of the Native Title Act, which increased Aboriginal land rights and set up tribunals to look into Aboriginal land claims.

But in 2007 the Australian government took back some of the autonomy it had granted Aboriginal communities in the Northern Territory after the government found widespread child abuse at indigenous settlements. Specifically, the government seized control of alcohol and welfare-payment distribution, as alcohol abuse was considered a major contributing factor to the abuse. [44]

In Latin America between the 1960s and 1980s, indigenous peoples were buffeted by a power struggle between militant leftist groups and autocratic, often military-backed, right-wing governments. Peru's indigenous Amazonian communities greatly suffered at the hands of the Shining Path, a rebel Maoist group that controlled large parts of the country in the 1980s. Three-quarters of the 70,000 people killed during Peru's conflict with the Shining Path were Quechua-speakers.

In Paraguay, the country's 20 different indigenous peoples were nearly wiped out during the long dictatorship of Gen. Alfredo Strossner (1954-89), when their lands were aggressively confiscated for agricultural use and workers were brutally exploited. [45] In Guatemala, Mayans were associated with an anti-government insurgency in the 1970s, which prompted the government to conduct widespread massacres in Mayan villages.

A new, somewhat brighter era began in the late 1980s, when Latin American countries began transitioning from autocracies into pluralist democracies. In Chile, for example, after Gen. Augusto Pinochet's dictatorship ended in 1990, the new government recognized the distinctness of Chile's indigenous communities. In the 1990s Mexico's

C H R O N O L O G Y

60,000 B.C.- A.D. 900 *Indigenous peoples populate Australasia, America and the Arctic.*

60,000 B.C.-800 A.D. Aboriginal Australians migrate to Australia from Micronesia. . . . Inuit ancestors begin to populate North American Arctic. . . . Sami culture emerges in Scandinavia in 5,000 B.C. . . . Mayan civilization flourishes in Central America. . . . Maori migrate from Polynesia to New Zealand.

986-1768 *Europeans conquer and colonize indigenous lands.*

986 Norse explorer Erik the Red establishes first European settlement on Greenland.

1492 Italian explorer Christopher Columbus leads a voyage to the Americas on behalf of the Spanish government, marking the beginning of European colonization in the Americas.

1700s European whalers hunt and explore in the Arctic. . . . Russian fur traders and missionaries settle Alaska.

1760s British and Irish settlement begins in Australia and New Zealand.

1800s-1950s *Settlers of European descent assimilate indigenous peoples in the New World.*

1830 U.S. Congress passes Indian Removal Act, which forcibly relocates five large Indian tribes from the South to territory west of the Mississippi River.

1840 Maori tribal leaders sign Treaty of Waitangi with English settlers, establishing the terms for white settlement of the territory.

1887 Congress passes Dawes Act permitting the sale of Indian lands to non-Indians, further fragmenting Indian territories.

1880s Chilean authorities seize lands from the indigenous Mapuche in a so-called pacification campaign.

1901 Australia gains independence from Britain and institutes aggressive assimilation policy toward

Aboriginals, including forcibly removing children from their parents and putting them into institutions or foster homes.

1953 Denmark annexes its largely Inuit colony, Greenland.

1959 Alaska and Hawaii, both with large indigenous populations, become states and are fully integrated into the United States.

1960s-2011 *Indigenous peoples worldwide mobilize politically. Many governments replace assimilation policies with greater recognition and autonomy for indigenous peoples.*

1969 American Indians occupy Alcatraz Island in San Francisco Bay in effort to force U.S. government to give greater autonomy to Native Americans.

1979 Inter-American Court for Human Rights is established in Costa Rica, eventually ruling on indigenous-rights cases from Paraguay, Suriname, Guatemala and Brazil.

1987 Norway establishes Sami parliament. Sweden and Finland later follow suit.

1988 Congress passes Indian Gaming Regulatory Act, paving the way for Indians to set up casinos and fostering rapid growth in the casino industry and much-needed revenues for Indian communities.

1992 "Mabo" ruling by Australia's high court says Aboriginals have the right to claim title over traditional lands, triggering passage of the 1993 Native Title Act establishing tribunals to examine indigenous land claims.

2007 U.N. General Assembly approves Declaration on the Rights of Indigenous Peoples. Australia, Canada, New Zealand and the United States, which initially opposed it, later endorse the measure.

2008 Passage of a referendum grants enhanced autonomy to Greenlanders.

2011 Energy and tourism development plans on indigenous lands cause mounting tension between indigenous and nonindigenous populations in Brazil, Peru, Russia, Canada and Chile.

Aboriginals and Maori Took Different Paths

Political, cultural and social progress has been uneven.

New Zealand's Maori and Australia's Aboriginals are a study in contrasts. The two neighboring groups have asserted themselves differently — and been treated differently by their European colonizers — with varying degrees of political, cultural and sociological success.

For instance, only three Aboriginals have served in the national parliament during Australia's 110-year history. Two national Aboriginal representative bodies created in the 1970s and '80s were ultimately disbanded amid claims they did not truly represent the Aboriginals. The Maori, by contrast, have had specially designated seats in the New Zealand parliament for more than a century, and today their 15 percent representation in parliament corresponds to their population share. Aboriginals constitute just 2 percent of Australia's population.

Many of the 80 Aboriginal languages are on the verge of extinction, and only 30,000 Australian students are learning an indigenous language. [1] In New Zealand, the Maori language is also at crisis point, according to Valmaine Toki, a member of the U.N. Permanent Forum on Indigenous Peoples and a law lecturer at the University of Auckland, who is of Maori descent.

"At school, the proportion of Maori children participating in Maori-medium education [schools where Maori is the language of instruction] has dropped from a high point of 18.6 per cent in 1999 to 15.2 per cent in 2009," she says. Fewer young people speak Maori, she notes, so older native speakers are not replaced as they die.

The gap between the two groups is also less obvious with regard to social indicators. Social and economic conditions among the Maori put them at an "extreme disadvantage . . . across a range of indicators, including education, health and income," according to James Anaya, a Native American, who is the U.N. special rapporteur on the rights of indigenous peoples. After leaving secondary school, for example, only one in five Maori students is qualified to attend university. [2] Similarly, the Aboriginal and Torres Strait Islander peoples "continue to rank as the most disadvantaged peoples in Australia," particularly with regard to education, employment, health, life expectancy, domestic violence and child abuse, according to Jacqui Zalcberg, author of a paper on indigenous peoples in Oceania for the U.K.-based advocacy organization, Minority Rights Group International. [3]

As for securing land rights and control of natural resources, the Maori have had a head start, but the Aboriginals are catching up. In 1975, the New Zealand government set up the Waitangi Tribunal, which gave the Maori a legal forum to pursue land claims. By mid-2010, the tribunal was wading through 3,490 claims. "Overall, the Waitangi Tribunal has provided enormous benefits for all of New Zealand by helping to provide redress for Maori grievances," reported Anaya.

Australia's government created a similar legal forum for Aboriginals in 1993, spurred on by a landmark 1992 court ruling in the "Mabo" case, which overturned previous case-law by insisting that Aboriginals had the right to claim title to their traditional lands. So far, Aboriginals have succeeding in reclaiming some of their lands in the 145 tribunal rulings. [4]

There have been bumps along the road for both peoples, such as the 2004 Foreshore and Seabed Act in New Zealand, which limited the Maori's ability to claim shoreline areas. The government in 2009 agreed to repeal the act after fierce Maori opposition, but Parliament has yet to repeal the measure.

Mayans created about 30 autonomous municipalities in the southern state of Chiapas as part of the so-called Zapatista insurgency. Ancestral government policies — including communal land ownership, indigenous education and the practice of traditional medicine — were restored. Although the Mexican government did not recognize the autonomy of the new municipalities, it did not use military force to suppress them.

Aboriginals — Australia's original inhabitants — have lived on their homelands for more than 50,000 years, having migrated there from Micronesia, while the Maori are believed to have arrived a little over 1,000 years ago from Polynesia. But after the British and Irish began to arrive in New Zealand and Australia in the 1800s, both populations plummeted — almost to the point of extinction by 1900. Both native populations have rebounded in recent decades, as the governments replaced assimilation policies with an acknowledgement of their right of self-determination.

Australia has recently shown itself a leader in making amends for historical injustices. In February 2008, Prime Minister Kevin Rudd delivered a lengthy and heartfelt apology to Aboriginal peoples for previous governments' policies of removing Aboriginal children from their parents. The forcible placement of Aboriginal children in state-run institutions or with non-Aboriginal foster parents was part of a policy aimed at assimilating Aboriginals into white Australian society. Rudd then instituted several policies aimed at improving the Aboriginals' lives.

The Closing the Gap program, for example, requires the government to make detailed yearly status reports on Aboriginals' status and establish concrete targets in areas such as health services, school attendance and employment training. [5] The targets include closing the 10-year gap in life expectancy between indigenous and nonindigenous populations within a generation and halving child mortality rates by 2018. [6]

— *Brian Beary*

A Maori dancer performs during a traditional welcoming ceremony for the Australian rugby team in Auckland, New Zealand, on Sept. 6, 2011. The Maoris have achieved greater political representation than Australia's Aboriginals.

[1] "Indigenous Language Programmes in Australian Schools — A Way Forward," Australia Department of Education, November 2008, pp. x-xii, www.dest.gov.au/NR/rdonlyres/FBEAC65B-3A11-41F0-B836-1A480FDD82F9/25487/LPfinal130109NP.pdf.

[2] James Anaya, "Report of the Special Rapporteur on the Rights of Indigenous Peoples, Addendum, The situation of Máori People in New Zealand," United Nations, Feb. 17, 2011, http://unsr.jamesanaya.org/docs/countries/2011_report_new_zealand_advanced_version.pdf.

[3] Joanna Hoare, ed., "State of World's Minorities and Indigenous People 2011 (Events of 2010)," Minority Rights Group International, July 6, 2011, p. 174, www.minorityrights.org/10848/state-of-the-worlds-minorities/state-of-the-worlds-minorities-and-indigenous-peoples-2011.html.

[4] "National Perspective," Native Title Tribunal, www.nntt.gov.au/Native-Title-In-Australia/Pages/National-Perspective.aspx.

[5] Kevin Rudd, "Tjurkurpa: For the Indigenous People of the World," speech at Adelaide Town Hall, July 26, 2011, www.foreignminister.gov.au/speeches/2011/kr_sp_110726.html.

[6] "Closing the Gap — Prime Minister's Report 2011," Government of Australia, February 2011, www.fahcsia.gov.au/sa/indigenous/pubs/closing_the_gap/2011_ctg_pm_report/Pages/part_a.aspx.

In Norway, the Sami sought to mobilize politically in the 1970s after plans were announced for a hydropower project on the Alta River, which would have interfered with their fishing and reindeer herding. Although they failed to halt the power project, the Sami campaign — including hunger strikes outside parliament — ultimately persuaded the government to establish a Sami parliament in 1987.

Levels of Autonomy Vary

Indigenous peoples around the world have achieved varying degrees of autonomy or self-government, some only recently. For instance, the Greenlandic Inuit have enjoyed an increasing degree of autonomy since 2008, when its home-rule government was allowed to operate independently from Denmark in nearly all matters except defense. Many of Canada's Inuit, meanwhile, live in a special Inuit-majority province called Nunavut, created in 1999 under its "provincial autonomy" style of government.

Selected Examples of Indigenous Self-Government

- Tribal government on government-approved reservations (American Indians)
- Provincial or territorial autonomy (Canadian Inuit, Nicaraguan Miskito)
- Self-declared autonomous municipalities (Zapatista rebels in southern Mexico)
- Enhanced autonomy (Greenlandic Inuit)
- Indigenous parliaments (Sami in Norway, Sweden and Finland)
- Designated seats in national parliament (Maori in New Zealand)

Source: Brian Beary

Sweden and Finland, with smaller numbers of Sami, followed suit, and in 2000 the three Sami parliaments formed the joint Sami Parliamentary Council. Further west, Greenland was granted its own parliament in 1979; and in 2008 a referendum to grant Greenlanders further autonomy was approved by 76 percent of voters. [46]

International Forums

While indigenous peoples historically tended to negotiate with colonial and later national governments, the emergence of international justice and similar concepts has prompted native peoples to advocate for their rights in international forums. In the 1920s, for instance, an indigenous Canadian group made its case for self-government to the League of Nations, only to see Britain take the issue off the agenda by declaring it an internal matter.

When the League of Nations was succeeded after World War II by the United Nations, Bolivia tried unsuccessfully to create a panel to study the social problems of aboriginal populations. [47] In 1982, the United Nations formed a Working Group on Indigenous Populations. [48] The International Labour Organization, another U.N. agency, adopted a landmark treaty in 1989 recognizing indigenous

peoples' right to control their cultures, economic development, language and religion. [49] In 2000, the U.N. established the Permanent Forum on Indigenous Issues, which held its first meeting in 2002.

A major breakthrough on the international stage occurred on Sept. 13, 2007, when — after more than 20 years of negotiations — the U.N. General Assembly passed the Declaration on the Rights of Indigenous Peoples, approved by 144 countries.* [50]

In April 2009 Australia reversed its earlier opposition and endorsed the declaration, with New Zealand, Canada and the United States following suit in 2010. They carefully qualified their support by declaring that they would apply the declaration only within the limits of existing legal and constitutional frameworks.

According to Lightfoot at the University of British Columbia, the declaration has had "very limited" impact so far, as is generally the case with human rights declarations. However, "it will hopefully grow over time," she says.

Bolivia, a leading advocate of the declaration, and Ecuador have since enshrined the declaration in their constitutions, while Belize's high court has cited it in a case. The World Conference on Indigenous Peoples in 2014 will examine how to meet the goals set out in the declaration.

On a regional level, the Inter-American Court for Human Rights — established in 1979 in Costa Rica — has heard indigenous-related cases from many countries, including Paraguay, Suriname, Guatemala and Brazil. It has moral and political authority over such cases because regional governments have signed the American Convention on Human Rights, the core document interpreted by the court.

"Indigenous peoples are using the courts effectively," says the International Center for Transitional Justice's Gonzalez. In fact, some Mayans recently pursued claims

---

* Eleven countries abstained, and four nations — Australia, Canada, New Zealand and the United States — opposed it, mostly because they feared its impact on control of natural resources.

in Spanish courts, he notes, because Spain applies the principle of universal jurisdiction, meaning it hears cases involving human rights violations that allegedly occurred outside of its territory.

CURRENT SITUATION

Development Dilemma

The rising demand for natural resources found in their homelands is a significant challenge facing indigenous peoples today. Tensions are inevitable, given the reluctance of national governments to give indigenous groups a veto over local development projects.

In Danish-owned Greenland, exploration of subsurface resources is intensifying, with the Scottish oil-drilling company Cairn Energy moving 600 foreign workers each month to the town of Aasiaat in Disko Bay. [51] In Russia, the state-owned gas company Gazprom is building pipelines that would cut through ancestral lands of the Evenks, a small indigenous nation. In Canada, oil sands operations threaten to pollute the Athabasca River, which runs through lands occupied by the Athabasca Chipewyan and Mikisew Cree peoples. [52] In Mexico, a Spanish company is installing 410 wind turbines that encroach on the homelands of the Binniza and Huaves peoples in the Tehuantepec Isthmus.[53]

In South America, both Peru and Brazil are proceeding with plans to build hydropower stations that could flood indigenous communities and destroy tropical rainforests. [54] The Peruvian government also plans to give oil and gas companies access to lands occupied by a remote Indian nation in the Kugapakori Nahua Nanti nature reserve, which lies about 60 miles from the 15th-century Inca settlement of Machu Picchu. [55] Machu Picchu, Peru's biggest tourist attraction, attracted 800,000 visitors in 2010 and provides 70 percent of Peru's tourism revenue.

In Chile, the government is trying to convert its Easter Island territory, located in the Pacific Ocean 2,000 miles west of the Chilean mainland, into a tourist attraction centered around the island's 887 giant carved stone heads, known as Moais. Although the island was annexed by Chile in 1888, the Rapa Nui natives' opposition to Chile's occupation of their lands has resulted in regular and sometimes violent clashes, as well as a lawsuit filed with the Inter-American Commission on Human Rights. [56]

Most indigenous peoples want to be consulted before decisions are made regarding their resources. "There is no federal framework for getting prior consent," says Chief Atleo, from the Assembly of First Nations in Canada. "There is no national plan for energy. Instead, we have a patchwork of jurisdictions."

Indigenous groups are not universally opposed to resource development. For example:

- The Inuit of Greenland are keen to allow the extraction of oil and gas on their territory, which they see as crucial to their becoming more self-sufficient.
- Canada's Inuit, who are zealously trying to safeguard their right to trade in sealskins, have sued the European Union over its decision to ban sealskin imports. [57]
- Argentina's Guaraní Mbyá indigenous community, near the city of Puerto Iguazu and its spectacular Iguazu waterfalls, is developing — with funds from both Argentina and Canada — a tourism industry centered around its traditional culture. [58]
- In Brazil, the Suruí, a 1,300-member Amazon people, have forged a partnership with the government and the U.N. that will help them preserve some 925 square miles of rainforest and conduct carbon-friendly agriculture. [59]

Meanwhile, Native Americans' successful development of casinos on their reservations has produced remarkable results. Revenues from the still relatively young industry have grown rapidly.

"There has not been much downside" to the industry's growth, says Assistant Secretary Laverdure, "apart from the social ills associated with gambling."

But some U.S. lawmakers want tighter controls over how the casino revenues are used. After a 2006 U.S. District Appeals Court ruling limited the U.S. government's oversight powers on Indian-run casinos, Arizona Republican Sen. John McCain called for new legislation allowing the federal government to more closely scrutinize gaming operations. [60] But Indian representatives are generally opposed to changing the status quo.

Jamie Hummingbird, chairperson of the National Tribal Gaming Commissioners/Regulators, says a 1988 law that gives tribal governments the exclusive right to regulate their gaming industries provides a "stable framework."

Keith Anderson celebrates his Cherokee and Catawba heritage by competing in the men's traditional dance category at a Native American Pow-Wow in King William, Va. The Cherokee were among five Southern tribes forcibly moved to Indian Territory west of the Mississippi River after Congress passed the Indian Removal Act of 1830. Many Indians died on the journey, known as the "trail of tears."

Further, he concludes, "If it ain't broke, don't fix it." [61]

Going to Court

Indigenous peoples continue to assert their identities and achieve their political goals through legal avenues.

For example, in April 2011 Sweden's Supreme Court ruled that Sami reindeer herders could continue to allow their animals to graze in the forests of northern Sweden, despite objections from more than 100 landowners. The Sami won because they proved that their ancestors had grazed reindeer on the land since time immemorial. [62]

In Australia, more than 400 legal claims by Aboriginals to secure native title to their traditional lands are being processed. Although the government is trying to settle the claims through negotiation, many of the cases are being referred to the National Native Title Tribunal. [63]

Efforts continue in the U.S. Congress to grant native Hawaiians some form of political autonomy. Sen. Daniel Akaka, a Democrat from Hawaii, introduced a bill in March that he says "would simply put native Hawaiians on equal footing with American Indians and Alaska Natives." The bill would create a government specifically for those people registered on a still-to-be-compiled Native Hawaiian roll. [64]

Meanwhile, in Canada about 70 land claims and self-government negotiations are ongoing between the government and indigenous peoples, while 17 agreements have been concluded with 27 communities. A typical agreement takes up to 25 years to conclude. [65]

In Latin America, at least 10 countries have set up Truth Commissions to explore human rights violations committed by previous regimes, often against indigenous peoples.* [66]

"The trend has received a mixed reception, both among transitional justice practitioners and Indigenous rights activists," according to Joanna Rice, associate of the Truth and Memory Program at the International Center for Transitional Justice. [67]

Critics say the commissions merely give guilty parties a chance to say that the past is over and that any demands for legal redress should be dropped. On the other hand, the commissions can provide a forum to raise critical indigenous issues, such as land reform, economic rights and cultural preservation, Rice notes.

Social Problems

While indigenous groups are making progress on the political front, the social situation continues to be dire.

In Latin America, poverty rates remain significantly higher among indigenous populations than nonindigenous. In a report on malnutrition in Peru, UNICEF health officer Mario Tavera noted that "the gaps are large and have widened . . . one out of two [indigenous] children has chronic malnutrition," compared to the national rate of 18 percent for children under the age of 5. [68]

_____

* Latin American countries with Truth Commissions include Bolivia, Brazil, Chile, Ecuador, El Salvador, Guatemala, Panama, Paraguay, Peru and Uruguay.

Should indigenous peoples be educated in their own languages?

YES
Jon Todal
Professor of Sociolinguistics
Sami University College Guovdageaidnu,
Norway

Written for *CQ Global Researcher,* September 2011

The living conditions of indigenous peoples vary across the world. In some countries they are integrated into society, while in others they are marginalized. Despite these differences, indigenous peoples share many experiences, including the attempt by nation-states to eradicate indigenous languages.

Since the 19th century countries have used schools to achieve monolingualism, or "one state — one language," and all teaching in compulsory education was in the majority language.

As a result, indigenous children struggle more at school than children from the majority population, because they must learn not only their subjects but also a new language. The policy has signaled that indigenous languages are not valued, and such negative school experiences account in part for why indigenous peoples have a lower level of education than majority peoples.

One response among indigenous peoples has been to reject schooling as irrelevant, leading to low levels of education. Another strategy has been to adjust to the schools' values. For example, parents may stop speaking the indigenous language with their children at home so that by the time the children start school they are more on a par with majority children. But this strategy halts the intergenerational transmission of indigenous languages, and the languages become endangered. In other words, both these strategies (rejection and adjustment) have a negative impact on indigenous societies.

A third strategy — to make schools in indigenous areas adjust to the children's language and culture — has produced good results. It is now supported in Scandinavia, for example, where the indigenous Sámi people can receive primary education in Sámi as a separate subject, and they may choose to have Sámi as the language of instruction in other subjects. The level of education among the Sámi is no longer lower than among the majority peoples in Scandinavia, and the Sami language has been strengthened.

Those advocating indigenous peoples receiving education in their own language can find support for their view in international conventions. However, these formal rights are not the main issue. They key points are that education in indigenous languages gives children a positive experience of their own culture and also strengthens the traditional indigenous languages. In this way children are better prepared for life both in the wider society and in the indigenous society.

For this reason education in their own language must be an important right for all indigenous peoples.

NO
Helen Hughes
Emeritus Professor and Fellow Research School
of Asia and the Pacific, Australian National
University, Canberra, and Senior Fellow, Centre
for Independent Studies Sydney, Australia

Written for *CQ Global Researcher,* September 2011

Open ended, this is a nonsensical question. However desirable for children to learn to read and write in their mother tongues, in many situations it is impractical. In Papua New Guinea, for example, a developing country with just under 7 million people, it has not been possible to train teachers and develop reading materials in the more than 800 indigenous languages spoken there.

Pretending to do so has contributed significantly to the country's failure of education. After nearly 40 years of independence, education is in crisis, with only about 20 percent of the population literate.

Some languages are dying out — not only in Oceania, but also in the Americas, India, China and many other parts of Asia and Africa — while new ones, such as Bahasa Indonesia, have been evolving. Countries must decide on language teaching that is best for their inhabitants, and this usually means compromises between resources and ideals.

Children must become articulate and literate in the principal language or languages of their country so they can function in its economy and society. They have to be able to qualify for jobs, participate in democratic decision-making and contribute to civil society. In countries made up of disparate groups, a national language or languages can make a contribution to stability, equity and economic and social development.

Fortunately, research on the human brain has demonstrated that children can absorb new languages at very early ages and can absorb several languages simultaneously when very young. Research also shows that linguistic development makes a special contribution to the development of children's brains. Teaching several languages simultaneously in preschools that take in children at 3 years of age and (even earlier) has made a multilingual approach to teaching languages possible.

Equality of opportunity demands quality education from very early years so that children are fully articulate and literate by the end of their primary education in a country's principal language or languages. The extent to which it is sensible to teach mother or traditional tongues in practice depends on a range of factors, including the extent to which such languages are developed and used, a country's resources and parents' wishes. There is no one-size-fits-all model.

Inuit hunter Pitseolak Alainga (left) explains native seal hunting techniques to Canadian Finance Minister Jim Flaherty in Iqaluit, Canada, on Feb. 6, 2010. The Arctic's Inuit worry about a resource grab by outsiders as the polar ice caps melt, making their region more accessible to international interests keen to develop the area's abundant oil and minerals.

In New Zealand, "Maori are over-represented as victims and perpetrators of family violence and are less likely to report family violence or to access existing services," says Valmaine Toki from the U.N. Permanent Forum on Indigenous Issues.

The Australian government recently reported that "progress is being made" in closing the gaps between indigenous and nonindigenous populations on several key measurements, with significant improvements in child mortality in recent years. [69] The government's 2007 take-over of the management of Aboriginal communities in the Northern Territory has been loosened somewhat under a new law that took effect on July 1, 2010. Although the core 2007 framework has been kept in place, Aboriginal communities now have more flexibility in applying alcohol restrictions.

In the United States, the Tribal Law and Order Act of 2010 aimed to boost tribal governments' policing resources in order to address the inadequate state of law enforcement services on Indian reservations. [70] Currently, only 3,000 Indian police officers patrol 56 million acres of Indian land, which is 48 percent fewer than the average for the rest of the country. The new law aims to address this shortfall by, among other things, expanding police training opportunities and extending the hiring age

of police officers from 37 to 47 in hopes of encouraging more retired Native American military officers to join. [71]

Those understaffed tribal police forces face a growing gang presence. Some 225 youth gangs — many involved in drug trafficking — operate in the Navajo Nation alone, which has a population of 250,000. On Pine Ridge, a Lakota Indian reservation in South Dakota, 39 gangs and 5,000 gang members have been identified in a population of 50,000. And Hispanic gangs have established a foothold on the Colville reservation in Washington State. [72]

OUTLOOK
Preserving Nationhood

The future of many indigenous languages is in doubt, although there is cause for cautious optimism in some places.

In Bolivia, President Morales has set up three indigenous language universities for Guaraní, Quechua and Aymara-speakers and is requiring government officials to learn one of the nation's 36 indigenous languages. In Suriname, where the indigenous represent 4 percent of the population, there are plans to teach children from the Konomerume community some subjects in their native language rather than the official Dutch language. [73]

In Greenland, Inuit is now being spoken in schools, homes, the media and churches, with Danish prevailing only within the government administration. In Norway, the government has said, "it may . . . be necessary to take active steps to repair the damage inflicted on indigenous cultures and languages, and to lay the foundation for linguistic and cultural revitalization." [74]

But in the United States, there is a general concern that indigenous languages are dying out. "There seems to be less and less of them spoken," says Laverdure from the Indian Affairs Department. While a majority of his own nation, the Crow, speaks the native language every day, that is more the exception than the rule for Indian nations, he says. Generally, only the older people speak the native languages.

Canada's Chief Atleo says his top priority is including the 52 indigenous Canadian languages into the country's education system. However, with little funding and a patchwork policy framework, he concedes it will be an uphill battle.

In New Zealand, the Maori television channel now has an average monthly audience of more than 1.6 million viewers, yet only 23 percent of Maori and 4 percent of New Zealanders can speak conversational Maori. [75] The government is not doing enough to provide for the use of Maori in courts and government departments nor has it trained enough teachers in Maori-medium education, says Toki, of the U.N. Permanent Forum on Indigenous Issues.

Intermarriage between indigenous and nonindigenous populations is expected to continue. In some countries, such as the United States and Australia, the rise in census figures for the indigenous population is seen as a sign that a growing number of people of predominantly European ancestry are now acknowledging their aboriginal roots.

However, that does not necessarily mean that indigenous peoples are likely to shed their distinct identity and assimilate. For example, First Nation peoples are beginning to identify who belongs to their community. Presently, the Canadian government makes those determinations. "We would like to change this system," says Chief Atleo, of the Ahousaht Nation near Vancouver Island in Canada.

While there is near-universal support among indigenous peoples for self-determination, few actually want to secede and form an independent country. When a group of disaffected Lakota American Indians, led by veteran activist Russell Means, declared an independent Lakota Republic in December 2007, the reaction from other Indians was decidedly muted. [76]

In Nicaragua, a small group of Miskito have been calling for independence, says Rev. Bent, who has been a Moravian preacher on the Atlantic coast for 25 years. "But they are not taken seriously," he says. "Really, they are just frustrated because autonomy has not come fast enough."

Greenland's Inuit are a possible exception: They may try to expand upon the enhanced autonomy they won in 2008 by moving toward full independence. But some other indigenous peoples want to emulate what Greenlanders already have accomplished.

"We are not looking for independence," says Victoria Hykes-Steere, an Alaska Native and autonomy advocate. "We would like to follow the Greenland model, where they still have ties to Denmark." She believes indigenous peoples should have more autonomy over such things as the right to hunt and trade in marine mammals like walruses and seals.

Thus, while the self-determination argument has, to some extent, been legally won by indigenous peoples, this may turn out to be a hollow victory if it doesn't translate into securing control over their natural resources, ensuring the survival of their culture and improving the economic conditions of their societies.

As Atleo of the Assembly of First Nations puts it, "We are moving in the right direction — we are being consulted more — but a lot more needs to be done."

NOTES

1. Jenny Macklin MP, Australian Minister for Families, Housing, Community Services and Indigenous Affairs, "Building the foundations for change," address to the Sydney Institute, Aug. 9, 2011, www.jennymacklin.fahcsia.gov.au/speeches/2011/Pages/building_funda tion_change_address_sydney_09082011.aspx.

2. Joanna Hoare, ed., "State of World's Minorities and Indigenous People 2011 (Events of 2010)," Minority Rights Group International, July 6 2011, p. 113, www.minorityrights.org/10848/state-of-the-worlds-minorities/state-of-the-worlds-minorities-and-indigenous-peoples-2011.html; Peter Katel, "American Indians," *CQ Researcher*, April 28, 2006, updated July 2010; Inuit Tapiriit Kanatami (ITK), "Health Indicators of the Inuit Nunangat within the Canadian Context 1994-1998 and 1999-2003," www.itk.ca/sites/default/files/20100706Health-Indicators-Inuit-Nunangat-EN.pdf.

3. Kathrin Wessendorf, (ed.), "The Indigenous World 2011," The International Work Group for Indigenous Affairs, May 2011, p. 10, www.iwgia.org/iwgia_files_publications_files/0454_THE_INDIGENOUS_ORLD-2011_eb.pdf.

4. *Ibid.*

5. Jeff J. Corntassel and Tomas Hopkins, "Indigenous 'Sovereignty' and International Law: Revised Strategies for Pursuing 'Self-Determination,' " *Human Rights Quarterly*, May, 1995, pp. 343-365. Corntassel teaches indigenous governance at the University of Victoria in Canada and Primeau teaches international relations at the Tecnologico de Monterrey in Mexico.

6. Hoare, *op. cit.*, p. 176.

7. U.S. Sen. Daniel Akaka, opening remarks at hearing entitled "Native Women: Protecting, Shielding, and Safeguarding Our Sisters, Mothers, and Daughters," U.S. Senate Committee on Indian Affairs, July 14, 2011.

8. Remarks made at hearing entitled "Native Women: Protecting, Shielding, and Safeguarding Our Sisters, Mothers, and Daughters," U.S. Senate Committee on Indian Affairs, July 14, 2011.

9. James Anaya, "Report of the Special Rapporteur on the rights of indigenous peoples, Addendum, The situation of Maori People in New Zealand," United Nations, Feb. 17, 2011, http://unsr.jamesanaya.org/docs/countries/2011_report_new_zealand_advanced_version.pdf.

10. Hoare, *op. cit.*

11. Kevin Rudd, Prime Minister of Australia, "Apology to Australia's Indigenous Peoples," Feb. 13, 2008, www.aph.gov.au/house/rudd_speech.pdf.

12. Sen. Daniel Akaka, opening remarks at oversight hearing on "Enforcing the Indian Gaming Regulatory Act —The Role of the National Indian Gaming Commission and Tribes as Regulators," U.S. Senate Indian Affairs Committee, July 28, 2011. For background, see Patrick Marshall, "Indian Casinos Rake in Billions," in "Gambling in America," *CQ Researcher*, March 7, 2003, pp. 214-215.

13. Maria Railaf Zuniga, speech given at a European Parliament conference entitled, "The Mapuche in Chile: Indigenous Communities in Modern Latin American States," March 25, 2011, www.unpo.org/downloads/187.pdf.

14. "Indigenous and Tribal Peoples, Convention No. 169," International Labour Organization, www.ilo.org/indigenous/Conventions/no169/lang--en/index.htm.

15. Alexandra Garretón, "Nequén Courts Rule in Favor of Mapuche," *The Argentina Independent*, March 9, 2011, www.argentinaindependent.com/currentaffairs/newsfromargentina/neuquen-courts-rule-in-favor-of-mapuche-/.

16. "Circumpolar Inuit Launch Declaration on Arctic Sovereignty," press release, Inuit Circumpolar Council, April 29, 2009, www.inuitcircumpolar.com/files/uploads/icc-files/PR-2009-04-28-CircumpolarInuitLaunchDeclarationonArcticSovereignty.pdf.

17. See Brian Beary, "Race for the Arctic," *CQ Global Researcher*, Aug. 1, 2008, pp. 213-242.

18. "First Nations Land Management (FNLM) Act Background," Aboriginal Affairs and Northern Development Canada, Factsheet, April 2011.

19. Hoare, *op. cit.*, p. 101.

20. *Ibid.*

21. Lars-Anders Baer, "The Autonomy of the Sami Parliaments," *Gáldu*, May 25, 2011, www.galdu.org/web/index.php?odas=5248&giella1=eng.

22. Brian Beary, *Separatist Movements — A Global Reference*, CQ Press, 2011.

23. Wessendorf, *op. cit.*

24. Akaka, "Native Women: Protecting, Shielding, and Safeguarding Our Sisters, Mothers, and Daughters," *op. cit.*

25. Constanza Vieira, "Colombia: Native Groups Mobilise Against Escalation of War," IPS, July 22, 2011, www.galdu.org/web/index.php?odas=5326&giella1=eng.

26. Hoare, *op. cit.*

27. *Ibid.*

28. Namaka Rawlins, testimony, "In Our Way: Expanding the Success of Native Language & Culture-Based Education," U.S. Senate Committee on Indian Affairs, May 26, 2011, http://indian.senate.gov/hearings/hearing.cfm?hearingid=e655f9e2809e5476862f735da16d6c3a&witnessId=e655f9e2809e5476862f735da16d6c3a-1-0.

29. Larry Lasley, testimony, *ibid.*

30. Rainer Grote, "On the Fringes of Europe: Europe's Largely Forgotten Indigenous Peoples," *American Indian Law Review*, Vol. 31, No. 2, (2006/2007), pp. 425-443.

31. "Bringing them Home: Report of the National Inquiry into the Separation of Aboriginal and Torres Strait Islander Children from Their Families, April 1997," Australian Human Rights Commission, www.hreoc.gov.au/social_justice/bth_report/report/index.html.

32. Helen Hughes and Mark Hughes, "Gap worse for remote indigenous," *The Australian*, Sept. 3, 2008, www.theaustralian.com.au/politics/opinion/gap-worse-for-remote-indigenous/story-e6frgd0x-1111117374575.

33. For more information, see "World Directory of Minorities and Indigenous Peoples," Minority Rights Group International, www.minorityrights.org/directory.

34. Corntassel and Hopkins, *op. cit.*, pp. 343-365.

35. *Ibid.*, pp. 344-345.

36. Sheryl Lightfoot, "Ojibwa," in Richard T. Schaefer, ed., *Encyclopedia of Race, Ethnicity, and Society*, DePaul University, SAGE Publications, 2008, pp. 995-998.

37. Mary C. Hurley, "The Indian Act," Library of Parliament (Canada), Oct. 4, 1999, http://dsp-psd.pwgsc.gc.ca/Collection-R/LoPBdP/EB/prb9923-e.htm.

38. Anaya, *op. cit.*

39. "Bringing them Home," *op. cit.*

40. Troy R. Johnson, *We Hold The Rock: The Indian Occupation of Alcatraz, 1969 to 1971* (1991).

41. For text of the resolution, see www.digitalhistory.uh.edu/native_voices/voices_display.cfm?id=96.

42. See Oystein Steinlien, "The Sami Law: A Change of Norwegian Government Policy Toward the Sami Minority?" *The Canadian Journal of Native Studies*, 9(1), pp. 1-14, www2.brandonu.ca/library/cjns/9.1/Steinlien.pdf.

43. Johnson, *op. cit.*

44. "Northern Territory Emergency Response (NTER) Redesign," factsheet, Government of Australia, www.fahcsia.gov.au/sa/indigenous/progserv/ctgnt/ctg_nter_redesign/Pages/default.aspx.

45. Interview with Eduardo Gonzalez, International Center for Transitional Justice, Aug. 1, 2011.

46. "Greenland Vote Favors Independence," Agence France-Presse, *The New York Times*, Nov. 26, 2008 www.nytimes.com/2008/11/26/world/europe/26greenland.html.

47. E. Lutz and N. Ledema, "Addressing indigenous rights at the United Nations," *Cultural Survival*, Fall 2004, www.culturalsurvival.org/publications/cultural-survival-quarterly/united-states/addressing-indigenous-rights-united-nations.

48. Corntassel and Hopkins, *op. cit.*, pp. 343-365.

49. Lutz and Ledema, *op. cit.*

50. "United Nations Declaration on the Rights of Indigenous Peoples," Sept. 13, 2007, www.un.org/esa/socdev/unpfii/en/declaration.html.

51. Wessendorf, *op. cit.*, p. 64,

52. *Ibid.*, p. 63.

53. *Ibid.*

54. *Ibid.*

55. "Machu Picchu celebrations just 100km from uncontacted tribes," *Survival International*, July 20, 2011, www.survivalinternational.org/news/7496.

56. Haider Rizvi, "Easter Islanders Seek U.N. Intervention in Dispute with Chile," IPS, Jan. 22, 2011, www.galdu.org/web/index.php?odas=5085&giella1=eng.

57. Wessendorf, *op. cit.*

58. Clarinha Glock, "Guarani Effort to Strengthen Culture Through Tourism," IPS/Tierramérica, Jan. 25, 2011, www.galdu.org/web/index.php?odas=5093&giella1=eng.

59. Steve Zwick, "Brazil's Indigenous Surui Establish First Indigenous Carbon Fund," *Ecosytem Marketplace*, Dec. 3, 2010, www.ecosystemmarketplace.com/pages/dynamic/article.page.php?page_id=7871&section=news_articles&eod=1.

60. The case was *Colorado River Indian Tribes v. National Indian Gaming Commission*, 05-5402 (D.C. Cir. 2006).

61. "Enforcing the Indian Gaming Regulatory Act — The Role of the National Indian Gaming Commission and Tribes as Regulators," *op. cit.*

62. Peter Vinthagen Simpson, "Sami win long fight for reindeer grazing rights," *The Local* (Sweden's news in English), April 27, 2011, www.allvoices.com/s/event-8906845/aHR0cDovL3Jzcy50aGVsb2Nhb-C5zZS9jLzY1Ni9mLzgzNTkvcy8xNDc0MDM1MC9sLzBMMMFN0aGVsb2NhbDBCc2UwQzMzNDMwQTBDMjBBMTEwQTQyNzBDL3N0b3J5MDEuaHRt.

63. "Information on Native Title," Attorney General's Office, Government of Australia, www.ag.gov.au/www/agd/agd.nsf/Page/Indigenous_law_and_native_titleNative_title.

64. "Akaka, Hawaii Delegation reintroduce Native Hawaiian Government Reorganization Act," Office of U.S. Sen. Daniel Akaka, March 30, 2011, http://akaka.senate.gov/press-releases.cfm?method=releases.view&id=66dc8f8c-9f3a-4ddb-b89d-7e7329758c44.

65. "Fact Sheet: Comprehensive Land Claims," Aboriginal Affairs and Northern Development Canada, Government of Canada, February 2010, www.ainc-inac.gc.ca/eng/1100100016296.

66. "Truth Commission Digital Collection," United States Institute of Peace, www.usip.org/publications/truth-commission-digital-collection. For background, see Jina Moore, "Truth Commissions," *CQ Global Researcher*, Jan. 1, 2010, pp. 1-24.

67. Joanna Rice, "Indigenous Rights and Truth Commissions," *Cultural Survival*, Spring 2011, www.culturalsurvival.org/publications/cultural-survival-quarterly/none/indigenous-rights-and-truth-commissions.

68. Ángel Páez, "Malnutrition Has an Indigenous Face in Peru," IPC, Jan. 19, 2011, www.galdu.org/web/index.php?odas=5080&giella1=eng.

69. "Closing the Gap — Prime Ministers Report 2011," Government of Australia, February 2011, www.fahcsia.gov.au/sa/indigenous/pubs/closing_the_gap/2011_ctg_pm_report/Pages/part_a.aspx.

70. Full text of act is found at www.justice.gov/usao/az/IndianCountry/Tribal%20Law%20%20Order%20Act%202010.pdf.

71. "Summary and Explanation of Provisions in the Tribal Law and Order Act of 2010," Mapetsi Policy Group, www.narf.org/nill/resources/TLOA/tloamapetsi.pdf.

72. "Hearing on the Crime and Law Enforcement Situation in Indian Country," U.S. Senate Committee on Indian Affairs, July 30, 2009.

73. Wessendorf, *op. cit.*

74. "The Foundation for Sami policy," Ministry of Government Administration, Reform and Church Affairs (Norway), www.regjeringen.no/en/dep/fad/Selected-topics/Sami-policy/midtspalte/the-foundation-for-sami-policy.html?id=87039.

75. Anaya, *op. cit.*

76. Beary, *op. cit.*

BIBLIOGRAPHY

Selected Sources

Books

Beary, Brian, *Separatist Movements —A Global Reference*, **CQ Press, 2011.**
The world's most significant autonomy movements, which are often led by indigenous peoples — including the Inuit, Maori, Mapuche, Mayans and Sami — are covered in this handbook by the author of this *CQ Global Researcher* report.

Hemming, John, *The Conquest of the Incas*, **Mariner Books, 2003.**
A Canadian explorer and expert on indigenous peoples of the Amazon recounts the brutal history of the Spanish conquest of Peru's Incas in the 16th century.

Mackey, Eva, *The House of Difference: Cultural Politics and National Identity in Canada*, **University of Toronto Press, 2002.**
A professor of anthropology at Carleton University in Canada examines Canada's relationship with its indigenous peoples, arguing that — despite its reputation for multiculturalism — the government has not promoted genuine autonomy for indigenous nations.

Maddison, Sarah, *Black Politics: Inside the Complexity of Aboriginal Culture*, **Allen & Unwin, 2009.**
A fellow at the University of New South Wales critically explores Australian Aboriginal politics, highlighting tensions within the community's leadership over the past 25 years.

Mutu, Margaret, *The State of Maori Rights*, **Huia Publishers, 2011.**
These articles, written between 1994 and 2009 by the head of the Department of Maori Studies at the University of Auckland, provide the Maori perspective on hot-button issues such as land rights.

Articles

Corntassel, Jeff J., and Tomas Hopkins, "Indigenous 'Sovereignty' and International Law: Revised Strategies for Pursuing 'Self- Determination,' " *Human Rights Quarterly*, **Vol. 17, No. 2, May 1995, pp. 343-365.**

The authors contend that modern state governments create a double standard when they claim the right of self-determination for themselves while denying it to their indigenous communities.

Grote, Rainer, "On the Fringes of Europe: Europe's Largely Forgotten Indigenous Peoples," *American Indian Law Review,* **Vol. 31, No. 2, 2006/2007, pp. 425-443.**
Instead of discussing the Americas and Australasia, which typically receive attention in discussions of indigenous rights, Grote looks at how indigenous groups in Europe, such as the Sami, are asserting their autonomy.

Rice, Joanna, "Indigenous Rights and Truth Commissions," Cultural Survival, Spring 2011, www.cultural survival.org/publications/cultural-survival-quarterly/none/indigenous-rights-and-truth-commissions.
An associate at the International Center for Transitional Justice explores whether so-called truth commissions, set up to look into dark chapters in a country's past, truly help indigenous peoples.

Reports and Studies

"Bringing them Home," Government of Australia, April 1997, www.hreoc.gov.au/social_justice/bth_report/report/index.html.
This sensational and groundbreaking Australian government report, issued after a national inquiry into an earlier government policy that separated Aboriginal children from their families, prompted the government to issue an official apology to the Aboriginals.

Anaya, James, "The situation of the Maori People in New Zealand," United Nations, Feb. 17, 2011, http://unsr.jamesanaya.org/docs/countries/2011_report_new_zealand_advanced_version.pdf.
Following a 2010 visit, the United Nations Special Rapporteur on the Rights of Indigenous Peoples assesses the progress made by New Zealand's Maori.

Hoare, Joanna, ed., "State of World's Minorities and Indigenous People 2011," Minority Rights Group International, July 6, 2011, www.minorityrights.org/10848/state-of-the-worlds-minorities/state-of-the-worlds-minorities-and-indigenous-peoples-2011.html.
A comprehensive report from a British-based nongovernmental organization charts the main events in 2010 that affected minorities and indigenous peoples.

Hurley, Mary C., "The Indian Act," Library of Parliament (Canada), Oct. 4, 2009, http://dsp-psd.pwgsc.gc.ca/Collection-R/LoPBdP/EB/prb9923-e.htm.
The Canadian government's parliamentary research unit assesses the legacy of the 1876 Indian Act, the key legislation regulating Canada's relationship with its First Nation peoples.

Wessendorf, Kathrin, ed., "The Indigenous World 2011," The International Work Group for Indigenous Affairs, May 2011, www.iwgia.org/iwgia_files_publications_files/0454_THE_INDIGENOUS_ORLD-2011_eb.pdf.
A Copenhagen-based advocacy group gives a comprehensive, country-by-country status report on indigenous peoples around the world.

For More Information

Bureau of Indian Affairs, Office of Public Affairs, Department of the Interior, MS-3658-MIB, 1849 C St., N.W., Washington, DC 20240; (202) 208-3710; www.bia.gov. The main U.S. government department responsible for matters concerning American Indians and Alaska Natives, established in 1824.

Center for World Indigenous Studies, PMB 214, 1001 Cooper Point Rd., S.W., #140, Olympia, WA 98502-1107; (360) 450-5183; www.cwis.org. An independent research and education organization that studies social, economic and political issues.

Cultural Survival, 215 Prospect St., Cambridge, MA 02139; (617) 441-5400; www.culturalsurvival.org. Nongovernmental organization that helps to raise public awareness of indigenous issues.

Gáldu Resource Center for Indigenous Peoples, Hánnoluohkká 45, N-9520 Guovdageaidnu-Kautokeino, Norway; 47 78 44 84 00; www.galdu.org. Funded by the Norwegian government, the center maintains a comprehensive database of news articles on indigenous peoples around the world.

International Center for Transitional Justice, 5 Hanover Square, Floor 24, New York, NY 10004; (917) 637-3800; http://ictj.org. A nonprofit organization that aims to address legacies of massive human rights violations and build civic trust in state institutions as protectors of human rights.

International Work Group for Indigenous Affairs, Classensgade 11 E, DK 2100, Copenhagen, Denmark; 45 35 27 05 00; http://iwgia.org. A human rights organization that supports indigenous peoples' self determination, right to territory, control of land and resources, cultural integrity and right to develop.

United Nations Permanent Forum on Indigenous Issues, United Nations, 2 U.N. Plaza, Room DC2-1454, New York, NY 10017; (917) 367-5100; www.un.org/esa/socdev/unpfii. Studies indigenous issues related to economic and social development, culture, the environment, education, health and human rights.

Unrepresented Nations and Peoples Organisation, Laan van Meerdervoort 70, 2517 AN The Hague, The Netherlands; 31 (0)70 36 46 504; www.unpo.org. A nongovernmental umbrella group that promotes the rights of indigenous peoples, minorities and unrecognised or occupied territories.

Voices From Abroad:

CATHY FREEMAN

Aboriginal athlete and 2000 Olympic gold medalist, Australia

The difficult past

"There's still an aura of racism and hatred and loathing. It's hard because it does bring up the past. Everyone's country has got a past they don't feel good about."

The Boston Globe, September 2010

BAN KI-MOON

Secretary-General, United Nations

A benefit to all

"The United Nations Declaration on the Rights of Indigenous Peoples finally has the consensus it deserves. Now we need to make the declaration's principles a reality. . . . We must end the oppression, and we must ensure that indigenous peoples are always heard."

Speech before Permanent Forum on Indigenous Issues, May 2011

Dario La Crisis/Dario Castillejos

SANJEEB DRONG

General Secretary, Bangladesh Indigenous Peoples Forum, Bangladesh

Self-identification is key

"No state can impose any identity on any people or community. This is a violation of human rights. Self-identification is considered as a fundamental criterion for the identification of indigenous and tribal peoples."

Daily Star (Bangladesh), June 2011

TEDDY BRAWNER BAGUILAT

Chairman, House Committee on Natural Cultural Communities, Philippines

Slow progress

"There is today intense demand by indigenous communities to evaluate and review the implementation of IPRA (Indigenous Peoples Rights Act). Our indigenous peoples have reported persistent violations of their Free and Prior Informed Consent requirement, the hasty manner in the approval of mining explorations, deployment of the military as a security force to mining and the unacceptably slow titling of their ancestral domains."

Philippine News Agency, August 2011

BEDE HARRIS

Senior Law Lecturer, Charles Sturt University, Australia

Stating the obvious

"A statement 'recognising' the existence of indigenous people would be simply to state the obvious, and would be no more useful than adding to the constitution a statement that Australia is in the Southern Hemisphere or that the sky is blue."

Canberra Times (Australia), November 2010

ADOLFO CHAVEZ

Leader, Indigenous Peoples' Confederation, Bolivia

Ready for battle

"We want to live in peace, with development that respects our lands. Your shovels will crash into our children. That is why you do not want a binding consultation. So our spears and arrows will be ready for the mechanical diggers [that] want to destroy our virgin territory."

The Independent (England), August 2011

MARIA TOMASIC

President, Royal Australian and New Zealand College of Psychiatrists, Australia

Long overdue

"The fact that our constitution does not recognise indigenous Australians is inexcusable, and it is an admirable move for the current government to move to remedy this. Constitutional acknowledgement of indigenous people is long overdue."

Australian Associated Press, October 2010

KENNETH DEER

Mohawk Indian, Canada

'It's up to us'

"As indigenous peoples it's up to us to hold Canada's feet to the fire on this Declaration. I'm cautiously optimistic. I'm not doing cartwheels, but we have to use it in the most positive way to advance the rights of indigenous peoples."

Indian Country Today (United States), November 2010

13

Future of the Euro

Sarah Glazer
Jason McLure

An election worker counts ballots after Ireland's general election on Feb. 25, in which the ruling party suffered a crushing defeat amid public anger over the country's economic crisis. Ireland's new prime minister, Enda Kenny, resisted pressure at an EU summit the following month to raise Ireland's low corporate tax rate — which attracts corporations like Google to Dublin — as the price for lowering the interest rate charged by the EU to Ireland for its bailout.

From *CQ Researcher*,
May 17, 2011
Updated March 16, 2012

When two German lawmakers suggested last year that Greece sell off some of its islands and artworks in exchange for a bailout from the European Union, the suggestion caused much hilarity in the European press.

"We give you cash, you give us Corfu . . . and the Acropolis too," cackled a headline in the German newspaper *Bild*. The British *Guardian* couldn't resist calling the proposal "My Big Fat Greek Auction," noting a Greek island could be picked up for as little as $2 million.

Dimitris Droutsas, Greece's deputy foreign minister, was not amused. "Suggestions like this are not appropriate at this time," he told German television. [1]

The dust-up epitomized the conflicts between the weak and the economically strong economies in the eurozone — the 17 European Union (EU) members that have adopted the euro as their currency. The tensions have escalated over the past year as Greece, Ireland and Portugal have received handouts from their EU brethren to help deal with domestic debt and budget crises. Now Greece apparently will need even more money to finance its debt, aggravating tensions and raising questions about whether richer countries will support yet more loans.

"The political understandings that underpin the European Union are beginning to unravel," declared *Financial Times* columnist Gideon Rachman on April 17, the day Finland's nationalist True Finns party — which had campaigned strongly against a bailout for Portugal — made spectacular gains in the general election. The victory intensified doubts at the time over whether Europe could agree

Eurozone Powers Most of EU Economy

Seventeen of the 27 European Union (EU) members, representing a population of about 330 million, have adopted the euro currency. Seven other countries are expected to join the eurozone over the next seven years. Euro countries account for 75 percent of the EU's gross domestic product, making the euro the world's second-most-important currency after the U.S. dollar. Sweden, Denmark and the United Kingdom have declined to join the eurozone. Portugal, Ireland and Greece are experiencing debt problems and have asked for bailouts. Some worry Spain could be next.

The European Union and the Eurozone

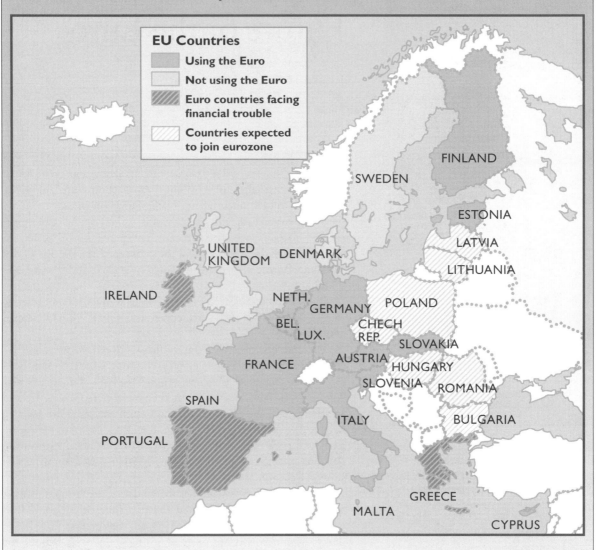

EU Countries

- Using the Euro
- Not using the Euro
- Euro countries facing financial trouble
- Countries expected to join eurozone

Source: European Commission

Map by Lewis Agrell

on a solution to the debt crisis, since bailouts require unanimous approval by all 17 members of the eurozone. [2] Those fears were calmed, somewhat, when Finland's Parliament voted May 12 to support the Portugal bailout. But the vote came amid growing opposition in Germany to a possible second bailout for Greece and concerns that all three countries could make return visits to the euro till.

"My fear is the euro could sow seeds of division between members," says Simon Tilford, chief economist at the Centre for European Reform, a London think tank. "My question for the euro is whether it was ever realistic for such a heterogeneous group of nations," he says.

The growing resentments between rich and poor countries feed into a lingering question that has plagued the eurozone experiment since it was created in 1999: Can a common market like the eurozone function without a common government? In the United States, points out Harvard Business School professor of business administration David Moss, "There is a lot of anxiety and anger that Americans feel in bailing out Wall Street banks, but at least they're American banks." In the eurozone, a German voter is just as likely to be asked to bail out the Greek government — or, ultimately, to shore up a Greek bank.

The current crisis grew out of the inability of highly indebted governments like Greece, Ireland and Portugal to raise enough money in the bond markets to pay their debts and government obligations after the global recession sent tax revenues plunging. It began a year ago, when Greece — facing default after revelations that the nation's finances were in much worse shape than the previous administration had claimed — received a €110 billion ($145 billion) bailout loan from the EU and the International Monetary Fund (IMF). Then in November, Ireland — whose hyper-inflated housing bubble burst during the world credit crisis — received a

€67.5 billion ($88.42 billion) EU/IMF rescue. Finally, Portugal's Socialist government last month came to the EU hat in hand, realizing it would not be able to pay its bondholders this June. On May 3, the EU and IMF agreed to loan Portugal €78 billion ($115 billion). The May 14 arrest of IMF Managing Director Dominique Strauss-Kahn on charges of the attempted rape of a New York hotel maid could complicate upcoming EU/IMF talks over revamping Greece's bailout loan, since he was a crucial figure in arranging the bailouts for the three countries. [3]

Despite the bailouts, interest rates for loans to Greece and Portugal have continued to soar, effectively preventing them from resuming normal borrowing. "Apparently bond traders are skeptical of whether those [bailout] guarantees will be sufficient and whether the Germans and other Europeans will stand behind larger and larger guarantees, if they become necessary," says Moss.

In exchange for the bailouts, the EU is demanding painful austerity measures that some economists say could trigger

Failing Economies Loaded With Debt

Portugal, Ireland, Greece and Spain failed last year to meet the European Union (EU) goal of limiting countries' public debt to 60 percent of national output, or gross domestic product (GDP). Greece's debt-to-GDP ratio was the EU's highest, at 144 percent of GDP. Nordic countries such as Finland and Sweden had far lower ratios. But Germany, critical of countries with high debts, had a higher ratio than Spain. By comparison, the U.S. debt was 58.9 percent of GDP — just below the EU target.

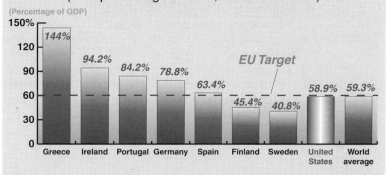

Public Debt for Select Countries
(as a percentage of GDP, 2010 Estimates)

Source: "Public Debt," *The World Factbook,* Central Intelligence Agency, May 2011

"Desperate Generation" Hits the Streets in Portugal

Youths complain of low pay, few jobs.

Twenty-three-year-old João Moreira considered himself lucky to get a job as a school teacher after obtaining his master's degree in education in Porto, Portugal's second-largest city.

But he was appalled when he discovered that he would earn less than the minimum wage. At €330 a month ($440) he is forced to live at home with his mother in his second year of teaching high-school students.

On March 12, Moreira and other recent university graduates used Facebook to organize street demonstrations to protest the dismal economic conditions facing his generation. The protests attracted between 300,000-400,000 demonstrators in Portugal's 10 major cities, surprising even the organizers themselves.

The organizers, all in their 20s, called themselves *geração à rasca* — loosely translated as the "desperate generation" or "generation in a jam." They say they were inspired by the Portuguese band Deolinda's popular song "What a Fool I Am," whose lyrics, "I'm from the unpaid generation," spoke to their precarious work situation.

"There are no jobs for young people in Portugal, and when you have a job, you have a job like mine — a low-paid job," says Moreira. "We can't see a future for ourselves; we have no prospects." Two of his fellow organizers were headed to wealthier countries — Germany and Denmark — to work.

Besides unemployment, demonstrators complained about the lack of job security. The number of so-called "green receipts" jobs — temporary consultant jobs without benefits — has swelled, and the protesters say many are trapped in these jobs for years. Youths also complain of another form of exploitation in their eyes: unpaid or low-paid internships.

"We have 35-year-olds who graduated 10 or 15 years ago who are still in internships because there's no other way of getting into the job market," says Paula Gil, 26, a petite, serious-eyed organizer of the Lisbon protests, who has a master's degree in international relations and is working in a year-long paid internship with a nongovernmental, international development organization.

"It is slavery," when you're working for free, says Gil. In a paid internship like hers, she says, payroll taxes take 50 percent of her pay even though "you don't get access to unemployment insurance or sick leave, you can be fired at any time and you don't get social security benefits."

Such dead-end jobs delay young people's decisions, experts note. "They can't marry because banks won't give them a mortgage," further contributing to Portugal's low fertility rate, observes Ana Catarina Santos, a political journalist for TSF, a radio news station in Lisbon. [1]

But not all university graduates foresee such a grim future. Several graduate students in economics at Nova University School of Business and Economics in Lisbon — Portugal's most selective business school — are optimistic about finding jobs, but expect they probably will have to go abroad to find their "dream job." None had attended the recent demonstrations.

Employers are simply trying to get around Portugal's rigid labor and benefit rules that make it expensive to hire and difficult to fire employees, these students say, echoing

up to 10 more years of recession and huge cuts in treasured pension, unemployment, education and health-care programs. Nevertheless, although EU officials in Brussels insist such budget-cutting conditions will prevent defaults, investors recently have come to believe that a Greek default is "inevitable," according to the *Financial Times.* [4]

Indeed, some experts foresee the collapse of banks in wealthier nations like Germany, which loaned billions to the four faltering countries — Portugal, Ireland, Greece and Spain (known by their acronym, the PIGS) — during the credit boom years. Because of those banks' high exposure to troubled governments' bonds, EU leaders want to stave off default at all costs, experts say. The EU's solution is "a Ponzi scheme [that] could in theory go on forever," the former governor of Argentina's central bank, Mario Biejer, recently charged, suggesting that the view of the European Union, which is expected to demand that Portugal move towards a more flexible labor market. Those labor laws need to change, says Nova student Rafael Barbosa, 21. "When you march against symptoms, nothing will get done," he says.

"It is very difficult for a boss to fire a worker in Portugal because they're protected by law by unions and lawyers," explains Santos, coauthor of the 2010 book, *Dangerous Ideas to Save Portugal.* Under existing law, if an employer fires a worker the boss must pay close to twice the employee's salary for every year worked, Santos notes. If the employer tries to challenge the requirement in court, it could take up to 10 years to get through the appeal process.

Indeed, there's "a cultural expectation" among the Portuguese that they'll have a job for life, especially in the bloated government sector, Santos says. It's partly a legacy of the 1974 revolution against the 42-year dictatorship of António de Oliviera Salazar and of the socialist rhetoric in liberated Portugal's constitution, which strongly guarantees workers' rights. About 13 percent of Portugal's workforce is employed in government jobs, from which it is almost impossible to be fired, according to Santos.

But Portugal's recently requested bailout from the European Union will likely require reform of the country's rigid labor rules — similar to recent labor reforms in Spain — and reductions in worker benefits.

Portugal also has suffered from a decade of poor economic growth, largely the result of its failure to improve the productivity of industries like textiles, which have become increasingly uncompetitive in the face of cheap Chinese exports.

Protest leaders have steered clear of offering political solutions to these economic realities. Their primary purpose, they say, was to start a discussion at the grass roots. They presented parliament with hundreds of survey sheets filled out by protesters, who were asked to suggest solutions. It's unclear what kind of reception their proposals, which Santos expects to be "a bit utopian," will receive from

Protesters in downtown Lisbon are just some of the 300,000-400,000 demonstrators who took to the streets of 10 major cities in Portugal on March 12, 2011, to protest the lack of job opportunities for young people. The turnout surprised even the organizers, who used Facebook to advertise the protests.

the new government after the June 5 elections. The new government will have to devise a strict austerity package to meet EU bailout conditions.

Still, the March demonstrations, notable for their lack of violence, touched a chord among other generations, too. "You could see a 40-year-old mother worried that her sons were unemployed, and you could see pensioners who earn only €300 a month," reports Santos. "It was diverse — each group protesting a different thing, a bit messy but very genuine. It showed Portuguese society has a lot of problems."

— *Sarah Glazer*

[1]The fertility rate refers to the average number of children born per woman in the population during her life. From 2005-2010, Portugal's fertility rate averaged 1.38 children per woman. A fertility rate below 1.8 is considered insufficient to replace the current population. For fertility rates, See "Pensions at a Glance, 2011," Organisation for Economic Co-operation and Development, 2011, p. 163.

accepting a default might be "preferable to increasing the burden on future taxpayers." [5]

The eurozone was conceived as a way to turn the European Union into a formidable world economic power. [6] But the current crisis has highlighted what some economists say is the system's inherent weakness: the failure to form a United States of Europe with overarching power to balance the vast differences in wealth between the poor

South and the rich North. The euro imposed a single currency on diverse countries without creating a centralized government with the power to collect taxes and decide how to spend them.

Ardent proponents of the euro knew from the beginning that eventually they would have to create "a federal fiscal system," says British economic historian Niall Ferguson, author of *The Cash Nexus* and a professor of

Budget Deficits Hobble Troubled Euro Countries

Portugal, Ireland and Greece are experiencing both debt crises and budget deficits. Greece and Portugal have the biggest deficits — more than 10 percent of their national output, or gross domestic product (GDP). The European Union recommends that member countries' budget shortfalls not exceed 3 percent of GDP. The U.S. budget deficit is 3.4 percent of GDP. Finland, Germany and the Netherlands have budget surpluses.

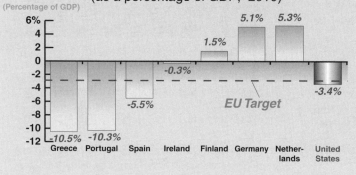

Budget Deficits (or Surpluses) for Select Countries (as a percentage of GDP, 2010)

(Percentage of GDP)

Source: Organisation for Economic Co-operation and Development

[debt- and budget-cutting] adjustment,' " says Desmond Lachman, resident scholar at the American Enterprise Institute (AEI), a conservative think tank in Washington. Or the Germans will simply "get tired of financing this."

The conflict already has had serious political repercussions for leaders in the eurozone. In February, the Irish government fell. A month later Portugal's Socialist Prime Minister José Sócrates was forced to resign. Also in March, German Chancellor Angela Merkel's Christian Democratic Party lost a crucial provincial election in a former party bastion — a loss partly blamed on German voters' resistance to paying higher taxes to rescue crisis-ridden Greece and Ireland. [9]

"The German voter has had enough of writing checks for people in the rest of Europe that he or she regards as lazy," says Ferguson.

Brussels diplomats refer to the tension between what countries must give up to make a common currency work and what is politically feasible as "Juncker's curse," after Luxembourg Prime Minister Jean-Claude Juncker's quip, "We all know what to do, but we don't know how to get re-elected once we have done it." [10]

However, that logjam may have broken, say EU diplomats, citing the recent bailouts and efforts to more closely monitor weaker states' balance sheets to prevent future disasters. "We are strengthening and broadening the surveillance framework of the euro in ways that would not have been thought possible before this crisis," maintains Silvia Kofler, minister counselor and head of press and public diplomacy at the EU delegation to the United States.

Yet, those very budget-cutting, debt-reducing measures could force the weaker countries to desert the euro, some fear. At some point, the troubled countries "are going to say, 'We're going through these tremendous recessions in order to pay interest to foreign bankers.' That's a very difficult political sell to maintain," observes Lachman.

And, unlike the U.S. dollar regime, the EU has no common military or coercive power that could be used to

history at Harvard. "But they didn't say it publicly, because no ordinary voter wants to be in the United States of Europe."

"Politicians knew that they risked running afoul of voters if they surrendered too much sovereignty," writes Mary Elise Sarotte, a professor of International Relations at the University of Southern California. [7] Instead, member countries have continued to guard jealously their power to tax and spend.

The recent deals among EU countries in the wake of the crisis show that member states continue to be reluctant to surrender sovereignty "in key areas such as pensions, labor and wage policy, or taxation," said the European Policy Centre, a Brussels think tank. [8]

EU diplomats say the current crisis presents an opportunity to fix those weaknesses. But some experts say the price demanded by the EU — austerity budgets and repayment of huge loans to the EU — will be so high that debt-laden countries like Portugal, Greece and Ireland will eventually abandon the euro currency.

"It's a question of time before the Irish or the Greeks or the Portuguese say, 'We can't do any more of this force member states to stay in the eurozone, notes Harvard's Moss. "In this country, an attempted secession was put down by force during the Civil War. One has to wonder whether there is a limit to how far integration can go in Europe without a common government and without the threat of coercive power."

"The euro is like a sick patient on the couch, and the doctors don't agree on the diagnosis or prescription," Charles Grant, director of the Centre for European Reform, told a London School of Economics audience on March 15. And the crisis, he noted, comes as Europe's military and diplomatic power are dwindling, along with its economic competitiveness.

The fallout from the crisis has been multifaceted. The seven other EU members expected to adopt the euro sometime in the next seven years may now be less willing to abandon their own currencies. [11] And EU enthusiasm for admitting new, less prosperous countries appears to have cooled somewhat. Meanwhile, right-wing nationalist parties — many of them skeptical of the euro and opposed to helping struggling neighbors — are making big strides across Europe.

Is the eurozone headed for yet more internal conflict or greater unity? Here are some of the questions being posed in governments, academia and the international community:

Will the Eurozone survive in its current form?

Even before Portugal was bracing for a new round of budget cuts in exchange for an EU bailout, some experts were predicting the eurozone's poorest country would defect if the EU's budget discipline became too draconian.

Current EU budget rules require member countries to reduce their public debt to no more than 60 percent of national output — or gross domestic product (GDP) — and to keep their budget deficits from exceeding 3 percent of GDP. [12]

Portugal, Ireland, Greece and Spain have a long way to go to meet those goals. And reaching them could take up to 10 years of stunted economic growth while they pay back their debts, slash their budgets and raise taxes, some economists say.

Such strict budget and debt ceilings, however, will block the PIGS from using economic tools governments historically have utilized to lift their nations out of recession: deficit spending to stimulate the economy.

"These countries are now forced in a vicious way to use austerity when you shouldn't have it; austerity makes things worse and undermines the political basis of the support you need for the eurozone," says Paul De Grauwe, a professor of economics at the University of Leuven, in Belgium.

Indeed, AEI's Lachman predicts that Greece, Ireland, Portugal and probably Spain will drop out of the eurozone because they won't be able to survive the inevitable years of recession that will follow such austerity programs.

The eurozone "can't survive in its present form," he says. "For me, it's a question of just the timing when that occurs."

Others, such as EU diplomat Kofler, consider the idea of defection "really difficult to take seriously." If a nation left the euro, she says, its "existing debt level would remain in euros, regardless of what new currency it introduced after leaving the euro area." Since the new currency likely would devalue against the euro — by 50 percent according to some estimates — the cost of paying back interest and principal on the existing debt would "skyrocket," she predicts. [13] The result would be steep inflation, collapsed banking sectors and the flight of capital, EU officials warn. [14]

Irish economist David McWilliams, however, advocates that Ireland leave the euro and pay back its debtors in a new devalued Irish currency, essentially forcing debtors to accept a loss. Adopting a new, weaker currency, McWilliams predicts, would make Ireland "cheaper overnight for people to do business in." [15]

Yet, even an early euroskeptic like economist Ferguson considers exiting too expensive and unlikely, partly because of a widely expressed fear of crisis contagion.

Others cite practical problems like printing new currency and redesigning vending machines. De Grauwe, another early euroskeptic, says these arguments remind him of the stories of Soviet couples who wanted to divorce but couldn't because of the impossibility of finding a second apartment. "You were condemned to stay together, and you hated each other. If that's the future of the eurozone, I'm not optimistic," he says. "In the end, the [weaker countries] will say, 'To hell with it: Even if the practical problems are high, we just don't want it anymore.'"

On the other hand, De Grauwe and other euroskeptics have suggested, stronger economies like Germany are suffering from "integration fatigue" and might leave the eurozone to avoid paying bailout costs. Euro defenders counter that richer countries won't let a collapse happen if only for their own self-interest: Bailouts for Greece help German banks, which own large amounts of the PIGS' debt in the form of government bonds and loans. If any one of the troubled countries defaults and leaves the euro, German banks would suffer huge losses. [16]

By sharing the euro with poorer economies, Germany also benefits from using a weaker currency, making its exports cheaper than if German exports were priced in a more expensive deutschmark. "It's a great advantage; that's why they'll never leave it," says Carlo Bastasin, an economist and senior fellow at the Brookings Institution, a moderate think tank in Washington.

Observers on both sides say the eurozone is at a critical political juncture. The current crisis is "analogous to the New Deal period in the United States," says Simon Hix, a professor of European and Comparative Politics at the London School of Economics. "There were huge battles over whether the U.S. government would take on . . . fiscal responsibilities [for other states,] because until then the U.S. federal budget was tiny."

And despite the current raging debate, Hix maintains, there's a surprising amount of consensus among political rivals about accepting the EU's new levels of austerity. Even in Portugal, the opposition Social Democratic Party — which is favored to win the June election and which helped sink the government's last austerity package — has accepted the need for bailout austerity.

"If that broad level of consensus carries on in Europe among voters like this, we have a good chance of getting through this," Hix says, "because you have publics that are willing to accept the tough political decisions needed to make these things work."

Skeptics, however, think the strains of trying to yoke such different economies to the euro are fomenting, not calming, new political tensions. "You're getting two Europes: the North that is doing OK and the South that is going down the drain," says Lachman. "That's not the way to have a political union."

Are some countries worse off under the euro?

When it comes to Ireland's current economic crisis, the government's biggest mistake was joining the euro in the first place, according to Sean Barrett, an economist at Trinity College, Dublin.

"Since joining the euro we've conducted an experiment by blowing up the laboratory," he says, pointing out that Ireland went from full employment and a balanced budget before adopting the euro to 14.5 percent unemployment and insolvency today.

As Nobel Prize-winning American economist Milton Friedman warned in 2001, countries need different monetary policies depending on whether their economies are fast-growing and inflationary — which need higher interest rates to cool them down — or slow-growing, needing low rates to help heat up the economy by encouraging borrowing, investment and consumption. [17]

Today Friedman's predictions seem prescient. Known during boom times as the "Celtic Tiger," Ireland was growing exponentially on a virtual tsunami of cheap money during the 1990s-2000s, which triggered a disastrous property bubble. The government should have raised interest rates to slow down the borrowing frenzy, euro critics say, but it no longer had that power since the European Central Bank (ECB) sets interest rates for the euro countries.

"Ireland needed to cool down in the years after it joined the euro, but Germany needed to warm up," notes Barrett. Now the situation is reversed, with the European Central Bank responding more to Germany's fast-growth situation than to Ireland's dismal recession.

ECB President Jean-Claude Trichet encountered a storm of criticism — mainly from Ireland and Spain — when the bank on April 7 raised Europe's interest rates by a quarter of a percentage point to 1.25 percent. The increase was expected to hit the two countries especially hard because of the large number of homeowners with variable-rate mortgages. [18]

"There's a double whammy [in Ireland] for homeowners in that the main banks here can increase their rates but also the European Central Bank can increase its rates," which are reflected in variable-rate mortgages, says Aoife Walsh, spokesperson for Respond! Housing Association, which advises Irish homeowners.

By contrast, Germany welcomed the interest rate hike as a way to cool inflation. Trichet said his action was aimed at the eurozone as a whole, where inflation has exceeded the bank's 2 percent target.

Adopting the euro also meant governments could no longer devalue their own currencies — a primary tool nations use to recover from a recession because it makes their exports cheaper and therefore more competitive. When Ireland devalued its currency, the punt, during its 1990s recession, Barrett notes, it stimulated "pretty strong growth."

In addition, say economists, the EU's Germanic obsession with living within one's budget has shifted attention away from encouraging economic growth, which would require deficit spending.

Portugal, for example, has suffered from a decade of slow growth. After years as Europe's sweatshop, selling cheap shoes and textiles, Portugal recently has found itself underpriced by China. And Portugal's failure to reconfigure its industries as high-end, high-fashion brands, as Italy has done, has forced many small companies to shut down and others to suffer. But that kind of investment seems unlikely when demand is low and the cost of borrowing is high.

During the boom years, with exceptionally low interest rates, those in the weaker eurozone countries were practically "paid to borrow," says Tilford, of London's Centre for European Reform. The resulting borrowing-fueled consumption disguised both the lack of underlying growth and the need for structural reforms, such as making hiring and firing more flexible.

"Spain, Italy and Portugal saw the euro as a way of avoiding reforms and being free of currency crises, but it doesn't shield them from the credit crisis," he says.

By contrast, some non-euro EU economies — notably Sweden, Poland and Britain — grew faster in 2010 than eurozone countries. [19] The U.K. also has embarked on an austerity budget, but it can devalue its currency to make its exports more competitive, which the euro countries aren't free to do.

Other economists say the euro is being blamed unfairly for an economic crash that had more to do with the international credit crisis and the failure of domestic regulators. In the case of Ireland, "joining the euro meant we had greater access" to funding from abroad, acknowledges Philip Lane, a professor of economics at Trinity College, Dublin. German banks lent to Irish banks at low rates, who in turn lent cheaply and recklessly to property developers and homeowners. But, "That doesn't mean we had to take it up. It's the role of the regulator to be the grown-up," he says, by requiring a sensible fit between the income of the borrower and the value of the property, something Ireland's regulators failed to do.

"The world was awash in credit," he says, and borrowing standards were being loosened internationally. Iceland, for example, experienced a phenomenal credit crash even though it wasn't on the euro, he points out.

Once Ireland got into trouble, he notes, it benefited from eurozone membership by being able to borrow from the European Central Bank when borrowing in the bond markets became too expensive.

John Fitz Gerald, an economist at the Economic and Social Research Institute, a think tank in Dublin, says his group warned as early as 1996 that once on the euro the Irish government would have to take other steps to cool borrowing, like taxing homeowners' mortgage-interest payments.

"It's not rocket science," he says, but the government paid no attention. "Don't blame the euro for bad government. Bad government gives you bad results."

Will the EU approach solve the debt crisis?

"Trouble paying your debt? Here borrow some more: How about $80 billion?" asked the *Financial Times* the day after Portugal asked the EU for a $119 billion loan. The eurozone's policymakers should ask themselves whether overindebted Portugal, Ireland and Greece can really do everything expected of them in drastic austerity plans and still pay back their EU loans on time, the *FT* warned. [20]

Some economists say the EU bailout formula "shows no sign of working," according to *The New York Times*, and some say it's making the problem worse. [21]

Under the weight of steep budget cuts over the past two years, the EU's first bailout recipient, Greece, has suffered a 6-percent contraction in real GDP, while Ireland's economy has shrunk by 11 percent. "This is now seriously undermining those countries' tax bases as well as their political willingness to stay the course of [budget-cutting] adjustment," concluded AEI's Lachman. [22] In fact, he predicts, under the EU's prescription, Greece's economy "will collapse."

Already, "Greece has basically ground to a halt," *FT* writer Vincent Boland said on May 9, after the euro plunged on rumors Greece was in so much trouble it would leave the eurozone. [23]

The EU insistence on governments living within their budgets has deprived these countries of deficit spending, says the University of Leuven's De Grauwe. Deficit

New York City detectives hold IMF Managing Director Dominique Strauss-Kahn after he was arrested on May 15 and charged with the attempted rape of a hotel chambermaid. Strauss-Kahn, who was held without bond, was a crucial figure in advocating the bailouts for Greece as well as Ireland and Portugal, and his arrest could complicate upcoming EU/IMF talks over easing the terms of Greece's bailout loan.

spending is used by governments to "make sure those who are unemployed have some purchasing power to buy goods and services to permit the economy to start growing again," he says. "You don't do that only out of altruism, but also out of a rational calculus that it stabilizes the economy."

Eurozone ministers acknowledged on May 8 that Greece's bailout was insufficient and that the government would need more EU cash to pay its debts into next year. EU ministers planned to meet in May to find a solution, since it was clear Greece could not borrow in the bond markets at the prohibitively high interest rates it was being charged. Amid heightened speculation that Greece would default, eurozone leaders said they were also considering easing Greece's repayment terms. [24]

That renewed crisis — a year after Greece received its bailout, plus Ireland's recent request for easier payback terms — signal that the bailout approach is failing, critics say. "Greece and Ireland are already bailed out and look like they won't be able to finance themselves next year," because of skyrocketing borrowing costs, says Raoul Ruparel, an analyst at Open Europe, a London think tank focused on the European Union.

Increasingly, some prominent economists are urging that these countries need a restructuring — a polite term for default.

"There needs to be a frank acknowledgement that these debts are unsustainable," says University of California, Berkeley, economist Barry Eichengreen. So far, he says, the EU's emphasis on budget cuts is "reducing the cost of everything but the debt; that's another reason why the current strategy will not work."

With an orderly debt restructuring, much like a personal bankruptcy, the EU could tell the countries' creditors, or bondholders, that if they don't want to suffer a total loss from a likely default, "take 60 cents on the dollar plus a guarantee that this debt is secure" — backed by the full faith and credit of the eurozone member countries.

Once the debt load is reduced in this manner, Eichengreen says, countries like Greece and Ireland can grow again.

A default — or restructuring — would actually be cheaper for Portugal than the current EU-style bailouts, argues a recent paper by Open Europe's Ruparel. The country's overall debt burden would decline, eventually driving down the nation's borrowing costs. It would also shift some of the burden of the loss that default inevitably brings to investors, who would not get back all their money, and away from taxpayers who now are bearing the burden of repaying their government's loans in full. [25]

Ruparel says much of the opposition to restructuring comes from the banking sector, "particularly in Germany, where banks are heavily exposed to these [troubled] countries. The government knows if a restructure were to happen, the banks would suffer serious losses."

In their 2011 book, *This Time Is Different*, American economists Carmen M. Reinhart and Kenneth S. Rogoff find that sovereign defaults have been a common government feature for more than eight centuries. Reinhart says a default could end the market speculation that escalates governments' borrowing costs — and their pain — once and for all. "You may be postponing going to the dentist, and it is not going to be a pretty experience, " says Reinhart, "but once you do, it's over and you move on."

Some economists are horrified by the idea of letting any country default, because they fear failures would spread like a contagious virus. For example, if Portugal defaulted many experts fear Spain, whose banks have high exposure to Portuguese government bonds, would be the next to fall.

Italian economist Bastasin says, "It would be politically disruptive and have terrible consequences on those countries."

EU diplomats have strongly resisted any suggestion of default or restructuring for Greece or Portugal. The EU does not contemplate the possibility of restructuring until 2013, when the EU proposes to establish a permanent bailout fund — the European Stability Mechanism (ESM).

Critics say that's too little too late. And most observers agree the fund wouldn't be big enough to bail out a large economy like Spain. Some experts say they won't worry about the eurozone's future until Spain, a much bigger economy than any of the other PIGS, appears to be in serious trouble. As in Ireland, Spain's housing bubble — concentrated in coastal resort/retirement areas — pulled down home prices. Spanish savings banks are heavily exposed to domestic property losses, so a sharp decline in housing prices could trigger difficulties that could spread to the eurozone. However, Spain has begun to reform its extremely rigid labor market and enacted deficit-controlling cost-cutting measures. So far Spain's borrowing costs have remained below 5 percent, far less than the other PIGS' double digit rates. [26]

Officials in Brussels say the new proposed bailout fund, created from contributions and guarantees from all eurozone countries — represents the kind of "fiscal union" the eurozone has long been criticized for lacking. But De Grauwe, author of the classic textbook *Economics of Monetary Union*, now in its eighth edition, disagrees.

"It's a far cry from the kind of budgetary union the United States would have with automatic transfers" from one state to another, he says. "The ESM is a mechanism to manage crisis not to prevent crisis."

Ironically, when the fund was first proposed last year, it triggered a crisis of its own after investors learned it contemplated restructuring after 2013. Private holders of government bonds feared a default would cost them money. The borrowing costs for struggling eurozone members surged on that news.

As De Grauwe puts it, each time a new country runs into trouble, "we fight, then the markets are uncertain what's going to happen. As a result, they dump bonds of countries in trouble, and we get involved each time in a major financial crisis."

Some economists would favor the introduction of a so-called eurobond, which would be backed by all the countries

Weeds grow unchecked in the streets and yards of new houses offered at discount prices in Ballindine, County Mayo, Ireland — remnants of the country's hyper-inflated housing bubble that caused average home prices to nearly triple. When the bubble burst, home prices and tax revenues plummeted and Ireland's debt and interest rates skyrocketed, forcing it to seek an EU/IMF rescue.

of the eurozone. That would avoid the kind of market attacks on individual countries' bonds that have occurred in the past year. De Grauwe sees a eurobond as a partial step toward the political union the eurozone has always lacked, yet "more realistic than full budgetary union like in the U.S."

BACKGROUND

Bending Union Rules

History offers few examples of successful efforts among nations to share a single currency on the scale of today's eurozone. It does offer, however, "several examples of monetary unions between sovereign states disintegrating," writes historian Ferguson in his 2001 history of money, *The Cash Nexus*. [27] The unions usually fell apart when one member suffering from deficits bent the rules and began printing its own money, essentially devaluing the currency.

The closest precedent to the eurozone, the so-called Latin Monetary Union (1865-1927), made the coinages of six European governments freely exchangeable within a single area that encompassed France, Belgium, Switzerland, Italy, the Papal States and Greece. Like the eurozone, the Latin Union began with a political motivation — the dream of a "European Union."

Eventually the extravagance of the Italian and Papal governments became too costly for the other member

C H R O N O L O G Y

1945-1959 *In aftermath of World War II, European leaders decide to forge greater economic cooperation to prevent more bloodshed.*

1951 Six countries (France, Germany, Italy, the Netherlands, Belgium and Luxembourg) agree to run coal and steel industries under a common pact to prevent one country from forging weapons to use against another.

1957 The six coal and steel compact nations adopt Treaty of Rome, creating the European Economic Community (EEC) — the "Common Market" — to allow free movement of goods and people across borders.

1960-1979 *Economic growth and trade grow rapidly; EEC expands.*

1968 The six EEC members remove customs duties among themselves.

1973 Denmark, Ireland and U.K. join the EEC.

1980s *Berlin Wall falls; Germany agrees to monetary union; EEC membership expands.*

1980 Greece joins EEC, bringing membership to 10.

1986 Portugal and Spain become EEC's 11th and 12th members.

1988 Single Market Act commits to a European monetary union but no deadline for achieving it.

1989 Berlin Wall falls. France approves German reunification in exchange for German agreement to establish a common European currency.

1990s *European Monetary Union and euro established.*

1992 Treaty — signed at Maastricht, Netherlands — re-names EEC the European Community under the newly created European Union (in 2009 the EC is absorbed into the EU), commits it to monetary union by 1999 and sets rules for participating countries.

1997 Stability Pact establishes stricter maximum debt and budget deficit targets for EU members, but they're never enforced.

Jan. 1, 1999 Euro introduced in 11 countries for commercial/financial transactions, but U.K. retains the British pound as its currency.

2000s *World financial crisis dries up credit; housing bubbles burst in Ireland, Spain; EU bails out Greece, Ireland.*

2001 Greece becomes 12th country to join euro but its financial qualifications are later found deceptive.

2002 Euro notes and coins introduced into general circulation.

September 2008 Major financial crisis strikes Europe, as mortgage, credit and housing bubbles burst; Lehman Bros. fails; Irish government guarantees banks' deposits and bonds.

2009 Greece's new government reveals budget deficit is twice what the previous government had reported.

2010 EU and IMF bail out Greece with €110 billion ($160 billion) loan. EU approves new lending to euro countries to prevent the financial crisis from spreading. . . . EU agrees to bail out Ireland (Nov. 28).

2011 José Sócrates' Socialist government in Portugal collapses after his austerity package fails to pass (March 23). . . . EU summit agrees to establish permanent bailout fund to safeguard euro and help struggling countries (March 24-25). . . . Portugal asks EU for bailout (April 6). . . . Greek borrowing costs soar on news it failed to meet its EU deficit-reduction target. Borrowing costs for Portugal and Ireland reach euro-era highs on fears all three countries might default (April 27). . . . EU discusses more aid for Greece (May 7-9). . . . Finnish Parliament supports Portugal bailout, despite opposition from nationalist True Finns party (May 12). . . . IMF head Dominique Strauss-Kahn is arrested for attempted rape in New York, complicating bailout negotiations (May 14). . . . Portugal general election scheduled (June 5). . . . Portugal must redeem €7 billion ($10 billion) in maturing bonds; bailout loan seen as crucial (June 15).

August 2011 Yields on government bonds from Spain and Italy rise sharply – indicating investors are losing faith in their ability to repay loans. European Central Bank responds by purchasing billions of euros in bonds from the two countries

November 2011 Italian Prime Minister Silvio Berlusconi resigns after failing to quell concerns about his country's solvency. Economist Mario Monti is appointed as successor, and Italy's parliament passes an austerity package.

December 2011 French President Nicolas Sarkozy and German Chancellor Angela Merkel announce their support for a new treaty with stringent budgetary rules to prevent future crises.

January 2012 Credit rating agency Standard & Poor's downgrades the debt of France, Italy, Spain and nine other European countries, citing the EU's failure to resolve the region's economic crisis. It also downgrades the euro's stability fund because of concerns about the financial stability of governments that have guaranteed funding to it.

February 2012 Demonstrators burn buildings in central Athens to protest government austerity measures.

March 2012 Following the protests in February, Greece and other European governments agree to the terms of a second bailout – worth 130 billion euros –requiring further austerity. In addition, private bondholders agree to write down the value of the 206 billion euro Greek debt they hold by more than half. Still many analysts say the country will be unable to pay even this lower debt.

states. The Papal government financed its debts by debasing its coinage, while Italy issued its own paper currency. Under these strains, the union had effectively stopped functioning by World War I and was pronounced dead, belatedly, in the 1920s. [28]

In more recent times, several unions have been short-lived. Around the time of the fall of the Berlin Wall, three separate monetary unions — one among the former members of the Soviet Union, and one each among the countries that make up the former Yugoslavia and Czechoslovakia — broke apart after weaker members raised revenue by printing money. Looking back at that history, Ferguson predicted in 2001 that "the strains caused by unaffordable social security and pension systems," which would grow with Europe's aging population, could similarly break up the eurozone. [29]

Governments have long used the tactic of debasing their currencies — which spurred many of the past breakups — to reduce their debts. Ancient Roman emperors had reduced the silver content of the denarius coin by nearly 99 percent between the reign of Marcus Aurelius and the time of Diocletian. Struggling to pay his debts, King Henry VIII in the 1540s reduced the gold and silver content of England's new coins, giving them a face value twice that of the metal they contained. [30]

Today, printing more paper money to devalue one's currency is a technologically advanced way of debasing coinage. But eurozone governments lost the option of devaluing their currency when they adopted the euro — a loss that has exacerbated their current troubles.

Bloodshed Averted

After World War II, European leaders were determined to prevent future bloodshed by creating greater cooperation among their nations. In 1951 six countries — France, Germany, Italy, Netherlands, Belgium and Luxembourg — agreed to run their coal and steel industries under a common plan so no country could create weapons against another. For the first time, the six nations agreed to give up some of their sovereignty in a common effort.

Following the success of the coal and steel treaty, the six nations in 1957 signed the Treaty of Rome, creating the European Economic Community (EEC) or Common Market, pledging cooperation in the free movement of goods, services and people across borders. [31]

Throughout the 1960s and into the '70s, the EEC continued to break down trade barriers and add new members. In 1968 the six Common Market countries removed customs duties on goods imported across their borders. Trade grew rapidly both among the six and with the rest of the world. [32]

By 1988, the Single Market Act contained a commitment to monetary unification but included no deadline for introducing it. The deciding event came in 1989

Ireland Struggles With Public and Private Debt

"Reckless lending" and cronyism are blamed.

According to a joke told around Dublin these days, second prize for winning the Irish sweepstakes is five apartments. First prize? Zero apartments.

It's a painful truth that during Ireland's roaring "Celtic Tiger" years, the entire country was caught up in a property-buying frenzy and easy credit — until it all ended in the economic crash of 2008-09.

Since property values plummeted, one of every two homeowners is in "negative equity," with the amount they owe on their mortgage greater than the value of their house. Many families can't pay their debts because they have lost a job, had their salary cut or seen their house value drop by 50 percent from the peak.

"We've seen cases of middle-income families that have their own mortgage to pay plus three more mortgages" on houses they bought to rent out, says Paul Joyce, senior policy researcher at Free Legal Advice Centers (FLAC) in Dublin, a network of volunteer lawyers that advises people on how to get out of debt. During the boom years, investment advisors regularly touted property purchases as a nest egg for retirement, he says. But potential tenants and homebuyers have evaporated, including the immigrant construction workers who returned to Eastern Europe when the housing industry collapsed.

The stories of property magnates and government regulators drinking together at lavish racetrack fundraisers for Fianna Fáil, the previous government's party, are rife — a relationship many blame for a housing bubble the government either didn't see coming or didn't want to burst. [1] "It was cronyism at its worst," says Joan Collins, a member of Parliament who represents Dublin's South Central neighborhood, one of Ireland's poorest. She blames "all this madness" on tax breaks the Fianna Fáil government gave developers to build new housing, hotels and private hospitals.

Less well-known is the extent to which the government turned to private developers to build public housing. The wreckage of that failed effort can be seen at St. Michael's public housing complex in Dublin, where a developer demolished eight of 10 apartment blocks, then walked away bankrupt when the economy crashed, leaving a vast wasteland and former tenants scattered into temporary rentals. "Now a community has been devastated," Collins says.

At one of Dublin's largest public housing complexes, Dolphin House, where residents had long complained of backed-up sewage seeping into their 1940s-era apartments, the City Council also turned to a developer for the solution. The developer planned to replace the existing 436 apartments and build an additional 600 private apartments to be sold to well-heeled professionals, since the location is desirable — just five minutes by light rail from downtown. [2]

The residents were still in the planning stage when the housing bubble burst. The developers vanished. "We missed the boat," admits Veronica Lally, 41, a resident of Dolphin House. "The Dublin City Council is bankrupt. There's no money to maintain these properties," she says, holding little hope for repair of the archaic plumbing system.

Like many Irish taxpayers, Lally, a community employment adviser, expresses rage that she'll be paying thousands of euros in taxes "for a developer that was greedy" and the ensuing bank crisis. She holds government, developers and trade unions equally responsible. [3]

"They got into bed the three of them and ripped the heart out of this country; and young people are shipping off to America and Australia — all our good talent going, because there's nothing here for them," she continues. Now the bankers must be bailed out and the money the government borrowed from the European Union to prop up the banks "paid back to Europe."

Like Dublin's council, the national government made the mistake of failing to build up its budget surpluses during the good times for a rainy day, some economists say.

with the fall of the Berlin Wall and the prospect of a reunified Germany for the first time in 40 years. [33]

Germany's reunification required the consent of the four post-World War II occupying powers: France, Britain, the United States and the Soviet Union. When Germany sought French approval for reunification, the creation of a European monetary union — something long sought by France as a way to increase

"The government should have targeted the housing market by taxing mortgage interest payments. Instead they subsidized mortgage interest payments," says John Fitz Gerald, an economist at the Economic and Social Research Institute, a Dublin think tank. If the government had followed his advice, "they would have given households higher interest rates de facto," he says, which would have made households more cautious about taking on too big a mortgage. Then, "when the economy slowed down, the government would have had a surplus they could have used."

"Reckless lending" by banks is a common phrase heard in Ireland these days. Many blame the failed Anglo-Irish Bank for its maverick lending strategy of dropping traditional credit requirements, such as putting a down payment on a home mortgage — a practice that put pressure on other Irish banks to do the same.

Besides middle-class homeowners, Ireland has a new and growing working class saddled with exorbitant amounts of personal debt, often piled up on multiple credit cards. "A lot of people in working-class areas had access to subprime lenders and to credit they wouldn't have had before," Joyce says. "A lot of individuals won't be able to pay the money back; it was lent quite recklessly with very little regard to lending standards."

Ireland's debt problem is compounded by the fact that the country lacks modern bankruptcy laws that would allow an individual to wipe out his personal debts, Joyce says. And "non-recourse" lending, common in the United States, is totally unknown in Ireland. It allows a homeowner to mail his keys back to the bank and walk away without paying the rest of the mortgage. Even if an Irish bank forecloses on a house and sells it — typically for a fraction of its original value — the homeowner is still responsible for the remainder of the mortgage.

"That's really why people are concerned," says Aoife Walsh, spokesperson for Respond! Housing Association, which advises troubled homeowners. "They know that not only could they lose the roof over their heads, but they'll have this massive debt hanging over them for the rest of their lives."

Although the new Fine Gael/Labour coalition government elected Feb. 25 has pledged to "fast-track" personal bankruptcy reform, no legislation is pending yet. The

Community organizer Wally Bowden stands in front of an abandoned building at Dolphin House, a public housing complex in Dublin, Ireland. A developer had planned to renovate the complex, add profit-making apartments and turn the building into a private clinic. When the property market crashed, the developer abandoned the project.

International Monetary Fund's bailout loan for Ireland, however, called for such legislation to be introduced by March 2012.

— Sarah Glazer

[1]Christopher Caldwell, "Not Too Big to Fáil," *The Weekly Standard*, Feb. 21, 2011, www.weeklystandard.com/articles/not-too-big-f-il_547416 .html.

[2]"Dolphin Decides: The Final Report," Dolphin House Community Development Association, 2009, p. 8, www.pcc.ie/dolphindecides/ dolphin.html.

[3]The bill to the government for bailing out Irish banks reached €70 billion in March, equal to €17,000 for each citizen. See Larry Elliott and Jill Treanor, "Ireland forced into new €21 billion bailout by debt crisis," *Guardian*, March 31, 2011, www.guardian.co.uk/world/2011/ mar/31/ireland-new-bailout-euro-crisis?INTCMP=SRCH.

its own political influence — became France's quid pro quo.

"Now that Germany's land area, population and economic capacity were set to expand at a stroke, it became even more urgent to lock it into Europe" to prevent German imperial ambitions — which had flourished during two world wars — from re-emerging, writes University of California economist Eichengreen. [34]

Strikes and Protests

A man hauls around fake euro notes (top) during a demonstration in Seville called by Spanish unions on June 8, 2010, to protest government austerity cuts. Garbage went uncollected and hospital services were limited throughout the country as thousands of public workers protested the cuts, designed to reduce Spain's deficit. BBVA is Spain's second-largest bank. In Athens, Greece, a cardboard coffin symbolizes the death of the euro during a protest march on March 30, 2010 (bottom). Government austerity measures in Greece have sparked several general strikes and street protests.

Why was France so committed to a monetary union? Ferguson notes that one ardent single-currency proponent, French Socialist Jacques Delors, thought the euro would protect Europe's extensive welfare state because all members would be tied to the same highly taxed, "centralized, redistributive and, in some ways, socialist system." [35]

Paradoxically, the eurozone's political leaders have taken more of a free-market approach, judging by recent EU requirements that debt-laden economies slash their social-welfare benefits and reduce expensive payroll taxes paid by businesses for those benefits. "When the countries joined, they effectively signed up to much more liberal [free-market] economic policies — free trade and flexible labor markets — but they don't seem to realize that" or acknowledge it to their voters, says Tilford of London's Centre for European Reform.

Of course, there were also some mutual benefits, even for Germany. "What you got was lower borrowing costs for the indebted nations and a weaker currency for Germany," says Ferguson. That meant German exports were cheaper, making them more competitive.

Until the last 50 years, most Western European countries were not economically viable on their own, and some, like Britain and France, used colonial empires to fuel their domestic economies, points out London School of Economics professor Hix. The Common Market, and later the EU, accomplished the same thing without bloodshed.

Indeed, without the creation of this internal market, the German, French, British and Italian economies "would not be large enough to sustain the standards of living which their citizens take for granted," Hix writes. [36]

Birth of the Euro

On Feb. 7, 1992, the Treaty on European Union was signed by the members of the Common Market, under the renamed European Union, at Maastricht, Netherlands. The treaty established rules for a single currency and set 1999 as the deadline for introducing the euro. Britain was exempted from the currency, while Denmark was to decide by referendum.

Both Britain and Denmark obtained legal exemptions from joining the euro. Denmark, a small but proud country, voted in 2002 not to join the euro. [37] Under Conservative Prime Minister John Major, Britain had participated in an earlier version of monetary union, the European Monetary System. But after a speculators' attack on the pound, Britain took its currency out of the joint system in 1992. "Tony Blair could credit his victory in the 1997 general election to the damage done to the Conservative government of John Major by the 1992 crisis," Eichengreen writes.

The so-called Maastricht Criteria set conditions for participating in the monetary union, including caps on budget deficits (no more than 3 percent of GDP), public debt (no more than 60 percent of GDP) and limits on inflation and long-term interest rates. But members had trouble following these conditions.

As the University of Southern California's Sarotte has observed, "Policymakers wanted the new currency to succeed and started using the number of members and applicants as an oversimplified metric of success, thereby allowing weaker economies to join without due scrutiny. Such laxness allowed the entry not only of members with debt-to-GDP ratios well in excess of 60 percent (Belgium, Italy) but also of applicants such as Greece, which not only flouted the rules but also falsified its records." [38]

Once accepted into the union, weaker member states could borrow at roughly the same interest rate as Germany, due to the European Central Bank's practice of treating the sovereign debt of all eurozone members equally. This meant that spending increased without regard to what the countries could actually afford.

The budgeting criteria were strengthened, at least in theory, at the request of the Germans in a 1997 Stability Pact, which established fines on those who violated the criteria. But fines have never been imposed, so the Maastricht Criteria have been observed mostly in the breach — even by the Germans.

After German reunification, the high cost of economic reconstruction in East Germany drove up Germany's borrowing costs, forcing Germany to ask, humiliatingly, for lenient implementation of the Stability Pact it had instigated. The EU agreed. Afterward, it was much harder for subsequent German governments to act in a holier-than-thou fashion toward any other member with economic woes. The fact that the French also found themselves in a fiscal hole for much of the 1990s only compounded the problem.

Thus, the Maastricht Criteria were only minimally enforced. But some experts say the caps were unrealistic from the outset. "The aging population of Europe plus the welfare state translated into deficits that were going to be way larger than 3 percent of GDP," says Ferguson, who predicted in 2000 that problems would surface within a decade.

On Jan. 1, 1999, the euro was introduced in 11 countries for commercial and financial transactions. Notes and coins entered general circulation in 2002.

Bubbles and Bailouts

When Greece became the 12th country to adopt the euro in 2001, no one guessed that it held the seeds of a disaster that would severely test the future of the monetary union.

Three years later it was discovered that Greece's financial reports, which had seemed to meet the eurozone's conditions for entry, were inaccurate. And in 2009 Greece's new Socialist government revealed that the national budget deficit would be 12.7 percent of GDP — twice the previous government's estimate, and more than four times larger than the EU's target.

The announcement caused Greece's bond rating to plummet, and the risk of a default surfaced for the first time. This occurred as an international credit and financial crisis was building in 2007 and became official in September 2008, when Lehman Brothers, a big U.S. investment bank, collapsed, and credit dried up around the world.

Starting as early as 2005, imbalances were already building between stolid, economically successful Germany and weaker economies in southern eurozone countries on such crucial measures as competitiveness, trade surpluses and deficits.

With a Greek default looming and fears that such a crisis might prove contagious, European heads of state on April 11, 2010, agreed to establish a crisis mechanism to safeguard the zone's financial stability by lending funds to member states in serious financial distress. On May 2, it was announced that Greece would receive an EU/IMF bailout loan of €110 billion. [39]

On May 9, 2010, officials established the European Financial Stability Facility (EFSF) — a three-year, €440 billion ($592 billion) fund to lend to troubled euro countries (other than Greece). That would be supplemented with a €250 billion ($337 billion) IMF commitment. After recent growing concerns that the fund's lending capacity might be insufficient, EU leaders this March committed themselves to finding a compromise by the summer to boost its lending ability. [40]

Last July 23 the EU announced the results of its "stress tests" on 91 European banks to determine whether the banks were resilient enough to weather future economic shocks. All but seven passed the tests, which the EU represented as a sign of the banks' solidity. [41] But the spectacular crash just a few months later of several Irish banks raised skepticism about the value of future tests.

Between 2003 and 2007 Ireland experienced a property-driven boom. By 2007, average house prices were nearly triple 2000 levels. The Irish economy became increasingly dependent on the construction sector — representing almost a quarter of its economy. By 2007, government revenues were heavily dependent on windfall taxes from the housing market.

When the housing bubble burst, tax revenues plummeted, ending a decade of budget surpluses. [42] But none of this could have happened without German banks lending to Irish banks cheaply and massively.

"People have not commented enough on how unusual it is for banks to get their growth driven by lending from other banks," says William Black, associate professor of economics and law at the University of Missouri, Kansas City, and a former senior financial regulator during the U.S. savings and loan crisis of the 1980s.

As a result, Irish banks grew to be much larger, relative to Ireland's small economy, than U.S. banks. [43]

By the end of September 2008, troubled Irish banks were unable to access financial markets, which were frozen by the international credit crunch. The government agreed to a blanket guarantee on all the banks' deposits as well as to most private bondholders of the six major banks — a move that has been severely criticized for essentially putting the entire burden for bank losses on Irish taxpayers. [44]

Black, an outspoken critic of the move, says bondholders who made risky investments are "supposed to be wiped out. To do anything else is to give people a complete bonanza."

Throughout 2010, the impact of the Greek sovereign debt crisis, coupled with the market's realization that Ireland's generous bank guarantees would severely strain its finances, sent interest rates on Irish government bonds soaring. By autumn it was clear the country was running out of money and was effectively shut out of the financial markets. The government had no choice but to seek help from the new EU bailout fund.

On November 28, the EU and the IMF agreed to bail out Ireland, the second eurozone member to come hat in hand. Under the agreement, it would receive a loan of €67.5 billion ($88.42 billion). [45]

CURRENT SITUATION

Cutting Deals

Eurozone leaders are taking steps to shore up the eurozone's struggling members and will meet in June to put the finishing details on a permanent fund to help future governments that run into difficulty.

But troubles continue to plague countries that have received bailouts and embarked on austerity programs. In April and May, the bond markets were punishing both Ireland and Greece with double-digit interest rates, even as steadfast Germany was paying only around 3.4 percent on its government debt. [46]

Nearly a year after Greece received its bailout deal, its borrowing costs on April 14 had soared to more than 13 percent on 10-year government bonds — the highest since it joined the euro in 2001. The surge followed suggestions by German Finance Minister Wolfgang Schäuble that Greece might have to restructure (default on) its debt. Thus, it appeared increasingly likely that the Greek government would be shut out of the financial markets in 2012, when it needs to raise €25-30 billion ($35 billion-$43 billion). [47]

With a national debt mounting to more than 150 percent of GDP, Greece appeared condemned to years of zero growth and recession, fueled by deep spending cuts and tax increases. [48] Its jobless rate rose to 15.1 percent in January, the highest level since 2004, when the country's national statistics agency began collecting unemployment figures. [49] Given the dismal statistics, European officials admitted on May 7 that Greece probably would need a new cash bailout of tens of billions of euros, possibly with easier repayment terms. [50]

However, EU officials continued to resist any talk of a Greek restructuring plan, even though market speculation that a default was inevitable intensified on May 9, as interest rates on Greek bonds continued to rise. [51]

And in the week following the flurry of EU meetings on the Greek crisis, German leader Merkel, facing opposition to any further bailouts from her junior coalition party, the Free Democrats, denied that Germany was ready to give Greece more aid. She said she was awaiting an EU report on the situation due in June. [52]

EU leaders had already agreed on March 11 to reduce Greece's bailout interest rate by 1 percentage point and extend the payback period to 7.5 years. In exchange, the EU demanded that Greece privatize government assets to yield €50 billion ($69 billion) by 2015 — which led to the German politicians' suggestion, mocked in the press, that Greece sell some of its islands and art treasures. [53]

Some economists said the €50 billion target, amounting to about 20 percent of Greek GDP, would be

Would Ireland have been better off without the euro?

YES

Sean Barrett
*Senior Lecturer, Economics Department,
Trinity College, Dublin, Ireland*

Written for *CQ Global Researcher,* May 2011

Ireland joined the euro as a political gesture to a currency that accounted for less than a third of its trade. University of Chicago economist Milton Friedman warned in the Irish Times on Sept. 5, 2001, that "the euro was adopted really for political purposes, not economic purposes, as a step towards the myth of the United States of Europe. In fact I believe that its effect will be exactly the opposite. The need for different policies like tightening monetary policy in Ireland or a more flexible monetary policy in Italy will produce political tensions that will make it more difficult to achieve political unity."

Today these tensions have increased German reluctance to fund further rescues after Greece and Ireland. Germany needs higher interest rates in order to curb inflation. Ireland needs lower interest rates to tackle a 14.5 percent unemployment rate. The peripheral countries need a weaker euro to grow, but the euro is strengthening. When Ireland joined as a full-employment, solvent country it did not need either reduced interest rates or the large capital inflow arising from membership.

Friedman was pessimistic about any way out for Ireland. "Ireland is stuck with the euro. How would you break out, and start all over again to establish a new monetary system, the punt?* You are not going to give it up. You have locked yourselves together and thrown away the key."

Having joined the euro without economic analysis, Ireland then celebrated a hard-currency union with soft-currency policies. The Organisation for Economic Co-operation and Development's (OECD) 2008 "Report on Public Management in Ireland" found that between 1995 and 2005 the public-expenditure policies in Ireland and Germany were polar opposites. Real annual public expenditure in Ireland increased by 5 percent a year and contracted by 0.5 percent a year in Germany. Ireland lacked fiscal discipline.

Meanwhile, less than 2 percent of the massive capital inflow resulting from euro membership was invested in industry and agriculture. Ireland had the highest home-price increases in the OECD countries, with Dublin second-hand house prices rising from €104,000 ($121,000) in 1997 to €512,000 ($645,000) in 2006.

Ireland joined the euro without analysis, pursued economic policies the opposite of those of Germany — the bulwark of the euro — and has no exit strategy. It is a lethal policy combination.

---

*The Irish pound also is known as the punt.

NO

Philip R. Lane
*Professor of International Macroeconomics,
Trinity College Dublin, Ireland*

Written for *CQ Global Researcher,* May 2011

At a superficial level, membership in Europe's Economic and Monetary Union (EMU)* may seem to have directly contributed to the boom-bust cycle in Ireland. However, had Ireland not joined the euro, the current banking crisis could have been amplified by a currency crisis. Moreover, an independent currency would not have offered a guarantee against the onset of the mid-2000s credit boom.

The credit boom affected many non-euro economies in Europe, including Iceland and countries in Central and Eastern Europe. In addition, many nations have experienced twin banking and currency crises, in which collapsing currencies raised the local burden of foreign-currency debts, inducing a more severe crash. Moreover, even under an independent monetary policy, it is not clear that the central bank would have been able to neuter the housing boom solely through its interest rate policy, since a large interest rate hike might have caused a big recession without cooling down the housing market.

Membership in the monetary union also has provided considerable stability during this crisis period. Most directly, the European Central Bank has provided substantial cheap funding to Irish banks during the crisis. In contrast, non-euro countries such as Latvia and Iceland suffered far harsher crises, since these economies had no similar source of external funding. In addition, highly indebted Irish households have benefited from low ECB interest rates during the crisis.

However, it is important to emphasize that Ireland took excessive macroeconomic risks during the first decade of the single currency, particularly by failing to regulate the banking sector to guard against systemic risk factors. This was especially problematic under the EMU, because Irish banks' newly expanded access to area-wide financial markets amplified the scope of their risk-taking. In addition, Ireland's fiscal policy was insufficiently counter-cyclical. These twin policy weaknesses both failed to curb the boom and exacerbated the scale of the crisis. Ireland learned a harsh lesson from the crisis: It should never again tolerate weak banking regulation or imprudent fiscal policies. Indeed, Ireland is now undergoing extensive institutional reforms in order to ensure that such a crisis does not recur in the future.

---

*The EU-established monetary system that introduced the euro.

difficult to reach. As Greece was headed for a revamped bailout in May, European leaders complained that the government's delay in selling off its public holdings was one reason it failed to meet its deficit-reduction target. Intense opposition from public unions over cost-cutting measures also has hampered Greece from meeting EU budget targets. [54]

In March Ireland had refused a similar deal — reducing its bailout loan interest rate — when told it would have to eliminate its corporate tax haven in return. In the wake of the Greek crisis in May, Irish Prime Minister Enda Kenny was intensifying pressure on EU leaders to reduce Ireland's interest bill, saying there was a question as to whether Ireland could repay its bailout loan at the current rate. But in exchange he was once again expected to face pressure from French leaders to "harmonize" Ireland's corporate tax system with the rest of the EU. [55]

France fears that lower-tax regimes like Ireland's could undercut France's own ample social welfare state, says Hix, of the London School of Economics. "In France, a lot of the costs of their generous social welfare state are imposed on business in corporate taxes and in unemployment insurance paid by business," he notes.

Despite the deals cut in early March, EU leaders failed to calm the markets. As the details of the deal trickled out in early March, Moody's downgraded both Greece's and Spain's credit ratings, citing increased risk of default (Greece), and higher estimates of the Spanish banking system's capital needs.

On March 23 Portugal's prime minister resigned after Parliament failed to approve his party's fourth austerity package. The failure was blamed on lack of cooperation from opposition Social Democrats, who are favored to win the June 5th general election.

Then in the run-up to the EU's March 24-25 summit on Portugal's bailout, Portugal's credit rating was downgraded by both the Moody's and Fitch ratings agencies. Standard & Poor's went further, downgrading Portugal's bonds to one notch above junk status on March 29. The actions sent Portugal's borrowing costs soaring, forcing the country's caretaker government to seek a bailout loan in April. [56]

In late March eurozone leaders also agreed to create a permanent rescue fund, the European Stability Mechanism (ESM), which in 2013 would replace the temporary fund known as the EFSF. It would have an effective lending capacity of €500 billion ($688 billion). But leaders postponed decisions on the funds' details, saying the effective lending capacity of the temporary fund and of the permanent facility would be finalized by the end of June. [57]

Eurozone leaders also agreed on the so-called Euro Plus Pact — touted earlier in the year by French and German leaders as the Competitiveness Pact — which commits eurozone countries to closer economic cooperation. In provisions that go to the heart of nations' traditional sovereignty, the pact calls on participating states to limit public-sector wage increases, lower taxes on labor, develop a common corporate tax base, revise pension systems with an eye to future costs and establish some form of debt brake in their national fiscal rules.

Both the French and Germans claimed victory, even though the pact did not include any enforcement mechanisms — such as fines or sanctions — included in the original German proposal.

"They've totally watered down the idea that they should all coordinate what they do in their domestic policy," says Hix. "They'll monitor what each other [does] but in a very soft-power way. There's no way they're going to enforce sanctions on what people do with their labor market policies and their tax policy."

By June, new bank stress tests are expected to be carried out by the EU's newly created European Banking Authority, but some observers doubt they will be tough enough to restore confidence in Europe's banking system. The EU's 2010 stress tests were widely criticized when only seven of 91 banks failed the tests. All of Ireland's banks passed the tests, for instance, yet by year's end they required huge bailouts. [58]

Government Killer?

Whether or not the euro is a "government-killing mechanism" as historian Ferguson terms it, several recent government defeats have been attributed to the sovereign debt crises in the euro countries.

In Spain, where unemployment is running at 20 percent, the austerity program arguably made the Socialist Prime Minister José Luis Rodríguez Zapatero so unpopular he has said he won't run for a third term.

Right-wing populist parties — which combine their anti-bailout messages with anti-immigrant sentiments — have made gains, especially in countries with stronger economies. The most recent sign of rising nationalism occurred May 12, when Denmark re-erected border controls with other EU countries, a measure pushed by the right-wing, anti-immigrant Danish People's Party. The action came just as EU interior ministers agreed to reinstate passport controls among 22 EU countries that since 1995 have enjoyed unfettered travel. The measure was designed to restrict the recent flood of North African immigrants fleeing political upheavals and followed an earlier spat between Italy and France over whether the rising tide of Tunisian immigrants arriving on Italy's shores should be able to migrate easily to the other EU countries. [59]

On March 23, the Socialist government of Portuguese Prime Minister Sócrates collapsed after it could not muster support for a fourth austerity package in Parliament. The opposition Social Democrats, now favored to win the June 5 election, particularly opposed cuts that fell hard on pensioners. [60]

Concern about Portugal's ability to pay €7 billion ($10 billion) on bonds maturing on June 15 led to the government's request in April for an EU rescue package, because the newly elected government was not expected to be in place in time for the June deadline. [61] EU officials hoped to approve a final Portuguese rescue package amounting to €78 billion ($115 billion) at a May 16 meeting of eurozone finance ministers. [62] But Finland's finance minister warned that the package must be "harder and more comprehensive than the one the parliament voted against," which included a tax of up to 10 percent on pensions over €1,500 a month and a freeze on smaller pensions. [63]

The latest potential setback for a resolution of the debt crisis came in mid-April, when the True Finns party, which campaigned against a bailout for Portugal, made spectacular gains in the general election. With their jingoistic motto, "The Finnish cow should be milked in Finland," the party rose to a 19 percent share of the vote from only 4 percent in 2007, making it a close third behind the two leading parties. Finland, unlike other countries, requires parliamentary approval to take part in bailouts, which require unanimous support of all 17 eurozone members. [64]

However, on May 12, Finland's Parliament voted to support Portugal's bailout, after the conservative NCP party agreed with the Social Democrats to include conditions requiring Portugal to sell off assets to repay EU

countries and to begin talks with private investors. [65] Nevertheless, the True Finns' gains had already triggered a renewed outbreak of the sovereign debt crisis in the eurozone, as the costs of borrowing for debt-laden countries like Greece rose to record levels again.

On May 9, Standard & Poor's downgraded Greece's bond status further into junk status territory — from BB- to B — saying Greece may need to renege on at least half of its $327 billion ($470 billion) debt mountain, implying big losses for investors. [66]

OUTLOOK

Nationalist Obstructionism?

The recent rise of nationalist parties in Europe raises questions about how willing prosperous Europeans will be to bail out their poorer brethren, but also, more broadly, how much unity Europe really wants. Anti-EU rhetoric coupled with anti-immigrant right-wing messages make it appear that this is "Europe's own Tea Party moment." [67]

If nationalism holds sway in any country, a single government could block the rescue packages. Most EU supporters were confident that an effort to put the bailout funds on a firm legal ground, via a pending amendment to remove the EU treaty's prohibition on bailouts, will be approved. But one country could block the change. [68]

In addition, unanimous approval is needed to loan money to any troubled country after 2013, when the permanent bailout fund is set to open. This provision was aimed at reassuring richer eurozone countries like Austria, Finland, Germany and the Netherlands that they can't be forced to provide loans. [69]

Nationalists in debt-laden countries may argue that the bailout austerity measures are too harsh. Will voters stand for such harsh cuts? Ana Caterina Santos, a journalist for the Portuguese radio news station TSF, thinks they will.

"What scares us most is Greece — we don't want to be seen as Greek people," with all the connotations of the profligate southern stereotype, she says. "We have this idea: We Portuguese are more European than the Greeks. [W]e want to prove we can change."

That could be harder than people think. Most Portuguese see free health and education as two sacred untouchables, according to Santos. Unfortunately, that's where the big savings can be found, experts say, along with pensions, which are already very low by European standards.

Europe's lack of unity was further underscored in mid-April when Hungarian Prime Minister Viktor Orbán, whose country currently holds the EU presidency, said the EU's willingness to welcome new members was weaker than at any time in past 15 years. [70]

But the euro's troubles have also given some EU members pause about whether they're ready to adopt the currency, legally a requirement of EU membership (except for Britain and Denmark, which have legal exemptions.)

"The Poles and the Czechs continue to say, 'We'll join.' But they're not going to rush into it," predicts economist Tilford.

"The walking-wounded banks are the second part of the crisis," predicts Ferguson. "Before the end of this year, we'll have to sit down and admit which banks in Europe are bust."

As the continent struggles with the economic crisis, Europe's inferiority complex about its shrinking importance, squeezed between the great economic powers of China and the United States, has intensified. "[W]ill Europe be unable to cope with the dynamism of other regions of the world and be paralyzed at home by national populism and selfishness, leading it to resign itself to being nothing more than a regional power?" Michel Barnier, EU commissioner for the internal market, asked on May 9.

He urged the European Union to move toward greater cooperation, including adopting a common defense policy. "Will Europe be a continent under the influence of the United States, China and even of Russia?" he asked. [71]

To the contrary, according to American economist Eichengreen, the euro — alongside the dollar and the Chinese renminbi — will be one of the three currencies that will dominate world trade in the future. Already, the euro is widely used outside of the eurozone. Some 37 percent of all international bonds are in euros, according to Eichengreen, partly to appeal to European investors.

But what about Europe's failure to come up with an overarching federal government like that in the United States? Won't that hold the eurozone back?

"There are different flavors of capitalism and different flavors of monetary union," says Eichengreen. In his view, European countries "don't need to turn into a United States of Europe to make a monetary union work."

The eyes of the world are on Europe to see what kind of recipe for unity it will devise and whether it will work.

UPDATE

The leaders of the 17 European governments that use the euro —faced with the prospect of a chaotic Greek default that would roil financial markets, destabilize their currency and collapse banks — blinked.

On March 15 the eurozone leaders approved a second bailout in two years for Greece, authorizing 130 billion euros ($170 billion) that allows the troubled Mediterranean government to continue making some payments to its bondholders. Opening the way for the bailout was a deal just a week earlier in which investors owning 96 percent of the country's privately held debt agreed to write down, or forfeit, more than 100 billion euros of the 206 billion owed to them by the country – the largest debt restructuring in history. [72]

For the moment the move headed off a potential contagion that could have threatened the finances of other shaky European debtors, including Portugal, Spain and Italy. And for Greece the price of the latest bailout was high. In return for cash from the European Union, Greece agreed to reduce its minimum wage 22 percent and lay off 150,000 government workers by 2015. The belt tightening comes as the country contends with a crippling 21 percent unemployment rate — including half its young adults out of work — and just a month after rioters burned more than 80 buildings in Athens to protest austerity measures. [73]

The EU's move was the latest effort by European leaders to end a debt crisis that has stalled the continent's economic growth, upset world stock markets and helped topple governments in Ireland, Portugal, Greece and Italy. The 2-year-old crisis has deepened over the past nine months, affecting more nations and leading policymakers to greater commitments to stave off sovereign, or government, defaults. Even economically stable countries such as France and Austria have seen their credit ratings — a measure of their ability to pay back loans — downgraded.

In late 2011, the crisis led the European Central Bank to issue a 489 billion euro ($639.3 billion) "wall of cash" to the continent's banks at just 1 percent interest.[74] The unprecedented move was aimed at halting panic in the market that could freeze lending between banks and cut off credit to businesses.

European governments and the International Monetary Fund are considering increasing the size of a separate emergency bailout fund, known as the European Financial Stability Facility, for other countries that may face default. At the same time, Germany and France, Europe's two largest economies and the most powerful political forces in the zone, are pushing for a fiscal union requiring individual governments' spending and revenues to be closely monitored and coordinated.[75]

Ireland, Portugal and Greece experienced rapid growth in the 1990s after joining the eurozone, but in the wake of the global economic crisis that growth has proved illusory. Much of it was built on cheap loans from banks in Germany and the stronger economies in northern Europe.

Now Germany, France and other European nations are themselves threatened by the crisis since defaults by other European governments could bankrupt some of their largest banks. Nonetheless, resolving the situation has been complicated by the insistence of Germany and some other creditor nations that debtors already mired in recession must further cut spending, a demand widely seen as likely to exacerbate their economic woes and heighten social strife.

Analysts say the latest bailout won't be enough to save Greece from a major default on its debt in the future, and some argue it won't save the euro itself. "This latest bailout isn't going to last very long," says Desmond Lachman, a fellow at the American Enterprise Institute, a conservative think tank, and a former managing director at the investment firm Salomon Smith Barney. "It is only months before Greece starts defaulting on its official debt. I just think it's a slow-motion train wreck."

Indeed, even the principal backers of the latest bailout seem to have serious doubts about its efficacy. Almost immediately after the deal was announced, newspapers obtained a leaked report by economists from the EU, International Monetary Fund (IMF) and European Central Bank suggesting that the proposed spending cuts would only sink Greece further into recession, thereby slashing tax revenues, worsening government deficits and accelerating the country's insolvency.

The leaked report also suggested that the Greek debt restructuring by private lenders, which included a default on some of the money Greece owed, could prevent the country from being able to borrow from the private sector again for years.[76]

With the eurozone expected to enter recession this year, Greece isn't the only country about which economists are pessimistic. Portugal, which received a 78 billion euro bailout in May, has implemented all of the government spending cuts and tax hikes demanded by the EU and IMF. Still, the ratio of the country's gross domestic product (GDP) to its debt, a broad measure of overall indebtedness, has worsened because the economy has shrunk. At the time of the bailout its debt was 107 percent of its economic output. Next year it's expected to reach 118 percent.[77]

Italy also faces trouble. With its parliament forced by the European Union to adopt austerity measures, Prime Minister Silvio Berlusconi resigned after dominating Italian politics for the last 17 years. The austerity steps included raising the country's value-added tax (a form of sales tax); freezing government salaries; increasing the retirement age for women; and imposing new taxes on energy. Still, 34 Italian banks saw their credit ratings downgraded in February. The Standard & Poor's rating agency said the Italian government's difficulties in borrowing in the international market posed risks for Italian government debt held by the country's banks.[78]

In Ireland, which received an 85 billion euro bailout in 2010, the government has met its obligations to slash its budget deficit and shrink its banks. But it still may need an additional 24 billion euros to meet its 2014 debt payments, and IMF, European Commission and European Central Bank officials are now forecasting that the economy will grow at a paltry 0.5 percent this year.[79]

Like Ireland, Spain has been considered a star at implementing austerity. In 2011, its socialist government increased the retirement age, slashed pay for government workers and ended a subsidy for women who give birth.[80] Even as the moves trimmed the gap between government spending and revenues, unemployment has remained stubbornly high, particularly for the young. Among those age 24 and under, the unemployment rate is 46 percent, and joblessness is forecast to rise this year.[81]

Analysts agree that the European Central Bank's "wall of cash" last year has helped keep banks in Spain and Italy afloat and headed away from a credit crunch that would have halted lending to businesses. But there is no consensus as to whether the eurozone has permanently contained the crisis.

Italy is likely to experience strikes and other social strife as it implements economic reforms in the comings months, says Jacob Funk Kirkegaard, a Danish research fellow at the Peterson Institute for International Economics in Washington. Despite the likely bumps in the road, the outlook for the eurozone's third-largest economy is now positive. "I think fears about Italy becoming an insolvent country will gradually disappear," he says. "I think Italy is well on its way to bailing itself out through reforms."

As a result of the economic integration resulting from the crisis, Kirkegaard foresees countries that are currently outside the eurozone joining over the next decade in order not to be left out of the continent's key economic decisions. "In a five-year time horizon you'll see a number of other countries joining, such as Poland, Latvia and maybe Sweden and Denmark," he says. "They will really pay a political price for being on the outside. If you're a small country like Denmark, the reality is you will probably have a better chance of blocking something that comes from France and Germany that is vital to your national interest if you're on the inside."

Others are more bearish. The austerity efforts by Spain, Italy and Portugal are likely to result in shrinking economies, slower tax growth and radicalized politics as joblessness grows and opportunity wanes, says AEI's Lachman, who foresees the euro collapsing.

"In my view, this is insanity," he says. "You have countries moving into recession, and you require that they reduce spending. A country like Spain that has to cut its budget by 3 percent of GDP in the middle of a credit crunch, when its external partners are weak and in the middle of a housing bust — it's going to deepen the recession."

The next major hurdle is likely to be another Greek default. But it remains to be seen whether that means Greece will be forced to abandon the euro and bring back its own currency, or whether it will trigger a panic and mass sell-off of Portuguese, Spanish or Italian debt. If history is a guide, however, the EU is likely to do just enough to avoid a disaster while failing to end the crisis, some analysts say.

"If there is some intelligent principle behind this approach, rather than mere flailing incompetence, it would sound like this: 'Let's build this manageable problem up into a crisis capable of vast destruction that we might be unable to control. That will create the fear needed to force some real improvements in economic policy,' " wrote financial journalist Clive Crook, a senior editor at *The Atlantic* and a critic of the response to the crisis by Germany and other creditor nations.

"When panic gripped the markets recently and bond yields surged, the solvency of Spain and Italy — plainly capable of servicing their debts under conditions of no panic — was called into question," Crook continued. "It beggars belief that the EU is willing to let the fear of a calamity on such a scale persist, when there's no need. But it has been willing, and still is." [82]

NOTES

1. Julia Finch, "Greece Told to Sell off Islands and Artwork," *Guardian*, March 4, 2010, www.guardian.co.uk/world/2010/mar/04/greece-greek-islands-auction.

2. Gideon Rachman's Blog, "The European Union in Deep Trouble," *ft.com*, April 17, 2011, http://blogs.ft.com/rachmanblog/2011/04/the-european-union-in-deep-trouble/.

3. "Wires: Portugal Agrees to Bailout Loan," *ft.com*, May 3, 2011, http://ftalphaville.ft.com/blog/2011/05/03/558136/wires-portugal-agrees-to-bailout-loan/. Robin Harding, *et al.*, "IMF head's arrest hits debt talks," *Financial Times*, May 15, 2011, www.ft.com/cms/s/0/415d008c-7e97-11e0-9e98-00144feabdc0.html#ixzz1MX9YTphe.

4. "Jump in Greek Yields Spurs Restructure Talk," *Financial Times*, May 3, 2011, www.ft.com/cms/s/0/6cd219e4-75a7-11e0-80d5-00144feabdc0.html#axzz1LUBTvdlc.

5. Mario Biejer, "Europe is running a giant Ponzi scheme," *Financial Times*, May 5, 2011, www.ft.com/cms/s/0/ee728cb6-773e-11e0-aed6-00144feabdc0.html#axzz1LUBTvdlc.

6. Estonia became the 17th country to adopt the euro on Jan. 1, 2011. Under EU law, all other members of the 27-nation EU — except for Britain and Denmark — are required to adopt the euro after meeting the budgetary and economic criteria set by the European Union.

7. Mary Elise Sarotte, "Eurozone Crisis as Historical Legacy," *Foreign Affairs*, Sept. 29, 2010, www.foreign affairs.com/print/66715?page-2.

8. "A Quantum Leap in Economic Governance; But Questions Remain," European Policy Centre, March 28, 2011, pp. 8-9, www.epc.eu/documents/uploads/pub_1247_post-summit_analysis_-_28_march_2011.pdf.

9. The state is Baden-Württemberg. A similar defeat occurred in Rhineland-Palatine. See "Germany: The Lights Go Out," *Financial Times*, March 28, 2011, www.ft.com/cms/s/0/828b8746-596b-11e0-bc39-00144feab49a.html#axzz1JCQeKBqX. Also see, "Angela's Trauma," *The Economist*, March 28, 2010, www.economist.com/blogs/newsbook/2011/03/germanys_regional_elections?page=1.

10. "The Quest for Prosperity," *The Economist*, March 15, 2007, www.economist.com/node/8808044.

11. For background, see "Europe Will Work," *Nomura Global Economics*, March 2011, p. 19, www.nomura.com/europe/resources/pdf/Europe%20will%20work%20FINAL_March2011.pdf.

12. GDP is the total value of an economy's output of goods and services. It is considered a key indicator of economic growth.

13. It's estimated that the new currencies of Spain, Portugal and Ireland would fall as much as 50 percent and Greece's as much as 80 percent. See Simon Tilford, "How to Save the Euro," Centre for European Reform, September 2010, p. 14, www.cer.org.uk/pdf/essay_euro_tilford_14sept10.pdf.

14. *Ibid.*

15. David McWilliams, "Ditching the Euro Could Boost Our Failing Economy," May 6, 2009, www.davidmcwilliams.ie/2009/05/06/ditching-the-euro-could-boost-our-failing-economy.

16. "Europe's Banks: Follow the Money," *The Economist*, April 16, 2011, p. 80, www.economist.com/node/18560535?story_id=18560535&CFID=168405116&CFTOKEN=43737452.

17. See Conor O'Clery, "U.S. Economist Expounds on Great Euro Mistake," *The Irish Times*, Sept. 5, 2001, p. 17, www.irishtimes.com/newspaper/archive/2001/0905/Pg017.html#Ar01700.

18. "Trichet Defends ECB Rate Increase," *Financial Times*, April 7, 2011, www.ft.com/cms/s/0/e4c95f16-6143-11e0-ab25-00144feab49a.html#axzz1Ipf7zFRy.

19. www.economist.com/blog/dailychart/2010/12/Europes_economies.

20. Lex, "Portugalling: Debts are Not Sustainable," *Financial Times*, April 7, 2011, www.ft.com/cms/s/3/26efc574-6126-11e0-8899-00144feab49a.html#axzz1Ipf7zFRy.

21. Steven Erlanger, "In Portugal Crisis, Worries on Europe's 'Debt Trap,' " *The New York Times*, April 8, 2011, www.nytimes.com/2011/04/09/world/europe/09portugal.html?_r=1&scp=1&sq=%22In%20Portugal%20Crisis,%20worries%20on%20europe%27s%20debt%20trap%22&st=cse.

22. Desmond Lachman, "Waiving the Rules for Portugal," *Financial Times*, April 7, 2011, www.ft.com/cms/s/0/e44bab88-6103-11e0-8899-00144feab49a.html#ixzz1JIf33xid.

23. The rumors were denied by both Greek and EU officials. See "Video: Greece Needs Revised Bailout," *ft.com*, May 9, 2011, http://video.ft.com/v/936381701001/Greece-needs-revised-bail-out.

24. Peter Spiegel, *et al.*, "European Officials to Revamp Greek Aid," *Financial Times*, May 8, 2011, www.ft.com/cms/s/0/b445945c-7978-11e0-86bd-00144feabdc0.html#axzz1LrivhFKc.

25. Raoul Ruparel, "Stopping the Rot? The Cost of a Portuguese Bail-Out and Why it is Better to Move Straight to Restructuring," Open Europe, March 2011, www.openeurope.org.uk/research/portugalrestructure.pdf.

26. FT Alphaville, "A Proclamation from Spain's Ministry of Public Works," *Financial Times*, May 11, 2011, p. 35. Also see Martin Wolf, "The Eurozone's Journey to Defaults," *Financial Times*, May 11, 2011, p. 15.

27. Niall Ferguson, *The Cash Nexus: Money and Power in the Modern World 1700-2000* (2001), p. 340.

28. *Ibid.*, pp. 334-335.

29. *Ibid.*, p. 336. For background, see Alan Greenblatt, "The Graying Planet," *CQ Global Researcher*, March 15, 2011, pp. 133-156; and Sarah Glazer, "Social Welfare in Europe," *CQ Global Researcher*, Aug. 1, 2010, pp. 185-210.

30. Ferguson, *op. cit.*, p. 150.

31. For background, see B. W. Patch, "European Economic Union," *Editorial Research Reports*, March 27, 1957, available at *CQ Researcher Plus Archive.*

32. For background, see I. B. Kobrak, "Common Market: Start of a New Decade," *Editorial Research Reports*, Feb. 8, 1967, available at *CQ Researcher Plus Archive.*

33. For background, see Mary H. Cooper, "A Primer on German Reunification," *Editorial Research Reports*, Dec. 22, 1989, available at *CQ Researcher Plus Archive.*

34. Barry Eichengreen, *Exorbitant Privilege* (2011), pp. 88-89.

35. Delors later became president during the 1980s of the European Commission, a policy-setting branch of the then-Common Market and later the EU, whose membership consists of one commissioner per member state. The presidency of the commission has been compared to the post of prime minister in a parliamentary government.

36. Simon Hix, *What's Wrong with the European Union & How to Fix It* (2010), pp. 10-11, 15.

37. See www.worldpress.org/Europe/232.cfm.

38. Mary Elise Sarotte, "Eurozone Crisis as Historical Legacy," *Foreign Affairs*, Sept. 29, 2010, www.foreign affairs.com/print/66715?page=2.

39. The $110 billion package, formally agreed to May 10, 2010, consists of $80 billion from euro area countries and $30 billion from the IMF.

40. "A Quantum Leap in Economic Governance, but Questions Remain," European Policy Centre, March 28, 2013, p. 4, www.epc.eu/documents/uploads/pub_1247_post-summit_analysis_-_28_march_2011.pdf.

41. Patrick Jenkins, "Seven Banks Fail EU Stress Tests, *Financial Times*, July 23, 2010, www.ft.com/cms/s/0/c14b9464-9678-11df-9caa-00144feab49a,s01=2.html#axzz1LsWojoIn.

42. Constantin Gurdgiev, *et al.*, "The Irish Economy: Three Strikes and You're Out?" Social Science Research Network, March 6, 2011, http://ssrn.com/abstract=1776190.

43. "How Ireland's Bank Bailout Shook the World," National Public Radio, Nov. 23, 2010, www.npr.org/blogs/money/2010/11/23/131538931/how-the-irish-bank-bailout-shook-the-world.

44. Gurdgiev, *op. cit.*

45. The total rescue package came to $85 billion, including $17.5 billion from the Irish government. Of the $67.5 billion in external assistance: $22.5 billion came from the European Financial Stability Mechanism (EFSM) contributed by EU members; $22.5 billion from the International Monetary Fund (IMF); and $22.5 billion from the European Financial Stability Fund (EFSF) and bilateral loans contributed by eurozone members.

46. See Landon Thomas Jr., "In U.K. Budget Cuts, Test Case for America," *International Herald Tribune*, April 15, 2011, p. 1.

47. Jennifer Hughes, "Greek debt hit by restructuring fears," *Financial Times*, April 14, 2011, www.ft.com/cms/s/0/086d7be6-667b-11e0-ac4d-00144feab49a.html#axzz1JVwZGUMq.

48. "Reuters Breaking Views: Not Yet Time for a Greek Restructuring," *International Herald Tribune*, April 15, 2011, p. 18. See Erlanger, *op. cit.*, for 150 percent figure.

49. "Greece Hit by Fear of Debt Overhaul," *International Herald Tribune*, April 15, 2011, p. 15.

50. Steven Erlanger, "Greek Leader Irked by Speculation on Debt," *The New York Times*, May 7, 2011, www.nytimes.com/2011/05/08/business/global/08greece.html?scp=1&sq=erlanger%20greece&st=cse.

51. *Ibid.* Also See Richard Milne, "S&P Cuts Greece Rating Two Notches," *Financial Times*, May 9, 2011, www.ft.com/cms/s/0/3997499c-7a47-11e0-bc74-00144feabdc0.html#axzz1LrivhFKc.

52. Judy Dempsey, "Germany Rejects Talk of Easing Bailout Terms," *The New York Times*, May 10, 2011, www.nytimes.com/2011/05/11/business/global/11euro.html.

53. Ralph Atkins and Kerin Hope, "Greek Goal of Return to Market in Doubt," *Financial Times*, April 13, 2011, www.ft.com/cms/s/0/c08e2970-65f2-11e0-9d40-00144feab49a.html#axzz1LsWojoIn.

54. Kerin Hope, "Greece in Line of Fire over Inability to Hit Targets," *Financial Times*, May 9, 2011, www.ft.com/cms/s/0/889c47f4-7a60-11e0-af64-00144feabdc0,s01=1.html#axzz1LrivhFKc.

55. Philip Inman, "EU Under pressure to Slash Ruinous Irish and Greek Bailout Bills," *Guardian*, May 9, 2011, www.guardian.co.uk/business/2011/may/09/eu-pressure-slash-irish-greek-bailout-bills?INTCMP=SRCH.

56. European Policy Centre, *op. cit.*, p. 2.

57. *Ibid.*

58. *Ibid.*, pp. 11-12.

59. The May 12 proposal, described as a "last resort" for emergencies, still needs approval from EU prime ministers and the European Parliament. See Ian Traynor, "Europe Moves to End Passport-Free Travel in Migrant Row," *Guardian*, May 12, 2011, www.guardian.co.uk/world/2011/may/12/europe-to-end-passport-free-travel.

60. Raphael Minder, "Austerity Debate Fells Portugal's Premier," *The New York Times*, March 23, 2011, www.nytimes.com/2011/03/24/world/europe/24portugal.html?_r=1&scp=3&sq=Socrates%20resigns&st=cse.

61. Peter Wise, "Portugal's Borrowing Costs Rise," *Financial Times*, April 15, 2011, www.ft.com/cms/s/0/6a38d2a0-675f-11e0-9bb8-00144feab49a.html#axzz1JVwZGUMq.

62. For Portugal's $78 billion package, the EU has pledged a total of $52 billion; the IMF contribution will be $26 billion over three years. See, IMF Survey Magazine, "IMF Outlines Joint Support Plan with EU for Portugal," May 6, 2011, www.imf.org/external/pubs/ft/survey/so/2011/INT050611A.htm.

63. Peter Wise, "Portuguese Prepare for Tighter Belts," *Financial Time*, April 8, 2011, www.ft.com/cms/s/0/4067461c-6211-11e0-8ee4-00144feab49a.html#axzz1JVwZGUMq.

64. See "Frustrated Finland," *Financial Times*, April 18, 2011.

65. "Finnish Parties Agree to Support Bail-out for Portugal," BBC News, May 12, 2011, www.bbc.co.uk/news/world-europe-13372218.

66. Inman, *op. cit.*

67. Peter Spiegel, "Anger Begins to Infect Europe's Prosperous Core," *Financial Times*, April 11, 2011, www.ft.com/cms/s/0/c9ec3d9e-6463-11e0-a69a-00144feab49a.html#axzz1JUlJGMDc.

68. The amendment is needed to counter challenges that have already arisen in German courts. See European Policy Centre, *op. cit.*

69. European Policy Centre, *op. cit.*, p. 5.

70. Stephen Castle, "Hungary Urges Balkan E.U. Entry," *The New York Times*, April 14, 2011, hwww.nytimes.com/2011/04/15/world/europe/15iht-hungary15.html?_r=1&scp=1&sq=Stephen%20Castle%20Hungary&st=cse.

71. Stephen Castle, "EU Official Urges More Unity," *The New York Times*, May 9, 2011, www.nytimes.com/2011/05/10/world/europe/10iht-union10.html?_r=1&emc=tnt&tntemail0=y.

72. Maria Petrakis and Rebecca Christie, "Greece Pushes Bondholders Into Record Debt Swap," Bloomberg News, March 9, 2012, www.bloomberg.com/news/2012-03-09/greece-debt-swap-tops-95-level-to-trigger-forced-bondholder-participation.html

73. Renee Maltezou and David Stamp, "Athens Mayhem Raises Fears of Greek Social Explosion," Reuters, Feb. 13, 2012, www.reuters.com/article/2012/02/13/us-greece-violence-idUSTRE81C1OK20120213.

74. Eva Kuehnen, "ECB Wall of Cash Averts Credit Crunch," Reuters, Feb. 27, 2012, www.reuters.com/article/2012/02/27/us-ecb-m-idUSTRE81Q0XP20120227.

75. "Germany, France in Push for Fiscal Union to Save Euro," *Agence France-Presse,* Dec. 2, 2011, http://

timesofindia.indiatimes.com/business/international-business/Germany-France-in-push-for-fiscal-union-to-save-euro/articleshow/10961434.cms.

76. Peter Spiegel, "Greek Debt Nightmare Laid Bare," *Financial Times,* Feb. 21, 2012, www.ft.com/intl/cms/s/0/b5909e86-5c0f-11e1-841c-00144feabdc0.html#axzz1nKVMZVeh.

77. Landon Thomas Jr., "Portugal's Debt Efforts May Be a Warning for Greece," The *New York Times*, Feb. 14, 2012, www.nytimes.com/2012/02/15/business/global/portugals-debt-efforts-may-be-a-warning-for-greece.html.

78. Nicole Bullock, Telis Demos and Vivianne Rodrigues, "S&P Downgrades Ratings of 34 Italian Banks," *Financial Times,* Feb. 10, 2012, www.ft.com/cms/s/0/cbdf0702-5428-11e1-bacb-00144feabdc0.html#axzz1nbp0XY1k.

79. Padraic Halpin, "Dim Growth Prospects Overshadow Irish Success," Reuters, Jan. 19, 2012, www.reuters.com/article/2012/01/19/ireland-bailout-idUSL6E8CJ2K920120119.

80. Edward Cody, "Socialists Cut Spain's Welfare State, Riling Spaniards," The *Washington Post,* May 20, 2011, www.washingtonpost.com/world/europe/socialists-cut-spains-welfare-state-riling-spaniards/2011/05/19/AFr6go7G_story.html.

81. Edward Cody, "Spain Faces Unemployment Pain After Embracing Austerity in European Crisis," *The Washington Post,* Feb. 17, 2012, www.washingtonpost.com/world/europe/spain-faces-unemployment-pain-after-embracing-austerity-in-european-crisis/2012/02/09/gIQA8qsVJR_story.html.

82. Clive Crook, "Greek Deal Leaves Europe on Road to Disaster," Bloomberg, Feb. 22, 2012, www.bloomberg.com/news/2012-02-23/greek-deal-leaves-europe-on-the-road-to-disaster-clive-crook.html.

BIBLIOGRAPHY

Selected Sources
Bibliography

Eichengreen, Barry, *Exorbitant Privilege: The Rise and Fall of the Dollar***, Oxford University Press, 2011.**
A professor of economics and political science at the University of California, Berkeley, predicts that the euro will become one of three leading international currencies along with the dollar and the Chinese renminbi.

Ferguson, Niall, *The Cash Nexus: Money and Power in the Modern World, 1700-2000***, Penguin, 2001.**
A Harvard professor of international history, who predicted 10 years ago that the eurozone would run into problems, finds that prior attempts to form monetary unions have failed.

McWilliams, David, *Follow the Money: The Tale of the Merchant of Ennis***, Gill & Macmillan, 2010.**
In this amusing account of Ireland's economic crash, an Irish columnist says the previous government's finance minister was clueless about how to respond and predicts Ireland will become "a large debt-servicing machine for a generation."

Reinhart, Carmen M., and Kenneth S. Rogoff, *This Time Is Different: Eight Centuries of Financial Folly***, Princeton University Press, 2009.**
An economist at the Peterson Institute for International Economics (Reinhart) and a Harvard University professor of economics find that government defaults have been surprisingly frequent over time in their study of 66 countries.

Articles

Erlanger, Steven, "In Portugal's Crisis, Worries on Europe's 'Debt Trap,' " *The New York Times***, April 8, 2011, www.nytimes.com/2011/04/09/world/europe/09portugal.html?_r=1&scp=2&sq=steven%20erlanger%20euro&st=cse.**
Economists fear Portugal will follow Greece and Ireland into a "debt trap."

Heise, Michael, "Why the Euro Will Survive," *The Wall Street Journal***, Jan. 6, 2011, http://online.wsj.com/article/SB10001424052748704723104576061440431381526.html.**
The chief economist at Germany's giant Allianz insurance company says breaking up the eurozone would hurt

its members, and budget retrenchment for debt-ridden countries will help them in the long run.

Lachman, Desmond, "Waiving the Rules for Portugal," *Financial Times*, **April 7, 2011.**
A resident fellow at the American Enterprise Institute says austerity budgets imposed on bailout countries like Greece and Ireland are making it harder for those economies to recover.

Lewis, Michael, "When Irish Eyes are Crying," *Vanity Fair*, **March 2011, www.vanityfair.com/business/features/2011/03/michael-lewis-ireland-201103.**
In his usual amusing style, journalist Lewis describes how Ireland got into its current economic mess.

McNamara, Kathleen R., "Can the Eurozone be Saved?" *Foreign Affairs*, **April 7, 2011, www.foreignaffairs.com/articles/67710/kathleen-r-mcnamara/can-the-eurozone-be-saved.**
The director of Georgetown University's Mortara Center for International Studies says the eurozone has failed to create the kind of unified federal government necessary for a monetary union to work, but that a common eurobond will solve the problem.

Münchau, Walter, "The Eurozone's Quack Solutions Will Be No Cure," *Financial Times*, **April 24, 2011.**
A respected economics columnist says the eurozone's solutions to the debt crisis will not calm the bond market's fears.

Reports and Studies

"Europe Will Work," Nomura, March 2011, www.nomura.com/europe/resources/pdf/Europe%20will%20work%20FINAL_March2011.pdf.
Asia's largest global investment bank concludes that the eurozone probably will not break up but needs to strengthen its governance.

"A Quantum Leap in Economic Governance — But Questions Remain," European Policy Centre, March 28, 2011, www.epc.eu/pub_details.php?cat_id=5&pub_id=1247.
This summary of the European Union's March summit agreements on how to tackle the euro debt crisis includes criticisms of the proposed solutions.

Ruparel, Raoul, "Stopping the Rot? The Cost of a Portuguese Bail-Out and Why It Is Better to Move Straight to Restructuring," Open Europe, March 2011, www.openeurope.org.uk.
It would be cheaper for Portugal to default than to accept a bailout loan from the European Union, concludes an analyst at the London think tank Open Europe.

Tilford, Simon, "How to Save the Euro," Centre for European Reform, September 2010, www.cer.org.uk/about_new/about_cerpersonnel_tilford_09.html.
The gap between the rhetoric of integration and the reality of national interests is proving lethal to the eurozone, argues the chief economist for a London think tank.

For More Information

Centre for Economic Policy Research, 77 Bastwick St., London EC1V 3PZ, United Kingdom; +44 (0)20 7183 8801; www.cepr.org. Network of more than 700 European researchers who study issues such as the euro. Has set up VoxEU.org website for commentary by leading economists.

Economics Without Boundaries With David McWilliams; www.davidmcwilliams.ie/2010/09/08/economics-without-boundaries-with-david-mcwilliams. Blog of Irish economics columnist who has been highly critical of the government's handling of Irish debt and economic crisis.

European Council, Rue de la Loi 175, B-1048 Brussels, Belgium; (32-2) 281 61 11; www.european-council.europa.eu/home-page.aspx?lang=en. Composed of the heads of member states of the European Union; defines the general political directions and priorities of the EU; posted the March 25 summit agreement on the euro at www.consilium.europa.eu/uedocs/cms_data/docs/pressdata/en/ec/120296.pdf.

European Union, http://europa.eu/index_en.htm. Web portal that links to all EU agencies.

European Union Delegation to the United States of America, 2175 K St., N.W., Washington, DC 20037; (202) 862-9500; www.eurunion.org/eu. Provides information about the EU to Americans.

European Policy Centre, Résidence Palace, 155 rue de la Loi, B-1040, Brussels, Belgium; +32 (0) 2 231 0340; www.epc.eu. Independent Brussels think tank devoted to European integration.

Open Europe, 7 Tufton St., London SW1P 3QN, U.K.; (44) 207 197 2333; www.openeurope.org.uk. Independent think tank with offices in London and Brussels.

Respond! Housing Association, Airmount, Dominick Pl., Waterford, Ireland; (353) 0818 357901; www.respond.ie. Ireland's largest nonprofit public housing association; has built nearly 5,200 homes nationwide for traditional families, single-parent families, the elderly, homeless and disabled.

Voices From Abroad:

DOMINIQUE STRAUSS-KAHN

Former Managing Director, International Monetary Fund

Praise Greece

"The Greek government should be commended for committing to an historic course of action that will give this proud nation a chance of rising above its current troubles and securing a better future for the Greek people."

The Boston Globe, May 2010

ANGELA MERKEL

Chancellor of Germany

Germany is ready

"We now have a mechanism of collective solidarity for the euro. And we all are ready, including Germany, to say that we now need a permanent crisis mechanism to protect the euro."

The Washington Post, November 2010

OLLI REHN

Commissioner for Economic and Monetary Affairs, European Commission

Containing the fire

"The recovery is taking hold, and it is progressing, but at the same time it is essential that we contain the financial bush fires so that they will not turn into a Europe-wide forest fire."

Thai Press Reports, December 2010

SIMON TILFORD

Chief Economist, Centre for European Reform, United Kingdom

Euro's Survival

"I don't think it's sustainable in the absence of a much greater degree of political and economic integration. It's very hard for any economy to flourish in the teeth of fiscal austerity of this magnitude — let alone those that can't devalue."

The New York Times, November 2010

SIMON WARD

Chief Economist, Henderson Global Investors United Kingdom

Weak won't leave

"I don't believe that the weak countries will leave the euro. If it's anyone it'll be Germany, which is worried about financing the bailouts, so it may be attractive for it to return to the deutschemark."

Express on Sunday (U.K.), November 2010

MARKUS KERBER

Professor of Finance, Berlin Technical University, Germany

Germany is not alone

"German guilt has been turned into too much money over too many years. But this is over. All of a sudden Germans are grasping the figures. The Dutch and the Austrians are fundamentally in the same situation. They don't want to see the monetary union turn into a transfer union."

The Christian Science Monitor, May 2010

COLM MCCARTHY

Lecturer in Economics, University College Dublin, Ireland

Blame the real estate bubble

"The credit-fuelled property bubble is the direct and indirect source of Ireland's debt crisis. If the bubble had been prevented by the bankers or their regulators, Ireland would now be suffering a mild recession rather than an existential threat to economic sovereignty."

Sunday Independent (Ireland), November 2010

FRANÇOIS FILLON

Former Prime Minister, France

Greece is unique

"Portugal's situation is nothing like that of Greece. . . . There is no reason to speculate against Spain and Portugal. . . . These countries' debt is perfectly within the average for the eurozone."

Daily Telegraph (England), May 2010

NICOLAS VERON

Economist, Belgium

Remaining intact

"The market perception now is the eurozone is not going to break up. We can safely say that if a country left the euro, it would be economically disruptive."

The Associated Press, December 2010

14

The Resource Curse

Jennifer Weeks

Chinese President Hu Jintao welcomes the president of Equatorial Guinea, Teodoro Obiang Nguema Mbasogo, to a 2006 summit in Beijing on China-Africa cooperation. The tiny, oil-rich West African nation is often cited as an example of the resource curse. Obiang reportedly has amassed a $65 billion personal fortune while his country ranks near the bottom on the U.N.'s economic development scale. Critics say China, now Africa's largest trading partner, turns a blind eye to corruption or repression by its resource-rich African trading partners.

From *CQ Researcher*, Dec. 20, 2011

AFP/Getty Images/Goh Chai Hin

C rowds danced in the streets when Libyan dictator Moammar Gadhafi was killed in October, following a bloody, six-month uprising. During his 42-year reign, Gadhafi had made Libya into a global scourge that sheltered terrorists, sponsored clandestine chemical and nuclear weapons programs and intervened in neighboring countries' civil wars. At home he presided over what Human Rights Watch called "an appalling catalogue of human rights abuses," including political arrests, torture and executions. [1]

But more outrage was still to come. The day after Gadhafi's death made global headlines, officials revealed he had stashed more than $200 billion in cash, gold and investment accounts around the world. The hoard, roughly twice as large as Libya's annual economic output, was also twice as much as investigators previously believed he had stolen. Moreover, he had amassed the assets "at a time when Libyans were struggling for the money they needed for schools, hospitals and all sorts of infrastructure," said an unnamed source close to Libya's transitional government. [2]

Even before this latest disclosure, Gadhafi's long tenure in Libya was often cited as a textbook example of the "resource curse." Coined by economists, the controversial term refers to developing countries that have abundant extractable resources — such as oil, gas or minerals — but lag behind other nations economically. When a country exports valuable raw materials, it earns enormous revenues — dubbed "rents" by economists — which can be invested in its overall development and well-being. Or, according to proponents of the resource curse theory, those revenues can trigger graft, corruption and even outright theft of public funds by officials and their cronies. [3] Resource windfalls also can be used to hire and arm

Africa and Middle East Rely Most on Extractive Industries

At least 40 nations derive at least 50 percent of their export revenues from oil, gas and mining; most are in Africa and the Middle East. Twenty-eight of those countries derive 75 percent or more from the export of extractable resources.

Exports Derived From Extractive Industries
(as a percentage of total exports, by country, 2007-2009)

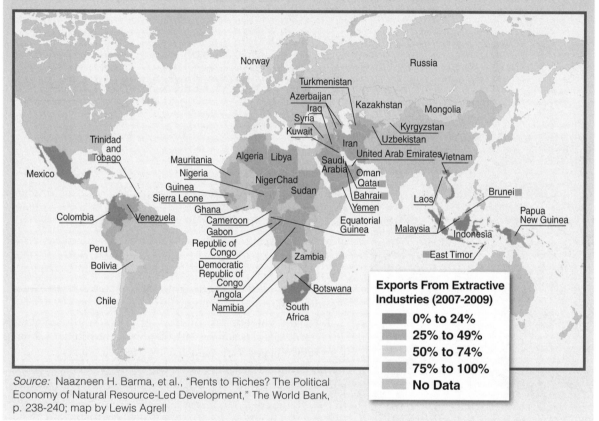

Exports From Extractive Industries (2007-2009)
- 0% to 24%
- 25% to 49%
- 50% to 74%
- 75% to 100%
- No Data

Source: Naazneen H. Barma, et al., "Rents to Riches? The Political Economy of Natural Resource-Led Development," The World Bank, p. 238-240; map by Lewis Agrell

powerful security forces, which help to keep dictators in power and relegate democracy to a back burner.

"Oil has sustained the rule of tyrants" in the Middle East and North Africa, University of Western Ontario Professor Peter Fragiskatos said shortly before Gadhafi's death. "In place of taxes — and the calls for democracy and representative government that they usually give rise to — the Gadhafi regime used oil profits to maintain its power. Flush with cash, the only real requirement it needed to fulfill was to adequately fund a security and military force that could silence any signs of dissent." [4]

While oil and mineral exports have spurred strong economic growth in some developing nations, "too often, oil money intended for a nation's poor ends up lining the pockets of the rich or is squandered on showcase projects instead of productive investments," Sens. Richard Lugar, R-Ind., and Benjamin Cardin, D-Md., wrote last April. [5]

Many countries blessed with abundant natural resources earn a large percentage of their income from extractive industries. Oil and gas account for nearly half of Norway's exports; Botswana earns 70 percent of its export revenues from diamonds and Chile gets roughly half of its export earnings and a third of government revenues from copper. [6]

The resource curse has not affected all countries with large oil, gas or mineral reserves. Norway, Botswana and Chile, for instance, have used their earnings to promote economic growth, address social needs and stabilize their economies.

But then there are countries such as Nigeria, widely considered a prime example of the resource curse. Oil deposits in Nigeria's Niger Delta generate 80 percent of current government revenues and have been the country's main income source since the 1970s. [7] But oil revenues have improved the lives of few Nigerians: Some 70 percent of the country's 155 million citizens live in poverty, two-thirds lack access to basic sanitation and life expectancy is less than 48 years. [8]

"Nigeria has had 40 years of oil but for the first 30 years it wasted the proceeds from that oil," former International Monetary Fund chief Dominique Strauss-Kahn said in 2008. [9]

Development Varies in Resource-Rich Countries

Among the 28 countries that depend on oil, gas and minerals for at least 75 percent of their export revenues, Brunei has the highest level of development, based on quality-of-life indicators such as life expectancy, literacy and education. Seven of the top 10 countries are in the Middle East and North Africa. Among the bottom 10, eight are in Sub-Saharan Africa, including the Democratic Republic of Congo, which ranks lowest.

Development Indexes for Resource-Dependent Countries, 2011
(on a 0-1 scale, with 1 being the most developed)

Most Developed		Least Developed	
Brunei	0.838	Dem. Republic of Congo	0.286
Qatar	0.831	Niger	0.295
Bahrain	0.806	Chad	0.328
Saudi Arabia	0.770	Sierra Leone	0.336
Kuwait	0.760	Guinea	0.344
Libya	0.760	Sudan	0.408
Trinidad and Tobago	0.760	Nigeria	0.459
Venezuela	0.735	Yemen	0.462
Iran	0.707	Papua New Guinea	0.466
Oman	0.705	Angola	0.486

Sources: "International Human Development Indicators," U.N. Development Programme, 2011, hdr.undp.org/en/data/map/; Naazneen H. Barma, et al., "Rents to Riches? The Political Economy of Natural Resource-Led Development," The World Bank, pp. 238-240

In addition to increasing corruption, rich natural resources also tend to "exacerbate poverty and increase conflict," says Ian Gary, senior policy manager for extractive industries at Oxfam America, a global relief and development advocacy group. "In countries with weak governments or that are just emerging from conflict, the impacts are likely to be especially profound," he adds. Some observers predict that Libya will have trouble forming a stable democratic government because rival factions will fight for control of the country's oil industry.

But many experts reject the theory of a resource curse. "It's a myth," says Calestous Juma, founding director of the African Centre for Technology Studies in Nairobi, Kenya, and a professor at the Harvard Kennedy School of Government. "It scapegoats extractable resources instead of looking at the real drivers of economic growth,

which are human capabilities. If you don't invest in those, you're not going to grow, and you're going to waste whatever resources you have."

Ever since dozens of countries became independent after World War II, development experts have been trying to identify factors that promote economic growth and understand why some countries have made great progress while others have not. Most acknowledge that suddenly having to handle vast deposits of natural resources is a challenge for fledgling countries.

"It's like winning the lottery," says Charles Kenny, a senior fellow at the Center for Global Development in Washington. "All of a sudden you're a lot richer than you used to be. Some people handle that very sensibly: They invest it. Others rush out and buy a house or a big boat that they can't afford to maintain, and then the money runs out and their lives aren't any better in the long term."

How to Successfully Manage Resource Wealth

Resource-rich role models focus on accountability and the long term.

Some countries with abundant resources have avoided the resource curse by using their wealth to promote economic growth and meet social needs. Although each country's situation is different, successful cases share some common elements: strong democratic institutions and a focus on the long-term future.

Norway earned most of its income from shipping and fishing before oil was discovered in its coastal waters in 1970. Today oil accounts for almost half of Norway's exports and more than 30 percent of state revenue. The nation's Government Pension Fund (actually a reserve for oil revenues) was valued at $560 billion as of mid-December 2011 — the second-largest such reserve in the world. [1]

From the outset, observers say, Norway has managed its oil wealth with a focus on the future. The government awarded drilling permits slowly to stretch resources out over time, even as production declines, to generate funds for public pension costs as workers retire. [2] All revenues go into the oil trust fund. Only interest from the fund can be spent, while the principal is saved. [3]

"We cannot spend this money now; it would be stealing from future generations," said Norwegian economist Eirik Wekre in 2009, during the global recession. [4]

Five thousand miles to the south in southern Africa, land-locked Botswana is another successful resource-rich country, but with a very different background. A British colony called Bechuanaland, it was one of the world's poorest countries when it became independent in 1966. But it also has diamond mines, which generate 70 to 80 percent of export earnings and about half of government revenues.

And like Norway, Botswana has managed its earnings with discipline and a focus on the future. Today it is a middle-income country and is viewed as one of the best credit risks in Africa. [5]

Many factors helped Botswana perform so well. Before and during its colonial period, the country had lower levels of ethnic conflict than many other parts of Africa. When it became independent, the government focused on building up health, education and infrastructure systems and worked to diversify the economy. And when diamond revenues began to flow, the government demanded 50 percent of the profits and invested them in long-term needs. [6]

Importantly, Botswana also has strong democratic institutions such as regular and fair elections, independent courts and a free press — all of which help prevent corruption and hold government officials accountable. [7]

"By and large Botswana's political elite has been frugal and accountable to the people," writes Hippolyte Fofack, a fellow of the African Academy of Sciences in Nairobi, Kenya. "These attributes have enabled these leaders to withstand a culture of rampant greed that has done so much to undermine the development process in the rest of the continent." [8] According to Transparency International, Botswana is perceived as the least corrupt country in Africa. [9]

In Latin America, Chile has prospered from its copper wealth, even during several decades of political turmoil. Socialist President Salvador Allende nationalized the country's copper mines in 1971, but he was overthrown in a 1973 coup and replaced by a repressive military government that ruled until elections took place in 1990.

To deter leaders from wasting their countries' newfound riches, many advocacy groups support publicizing all transactions between governments and extractive industries, such as mining or energy companies. Once citizens know how much the country is being paid for its resources, the argument goes, they will demand a larger share.

Others suggest strengthening anti-bribery policies and promoting simple, fair rules for competitive bidding on contracts to develop the resources. Still others recommend strengthening the rights of local communities affected by large extractive projects.

"We view a large endowment of hydrocarbons and minerals as an opportunity to transform development prospects," said Helen Clark, director of the United Nations Development Programme (UNDP). "Extractive industries can create the wealth required to do that if they are managed properly and their proceeds are fairly distributed." [10]

Although the military regime suppressed many democratic freedoms, it diversified Chile's economy and managed the copper industry effectively. Economic conditions improved further after the country transitioned to democracy. [10]

Chile created a Copper Stabilization Fund in 1985 to invest copper revenues and help to insulate the country from fluctuating commodity markets. The fund is used to absorb excess revenues when copper prices are high and supplement the national budget when prices are low. [11] Currently, the fund is valued at $21.8 billion.

— *Jennifer Weeks*

[1]"Norway," The World Factbook, Central Intelligence Agency, https://www.cia.gov/library/publications/the-world-factbook/geos/no.html; "Norway Government Pension Fund Global," Sovereign Wealth Fund Institute, www.swfinstitute.org/swfs/norway-government-pension-fund-global/.

[2]"Norway Government Pension Fund Global," *ibid.*

[3]Alex Blumberg, "How to Avoid the Oil Curse," NPR, Sept. 6, 2011, www.npr.org/blogs/money/2011/09/06/140110346/how-to-avoid-the-oil-curse.

[4]Landon Thomas, Jr., "Thriving Norway Provides an Economics Lesson," *The New York Times*, May 14, 2009, www.nytimes.com/2009/05/14/business/global/14frugal.html.

[5]"Botswana," *The World Factbook*, Central Intelligence Agency, https://www.cia.gov/library/publications/the-world-factbook/geos/bc.html.

[6]Daron Acemoglu, Simon Johnson and James A. Robinson, "An African Success Story: Botswana," July 11, 2001, pp. 9-17, www.colby.edu/economics/faculty/jmlong/ec479/AJR.pdf.

[7]"Avoiding the Resource Curse: What Can We Learn from the Case of Botswana?" Transparency International, (undated), http://eadi.org/gc2005/confweb/papersps/Peter_Eigen.pdf.

[8] Hippolyte Fofack, "How Botswana Avoided the 'Resource Curse,'" *African Business*, February 2009, http://findarticles.com/p/articles/mi_qa5327/is_350/ai_n31377446/?tag=content;col1.

[9]"Transparency International Corruption Perception Index 2011," Transparency International, http://cpi.transparency.org/cpi2011/results.

[10]Goril Havro and Javier Santiso, "Benefiting the Resource Rich: How Can International Development Policy Help Tame the Resource Curse?" Institute of Development Studies, University of Sussex, January 2011, pp. 22-27, www.acp-eu-trade.org/library/files/Havro%20&%20Santiso_EN_090211_IDS_Benefiting%20the%20Resource%20Rich.pdf.

[11]"Social and Economic Stabilization Fund," Sovereign Wealth Fund Institute, www.swfinstitute.org/swfs/social-and-economic-stabilization-fund/.

An oil platform in the vast Statfjord oil and gas field, about 125 miles off the coast of Norway, is partly owned by the Norwegian government. Norway is considered a model for wise management of oil wealth.

As developing countries, international lenders and advocacy groups debate the resource curse, here are some issues they are considering:

Is there a resource curse?

The resource curse theory was originally proposed by British economist Richard Auty, who argued in 1993 that mineral resources could distort producing countries' economies by making them prone to factors like sudden price swings and "Dutch disease," which occurs when sudden windfall profits from resource exports cause the value of a country's currency to escalate. [11]

Other social scientists soon began applying the idea more widely and finding broad correlations between resource wealth and poverty in developing countries. For example, in 2001 UCLA political scientist Michael Ross found that 12 of the world's 25 most mineral-dependent nations and six of the 25 most oil-dependent countries

AFP/Getty Images/Pius Utomi Ekpei (both)

Nigeria's Resource Woes

The resource curse is dramatically visible in Nigeria, the world's 10th-largest oil-producing country. Critics say corrupt officials have squandered the nation's oil wealth rather than build infrastructure or improve the lives of average citizens, seen clinging atop a packed train passing through a Lagos shantytown (top). In Nigeria's oil-rich Niger Delta (bottom) a man surveys damage from an oil spill on June 24, 2010. Critics say the region suffers from pollution caused by oil production but has received few benefits.

were classified by the World Bank as among the poorest and most-indebted nations in the world. [12]

Other scholars argued that resource dependence stunted countries' political development as well as their economies. Stanford University political scientist Terry

Lynn Karl argued that in "petro-states," government power became highly centralized and leaders tended to over-rely on spending oil money to solve political and economic problems. Subsequent economic troubles like Dutch disease, Karl contended, did not explain underdevelopment in oil-rich states; rather, she argued, they were an outcome of poor management by governments that cared more about keeping oil money flowing than building healthy economies. [13]

Today the resource curse theory is widely cited in political and development circles, including institutions such as the World Bank and the U.N. But many experts don't see a causal link between resource wealth and poverty. In fact, based on more recent studies, some argue that countries with extractable resources are more likely to prosper than lag.

"On balance, countries that have found extractable resources are wealthier than those that haven't," says Center for Global Development fellow Kenny. "If you want to know why a country is or isn't democratic, look at its history and culture, not at what fraction of its income comes from oil." [14]

A book co-published by the World Bank in 2007 concluded that natural resource industries can become engines of economic growth, especially if nations develop those industries using advanced technologies and invest in worker training and education — what economists call "human capital."

The book cited Sweden and Finland, which are wealthy today but were among Europe's poorest countries in the mid-19th century. Their growth was powered by expanding and continually upgrading extractive industries such as timber and iron ore mining, then eventually diversifying into manufactured products and services. (Nokia, the Finnish telecommunications giant, started out as a pulp and paper mill in 1865, then gradually expanded into rubber, cable and wire, and finally electronics.) Both countries spent many years improving skills and knowledge in their key industries. [15]

"Development is an outcome of human capabilities," says Harvard's Juma. "Some countries without natural resources have grown because they realized that their biggest resource was human beings. We need a vision of economic transformation that focuses on key drivers of growth, and on using revenues from extractive resources well."

Indeed, some extremely poor but resource-rich countries have used their resource wealth to strengthen other sectors and promote future growth in key industries or geographic regions. Malaysia, which has large oil and gas resources, followed that path.

"If we go back 40 years, Malaysia looked just like Africa. It was resource rich, it had all sorts of social problems, a lot of social tensions, and people were forecasting the worst," said Oxford University economist Paul Collier. But Malaysian leaders used oil money to improve infrastructure and services in poor areas so they could attract industry. "Penang used to be a dirt-poor fishing area. It is now a world-beating electronics center because the government put in the physical infrastructure and the social infrastructure that made the Penang area attractive for skilled people to go to," Collier observed. [16]

Malaysia's experience contrasts starkly with Equatorial Guinea, a West African nation that earns nearly all of its export revenues from oil. The country's estimated per capita income was $36,600 in 2010, 29th in the world, but virtually none of that wealth enters the economy. [17] President Teodoro Obiang Nguema Mbasogo, who seized power in a military coup in 1979, reportedly has amassed a $65 billion fortune from state revenues in personal bank accounts. [18] Unemployment stands at 22.3 percent, the infant mortality rate is 16th-highest worldwide, and less than half of the population has access to clean drinking water. [19]

Such cases lead many experts to focus on the quality of governance in resource-rich countries, rather than on the resources themselves. "Resources can be a boon, depending on how countries manage the income and how their political systems use it over time," says Nina Merchant, assistant director for economic reform and development with the San Francisco-based Asia Foundation. "Having an established democracy and a tradition of transparency are very valuable. Checks and balances within the government are important too."

China Generates Most Resource Wealth

China generated over $550 billion — more than any other country — by exporting natural resources in 2008, mainly from coal. Russia generated nearly as much, $542 billion, while the United States ranked third. Four oil-rich Middle Eastern countries were among the top 15. The resource curse is less likely to affect large countries with multiple exports, such as China or the United States, than a small country that depends heavily on exports of a single resource.

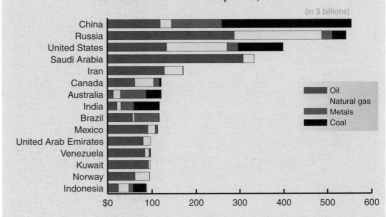

Countries Generating the Most Revenue from Natural Resource Exports, 2008

Source: Kai Kaiser and Lorena Vinuela, "Where the Extractive Resource Rents Are?" The World Bank, 2011

Many recent studies have focused on building strong political institutions that can block harmful actions such as bribery and looting of public treasuries. [20]

"By the 1970s [when oil was discovered in the North Sea] Norway had a long tradition of democratic governance and a bureaucracy that could manage the oil sector, so it's not surprising that it has managed its oil wealth relatively well," says Oxfam America's Gary. "In Liberia or Chad, there is very little, if any, rule of law."

Can transparency break the resource curse?

In many resource-rich developing countries, little information is available about how much money the nation receives from its oil, gas or mining operations and how that money is spent. Many anti-poverty and citizens' groups say making these transactions public will reduce opportunities for bribery and corruption and help citizens hold government accountable.

Rating Resource-Rich Countries on Transparency

What happens to the money that oil, gas and mining companies pay governments and government-linked entities? Does it fund improvements or line the pockets of officials? The Extractive Industries Transparency Initiative (EITI) sets standards for increasing transparency in such transactions. Twelve countries comply with the standards, while 23 have been designated as candidates. Candidate countries must meet five requirements, such as committing to increase transparency and developing a comprehensive transparency plan.

EITI Compliant and Candidate Countries

Compliant Countries		
Azerbaijan	Liberia	Nigeria
Central African Republic	Mali	Norway
Ghana	Mongolia	Timor-Leste
	Niger	Yemen*

Candidate Countries		
Afghanistan	Gabon	Mozambique
Albania	Guatemala	Peru
Burkina Faso	Guinea	Republic of the Congo
Cameroon	Indonesia	Sierra Leone
Chad	Iraq	Tanzania
Cote d'Ivoire	Kazakhstan	Togo
Democratic Republic of the Congo	Madagascar*	Trinidad and Tobago
	Mauritania	Zambia

* Suspended because of doubts that the country could meet the standards.

Source: "EITI Countries," Extractive Industries Transparency Initiative, November 2011, eiti.org/countries

In 2002 a coalition of anti-poverty groups such as Oxfam and Save the Children and organizations promoting good governance, such as the Open Society Institute, launched the Publish What You Pay (PWYP) campaign. It called on natural resource companies to disclose all of their payments to governments in countries where they operate. Headquartered in London, PWYP now has 650 member groups in 59 countries, including prominent organizations like Catholic Relief Services and Human Rights Watch.

"Oil, gas and mining revenues should form the basis for development and improve the lives of ordinary citizens in resource-rich countries," says Marinke van Riet, PWYP's international director. "Revenue flows from extractive industries are almost 10 times bigger than global aid flows, but the resource-richest countries are often mired in poverty, corruption and conflict."

A centerpiece of the PWYP campaign, the Extractive Industries Transparency Initiative (EITI), commits participating companies to regularly publish how much they pay to individual governments, which are in turn expected to disclose those revenues. Independent "validators" (preapproved audit and consulting firms), selected by national stakeholder panels, then reconcile the numbers provided by the corporations with those released by the government, ensuring that all members are held to the same standard. [21]

Leaders of the G20 group of leading world economies endorsed the EITI in 2009, and this fall President Obama announced that the United States would participate in the initiative "so that taxpayers receive every dollar they're due from the extraction of natural resources." [22] Major companies implementing the pledge include Alcoa, BP, Chevron, ExxonMobil, Pemex, Qatar Petroleum and Shell. [23]

The United Kingdom is a notable holdout, even though former Prime Minister Tony Blair helped launch the EITI in 2002. Last September a U.K. government spokesman said Britain strongly supports transparency but that it was not appropriate for the U.K. to implement the EITI because it was not a "resource rich" country. [24] Critics derided this position.

"So much for a commitment to transparency by this government," said Richard Murphy, a British tax expert and antipoverty activist. "This is about keeping their friends in shady places happy." [25]

But others disagree with the EITI's approach. "I don't believe in the naming-and-shaming strategy," says Harvard's Juma. "Simply exposing corporations without offering both sides ways to make these arrangements [between companies and governments] more mutually beneficial isn't helpful." Instead, Juma urges large mining companies to put the money to work themselves by setting up universities and vocational and professional training institutes in countries where they have operations, to help build up local skills.

"Conversations like that are more interesting than simply making information public," he says.

PWYP supports adding mandatory disclosure requirements to national stock market regulations and global accounting standards, in addition to voluntary measures such as the EITI. The group also wants the World Bank, the International Monetary Fund and regional development banks to require public disclosure of revenues and contracts for all extractive projects that they fund. [26]

Mandatory disclosure policies like this "will shed light on extractive companies' payments to governments and allow ordinary citizens to scrutinize both companies and governments," says PWYP's van Riet.

Section 1504 of the Dodd-Frank Wall Street Reform and Consumer Protection Act, enacted in July 2010, requires all oil, gas and mining companies listed on U.S. stock exchanges (which include most international resource companies) to file annual public reports listing any payments made to the U.S. or foreign governments on a project-by-project and country-by-country basis. The U.S. Securities and Exchange Commission proposed rules in late 2010 to implement the new law. [27] Anti-poverty and human rights groups strongly support the requirement, along with many investment funds. But some large corporations say it creates burdensome requirements that are not worth the cost.

For example, ExxonMobil estimates that complying with Section 1504 will cost it $50 million a year and argues that disclosing project payments "would substantially expand the volume of financial data reporting, with little to no added benefit to investors." The company also contends that resource-exporting countries are likely to award contracts to companies that are not subject to "overly detailed, disaggregated public reporting," in order to protect sensitive commercial information, so companies covered by Section 1504 will be less competitive. [28]

But Sens. Lugar and Cardin, the authors of Section 1504, say extending disclosure requirements beyond voluntary measures like the EITI is in the national interest.

Diamond cutters in Gaborone, Botswana, show why the country is seen as a model of wise resource management. Rather than continuing to export only rough diamonds, the government encourages diamond companies to train local cutters, creating thousands of jobs and boosting the value of diamond exports.

"Increasingly, the economic and energy security of Europe and the United States is tied to stability and sustainable growth in developing nations," the two wrote last spring. "A concerted global effort, led by Europe and America, to end the secrecy that often surrounds energy development is a good place to start." [29]

Is foreign aid the real curse?

Many resource-poor developing countries have struggled with the same challenges that often are attributed to resource-rich countries — slow economic growth and corruption. Some scholars and policymakers argue that foreign aid impedes development, much as wealth from natural resources often fails to improve the quality of life in developing nations.

Like revenue from resource exports, economists see foreign aid as a type of "rent" — or money received in return for little work. When governments receive large amounts of foreign aid, some scholars say, they have less incentive to collect taxes, making leaders less accountable to citizens.

"Foreign aid damages the political institutions of the country by reducing democratic rules," two World Bank economists wrote in a 2005 study: "Since most foreign aid is not contingent on the democratic level of the recipient countries, there is no incentive for governments to keep a good level of checks and balances in place."

After reviewing data on more than 100 countries over 40 years, they found that political institutions were less democratic in countries that depended heavily on foreign aid. [30]

This issue looms particularly large today in Pakistan, where a fragile democracy is struggling to manage a fractured and politically unstable country. [31] A frontline nation in the "war on terror," Pakistan has received more than $22 billion in U.S. military and economic aid over the past decade but is widely viewed as a failing state. [32] The International Crisis Group, an independent organization dedicated to resolving conflict, describes Pakistan's electoral, judicial and criminal justice systems as "dysfunctional," and the U.N. Development Programme ranked Pakistan 145th from the top out of 187 countries in its 2011 "Human Development Report," which measures social indicators such as health and education. [33]

Imram Khan, an opposition politician and a legendary former member of Pakistan's national cricket team, has called for an end to U.S. and British aid to his country. "Aid has been a curse for Pakistan," Khan said in September. "It is not helping the people, it is disappearing in corruption." [34] Khan wants to end Pakistan's role in the war on terror, asserting, "We're basically using our army to kill our own people with American money." [35]

Anti-poverty advocates say foreign aid can fill important gaps when directed to areas of real need. "If the money is completely fungible and there are problems with corruption or democracy in the recipient country, aid can have effects similar to the resource curse," says Oxfam America's Gary. "But if aid is specifically targeted in ways that benefit local populations or goes to civil society groups instead of governments, then the analogy falls apart."

Many nonprofit organizations raise money and spend it directly in developing countries, bypassing the central governments. Justin Byworth, chief executive of World Vision UK (an international Christian humanitarian aid organization), strongly rejected Khan's criticism of foreign aid to Pakistan. In 2010, Byworth wrote, the British public donated nearly $100 million when Pakistan was ravaged by catastrophic flash floods.

"Donations have been well-spent on providing food, shelter, clean water and health care to more than 1.5 million flood-affected people across three of Pakistan's four provinces," Byworth said. "How are things ever meant to improve by robbing families, already living in poverty, of foreign aid — of a temporary roof over their head, of food in their children's mouths or the chance to rebuild their livelihoods?" [36]

Critics also say foreign aid promotes a culture of poverty and dependence. After a devastating earthquake in January 2010, aid poured into Haiti, one of the world's poorest countries. But some observers said Haitians needed to take more control over rebuilding their own country. [37]

"If we really want to change, this is the time for the international community to work with the state . . . and government to build their own capacities. If we don't do that now, we will be here for the next 200 years addressing these issues," said Edmond Mulet, director of the U.N. mission in Haiti. [38]

BACKGROUND

Colonial Legacies

Many of today's developing nations once were colonies, often harshly ruled by powerful countries. Starting in the late 1400s European nations began claiming territories in the Americas, Africa and Asia. Some sought new trading markets, others wanted to spread Christianity, but most hoped to harvest valuable resources.

For example, by the 1500s English, French, Spanish and Portuguese fishermen were crossing the Atlantic to harvest vast schools of cod off the coast of Canada. [39] Much exploration across North America in the 17th and 18th centuries was spurred by competition among English, French and Dutch explorers to control the lucrative fur trade. And Spain colonized the Americas in search of gold and silver, which it found in great quantities in Peru and Mexico. Untold numbers of native peoples in both countries were killed, enslaved or died of diseases carried west by Spanish explorers.

Humans also became a widely traded commodity. Starting in the 1400s, roughly 12 million people were shipped from Africa to European colonies in the New World. [40] Many were part of the infamous "triangle trade," in which finished goods were sent from Europe to Africa; slaves were taken from Africa to the Caribbean and the Americas, and agricultural products from the

CHRONOLOGY

1940s-1950s *Newly independent countries seek earnings from natural resource exports.*

1945 With the end of World War II, former colonies in Asia and Africa begin to gain independence.

1953 Kuwait forms the first non-U.S. sovereign wealth fund to manage its oil revenues and invest them for citizens' benefit.

1956 China provides its first aid to African countries.

1960s-1980s *Some countries prosper from extractive industries, but development lags in many regions.*

1960 Influential American economist W.W. Rostow publishes *The Stages of Economic Growth*, which focuses on capital investments to build up economies.

1971 DeBeers, the world's leading diamond producer, begins mining in Botswana under a joint venture with the government.

1973 Arab oil embargo quadruples world oil prices, triggering a massive flow of wealth to oil-producing countries.

1977 Foreign Corrupt Practices Act bars U.S. citizens or corporations from making illegal payments to foreign governments or entities.

1986 World oil prices collapse due to a supply glut, triggering economic shocks in Mexico, Venezuela, Nigeria and other oil-dependent countries.

1988 Economists begin studying the phenomenon of low economic growth in resource-rich countries.

1990-2000 *The "resource curse" theory is debated.*

1992 U.N. Conference on Environment and Development criticizes environmental impacts of conventional development theory and calls for a more sustainable approach.

1993 British economist Richard Auty publishes the first book advancing the resource curse thesis.

1995 Nigeria executes activist Ken Saro-Wiwa for protesting oil industry damage to his home region, triggering international sanctions. . . . Russian President Boris Yeltsin privatizes oil and gas holdings for a fraction of their value, creating a powerful class of oligarchs.

1999 Organisation for Economic Co-operation and Development says bribing public officials in international business transactions should be a crime.

2000 World leaders adopt U.N.'s Millennium Development Goals, a set of targets for reducing extreme poverty by 2015. China and African nations establish the Forum on China-Africa Cooperation, linking aid and economic cooperation.

2001-Present *Advocates push for more local control and public disclosure about resource extraction.*

2002 Activists launch the Publish What You Pay initiative, which calls for companies to disclose payments and governments to disclose earnings from extractive industries. . . . British Prime Minister Tony Blair proposes the Extractive Industries Transparency Initiative (EITI), a voluntary disclosure standard for companies and governments involved in oil, gas and mining.

2004 World Bank pledges to invest more selectively in extractive industries and require revenue transparency as a condition for new investments.

2008 World Bank withdraws support for an oil pipeline from Chad to Cameroon after Chad flouts pledges to use oil revenues to reduce poverty.

2010 Congress passes Dodd-Frank law, including a requirement for energy and mining companies listed on U.S. stock exchanges to publish annual reports listing their payments to governments.

2011 President Barack Obama pledges to sign EITI; Britain says it supports transparency but will not sign.

Government Commodity Funds Control Trillions

Unique "Alaska model" pays residents yearly dividends.

Many resource-rich countries — and several U.S. states — have created government-owned funds to manage revenues from the sale of valuable natural resources. [1] Known as sovereign wealth funds, these accounts can serve diverse purposes, such as paying for specific national priorities or insulating the economy from fluctuating commodity prices. In a unique twist that has become known as "the Alaska model," they can also be used to make direct payments to citizens.

According to the Nevada-based Sovereign Wealth Fund Institute, the world's 54 largest sovereign wealth funds control more than $4.7 trillion in assets. More than half of this amount ($2.6 trillion) comes from oil and gas revenues. Another $33.8 billion comes from the sale of other commodities, such as copper, phosphates and diamonds. The rest comes from non-commodity sources, such as official foreign currency operations and fiscal surpluses. Since 2005 at least 20 funds had been created as of December, partly in response to high oil and gas prices. [2]

Some funds invest heavily in overseas entities. For example, the sovereign fund managed by the oil-rich Middle Eastern emirate of Qatar owns Harrods, London's flagship luxury department store, along with shares in European banks, power companies, ports and several French and Spanish soccer teams. [3] Norway's $560 billion oil fund owns 2 percent of all European stocks, making it the largest equity investor on the continent. [4] During the global recession of 2008-2009, sovereign funds pumped billions of dollars in much-needed capital into Citigroup, Barclays and other Western banks and private investment firms — in some cases reaping handsome profits. [5]

Every sovereign wealth fund has its own rules and goals. Some operate under strict laws that direct investments toward specific sectors and provide the public with extensive

information about the holdings and investment policies. Others are much less transparent. Some have wasted much of their wealth. Libya set up a sovereign fund in 2006 under the control of Seif al-Islam el-Gadhafi, one of Moammar Gadhafi's sons; it was poorly managed and lost millions of dollars on investments. [6]

In late September the fund's new director, Rafik Nayed, put all new investments on hold while the staff tried to sort out past deals. "The dark cloud of poor governance and corruption of the previous regime will be with us for a long time unless there is a comprehensive review," Nayed said. [7] The U.S. Securities and Exchange Commission and the U.K.'s Serious Fraud Office are investigating whether U.S. and British banks paid bribes to sovereign wealth fund managers in Libya and elsewhere to win their business. [8]

Alaska has taken an unusual approach with its Permanent Fund, which manages the state's oil and gas revenues. Created through a 1976 state constitutional amendment, the fund must receive at least 25 percent of all state earnings from oil production, and the money must be invested in stocks, bonds, real estate and other assets that generate income. Its principal cannot be spent unless Alaskans vote to do so.

Each year income from those investments is used to pay direct dividends to state residents. Over the past decade annual dividends have ranged from $845 to $2,069 per person; the amount is based on an average of the past five years of earnings. [9] Some earnings are also used to protect the fund against inflation. Remaining earnings can be spent by the legislature but historically have been reinvested in the fund.

"When the fund was created, most people thought the state legislature needed to be constrained. They may have been right, because legislators had spent most of Alaska's early oil revenues," says Gerald McBeath, a political science

Americas like sugar, rum, cotton and tobacco were shipped back to Europe. [41]

In the late 18th century, Spanish, French and Portuguese colonies in the Americas began rebelling

against imperial control. Haiti won independence from France in 1804, and by the mid-1820s Venezuela, Colombia, Ecuador, Paraguay, Chile, Peru and Bolivia had all broken away from European overlords and professor at the University of Alaska at Fairbanks. "Now Alaskans expect a dividend every year. Any politician who ran for office proposing to use the Permanent Fund to pay for state government operations would go down to a quick defeat."

Some development experts say paying direct dividends from oil revenues, Alaska-style, would benefit the poor and make governments more accountable in countries emerging from autocratic rule, such as Libya and Iraq, or struggling to manage newfound resource wealth.

"Rather than put the funds into the budget (and hope that they trickle down to the people), or into a savings fund (and hope they are used wisely in the future), this would put the cash directly into the hands of the people," writes Todd Moss, vice president and senior fellow at the Center for Global Development in Washington, D.C. [10]

Although the Permanent Fund Dividend provides a big yearly boost to Alaska's economy, Alaskans are not highly attuned to state government, McBeath points out, because Alaska earns so much money from oil it doesn't have a sales or income tax. "People here aren't vested in the government's actions because they're not paying for them," he says.

An economist might not see a conflict in paying dividends to citizens, then charging them income tax. [11] But in Alaska, when someone proposes restoring an income or sales tax, "Legislators typically say that it would be confusing to tax residents on the one hand and give them money with the other," says McBeath.

— *Jennifer Weeks*

Gov. Sean Parnell, R-Alaska, reveals the amount of this year's Alaska Permanent Fund Dividend checks on Sept. 20. The fund receives at least 25 percent of all state earnings from oil production and uses the income from investments to pay direct dividends to state residents.

[5] Eric Dash, "Big Paydays for Rescuers in the Crisis," *The New York Times*, Dec. 7, 2009, www.nytimes.com/2009/12/07/business/global/07bank.html.

[6] Landon Thomas, Jr., "Libya's Hidden Wealth May Be Next Battle," *The New York Times*, March 3, 2011, www.nytimes.com/2011/03/04/business/global/04sovereign.html?pagewanted=all; David Rohde, "Western Funds Are Said to Have Managed Libyan Money Poorly," *The New York Times*, June 30, 2011, www.nytimes.com/2011/07/01/business/global/01libya.html.

[7] Margaret Coker, "Libya's Sovereign Fund Seeks Investment Probe," *The Wall Street Journal*, Sept. 23, 2011, http://online.wsj.com/article/SB10001424053111904563904576587041911379606.html.

[8] Lindsay Fortado, "U.K. Prosecutors to Assist U.S. on Fund Bribery Probes," *BusinessWeek.com*, June 29, 2011, www.bloomberg.com/news/2011-06-29/u-k-prosecutors-to-assist-u-s-on-wealth-fund-bribery-probes.html.

[9] "An Alaskan's Guide to the Permanent Fund," Alaska Permanent Fund Corporation, p. 26, www.apfc.org/home/Media/publications/2009AlaskansGuide.pdf.

[10] Todd Moss, "Oil to Cash: Fighting the Resource Curse Through Cash Transfers," Center for Global Development, *Working Paper 237*, January 2011, p. 7, www.cgdev.org/files/1424714_file_Oil2Cash_primer_FINAL.pdf.

[11] *Ibid.*, p. 7.

[1] The U.S. states with sovereign wealth funds are Alaska, Texas, New Mexico and Wyoming.

[2] "Sovereign Wealth Fund Rankings," Sovereign Wealth Fund Institute, October 2011, www.swfinstitute.org/fund-rankings/; also see "What is a SWF?" www.swfinstitute.org/what-is-a-swf/.

[3] Julia Werdiger, "Qatar Holding Buys Harrods Store," *The New York Times*, May 9, 2010, www.nytimes.com/2010/05/10/business/global/10harrods.html; Sarah Hamdan, "Qatar Shows Faith in Europe," Sept. 14, 2011, www.nytimes.com/2011/09/15/world/middleeast/qatar-shows-faith-in-europe.html.

[4] Andrew Ward, "Norway's Sovereign Wealth Fund Optimistic on Europe," *Financial Times*, June 13, 2011, www.ft.com/cms/s/0/5f1e4ace-958d-11e0-8f82-00144feab49a,s01=1.html#axzz1f78NIWkr.

declared independence. Fifty years of foreign intervention and border conflicts followed, as Spain, Britain, France and the United States, itself newly independent, competed for markets and influence in the fledgling South American countries. As young governments struggled to contain violence, pass modern laws and separate church and state functions, the economies of the new Latin American nations stagnated. [42]

A similar pattern played out in Africa. European industrial powers, seeking raw materials and markets for their finished goods, colonized nearly the entire continent starting in the late 19th century. Some colonies' economies centered on large-scale farming; in others, such as the Belgian Congo (now the Democratic Republic of Congo), rulers forced Africans to extract copper and other resources, such as rubber. The brutal tactics used during the rule of Belgium's King Leopold II became an international scandal in the early 20th century.

"I have seen natives with one hand cut off and I have seen them with both cut off, and in many cases the poor victims were children," said Canadian missionary the Rev. Dr. William H. Leslie, in a 1909 interview with *The New York Times*. Much of the cruelty, he explained, was designed "to impress upon the blacks the necessity of their bringing to market the rubber wanted by their persecutors, and to emphasize the dire results" if they failed to do so. [43] International outrage over the revelations ultimately led the Belgian government to force Leopold to relinquish his ownership of the colony.

Colonial governments typically spent little on infrastructure and nothing on education or social needs. [44] In Africa, centuries of slave trading fractured relationships between ethnic groups and further weakened local political systems, leaving many parts of the continent unprepared for independence. [45]

Launching New Nations

After World War II European colonial powers were economically devastated and faced years of rebuilding at home. As their overseas empires broke up, more than 70 colonies in Africa, Asia, the Middle East and the Pacific became independent between 1945 and the 1970s. Some transitions were relatively calm, while others — such as in Algeria, Angola and Vietnam — involved years of bloody conflict.

The new countries needed to develop their economies in order to pay for roads, bridges, transportation systems, health care and education. Most had few educated workers and little capital. Countries with valuable extractable resources seemed like the lucky ones.

That was especially true for countries with oil, as postwar energy demand rose in the United States and Western Europe. Major oil companies pressed for new access to oil fields in the Middle East. Oil-rich countries' earnings swelled, but their governments struggled to deal with fluctuating global oil prices and to negotiate as equals with powerful foreign companies, which provided the capital needed to get oil out of the ground.

Even after exporters founded the Organization of Petroleum Exporting Countries (OPEC), "the oil reserve in the ground actually belonged by contract to the oil companies — known as the concessionaires — thus limiting the countries' control," writes energy consultant Daniel Yergin in *The Prize*, his best-selling book on the oil industry. Moreover, he notes, exporting countries were competing with one another, so "they had to worry about holding onto markets in order to maintain revenues. Thus, they could not afford to alienate the companies on which they depended for access to those markets." [46]

Through the 1960s and '70s Western economists asserted that investment drove economic development. In his classic 1960 book, *The Stages of Economic Growth*, Walt Rostow — an influential advisor to presidents John F. Kennedy and Lyndon B. Johnson — described a "take-off" point when countries were politically and socially ready to modernize and investment reached 10 percent or more of the nation's income. At that point, he argued, growth would ripple from sector to sector through the economy.

"During the take-off, new industries expand rapidly, yielding profits, a large proportion of which are invested in new plants; and these new industries, in turn, stimulate . . . a further expansion in urban areas and in other modern industrial plants," Rostow wrote. "In a decade or two both the basic structure of the economy and the social and political structure of the society are transformed in such a way that a steady rate of growth can be, thereafter, regularly sustained." [47]

Uneven Results

In 1970 more than 80 per cent of the average export earnings in developing countries came from extractable commodities. [48] Many of these nations wanted to gain control over their resources and retain more of the revenues that were flowing to multinational corporations.

Over the next decade Venezuela, Libya, Nigeria, Iraq, Saudi Arabia and other major oil exporters nationalized at least some of their production. Other countries, including Chile, Zambia, Mauritania, Peru and Guyana nationalized their mining industries. [49]

Nonetheless, from 1980 to 2000 overall growth slowed drastically in low- and middle-income countries. [50] Many factors contributed, including two global oil "shocks" in the 1970s, recessions in wealthy countries in the 1980s and debt crises at roughly the same time in many developing countries.

Analysts wondered, however, why some countries were hit harder than others — or, as Harvard economist Dani Rodrik put it, "Where did all the growth go?" [51]

Some scholars pointed out that, paradoxically, many resource-rich countries were growing more slowly than countries with few natural resources. For example, many Latin American and African countries with large reserves of oil, copper, or other commodities were stagnating, while Asian countries without similar endowments were growing and industrializing rapidly — a process the World Bank dubbed "the East Asian Miracle." [52]

In 1993 British economist Auty observed that mining sectors in developing countries had strong "enclave tendencies." In other words, they relied mainly on capital from foreign investors, employed few local workers and usually shipped ore out of the country for further processing. They did not generate growth in local economies — contrary to predictions from experts like Rostow.

Auty also described a problem that economists dubbed "Dutch disease," in which sudden windfalls from the extractive sector distorted local economies and made other exports, such as agricultural products, less competitive. [53]

In another study, Harvard economists Jeffrey Sachs (who would later become a senior World Bank advisor) and Andrew Warner surveyed 95 countries, and found that those relying heavily on natural resource exports grew more slowly in the 1970s and '80s than others. [54] Other analysts began pointing out political repercussions from resource wealth, linking it to bribery (to win lucrative extraction contracts), graft and violence. [55]

In oil-rich Nigeria, for example, a local resistance movement developed in 1990 among the Ogoni people of the Niger Delta region, who contended that oil production in their homeland was causing massive environmental damage but that local communities were not receiving any economic benefits. When the Ogoni demanded payments in 1992 from oil companies

> **"We have had some bitter experiences with gold, and we do not want to go down that road again."**
>
> **— Joe Oteng Adjei,
> Energy Minister, Ghana**

working in their region, plus control over local oil rights, Nigeria suppressed the movement with military force.

Two years later acclaimed author Ken Saro-Wiwa, the leader of the main Ogoni-rights group, was arrested along with eight colleagues. In 1995 they were executed, triggering global outrage. [56] Shell Oil, which had major operations in the delta, was accused of conspiring with the government to capture and execute the protesters. The company denied the charges but later paid $15.5 million to settle a lawsuit filed by relatives of the victims. [57]

Another horrific example of resources fueling conflict emerged in Angola, Sierra Leone, Liberia and the Democratic Republic of Congo — the trade in "conflict diamonds" or "blood diamonds." In all four countries, rebel groups fighting civil wars against the national governments financed their causes during the 1990s partly by harvesting rough (uncut) diamonds and trading them for money or weapons. [58]

Although illicit diamonds represented only a small share of the global diamond industry, they financed bloody conflicts that killed and maimed millions of people. After repeated U.N. sanctions against the offending countries failed to curb the blood diamond trade, national governments and diamond producers in 2002 created a voluntary certification system called the Kimberley Process (named for a city in South Africa), in which members pledged to trade only with other members, and all diamonds were certified as coming from nonconflict zones. [59]

This approach yielded some progress: Notably, Congo was expelled from the Kimberley Process in 2004 after failing to account for large quantities of rough diamond exports. But the system was dogged by concerns about data quality and effective enforcement. Some source countries like Sierra Leone and Liberia did not have enough trained personnel or equipment to monitor their diamond industries effectively, even with international aid. [60]

Seeking Solutions

By the late 1990s, pressure on corrupt governments had begun to build. In 1999 a report by the British advocacy group Global Witness charged that government agencies in Angola were embezzling oil money and using it to fund a civil war against the UNITA rebel group. [61] Human Rights Watch subsequently calculated that $4.2 billion in oil revenues had disappeared from Angola's treasury from 1997 to 2002, a figure equivalent to all government spending on social programs in the same period. [62]

The findings spurred the creation of the Publish What You Pay campaign, urging natural resource companies to disclose payments to governments. PWYP helped draft the Extractive Industries Transparency Initiative, or EITI, a voluntary pledge by governments and extractive companies to disclose payments and receipts.

"Secrecy over state revenues encourages ruling elites to mismanage and misappropriate money rather than invest in long-term development," said financier and philanthropist George Soros in support of the PWYP campaign. "This is a real chance to promote good fiscal governance and help tackle worldwide poverty." [63]

Other advocates targeted global lenders. In 2000 environmental organizations called on the World Bank and other international financial institutions to stop funding new fossil fuel and mining projects in environmentally sensitive areas. "Oil, gas, and mining operations have left a legacy of ecological destruction and social upheaval on the world's poorest in the 20th century," said Ricardo Navarro, chairman of Friends of the Earth International. [64]

In response, the World Bank commissioned a study of its support for mining and energy projects. The "Extractive Industry Review," completed in 2003, urged the bank to make sure its projects benefit local communities, focus more strongly on environmental and social impacts and protect human rights more effectively. It also recommended ending World Bank support for oil and coal projects by 2008. [65]

World Bank leaders accepted the broad recommendations but did not end support for fossil fuel projects. The bank's focus began to shift toward helping countries leverage extractive-industry projects to reduce poverty. Some critics said, however, that the bank was not moving quickly enough or setting adequately specific policies to protect the rule of law and human rights in extractive sectors. [66]

CURRENT SITUATION

Millennium Goals

Although some resource-rich states still lag sharply behind others on important development indicators like life expectancy and education, nearly all developing countries are making measurable progress.

For the past decade world leaders have measured improvements in developing countries against a set of targets called the Millennium Development Goals (MDGs), which were adopted by the United Nations in 2000 and are designed to promote sharp cuts in levels of extreme poverty worldwide by 2015. As that date draws near, many measurements indicate that living conditions are improving widely in the developing world.

MDG targets are defined by specific quantitative benchmarks. For example, one measurement toward the goal of ending poverty and hunger is to halve the proportion of people who live on less than $1 per day between 1990 and 2015. [67] According to the U.N., the world is on track to meet that target. Progress is lagging on other goals, such as providing universal primary education and improving maternal health. [68]

But even countries that may not reach the extremely ambitious goals are making important progress, including some resource-dependent nations. For example, in 2010 Nigeria reported that it had reduced infant mortality 25 percent and under-5 mortality 20 percent over two years; raised youth literacy from 64 percent to 80 percent in eight years; and nearly eliminated polio. President Goodluck Jonathan predicted that "in the next five years we will have the solutions and the political will to make meeting the MDGs by 2015 a reality." [69]

The U.N.'s 2011 Human Development Index — which ranks countries by their health, education and living standards — shows no automatic correlation between resource dependence and a country's level of development. [70] Several resource-dependent countries receive low human development scores — notably, Angola and Nigeria.

But many rate higher. Resource-rich countries in the medium human development category include Botswana, Ghana and the Republic of Congo. Moving upward, Saudi Arabia, Mexico, Venezuela, Iran and Libya all are ranked as highly developed, although Libya's ranking fell sharply during its recent civil war. And some resource-dependent nations are very highly developed, such as Norway (the world's top-ranking nation), the United Arab Emirates, Qatar, Bahrain and Chile.

The index was created by Pakistani economist Mahbub ul Haq to measure national development in a broader way than simply comparing income levels and economic growth rates. "[P]eople and their capabilities should be the ultimate criteria for assessing the development of a country, not economic growth alone," the U.N. Development Programme states. [71]

Learning from the Past

Some nations just starting to develop newfound resources are moving carefully, seeking to avoid problems commonly attributed to the resource curse. The issue looms large in Ghana, where several large offshore oil fields have been discovered since 2007. Ghana has been a gold-mining center for a century, but gold income has done little to boost development. Now, many observers say, Ghana has an opportunity to do better.

"We have had some bitter experiences with gold, and we do not want to go down that road again," Ghanaian Energy Minister Joe Oteng Adjei said recently. [72]

Good-government advocates in Ghana have united in a coalition called the Civil Society Platform to push for transparency and accountability in the nation's oil and gas operations. Last spring the group issued a report card that gave Ghana a C on its readiness to manage the oil sector. National leaders welcomed the report and civil groups' input. [73]

"The government has been forced to open up its doors and deal with nongovernment organizations," says Richard Hato-Kuevor, who oversees Oxfam America's extractive industry programs in Ghana. Advocacy groups want more than attention, he says. They want oil revenues to fund a national development program.

"A national agenda would ensure that oil revenues feed into an overall plan, even if [political] parties change," says Hato-Kuevor. "We need to shore up agriculture,

Getty Images/Bloomberg/Morten Andersen

The El Teniente copper mine and processing plant near Rancagua, Chile, is owned and operated by the world's largest copper producer, Corporacion Nacional del Cobre de Chile (Codelco). Chile, which gets half its export earnings and a third of government revenues from copper, created a Copper Stabilization Fund in 1985 that invests copper revenues and insulates the country from fluctuating commodity markets. The fund currently is valued at $21.8 billion.

infrastructure and health. The challenges are enormous, and priorities haven't been spelled out. We've had lots of talk about the need for a national development plan, but no concrete initiatives yet."

East Timor (now called Timor-Leste), an island nation occupied by Indonesia from 1975 until 1999, also has offshore oil and gas deposits. The country is rebuilding from pre-independence riots, which destroyed much of its infrastructure before international peacekeeping forces suppressed the violence. Although East Timor is not one of the world's large oil producers, it is highly resource-dependent: Virtually all of its income comes from oil.

What Is "Dutch Disease"?

One of the first symptoms that economists attributed to the resource curse is an economic syndrome, "Dutch disease," named for events that occurred when the Netherlands discovered vast natural gas deposits in the North Sea in the 1960s. The phenomenon occurs when:

- A country earns large revenues from oil, gas or minerals;
- The inflow of wealth makes its currency appreciate in value;
- The more expensive currency makes the country's other exports too pricey for foreign buyers;
- The nonextractive sectors of the export economy wither.

The country's legal framework for oil production, taxation and revenue management (based on the Extractive Industries Transparency Initiative) has earned widespread international praise. The government has created an $8 billion sovereign petroleum fund, and leaders are working to stimulate other areas of the economy, such as agriculture and tourism. [74] But advocates worry that it may be hard for such a fragile democracy to focus on long-term investments instead of spending money in politically expedient ways.

"Since 2004, the number of civil servants has mushroomed, as have their salaries," says Silas Everett, the Asia Foundation's country representative in East Timor. "But they are not delivering service more effectively. That contributes to a growing divide between the urban elite in Dili [the capital] and the rural poor, which could be destabilizing, especially if we do not see parallel growth in the non-oil economy."

Wealthy countries such as Norway have offered East Timor advice on managing its oil wealth, but experiences in such advanced countries have limited relevance to the Timorese. "East Timor is on its own path and is rightly picking and choosing the advice it takes," says Everett.

China, Africa and the Resource Curse

Africa's largest trading partner today is a developing country: China. According to a white paper by China's cabinet, trade between China and Africa has grown from $12.14 million in 1950 to nearly $115 billion in 2010. [75]

Much of the trade consists of natural resource exports from Africa to China, which needs oil to fuel its booming economy and raw materials for its factories. In turn, China sends workers and manufactured goods to Africa. It is also providing aid and is building infrastructure projects such as bridges, health clinics, railways and water treatment plants.

Many observers question whether these relationships benefit African countries in the long run. Critics claim China trades freely with repressive governments, engages in bribery to win contracts and undercuts local African industries with cheap exports. In addition, its commercial relationships with African countries usually are not transparent. [76]

China's goals in Africa are "to elbow out all foreign companies and gain access to Africa's resources at cheap prices; canvas for African votes at the U.N. in its quest for global hegemony . . . and seek new markets for Chinese manufactures as European markets become saturated with Chinese goods," Ghanaian economist George Ayittey, a professor at American University in Washington, said in a 2010 debate. [77]

But others say African countries benefit from their trade with China and that trading ties do not lock them into exporting unprocessed raw materials. "China has committed itself to the whole continent, even countries that are not mineral exporters," says Harvard's Juma. "They have removed tariffs on African exports, and a lot of African businesses are investing in China. The next step is for China to start manufacturing in Africa, which is beginning to happen."

World Bank President Robert Zoellick has urged China to transfer manufacturing jobs to Africa and to help Africa improve its food production. [78]

Some Chinese activities in Africa's extractive industries have drawn strong criticism. In Zambia, for example, where China has invested heavily in copper mines, many critics say conditions at Chinese-owned sites persistently violate local health, safety and labor laws. [79]

But Chinese leaders are learning from those mistakes, Juma says. "They underestimated public perceptions and didn't have good control over Chinese businesses there, which are state-run but highly autonomous," says Juma. "China also didn't share knowledge well in areas like raising poultry. Africans should make the effort to figure out how to leverage Chinese knowledge."

Will the resource curse stifle democracy in Libya?

YES Paul Frijters
Professor of Economics University of Queensland Australia

Written for *CQ Global Researcher*, December 2011

NO Ian Vasquez
Director, Center for Global Liberty and Prosperity, Cato Institute Washington, D.C.

Written for *CQ Global Researcher*, December 2011

If any Arab country could pull off a modern democracy it might be Libya, with its relatively high per capita gross domestic product, high urbanization rate, minimal government debt and projected revenues higher than expenses.

The danger is the resource curse. A vast amount of natural resources is like a large pile of juicy bones before a pack of hungry dogs. If the pack is well-organized and united around a common goal, some bones get used immediately, but the rest are stored for the future. Without that common goal, the mere presence of the pile destabilizes the pack, and each animal fights for control.

Norway is an example of a united pack, storing much of its oil wealth in a sovereign fund that invests oil revenues in overseas equities — relieving some pressures on the Norwegian currency and keeping its non-oil businesses competitive. This is clearly what Libya should do.

Nigeria is an example of a divided pack, where tribe fights tribe, religion fights religion, North fights South and armies fight militias for control of the country's oil. Dictator after dictator looks after his own group, while a high exchange rate makes it difficult to jump-start other businesses.

Libya resembles the divided pack. Members of the National Transitional Council are mainly loyal to their own regional identities. Land holdings are primarily based on family and community ties. Cities have strong independent histories and are made up of overlapping tribe-like communities. Whole cities, tribes and clans made collective decisions whether or not to oppose Moammar Gadhafi. The victors are now clamoring for their share of the spoils.

Who is going to deny them? None of these groups will trust the others, so each would raid a national future fund for its own benefits. There might be some prestige projects (like "broadband for all"), but every check and balance in the system gets manned by individuals who first identify with their own group. Deal-makers on the side of the oil companies are forging political connections with these groups to safeguard their own interests.

So there will be an election, followed by a gradual sifting-out of alliance members who are not needed to retain power. The best jobs will go to a smaller in-group defined by family, ethnicity and region. That group will subvert the democratic process, making Libya a kind of small Egypt with oil — a mini-Russia at best.

With the fall of Moammar Gadhafi, Libyans can build a society on principles diametrically opposed to those that propped up the late dictator's oil-based regime. The challenges are large, but, as other countries have shown, they can be met.

Libya's biggest problem is the so-called natural resource curse. Revenues from oil and gas represent more than half of Libya's economy. Unfortunately, in developing countries with weak institutions, such resources tend to be channeled through and usually monopolized by government, which then becomes corrupted, unresponsive to citizens' needs and less interested in advancing policies and institutions that create wealth for all.

That's certainly been the case in Libya. Since the early 1980s, the country of 6.5 million people received more than $450 billion in oil revenues. Yet economic, civil and political liberties have long been repressed, the state became the major employer, a third of the workforce is unemployed, a third of Libyans live below the poverty line and the World Bank says the rule of law is weaker in Libya than in about 80 percent of countries around the globe.

Not all resource-rich countries suffer from the curse, however. Chile overcame it, and diamond-rich Botswana avoided it. What sets successful countries apart from the rest? The Fraser Institute studied indicators of economic freedom, including rule-of-law measures, to find out. On a scale of 0 to 10, where 10 represents better institutional quality, the institute found a resource curse threshold of about 6.9 — the level above which countries broke the so-called curse. Thus, more economic freedom turns the curse into a blessing.

Libya is far below the point at which it could take advantage of its riches to make its people rich. Its new leaders would do well by significantly increasing the economic freedom of their people through reforms, such as eliminating burdensome regulations and securing private-property rights, including those for oil. Such moves would increase the government's legitimacy. After all, as Arab scholars point out, the Arab Spring began when Tunisian street vendor Muhammad Bouazizi set himself on fire after being denied the economic freedom to sell his goods — a grievance with which Libyans widely identify.

No iron law says Libya must remain cursed. The only barriers are ideological and political. Although often formidable, in this case they can be overcome by skillfully appealing to popular sentiment.

American University professor of international development Deborah Bräutigam, who has done research in more than a dozen African countries, agrees some concerns are well-founded. However, she argues, China's involvement in Africa is often exaggerated and presented in alarmist terms. Chinese investments and credits, which often are repaid in oil or other resources, "can directly channel mineral riches into development projects," Bräutigam writes. "This is a practical way to address the 'natural resource curse' that plagues so many African countries." [80]

OUTLOOK

Awareness Grows

As demand for natural resources increases in large emerging economies such as China and India, experts predict that managing extractive industries will continue to challenge governments in many developing countries. But they also believe awareness of the resource curse is growing, and that citizens are becoming more willing and able to hold governments accountable for resource wealth.

"Ten or 15 years ago, hardly anyone talked about the problems of resource-rich countries, even though they affected something like 1.5 billion people who were living on less than $2 per day," says Oxfam America's Gary. "Ten years from now, countries will definitely still be grappling with these effects, but policies to address them — like disclosure and protection of local rights — will be a lot stronger too."

That prediction is supported by broad political trends across the developing world. Not only are economies growing and living conditions improving in many countries but citizens increasingly are demanding the right to choose their leaders, voice opinions and criticize their governments. The Arab Spring revolts in Tunisia, Egypt, Yemen and Libya, for example, were fuelled in large part by deep popular resentment against tyrannical leaders and economic stagnation. [81]

"There are large parts of the world where rights remain severely and often violently curtailed — not least in China — but the global trend is away from autocracy and toward respect for civil and political rights," writes Kenny of the Center for Global Development. [82] And when governments respect those basic rights, it becomes easier for citizens to demand more transparency and fairness in budget-making and spending national wealth.

U.N. Development Programme Administrator Clark lists three key ways in which income from natural resources can promote human development instead of obstructing it:

- There should be transparency in contracting, managing the revenues and deciding how to spend them.
- Community groups should be included from the early stage, so benefits are shared as widely as possible.
- Nations need to strike a balance between short-term needs and long-term goals as they decide how to spend their revenues.

If countries learn from past successes and failures, Clark contends, they will find that the resource curse is not inevitable. And countries that are just starting to develop extractive resources today have an opportunity to create strong systems for managing them.

"There is a window now for these countries to design policies that will avoid the resource curse," she said. [83]

NOTES

1. Peter Bouckaert, "Human Rights Must Be Cornerstone of Libya's Law," Human Rights Watch, Oct. 20, 2011, www.hrw.org/news/2011/10/20/human-rights-must-be-cornerstone-libyas-law.

2. Paul Richter, "As Libya Takes Stock, Moammar Kadafi's Hidden Riches Astound," *Los Angeles Times*, Oct. 21, 2011, http://articles.latimes.com/2011/oct/21/world/la-fg-kadafi-money-20111022.

3. Economists define rents as "payment to a factor of production in excess of what is required to keep that factor in its present use" — for example, royalties that an energy company pays to a government in return for developing that government's oil or mineral resources. David R. Henderson, "Rent Seeking," *Concise Encyclopedia of Economics*, www.econlib.org/library/Enc/RentSeeking.html.

4. Peter Fragiskatos, "Will Libya's Oil Again Prove Its Curse?" *Le Monde Diplomatique* (English edition), Oct. 10, 2011, http://mondediplo.com/blogs/will-libya-s-oil-again-prove-its-curse.

5. Senator Richard Lugar and Senator Ben Cardin, "Libya: The Resource Curse Strikes Again," *Huffington Post*, April 20, 2011, www.huffington-post.com/sen-dick-lugar/libya-the-resource-curse-_b_851672.html.

6. "Background Note: Norway," U.S. Department of State, www.state.gov/r/pa/ei/bgn/3421.htm, and "Background Note: Botswana," www.state.gov/r/pa/ei/bgn/1830.htm; "Falling Copper Prices Hurt Chile," *Forbes.com*, Dec. 10, 2008, www.forbes.com/2008/12/09/chile-copper-budget-cx_1210oxford.html.

7. "Background Note: Nigeria," U.S. Department of State, updated Oct. 20, 2011, hwww.state.gov/r/pa/ei/bgn/2836.htm.

8. *The World Factbook*, U.S. Central Intelligence Agency, https://www.cia.gov/library/publications/the-world-factbook/geos/ni.html.

9. "Nigeria 'Wasted' 30 Years of Oil Income: IMF Chief," Agence France-Presse, Feb. 27, 2008, http://afp.google.com/article/ALeqM5gJwbeZbjEqJqmme3BNcM48u8BXxQ?docId=080227183452.6tbz6hoq&index=0.

10. Helen Clark, "Avoiding the resource curse: Managing extractive industries for Human Development," U.N. Development Programme, Oct. 20, 2011, www.beta.undp.org/undp/en/home/presscenter/speeches/2011/10/20/helen-clark-avoiding-the-resource-curse-managing-extractive-industries-for-human-development-.html.

11. Richard Auty, *Sustaining Development in Mineral Economies: The Resource Curse Thesis* (1993).

12. Michael Ross, "Extractive Sectors and the Poor," Oxfam America, October 2001, p. 7, www.oxfamamerica.org/publications/extractive-sectors-and-the-poor.

13. Terry Lynn Karl, *The Paradox of Plenty: Oil Booms and Petro-States* (1997), pp. 6-7, 16-18.

14. For more analysis and links to multiple studies, see Charles Kenny, "What Resource Curse?" *Foreign Policy*, Dec. 6, 2010, www.foreignpolicy.com/articles/2010/12/06/what_resource_curse?print=yes&hidecomments=yes&page=full.

15. Daniel Lederman and William F. Maloney, eds., *Natural Resources: Neither Curse Nor Destiny* (2007), chapters 6-8, http://siteresources.worldbank.org/INTTRADERESEARCH/Resources/D.Lederman_W.Maloney_Natural_Resources_book.pdf.

16. "Resource-Rich Countries Can Learn From History, Says Collier," IMF survey, Sept. 27, 2011, www.imf.org/external/pubs/ft/survey/so/2011/INT092711B.htm.

17. "Equatorial Guinea," *The World Factbook*, U.S. Central Intelligence Agency, https://www.cia.gov/library/publications/the-world-factbook/geos/ek.html.

18. "Leadership Africa: Who Is Next on the 'Hit List'?" *Black Business Quarterly* (South Africa), Nov. 7, 2011, www.bbqonline.co.za/articles/politics/local/450-leadership-africa; Kevin Johnson, "Probe of Alleged Extortion Targets Son of African Leader," *USA Today*, Nov. 9, 2011, www.usatoday.com/news/washington/story/2011-11-07/probe-west-african-leaders-son/51109220/1.

19. CIA *World Factbook*, *op. cit.*

20. Paul Stevens and Evelyn Dietsche, "Resource Curse: An Analysis of Causes, Experiences and Possible Ways Forward," *Energy Policy*, Vol. 36 (2008), pp. 59-60.

21. See "Extractive Industries Transparency Initiative," EITI, http://eiti.org/eiti.

22. "G20 Leaders Express Their Support of Participation in EITI," EITI, http://eiti.org/news-events/g20-leaders-express-their-support-participation-eiti; "Opening Remarks by President Obama on Open Government Partnership," Sept. 20, 2011, www.whitehouse.gov/the-press-office/2011/09/20/opening-remarks-president-obama-open-government-partnership.

23. Details at http://eiti.org/supporters/companies.

24. Sean O'Hare, "UK Refuses to Sign Up to Oil, Mining and Gas Transparency Initiative," *The Telegraph*, Sept. 21, 2011, www.telegraph.co.uk/finance/personalfinance/offshorefinance/8779905/UK-refuses-to-sign-up-to-oil-mining-and-gas-transparency-initiative.html.

25. Richard Murphy, "Pure Hypocrisy from the UK By Refusing to Join the Extractive Industries

Transparency Initiative," *Tax Research UK*, Sept. 22, 2011, www.taxresearch.org.uk/Blog/2011/09/22/pure-hypocrisy-from-the-uk-by-refusing-to-join-the-extractive-industries-transparency-initiative/.

26. For details see Publish What You Pay, www.publish whatyoupay.org/activities/advocacy.

27. "Disclosure of Payments by Resource Extraction Issuers," *Federal Register*, Dec. 23, 2010, pp. 80978-81002, www.sec.gov/rules/proposed/2010/34-63549fr.pdf.

28. Comments submitted by ExxonMobil Vice President and Controller Patrick T. Mulva, Oct. 25, 2011, www.sec.gov/comments/s7-42-10/s74210-112.pdf; full database of public comments is at www.sec.gov/comments/s7-42-10/s74210.shtml.

29. Lugar and Cardin, *op. cit.*

30. Simeon Djankov, Jose G. Montalvo, and Marta Reynol-Querol, "The Curse of Aid," Universitat of Pompeu Fabra, April 2005, www.econ.upf.edu/docs/papers/downloads/870.pdf (quotes on p. 3).

31. For background see Marcia Clemmitt, "U.S.-Pakistani Relations," *CQ Researcher*, Aug. 5, 2011, pp. 653-676, and Robert Kiener, "Crisis in Pakistan," *CQ Global Researcher*, December 2008, pp. 321-348.

32. "Direct Overt U.S. Aid Appropriations and Military Reimbursements To Pakistan, FY 2002-FY2012," Congressional Research Service, Aug. 9, 2011, www.fas.org/sgp/crs/row/pakaid.pdf.

33. See International Crisis Group reports at www.crisis group.org/en/regions/asia/south-asia/pakistan.aspx; "Human Development Index, 2011," U.N. Development Programme, http://hdr-undp.org/en/statistics/.

34. "Imram Khan Calls for Britain to Cut Aid to Pakistan," BBC News, Sept. 26, 2011, www.bbc.co.uk/news/uk-15055738?print=true; "World Vision's Message to Imram Khan: Aid is a Blessing, Not a Curse," www.worldvision.org.uk/server.php?show=nav.4027.

35. "U.S. Aid is a Curse: Imram Khan," *Pakistan Today*, Sept. 19, 2011, www.pakistantoday.com.pk/2011/09/us-aid-is-a-curse-imran-khan/.

36. "World Vision's Message to Imram Khan: Aid is a Blessing, Not a Curse," World Vision, www.world vision.org.uk/server.php?show=nav.4027.

37. For background see Peter Katel, "Haiti's Dilemma," *CQ Researcher*, Feb. 18, 2005, pp. 149-172.

38. Jason Beaubien, "Foreign Aid a Blessing, curse For Struggling Haiti," NPR, March 30, 2010, www.npr.org/templates/story/story.php?storyId=125343322; see also Jonah Goldberg, "Haiti's True Curse," *The New York Post*, Jan. 20, 2010, www.nypost.com/p/news/opinion/opedcolumnists/haiti_true_curse_b2j XL3a8JoXWcLSC8wzuQI, and Peter Worthington, "Haiti's Curse," *Toronto Sun*, Nov. 23, 2010, www.torontosun.com/comment/columnists/peter_wor thington/2010/11/23/16285551.html.

39. Mark Kurlansky, *Cod: A Biography of the Fish That Changed the World* (1997), pp. 48-52.

40. Nathan Nunn, "The Long-Term Effects of Africa's Slave Trades," *Quarterly Journal of Economics*, February 2008, p. 143, www.economics.harvard .edu/faculty/nunn/files/empirical_slavery.pdf.

41. "Triangular Trade," Understanding Slavery Initiative, www.understandingslavery.com, and Boston Tea Party Historical Society, "Triangular Trade in New England Colonies," www.boston-tea-party.org/triangular-trade.html.

42. Robert H. Bates, John H., Coatsworth, and Jeffrey G. Williamson, "Lost Decades: Postindependence Performance in Latin America and Africa," *Journal of Economic History*, Vol. 67, No. 4 (December 2007), pp. 923-36.

43. "Tells of Atrocities in Belgian Congo," *The New York Times*, Nov. 24, 1909, http://query.nytimes.com/mem/archive-free/pdf?res=F10C14F83D5412738D DDAD0A94D9415B898CF1D3.

44. *Ibid.*

45. Nunn, *op. cit.*

46. Daniel Yergin, *The Prize: The Epic Quest for Oil, Money, and Power* (1991), pp. 523-524.

47. W.W. Rostow, *The Stages of Economic Growth: A Non-Communist Manifesto* (1960), chapter 2, online at www.mtholyoke.edu/acad/intrel/ipe/rostow.htm.

48. Michael L. Ross, "The Political Economy of the Resource Curse," *World Politics*, Vol. 51 (January 1999), pp. 297-298, www.sscnet.ucla.edu/polisci/faculty/ross/paper.pdf.

49. For background, see Peter Behr, "Energy Nationalism," *CQ Global Researcher*, July 1, 2007, pp. 151-180.

50. Rebecca Ray, "Turning the Page: Are Developing Countries Bouncing Back From 20 Years of Economic Stagnation?" Center for Economic and Policy Research, April 15, 2011, www.cepr.net/blogs/cepr-blog/turning-the-page-are-developing-countries-bouncing-back-from-20-years-of-stagnation.

51. Dani Rodrik, "Where Did All the Growth Go? External Shocks, Social Conflict, and Growth Collapses," Centre for Economic Policy Research, January 1998, www.cepr.org/pubs/new-dps/dplist.asp?dpno=1789.

52. *The East Asian Miracle: Economic Growth and Public Policy*, World Bank (1993).

53. Richard M. Auty, *Sustaining Development in Mineral Economies: The Resource Curse Thesis* (1993), pp. 3-6, 14-17.

54. Jeffrey D. Sachs and Andrew M. Warner, "Natural Resource Abundance and Economic Growth," Harvard University, November 1997, www.cid.harvard.edu/ciddata/warner_files/natresf5.pdf.

55. See, for example, Terry Lynn Karl, *The Paradox of Plenty: Oil Booms and Petro-States* (1997).

56. Howard W. French, "Nigeria Executes Critic of Regime; National Protest," *The New York Times*, Nov. 11, 1995, www.nytimes.com/1995/11/11/world/nigeria-executes-critic-of-regime-nations-protest.html?scp=9&sq=saro-wiwa&st=cse.

57. Ed Pilkington, "Shell Pays Out $15.5m Over Saro-Wiwa Killing," *The Guardian*, June 8, 2009.

58. Louis Goreux, "Conflict Diamonds," *Africa Region Working Paper Series No. 13*, World Bank, March 2001, www.worldbank.org/afr/wps/wp13.pdf; Michael Fleshman, "Targeting 'Conflict Diamonds' in Africa," *Africa Recovery*, January 2001, www.un.org/ecosocdev/geninfo/afrec/subjindx/144diam.htm.

59. Vivienne Walt, "Diamonds Aren't Forever," *Fortune*, Dec. 7, 2006, http://money.cnn.com/magazines/fortune/fortune_archive/2006/12/11/8395442/index.htm.

60. "Conflict Diamonds: Agency Actions Needed to Enhance Implementation of the Clean Diamond Trade Act," Government Accountability Office, September 2006, www.gao.gov/new.items/d06978.pdf.

61. "A Crude Awakening: The Role of the Oil and Banking Industries in Angola's Civil War and the Plunder of State Assets," Global Witness, 1999, www.globalwitness.org/sites/default/files/pdfs/A%20Crude%20Awakening.pdf.

62. "Angola: Account of Missing Oil Revenues," Human Rights Watch, Jan. 11, 2004, www.hrw.org/en/news/2004/01/11/angola-account-missing-oil-revenues; World Bank Development Indicators, in 2010 dollars.

63. "George Soros and NGOs Call For Rules To Require Corporations To Disclose Payments," Global Witness, June 13, 2002, www.globalwitness.org/library/publish-what-you-pay.

64. "International Environmental Group Calls On World Bank To Stop Funding Oil, Gas, and Mining Projects," Friends of the Earth International, Sept. 25, 2000, www.foei.org/en/media/archive/2000/press stopmining.html.

65. "Striking a Better Balance: The Extractive Industries Review," executive summary, World Bank, 2003, http://irispublic.worldbank.org/85257559006C22E9/All+Documents/85257559006C22E985256FF600682 0D2/$File/execsummaryenglish.pdf.

66. "Slow Progress on World Bank's Oil, Gas and Mining Commitments," Bretton Woods Project, June 13, 2005, www.brettonwoodsproject.org/art-235789; Shannon Lawrence and Nikki Reisch, "The World Bank, The Extractive Industries Review, and Governance: Evaluating the Bank Group's Implementation of Its Commitments," Environmental Defense and Bank Information Center, January 2006, http://bankwatch.org/documents/bic_eir_review.pdf.

67. "Millennium Development Goals," United Nations, www.un.org/millenniumgoals/bkgd.shtml (click on specific goals for quantitative targets).

68. "The Millennium Development Goals Report 2011," United Nations, www.un.org/millenniumgoals/pdf/%282011_E%29%20MDG%20Report%202011_Book%20LR.pdf, (see p. 6, for progress on poverty reduction).

69. "Nigeria Millennium Development Goals Report 2010," U.N. Development Programme, 2010, pp. 1, 6-7, www.undp.org/africa/documents/mdg/nigeria_2010.pdf.

70. "Human Development Index," United Nations Development Programme, http://hdr.undp.org/en/statistics/hdi/; rankings are from Table 2, "Human Development Index Trends," http://hdr.undp.org/en/media/HDR_2011_EN_Table2.pdf.

71. "Frequently Asked Questions about the Human Development Index," U.N. Development Programme, p. 1, http://hdr.undp.org/en/media/FAQs_2011_HDI.pdf.

72. "Game Changer or Resource Curse?" *Business Times Africa Magazine*, October 2010, www.businesstimesafrica.net/btm/details.cfm?tblNewsCatID=4&prodcatID=6&tblNewsID=429. See also "Ghana's Big Test," Oxfam America, Feb. 13, 2009, www.oxfamamerica.org/publications/ghanas-big-test; Kofi Bentil, "Oil Revenues Commission — How Ghana Can Avoid the Resource Curse," *Ghanaian Journal*, Oct. 29, 2009, www.theghanaianjournal.com/2009/10/29/oil-revenues-commission-how-ghana-can-avoid-the-resource-curse/; and "Ghana: Oil Opportunity," *New Africa Analysis*, May 9, 2011, http://newafricaanalysis.co.uk/index.php/2011/05/ghana-oil-opportunity/.

73. Patrick Ezeala, "Oil in Ghana: Civil Society Groups Launch Country's Readiness Report Card," Oxfam America, April 19, 2011, www.oxfamamerica.org/articles/oil-in-ghana-civil-society-groups-launch-countrys-readiness-report-card.

74. "East Timor Country Brief," Department of Foreign Affairs and Trade, Government of Australia, www.dfat.gov.au/geo/east_timor/east_timor_brief.html.

75. "China-Africa Economic and Trade Cooperation," Information Office of the State Council, People's Republic of China, Dec. 23, 2010, http://english.cri.cn/6909/2010/12/23/2741s611673.htm.

76. For background, see Karen Foerstel, "China in Africa," *CQ Global Researcher*, Jan. 1, 2008, pp. 1-26.

77. "Africa and China," *The Economist*, Feb. 16, 2010, www.economist.com/debate/days/view/466, (George Ayittey, "Against the Motion").

78. "World Bank, China May Cooperate to Transfer Manufacturing Jobs to Africa," Bloomberg News, Sept. 5, 2011, www.bloomberg.com/news/print/2011-09-05/world-bank-china-may-cooperate-to-transfer-manufacturing-jobs-to-africa.html.

79. Kelvin Kachingwe, "Controversial Chinese Firm Given Another Copper Mine," Inter Press News Service Agency, June 2, 2009, http://ipsnews.net/africa/nota.asp?idnews=47065; " 'You'll Be Fired If You Refuse': Labor Abuses in Zambia's Chinese State-Owned Copper Mines," Human Rights Watch, Nov. 3, 2011, www.hrw.org/reports/2011/11/03/you-ll-be-fired-if-you-refuse.

80. Deborah Brautigam, *The Dragon's Gift: The Real Story of China in Africa* (2010), p. 307.

81. For background, see Roland Flamini, "Turmoil in the Arab World," *CQ Global Researcher*, May 3, 2011, pp. 209-236.

82. Charles Kenny, *Getting Better: Why Global Development is Succeeding — And How We Can Help the World Even More* (2011), p. 87.

83. Helen Clark, *op. cit.*

BIBLIOGRAPHY

Selected Sources
Books

Collier, Paul, and Tony J. Venables, *Plundered Nations? Successes and Failures in Natural Resource Extraction*, Palgrave Macmillan, 2011.
Two Oxford University economists show how eight different countries have managed their natural resources.

Humphries, Macartan, Jeffrey D. Sachs and Joseph E. Stiglitz, eds., *Escaping the Resource Curse*, Columbia University Press, 2007.
Three Columbia University professors, including a Nobel laureate in economics (Stiglitz), edit essays advising leaders in resource-rich countries on how to maximize revenues.

Kenny, Charles, *Getting Better: Why Global Development is Succeeding — And How We Can Improve the World Even More*, Basic Books, 2011.
A senior World Bank economist explains how conditions for the poor are improving and how to speed progress.

Luong, Pauline Jones, and Erika Weinthal, *Oil Is Not a Curse: Ownership Structure and Institutions in Soviet Successor States*, Cambridge University Press, 2010.
Two political scientists compare the behaviors of five oil-rich former Soviet states and conclude that private management of resources is better than government control.

Articles

"Africa and China," *Economist.com*, 2011, www.economist.com/debate/overview/165.
A multipart online debate over the impact of China's involvement in Africa, which centers on a booming trade in oil and other raw materials.

Eligon, John, "Global Witness Quits Group on 'Blood Diamonds,' " *The New York Times*, Dec. 5, 2011, www.nytimes.com/2011/12/06/world/africa/global-witness-quits-group-on-blood-diamonds.html?scp=1&sq=blood%20diamonds&st=cse.
A leading international advocacy group has withdrawn from the global agreement to regulate the "blood diamond" trade, saying the system is poorly enforced.

Lugar, Dick, and Benjamin Cardin, "Libya: The Resource Curse Strikes Again," *Huffington Post*, April 20, 2011, www.huffingtonpost.com/sen-dick-lugar/libya-the-resource-curse-_b_851672.html.
Two U.S. senators assert that the resource curse affects importing as well as exporting countries by fostering poverty and autocratic governments, which helps keep world oil markets unstable.

O'Hare, Sean, "UK Refuses to Sign Up to Oil, Mining and Gas Transparency Initiative," *The Telegraph*, Sept. 21, 2011, www.telegraph.co.uk/finance/personalfinance/offshorefinance/8779905/UK-refuses-to-sign-up-to-oil-mining-and-gas-transparency-initiative.html.
The United Kingdom's government says it strongly supports transparency, but will not join a global disclosure initiative because it is not a "resource-rich" country.

Otis, John, "Report Card: 12 Years of Hugo Chavez," *GlobalPost*, July 18, 2011, www.globalpost.com/dispatch/news/regions/americas/venezuela/110715/chavez-poor-social-welfare-reelection.
Unemployment and poverty have fallen under populist Chavez, but critics say he has mismanaged oil earnings and could have achieved much more.

Reports and Studies

"Lifting The Resource Curse: How Poor People Can and Should Benefit from the Revenues of Extractive Industries," Oxfam Briefing Paper 134, Oxfam International, December 2009, www.oxfam.org/en/policy/lifting-resource-curse.
International antipoverty advocates recommend more transparency and accountability to ensure that natural resource revenues are shared fairly and used to address basic needs.

"Promoting Revenue Transparency: 2011 Report on Oil and Gas companies," Transparency International, www.transparency.org/publications/publications/other/prt_2011.
A growing number of oil and gas companies are publishing information about how much money they pay their foreign government partners.

Moss, Todd, "Oil to Cash: Fighting the Resource Curse through Cash Transfers," Center for Global Development Working Paper No. 237 (January 2011), http://cgdev.org/files/1424714_file_Oil2Cash_primer_FINAL.pdf.
Countries seeking to manage new resource wealth should consider making direct cash payments to citizens, according to a Washington think tank.

Pineda, José, and Francisco Rodriguez, "Curse or Blessing? Natural Resources and Human Development," United Nations Development Programme, Human Development Reports, Research Paper 2010/04 (June 2010), http://hdr.undp.org/en/reports/global/hdr2010/papers/HDRP_2010_04.pdf.
Two senior UNDP researchers find that natural resource endowments have had a net positive impact on human development since 1970, mainly by helping to improve health and education.

For More Information

Asia Foundation, 465 California St., 9th Floor, San Francisco, CA 94104; 415-982-4640; www.asiafoundation.org. A nonprofit organization that works to develop a peaceful, prosperous, just and open Asia-Pacific region.

Center for Global Development, 1800 Massachusetts Ave., N.W., Washington, DC 20036; 202-416-4000; www.cgdev.org. A self-described "think and do" tank that conducts research and develops policy proposals designed to improve conditions for poor people in developing countries.

Extractive Industries Transparency Initiative, International Secretariat, Ruselokkveien 26, 0251 Oslo, Norway; +47 2224 2105; www.eiti.org. A nonprofit organization that oversees implementation of the Extractive Industries Transparency Initiative, a global disclosure standard for international oil, gas and mining companies.

Oxfam International, Oxfam House, John Smith Drive, Cowley, Oxford, OX4 2JY, United Kingdom; +44 1865 47 3727; www .oxfam.org. An international confederation of advocacy groups working in 98 countries to find solutions to poverty and injustice.

Publish What You Pay, c/o Open Society Foundation — London, 4th Floor, Cambridge House, 100 Cambridge Grove, London W6 OLE, United Kingdom; +44 20 7031 1616; www.publishwhatyoupay.org. A global network of organizations that advocate disclosing information about extractive industry contracts and revenues.

Sovereign Wealth Fund Institute, 2300 West Sahara Ave., Suite 800, Las Vegas, NV 89102; www.swfinc.com. A private corporation that studies sovereign wealth funds and their impact on global economics, politics, financial markets, trade and public policy.

World Bank, 1818 H St., N.W., Washington, DC 20433; 202-473-1000; www.worldbank.org. Two agencies (the International Bank for Reconstruction and Development and the International Development Association) that provide financial and technical assistance to developing countries around the world.

Voices From Abroad:

ISRAEL AYE

Partner, Sterling Partnership Legal Practitioners, Nigeria

Irresponsibility is the curse

"Oil is not a curse. I know people who have been blessed with it. It will be a curse for those who have been irresponsible in managing it. Oil can be good to you if you are good to it and bad to you if you are bad at it. It is a matter of being a responsible steward."

East African Business Week (Uganda), August 2011

HANY BESADA

Senior Researcher, North-South Institute, Canada

Libya's challenge

"In the lawless and long-marginalized southern regions, tribal groups with ties to Libya's neighbors, or with tribal affiliations to Gadhafi's former regime, will expect greater access to the country's resource wealth as the price of cooperation with the new government in Tripoli. Finding the right balance among these competing interests, without succumbing to the temptation of recentralizing power, will be an immense challenge for whatever governing coalition emerges from Libya's chaotic political scene."

Korea Times (South Korea), November 2011

WINNIE NGABIIWE

Chairwoman, Publish What You Pay, Uganda

Transparency's role

"Ugandans are nervously looking across to neighbors in the Democratic Republic of Congo and wondering if they are heading down the same road, where natural resources have been a curse rather than a blessing. Of course, transparency itself cannot deliver perfect oil governance — it is a means to an end. It is vital that once published, the information is used in the right way."

The Independent (Sierra Leone), April 2011

La Vanguardia, Spain/Kap

RICHARD DOWDEN

Executive Director, African Royal Society, England

Scaring off investors

"After oil and corruption, which are closely linked, I would say that Nigeria's reputation in the past still puts off investors and tourists. . . . Perceived or real unfairness in the system of resource allocation has led to fierce competition for success — or just survival. I would say that the competitive, creative spirit this creates is far more powerful than in any other country in the world."

Daily Champion (Nigeria), September 2011

BRENDAN O'DONNELL

Senior oil campaigner, Global Witness, England

Transparency in Libya

"Libya currently stands at a crossroads in several senses. One of the best ways to ensure it takes the path of peace and prosperity is to bring transparency to its oil sector. By drawing a line under Gaddafi-era corruption and the mismanagement of public wealth, the NTC (National Transitional Council) could champion resource justice in the transitional constitution and set a great precedent for Libya's future."

Guardian Unlimited (England), August 2011

IMRAN KHAN

Chairman, Pakistan Tehreek-e-Insaf (political party), Pakistan

Disappearing aid

"Unfortunately, aid has been a curse for Pakistan. It is not helping the people, . . . It is probably disappearing in Swiss bank accounts, or it's going into the army. If we have aid which keeps feeding these governments, it's

propping them up. If we don't have aid, we will be forced to make the reforms and stand on our own feet."

Daily Mail (England), September 2011

SIMONA MARINESCU

Senior Economist, United Nations Development Programme, Iraq

Escaping the oil trap

"The restructuring of state-owned enterprises is required because this (Iraqi) economy needs to move out of this oil trap as quickly as possible."

The Christian Science Monitor, May 2011

15

Rising Food Prices

Sarah Glazer

Traders signal their orders in the "wheat pit" at Chicago's Mercantile Exchange, which sets global prices for the world's four major grains — wheat, corn, rice and soybeans. Some economists blame commodities speculators and the rising demand for biofuels for rising food prices. Others blame poor weather, an imbalance between supply and demand and low surplus stocks.

From *CQ Researcher*,
Oct. 18, 2011

L ast December a 26-year-old Tunisian who dreamed of saving enough money to buy a car went into the street to sell vegetables and fruit from his cart in the dusty town of Sidi Bouzid. Although he was accustomed to being bullied by police, he couldn't take it anymore after a policewoman confiscated his produce, slapped him, spat at him and insulted his dead father.

In protest, Mohammed Bouazizi went to the municipal government building on Dec. 17 and set himself on fire — an immolation that set off a chain of angry street protests that spread across the Arab world. [1]

To Rami Zurayk, an agronomy professor at the University of Beirut, it was no coincidence that the so-called Arab Spring began in a rural area where a drought and scarce water are making it harder for farmers to make a living. Frustrated young men with no prospects in farming set out for better opportunities in the cities, only to find no work and high food prices — since more than half of the food in the Middle East and North Africa is imported. [2]

"Although the Arab revolutions were united under the slogan 'the people want to bring down the regime' not 'the people want more bread,' food was a catalyst," according to Zurayk. [3] "I think that the prices of food mobilized people." [4]

As protests engulfed one Arab country after another in the ensuing months, a widely photographed demonstrator in the Yemeni capital of Sanaa showed up with baguettes and an uncooked chapatti taped to his forehead. In Egypt, Tunisia and Yemen, demonstrators carried pots and pans and brandished baguettes to protest high food prices.

Poor Nations Hit by Big Price Spikes

Several of the poorest countries in Africa, Asia and Latin America are grappling with food prices for key commodities such as maize, wheat and potatoes that are more than twice last year's prices. In Somalia and Uganda, some prices have nearly tripled. At the same time, prices have dropped for certain commodities in some cities in other countries — such as the prices for potatoes in Santiago, Chile, and cassava flour in Bangkok, Thailand.

Price Changes for Key Commodities, 2010 to 2011

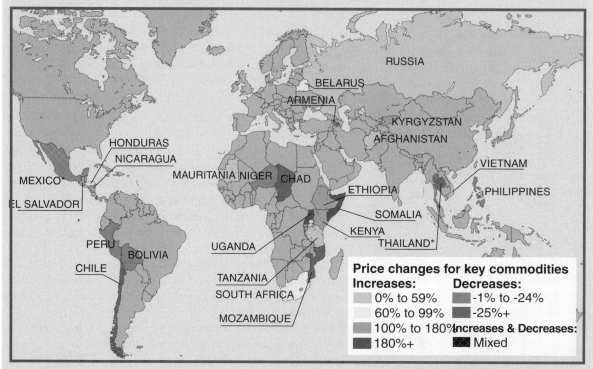

Price changes for key commodities

Increases:	Decreases:
0% to 59%	-1% to -24%
60% to 99%	-25%+
100% to 180%	**Increases & Decreases:**
180%+	Mixed

* In Mexico, maize prices rose in Culiácan but fell in Mexico City. In Bangkok, Thailand, cassava prices fell more than 25 percent, while maize fell less than 10 percent.

Source: "Global Food Price Monitor," Food and Agriculture Organization of the United Nations, September 2011, www.fao.org/giews/ english/gfpm/GFPM_09_2011.pdf . Map by Lewis Agrell

While most Western accounts described the demonstrations as political protests against authoritarian governments, economists pointed out that rising food prices coupled with high unemployment helped ignite already-smoldering discontent. Many pointed to a chain of events that began with Russia's worst drought in a century in the summer of 2010, killing one-third of the wheat crop and leading the government to ban wheat exports to keep domestic food prices down. [5]

Shortly after the export ban, bread prices surged in Egypt, Russia's biggest wheat customer and one of the world's largest food importers. Egypt was forced to import higher-priced wheat from the United States, putting financial pressure on already-strapped Egyptian families, who typically spend about 40 percent of their income on food (compared to less than 10 percent in U.S. households). [6]

Frustrated by high food prices, unemployment and repressive governments, young Egyptians gathered to protest in Cairo's Tahrir Square in late January, joining the chain of protests that had begun in Tunisia. In Algeria, protests that broke out in late December were a direct response to record prices for bread, milk and sugar and high unemployment. By the time the so-called Arab Spring protests ended in Tunisia, Egypt and Libya, the leaders of those countries had been deposed or were on the run. [7]

"The kind of prices we have can only contribute to more political instability and problems in countries that are poor and import food," says Abdolreza Abbassian, senior grains economist at the U.N. Food and Agriculture Organization (FAO) in Rome.

"We have been emphasizing that these high prices are not one event; these are the prices we'll have to live with — not like the past," he continues. "This has taken poorer countries by surprise who are used to decades of low prices."

Biofuels Linked to Future Food Price Hikes

The anticipated global expansion of biofuels by 2020 will significantly increase food prices for select commodities, according to ActionAid, a Johannesburg-based humanitarian group. Prices for the oilseeds (such as canola, safflower and mustard, all of which are used to make biodiesel) will rise by nearly 80 percent. Prices for sugarcane and maize — used in other biofuels — are expected to rise by 65 and 41 percent, respectively.

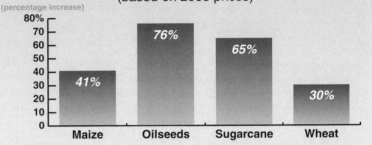

Projected Food Price Hikes by 2020 Due to Biofuels Expansion (based on 2008 prices)

Source: "Meals Per Gallon: The Impact of Industrial Biofuels on People and Global Hunger," ActionAid, January 2010, www.actionaid.org.uk/doc_lib/meals_per_gallon_final.pdf

Other experts agree that higher food prices aren't going away. In February, world food prices reached record levels, following eight consecutive months of increases. Wheat traded at $8.50 to $9 a bushel — more than twice the $4 price in July 2010. [8] Corn prices had nearly doubled from the year before. [9] Although prices have declined slightly since their peak in February, they remain near the 30-year record set in 2008, which sparked global food riots.

Normally, farmers benefit from high crop prices. Indeed, since June 2010, some 24 million farmers in low- and middle-income countries have escaped extreme poverty as a result of rising food prices, according to the World Bank. But the sudden price swings caught many small farmers in developing countries by surprise, making it difficult to boost their plantings to benefit from the higher prices, even as their own family food costs were skyrocketing.

The 24 million farmers who have benefited from higher prices have been dwarfed by the 68 million others, including city-dwellers, who fell below the $1.25-a-day poverty line set by the World Bank. The net result:

An extra 44 million people have fallen into extreme poverty in response to higher food prices. [10]

Although prices for the four major world grains — wheat, corn, rice and soybeans — are set at the Chicago Mercantile Exchange, the effect of rising prices differs enormously around the globe. In the United States, "if the price of wheat doubles, a loaf of bread goes from $2 to $2.10, because most of what we eat is packaging and transportation. But if you live in northern India or Pakistan, and you go to the market and buy wheat, bring it home and grind it into flour and make chapattis, the price for your bread basically doubles," explains Lester Brown, an environmental activist and founder of the Earth Policy Institute, an environmental research organization in Washington, D.C.

And once the price of a major grain goes up, consumers often substitute another — such as corn — causing all grains to rise together.

"The era of cheap prices is over," says Brown, who sees high prices as a sign that climate change already is making it harder to grow food.

Food prices are rising for several reasons, and everyone has a favorite culprit. But in agriculture, it's usually

Could That Seed in a Jar Save Mankind?

Ancient plants could save millions from starvation.

A few years ago, Israeli scientists took University of Minnesota agricultural economist Philip G. Pardey on a drive around Israel to see some plants. But not just any plants. The unimpressive, weedy-looking plants were the wild wheat from which our biblical ancestors made their bread.

Those ancient plants may be all that stands between a fungal disease that threatens 90 percent of the world's wheat crop and the survival of millions of people if the disease jumps to other continents. A fungus called stem rust regularly devastated wheat crops throughout the world until the late 1960s, when a resistant wheat variety was found. Then in 1999, a strain of stem rust in Uganda — Ug99 — was found to have overcome that resistance. [1]

But many of the wild, biblical wheat varieties are resistant to Ug99, according to Pardey. And it would be "really valuable" if someone could figure out which variety has the gene that is resistant to the disease, he says.

For scientists at the Kew Millennium Seed Bank in West Sussex, south of London, the search is a race against time. Although seed banks exist around the world, Kew is collaborating with more than 50 countries worldwide on the largest-ever effort to collect and conserve wild plant species.

As part of a 10-year program, Kew researchers first hope to save the wild relatives of 16 major food crops — including staples like rice, wheat and sweet potatoes. Then the scientists will help breeders find valuable traits — such as resistance to drought and disease — that can be bred into conventional crops.

Kew plans to preserve seeds for up to hundreds of years, depending on the species, in its modern, glass and concrete building that functions like a time capsule. The seeds can be protected in a vault designed to withstand earthquakes and nuclear accidents, and the building has state-of-the-art facilities for seed-drying and cold storage.

But Kew's secret weapon is the old-fashioned Mason jar, complete with orange rubber ring. After extensive testing, the jars were found to keep seeds the driest.

To preserve the seeds of heirloom plant varieties in danger of disappearing, Kew's scientists train farmers and home gardeners around the world to save seeds in Mason jars with a bit of charcoal or rice to keep them dry.

"We want to get away from the idea that a seed bank is just for saving seeds long into the future," says Kew International Projects Coordinator Kate Gold. Kew is part of a broad international effort to save indigenous vegetables in places like sub-Saharan Africa. As diets shift toward processed, Western foods, traditional recipes for nutritious, local vegetables are being lost, along with the habit of growing them.

"If you walk into a grocery store in Dakar [Senegal] or Abidjan [Ivory Coast] you find very few local products; you'll find boxed milk from Belgium and rice from Thailand," says Danielle Nierenberg, an expert on livestock and sustainable agriculture at the Worldwatch Institute, who has documented efforts to reclaim locally grown foods in 25 sub-Saharan countries. [2] "Indigenous vegetables have been long ignored by research institutes, consumers and farmers because they're considered poor people's foods — or even weeds — so people have lost their taste for them."

Yet such vegetables often are an important source of micronutrients like Vitamin A, zinc and iron. In school gardening projects, young Africans are re-discovering the tastes of their grandparents by learning to make traditional recipes, according to the institute, which promotes sustainable development.

a combination of poor weather, an imbalance between supply and demand and low surplus stocks. Some also blame the rising worldwide demand from biofuels (fuel made from corn, sugarcane or other plants), which will consume 40 percent of the U.S. corn crop this year — up from 31 percent in 2008-2009. Since the 1970s the government has been mandating a minimum amount of ethanol be blended into the nation's motor fuel supply and has offered tax incentives to petroleum refiners for adding up to 10 percent ethanol to each gallon of gasoline they sell. U.S. transportation fuels must contain a minimum of 12.6 billion gallons of corn-based ethanol this year, creating a guaranteed share of the motor fuels market for ethanol, originally intended to be roughly 10 percent. This has triggered a surge in demand for corn, the main ingredient of U.S.-produced ethanol. Thus,

Kew often finds plants in danger of disappearing by talking to community members who remember eating them. In western Kenya, for instance, Kew researchers discovered 50 plants whose existence and preparation were known only to village elders.

In Zambia, horticulturalist Mary O. Abukutsa-Onyango of Nairobi's Jomo Kenyatta University of Agriculture, has reintroduced farmers to vegetables that can survive in the marginal, arid soils of Kenya's lowlands. Many of the approximately 200 indigenous plants used by Kenyans in the past now "are either unknown or extinct," she laments. [3]

Kew scientists also hope to find plants that are resilient to climate change, such as a wild rice relative that flowers at night when it is cooler. If future temperatures rise even a few degrees, rice yields would drop by 30 to 40 percent. But if night-flowering characteristics were incorporated into farmed rice, millions of tons could be saved.

"If we lose all our natural resources, we don't know what options we're cutting off for the future," says biologist Ruth Eastwood, who coordinates Kew's program to collect wild relatives of conventional crops.

Most seed banks have no way of knowing whether the thousands of seeds they hold have valuable traits, and government funding for the necessary genetic research has been lacking. "If the seeds are sitting in the seed bank and you have no genetic information about them, they're effectively worthless," says Pardey.

Still, seed-savers like those at Kew are "real heroes" to Jonathan A. Foley, a climate scientist and director of the University of Minnesota's Institute on the Environment. Since agriculture began 10,000 years ago, thousands of crops have been lost. In fact, only 12 species contribute 80 percent of humans' total dietary intake today, compared to the more than 7,000 that were used at some point in history. [4]

"Throwing away the knowledge of previous generations is a huge loss to civilization," says Foley. "Who knows when the seeds might be valuable [in resisting] climate change or the next disease?"

— *Sarah Glazer*

At England's Kew Millenium Seed Bank, Moctar Sacandé, international project coordinator for Africa, displays a fruit from the African baobab tree that is rich in vitamin C and calcium. Kew is storing seeds of wild foods like the baobab in hope of saving those with valuable traits from extinction.

[1] Brendan I. Koemer, "Red Menace," *Wired*, Feb. 22, 2010, www.wired .com/magazine/2010/02/ff_ug99_fungus/.

[2] "State of the World 2011," Worldwatch Institute, www.worldwatch .org/sow11.

[3] *Ibid.*, p. 34.

[4] Zareen Bharucha and Jule Pretty, "The Roles and Values of Wild Foods in Agriculture," *Philosophical Transactions of the Royal Society B*, 2010, pp. 2913-2926, http://rstb.royalsocietypublishing.org/content/365/1554/2913 .full.pdf.

world corn prices now increasingly are linked to the rising price of oil. [11]

Others blame rising prices on the growing influence of commodities speculators. In January, French President Nicolas Sarkozy said commodities speculation was "extortion" that was "pillaging the poor." [12] Both the European Union and the G-20 nations are considering curbing speculators, just as the United States did last year when it enacted the Dodd-Frank Wall Street Reform Act. But some anti-poverty activists say the EU and G-20 proposals already are being watered-down due to opposition from the United Kingdom and the financial industry. [13]

Nevertheless, some long-term trends are sure to keep prices high, including the burgeoning world population, increasingly hotter, drier weather and a growing global appetite for grain-intensive meat among consumers in emerging economies such as China. To meet this growing demand, the planet's farmers will need to approximately double their output over the next 40 years in order to feed the additional 2 to 3 billion people projected for 2050, according to the FAO.

However, the rate of growth in agricultural production has been slowing in recent years compared to the hyperproductive 1960s-80s, when the so-called Green Revolution helped some countries' farmers boost their yields each year with new fertilizers and modern techniques. Globally, agricultural output has grown by 2.3 percent per year since 1961. But over the next 20 years, production growth is expected to fall to 1.5 percent a year, then plummet to less than 1 percent in the two decades leading up to 2050, the year world food demand is expected to double, the FAO says. [14]

And because of the heavy toll agriculture is taking on the environment, feeding the planet will only get more difficult, experts say. "The rise in demand from population growth, growing affluence and biofuels are on a collision course with our ability to produce food," says Jonathan A. Foley, director of the Institute on the Environment at the University of Minnesota.

Agriculture is now the main human-created threat to the environment, Foley contends. A high-tech menu of fertilizer-dependent improvements introduced by American agronomists to the developing world in the 1960s may have increased yields, but it also is exhausting and degrading soil and water supplies, some experts say.

"We've got to get back to some sustainable level globally; otherwise we'll go extinct sooner or later, like every other species has," says University of Nebraska agronomist Charles A. Francis, a visiting professor of agroecology at the Norwegian University of Life Sciences in Aas. Agroecology incorporates environmental stewardship into farming.

New biotechnology advances conceivably could increase crop yields. But some experts say it's time to start thinking locally, using what the World Bank calls "climate-smart agriculture" — finding local, traditional farming techniques and indigenous food plants that are well suited to hot, dry climates, particularly if future weather patterns move in that direction.

Droughts like the one causing famine in Somalia and near-famine conditions in Ethiopia will become more common, some experts predict. African farmers, who for centuries planted their crops on June 24 — confident

that the rainy season would arrive within a week or two — now "have no idea whether the rains will start in May, June, July or even August," reports American agroecologist Roland Bunch. [15]

"The reality is we have to double production by 2050 or so, and we have to completely halt almost all the environmental damage from large-scale agriculture without giving it up," says Foley. More planet-warming carbon is emitted when tropical rain forests are cleared for farming than is emitted by all forms of transportation worldwide, he points out.* In a paper for the November issue of *Scientific American*, Foley says the world could halt further expansion of farmland while still satisfying the need to double agricultural production by mid-century — if it adopts ecological practices. [16]

"It's at least physically possible to do it," he says. "Whether it's politically tenable is another question."

As scientists, governments and activists debate how to provide enough food at affordable prices without damaging the environment, here are some of the questions being debated:

Are government incentives for biofuels driving up food prices?

This year for the first time in history, more American corn is going to ethanol refiners than to poultry and livestock producers, accounting for 40 percent of this past year's crop, according to the U.S. Department of Agriculture. [18] Meanwhile, world corn prices in July were up 90 percent over the same time a year ago. [19]

Since 1978, when corn prices were at rock bottom, the U.S. government has been promoting development of a corn-to-ethanol industry as a way to provide both a new market for American corn and a clean, renewable source of motor fuel. Between 1980 and 2000, the industry received some $19 billion in tax breaks alone, according to the Government Accountability Office. The three major incentives have been a tax credit to oil refiners to blend ethanol into gasoline, a tariff to block cheaper imported ethanol (mainly from Brazil) and a mandate to produce enough ethanol to make up about 10 percent of the automotive fuel supply. In some cases the biofuel subsidies have

---

* When tropical forests are cleared for farming, they are often burned down, releasing large amounts of carbon. In addition, the cleared forests are no longer there to absorb carbon dioxide from the atmosphere. [17]

been so generous that on a per-gallon basis, they have exceeded the total cost of the gasoline being replaced by the biofuel. In 2010, ethanol incentives cost American taxpayers $7 billion in tax credits, tariffs and other incentives. [20]

American taxpayers "get to pay twice," says Brown, of the Earth Policy Institute. "Once on April 15th and then at the supermarket checkout counter," in the form of higher food prices.

As the world's largest corn producer, the United States traditionally has set world corn prices. And because corn is one of the world's main food staples, U.S. ethanol policy significantly affects world food prices, say critics of the policy. [21] "You can't take 40 percent of the U.S. corn crop and divert it to ethanol and not expect to have a price effect," says C. Ford Runge, a professor of applied economics and law at the University of Minnesota. He estimates that up to a third of the record world food prices in 2007-08 were caused by government ethanol policies.

Farmers, feed companies and their supporters lobbied hard for the ethanol subsidies — adopted in the 1970s and '80s, when corn prices were around $2 a bushel (vs. almost $7 for most of this year) and farmers were barely breaking even. The program was designed to boost corn prices, Runge contends. "To deny this is what happened is disingenuous," he says. "This was the idea — and it worked."

European governments eventually adopted similar incentives, and today subsidies for EU farmers to produce biofuels total more than $5.3 billion annually, according to ActionAid, a nonprofit based in Johannesburg devoted to fighting hunger and poverty. [22] The Brazilian government also has a heavily subsidized biofuels industry, based on sugarcane.

The FAO and other international organizations recommended in a June report that G-20 governments remove their biofuels mandates and subsidies. Subsidies are encouraging the diversion of crops from food to fuel and pushing food prices up, the report said. And as government biofuels policies link crop prices ever closer to the price of oil, the report noted, abrupt rises in the price of oil can increase food price volatility, making it hard for farmers to know how much to plant. [23] The United States and Brazil successfully lobbied against the recommendation when the G-20 met in June, and the final communiqué was watered down significantly. [24]

"In the FAO, we do feel that biofuels policies — and export restrictions — have played a part in leading to

An Indian policeman beats a demonstrator during a protest against rising inflation in New Delhi on Feb. 24, 2011, when food inflation was running at more than 11 percent in India. Consumer prices for food had risen by 80 percent in six years, according to the Credit Suisse investment house.

higher and more volatile prices," says David Hallam, director of FAO's markets and trades division. However, "whether the impact of biofuels on prices is 15, 20 or 30 percent is difficult to pin down."

Bruce Babcock, an agricultural economist at Iowa State University, downplays the impact of biofuels subsidies — so far. Until now, he says, the subsidies have had only a "modest" effect on world corn prices — about 7 percent in 2007 — and even less on U.S. retail food prices. But in 2011, world corn prices will be about 17 percent higher than they would have been if ethanol subsidies were eliminated, he estimates. That bigger price effect for this year, he says, is due to today's tight market conditions: Ethanol is in high demand when oil prices are high — as they are now. [25]

Babcock maintains that today's high oil prices alone give the industry plenty of incentive to produce, even without government hand-outs. But would the ethanol industry even exist without government mandates?

"If ethanol hadn't expanded, corn would have been so cheap compared to gasoline that someone would have figured out, 'My gosh, I can make a fortune buying this cheap corn and turning it into a substitute for gasoline and selling it,' " he says.

Rob Vierhout, secretary-general of the Brussels-based European Renewable Ethanol Association (ePURE), says food export bans — such as the one Russia imposed on its wheat in 2010 and 2011 — have done more to drive up world food prices than biofuels subsidies.

But Timothy D. Searchinger, a research scholar and lecturer in public and international affairs at Princeton University's Woodrow Wilson School, counters, "If it weren't for biofuels, you wouldn't have had the run-up in prices and the fear that made countries [like Russia] put on export controls," because heads of state "know that governments fall when food prices get too high."

Still, if biofuel mandates and subsidies were removed tomorrow, world corn prices — and food prices in general — would crash, say some experts. "If you were to dismantle mandates overnight you would suddenly be left with over 100 million tons — if not more — of grains, which could result in a complete collapse of world grain prices, sending shock waves to farmers across the world and bankrupticies," warns FAO economist Abbassian.

"The kinds of things I see do not justify to me that making biofuels from corn makes either economic or environmental sense, but now that we have established the sector it will be adding another fuel to farmers' problems if we dismantle it overnight," he warns.

Are commodity speculators causing high and volatile food prices?

Commodity speculators have been blamed as the main culprits behind skyrocketing food prices by French President Sarkozy, the U.N. special rapporteur on the right to food and EU Commissioner Michel Barnier, who has called such speculation "scandalous." [26]

Paradoxically, Chicago's commodities markets were established to provide price stability for farmers faced with unpredictable harvests and to large grain buyers, such as flour mills, seeking to nail down a price before harvest time. Over the last 15 years, however, participation by speculators without any role in farming or food processing has risen from just 12 percent of the market to 60 percent today, according to the London-based activist group World Development Movement, which campaigns against global poverty. [27]

"Food prices at historic levels are being driven by financial speculators," says Murray Worthy, author of the recent report for the group. "We definitely think there's much more rapid price inflation" as a result. He says large index funds are most to blame.

Since Congress deregulated the commodities market in 2000, index funds for a basket of commodities have risen in popularity, especially for investors seeking a safe haven from the stock market.

Commodity markets traditionally work on short-term futures contracts. When Farmer Brown plants his corn crop in April, he enters into a contract, with, say, General Mills, to deliver corn at $7 per bushel on September 30, cushioning himself against a possible drop in the price below $7 during that five-month period. Unlike farmers and grain buyers, pension funds tend to be in the market for long-term gains; so each time a short-term contract expires the funds buy a new one.

Critics say index funds encourage a speculative environment independent of the traditional market "fundamentals," such as the size of the corn harvest or how much market demand exists for a crop.

"You have a pension fund that buys into commodities and wants to hold the portfolio for 5-10 years, and every month they have to re-buy the contract just to keep their bets on the table," says David Frank, research director of Better Markets, a nonprofit group in Washington that advocates stricter regulation of commodities. "Since everyone else in the marketplace knows they have to buy these contracts [each month], it basically pushes up the prices synthetically in advance of the pension-fund buying. So you see this long-term upward creep of prices."

The monthly buying and selling of contracts creates a volatile, "whipsaw effect" on prices, destroying farmers' and grain buyers' ability to plan, according to Frank and other critics. Congress bought their argument when it passed the Wall Street reform act, which limits the share of a market that can be held by either individual speculators or by a class of speculators. Those caps are known as "position limits."

Kenneth Raisler, general counsel of the Commodity Futures Trading Commission (CFTC) during the Reagan administration, says concern about speculation is based on a misunderstanding of the market. The commodities market has always relied on speculators to play a useful role — assuring farmers of future revenues by agreeing to buy the actual crop, for example. And commodities investments are time-limited, Raisler says, because the contracts have an expiration date. So commodities investments can't be exerting the long-term upward pressure on prices that critics describe, he says.

"It is fair to say that the CFTC's initiative around position limits and Congress' discussion was built on misinformation and the political impact of the information," he says. "I think the position limit regulations are potentially very destructive of the U.S. markets. I don't think there's any evidence that driving these people out of the market is a good thing."

University of Massachusetts Professor of Economics Robert Pollin, who has testified in favor of speculation limits, agrees speculators can play a useful insurance role for farmers — but only up to a point. The more the commodities market starts to look like the financial markets, the more trouble he sees ahead.

Such markets "are easily overtaken by speculative bubbles, and that's what we're witnessing now," he says. "We've turned the commodities market into a securities market vulnerable to the forces of psychology and bubble speculation."

A blizzard of academic and industry papers debating speculators' impact on food prices has left even FAO experts somewhat bewildered. So far the studies are "giving us completely indecisive results as to who is at fault here," says FAO economist Abbassian.

"We don't feel what people call speculation is the root cause of the price movements we've seen," but it does cause more short-term swings and exaggerated short-term price hikes, says the FAO's Hallam.

As a result, Abbassian says, the G-20's next step "is not about regulation; it's about knowing more about what goes on in that market and how the market actors benefit from all these derivatives." The G-20 is developing an expanded information system showing who is trading what in the market — copied from U.S. legislation.

In recent years, as pension funds and others invested dollars on a scale never seen before, commodities index fund holdings swelled from $13 billion in 2003 to $317 billion in 2008. [28] "Your retirement fund dollars are helping to make decisions that affect the world's poorest people," says Alan Bjerga, an agricultural policy reporter for Bloomberg News and author of a new book

Food Prices Soared in Past Decade

World food prices have risen significantly since 2000, with cereals now costing 145 percent more than the 2002-04 average and 75 percent more than the overall 2010 price. Prices for both cereals and food fell slightly in 2009, as supplies rose, but have jumped since then. By this September prices had exceeded their 2008 peak, when food riots erupted around the world.

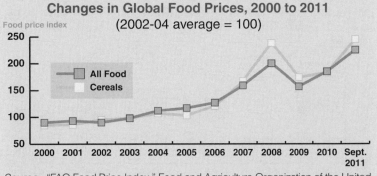

Source: "FAO Food Price Index," Food and Agriculture Organization of the United Nations, October 2011, www.fao.org/worldfoodsituation/wfs-home/foodprices index/en/

Endless Appetites: How the Commodities Casino Creates Hunger and Unrest.

Historically, he points out, the value of corn has been based on the number of people who need to eat it. Now, he says, it's based on what "these investors need to save for their retirement. The meaning of corn has changed."

Can farmers meet increasing demands for food at affordable prices?

Over 200,000 people will sit down to dinner tonight who weren't there last night, and many will be facing empty plates. That's how environmental activist Brown describes the inexorable rise in the planet's population. [29]

World population growth is expected to increase the demand for food by 70-100 percent by 2050, according to the FAO. [30] To meet that demand at affordable prices, farmers would need to boost the number of bushels they harvest per acre, something they've been able to do since modern farming techniques were introduced during the Green Revolution of the 1950s and '60s.

But those near-miraculous jumps in annual yields in the '50s and '60s were significantly smaller by the 1990s. "The miracle of the Green Revolution has been slowly running out of gas for the last few years," says environmental scientist Foley.

Food Prices Skyrocketed in Past Year

Prices for many food commodities, including maize, sugar and wheat, have increased by 50 percent or more over the past year — rising even more than the price of crude oil. The price of maize, a primary ingredient in ethanol as well as a staple in developing countries, nearly doubled as growers began diverting more of it to biofuels production.

Price Increases of Key Commodities, July 2010-July 2011

(percentage increase)

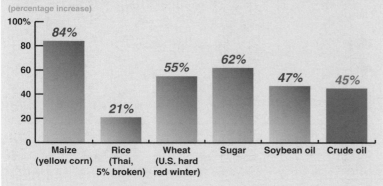

Source: "Food Price Watch," World Bank, August 2011, siteresources. worldbank.org/INTPOVERTY/ News and Events/22982477/Food-Price-Watch-August-2011.htm

Economist Philip G. Pardey, director of the University of Minnesota's International Science and Technology Practice and Policy Center, also says it's "questionable" whether farmers can satisfy the world's food needs by mid-century. Yet he says it's not a technical constraint but a policy problem — the U.S. government has been ratcheting down spending on agricultural research over the past three decades — from 4 percent annual growth in the '60s to less than 1 percent today.

"When you spend money on research and development, it takes decades for that technology to be commercialized and find its way to farmers' fields; so slowdowns in spending in the late 1960s, '70s and '80s started to show up in the '90s as a slowdown in productivity growth," Pardey says.

"If research is slowing down here in the U.S., it has a direct impact on global food and feed supplies," he continues, because as the largest exporter of corn and wheat and the third largest exporter of soybeans, the United States dominates global agriculture. [33]

On a global basis, Foley calculates, crop yields have only grown about 20 percent in the past two decades — far from the galloping increases needed to double production by mid-century.

The Earth Policy Institute's Brown, an agricultural scientist by training, is pessimistic about the potential to increase fertility per acre. In Japan, rice yields have been flat for 14 years; and a similar plateau is found in wheat yields in Europe. [31]

"Farmers have caught up with science," he says. "We may be beginning to press against the limits of science."

At the optimistic end of the spectrum, the seed company Monsanto has pledged by 2030 to double corn and soybean yields from 2000 levels. The challenge looks daunting. If yields don't improve, the company projects, 300 million acres of additional farmland will need to be brought into production by that year to keep up with demand. [32]

Monsanto says it can fulfill its pledge through a combination of better farm management and advanced biotechnology techniques.

On a global basis, agricultural spending will need to increase by about $85 billion per year to meet the growing demand, the FAO has estimated. "It's an interesting question where that will come from, [since] we see spending on agriculture R&D declining in most countries," says FAO economist Hallam.

Some scientists worry about how to grow food on a climate-challenged planet with rising temperatures and dwindling rainfall. Most of the water humans draw from rivers and aquifers already is being used for irrigation, and much of that has been contaminated with fertilizers, herbicides and pesticides.

Rising temperatures could mean fewer or no crops in many areas. Each 1-degree Celsius rise in temperature above the optimum during the growing season will mean about a 10 percent decline in grain yields at harvesttime, Brown estimates. [34]

"We're moving into a more unstable period," says University of Nebraska agronomist Francis. "We've got a huge global population dependent on benign climate, good agricultural conditions plus exploitation of fossil fuels, and we're heading into a whole new territory with limited fossil fuels, limited fresh water."

Some forecasting models have suggested that growing conditions in cooler areas of the world could benefit from increased temperatures. But the models don't take into account the vast expense of irrigation that would be needed if weather got drier, says Wolfram Schlenker, an economist at the School of International and Public Affairs at Columbia University in New York City. "If it gets warmer, and Iowa gets more like Mississippi and less like California, it's unambiguously not a benefit," he says. "The biggest challenge we have, if you talk to breeders like Monsanto, is we need to reduce plant sensitivity to extreme heat. But . . . we haven't seen it happening in the past."

Could the answer come from new breeds of plants born of biotechnology? Francis doesn't think so. Genetic modification, he says, has been "vastly overblown." [35]

"It's not going to solve the world's food problems and has done nothing to push up yield potential so far," he says, while acknowledging that biotech's pest-resistant, herbicide-resistant varieties have helped some farmers with weed and insect problems.

Food experts like Hallam say most of the increased production will have to come from the least productive farms in places like Africa, Central America and Eastern Europe — where yields are far below their theoretical potential and could be boosted with better seeds, more fertilizer and irrigation. In his forthcoming article in *Scientific American*, Foley estimates that closing this gap for the world's top 16 crops could increase total food production by 50 to 60 percent. [36]

But some agronomists are skeptical that Western technology and its promise of fantastic yields are always transferable to places with different soil conditions and weather. Francis advocates shifting to a local approach, using home-grown techniques and fewer fossil fuels.

Although agricultural production could be boosted by clearing more land and using more water or chemicals, the planet can't take much more of that kind of degradation, say experts like Foley. Agriculture is the largest single source of climate-altering greenhouse gas emissions, mostly because expanding farming destroys tropical rain forests. Methane released from animals

and nitrous oxide from overfertilized soils also contribute carbon emissions. [37]

Foley and an international team of experts have developed a five-point plan that he says would meet the planet's food needs by mid-century without degrading the environment. [38] Some of the proposals, such as using irrigation more efficiently and reducing food waste, are not controversial. But others, like eating less meat or halting the clearing of forests for farmland, will be a hard sell, especially as more of the world's people can afford a good steak.

BACKGROUND

Investing in Food

In the 1930s, North America was a small grain exporter. By 1966, North American grain exports had increased twelvefold — to nearly 60 million tons. [39] As the continent became the global center of the grain trade, changes in U.S. production would have huge impacts on international prices and food supply. [40]

Columbia University economist Schlenker compares America's dominance in the world food market to Saudi Arabia's outsized influence on global oil markets. Yet Saudi Arabia only produces about 8 percent of the world's oil, while the United States produces almost a quarter of the four grains that provide 75 percent of the world's calories: corn, wheat, rice and soybeans. [41]

"So the United States is really driving the market globally," he says.

America eventually came to dominate the world grain market — rather than even bigger 19th-century grain producers like the Ukraine — thanks to its railroad and canal transportation system.

The creation of a permanent futures exchange in 1874 — the Chicago Produce Exchange, the forerunner of today's Chicago Mercantile Exchange — came in the wake of wild fluctuation in the prices of wheat, partly as a result of the Civil War. It created a way for a farmer to hedge against poor prices at harvest by setting a good price in a "forward contract" for the date of delivery. The merchant who sold him the contract hoped the market price on the delivery date would be higher, leaving him with a profit. [42]

Over the years, as speculators were accused periodically of manipulating the commodities market, several laws were passed to regulate the industry. The Commodities Exchange Act of 1936, for instance, limited the number of contracts a speculator could hold, and the Commodity Futures Trading Commission, the market's regulatory agency, was created in 1974.

In 1991, a commodities trader at Goldman Sachs came up with the idea of creating an index that would track prices for a "basket" of commodities, allowing the buyers of the so-called index fund to speculate. But the fund was limited in how much trading it could do because of speculative limits dating back to 1936. Goldman asked the CFTC for an exemption from the limits, and the agency, controlled by free-market advocates appointed by President George H. W. Bush, agreed.

In 2000, the Commodity Futures Modernization Act, passed by Congress at the end of the Clinton administration, exempted most over-the-counter derivatives — contracts negotiated between two parties — from the CFTC's oversight.

Trading soared. The number of futures and options traded on commodity exchanges quintupled between 2002 and 2008. [43]

Commodities looked increasingly attractive to pension funds, hedge funds and portfolio managers because other markets were drying up: The dot.com bubble had burst, the stock market plunged soon after and the U.S. housing market collapsed in 2007-08 when the subprime crisis hit. [44] And, as U.N. Rapporteur on the Right to Food Olivier de Schutter has described it, the growing attraction to commodities as sound investments can be explained by the simple belief that people "will always have to eat." [45]

Yet as the market grew, commodity prices appeared to some experts to be increasingly divorced from market fundamentals of supply and demand. "Over the years of deregulation, we've established a virtual market out there, and farmers are getting frustrated when they see [commodity price] changes are not always reflecting the actual fundamentals," FAO economist Abbassian says.

Green Revolution

In 1944, an American agronomist, Norman E. Borlaug, went to Mexico to help farmers boost their wheat crop under a partnership between the Rockefeller Foundation and the Mexican government. The wheat varieties introduced by Borlaug doubled yields in Mexico, and Borlaug's efforts soon became a worldwide movement, later dubbed the Green Revolution.

Borlaug, who received the Nobel Peace Prize for his work in 1970, became known as the father of the Green Revolution, widely acknowledged for boosting crop yields by bringing modern farming techniques, such as fertilizers and irrigation, to South America and Asia.

Wheat varieties dependent on fertilizer, like those that had been successful in Mexico, were introduced in the early 1960s in India and Pakistan, tripling yields there. The success with wheat was soon repeated with rice. The semidwarf rice variety IR8, developed by the International Rice Research Institute in the Philippines, tripled the tons per acre harvested in India between 1961 and 1970 and turned India into one of the world's leading rice producers. The high-yielding "miracle rice" was credited with saving millions from famine. [46]

Luckily, the Green Revolution emerged in Asia just before the 1972-74 world food crisis. The continent — by then enjoying bigger local harvests — was protected from the worst impacts of the price hikes. [47]

By the 1990s, nearly 75 percent of the rice grown in Asia came from Green Revolution seeds, along with about half the wheat planted in Africa, Latin America and Asia and about 70 percent of the world's corn. [48]

Meanwhile in China, agricultural productivity began to improve in the 1970s after the government made major policy changes and adopted technological innovations. Between 1978 and 1984, the Chinese Communist Party adopted economic reforms and reintroduced family farming. After more than 30 years of collective agriculture, small farmers were allowed to grow their own food and market their surplus. (This was an ideological reversal from Mao Zedong's disastrous Great Leap Forward, which aimed to increase industrial production by diverting thousands of peasants from private farms to factory work and converting their farmland to collective farming operations. Harvests plummeted, leading eventually to the great famine of 1959-61, which left an estimated 30 million dead.) [49]

The reforms returned more than 95 percent of China's farmland to approximately 160 million households, increasing rural incomes by 137 percent, reducing

CHRONOLOGY

1940s *Rockefeller Foundation begins funding crop research in Mexico that will evolve into a worldwide Green Revolution.*

1944 American agronomist Norman Borlaug teaches modern techniques to Mexican farmers, boosting wheat crops and launching Green Revolution.

1950s-1970s *China's collective farming experiment fails disastrously. Green Revolution boosts crop yields in developing countries. . . . United States becomes major grain exporter; China reintroduces family farming; Soviets expand livestock production, boost grain imports; Brazil improves its grasslands.*

1959-61 Collective farming in China causes deaths of 30 million Chinese due to famine.

1972-74 World food prices hit record highs after Soviet Union buys record amounts of U.S. wheat.

1973 Arab oil embargo contributes to rising food prices as farmers' costs of oil-based fertilizer, fuel skyrocket.

1975-76 Brazil launches its program to make ethanol from sugarcane, mandating that it be blended with gasoline to power a fuel-flexible auto fleet.

1978 U.S. Congress exempts ethanol from gasoline taxes.

1980s *United States and Europe have food surpluses; world corn prices hit record lows; ethanol incentives gain traction in United States.*

1990s *Market reforms after collapse of Soviet Union help reduce Russia's need for grain imports. . . . New speculators enter U.S. food commodities markets; share of world's hungry declines.*

1991 U.S. investment bank Goldman Sachs creates first index fund to track basket of commodities. . . . Soviet Union disbands on Dec. 31, 1991.

1998 Russia becomes net exporter of wheat for first time in quarter-century.

2000s *World food prices spike to record highs twice, triggering riots in 2008. . . . Congress deregulates commodity trading. . . . Russia becomes major wheat exporter.*

2000 Congress exempts most over-the-counter derivatives contracts from government oversight; commodities trading soars.

2006 United States passes Brazil as world's leading producer of ethanol.

2007 U.S. Congress mandates a tripling in production of renewable biofuels by 2022.

2007-2008 World food prices hit record high due to rising energy costs, falling grain stocks. Food riots break out in 60 countries.

2010s *Arab Spring revolutions follow spike in food prices. . . . Congress imposes curbs on commodities speculation. . . . Ethanol production absorbs 40 percent of U.S. corn crop.*

2010 After worst drought in a century, Russia bans wheat exports. . . . Bread prices surge in Egypt, Russia's largest wheat customer. . . . President Obama signs Dodd-Frank bill curbing speculation in commodities market.

Jan. 4, 2011 Street vendor Mohammed Bouazizi dies after setting himself on fire in protest, spurring revolution in Tunisia.

Jan. 25, 2011 Street demonstrations spread to Egypt, partly in response to high food prices, leading to overthrow of President Hosni Mubarak. . . . Protests and demonstrations break out throughout the Middle East.

February 2011 World food prices hit all-time high and then decline only slightly.

Nov. 3-4, 2011 G-20 nations scheduled to meet in Cannes, France; commodity-speculation measures are on agenda.

Can Ecological Farming Feed the World?

Ancient techniques are replacing conventional methods.

Thirty women gathered under a shade tree in the Malawi village of Koboko to answer questions from an American visitor about the biggest problem they face in producing enough food to feed their children.

The answer was surprising to consultant Roland Bunch, a prominent advocate of ecological farming practices. He was expecting to hear about the devastating droughts that had reduced people in Malawi to eating tree bark.

"Our soil is tired out. And it's getting worse every year," said one of the women. Soon others chimed in. "Our soil has become so hard that even when it rains, the water just runs off." Despite enough rain, one woman said she harvested only 27 bags of corn, compared to 35 the previous year. [1]

Over the following year, Bunch heard the same story in five other African countries — Zambia, Kenya, Uganda, Mali and Niger: Harvests were crashing, dropping 15 to 25 percent a year. Whole villages had been compelled to move in search of more fertile land; some were turned back by force at the borders by police.

Droughts and depleted soil are affecting much of eastern Africa, producing famine in Somalia and near-famine in Ethiopia. Some international organizations recommend providing either free or subsidized chemical fertilizers, since a bag of fertilizer is unaffordable for most small farmers. But as a leading proponent of agroecology — a farming philosophy that focuses on protecting the environment — Bunch says chemical fertilizers won't solve the underlying problem: the loss of organic matter that makes soils fertile.

Loss of soil nutrients, he warns, threatens to cause widespread famine — a result of climate change-induced droughts, a dearth of animal manure and farmers' inability to allow some fields to lie fallow and replenish themselves. The farmers say they must farm all their land every year just to survive.

Instead of chemical fertilizers, agroecologists use cultivation methods dating back to the Roman Empire, such as "green manuring" — planting a variety of crops together and leaving some to rot on the soil's surface after harvest — and planting trees on cropland to provide cooling shade and fallen leaves that rot into organic matter.

In West Africa's arid Mali, for example, the cliff-dwelling Dogon ethnic group have tripled their millet output per acre by interspersing cowpea legume plants, which add to soil fertility, with their millet and having herders bring their cattle in to stay overnight in the fields, leaving behind their manure.

Green manure cover crops are being used by more than a million farmers worldwide, mostly in Central and South America. Brazil is integrating trees, crops and livestock in the same fields as part of its strategy to boost its already impressive agricultural yields on once infertile grasslands. [2]

However, some critics say, despite reports of improvements for small-scale farmers like the Dogon, organic farming methods produce less food per acre than the Midwest's large-scale conventional farms, with their heavy dependence on artificial fertilizer. Adherents of organic farming answer that no large-scale comparative studies have been done to answer the question scientifically. Yet even those

rural poverty by 22 percent and increasing grain production by 34 percent. [50]

Russia's shift from wheat importer to leading wheat exporter also was shaped by its transition from a communist regime to a market economy, beginning in the early 1990s.

In the 19th century, the Russian Empire was the world's major wheat exporter thanks to a rich vein of black earth stretching through the Ukraine, Russia and southwest Siberia. Communism radically undermined that, however. Josef Stalin's forced collectivization of farms in the Ukraine destroyed the landowner farming

class and together with mass shipment of foodstuffs out of Ukraine to the Soviet Union resulted in the starvation deaths of 7 to 11 million Ukrainians in the 1930s. [51]

In the 1960s and '70s, Soviet leaders Nikita Khruschev and Leonid Brezhnev decided to improve the Soviet standard of living by increasing the population's consumption of meat and dairy products. To achieve this, the Brezhnev regime invested in large-scale livestock production and kept Soviet retail prices for meat virtually constant from the mid-1960s to 1990.

But, initially, the Soviet Union could not produce enough grain to support its growing livestock herds. In sympathetic to organic farming say it can't meet the planet's need to double food production in the next 40 years.

"You can't feed the world on organic broccoli," says Jonathan A. Foley, a climate scientist and director of the University of Minnesota's Institute on the Environment, noting that organic farming contributes less than 1 percent of today's agricultural production.

However, advocates of ecological agriculture point out, most of the world's farmland is cultivated by small farmers — not the agribusiness companies that account for most international trade. In addition, only 10 percent of the world's food is traded internationally, so low-cost ecological methods hold the most promise for improving small farms and local sustenance, they contend.

In a study of 286 projects in 57 developing countries that practiced some form of agroecology, Jules Pretty, an environment professor at England's University of Essex, found crop yields improved 79 percent, on average, over previous farming practices. [3]

Increasingly, as fertilizer gets more expensive, even large-scale Midwestern farms are practicing "no-tillage" methods — leaving crop waste behind to rot in the fields and replenish organic matter — and using satellite navigation to help spread fertilizer more efficiently and avoid wasteful double-dumping.

But acroecologists say even more radical change is required. "What we need now is more locally specific systems, unique to each place and environment — not the quick-fix menu offered by agribusiness out to sell products and not to feed the world," says Charles A. Francis, a visiting professor of agroecology at the Norwegian University of Life Sciences outside Oslo.

Many conventional farming techniques — such as those introduced during the Green Revolution in the 1960s and '70s — are becoming unsustainable in major food-producing areas like India's northwestern Punjab region, northern Mexico and Vietnam's Mekong Delta, where they are depleting and polluting groundwater, and pests and diseases are becoming resistant to chemical controls. [4]

"We don't want to drink all that stuff in the water and eat all that pesticide residue on food," Francis says.

But an international team headed by Foley proposes that in order to double global food production by 2050, when the world population is expected to reach 9 billion, both approaches will be necessary. Ecological practices will have to be incorporated into large-scale farming in order to boost yields while still protecting the environment. [5]

"Organic" is a feel-good label, but it doesn't necessarily tell you whether the farmer used water wisely or fostered biodiversity, Foley observes. The warring schools of organic and conventional farming, "need to put down our guns," he says. [6] "We don't have time for that anymore."

— *Sarah Glazer*

[1] Roland Bunch, "Africa's Soil Fertility Crisis and the Coming Famine," in "State of the World 2011," Worldwatch Institute, 2011, p. 59.

[2] *Ibid.*, p. 68. For Brazil, see "The Miracle of the Cerrado," *The Economist*, Aug. 26, 2010, www.economist.com/node/16886442.

[3] Worldwatch Institute, *op. cit.*, p. 20.

[4] *Ibid.*, p. 23.

[5] Jonathan A. Foley, *et al.*, "Solutions for a Cultivated Planet," *Nature*, Oct. 12, 2011, www.nature.com/nature/journal/vaop/ncurrent/full/nature10452.html.

[6] For background, see Kathy Koch, "Food Safety Battle: Organic Vs. Biotech," *CQ Researcher*, Sept. 4, 1998, pp. 761-784.

1972-73, to make up for its own poor grain crop, the Soviet Union secretly bought up most U.S. wheat exports at bargain prices — and even got American taxpayers to foot part of the bill through a farm subsidy. The so-called Great Grain Robbery sent world grain prices skyrocketing, and U.S. food prices jumped 18 percent. [52]

By the 1980s, the Soviets were the world's largest grain importers, much of it feed grain and soybeans from the United States.

The Soviet Union collapsed in 1991, and after the Russian Federation adopted market-oriented reforms in 1992 real wages fell and meat demand plummeted. Subsidies to livestock farmers were abruptly halted, contributing to the falling demand for feed grain. [53]

By 1998, however, Russia had become a net exporter of wheat for the first time in a quarter-century and remained a leading exporter through the 2000s. [54] By 2008-09, Russia was exporting all grains and was a major player in agricultural markets. [55]

Meanwhile, over the past 30 years Brazil has transformed itself from a net food importer to one of the world's great breadbaskets. Since 1996, it has increased its agricultural output ten-fold and now accounts for one-third of the world's soybean exports, second only to the United States.

Governments Set Biofuels Targets

Officials around the world are setting targets — some of them mandatory — for the use of renewable biofuels in transportation fuels. Some have specified a percentage of transportation fuels that should come from renewable fuels, while others established the number of gallons or tons to be produced. India wants 20 percent of transport fuels to come from biofuels by 2017, for instance, while the United States wants 36 billion gallons of biofuels produced by 2022 — the highest amount by far of any country. Diverting cropland to grow biofuels plants boosts food prices, critics say, but proponents say biofuels use only 5 percent of the world's food crops so they have only a "modest" effect on prices.

Biofuels Targets in Selected Countries
(as % of transport fuels or total volume to be produced)

Country	Biofuel target
European Union	10% by 2020
South Africa	4.5% by 2013
India	20% by 2017
Brazil	25% (of gasoline) and 5% (of diesel) by 2010
Canada	5% (of gasoline) by 2010; 2% (of diesel) by 2012
China	9.8 million tons (of ethanol) and 2 million tons (of biodiesel) by 2020
Japan	132 million gallons by 2010
United States	36 billion gallons by 2022

Source: "Meals Per Gallon: The Impact of Industrial Biofuels on People and Global Hunger," ActionAid, January 2010, www.actionaid.org.uk/doc_lib/meals_per_gallon_final.pdf

Its agricultural trade surplus has increased tenfold over the past decade, to more than $50 billion. [56]

Brazil used huge amounts of lime to reduce the acidity of the soil in its vast savannah grasslands, known as the *cerrado*, and brought in highyielding grasses to make it good for pasturing livestock. The area now accounts for 70 percent of Brazil's agricultural production. Brazil also crossbred soybeans, turning the traditionally temperate climate plant into a tropical crop. Recently, Brazilians have introduced some of the methods pushed by ecologists, such as growing trees between crop fields and "no-tillage farming," which leaves the husks of harvested crops to rot in the field to create fertile organic matter. [57]

From Surplus to Shortage

In recent history in the United States, overproduction was the perennial "farm problem." From the days of the Great Depression until the 1980s, American farmers experienced chronic surpluses and depressed prices, especially in wheat. To prop up prices, the federal government bought surplus crops and stored them or exported them as food aid to famine-stricken countries.

But by the 1970s, the government had found storing large stocks of surplus grain too expensive and took steps to reduce the surpluses. Grain reserves plummeted. As a result, even minor shocks to supply and demand could lead to dramatic price hikes.

Then harsh weather in 1972 and 1974, together with the massive grain purchases by the Soviet Union, created record spikes in world food prices.

Two other events helped contribute to a perfect storm for world food prices in the early 1970s. In 1971 President Richard M. Nixon devalued the dollar by taking it off the gold standard, making U.S. grain exports relatively cheap. World demand for American grain skyrocketed, and its price rose in response. [58] Then, in 1973 the Arab oil embargo caused world oil prices to skyrocket, causing general price inflation and increasing farmers' costs for petroleum-based fertilizer and transportation.

Surpluses and Low Prices

As more and more countries adopted high-yield Green Revolution seeds and farming techniques in the 1980s, food became plentiful and production grew faster than population growth. World food prices declined steadily in real terms. Most people assumed food would always be cheap, and many countries were lulled into depending on imports because they were a low-cost way of satisfying domestic food needs. By the end of the 1990s, the share of the world's population that was hungry would fall from a third to 20 percent. [59]

But cheap food was not good for American farmers. By the 1980s, corn prices were at record lows; a bushel of corn lost about one-fifth of its value over that decade. [60] Farm foreclosures proliferated throughout the Midwest as farmers found it hard to break even — despite the helping hand of government subsidies.

"Sometimes that was all your profit," says Boyd Smith, a farmer and farm manager in Lincoln, Neb. "A lot of times if your government payment was $20,000, that was your profit for the year. It was hard to make any money. . . . We were lucky to sell corn for $2 per bushel," he recalls, compared to the $7 price reached earlier this year. [61]

The strategy in the United States was to make "more production not higher prices the key to farmer income," writes Bjerga in his new book *Endless Appetites.* [62]

With each year, farmers like Smith were able to increase the number of bushels per acre through Green Revolution techniques. Lulled by these trends, governments began to cut back on agricultural research and development (R&D). Growth in U.S. agricultural R&D slowed from almost 4 percent per year in the 1960s and '70s to less than 1 percent today, according to the University of Minnesota's Pardey. Western aid for agricultural development to developing nations fell by almost half. [63]

Although yields per acre continued to grow, advances came at a much slower rate. The slowdown in spending occurred just as affluence in Asia began to rise, which would lead to more consumption of meat and grains.

"Our mindset was surpluses," explained Dan Glickman, former U.S. secretary of agriculture. "That just changed overnight." [64]

Prices Spike

With grain stockpiles low, prices doubled and in some cases tripled in 2007 and 2008. Once again (as in the 1970s) rising oil prices raised farmers' production costs, and a growing source of demand — biofuels — both reduced supplies and helped link the price of food even closer to rising fuel prices. Export restrictions and bad weather also contributed. [65]

Entire countries began hoarding food, and panic buying ensued, notably for rice. Food riots broke out in more than 60 countries, including Egypt, Haiti and Cameroon. [66]

In 2009, following the price spikes that began in 2007, an estimated 1 billion people went hungry for the first time.

Farmers responded to the higher prices by planting as much as they could, and healthy harvests in 2008 and 2009 helped to rebuild stocks. World prices declined in 2009, partly in response to the recession.

Last year, the U.S. Department of Agriculture predicted Russia would soon overtake the United States as the world's top wheat exporter by the 2010s because American farmers were shifting out of wheat to more profitable corn and soybeans. [67] But the department didn't count on the disastrous drought that hit Russia in mid-June 2010 and reduced its wheat crop by one-third. By Aug. 5, Russia had banned exports of wheat, barley, rye, corn and flour and then extended the ban into 2011. Wheat reached more than $8 a bushel — its highest price since 2008 — on the Chicago exchange.

The following month in Mozambique, where domestic wheat production covers only 5 percent of the country's needs, the cost for a sack of flour jumped 30 percent in one month. Protests erupted into riots, injuring 443 and killing 13, and forcing the government to reverse a hike in bread prices. [68]

By December 2010, the FAO announced, food prices had surpassed their 2008 peak.

That same month, vegetable seller Bouazizi set himself on fire in Tunisia, a country that imports twice as much food as it produces. Food prices were rising, and one-third of the work force was unemployed. Although Bouazizi's act of self-immolation was to protest police harassment, his burning in mid-December and his death on Jan. 4 triggered massive street protests that grew out of frustration over rising food prices, the lack of jobs and dissatisfaction with the government of President Zine El Abidine Ben Ali. Barely 10 days after the vegetable seller's death, Ben Ali fled on Jan. 15, and the government fell.

Meanwhile, Egypt, Russia's largest customer, was forced to buy more expensive American wheat after Russia banned wheat exports. The resulting spike in Egyptian food prices helped to spur the Jan. 25, 2011, uprising that would overthrow the regime in Egypt and trigger similar demonstrations and protests across the Arab World.

CURRENT SITUATION

Crisis Averted?

Although world food prices have dropped slightly since their all-time high in February, they remain above the record prices reached during the 2008 crisis, according to the FAO. [69]

High Food Prices Partly to Blame for African Hunger

It's not the "absence of food" but the price of it.

Sparse rains in East Africa have caused disastrous harvests and massive loss of livestock. The devastating drought has combined with skyrocketing food prices to create one of the world's worst hunger crises in decades, according to Save the Children, an independent global charity.

In Somalia, famine and ongoing civil conflict this year have forced tens of thousands of people to cross into neighboring Ethiopia and Kenya, further swelling already crowded refugee camps. [1] More than 12 million people are estimated to need humanitarian assistance in Somalia, Ethiopia, Kenya and Djibouti, according to the U.N.

By June prices for staples like corn had risen by as much as 107 percent over a year ago, according to the World Bank, due largely to low grain stocks, coupled with export restrictions imposed by Ethiopia and Tanzania. [2]

When staple prices jumped in May and June, it wasn't because a "complete absence of food" was causing widespread hunger but the high cost of food in the markets, says Michael Klosson, Save the Children's vice president for policy and humanitarian response, who recently returned from Ethiopia. "When you've got to feed your family, what do you do? You often substitute less nutritious food," he says, leading to malnutrition for the next generation. It also hurts children in other ways.

"Families have to spend so much on food, they forego health care," he continues. "Kids are pulled out of schools because families can't afford the fees and uniforms. Frequently kids have to go to work in situations that put them at risk."

Higher prices may be good for U.S. farmers, Klosson says, but in East Africa, "typically small shareholder families are not self-sufficient. They still have to buy food. It's not a win for them if food prices are going up."

— *Sarah Glazer*

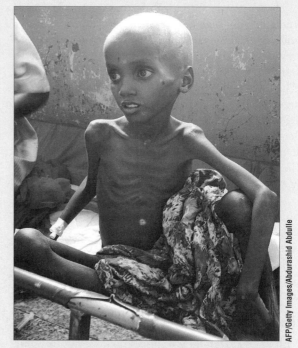

AFP/Getty Images/Abdurashid Abdulle

A severely malnourished child from southern Somalia is one of an estimated 12 million people in the Horn of Africa who need humanitarian assistance, according to the U.N. Skyrocketing food prices have contributed to one of the worst hunger crises in decades in the region.

---

[1] For background, see Jason McLure, "The Troubled Horn of Africa," *CQ Global Researcher*, June 1, 2009, pp. 149-176.

[2] World Bank, "Food Price Watch," August 2011, http://siteresources.worldbank.org/INTPOVERTY/News%20and%20Events/22982477/Food-Price-Watch-August-2011.htm#note5.

In the wake of export bans and disturbingly low global grain stocks, some experts — including FAO grain expert Abbassian — were warning at the beginning of the summer growing season that the 2008 disaster could be repeated.

"We have relatively good production, globally speaking, but not good enough to build inventories," Abbassian says. "As a result, we expect the 2011-12 season to be again one of quite strong price instability." The organization had

Are government biofuels incentives boosting food prices?

YES
Marie Brill
Senior Policy Analyst,
Anders Dahlbeck
European Campaigns Coordinator,
ActionAid International

Written for *CQ Global Researcher,* October 2011

NO
Rob Vierhout
Secretary-General European Renewable Ethanol
Association (ePURE)

Written for *CQ Global Researcher,* October 2011

Riots erupted and 100 million people fell into extreme poverty during the 2008 food crisis; last year another 44 million people joined them. The World Bank says biofuels account for 30 percent of the spikes in food prices, and new research blames government biofuel incentives as a contributing factor.

Global biofuels production has been driven largely by U.S. and European Union (EU) government incentives. EU blending mandates and financial incentives mean that about 9 percent of transport fuel will come from biofuels such as ethanol, biodiesel and biomass by 2020 — more than triple current levels.

Unable to meet this higher demand from domestic production, the EU imports biofuels, primarily from Brazil, but increasingly from Africa and Asia, where biofuel production often competes with food production. That generates food insecurity and helps reduce the global supply of arable land available for growing food. European biofuel production also risks diverting to developing countries the production of food for European consumers, putting further pressure on land and food supply.

Corn ethanol consumes 75 percent of U.S. federal renewable fuel dollars, benefiting from mandates, subsidies and a tariff on imports of foreign biofuel ingredients. This "incentive cocktail" inspired farmers to increase corn planting for ethanol. Today the United States burns 40 percent of its corn for fuel, more than is used for animal feed or human consumption.

American farmers are planting more corn, but weather shocks have depressed yields while growing demand for corn as food, feed and fuel have depleted stocks. Thus, corn prices are up. The United States controls more than 50 percent of the corn export market, tying U.S. corn prices to global prices. Global and local prices in developing countries are operating increasingly in tandem. In countries where food is heavily processed and transported, rising prices are broadly absorbed, mitigating the impact on consumers. Americans spend roughly 10 percent of their income on food, and 2011 prices will be up by only 4 percent. In import-dependent Uganda, however, the average consumer spends 63 percent of his income on whole foods, such as unprocessed grains, and the price of corn alone is 122 percent higher than last year. Such price increases devastate poor families.

Biofuels are not the only factor at play in rising food prices, but they're a key driver. Dropping artificial incentives can help relieve pressure on global food prices.

In 2008 record high food prices triggered riots in some parts of the world. At the same time, biofuels production increased, a sector that depends on policy supports to level the playing field with fossil fuels.

Certain groups were quick to blame the biofuels industry for condemning millions of people around the globe to starvation. Do away with biofuels incentives, and nobody has to go hungry, was the tune of the day.

But such thinking overlooks the fact that hunger is, unfortunately, not a recent phenomenon. We have seen famine in years where not a single drop of biofuel was produced.

In 2009 commodity prices fell back to almost pre-peak (2008) levels. But biofuels production continued to increase, demonstrating clearly that biofuels did not have a hand in the recent commodity price increases, or at least not the strong one that some interest groups wanted to make us believe.

While increased biofuel production induces an additional demand for the raw materials used to make biofuels, this link is generally both oversimplified and overestimated. It's oversimplified, because the industry is wrongly portrayed as producing only fuel, when in reality biofuel refineries yield many different high-value products that benefit the food chain. Co-products include, among others, protein-rich animal feed, food ingredients and carbon dioxide to carbonate drinks and improve horticultural practices.

The link is overestimated because demand from biofuel production is not the only thing causing prices for soft commodities, such as wheat, to go up. Speculation, bad weather and export restrictions also have an impact on food prices.

A myth is being created that biofuel production requires huge volumes of crops. But on a global scale, only a net 3 percent of all cereals are used for biofuels — too marginal to be the sole cause of fluctuation in commodity prices.

But, let's imagine that there was a price-effect induced by increased demand. This would provide an incentive for farmers in poorer regions to grow more crops. That seems a more sustainable way forward than exporting (dumping) the oversupply of commodities on African markets.

Higher yields and improved farming methods will ensure that supply can match demand, the very basis of price stability.

hoped for a 4 percent rise in global production to rebuild stocks but is now projecting only 3 percent growth, Abbassian says.

Whether a crisis develops, Abbassian says, depends partly on how much corn is produced in the United States, and the Agriculture Department recently revised estimates downward because of severe droughts in Texas and parts of the Midwest. Rice production in three big rice-producing countries — Cambodia, Egypt and China — is looking better than expected, he says.

"And that gives me a certain degree of confidence in saying the likelihood of a crisis in 2011-12 is probably less than we had in 2010-11," Abbassian says.

Although the Dodd-Frank legislation enacted last year was designed to curb commodities speculation, attention now is focused on how aggressive the Commodity Futures Trading Commission will be when it writes the regulations to enforce the law.

In an effort to curb commodities speculation by investors with no connection to the farming or food sectors, the law requires the agency to establish monthly limits on the amount of trading by speculators, both individually and as a group. [70]

After being deluged by at least 110 lobbying firms in the first quarter of this year (compared with 46 in the same period in 2010) the agency has delayed issuing regulations until the end of the year. [71]

Large banks are "spending a huge amount of money trying to undo [the proposals], shift the burden and delay the reforms that are targeted at them," Treasury Secretary Timothy Geithner recently told the House Small Business Committee. [72]

The U.S. rules-writing exercise is being closely followed in Europe, where similar curbs are under consideration. Recently though, according to several observers, enthusiasm has waned among European leaders who came out strongly for such limits last year.

Michel Barnier, the EU commissioner for internal market and services, proposed a regulation in September 2010 that borrows from Dodd-Frank, both in limiting the concentration of speculators and requiring mandatory reporting from those trading in over-the-counter derivatives.

Heidi Chow, an anti-hunger campaigner for the World Development Movement, calls these proposals "the key policy" for tackling speculation in the European Union.

However, Marc-Olivier Herman, Oxfam International's lead person on EU economic-justice policy, says Barnier already has "watered down" the proposal. Rather than setting out strict numerical limits on the positions speculators can hold, the proposal would give big market investors like pension funds a say in managing their positions, along the lines favored by Britain, according to Herman.

Another proposal pending before the European Commission would move unregulated trading of certain derivatives onto public exchanges, requiring reporting on their trading activity. It "will go a long way in achieving transparency of the huge over-the-counter market that caused the financial crisis," Herman says. But the proposal doesn't use that information to regulate the biggest traders, he says. "For Oxfam, the important issue is the relation between excessive speculation and food prices for poor countries. We believe [the EU] should be bolder because the potential harm is so great."

Similarly, G-20 members appear to be pulling back despite strong earlier statements by Sarkozy as France took over the G-20 presidency. "France [had] made strong comments about ways to curb speculation but came to the conclusion by the summer that the issue was market information," according to Abbassian.

When it comes to putting position limits on traders, says Chow, the British "are really resistant, and there's no real consensus among the G-20 countries about tackling it."

Action by the G-20 could come when finance ministers gather in Paris in mid-October or Nov. 3-4 at the G-20 summit in Cannes, France.

OUTLOOK

Climate Change

As food demand, energy prices and climate temperatures continue to rise over the long term, many experts say high food prices are here to stay.

Some are particularly worried by the impact of an increasingly affluent Chinese population, which already consumes about half the world's pork and whose per capita meat consumption grew 15-fold between 1960 and 2002. [73]

"That's going to have a huge impact on food prices," says Columbia University economist Schlenker. "That's part of why they've started buying land in Africa and other places; they want to secure their food supply." [74]

A recent report from the Worldwatch Institute, which found that global meat production tripled since the 1970s and is continuing to rise at a faster pace in 2010 than 2009, predicted that reduced pork supplies in Asia as a result of disease and expiring subsidies would translate into record pork exports from the United States to satisfy rising demand in South Korea, China and Japan. [75]

But other experts say China will satisfy most of its own demand within its borders, helped by some modest imports. Compared to Japan, which imports half its food, China only imports 1 percent, and isn't even among the world's top 10 food importers. [76]

Until 2005, China was a net exporter of food, according to the Paris-based Organisation for Economic Co-operation and Development. But in recent years, it has begun importing agricultural products, especially soybeans, on a large scale. [77]

"China will become a bigger net importer over the next 10 years, but it's a huge country and very worried about food security," says Scott Rozelle, an agricultural economist specializing in China at Stanford University's Freeman Spogli Institute for International Studies. "They don't want to become another Japan that imports half of its food. And they have relatively more agricultural resources to make sure that happens, so they're investing billions of dollars in research to increase productivity."

Some say cracks in China's self-sufficiency are just starting to show up. This year, one of every four soybean rows planted in the United States was being grown for Chinese export, and China's surprisingly large purchase of U.S. corn this summer prompted speculation that the Asian giant could become the biggest foreign buyer of American corn within the next 5-10 years. [78]

But FAO grain expert Abbassian is not worried about China's future demand. "China will eventually become an even bigger player in the world market in purchasing food," he says, but countries like Brazil, the United States and Argentina will be able to satisfy China's needs. "In 2020, we see China as a very modest importer of 5-6 million tons of grain, which is nothing for a country of over a billion people. Five to six million tons won't have any big impact on world markets."

If global temperatures rise and rainfall becomes less frequent, especially in already-arid regions, it will strain farmers' ability to continue producing increased yields, let alone meet current demand.

A recent widely discussed paper by Schlenker and Stanford University environmental scientist David B. Lobell finds that climate change has already knocked 3.8 percentage points off world corn yields and 5.5 percent off global wheat yields. [79]

Compounding these environmental problems, growing more crops for biofuels may worsen greenhouse gas emissions, rather than ameliorating them, according to two highly respected scientific groups on both sides of the Atlantic. In a report released in October, the National Academy of Science's National Research Council noted that clearing land to grow biofuel crops may "disrupt any future potential" for storing carbon in the soil. [80] In September, a scientific advisory committee to the EU also warned that clearing forests for biofuel crops releases "large stores of carbon into the atmosphere" and said EU governments had failed to take this into account when they began encouraging the production of biofuels. [81]

Farming already emits more greenhouse gases than all transportation combined. If agriculture continues on its conventional course, farmers will have to chop down more rain forests, destroy savannahs and pollute more waterways to grow enough food. But new interest in native crops, wild relatives of conventional crops, traditional sustainable cultivation and biotechnology discoveries may uncover plants that can survive amidst a warming climate and other challenges like the evolving resistance of pests and diseases to chemical controls. Increasingly, environmentalists and agricultural experts say it will be necessary to draw on both the wisdom of traditional farmers and the advances of modern agriculture to feed the world without destroying the planet.

"We're talking about the foundation of civilization," says Foley. "We can't afford to let anyone in the world go hungry. Hungry countries are unstable countries — places that could be very dangerous to the whole world."

NOTES

1. "Bouazizi," *Time*, Jan. 21, 2011, www.time.com/ time/magazine/article/0,9171,2044723,00.html.

2. World Bank, "Middle East and North Africa: Agriculture and Rural Development," 2008, http://web

.worldbank.org/WBSITE/EXTERNAL/COUNTR IESMENAEXT/0,,contentMDK:20528258~ pagePK:146736~piPK:226340~theSitePK:256299,00 .html.

3. Rami Zurayk, "Use your Loaf," *The Observer*, July 17, 2011, www.guardian.co.uk/lifeandstyle/2011/jul/17/ bread-food-arab-spring.

4. "The News Hour," PBS, Sept. 7, 2011, "Did Food Prices Spur Arab Spring?" www.pbs.org/newshour/ updates/world/july-dec11/food_09-07.html.

5. "Putin Says No Grain Exports Before 2011 Harvest," Reuters, Sept. 2, 2010, www.reuters.com/article/ 2010/09/02/us-russia-grain-idUSTRE68125 J20100902.

6. "Bread and Protests: The Return of High Food Prices," International Institute for Strategic Studies, March 2011, www.iiss.org/publications/strategic- comments/past-issues/volume-17-2011/march/ bread-and-protests-the-return-of-high-food-prices/ mobile-edition/?locale=en.

7. For background, see Roland Flamini, "Turmoil in the Arab World," *CQ Global Researcher*, May 3, 2011, pp. 209-236.

8. "Bread and Protests: The Return of High Food Prices," *op. cit.*

9. "Chinese Hunger for Corn Stretches Farm Belt," *The Wall Street Journal*, Aug. 17, 2011, http://online.wsj .com/article/SB1000142405311190355490457646 0300155681760.html.

10. World Bank, "Food Price Watch," February 2011, www.worldbank.org/foodcrisis/food_price_watch_ report_feb2011.html. Note: This increase occurred between June-December 2010.

11. These are USDA projections for the 2010/11 growing season, cited in World Bank, *op. cit.* The EPA recently approved plans to allow the use of 15 percent ethanol in newer cars. For the rule see www.epa.gov/otaq/ regs/fuels/additive/e15/index.htm#waiver. By law, the corn ethanol share of motor fuel must rise to 15 billion gallons by 2015. See Reuters, "Corn dominance to bend, not break," Sept. 30, 2011, http://us.mobile .reuters.com/article/environmentNews/idUSTRE78T 3CO20110930.

12. Alan Bjerga, *Endless Appetites* (2011), p. 78.

13. The G-20 is an economic forum for a group of 20 industrialized and developing countries.

14. Food and Agriculture Organization, *et al.*, "Price Volatility and Agricultural Markets: Policy Responses," Policy report to the G20, June 2, 2011, p. 15. Demand is projected to increase between 70 and 100 percent by 2050, while world population will increase from the current 7 billion to 9 billion, www.oecd.org/document /20/0,3746,en_2649_37401_48152724_1_1_1_374 01,00.html.

15. Worldwatch Institute, "State of the World 2011: Innovations that Nourish the Planet," 2011, p. 61.

16. Jonathan A. Foley, "Can We Feed the World & Sustain the Planet?" *Scientific American*, November 2011.

17. For background, see Doug Struck, "Disappearing Forests," *CQ Global Researcher*, Jan. 18, 2011, pp. 27-52.

18. Gregory Meyer, "U.S. Ethanol Refiners Use More Corn than Farmers," *Financial Times*, July 12, 2011, www.ft.com/cms/s/0/77dfcd98-ac9f-11e0-a2f3-00144 feabdc0.html#axzz1ZhlruBdj. Ethanol will use 40 percent of the corn crop from the 2010-11 growing season, which ended Aug. 31, 2011, according to USDA. Also see, David Biello, "Intoxicated on Independence: Is Domestically Produced Ethanol Worth the Cost?" *Scientific American*, July 28, 2011, www.scientificamerican.com/article.cfm?id=ethanol- domestic-fuel-supply-or-environmental-boondoggle& print=true.

19. Meyer, *op. cit.*

20. Biello, *op. cit.*

21. Javier Blas and Chris Flood, "Heavy U.S. Rains to Lower Corn Yields," *Financial Times*, June 10, 2011, www.ft.com/cms/s/0/b5a41a66-3714-11dd-bc1c- 0000779fd2ac.html#axzz1ZhlruBdj.

22. "Meals per Gallon," ActionAid, January 2010, p. 10, www.actionaid.org.uk/doc_lib/meals_per_gallon_ final.pdf.

23. "Price Volatility in Food and Agricultural Markets: Policy Responses," *op. cit.*, p. 27.

24. Javier Blas, "G20 Attacked on Food Crisis Plan," *Financial Times*, June 23, 2011, www.ft.com/ cms/s/0/aca4d56a-9da8-11e0-b30c-00144feabdc0 .html#axzz1ZuYetBKA.

25. Bruce A. Babcock, "The Impact of U.S. Biofuel Policies on Agricultural Price Levels and Volatility," International Centre for Trade and Sustainable Development, June 2011, Issue Paper No. 35, p. viii, http://ictsd.org/downloads/2011/06/babcock-us-biofuels.pdf. The 17 percent is the average result across 500 alternative future scenarios for 2011-12, modeled with varying supply/demand conditions, Babcock explained in an interview.

26. Murray Worthy, "Broken Markets: How financial market regulation can help prevent another global food crisis," World Development Movement, September 2011, www.wdm.org.uk/stop-bankers-betting-food/broken-markets-how-financial-regulation-can-prevent-food-crisis. Also see Peggy Hollinger and Javier Blas, "French Anger at Speculators Hits G20 Hopes," *Financial Times*, Feb. 3, 2011, www.ft.com/cms/s/0/d487b732-2efe-11e0-88ec-00144feabdc0.html#axzz1ZALNA6Sb. Also see: Olivier de Schutter, "Food Commodities Speculation and the Food Price Crises: Regulation to reduce the risks of price volatility," U.N. Special Rapporteur on the Right to Food, September 2010, www.srfood.org/index.php/en/component/content/article/894-food-commodities-speculation-and-food-price-crises.

27. Worthy, *op. cit.*

28. De Schutter, *op. cit.*, p. 3.

29. Lester Brown, "The Great Food Crisis of 2011," *Foreign Policy*, Jan. 10, 2011, www.foreignpolicy.com/articles/2011/01/10/the_great_food_crisis_of_2011. The number of additional diners each day cited in the article is 219,000.

30. "Price Volatility in Food and Agricultural Markets: Policy Responses," *op. cit.*, p. 10. FAO estimates that the global demand for food will increase between 70 and 100 percent by 2050.

31. Brown, *op. cit.*

32. Monsanto, "Producing More," www.monsanto.com/ourcommitments/Pages/sustainable-agriculture-producing-more.aspx.

33. Derek Headey and Shenggen Fan, "Reflections on the Global Food Crisis," International Food Policy Research Institute, 2010, p. 4, www.ifpri.org/publication/reflections-global-food-crisis.

34. Brown, *op. cit.*

35. For background, see Peter Katel, "Food Safety," *CQ Researcher*, Dec. 17, 2010, pp. 1037-1060; and David Hosansky, "Biotech Foods," *CQ Researcher*, March 30, 2001, *CQ Researcher*, 11, pp. 249-272.

36. Jonathan A. Foley, "Can We Feed the World & Sustain the Planet?" *Scientific American*, November 2011.

37. *Ibid.*

38. *Ibid.*

39. Headey and Fan, *op. cit.*, p. 82.

40. *Ibid.*

41. Michael Roberts and Wolfram Schlenker, "Identifying Supply and Demand Elasticities of Agricultural Commodities: Implications for the U.S. Ethanol Mandate," National Bureau of Economic Research, 2011. The United States produces roughly 23 percent of the four major grains worldwide, www.nber.org/digest/aug10/w15921.html.

42. Niall Ferguson, *The Ascent of Money* (2008), pp. 226-227.

43. de Schutter, *op. cit.*, p. 6.

44. For background, see the following *CQ Researchers*: Kenneth Jost, "Financial Crisis," May 9, 2008, pp. 409-432; Marcia Clemmitt, "Mortgage Crisis," Nov. 2, 2007, pp. 913-936; and David Masci, "Stock Market Troubles," Jan. 16, 2004, pp. 25-48.

45. de Schutter, *op. cit.*

46. "State of the World 2011," *op. cit.*, p. 30, 133-134.

47. Headey and Fan, *op. cit.*, p. 86.

48. For background, see Marcia Clemmitt, "Global Food Crisis," *CQ Researcher*, June 27, 2008, pp. 553-576.

49. Vaclav Smil, "China's Great Famine: 40 Years Later," BMJ, Dec. 18, 1999, www.bmj.com/content/319/7225/1619.full.

50. Worldwatch Institute, *op. cit.*, p. 13.

51. Askold Krushelnycky, "Stalin's Starvation of Ukraine," Radio Free Europe/Radio Liberty, 2003, www.ukemonde.com/news/rferl.html. Also see, www.historyplace.com/worldhistory/genocide/stalin.htm.

52. Bjerga, *op. cit.*, pp. 65-66. Also see, "Another Soviet Grain Sting," *Time*, Nov. 26, 1977, www.time.com/time/magazine/article/0,9171,919164,00.html.

53. "Food Security in the Russian Federation," Food and Agriculture Organization, www.fao.org/docrep/007/y5069e/y5069e03.htm.

54. Bjerga, *op. cit.*, p. 66.

55. William M. Liefert, *et al.*, "Russia's Transition to Major Player in World Agricultural Markets," *Choices*, second quarter 2009, www.choicesmagazine.org/magazine/article.php?article=78.

56. "Agricultural Policy Monitoring and Evaluation 2011," Organisation for Economic Co-operation and Development, 2011, p. 213, www.oecd.org/document/32/0,3746,en_2649_37401_48625184_1_1_1_37401,00.html.

57. "The Miracle of the Cerrado," *The Economist*, Aug. 26, 2010, www.economist.com/node/16886442.

58. Headey and Fan, op. cit., p. 89.

59. Justin Gillis, "A Warming Planet Struggles to Feed Itself," *The New York Times*, June 4, 2011, www.nytimes.com/2011/06/05/science/earth/05harvest.html?_r=3&ref=todayspaper&pagewanted=print.

60. Bjerga, *op. cit.*, p. 22.

61. For most of 2011 corn prices were above $7 a bushel but fell to $5.75 in early October. See Dan Piller, "Corn's Fall Continues," Oct. 3, 2011, *Des Moines Register*, http://blogs.desmoinesregister.com/dmr/index.php/2011/10/03/corns-fall-continues/.

62. *Ibid.*

63. Gillis, *op. cit.*

64. *Ibid.*

65. Headey and Fan, *op. cit.*, p. 89.

66. "Anti-government rioting spreads in Cameroon," *The New York Times*, Dec. 7, 2008, www.nytimes.com/2008/02/27/world/africa/27iht-27cameroon.10504780.html. Also See "Meals per Gallon," *op. cit.*, p. 14. Overall, world food prices increased by 75 percent. But the price for staple food grains like corn, rice and wheat jumped even more — on the order of 126 percent. For background, see Clemmitt, *op. cit.*

67. Bjerga, *op. cit.*, p. 66.

68. "Mass Arrests Over Mozambique Food Riots," BBC, Sept. 6, 2010, www.bbc.co.uk/news/world-africa-11198444. Also See, "Mozambique Bread Riots Spread as Police Shoot Protesters Dead," *Guardian*, Sept. 2, 2010, www.guardian.co.uk/world/2010/sep/02/mozambique-bread-riots-looters-dead?intcmp=239. Also see Bjerga, *op. cit.*, p. 68.

69. "FAO Food Price Watch," Food and Agriculture Organization, Oct. 6, 2011, www.fao.org/worldfoodsituation/wfs-home/foodpricesindex/en/.

70. de Schutter, p. 6. The act (PL 111-203) was signed July 21, 2010.

71. Josh Boak, "Wall Street Strikes at Regulations," *Politico*, July 10, 2011, www.politico.com/news/stories/0711/58644.html.

72. *Ibid.*

73. "Datablog: Meat Consumption per Capita," *Guardian*, Sept. 2, 2009, www.guardian.co.uk/environment/datablog/2009/sep/02/meat-consumption-per-capita-climate-change.

74. For background, see Jina Moore, "Resolving Land Disputes," *CQ Global Researcher*, Sept. 6, 2011, pp. 421-446; and Karen Foerstel, "China in Africa," *CQ Global Researcher*, Jan. 1, 2008, pp. 1-26.

75. Jesse Chang, "Meat Production and Consumption Continue to Grow," Vital Signs, Worldwatch Institute, Oct. 11, 2011, www.worldwatch.org/node/9055.

76. Headey and Fan, *op. cit.*

77. "Agricultural Policy Monitoring and Evaluation 2011," *op. cit.*, p. 223.

78. "Chinese Hunger for Corn Stretches Farm Belt," *The Wall Street Journal*, Aug. 17, 2011, *op. cit.*

79. David B. Lobell, Wolfram Schlenker and Justin Costa-Roberts, "Climate Trends and Global Crop Production Since 1980," *Science*, July 29, 2011, pp. 616-620, www.sciencemag.org/content/early/2011/05/04/science.1204531.abstract.

80. "Renewable Fuel Standard: Potential Economic and Environmental Effects of U.S. Biofuel Policy," National Research Council, 2011, p. 5, http://download.nap.edu/catalog.php?record_id=13105.

81. James Kanter, "Serious Error Found in Carbon Savings for Fuels," Green Blog, *The New York Times*, Sept. 14, 2011, http://green.blogs.nytimes.com/2011/09/14/serious-error-found-in-carbon-savings-for-biofuels/.

Also See: www.eea.europa.eu/about-us/governance/
scientific-committee/sc-opinions/opinions-on-scien-
tific-issues/sc-opinion-on-greenhouse-gas/view.

BIBLIOGRAPHY
Selected Sources
Books

Bjerga, Alan, *Endless Appetites: How the Commodities Casino Creates Hunger and Unrest*, Bloomberg Press, 2011.
The agricultural policy reporter for Bloomberg News explains the recent growth of commodities speculators in this fast-paced, entertaining account of the latest world food crises.

Worldwatch Institute, "State of the World Report 2011," Norton, 2011, www.worldwatch.org/sow11.
A collection of essays by experts, gathered by a Washington, D.C.-based environmental research organization, describes how the rediscovery of native vegetables and ecological farming methods in 25 sub-Saharan African countries is improving output.

Articles

Brown, Lester, "The Great Food Crisis of 2011," *Foreign Policy*, Jan. 10, 2011, www.foreignpolicy.com/articles/2011/01/10/the_great_food_crisis_of_2011.
Rising food prices and riots in the Middle East signal a broader environmental crisis that will make it harder to grow enough food, according to this environmentalist.

Foley, Jonathan A., "Can We Feed the World & Sustain the Planet?" *Scientific American*, November 2011, pp. 34-37.
University of Minnesota environmental scientist Foley explains how world food production could be doubled by 2050 without destroying the planet.

Gillis, Justin, "A Warming Planet Struggles to Feed Itself," *The New York Times*, June 4, 2011.
Scientists worry that warming temperatures from climate change will make it difficult to meet world food demand.

Kilman, Scott and Brian Spegele, "Chinese Hunger for Corn Stretches Farm Belt," *The Wall Street Journal*, Aug. 17, 2011, http://online.wsj.com/article/SB10001424053111903554904576460300155681760.html.
A surprise purchase of U.S. corn by China this summer raised speculation that the giant Asian country could become the largest importer of American corn as the Chinese appetite for meat grows.

Lobell, David B., Wolfram Schlenker and Justin Costa-Roberts, "Climate Trends and Global Crop Production Since 1980," *Science*, July 29, 2011, pp. 616-620, www.sciencemag.org/content/333/6042/616.full.html.
Researchers from Stanford and Columbia estimate that rising temperatures due to climate change have already reduced crop yields over the past 30 years in France, Russia, China and other countries.

Runge, C. Ford, "The Case against Biofuels: Probing Ethanol's Hidden Costs," *Yale Environment 360*, 11 March 2010, http://e360.yale.edu/feature/the_case_against_biofuels_probing_ethanols_hidden_costs/2251/.
A University of Minnesota professor of applied economics and law traces the U.S. ethanol industry's expansion since the powerful Midwestern farm lobby obtained government biofuel subsidies, which he says hurt both the environment and food prices for the poor.

Reports

"Financial Investment in Commodities Markets: Potential Impact on Commodity Prices and Volatility," Institute of International Finance, September 2011, www.iif.com/press/press+204.php.
This global association of large banks and investment managers counters the charge that new commodities speculators have boosted food prices and made them more volatile.

"Meals Per Gallon: The Impact of Industrial Biofuels on People and Global Hunger," ActionAid, 2010, www.actionaid.org.uk/doc_lib/meals_per_gallon_final.pdf.
European policies to expand biofuels production are pushing small farmers off their land and raising food prices in developing countries, according to this report from a Johannesburg-based group devoted to reducing global hunger and poverty.

"Price Volatility in Food and Agricultural Markets: Policy Responses," Food and Agriculture Organization, et al., June 2, 2011, www.oecd.org/document/20/0,3746,en_2649_37401_48152724_1_1_1_37401,00.html.
This report, prepared for the G-20, blames government biofuel mandates for driving up world food prices but says the jury is still out on whether commodities speculation also was boosting prices.

Headey, Derek and Shenggen Fan, "Reflections on the Global Food Crisis," International Food Policy Research Institute, Nov. 18, 2010, www.ifpri.org/pressroom/briefing/reflections-global-food-crisis.

An independent research institute blames the 2008 food crisis on rising energy costs, biofuels expansion, export restrictions and bad weather — not meat-eating in China.

Worthy, Murray, "Broken Markets: How Financial Market Regulation Can Help Prevent Another Global Food Crisis," World Development Movement, 2011, www.wdm.org.uk/stop-bankers-betting-food/broken-markets-how-financial-regulation-can-prevent-food-crisis.
This report from a London-based anti-poverty group blames the latest food crisis on commodities speculators.

For More Information

ActionAid International, 41 Rue du Commerce, 1000, Brussels, Belgium; 32 2502 40 28; www.actionaid.org/eu. Network of community groups around the world that advocates for rights for the poor; has been particularly active in reporting on "land grabs" by foreign biofuels companies that displace people in developing countries.

Earth Policy Institute, 1350 Connecticut Ave., N.W., Suite 403, Washington, DC 20036; 202-496-9290; www.earth-policy.org. An environmental organization founded by Lester Brown, an agricultural economist and expert on international agriculture, who has been called the guru of the global environmental movement.

Food and Agriculture Organization of the United Nations (FAO), Viale delle Terme di Caracalla, 00153 Rome, Italy; 39 06 57051; www.fao.org. A 191-member international organization that provides information about global food prices and supplies; focuses on improving nutrition levels and agricultural productivity.

Institute of International Finance, 1333 H St., N.W., Suite 800E, Washington, DC 20005-4770; 202-857-3600; www.iif.com. Represents world's largest banks and financial institutions in 70 countries; active on commodity speculation regulation.

International Food Policy Research Institute, 2033 K St., N.W., Washington, DC 20006; 202-862-5600; www.ifpri.org. Seeks sustainable solutions for ending hunger and poverty; one of 15 centers supported by the Consultative Group on International Agricultural Research, an alliance of 64 governments, private foundations and international and regional organizations.

Oxfam International, Suite 20, 266 Banbury Road, Oxford OX2 7DL, United Kingdom; 44 1865 339 100; www.oxfam.org. International confederation of 15 organizations working in 98 countries to find solutions to poverty and injustice.

Renewable Fuels Association, 425 Third Street, S.W., Suite 1150, Washington, DC 20024; 202-289-3835; www.ethanolrfa.org. Trade association for the renewable fuels industry in the United States.

World Development Movement, 66 Offley Road, London SW9 0LS, United Kingdom; +44 20 7820 4900; www.wdm.org.uk. Activist group working to defeat world poverty; [advocates ok???] commodities speculation regulation.

Worldwatch Institute, 1776 Massachusetts Ave., N.W., Washington, DC 20036; 202-452-1999; www.worldwatch.org. Independent research institute devoted to analyzing environmental issues of global concern.

Voices From Abroad:

HASSAN ZAMAN

Lead Economist, Poverty Reduction and Equity Group, World Bank

More than just agriculture

"Food security is about much more than food or agriculture. It's about ensuring adequate and nutritious food for every member of the household. This requires that people can afford to purchase nutritious food and so is clearly linked to income growth, particularly for the poor."

Pakistan Press International, February 2011

The Khaleej Times, UAE/Paresh Nath

ABDOLREZA ABBASSIAN

Food Economist, Food and Agriculture Organization, United Nations

More important to others

"High food prices are of major concern especially for low-income food deficit countries that may face problems in financing food imports and for poor households which spend a large share of their income on food. The only encouraging factor so far stems from a number of countries, where — due to good harvests — domestic prices of some food staples remain low compared to world prices."

This Day (Nigeria), February 2011

ALA'A AL DEEN MOUSA

Senior Researcher, Department of Economic Development, United Arab Emirates

Buffering prices

"For a country [United Arab Emirates] that imports so much of its food, a buffer stock is extremely crucial for times of crisis. Such stocks could even be used to absorb the shock of current high prices."

Gulf News (United Arab Emirates), March 2011

JOSETTE SHEERAN

Executive Director, World Food Program, United Nations

A reality for all

"We are on red alert, and we are continually assessing needs and reassessing plans and stand ready to assist. Rising food prices are a reality for the whole world, but they have the biggest impact on the poorest and most vulnerable populations."

UzReport (Uzbekistan), February 2011

NAZMEERA MOOLA

Director, Macquarie Bank, South Africa

Biofuel's drawback

"Estimates suggest biofuels have the potential to provide up to 27 percent of world transportation fuel by 2050. Unfortunately, biofuels often have a pernicious side-effect. They take food away from poor people by driving up the price of grains. Soaring food prices are far more disturbing to global political stability than rising energy prices. Ask many of the strongmen of the Middle East, or Marie Antoinette."

Financial Mail (South Africa), June 2011

414 INTERNATIONAL POLITICAL ECONOMY

DZULKIFLI ABDUL RAZAK

Vice Chancellor, Universiti Sains, Malaysia

A narrow focus
"Agricultural development focuses narrowly on increasing productivity rather than on the broader food and nutritional security of people. After all, freedom from hunger is the first requisite for sustainable human security."

New Straits Times (Malaysia), October 2011

JUDITH ROBERTSON

Director, Oxfam, Scotland

Hunger and history
"The food system must be overhauled if we are to overcome the increasingly pressing challenges of spiraling food prices, climate change and the scarcity of land, water and energy. We must consign hunger to history."

The Herald (Scotland), June 2011

ROBERT ZOELLICK

President, World Bank

Putting food first
"More poor people are suffering and more people could become poor because of high and volatile food prices. We have to put food first and protect the poor and vulnerable, who spend most of their money on food."

Guardian Unlimited (England), April 2011

16

Youth Unemployment

Reed Karaim

Rioting that lasted for five days in London and other British cities last summer was blamed in part on the lack of jobs — particularly among the young. Many believe if the issue of youth joblessness isn't addressed, countries around the globe will see further upheavals, but analysts differ on how closely youth unemployment can be connected to social unrest.

From *CQ Researcher*,
March 6, 2012

T he line of hopeful South Africans stretched for more than a mile. Many of the thousands standing outside the University of Johannesburg in January had come long distances and been waiting since the middle of the night.

But when the campus gate finally opened, the crowd surged forward so violently that a woman was trampled to death; several others were seriously injured.

In a country with a youth unemployment rate of 70 percent, the chance to get one of a few hundred openings at a South African public university is intensely competitive. For the prospective students — many accompanied by their parents — who rushed the gate, a college education is a crucial requirement for getting a decent job. [1]

The incident capped a year in which the frustrations of young people were on display from Tahrir Square in Cairo to the streets of Athens, Madrid and London. With youth unemployment stuck at staggering levels in many countries, finding work for an ever-growing number of jobless youths has become a pressing international issue, with economic prosperity, regime survival and social stability at stake.

While the average unemployment rate for people ages 15 to 24 stood at 12.6 percent worldwide in 2011, it was much higher in some individual countries, according to the International Labour Organization (ILO). The latest statistics for Spain and Greece, for instance, show youth joblessness rates of about 50 percent, and parts of the Middle East and North Africa had rates of more than 30 percent. [2] In both Europe, with a rate of 20.9 percent, and the United States, with an 18.4 percent rate, youth unemployment was about double the overall levels of joblessness. [3]

Youth Unemployment Highest in Arab World

Joblessness was higher among youths in the Middle East and North Africa over the past three years than in any other region and twice the global average of 12.7 percent, according to the most recent data available. Developed economies and the European Union also have above-average rates, with some individual countries — such as Spain and Greece — suffering from rates of around 50 percent.

Average Youth Unemployment Rates, by Region, 2008–2010

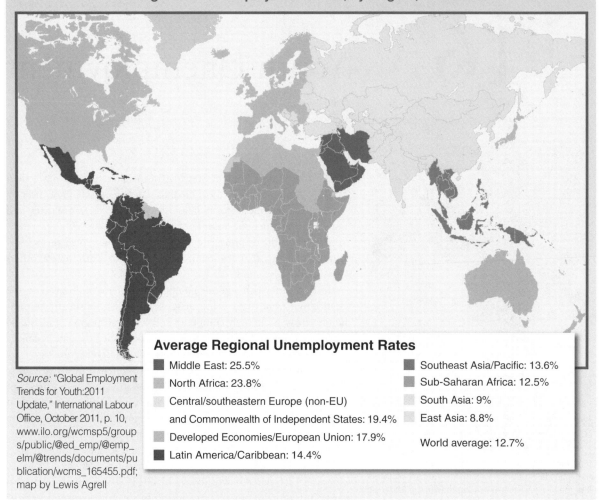

Average Regional Unemployment Rates

- Middle East: 25.5%
- North Africa: 23.8%
- Central/southeastern Europe (non-EU) and Commonwealth of Independent States: 19.4%
- Developed Economies/European Union: 17.9%
- Latin America/Caribbean: 14.4%
- Southeast Asia/Pacific: 13.6%
- Sub-Saharan Africa: 12.5%
- South Asia: 9%
- East Asia: 8.8%
- World average: 12.7%

Source: "Global Employment Trends for Youth:2011 Update," International Labour Office, October 2011, p. 10, www.ilo.org/wcmsp5/group s/public/@ed_emp/@emp_ elm/@trends/documents/pu blication/wcms_165455.pdf; map by Lewis Agrell

The difficulties facing young people looking for work are so severe that analysts describe the prospect of "a lost generation," whose delayed entry into the job market will leave them far behind, even after the world economy recovers. [4]

But experts disagree on how closely youth unemployment can be tied to social unrest. Most analysts see at least some link.

"There is a demonstrated link between youth unemployment and social exclusion that can translate into political and social instability," says Susana Puerto Gonzalez, officer-in-charge of the Geneva-based Youth Employment Network, a joint effort by the World Bank, ILO and United Nations to promote jobs for young people. "The inability to find employment creates a sense of uselessness and idleness that can trigger crime, mental health problems, violence and conflicts."

Educated young people were in the vanguard of the revolutions that marked the Arab Spring last year, which many observers say reflects dis-illusionment that Arab governments have failed to stimulate enough jobs for their growing youth populations. [5] "You grow up having faith in this idea that I'm going to study hard and get my college education and I'll be fine. But now they find out that isn't enough," says Sara Elder, an ILO economist in Geneva who studies youth employment. "The fallout of that is mistrust in the socioeconomic system, which is exactly what we're seeing."

Economists, demographers and political scientists debate the degree to which various factors cause high youth unemployment, but all agree the global economic downturn has played a leading role.

"At the peak of the crisis period in 2009, the global youth unemployment rate saw its largest annual increase on record," notes the ILO. Between 2008 and 2009, the rate rose from 11.8 to 12.7 percent — the largest annual increase over the 20 years of available global estimates. [6]

Young people usually are "the first out and the last in" during recessions, says Elder. Their lack of seniority makes them the easiest to let go, and their inexperience means companies are often reluctant to hire them when they begin refilling jobs.

Experts also point to more deeply rooted problems, particularly in the Middle East, parts of Europe and Southeast Asia. In Europe, for instance, generous job benefits and government policies that protect workers can make it more expensive to hire new employees. Wealthier societies also cushion the blow of unemployment, reducing the urgency

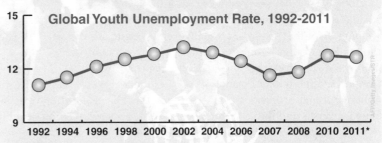

Youth Unemployment Remains High

Global youth unemployment declined during the economic boom in 2002-2007 and then began climbing again during the Great Recession. The projected 2011 rate is 12.6 percent — a full percentage point over the 2007 level, when unemployment fell almost to 1992 levels.

Global Youth Unemployment Rate, 1992-2011

*Projected

Source: "Global Employment Trends for Youth: 2011 Update," International Labour Organization, October 2011, p. 2, www.ilo.org/wcmsp5/groups/public/@ed_emp/@emp_elm/@trends/documents/publication/wcms_165455.pdf

of finding a job. "In developed countries, your parents are going to take care of you, the state is going to take care of you," notes Elder. "To some degree, you have the luxury of being unemployed."

Some analysts blame the problem on a disconnect between college curriculums and job markets in certain regions, notably the Middle East. Schools there "have been turning out people who are well-credentialed, but they don't have job skills," says Nader Kabbani, director of the Syrian Development Research Centre in Damascus.

In many developing countries, youth unemployment is driven in part by a surge in the number of younger citizens — what demographers call the "youth bulge" — which is particularly acute across the Middle East and North Africa. From Morocco to Iran, about 30 percent of the population is between the ages of 15 and 29, while only 20 percent of Western Europe's population is in that age group. [7]

Many countries in sub-Saharan Africa and South Asia also are seeing youth bulges, caused when death rates fall faster than birth rates. These increases in youth population pose a particular challenge.

"Two or three years ago, when people were really beginning to focus on the youth bulge, we talked about a billion new jobs being necessary to absorb the bulge," says William Reese, president of the International Youth Foundation, a worldwide youth development organization based in Baltimore, Md. "Well, about 90 percent of those billion jobs needed to be found in the developing world."

And while official unemployment numbers in many developing countries aren't as high as in Europe and the Middle East, analysts say that's often because people are scraping by in the "shadow" economy (which exists off the books), so they're only marginally employed and don't show up as seeking work. In developing countries, "people can't afford to be unemployed," says John Weeks, a distinguished professor of geography at San Diego State University and the co-editor of the book *The Youth Bulge: Challenge or Opportunity.* "If you're unemployed, you're dead."

Even when choices aren't that stark, millions of young people face difficult decisions as they confront their national job markets. For some, looking for work abroad has become the best option. Statistics on job-related migration are hard to come by, but economists and demographers agree it's gone up dramatically since the advent of the financial crisis.

For those who stay at home, frustration continues to mount, especially for the college educated, who once believed their degrees were a ticket to a better life. Abdul Rahim Momneh is one of a group of young Moroccans who stage almost daily protests in Rabat, the capital, with the hope of forcing their government to give them jobs.

"I have a degree, a master's degree in English," he said, "and I'm here . . . idle without a job, without dignity, without anything." [8]

As economists, demographers and political leaders try to deal with youth unemployment, here are some of the questions they are weighing:

Are we facing a "lost generation" of workers?

Analysts say the high unemployment rates for young people do not capture the full extent of the problem, because large numbers of young people have stopped looking for work.

In a report on youth employment, the ILO suggested the situation could lead to a " 'lost generation' made up of young people who detach themselves from the labour market altogether." And even those who eventually find work can suffer lasting consequences, the study said.

> *"I have a degree, a master's degree in English," he said, "and I'm here . . . idle without a job, without dignity, without anything."*
>
> — *Abdul Rahim Momneh, one of a group of youths who demonstrate almost daily in Rabat, Morocco, demanding jobs.*

"Numerous studies show how entering labour markets during recession can leave permanent scars on the generation of youth affected." [9]

The report touched off a wave of international commentary about the possibility that the lives of today's jobless youths could be permanently blighted. A delayed entry into the job market or a sustained period of unemployment early in someone's working life can have long-term consequences, which economists call "scarring."

Scarring occurs because wages rise for most people as they gain experience and seniority. Being unable to find work at the beginning puts people behind in their career track. "They will have lost precious time. Their skills will have depreciated. They're likely to have to accept jobs below their qualifications," says Glenda Quintini, an economist with the Organisation for Economic Co-operation and Development (OECD), a Paris-based coalition of 34 developed nations that works to promote democracy and free markets.

According to a British study, people who were unemployed for a year before age 22 were still earning 12 to 15 percent less — 20 years later — than they would have been earning if they'd not been unemployed. Shorter bouts of unemployment resulted in a smaller wage scar, but repeated periods of joblessness early in life had a cumulative effect that persisted for decades. [10]

"There are definitely going to be long-term consequences," Quintini says of the current rates of youth unemployment in many OECD nations.

Other analysts, however, believe young workers can catch up more quickly and say worries about a "lost generation" are exaggerated. "Young people who enter the labor market as a downturn is coming take about 10 years to catch up in wages," says Wendy Cunningham, a World Bank economist who formerly managed the

Helping Jobless Youth Develop "Soft" Skills

Punctuality and being a team player are highly valued.

Finding and holding down a job involves more than mastering a technical skill that is in high demand, say job-training experts. Equally important, they say, is having "soft" skills — the habits and social behaviors that make an employee a valuable part of the team.

Around the globe, in small programs and large, private groups are working to solve the youth unemployment problem, and helping young people develop soft skills is a big part of that campaign.

Two widely heralded approaches that have been the most effective are Entra21 — developed by the Baltimore-based International Youth Foundation (IYF), a worldwide youth development organization — and the smaller, Washington-based Education for Employment program.

With support from the Inter-American Development Bank (IDB) and the World Bank, both based in Washington, D.C., Entra21 has provided 20,000 young people with employment training and job placement services through 35 pilot projects in Latin America. The program targets "out-of-school, out-of-work teenagers," most of whom have attended school for only six or seven years, says William Reese, IYF president and CEO.

The youths receive 400-500 hours of training, including technical skills for jobs that are in high demand in the local community. Teens also receive training in life and professional skills, such as punctuality, working in teams and taking the initiative in problem-solving. The final stage is an internship with a company.

Initially, the World Bank and IDB thought teaching technical skills was the most important component of the program, Reese says. But employer surveys indicated that "all those softer things that are harder to put your finger on . . . were absolutely essential," he says.

The World Bank had hoped that at least 40 percent of the graduates would still be employed six months after graduating from the program. Instead, 55 percent were still employed and another 25 percent had gone back to school to get more training. "The bank was thrilled," Reese says.

Education for Employment, which has had similar results, operates on a smaller scale in the Middle East and targets "young people from very poor incomes and backgrounds," says Jamie McAuliffe, president and CEO. An applicant must have been out of work for six months and considered unlikely to find a job without the program.

Founded by Ron Bruder — a U.S. entrepreneur who became concerned about the lack of jobs for young Arabs after the 9/11 attacks — Education for Employment designs training courses for mostly mid-sized to larger private employers in the Middle East.

The program first started in Jordan in 2002 and now operates in six countries in the region. "We've graduated 2,500 young people and placed roughly 80 percent in jobs," says McAuliffe.

He attributes the program's success to the close working relationships the group has developed with potential employers, who commit to hiring acceptable trainees. As with Entra21, developing soft skills often turns out to be the "most critical and transformational" part of the program, McAuliffe says. "Time and time again our partners come back to us to say, 'We've just seen a real difference in the way your graduates are able to present themselves and operate in a business environment.' "

Education for Employment hopes to scale up its program in the next couple of years. McAuliffe says working with local partners has been critical for both financing and establishing credibility. And success depends on finding participants willing to be flexible about their future employment, he adds.

Economists debate the effectiveness of job-training programs, and critics say they show little long-term effectiveness. But Reese says he has found that the components of a successful youth jobs program include:

- Training in both professional and personal, or soft, skills,
- Providing the latest technical training based on local employer needs,
- Helping participants gain real-world experience through internships, and
- Providing job placement services.

"We know what works," says Reese. "What's missing is the political and financial commitment to take these things to scale."

— *Reed Karaim*

Thousands of students and parents push to get through the main gates at the University of Johannesburg in South Africa on Jan. 9, 2012, in a desperate attempt to register for the new academic year. A woman was trampled to death and several others were seriously injured during the stampede. In a country where 70 percent of the youths are unemployed and a college education is required to get a decent job, competition is stiff for one of the public university's few hundred openings.

children and youth division. "They do catch up, but not immediately."

Kabbani, at the Syrian Development Research Centre, has studied the impact of unemployment on young Syrians. He believes the long-term situation is not so bleak, particularly for young people in Europe and the Middle East, which have a substantial portion of the world's unemployed college graduates. "It's definitely a loss, but I wouldn't go so far to put it in generational terms," he says. "They're smart people; they're fairly well educated. Many of them will eventually catch up."

But as the global economic downturn drags on in Europe and elsewhere, some fear that when employers finally do return to hiring they will look toward the newest crop of graduates, bypassing those with lengthy periods of unemployment or a series of "make-do" jobs on their resumes. "There is some concern they will be skipped over," notes ILO economist Elder. That's what happened in Japan, which experienced rising youth unemployment in the 1990s and early 2000s. [11] In effect, many employers chose to start fresh with unscarred young workers.

And even if they return to the job force, workers may be "lost" as fully productive members of society in others ways. Studies show that prolonged joblessness can have long-term

mental health and even physical implications. A study in the 1980s found that many of the formerly unemployed suffered lingering feelings of failure and doubts about their abilities, which persisted after they returned to work. [12]

"The long-term scars of unemployment can be cruel, particularly as regards mental health, confidence and assertiveness," says Gonzalez, at the Youth Employment Network.

Unemployment also can affect life expectancy. A study of workers who lost their jobs in the 1970s and '80s found that they had a lower life expectancy, and the impact was greater for young unemployed workers. [13]

Other researchers say the mental-health impact of unemployment has been overstated and that even those who are unemployed for a lengthy period usually recover over time. [14] "In fact, most people cope well with this event and report few long-term effects on their overall well-being," said lead author Isaac Galatzer-Levy, a psychiatric researcher now at the New York University Langone Medical Center. [15]

However, Galatzer-Levy and his colleagues confined their study to the unemployed who were at least 21 years old. Younger people, they found, responded more poorly to not being able to find work.

In any case, lasting effects limiting the ability of younger workers to realize their full potential in life have ramifications that go beyond their individual struggles, say several analysts.

"You can imagine that there's a generation of young people in some countries that is scarred in this way, and that's very expensive for all of us," says Mattias Lundberg, senior economist in the Human Development Network at the World Bank. "If we have to sacrifice the economic gains from productive employment of young people, that's an enormous loss to the entire country."

Does education reduce youth unemployment?

A college education has long been considered the ticket to a better job. That belief is so fundamental it has fueled an explosion in the number of young people enrolling in higher education around the world. [16] "The literature is just plain overwhelming on the benefits of going to college," said Philip Altbach, director of the Center for International Higher Education at Boston College. [17]

But some analysts say youth unemployment trends in several countries indicate that higher learning no longer guarantees that a college graduate will be in more demand when he enters the job market. "There have always been expectations that a good education leads to a good career. This is no longer the case," says Gonzalez of the Youth Employment Network in Geneva. "The link between youth employment and education is more and more weak, as other factors come into play."

She cites unemployment trends in several Middle Eastern and North African countries that have invested heavily in education. The average number of years of schooling in the region "have grown nearly five times over the last five decades," she says. Yet the area's youth unemployment rates were among the highest in the world, even before the worldwide recession that began in 2008. In 2010, a quarter of the region's youths had no jobs, compared to the worldwide rate, which was half that. [18] Those countries now have "millions of young, educated unemployed," Gonzalez notes.

Higher education in these countries has not kept up with the changing nature of the job market, says Ragui Assaad, a professor of public affairs at the University of Minnesota, currently studying Egyptian labor market reforms in Cairo. Most of their economies have been government controlled and most of the best jobs — which provide better benefits and lifetime employment — were in government bureaucracies.

Today, however, only about 15 percent of college graduates in Egypt will be able to get a public-sector job, Assaad says, which remains the goal of most graduates. "This is the legacy of 40 years of policy in which the public sector was the dominant force in the economy," he says. "There was an implicit promise that anyone who got a college degree, or even a high school degree, would get a job in this sector."

Universities and students have reflected that bias by focusing on degrees, such as Arabic studies or English literature, that confer societal prestige but have little connection to the private job market, says Kabbani, of the Syrian Development Research Centre. Schools also have

Youth Joblessness is Double Adult Rate

The jobless rates for youths in Europe, Japan and the United States are more than twice the adult rates. Similar disparities exist in the developed countries that make up the Organisation for Economic Co-operation and Development (OECD).

Youth (15-24) and Adult (25-54) Joblessness in Selected Countries and Regions (First quarter, 2011)

* Includes Japan, United States, 21 EU countries and 11 other developed countries.

Source: "OECD Employment Outlook 2011," Organization for Economic Cooperation and Development, 2011, www.oecd.org/document/46/0,3746, en_2649_33729_40401454_1_1_1_1,00.html

poor job-placement services, and graduates have little idea what private employers require in terms of performance and behavior.

As a result, ironically, the more education you have in Egypt and other countries in the region, the more likely you are to be unemployed. Frustration over that realization played a significant role in the region's political upheavals last spring, observers say. "There is a sense of a broken social contract," says Assaad.

But the World Bank's Lundberg says inadequate education remains a barrier to productive employment in much of the developing world, particularly sub-Saharan Africa and South Asia, where secondary and higher education lags behind the rest of the world and illiteracy rates remain high. [19]

And even in other parts of the globe, labor experts say the right education still makes a big difference.

"It's not about the quantity of education, it's about the quality of education," says the World Bank's Cunningham. "We have the most educated youth ever, when you're talking about average education, but . . . we're increasingly hearing [from] employers that young people don't have the skills they want." Technical and

British musicians Ms. Dynamite and Charlie Simpson demonstrate in London, on Oct. 11, 2011, to help raise awareness of Britain's 1 million unemployed youths. The coalition government recently announced creation of a "Youth Contract" program to spend £1 billion subsidizing private youth employment, but some economists say government programs do little to increase jobs for young people.

vocational skills remain in high demand, she says, but vo-tech education programs often are stigmatized as a lesser career path.

The OECD's Quintini notes that the high number of unemployed youth means many European employers are placing a premium on educational attainment. "Having a secondary qualification [equivalent to a U.S. high school diploma] is now essential," she says. "The basic requirement is to reach that level of education. In fact, some countries are starting to impose compulsory education up to 18." And in the United States, research continues to indicate that college graduates are more likely to be employed. [20]

Still, it's not just the Middle East and North Africa where a diploma, even a college diploma, no longer means what it once did. China has strong economic growth with relatively low unemployment, but the number of Chinese students attending universities or other institutions of higher learning has mushroomed.

"Within the last 10 years, the share of China's population with higher education degrees has more than doubled," says Anke Schrader, a researcher at The Conference Board's China Center for Economics and Business in Beijing. Yet, even though the number of jobs in industries

requiring highly skilled labor — such as finance, scientific research and information technology — is growing rapidly, "China's overall employment base is still built largely on low-cost, low-skilled type work," she says.

At the end of 2010, the 9.3 percent official unemployment rate for college graduates was more than double the official average jobless rate in urban areas. Chinese official unemployment rates are calculated somewhat differently than in the West. With the annual output of graduates, "the urban labor market has not kept up with creating equal numbers of high-skilled, high-paid jobs for workforce entrants without work experience," she notes.

In several European nations, lack of economic growth and an entrenched, older work force has forced many college graduates to settle for temporary work or make-do jobs outside of their chosen professions. The situation is particularly difficult in Greece, Italy, Spain and Ireland. [21]

Iris Murumagi, 28, is grappling with the kinds of challenges often faced by even highly educated young people in those countries. She has a graduate degree in biology and previous work experience in microbiology in her native Estonia. After moving to Ireland to be near her boyfriend, she began applying for jobs last March.

"I applied for loads and loads of jobs," she says. "I applied for a job a day but got less than an interview a month."

After 10 months, Murumagi found work. "It's a fundraising job, asking people to sign up for charities," she says. "It's a tough job. It's not my profession or anything. But it's a job."

Should governments do more to address youth unemployment?

In Spain, more than half of the workers between ages 16 and 24 are unemployed — the highest youth unemployment rate in the developed world. [22] Nearly half of Greece's young people are unemployed, as are youths in Italy, Ireland and parts of Eastern Europe. [23]

With such high unemployment rates, it's not surprising that some of the most strident calls for increased government action on youth unemployment have come from inside the European Union. The European Youth Forum, an organization of national youth councils and nongovernmental youth groups from across the continent, has called for a "standardized youth guarantee that will offer young people a job, training or retraining within four months of unemployment." [24]

CHRONOLOGY

Early 20th Century *As world population explodes, economic growth manages to keep pace in the West. Swelling younger populations add to social unrest.*

1900 World population stands at 1.6 billion.

1930s U.S. and European birth rates fall during the Great Depression, when unemployment rates top 20 percent in developed nations.

1946-1964 Western world experiences baby boom after World War II ends.

Mid-to-Late 20th Century *China has a baby boom as it recovers from failed "Great Leap Forward" economic program.*

1964-1968 Led by baby boomers, youth protests break out in the West over civil rights and the Vietnam War.

1989 Chinese baby boomers' grown children demand greater freedom during demonstrations in Beijing's Tiananmen Square; army crushes the protests.

2000-2009 *Younger populations soar in the developing world. Youth unemployment drops during a booming economy but rises again as Great Recession strikes.*

2000 World population reaches 6.1 billion. Higher-education enrollment reaches 100 million worldwide, 200 times the number of a century earlier, providing the world with the largest educated pool of young job seekers in history.

2002-2007 Despite youth bulges around the world, youth joblessness falls during strong economic growth, reaching its lowest rate in 2007.

2008 Worst global economic downturn since the Great Depression takes hold. Youth unemployment begins to climb.

2009 Overall youth unemployment jumps from 11.8 to 12.7 percent, the biggest one-year increase on record, with some countries experiencing significantly higher rates.

2009 Ireland's youth joblessness triples in two years; 30,000 young Irish workers leave the country each year seeking work abroad.

October 2009 U.S. teen joblessness hits 27.6 percent, a post-WWII high.

2010-Present *Youth joblessness remains high. Social unrest, led by young people, spreads across Arab World.*

2010 World population reaches 6.9 billion, with most of the growth in developing countries, where half the population is under 25.

August 2010 International Labour Organization (ILO) warns of "lost generation" of youths due to lack of jobs.

Dec. 19, 2010 Mohammed Bouazizi, a 26-year-old Tunisian fruit seller, frustrated at police harassment, sets himself on fire. His act triggers Arab Spring protests and revolutions.

2011 Massive rallies protesting the lack of opportunity and injustice spread to Egypt, Algeria, Libya, Yemen and other countries, including Syria. Jobless Egyptian college graduates play leading role in ousting President Hosni Mubarak, toppled after 20 years in power. . . . In May, protests by jobless youths sweep across Spain as youth unemployment climbs past 45 percent. . . . Riots break out among young people in London and other English cities in August. Analysts debate how much high youth joblessness is to blame. By November, youth unemployment in Britain tops a record high 1 million, as joblessness reaches 21.9 percent among young people.

2012 ILO warns the world must create 600 million new jobs in the next 10 years to cope with existing unemployment and young people joining the workforce. . . . Youth unemployment in Spain reaches 51 percent, the highest in Europe. European leaders pledge on Jan. 30 to use untapped funds to address youth unemployment.

Desperate Youths Emigrate to Seek Work

But they don't always get a warm welcome.

Liam Allen, a 23-year-old Irishman who went to college to become a videographer, graduated into an Irish job market devastated by the global financial crash. "There's just no room in the industry for new people to come in," he says.

Determined to find a job in his profession, he chose the route embraced by a growing number of young people in many nations with high youth unemployment: He went abroad to search for work.

Youth joblessness in Ireland jumped from 9 percent in 2007 to 27.5 percent in 2010, but the International Labor Organization (ILO) believes it would be 19.3 percent higher if many Irish young people hadn't decided to remain in school or simply stopped looking for work. [1]

Migrating in search of a better life has a long tradition, of course, and had been on the rise even before the economic downturn. In the past, immigration primarily had been from developing to developed countries. Between 2000 and 2005-2006, the influx of migrants from Latin America and Africa into 34 developed nations jumped more than 30 percent, according to the Organisation for Economic Co-operation and Development in Paris. [2]

But the Great Recession and its aftermath changed the picture. Although overall numbers are hard to come by, analysts agree that job-seeking young Europeans increasingly are looking outside their national borders.

The National Youth Council of Ireland, for example, noted that between 2004 and 2009, the number of emigrants under 25 nearly doubled — from 15,600 to 30,000. [3] Spain, which has long been a magnet for immigrants from Spanish-speaking developing countries, recorded a net emigration of 50,000 people in 2011. Argentina, with its strong economy, is a popular destination, especially for Spanish-speaking emigrants. [4]

Greece, Italy and Portugal also are seeing a significant exodus. "Italy is one of the worst. There's absolutely no possibility of advancement for so many educated young people there, so they're just leaving," says Sara Elder, an economist with the International Labour Organization in Geneva, Switzerland. "They're all leaving, and they leave with a great sense of sadness."

At the same time, increased immigration has roused political passions in the countries where the job-seekers are moving. In Great Britain, MigrationWatch UK stirred up controversy when it blamed much of the country's youth unemployment problem on immigration from Eastern Bloc nations. The group pointed out that during the same period that British youth unemployment was rising by nearly 450,000, the number of Eastern European migrants working in the U.K. growing by 600,000. [5]

But Britain's Institute for Public Policy Research pointed out that immigration had been increasing for some time before youth unemployment soared and accused MigrationWatch of cherry-picking the years in order to blame foreigners for England's problems. [6]

In the United States, illegal migration remains a potent political issue, blamed by many for growing U.S. unemployment. But during the recession, government data indicate that illegal immigration was declining significantly when youth and overall unemployment in the United States was soaring. [7]

The group also has called for more scholarships to help young people go back to school and sufficient support through European government safety nets to keep young people from falling into poverty. Finally, the organization believes "young people should have the right to personalized career counseling and guidance . . . to help find a tailored solution to unemployment." [25]

But proposed programs for dealing with rising youth unemployment in Europe have faced a backlash from those who believe government should get out of the way of free enterprise. In Great Britain, the coalition government's announcement last winter of a "Youth Contract," designed to spend £1 billion subsidizing private youth employment drew a dismissive retort from Eamonn Butler, director of the Adam Smith Institute, a conservative think tank in London.

"Another . . . government 'initiative' is not the way to get young people into work," Butler said. Instead, he said the government should "reduce the cost and the risk that employers face when taking on young people. We

While the public often views immigrants as a threat and laments the exodus of its own young people, Wendy Cunningham, a World Bank analyst, notes the actual effects are less clear. Migrants often send significant amounts of money back home while filling labor needs in their new home countries.

"There's a big question about whether migration is good for the sending country and good for the receiving country," she says. "It's not at all settled."

As for Irishman Allen, he found a videographer job in New York City. But he was hardly alone. "I met a lot of people, Irish people, who left college over there and came to New York to find a job," he says. "It was crazy." Allen returned to Ireland after his visa expired but hopes to return to Manhattan, where his former employer has promised him a job as soon as he can get a new work visa. He is upbeat about his prospects, joking that leaving the country to look for work has become "almost a coming-of-age thing" in Ireland.

Yet, he also sums up the frustration of many young people when he compares his circumstances to those of past college graduates. "You look at those people who are five to 10 years senior, and you think, you guys just had it all," Allen says. "You came out at the right time."

— *Reed Karaim*

Getty Images/Joe Raedle

With high rates of unemployment in their home countries, many young people are going abroad to find work, such as Stephen Masterson, 23, from Northern Ireland, who found a construction job in Nantucket, Mass.

[3]"Youth Unemployment in Ireland: The Forgotten Generation," National Youth Council of Ireland, January 2011, www.youth.ie/sites/youth.ie/files/Youth_Unemployment_in_Ireland_web.pdf.

[4]Wolf Richter, "Europe's Youth Unemployment Crisis is Leading to an Exodus," *Business Insider*, Feb. 1, 2012, http://articles.businessinsider.com/2012-02-01/europe/31011916_1_immigrants-oil-and-diamonds-angola.

[5]Macer Hall, "East European Surge Blamed for 1M Young Britons Being On Dole," *The Daily Express*, Jan. 9, 2012, www.express.co.uk/posts/view/294457/East-European-surge-blamed-for-1m-young-Britons-being-on-dole.

[6]Matt Cavanaugh, "The right tries to blame youth unemployment on immigration — again," *The New Statesman*, Jan. 9, 2012, www.newstatesman.com/blogs/the-staggers/2012/01/immigration-unemployment.

[7]Julia Preston, "Number of Illegal Immigrants in U.S. Fell, Study Says," *The New York Times*, Sept. 1, 2010, www.nytimes.com/2010/09/02/us/02immig.html.

[1]"Global Employment Trends for Youth: 2011 update," International Labour Organization, 2011, p. 4, www.ilo.org/empelm/pubs/WCMS_165455/lang--en/index.htm.

[2]Sarah Widmaier and Jean-Christophe Dumont, "Are Recent Immigrants Different? A New Profile of Immigrants in the OECD based on DIOC 2005/06," Organisation for Economic Co-operation and Development, Nov. 29, 2011, www.oecd-ilibrary.org/social-issues-migration-health/are-recent-immigrants-different-a-new-profile-of-immigrants-in-the-oecd-based-on-dioc-2005-06_5kg3ml17nps4-en.

need to get rid of the minimum wage, which is pricing young people out of starter jobs, and radically cut back workplace regulation." [26]

But at an appearance in January at the World Economic Forum, ILO Director-General Juan Somavia said the size of the youth unemployment problem demands a wide-ranging response from both governments and the private sector. He suggested incentives to promote youth employment, including hiring subsidies, training grants and career guidance. [27]

Somavia rejected the notion that government regulations have made it too difficult for employers to hire or fire employees. "The problem is not the flexibility of the labor markets," he said. "The problem is how do we agree that job creation is the central objective of economic policy. The question is how do we change the mix of policies [to help young people] because if we continue this way, the issue of a lost generation is going to be real." [28]

James Sherk, a senior policy analyst in labor economics at the conservative Heritage Foundation think tank in Washington, says government job programs aren't the answer. "Most youth employment programs have been shown not to work," he told a joint U.S. congressional economic committee. [29]

Previous U.S. jobs programs such as Job Corps, Job Start and the Job Training and Partnership Act were ineffective, he said. And the record is even clearer across the Atlantic, he continued. "European nations have created far more extensive youth job programs than America has because they have much higher youth unemployment," he said. "Evaluations of these programs come to similar conclusions. Public training, wage subsidies and direct government job creation have generally not worked."

Sherk echoed Butler's call for a lower minimum wage and said reducing government barriers to entrepreneurship and wealth creation will spur employers to hire. "A stronger overall labor market is the best way to help young and low-skilled workers," he said.

The ILO sharply rejected that view in its 2011 update on youth unemployment. "It is not enough to give the economy a little boost and then step back and let the recovery take its own course to eventually absorb the bulk of young jobseekers. Such an approach might have worked if the current recession was not proving to be as deep and structurally rooted as it is," the report concluded.

"Short term fixes are not enough," it continued. "Sustained support of young people, through expansion of the social protection system, long-term investment in education and training, hiring subsidies to promote employment of young people, employment intensive investment, sectoral policy, etc., is needed now more than ever." [30]

European Union leaders recently announced plans to use part of 82 billion euros in untapped EU funds to address youth unemployment, although they did not specify what actions they might take except pledging to help establish apprentice programs. [31]

Still, the ILO's Elder has been encouraged by government proposals around the world to address the problem. "I do think they're trying," she says, citing President Obama's proposal, The American Jobs Act, which would provide tax credits for hiring the long-term unemployed and subsidize successful approaches to hiring low-income youth and adults. "Obama's doing a lot of what we would advise," she adds. "Targeting the long-term unemployed is a good idea."

The Youth Employment Network's Gonzalez, however, cautions that research into the impact of youth employment programs, including the U.S. Jobs Corps, indicates their benefits deteriorate over time — participants enjoy a boost from initial employment but show scant improvement in long-term earnings or employment.

"There is little evidence on what works to support young workers," she says, adding there is a need for careful evaluations "that can give us an idea of what and why certain interventions help youth to find or stay in a job."

BACKGROUND

Youth Bulges

Many countries had to deal with youth bulges in the 20th century, providing both lessons and warnings for countries struggling with the frustrations of unemployed youth today.

A youth bulge is not the same as having a young population. In fact, throughout most of human history, the average age of the population was younger than today, because disease and hardship killed many people before they could grow old. In *The Youth Bulge: Challenge or Opportunity*, the authors point out that, until the early 20th century, life expectancy was rarely more than 40 years and was closer to 20 in most societies. Infant mortality was so high women had to have many children just to keep the population from dying out. [32]

That began to change, first in Western nations, with advances in modern hygiene, sanitation and medicine. Increased prosperity and the establishment of relatively stable political systems also played a role. But the authors, San Diego State University's Weeks and adjunct professor of geography Debbie Fugate, note that children benefit the most when conditions improve and death rates decline. When infant and child death rates fall, families eventually begin having fewer children — but it takes a while for families to change their behavior.

The result is a youth bulge — a generation significantly larger than those before and after it, which moves through society as it ages like a pig in a python. The "baby boom" that followed World War II in America and other Western nations was one example. Japan experienced a similar boom at about the same time; Korea had one in the mid-1950s and a Chinese baby boom peaked in the late 1960s and early '70s. [33]

Youth bulges present challenges to a society throughout their existence. When the mass of young people begins moving into adult society and looking for work, a nation can find itself struggling to absorb the influx.

"A bulge in itself isn't a problem, a bulge coupled with a low job-growth rates is a problem," says the World Bank's Cunningham.

Indeed, Weeks, Fugate and others point out that in a vibrant economy a youth bulge can bring an infusion of energy and talent that leads to even greater prosperity, as occurred in the 1960s, when the baby boomers came of age in the West. "The economic progress made in these already-rich countries would not have been nearly so dramatic had [they] not responded positively to the challenges created by the baby boomers and turned those challenges into opportunities," Weeks and Fugate observe. [34] Japan, South Korea and China also managed to put youth bulges to work, benefiting their societies overall.

But many of those countries had advantages that countries now dealing with youth bulges lack: They were already comparatively wealthy and had free-market economies. Most were also democracies, generally more able to respond to the changing demands of their populations.

The economies in many less developed parts of the world have not been able to keep pace with their growing populations, a situation exacerbated because demographic shifts are occurring more quickly as medical knowledge and other advances rapidly move from country to country, Weeks notes. "The population of the average country in sub-Saharan Africa, for example, is currently growing at a rate of 2.5 percent per year," he and Fugate write. "These countries can expect that 41 percent of their population will be under age 15, with 68 percent under the age of 30." [35]

At that rate, a country's population doubles in 40 years, or about a generation and a half. Demographers and other analysts note that when a youth bulge presents the greatest potential for social disruption as it reaches the age range of 15 to 29 — old enough to take part in adult society but not necessarily to have settled into a job or family life. If such a generation feels alienated or unfairly treated, it may believe it has nothing to lose.

"It certainly is dry tinder, ready to burn. All it takes is a spark. Quite literally, that's what we saw in Tunisia," says Weeks, referring to the self-immolation of Tunisian

> *"They will have lost precious time. Their skills will have depreciated. They're likely to have to accept jobs below their qualifications."*
>
> *— Glenda Quintini, Economist, Organisation for Economic Co-operation and Development, Paris, France*

peddler Mohamed Bouazizi. The 26-year-old vegetable vendor set himself on fire after a policewoman confiscated his cart and officials refused to listen to his appeal, part of a pattern of harassment that had frustrated his efforts to support his family.

Bouazizi's death is widely seen as having triggered the Arab Spring. [36] The young people that spilled into the streets in Tunisia were at the forefront of a regional revolution, but they also harkened back to a long history in which young people have manned the barricades against what they perceived as injustice.

Joblessness and Unrest

Educated, frustrated youths were at the forefront of revolutions throughout modern history, according to Jack Goldstone, a sociologist at George Mason University School of Public Policy in Arlington, Va., who specializes in social movements. "It was true in the Puritan revolution in 1640s" in England, Goldstone says. "It was true in the French Revolution in the 1780s and all across Europe in the revolutions of 1848." But a large youth population does not necessarily mean social unrest or revolution, he points out.

However, youths are less patient with perceived injustice and inequality in a society and more prone to react, even in a wealthy democracy. A wave of civil rights and anti-war protests swept through the United States as the first American baby boomers reached adulthood in the 1960s.

But, he notes, educated young people can't sustain a revolution on their own. The 1989 Tiananmen Square protests were led by college-age Chinese born during a similar baby boom in China; but without the support of the larger public, their protest was crushed by the army. During the Arab Spring, however, educated young people were joined by working class people of all ages with similar

> *"There have always been expectations that a good education leads to a good career. This is no longer the case. The link between youth employment and education is more and more weak."*
>
> — Susana Puerto Gonzalez, Officer in charge, Youth Employment Network, Geneva, Switzerland

frustrations. "Then you have a situation in which the youth are kind of like a hammer pounding on a table that's already cracking," he says.

In the past, Goldstone notes, educated youths often were in the vanguard because they were attending university, which brought together a concentration of young people being educated to think about big issues. But in today's wave of unrest, social media such as Facebook and Twitter have replaced the college coffee shop. In the Middle East, "young people who had more education and more access and comfort with social media were concentrated in the cities," he says, "and they were the easiest to bring out."

While the technology has changed, many of the motives remain the same, however. In the revolutions that swept across Europe in the 1840s, young people were frustrated because they felt their progress was being blocked by privileged groups who monopolized wealth and power, Goldstone points out. While in the past, "it might have been nobility and church leaders" who monopolized power, in Arab countries today, "the privileged groups were cronies of the leaders."

Some analysts do not find a direct connection between high youth unemployment and social unrest or violence, while other studies find that a lack of opportunity played a role in the discontent, such as in last summer's riots in London. [37] The riots, which included widespread looting and arson over the course of five days, began after police shot Mark Duggan, a 29-year-old man in Tottenham, North London, during an arrest. But the protests soon spread to include other parts of London and other cities. Much of the violence was concentrated in poorer neighborhoods with higher rates of unemployment.

The OECD's Quintini sees further evidence in other violent protests. "There seems to be a relationship and a correlation," she says. "If you think of France and the social unrest we had a few years ago, you would have seen that it came from areas of high unemployment."

The ILO's Elder, however, notes that youth unemployment has been high in Arab nations for 30 years, and young people had remained largely passive about the situation. "You have to ask yourself what has changed," she says. "I would say the unemployment of young people is a definite factor, but there is something bigger that brought them out into the street, and that has to do with social networking and this movement of social democracy. They've realized they're not alone, and they've finally gotten over their fear."

Youth unemployment is higher in several European nations, including Spain and Ireland, than in the Middle East, yet protests in those countries have been relatively peaceful. The same is true in sub-Saharan Africa, which is experiencing youth bulges that are as transformative as those in the Arab world.

CURRENT SITUATION

Developed Nations

The Great Recession still casts a giant shadow over millions of unemployed youths, but today's youth unemployment also is tied to longer-term cultural and political problems. Until the global economy recovers, analysts say, youth unemployment also is likely to remain a significant problem, especially in countries with the worst youth joblessness.

But even when the economy recovers, other issues will remain, experts say, with different countries facing different types of labor market challenges. Europe, for instance, includes countries at both extremes of the youth unemployment picture. Spain and Greece have two of the highest youth joblessness rates, but the rates in Germany, Austria and the Netherlands — which have extensive apprenticeship programs — are under 10 percent. [38]

Apprenticeships give youths work experience before they enter the job market. In Germany, a quarter of employers provide apprenticeships and nearly two-thirds of students take advantage of them. Students in vocational schools work as paid, part-time employees for two to four years while in school. The government and the employer share the cost. At the end, most apprentices expect their positions to turn into full-time jobs. [39]

"It's creating high quality jobs and a very positive image for their vocational education system," says Quintini of the German apprenticeship system. "Even the best of their students will go into it, and at the end, they actually have a job waiting for them."

Spain, in contrast, adopted a system of "temporary" contracts for younger workers, essentially creating a separate category of employees who can be let go and replaced more easily than permanent employees. Because Europe's labor protection laws and generous job benefits make it difficult and expensive to hire and fire full-time employees, temporary contracts were supposed to make it easier for companies to give younger workers a chance, which could then lead to full-time employment.

Instead, says the World Bank's Cunningham, "What seems to be happening . . . is young people just live from temporary contract to temporary contract." Temporary workers get little chance to advance their careers, and the high EU administrative costs for hiring or firing an employee work against younger people when a full-time opening becomes available. "Employers feel safer hiring somebody with references, a background where they can observe their previous experience," Quintini says.

Studies also have found that some European youth unemployment is caused by "churning," or trying out different jobs before settling on a career, Cunningham notes. The relatively generous benefits of European welfare states cushion the blow of unemployment, allowing young people to be choosier. "A more generous social safety net allows you to search in better conditions, so it's not such a bad thing in one sense," says Quintini, "but it can create an incentive to remain unemployed for a longer time."

Often, in countries with the highest youth unemployment, the older, permanent employees have set up barriers to protect their jobs. For instance, a 1992 Greek law established higher payroll taxes for new employees (and their employers) than those paid by workers who already have a job. More than two-thirds of Greek employees are at least 43 years old, according to one tally. [40] An Italian plan to relax rules for laying people off, which the government hopes will make it easier to hire young people, has drawn heated union opposition.

"This would damage the rights of all workers in order to help the young," said Vincenzo Scudiere, an official with CGIL, Italy's largest union. [41]

Youths in Asia's developed economies have fared better than those in most European nations during the downturn. Japan and South Korea had youth unemployment rates of about 10 percent in the latest ILO report. [42] South Korea's economy has remained strong, while Japanese corporations traditionally avoid layoffs by offering early retirement and reducing hours or salaries. [43]

Although the U.S. labor market is generally considered more flexible than Europe's, the United States still had an 18.4 percent youth unemployment rate in 2010, nearly double the rate for the nation's overall labor force. [44] But youth unemployment in the United States is concentrated in a younger age group than in Europe.

"In the U.S. you see record levels of teenage unemployment, particularly concentrated among some minorities," says Quintini. In fact in October 2009, U.S. teenage unemployment reached 27.6 percent, the highest since World War II, according to the OECD. [45]

U.S. teenage unemployment began to decline in 2010, although it continued to climb for some minorities. The unemployment rate of African-American teenagers, for instance, reached 43 percent in the first 11 months of 2010. "Historically, youth in this group have had the worst prospects on the labour market," the OECD notes, "and the recent rise in unemployment increases the risk that they will withdraw from the labour market and remain trapped in inactivity for a number of years." [46]

Emerging Nations

China, Brazil and India — the three largest emerging world economic powers — all rebounded quickly from the global downturn. Yet, the sheer size of their populations (China and India are the two most populous nations in the world, while Brazil ranks fifth) presents a continuing employment challenge. Despite their growing economies, for example, large segments of their populations still earn mostly a subsistence living.

In India, for instance, more than half of the population works on farms, and 30 percent of the population was surviving on less than $1.25 a day. [47] Many work in the informal economy, so their employment does not figure into unemployment statistics. Youth and overall unemployment is estimated at around 10 percent, but the larger problem remains underemployment and the lack of education of poorer workers. [48]

Does high youth joblessness lead to political instability?

YES
Henrik Urdal
Senior Researcher, Peace Research Institute, Oslo, Norway, and Research Fellow, Harvard Kennedy School

Written for *CQ Global Researcher*, March 2012

NO
Mattias Lundberg
Senior economist for Human Development Network, Children and Youth, World Bank

Based on an address to the Alliance for International Youth Development in October, 2011

When Tunisian vegetable vendor Mohamed Bouazizi self-immolated in December 2010, he set fire to a movement that transformed the Arab world. Frustrated young people — like the underemployed 26-year old Bouazizi — fueled the Arab Spring with their rage against undemocratic governments whose failed policies have created some of the world's highest youth joblessness rates.

Demography links youth unemployment to political instability. Statistical studies indicate that exceptionally large youth populations — or "youth bulges" — are associated with an elevated risk of armed conflict and other forms of instability.

Studies also have shown that large youth bulges experience higher rates of joblessness, on average, than smaller ones. And when the labor market cannot absorb a sudden surplus of young job seekers, a large pool of unemployed youths will generate high levels of frustration that could morph into protest movements or rebel organizations.

What can governments do to avoid instability in the face of youth bulges? Notably, a plentiful youth population can be a demographic bonus, given the right conditions. For instance, large youth bulges accounted for a third of the miraculous economic growth of the "Asian Tiger" economies of South Korea, Taiwan and Singapore. The bonus opportunity arises as fertility declines, if that decline is accompanied by stable political conditions and the availability of educated workers.

Governments often respond to youth bulges by expanding education, which works, to some degree. An empirical analysis of 120 countries over 40 years showed that boosting secondary education significantly lowered a country's risk that a youth bulge would ignite conflict. But expanding education also can lead to "elite overproduction" if such expansion is not matched by job opportunities. The result can be a large group of politically and economically alienated but highly mobilizable youth. Arguably, that may have contributed to last year's Arab Spring, since the most educated Arab youths experienced the highest unemployment rates.

Youth bulges will continue to challenge frail governments. In troubled countries such as Afghanistan, Yemen and the Palestinian areas, the number of youth ages 15 to 24 will grow by more than 40 per cent over the next 10 years. Providing greater economic opportunities to youth will not only build the economy of these countries but also significantly reduce the risk of political instability.

Reports of joblessness and disaffection among youths are growing across the globe, from China to Egypt to London. Does this mean unemployed young people are prone to violence to achieve their goals and redress grievances?

After the World Bank completed the World Development Report in 2007, I went on a sort of book tour, and among the few things that came up in conversation everywhere — almost a refrain or chorus — were jobs and violence. Implicitly, and sometimes explicitly, the link was made between the two. This concern was uppermost in the minds of public officials: If we don't find something for the young people to do, they'll get angry and throw us out of office. Well, in many cases they were right.

That said, I want to refute the widely-held belief that unemployment among young people necessarily leads to violence. The argument makes intuitive sense — that young people are tempted to engage in violence — both as a mechanism for the expression of frustration and because unemployment lowers the opportunity cost of criminal and violent activity. There's even a new book on the "precariat" class — the growing pool of increasingly frustrated and ostensibly dangerous young people and migrants.

But this intuition is not borne out by the evidence. As Christopher Cramer's background paper for the 2011 World Development Report on violence said: "There is no remotely convincing evidence . . . to support the claim that unemployment is a mechanistic causal factor in violent conflicts in developing countries. The evidence on youth unemployment is even weaker."

So why does youth unemployment matter? It matters because it determines welfare, equity, productivity, growth, personal and collective identity and social cohesion. Unemployment at any point in life makes people unhappy. Unemployment while young lowers morale and self-esteem and increases the rate of depression; it makes people ill, increasing the likelihood of poor physical health, including heart disease, in later life. Unemployment in early life reduces lifetime earnings and increases the risk of future unemployment. This is costly for the young person and a waste to society.

These should be sufficient grounds for decisive policies to foster labor demand and structural shifts in employment, provide opportunities for expression and improve the lives of millions of young men — and especially young women — stuck at the bottom of the labor market pile.

Likewise, Brazil's economy has a huge informal sector, which is "the main labor market segment to receive the unemployed," even though "they do not want to be there," according to Cunningham. [49] Brazil's 2009 youth unemployment rate of 17.8 percent is roughly three times as high as the country's overall jobless rate. [50] And while the country has expanded private higher education dramatically in recent years, many young people still cannot find formal employment.

In Latin America, the overall youth unemployment rate was 18.5 percent in 2009, but the impact of the global recession is reflected in the fact that nearly 20 percent of young people in the region are neither studying nor looking for work, according to the ILO. "Fewer young people were looking for jobs . . . when [youths] perceive there are no jobs, they just don't look for one," said Jurgen Weller, an economist at the Economic Commission for Latin America and the Caribbean in Santiago, Chile. [51]

China has a complicated youth employment situation. The growing number of un- or under-employed college graduates present a challenge, but the continued growth in manufacturing has led to strong demand for unskilled labor, much of which is supplied by the ongoing migration of young people from rural areas to urban centers, where manufacturers seek young, affordable employees.

"To a certain degree this trend improves bargaining power for young, low-skilled workers" the China Board's Schrader observes. Overall unemployment rates remain remarkably low compared to other nations.

Developing Nations

Although countries as disparate as Egypt and Ethiopia often are grouped together as part of the developing world, their economies and educational systems are different enough that one cannot generalize about the youth unemployment problems.

In sub-Saharan Africa and the poorest parts of Latin America and Asia, the World Bank's Lundberg notes, youth unemployment is closely linked to the challenge of boosting overall economic development. Many of these countries have high illiteracy rates and largely agricultural economies. Their ongoing youth bulges are a huge challenge.

"Sub-Saharan Africa and South Asia . . . are the areas where the United Nations Population Division projects that virtually all population growth between now and the half century is going to occur," says San Diego State University's Weeks.

China's Huzhong University of Science and Technology graduates a small academic army — more than 7,780 students — on June 23, 2010, joining the more than 6 million students who graduated from college in China in 2010. The share of China's population with university degrees has more than doubled in a decade, but the country's employment base is still built largely on low-cost, low-skilled jobs. Thus, China's 9.3 percent unemployment rate for college graduates in 2010 was more than double the nation's average in the cities.

Vusi Gumede, an associate professor in development studies at the University of Johannesburg in South Africa, offers one of the harshest assessments of conditions for young people in the region. "The troubles confronting young people are, arguably, Africa's most vexing policy challenge," he wrote. "A striking common thread is that the young person in Africa is poor, unemployed, out-of-school, and living in a rural area — and possibly angry." [52]

Yet Lundberg notes that, despite high levels of youth unemployment, most of these countries so far have avoided the kind of mass unrest that occurred last year in the Middle East and North Africa. After last year's revolutions, young workers in that region face a vastly different political scene than they did just a year ago.

Yet, several cultural conditions that led to chronic high youth unemployment still remain, contributing to uncertainty about the future. Although educated youths were in the forefront of the mass protest movements that overturned governments from Egypt to Tunisia, surveys indicate that a majority of college graduates still hope to get a public sector job.

Cultural pride and family support make college graduates less likely to take a job that they feel is beneath their status. In the Middle East and North Africa there is "this kind of tolerance — the family structure is set up so you can just stay at home for years, not working, until you get a job," says Cunningham.

If Arab graduates want better job prospects, experts say, they must start looking for jobs in the private sector and adjust to lives without the guaranteed lifetime employment their parents enjoyed working for the government. They also will have to embrace a more entrepreneurial spirit and be willing to take on new career challenges, employment experts say.

But these changes won't be easy. "The question is, 'Can you, at a real basic level, renegotiate the social contract [and] change social norms?' " says Kabbani. "It's not just about another youth program."

Kabbani's research included a survey of young people in Syria, which found that despite the nation's political upheavals, roughly four out of five still felt they had a right to employment in the public sector. The persistence of old attitudes is also on display in Morocco's capital of Rabat where the regular protests by unemployed graduates are aimed at getting government jobs, not more opportunity in the private sector. And every so often, government responds by hiring some of the graduates.

Still, a euphoric feeling of new possibilities has gripped the young in several Middle Eastern countries after their successful protests last spring. Salmin Eljawhari, a 22-year-old from Benghazi, Libya, says many of her friends had looked for work for years, but "they didn't give up." She recently entered a dental training program herself, but she views the emergence of a new civil society in Libya as the most "beautiful" thing she has seen.

"The role of the youth in the Arab spring revolutions and especially in Libya was the most important, because they had the real desire for change," she says. "I am sure things will be better. Sure, it will take time. Maybe longer then we expect, but in the end we will take our rights and fight corruption everywhere to have a better future for us and for the next generation."

OUTLOOK

Global Resource

Whether it's in families or nations, the young are generally regarded as the best hope for the future. The recent youth unrest that has roiled many countries,

> **"So we have a billion young people, mostly underemployed," he says. "That's a wealth of human capital and talent that we'll find a way to take advantage of sooner or later."**
>
> **— Mattias Lundberg, Senior Economist, Human Development Network, World Bank**

particularly in the Middle East, has cast the young in a different light — frustrated and deeply skeptical of social and political structures they believe have limited their opportunities.

But many of the experts continue to see the current population of young people just beginning their working lives as a global resource. The World Bank's Lundberg notes that there are more than 1 billion people today between the ages of 15 and 25, the largest youth population in human history, with the great majority of them in developing countries. "So we have a billion young people, mostly underemployed," he says. "Wouldn't you think, if we take a step back, that's a fantastic opportunity? That's a wealth of human capital and talent that we'll find a way to take advantage of sooner or later."

While attention has been focused on the Arab nations and Europe, Lundberg notes that several African countries have been making progress in establishing civil societies and laying the groundwork for stronger, more diversified economies. He hopes these seeds will bear fruit 10 or 15 years down the road.

"Ethiopia is a good case in point," Lundberg says. "They've been investing in education and health. I really hope they will become better integrated into the world economy, and young people will be able to take advantage of the opportunities that come with that. I hope there are factory jobs in Ethiopia. That would be a fantastic outcome."

Looking at the future from Cairo, Professor Assaad believes things will get better. "I'm pretty optimistic, if you're looking that far down the road, because the youth bulge will translate into a high working population, with people in their productive years. They will have made the transition into the labor market, so demographically we're going to be in a better position than we are now."

Weeks, of San Diego State University, also sees some reason for optimism about the Middle East, pointing out that the birth rates already are declining in the region. But he is less optimistic about the future of sub-Saharan Africa and parts of Asia, where the vast bulk of population growth is projected to occur between now and 2050.

"You've got countries that are growing rapidly without an apparent job base that can support all these young people," he says. "The resources, at the moment, just aren't there."

In the developed world, an economic recovery is expected eventually to bring down unemployment. Once strong growth resumes, "there will be a sense of a much brighter future," Weeks predicts.

ILO economist Elder, however, points out that the toll for many jobless individuals will likely be felt for some time, citing studies showing it can take a decade to recoup lost earnings. "Even 10 years is quite significant," she says.

And even with a growing global economy, Cunningham believes many countries, particularly in Europe, will need to adopt new labor rules and approaches to help integrate young people into their job markets. Education and attitudes about work also must change to fully address the problem.

"There isn't a quick fix for the youth unemployment problem," she says. "We need to accept that there isn't, and this isn't going to change overnight. There just isn't a magic bullet."

NOTES

1. Lydia Polgreen, "Fatal Stampede in South Africa Points Up University Crisis," *The New York Times*, Jan. 10 2012, www.nytimes.com/2012/01/11/world/africa/stampede-highlights-crisis-at-south-african-universities.html.

2. "Global Employment Trends for Youth: 2011 Update," International Labor Office, 2011, p. 1, www.ilo.org/empelm/pubs/WCMS_165455/lang--en/index.htm. Also see "Eurozone unemployment hits Euro-era high," The Associated Press, Jan. 31, 2012, www.cbc.ca/news/world/story/2012/01/31/eu-record-unemployment.html.

3. "Unemployment Statistics," Eurostat website, Dec. 15, 2011, http://epp.eurostat.ec.europa.eu/statistics_explained/index.php/Unemployment_statistics. See also, *ibid.*, table 6.

4. Naomi Powell, "Europe's Lost Generation: No Jobs or Hope for the Young," *The Globe and Mail*, Sept. 10, 2011, www.theglobeandmail.com/report-on-business/international-news/european/europes-lost-generation-no-jobs-or-hope-for-the-young/article2228489/singlepage/. Also see "The jobless young: Left behind," *The Economist*, Sept. 10, 2011, www.economist.com/node/21528614.

5. For background, see Roland Flamini, "Turmoil in the Arab World," *CQ Global Researcher*, May 3, 2011, pp. 209-236.

6. "Global Employment Trends for Youth: 2011 Update," *op. cit.*, p. 1.

7. Edward Sayre and Samantha Constant, "The Whole World Is Watching, Why the Middle East's own "youth bulge" is key to the region's economic and political stability," *The National Journal*, Feb. 21, 2011, www.nationaljournal.com/magazine/why-the-middle-east-s-youth-bulge-is-key-to-the-regions-stability-20110221.

8. Deborah Amos, "In Morocco, Unemployment Can Be A Full-Time Job," Morning Edition, NPR, Jan. 27, 2012, www.npr.org/2012/01/27/145860575/in-morocco-unemployment-can-be-a-full-time-job.

9. Sarah Elder, *et al.*, "Global Employment Trends for Youth: Special issue on the impact of the global economic crisis on youth," International Labour Organization, August 2010, p. 1, www.ilo.org/wcmsp5/groups/public/@ed_emp/@emp_elm/@trends/documents/publication/wcms_143349.pdf.

10. Paul Gregg and Emma Tominey, "The Wage Scar from Unemployment," Centre for Market and Public Organisation, University of Bristol, 2004, www.bris.ac.uk/cmpo/publications/papers/2004/wp97.pdf.

11. "The Jobless Young: Left Behind," *op. cit.*

12. Stephen Fineman, "The middle class: Unemployed and underemployed," in Unemployment: Personal and social consequences, S. Fineman (ed.), Tavistock, 1987, p. 74.

13. Daniel Sullivan and Till Von Wachter, "Job Displacement and Mortality: An Analysis Using Administrative Data," *The Quarterly Journal of Economics*, August 2009, www.columbia.edu/~

vw2112/papers/sullivan_vonwachter_resubmission.pdf.

14. Isaac R. Galatzer-Levy, *et al.*, "From Marienthal to Latent Growth Mixture Modeling: A Return to the Exploration of Individual Differences in Response to Unemployment," *Journal of Neuroscience, Psychology and Economics*, 2010, Vol. 3, No. 2, http://apa.ba0.biz/pubs/journals/releases/npe-3-2-116.pdf.

15. Jeanette Mulvey, "Unemployment Has Little Long-term Effect on Mental Health," *Business News Daily*, Dec. 14, 2010, www.businessnewsdaily.com/490-unemployment-has-little-long-term-effect-on-mental-health.html.

16. For background, see Reed Karaim, "Expanding Higher Education," *CQ Global Researcher*, Nov. 15, 2011, pp. 525-572.

17. *Ibid.*, p. 559.

18. "Global Unemployment Trends for Youth: 2011 Update," *op. cit.*, p. 3.

19. "Human Development Report 2011," United Nations, Table 9, p. 158, http://hdr.undp.org/en/reports/global/hdr2011/download/en/.

20. "Education pays . . .," U.S. Bureau of Labor Statistics, www.bls.gov/emp/ep_chart_001.htm.

21. Fiona Ortiz and Feliciano Tisera, "Southern Europe's Lost Generation Stuck in Junk Jobs," Reuters, Oct. 17, 2011, www.reuters.com/article/2011/10/17/us-europe-junkjobs-idUSTRE79G4RJ20111017.

22. Fiona Govan, "Spain's lost generation: youth unemployment surges above 50 percent," *The Telegraph*, Jan. 27, 2012, www.telegraph.co.uk/news/worldnews/europe/spain/9044897/Spains-lost-generation-youth-unemployment-surges-above-50-per-cent.html.

23. "Eurozone unemployment hits Euro-era high," *op. cit.*

24. "Youth Employment in Europe: A Call for Change," The European Youth Forum, December 2011, p. 19, http://issuu.com/yomag/docs/a_call_for_change.

25. *Ibid.*

26. Eamonn Butler, "On Nick Clegg's 'youth contract,'" blog, Adam Smith Institute, Nov. 25, 2011, www.adamsmith.org/blog/welfare/on-nick-cleggs-youth-contract.

27. "Somavia puts the accent on youth employment in Davos," ILO News, Jan. 27, 2012, www.ilo.org/global/about-the-ilo/press-and-media-centre/news/WCMS_172255/lang--en/index.htm.

28. "Davos 2012 — Averting a Lost Generation" panel discussion, World Economic Forum, Jan. 27, 2012, www.livestream.com/worldeconomicforum03.

29. James Sherk, testimony before the Joint Economic Committee, U.S. Congress, June 1, 2010, www.heritage.org/multimedia/video/2010/05/sherk-cspan-5-26-10.

30. "Global Employment Trends for Youth: 2011 Update," *op. cit.*, p. 7.

31. "EU: Pledges Action on Youth Unemployment, Credit Flows," *The Wall Street Journal*, Jan. 30, 2012, http://online.wsj.com/article/BT-CO-20120130-711890.html.

32. John Weeks and Debbie Fugate, *The Youth Bulge: Challenge or Opportunity*, International Debate Education Association, March 2012, p. 3.

33. "China's population by age and sex in 1990," China-Profile, www.china-profile.com/data/fig_p_19a_m.htm.

34. Weeks and Fugate, *op. cit.*, p. 8.

35. *Ibid.*, p. 5.

36. Rania Abouzeid, "Bouazizi: The Man Who Set Himself and Tunisia on Fire," *Time*, Jan. 21, 2011, www.time.com/time/magazine/article/0,9171,2044723,00.html.

37. Matthew Taylor, Simon Rogers and Paul Lewis, "England rioters: young, poor and unemployed," *The Guardian*, Aug. 18, 2011, www.guardian.co.uk/uk/2011/aug/18/england-rioters-young-poor-unemployed.

38. "Table 1: Youth unemployment figures, 2008-2011Q3," Eurostat website, http://epp.eurostat.ec.europa.eu/statistics_explained/index.php/Unemployment_statistics.

39. "The jobless young: Left behind," *op. cit.*

40. "Youth unemployment in Mediterranean Europe: It's grim down South," *The Economist*, Sept. 11, 2011, www.economist.com/node/21528616.

41. Deborah Ball, "Italy Seeks to Tackle Youth Jobless Problem," *The Wall Street Journal*, Aug. 22, 2011,

http://online.wsj.com/article/SB100014240531119
0427900457652231182474953534.html.

42. "Global Employment Trends for Youth: 2011 Update," *op. cit.*, p. 4.

43. Kazushi Minami, "Tackling Youth Unemployment in Japan," Youth Think! Blog, World Bank, Nov. 16, 2010, http://youthink.worldbank.org/issues/employment/tackling-youth-unemployment-japan.

44. "ILO Youth Unemployment: 2011 Update," *op. cit.*, p. 13.

45. "OECD (2010) — Off to a Good Start? Jobs for Youth, United States," www.oecd.org/dataoecd/22/54/46729274.pdf.

46. *Ibid.*

47. "India Country Overview — September 2011," The World Bank, www.worldbank.org.in/WBSITE/EXTERNAL/COUNTRIES/SOUTHASIAEXT/INDIAEXTN/0,,contentMDK:20195738~pagePK:141137~piPK:141127~theSitePK:295584,00.html.

48. India profile, *The World Factbook*, Central Intelligence Agency, Jan. 12, 2012, https://www.cia.gov/library/publications/the-world-factbook/geos/in.html.

49. Wendy Cunningham, "Unpacking Youth Unemployment in Latin America," The World Bank, August 2009, http://inec.usip.org/resource/unpacking-youth-unemployment-latin-america.

50. "Youth unemployment rate, aged 15-24, both sexes," Millennium goal indicators, United Nations Statistics Division, http://unstats.un.org/unsd/mdg/SeriesDetail.aspx?srid=630&crid=76.

51. Sara Miller Llana, "Unemployment among Latin America youths fuels 'lost generation,' " *The Christian Science Monitor*, March 12, 2010, www.csmonitor.com/World/Americas/2010/0312/Unemployment-among-Latin-America-youths-fuels-lost-generation.

52. Vusi Gumede, "Policies letting the youth down in Africa," Vusi Gumede Thinkers Network, Aug. 5, 2010, www.vusigumedethinkers.com/pages/acpapers_log/8.html.

BIBLIOGRAPHY

Selected Sources

Books

Papademetrious, Demetrios, Madeleine Sumption and Aaron Terrazas, eds., *Migration and the Great Recession: The Transatlantic Experience*, Migration Policy Institute, June 15, 2011.
Case studies trace the disproportionate impact of the financial crisis on young people and the effect their emigration has on the receiving countries.

Standing, Guy, *The Precariat: The New Dangerous Class*, Bloomsbury USA, July 24, 2011.
A professor of social and policy sciences at the University of Bath in England believes the global economy has created a growing "precariat" class — people living precariously, often with a series of short-term jobs that offer little security or standing.

Weeks, John, and Debbie Fugate, eds., *The Youth Bulge: Challenge or Opportunity?* International Debate Education Association, March 1, 2012.
Two San Diego State University professors examine the ramifications of demographic "youth bulges" — disproportionately young populations.

Articles

"The Jobless Young: Left Behind," *The Economist*, Sept. 10, 2011, www.economist.com/node/21528614.
The article examines the long-term consequences of high youth unemployment, for both the jobless and society as a whole.

Allen, Katie, " 'Bad luck' generation will be blighted by youth unemployment for several years," *The Guardian*, Oct. 19, 2011, www.guardian.co.uk/business/2011/oct/19/generation-scarred-by-youth-unemployment.
The International Labour Organization says nearly 50 percent of young people are jobless in many countries.

Coy, Peter, "The Youth Unemployment Bomb," *Businessweek*, Feb. 2, 2011, www.businessweek.com/magazine/content/11_07/b4215058743638.htm.
The growing problem of youth unemployment around the world could cause social unrest.

Klein, Matthew, "Educated, Unemployed and Frustrated," *The New York Times*, March 20, 2011, www.nytimes.com/2011/03/21/opinion/21klein.html.
The uprisings in the Middle East and North Africa are a warning for the developed world, says a 24-year-old research associate at the Council on Foreign Relations.

Llana, Sara Miller, "Unemployment among Latin American youths fuels 'lost generation,'" *The Christian Science Monitor*, March 12, 2010, www.csmonitor.com/World/Americas/2010/0312/Unemployment-among-Latin-America-youths-fuels-lost-generation.
While official youth unemployment rates in Latin America are high, they do not include the high number of young people who have given up looking for work.

Taylor, Mathew, Simon Rogers and Paul Lewis, "England Rioters: Young, Poor and Unemployed," *The Guardian*, Aug. 18, 2011, www.guardian.co.uk/uk/2011/aug/18/england-rioters-young-poor-unemployed.
The writers examine the link between economic hardship and last summer's riots in London.

Wessel, David, and Chip Cummins, "Arab World Built Colleges, but Not Jobs," *The Wall Street Journal*, Feb. 5, 2011, http://online.wsj.com/article/SB10001424052748704709304576124320031160648.html.
The lack of opportunity for college graduates in many Arab countries played a role in the region's "Arab Spring" revolutions last year.

Studies and Reports

"Global Employment Trends for Youth: 2011 Update," International Labour Organization, October 2011, www.ilo.org/wcmsp5/groups/public/@ed_emp/@emp_elm/@trends/documents/publication/wcms_165455.pdf.
The report updates the ILO's exhaustive 2010 study on global youth employment trends, which examined how people aged 15 to 24 years fared during the economic recession.

"OECD Employment Outlook 2011," Organisation for Economic Co-operation and Development, Sept. 15, 2011, www.oecd.org/document/46/0,3746,en_2649_33729_40401454_1_1_1_1,00.html.
The latest annual assessment of labor market developments and prospects in the organization's 34 member countries focuses on youth unemployment.

Cramer, Christopher, "Unemployment and Participation in Violence," World Development Report 2011 background paper, Nov. 16, 2010, http://wdr2011.worldbank.org/sites/default/files/pdfs/WDR%20Background%20Paper%20-%20Cramer.pdf.
A professor of politics, economics and development at the University of London concludes that there is no firm evidence linking youth unemployment to violence and social instability.

For More Information

AFL-CIO, 815 16th St., N.W., Washington, DC, 20006; 202-637-5000; www.afl-cio.org. A federation of 56 national and international unions; maintains extensive information on youth work and unemployment.

European Union, 00 800 6789 1011; http://europa.eu/. A political and economic partnership between 27 European nations; website includes the latest statistics on unemployment and the responses of individual countries and EU itself.

European Youth Forum, Rue Joseph II Straat 120, B-1000 Brussels, Belgium; + 32 2 230 64 90; www.youthforum.org. An umbrella organization established by national youth councils and international nongovernmental youth organizations to tackle youth employment in Europe.

International Labour Organization, 4 Route des Morillons, CH-1211, Geneva 22, Switzerland; +41 (0) 22 799 6111; www.ilo.org. An U.N. agency that deals with labor issues and conducts research on employment and other labor issues.

International Trade Union Confederation, Boulevard du Roi Albert II, 5, Bte 11210 Brussels, Belgium; 32 (0) 2 224 0211; www.ituc-csi.org. International trade organization representing about 175 million workers in 151 countries; website includes an international "young workers" blog.

International Youth Foundation, 32 South St., Baltimore, MD 21202; 410-951-1500; www.iyfnet.org. A nonprofit organization that aims to help young people become productive, engaged members of society; has several job-training efforts in different parts of the globe.

Organisation for Economic Co-operation and Development, 2, rue André Pascal 75775, Paris Cedex 16, France; 33 1 45.24.82.00; www.oecd.org. Promotes economic and social well-being among its membership, consisting of 34 developed countries.

The World Bank, 1818 H St., N.W., Washington, DC 20433; 202-473-1000; www.worldbank.org. International financial organization that lends money to developing countries for anti-poverty programs; studies and supports jobs programs around the globe.

Voices From Abroad:

BAN KI-MOON

Secretary-General, United Nations

Start with the young

"Today we have the largest generation of young people the world has ever known. They are demanding their rights and a greater voice in economic and political life. We need to pull the U.N. system together like never before to support a new social contract of job-rich economic growth. Let us start with young people."

Gulf News (United Arab Emirates), February 2012

DAVID CAMERON

Prime Minister, United Kingdom

A continuing problem

"Of course today's unemployment figures are a matter of great regret, and it's a great regret particularly in terms of higher youth unemployment. Youth unemployment has been a problem in this country for well over a decade, in good years and in bad. . . . What we have to do is sort out all of the things that help young people get back into work."

Leicester Mercury (England), February 2011

ELIAS MASILELA

CEO, Public Investment Corp., South Africa

Impatience leads to problems

"We must look at the way we invest and take account of youth unemployment. If the youth become impatient, then it is very difficult to stop them."

Business Day (South Africa), September 2011

ALHAJI ALIKO DANGOTE

Chairman, National Job Creation Committee, Nigeria

A new Arab Spring?

"Our [Nigerian] youth are underemployed, unemployed or unemployable at the peak of their productivity. As we

have seen in the Maghreb countries of Tunisia, Egypt, Libya and now spreading to the Emirates of the Middle East, youth unemployment is a very effective catalyst for social unrest that has brought down entire governments."

This Day (Nigeria), April 2011

MARYAM HOBALLAH

Economist, Lebanon

The 'brain drain' solution

"The constraints on the economy, job market and business environment for the youth exacerbate Lebanon's 'Brain Drain.' The youth live in a society where they feel their basic needs are not met. The most logical solution is to leave Lebanon for a better life and become one more number in the ever-growing 'Brain Drain.' "

Daily Star (Lebanon), August 2011

CLARIS MADHUKU

Director, Platform for Youth Development, Zimbabwe

Political perceptions

"It would appear the bigger politicians are not interested in addressing this problem for fear they will not have ready youths to use, misuse, abuse and dump. The situation portrays youths as unorganised, violent and an undisciplined lot."

Financial Gazette (Zimbabwe), May 2011

PAUL BROWN

Director of Communications, The Prince's Trust (youth charity), England

A 'dripping tap'

"Youth unemployment is like a dripping tap, costing tens of millions of pounds a week through benefits and lost productivity. And, just like a dripping tap, if we don't do something to fix it, it's likely to get much worse."

The Independent (England), October 2011

SHARON NAKANDHA

Attorney, Uganda

Education's role

"We should also recognise that our education system is partly responsible for the problem of youth unemployment and therefore needs to be reviewed. The system is still archaic and unresponsive to Uganda's growing needs."

The Monitor (Uganda), June 2011

THABO KUPA

Board Member, National Youth Development Agency, South Africa

The youth must lead

"If we know we are 'sitting on a ticking' time bomb then surely we must tackle the problem of youth unemployment with the same vigour and dedication used to bring about the demise of apartheid. As the most affected group, young people are expected to take the lead in fighting against unemployment."

Sowetan (South Africa), October 2011

⦿SAGE research**methods**

The essential online tool for researchers from the world's leading methods publisher

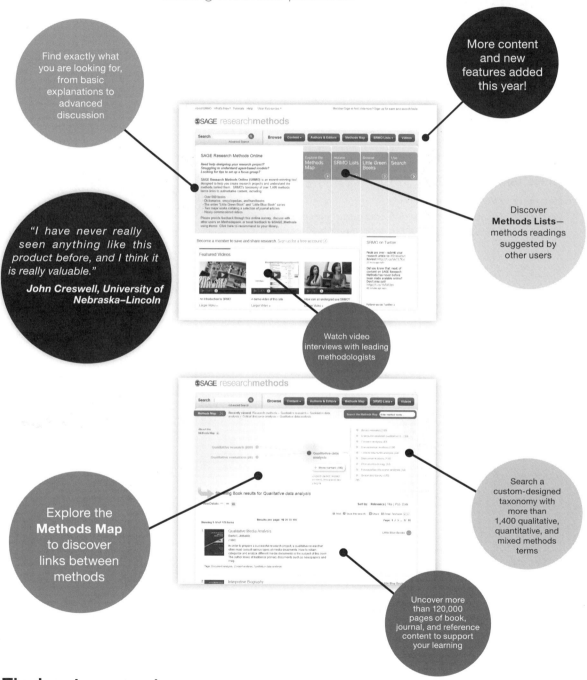

Find exactly what you are looking for, from basic explanations to advanced discussion

More content and new features added this year!

"I have never really seen anything like this product before, and I think it is really valuable."

John Creswell, University of Nebraska–Lincoln

Discover **Methods Lists**— methods readings suggested by other users

Watch video interviews with leading methodologists

Explore the **Methods Map** to discover links between methods

Search a custom-designed taxonomy with more than 1,400 qualitative, quantitative, and mixed methods terms

Uncover more than 120,000 pages of book, journal, and reference content to support your learning

Find out more at
www.sageresearchmethods.com